ELIZABETHAN CRITICAL ESSAYS

ELIZABETHAN CRITICAL ESSAYS

EDITED WITH AN INTRODUCTION

BY

G. GREGORY SMITH

VOLUME I

OXFORD UNIVERSITY PRESS

Oxford University Press, Ely House, London W.1

GLASGOW NEW YORK TORONTO MELBOURNE WELLINGTON
CAPE TOWN SALISBURY IBADAN NAIROBI LUSAKA ADDIS ABABA
BOMBAY CALCUTTA MADRAS KARACHI LAHORE DACCA
KUALA LUMPUR HONG KONG TOKYO

FIRST EDITION 1904
Reprinted lithographically in Great Britain by
LOWE AND BRYDONE (PRINTERS) LTD., LONDON N.W.10, from
sheets of the first edition 1937, 1950, 1959, 1964, 1967

PREFACE

THE purpose of these volumes is to collect the writings of the Elizabethan age which are concerned with Literary Criticism. The term is used in its most comprehensive sense, and permits the inclusion not merely of academic treatises on the nature of poetry or on more special problems of form, but of tracts and prefaces which express contemporary taste. Some of the texts, such as Harvey's and Nash's, are reproduced less for their matter than for their manner of approach. The work is therefore an attempt to recover, primarily in the words of the Elizabethans themselves, what then passed for critical opinion in literary circles. I hope the collection will commend itself as being fairly complete: the ingenious repetition of argument and illustration which runs throughout would show at least that we are in possession of the abiding topics.

Several of the texts have been reprinted, either individually or as parts of works, during the late century, and notably by Haslewood, Grosart, and Mr. Arber. In these, it may be said, the interest has been exclusively bibliographical and historical—a restriction perhaps inevitable in the plan of separate reprints. The advance in the study of Criticism has proved, however, that there are other, and perhaps more important, interests in this material, and that these are best served by treating it as a whole. In no other way can we find the historical perspective of what appears to be a 'mingle-mangle' of ill-con-

sidered, off-hand sayings, or better appreciate the
fact that in these we have the true beginnings of
English Criticism as a separate literary 'kind,' or
adequately understand how much of the classical
mood expressed in Dryden and his successors is the
natural and native outcome of these early specula-
tions. I have endeavoured, in the Introduction, to
discuss these general problems, and to show that the
texts here reprinted supply evidence for certain
conclusions.

It has been found convenient to use the epithet
'Elizabethan' in the strictest chronological sense,
and to exclude the earlier treatises of Coxe, Wilson,
and Sherry, and, with them, Fulwood's book of 1568,
which are either entirely rhetorical or merely anthological. By ending with Elizabeth's death-year, we
are denied the critical work of Ben Jonson,—other
than the earlier pieces which appear in the Appendix
to Vol. ii,—and all the work of Bacon: for though
the first edition of the *Essays* appeared in 1597,
the important reissues fall well within James's
reign. Moreover—considerations of space apart—
Jonson's and Bacon's *milieu* is Jacobean, and their
work introduces us to a later stage in the history of
criticism. In that work, with Bolton's *Hypercritica*,
Stirling's *Anacrisis*, Drayton's *Epistle to Reynolds*, and
others, there is ample material for another volume.
Yet we need not concern ourselves overmuch with
the chronological division. The defence of the limits
here chosen must be the mutual dependence of
the essays between Ascham's chapter on *Imitation*
and Daniel's *Defence*. It so happens that the date of
the latter falls in or about 1603.

All the writings in the body of the book are in prose. The contributions in verse, such as Daniel's *Musophilus*, Hall's *Satires*, or Peele's judgements on contemporaries, are either plainly supplementary or too occasional for the present purpose. These have been incorporated by way of illustration in the Notes. The extracts from Jonson's earlier criticism in verse and a passage from the *Returne from Parnassus* have been printed as an Appendix to Vol. ii, partly to elucidate certain matters, partly to make a link with the next period of English criticism.

In every case the texts have been taken from the originals, and have been carefully collated. I am responsible for the punctuation, and in several places for editorial emendation. The errors and confusion, which it is easier to note than to put right, are partly due to the carelessness or poor scholarship of some of the authors, but more frequently to the fact that the essays were printed without their consent, and were issued without correction, or were 'edited' by the compositors. Printer Jaggard once rounded on an author who had dared to complain, that he regretted his workmen had not been 'so madly disposed' as to 'have given him leave to print his own English.' For then, thought Jaggard (with what truth, it matters not), the complainer would have proved his incompetence. There is good reason to believe that in most cases the author never saw a proof of his work, and that in some no proof was pulled. Only in this way can we explain the appearance, if not always the meaning, of the gibberish in Lodge's *Defence*, or the eccentricities of Webbe and Meres, which are not unworthy of the genius whose *Butyrum et Caseum* disguised the names of Caesar's murderers. In one or two places the correction or suggested emendation of errors in the originals, which had escaped my scrutiny, will be found in the Notes. There must be others. For the transcription and collation of the texts in the Bodleian I am indebted to Miss L. Toulmin Smith, and of those in the British Museum to Mrs. Salmon.

As for the Notes, I hope I may claim for them, as Sir John Harington does for his, that they are not a 'work of supererogation'; though it is perhaps no defence or extenuation to state that the majority of the texts are here annotated for the first time. I shall be sorry if they are not explicit in showing my indebtedness to those who have helped me personally or by their writings. No venturer in this subject dare reckon without the learned author of the *History of Criticism*, or the American scholar who broke fresh ground in the remarkable volume on *Literary Criticism in the Renaissance.* To the thanks which I owe to them for my share of these public gifts, I add my hearty acknowledgement of not a few happy suggestions which our friendship has made possible. Mr. Nichol Smith, who very kindly read all the proofs, has supplied me with many interesting references, especially to the French critics. I would also thank the Secretary and Staff of the Clarendon Press for their ready co-operation at every stage of the work, and Mr. Doble, in particular, for helping me to the solution of some textual difficulties.

December 29, 1903.

CONTENTS OF VOL. I

INTRODUCTION

I.

IT is a commonplace that the age of Elizabeth was too great in creation to be even respectable in criticism. Many who see the bad logic and bad history of this popular formula have concluded not less adversely from a survey of the literary evidence. It is shown that the 'critical' writings are a mere miscellany of stray pamphlets, a 'gallimaufry' of treatises in the old rhetorical vein, tracts on prosody, or prefaces of abuse: and that the writers who disclose something of the critical temper were indifferent to the things which interest modern criticism, or indeed interested their own generation. For is it not remarkable that when Spenser and Sidney, not to speak of the lesser, turn critic, they have no eyes for the pageant of their stage, and but careless ears for the immortal music of contemporary verse; that they find the measure of dramatic excellence in Buchanan's *Jephthes* or Watson's *Absolon*, or the secret of English poetry in hobbling hexameters? And if Spenser redeemed his honour by giving us the *Faerie Queene* and Campion his in the *Books of Airs*, they have proved not so much how great they were as poets as how poor they were as critics. Sidney in his *Apologie*, to which of all these writings least exception can be taken, commends himself most when he strays from academic argument to raptures on the nobility of the Poet's calling.

This is altogether a superficial estimate. It is inadequate as a description of the critical activities which are crowded into the work of a single generation. The mere volume of the texts is evidence against the occasional character of the reflections; and their variety, far from showing the in-consequence of the amateur, proves a vitality of critical purpose. The persistent effort towards the understanding of the principles of Poetry is in itself an important fact which must prompt us, if it do nothing else, to discover its cause. Moreover, the modern dislike of the classical elements in the essays leaves unanswered the very per-tinent question why Elizabethan criticism is apparently out of touch with the literature of its age. And it passes by the important consideration of the bearing of this pre-Jonsonian material upon the doctrine of Dryden and his successors, who inherited more of Elizabethan tradition than it has been the custom to allow. Further, the experimental character of the work, taken as a whole, the tentative conclusions, the borrowings and reborrow-ings, the inconsistencies, are not without their positive value, especially as the age was itself conscious that it was but seeking its way. Nor must it be forgotten that English criticism had no English tradition, and little, if any, English material on which it could found a Poetic; and that it was at this time in England, and hardly earlier in Renaissance Europe, that Criticism *per se* first laid claim to rank as a literary 'kind' in the vernacular. It appears therefore more reasonable to look upon this ex-tensive and mixed collection of documents as an impor-tant body of evidence in the study of literary origins. In the perspective of these essays we may find something of that critical temper which is first made clear in Dryden, so justly named the Father of English Criticism; but we must not measure the quality of these early efforts, and even of Jonson's, by later experience, any more than we may look for a general canon governing the exercise of that temper. All is in the making: these remains are *Explorata* or *Discoveries—Timber* for the building of the

later edifice, of which Jonson drew the plans, but which he
could not complete.

It may be said that the recognition of this inchoate, and
to some extent irregular, character of Elizabethan criticism
is a serious objection to the treatment of the essays as a
whole, and makes their association in these volumes a mere
matter of convenience. What is common, it will be asked,
to Ascham on the imitation of classical authors, Gascoigne
on the making of verses, Nash on Gabriel Harvey, Sidney
in defence of 'poor Poetry,' Puttenham on rhetorical
figures, and Meres in his directory of writers? Can we
reconcile the purposes of the practical educationist, the
Bohemian, the college pedant, the rhapsodist, the courtier
who writes for courtiers? And what is the critical utility
of making neighbours of Gascoigne's random notes and
Puttenham's 'whole receipt of Poetry,' or King James's
juvenilia and Daniel's great *Defence*? The objection is
less valid than it would appear to be, though it may be
useful as a caution against making a too absolute 'composite' out of the variety. Recent study, especially on
the comparative side, has greatly increased our knowledge
of the relationship of phases which appear to be individual and incoherent. We have outlived the merely
antiquarian taste which happily prompted Haslewood to
collect certain of these tracts in his *Ancient Critical Essays*;
though there is in him some hint of their value as a
corporate study. 'Perhaps it may be confidently said,'
he wrote, 'that such a body of criticism as these tracts
collectively present, although few in number, is not anywhere to be found. Independent of rarity, intrinsic value
may justly entitle this volume, although a humble reprint,
to range with those of the Elizabethan æra[1].' This was
written nearly a century ago, and since then the editorial

---

[1] *Ancient Critical Essays upon English Poets and Poësy*, edited by
Joseph Haslewood (2 vols., 1811, 1815), II. xxii.

interest has been confined to the publication of some of these tracts either individually or in popular gatherings of kindred prose. The present collection brings these together again, and recovers others of not less importance. What justification there may be for restoring this comrade-ship, and for reasons other than that the Essays were written about the same time, the following pages will en-deavour to show.

II. THE PURITAN ATTACK.

Elizabethan criticism arose in controversy. The early Essays are 'Apologies' for Poets and Poetry against the attacks of a vigorous Puritanism. Some are direct answers to onslaughts on special forms or on individuals; all have the common purpose of upholding the usefulness and pleasure-giving power of Poetry. It is noteworthy that the greater forces which stimulated this literary defence were themselves unliterary. They are not represented in these volumes, except in the answers of their adversaries[1]. They denounce Poetry because it is often lewd, the theatre because it is a school of abuse: their argument is social, political, personal. Their importance—and it should not be underestimated—lies in the fact that they called forth a reasoned defence, and compelled their opponents to examine the principles of Poetry. They thus defined the first problem for English criticism. But they did more, by helping the critics, in their investigation of the bases of Poetry, to see that there was some excuse for the obloquy cast upon what had been written, and that some reform from within was necessary. The problem as it presented itself to Sidney and his friends was in general terms. Poetry is a good thing in itself: 'it is abused and does not abuse': if there be vice in it, it is the fault of 'poet-apes,' not of

---

[1] Occasional passages from Gosson are given in the notes to Lodge's reply. See the bibliography of the pamphlets, i. 61-3.

poets : let the vice be taken away. Thus, to a degree, the spirit of the extremer sort who would banish poets from the commonwealth passed into their opponents and made them severe judges of the literature which fell short of their ideal. There was not as yet any serious thought of the fixing of a canon, but the scrutiny of English habit which proceeded apace was, in the nature of things, the sure forerunner of a critical system. The achievement of this is, however, the tale of a later period. The Elizabethan mind was not, could not be, resolved on such discipline. Yet its efforts, though tentative, were not chaotic, for it established the preliminary positions that Poetry can justify herself, and that English Poetry must. And if the reader will keep this in view, he may escape some of the confusion which surrounds the double argument of the defenders against the ' Misomousoi ' or Poethaters, and against the 'rakehelly rout' of English rhymers.

The Puritan arguments fall into two main groups—the historical and moral. The former was the less urgent, though it may be undervalued because the other was debated with greater noise and persistency. There was, in the first place, the patristic tradition of the iniquity of stage-plays, songs, and merry tales, wrested with more or less exaggeration from Augustine, Tertullian, Cyprian, Lactantius, and Chrysostom. Passages of this mediaeval protest are quoted and requoted, not because Renaissance or Reformed England was in sympathy with the Fathers, or even knew their work at first hand, but because these satisfied the perennial instinct of that half of the nation which must be ascetic. The marked Puritanism of the Elizabethan age, to be traced alike in the *Faerie Queene* and in the abhorred plays, was but one phase of a condition which was constitutional rather than the literary infection of earlier theology and philosophy. It found support for its purposes in the alien and misunderstood past, and readily borrowed its phrases to clinch the argument. So, too, it turned to classical literature, and confounded the scholars and lovers of vain things with the dicta of Aristotle, or of Plato, the accredited expeller of poets from the ideal Commonwealth. It was a partisan selection ; and opponents of no greater scholarship found it easy to marshal other holy and learned adversaries, or to turn these very mentors to their own account. The Precisians, however, made a stronger point when they appealed to the Protestant antipathy to the so-called Dark Ages. It is clear to us that the blindness to the merits of the mediaeval romances is due less to a crazy dislike of what they chose to call their 'bold bawdry,' than to the fact that they were the work of 'abbey-lubbers' and 'wanton canons.' Even the courtier Puttenham boldly concludes : ' Thus what in writing of rhymes and registering of lies was the clergy of that fabulous age wholly occupied[1].' The Humanists joined with them in condemnation of the ' standing pool ' of English literature, though their nicer noses smelt ignorance rather than Papistry in its stagnant waters. But the chief support to this hatred of the fooleries and lies of the Muse lay in the record of English poetry. With the exception of Chaucer, and there was no reason why the sterner minds should except even him, there was little or nothing of poetry, as they knew it, to be commended, except by professional friendship, and certainly nothing sufficiently outstanding to win over the more open-minded of that party. The defenders are the first to admit this, but on that admission they founded an argument for the revival, not for the suppression of the Art.

The attack was, however, keener on the side of Morality, and it was led in two directions—against the playhouse and its associations, and against the foreign, especially the Italian, influences in society. The former

[1] i. 15.

are the immediate object. The Puritan pamphleteers inveigh rather than argue ; they are more concerned with
the social bearings of the playhouse than with the intrinsic immorality of the plays. They seldom condescend
to the literary question ; in their condemnation they are
but

> ' Rude foggie squires
> That knowe not to esteeme of witt or arte [1],'

and they are not too explicit in their production of evidence
against the theatre as a social institution. Gosson, who
has the exceeding enthusiasm of the pervert, defends his
position thus : ' Now if any man ask me why myself
have penned comedies in time past, and inveigh so
eagerly against them here, let him know that *semel insaniuimus omnes* : I have sinned, and am sorry for my
fault : he runs far that never turns ; better late than
never [2].' Such a plea, however effective it may have
proved by reason of its confidence, and however welcome
it must have been to cherished sentiments, was clearly inadequate for the settlement of even the narrowest issues.
It was not difficult for the opponents of the Puritans to
point out that all the vices of the playhouse, which
they themselves were not slow to condemn, were not an
argument against its continuation, much less against plays
and poetry.

There was more force in the protest against the Italianate
Englishman. Yet the Precisians state it in an indifferent
or occasional way, and do not see that it was perhaps the
best weapon in their armoury. Their more clear-sighted
opponents wrested it from their hands and used it for
their own purposes. To these, and not to the Puritans,
we must go for the best estimate of the risks which came
to English life and art from ' diabolical ruffs and wicked
great breeches full of sin.' The Puritans hate the over-sea

---

[1] *Pilgrimage to Parnassus*, v. (536–7).   [2] i. 369.

affectation because they find in it certain glaring evidences of Renaissance degeneracy, of loose living and filthy reading. They hardly touch the old problem whether Art may not, by its very exercise, tend to destroy itself. Ascham, the least bigoted in his Puritan sympathies, sees in the Italian books the undoing of both true doctrine and honest living, the opening of 'not fond and common ways to vice, but such subtle, cunning, new, and diverse shifts . . . as the simple head of an Englishman is not able to invent[1].' When he approaches nearest to the literary intention, as in his denunciation of rhyming, he vaguely concludes: 'And you that be able to understand no more than ye find in the Italian tongue, and never went farther than the school of Petrarch and Ariosto abroad, or else of Chaucer at home, though you have pleasure to wander blindly still in your foul wrong way, envy not others that seek, as wise men have done before them, the fairest and rightest way; or else, beside the just reproach of malice, wise men shall truly judge that you do so, as I have said and say yet again unto you, because either for idleness ye will not, or for ignorance ye cannot, come by no better yourself[2].' There is no criticism in these things: merely the old war against the Devil and his works, be he Italian or Englishman, rhymer or not, and the longing of saints and philosophers for the old simplicity. The constant appeal to the days of yore, when men were not yet schooled in abuse—to the England 'of our forefathers' time,' ere monkish tales of Sir Lancelot and Sir Tristram had infected our chivalry—is but the cry of the Gossons of every generation. In their zeal against playhouse ribaldry and Italian luxury some prayed for the Scriptural pastures, some for a new Scythia, where among valorous men even Poetry would be 'without vice, as the Phoenix in Arabia without a fellow[3].'

[1] i. 4.   [2] i. 33.   [3] i. 368.

It would, however, be an error to consider the Puritan attack as ineffectual zealotry. Though it was badly managed, though it erred by exaggeration, and was ignorant of the working values of the pleas which it advanced though (in Sidney's words), it fell out 'with these Poet-whippers, as with some good women, who often are sick, but in faith they cannot tell where[1],' it has more than an accidental bearing upon the development of Elizabethan criticism. That it was taken so seriously by the writers who had the cause of literature at heart gives it the importance of having to some extent determined the lines of their defence. Not merely were the Puritan positions, such as the appeal to history, directly met, but others of more specific character, such as the charges against the theatre and the denunciation of Italian influence, were transformed into essential topics in the ensuing discussion of literary principles. And, further, the Puritans called forth, and perhaps intensified, a latent sympathy with their ideals in some of the best and keenest of their professed opponents, even though their overstrainings prompted not a few hard sayings about the 'senseless stoical austerity,' and the inconsistency and confidence of the 'sour reforming enemies of art[2].' Ascham is strongly sympathetic; Sidney, who represents the most complete and positive qualities of Elizabethan criticism, gives a courtly hearing; Harington, who sees but a weak faction in those who from malice love not Poetry or from folly understand it not[3], must say that 'to us that are Christians, in respect of the high end of all, which is the health of our souls, not only Poetry but all other studies of Philosophy are in a manner vain and superfluous[4].' And William Vaughan, who will not have plays suffered in a Commonwealth, but defends Poetry,

---

[1] i. 180.   [2] The hardest hit (of many) at the Puritan is Jonson's. See *Discoveries* xii, ' *Hypocrita*.'   [3] ii. 195.   [4] ii. 197.

must yet have it after the purest pattern. 'Sundry times,' he says, 'have I been conversant with such as blasphemed Poetry, by calling it mincing and lying Poetry. But it is no marvel that they thus deride Poetry, since they stick not in this out-worn age to abuse the ministers of God by terming them bookish fellows and Puritans, they themselves not knowing what they mean[1].' There is likely to be some confusion here, in this enthusiasm for Poetry *and* Puritans.

It must be admitted that the main thesis of the Poet-whippers was not fully met by the Apologists. The controversy was carried on from different standpoints. The Puritans had in view the popular literature of the playhouse and of Paul's. As men of the people they spoke only of what interested the people. 'Poetry' with them meant Elderton and Tarlton, or bawdy sonnets; 'books' translations of the naughty tales of Italy; 'playgoing' the noisy delights of Shoreditch. The defence of Poetry was in the hands of courtiers and scholars who lived beyond the pale of Bohemia. To Sidney, Puttenham, or Harington those things which they admitted were pleasing neither to gentlemen nor Christians were not the sum of the matter. If Poetry was to be denounced because of this popular travesty, of which they professed to know little and for which perhaps they cared as little, it was necessary to show that she could be defended on broader and better grounds. Hence it is that each party, though in amiable agreement on the viciousness of Vice, argue for and against the claims of Poetry from different premises. And hence, too, our earlier critical literature presents the double paradox—that culture and learning, which were both the most competent force and the real agent in the development of criticism, took no serious heed to the truly national literature with which in the future that

[1] ii 326.

criticism must primarily concern itself: and, in the second place, that the defence was based largely on over-sea tradition and Italian practice, which in its more popular application was contemned by both sides. Thus Ascham, who hates things Italianate not less than the monkish *Morte Arthur*, justifies his literary theory by the canons of Italian Humanism in which he had been schooled. The Puritans in their anxiety to exile the too amorous Tuscan were the means of calling in his more learned, perhaps more respectable, brother to defend him against themselves.

III. THE DEFENCE.

The argument for the Defence falls into two main divisions—the historical testimony in favour of Poetry, and the excellence of its nature or character. There is, as we shall see, little originality in the general drift or in the illustrations. It is obvious that the Essayists are constantly borrowing from each other, and often verbatim: it is not less obvious from their selection and arrangement of the leading reasons that they are drawing from outside opinion[1]. There are of course degrees of adaptation—from the absolute 'scissors-and-paste' method of the *Palladis Tamia* to the happily disguised borrowings of the *Apologie for Poetrie*.

On the historical side there are three proofs of the goodness of Poetry: for when it is of hoary antiquity, is found with all peoples, and has enjoyed the favour of the greatest, it is surely good. To those who hold that in the earliest period of the national life men were rather doing things worthy to be written than writing things fit to be done[2], Sidney says, 'What that before time was, I think scarcely *Sphinx* can tell[3].' So thinks Lodge, when reflecting on the drama[4]; so Nash, quoting from Cicero[5]; so Puttenham,

---

[1] See infra, p. lxxi et seq.   [2] i. 187.   [3] Ibid.
[4] i. 80.   [5] i. 328.

when he says that the 'profession and use of Poesy is most ancient from the beginning, and not, as many erroneously suppose, after, but before any civil society was among men[1].' The Poets were the first lawgivers, the first philosophers, and, in due course, the first historians. It is a later refinement, specially commendable to King James VI and the courtier Puttenham, which denies them the right to treat of the grave matters of princes[2].

In all nations, too, there has been 'some feeling of Poetry[3].' As it was the most ancient, so was it the most universal. 'Which two points,' adds Puttenham, 'give to all human inventions and affairs no small credit[4].' Sidney and he have little difficulty in illustrating this by accounts of the poet-loving Turk, Indian, Dane, 'the Perusine, and the very cannibal[5].'

As for the approbation of Poetry by princes and the learned, the citations are certainly ample in Lodge[6], Sidney[7], Webbe[8], Puttenham[9], Harington[10], Chapman[11], and Meres[12]. 'But to speak of all those . . . were tedious, and would require a rehearsal of all such in whose time there grew any to credit and estimation in that faculty[13].' This favourite argument by testimonial[14] received an exaggerated importance from the fact that the Puritans had made so much of the opinions of the theologians and philosophers. The obvious retort was to count the votes on the other side : yet the defenders were not whole-hearted in the business. Harington, who feels that the defence of poetry is a supererogation, is content to say that he could bring in such an army of approvers 'as not only the sight but the very sound of them were able to vanquish and dismay the final forces of our adversaries[15].'

---

[1] ii. 6. [2] i. 221, ii. 33. [3] i. 153. [4] ii. 10. [5] Ibid.
[6] i. 70-1. [7] i. 192-3. [8] i. 232-3. [9] ii. 16-23. [10] ii. 195.
[11] ii. 302. [12] ii. 321-2. [13] i. 233.
[14] Of which Boccaccio's *De Genealogia Deorum* gives an early model. See infra, pp. lxxviii-ix. [15] ii. 195.

They based their defence with more confidence on the nature of Poetry, on its claims as a moral force and as an artistic pleasure.　In this section of their Apology they made their first critical experiments.　The argument is worked out on different lines; but in no single author, with perhaps the exception of Sidney, is a complete statement attempted.　The main points are these:—

(1) Poetry is of divine origin.　'Who thinketh not,' says Lodge, 'that it proceedeth from above? . . . It is a pretty sentence, yet not so pretty as pithy, *Poeta nascitur, orator fit*[1].'　All poets may not be holy[2], yet the poet, *per se*, is *vates*, diviner, foreseer, prophet[3].　He is possessed of the Platonic *furor*[4], or divine rapture[5].　Homer's poems were written 'from a free fury[6].'　*Est deus in nobis: agitante calescimus illo*[7].　Harington quizzically refuses to admit the point to debate by saying that Puttenham's 'parcels' of his own verse quoted in his treatise are themselves the best proof that poetry is a gift, not an art[8].

(2) Poetry is an art of imitation, and not a mere empiric of sound and form or the refashioning of traditional material. It is, as Sidney and others claim, ποίησις and μίμησις in a fuller sense than is allowed by their extremer opponents, or understood by the ordinary practitioners, or by young critics who could accept James VI's 'deciphering' of the perfect poet[9].　This appeal to Aristotelian doctrine, through Horace and especially through Scaliger and the Renaissance critics, is of first importance in its effect on the development of criticism in England.　It breaks fresh ground for the study of the bases of poetry: and it foreshadows the introduction of aesthetic theory.　Though the argument was classical in origin and classical in its first application, it contained *in gremio* the justification of romantic freedom[10].

[1] i. 70-1.　　[2] e. g. i. 71　　[3] i. 154.　　[4] ii. 3.　　[5] ii. 297.
[6] ii. 298.　　[7] See i. 232.　　[8] ii. 197.　　[9] i. 211.　　[10] Infra, p. lx et seq.

(3) The argument of the moral value of Poetry is to a great extent based on the mediaeval doctrine of the Allegory. 'For undoubtedly,' Wilson had said in his *Arte of Rhetorique*, 'there is no one tale among all the Poets, but under the same is comprehended some thing that pertaineth either to the amendment of manners, to the knowledge of truth, to the setting forth of Nature's work, or else to the understanding of some notable thing done. . . . The Poets were wise men and wished in heart the redress of things [1].' This idea runs throughout the essays, alike in the general theory, and in the method used in the interpretation of literary examples. There is, on the one hand, the plain statements of Lodge, following Campanus [2], or of Stanyhurst [3], or the more extreme attitude of Chapman, who upholds the views of Spondanus [4]: on the other, the more reasonable and historical explanation offered by Sidney and Harington. Between these two extremes there is perhaps more than a question of degree. In a sense there is a *volte-face*: or at least the turn has begun. The older view assumes that the *moralitas* is the kernel, and that the fable and poetic imaginings are an outside means to attract the reader to some hidden good. Or, to borrow the familiar Renaissance metaphors, common with the Elizabethans, Poetry is the sugar-coating of the pill, the candy with the dose of rhubarb. The sugar-coating or the candy is there, because there is the necessary pill or rhubarb. In other words, the allegorical usefulness of poetry is its *rationale*, and for that reason it is to be defended as a good thing. On the other hand, it is clear that with the progress of the general defence of Poetry this view becomes less important. Thus Sidney, though he refers to it in his claim for the poet as the right popular philosopher [5], makes little of it: and Harington, in his analysis of the allegorical senses in

[1] ed. 1562, f. 99ᵛ.   [2] i. 65.   [3] i. 136.   [4] ii. 297.   [5] i. 167.

which poetry may be read[1], rather emphasizes the attitude
of the weaker capacities who take but the pleasantness of
the story and the sweetness of the verse. The quite contrary position that imagination first constructs the fable,
and thereafter the poet or his commentator or his reader
finds the moral, could hardly be established until aesthetic
criticism had found its axioms. But we are not far from
it, certainly not far from the later theory of poetic freedom. The change was undoubtedly furthered by the
increasing attention by the critics to the pleasure-giving
function of Poetry. Nor must it be forgotten that the
allegorical enthusiasm of the age was of a secondary kind,
and that in so far as the majority of writers are interested
in the 'rind within the rind,' they often show no more than
emblematic or anagrammatic curiosity.

(4) In their rough definitions of the purpose of Poetry
the defenders are careful not to subordinate the *dulce* to
the *utile*. The end of Poetry is, with Sidney, 'to teach
and delight[2].' It is well known, says Nash, 'that delight
doth prick men forward to the attaining of knowledge,
and that true things are rather admired if they be included
in some witty fiction, like to pearls that delight more
if they be deeper set in gold[3].' Webbe's plea, which
he borrows by admission from Horace, is generally accepted. 'The perfect perfection of poetry is this, to
mingle delight with profit in such wise that a reader
might by his reading be partaker of both[4].' Puttenham
goes further in his account of the subject or matter of
Poetry[5] when he names, as one of its functions, 'the
common solace of mankind in all his travails and cares
of this transitory life'; and claims that 'in this last sort,
being used for recreation only, it may allowably bear
matter not always of the gravest or of any great commodity or profit, but rather in some sort vain, dissolute,

<hr>

[1] ii. 202-3. [2] i. 158. [3] i. 329. [4] i. 250. [5] ii. 25.

or wanton, so it be not very scandalous and of evil example[1].' Here the friends of poetry found their chief argument: and here too their adversaries, ever suspicious of pleasure, in argument or in practice, found the heresy. For this seductive power as readily leads men to like obscenity as to love honesty. Yet the defenders, though heartily admitting the danger, are in no doubt that the abuse cannot discredit the function or the excellence of its effects. ' In this their argument of abuse,' says Sidney, 'they prove the commendation[2].' The result of this consideration by the defence was that, though they did not go quite so far as to separate the *dulce* from the *utile*, they appeared to give a primary importance to the former. In Sidney's reiteration of the ' delightful teaching[3] ' he appears to be laying more stress on the pleasure than on the profit, and in the memorable passage on the Poet as Monarch he is still less equivocal. The Poet ' cometh to you with words sent in delightful proportion, either accompanied with, or prepared for, the well enchanting skill of music ; and with a tale for-sooth he cometh unto you, with a tale which holdeth children from play, and old men from the chimney corner[4].' Moreover, in Webbe's opinion, ' as the very sum or chiefest essence of Poetry did always for the most part consist in delighting the readers or hearers with pleasure, so, as the number of Poets increased, they still inclined this way rather than the other, so that most of them had special regard to the pleasantness of their fine conceits, whereby they might draw men's minds into admiration of their inventions, more than they had to the profit or commodity that the readers should reap by their works[5].' Puttenham caps his fore-quoted defence of toys by a more remarkable passage at the con-

---

[1] ii. 25.   [2] i. 187.   [3] e. g. i. 197, 200.
[4] i. 172.   [5] i. 235-6.

clusion of his quaint chapter on ' Proportion in Figure [1],'
and pushes the Puritan's logic *ad absurdum*.

> ' All is but a iest, all dust, all not worth two peason :
>   For why in mans matters is neither rime nor reason.'

The effect of this separation, or emphasis, of the
pleasure-giving function was undoubtedly to quicken the
theory of Poetry as an Art. We find hints of this in
Sidney [2], even in writers like Nash, who lay stress on
the ' profit' in the poetical account. ' Nothing is more
odious,' says the latter, ' than the artless tongue of a
tedious dolt, which dulleth the delight of hearing, and
slacketh the desire of remembering [3].' Yet the expression
of a general theory is but half-conscious : we shall see
the underlying principle more clearly in their practical
schemes of reform. Sidney, who reaches nearest to the
root of this matter, comes to it by natural sympathy rather
than by critical insight. When he points to the danger
of poesy which ' by the reason of his sweet charming
force can do more hurt than any other army of words [4],'
he has no inkling of the problem of the self-destruc-
tion of Art [5]. He is merely admitting that abuse is
possible.

In support of these views of the character of Poetry
the writers added the well-worn comparisons with Philosophy and History, and answered, in more or less stereo-
typed fashion, the charges of Agrippa [6], that poets are liars,
wantons, and wasters of wise men's time. The persistency of these comparisons is not less striking than their
lack of originality. The defensive character of the Essays
probably gave an undue importance to this line of argu-

---

[1] ii. 115–16.   [2] e.g. i. 183.   [3] i. 335.   [4] i. 187.
[5] Supra, p. xviii.
[6] Agrippa, who is named by Sidney, was not the first framer of these,
as Boccaccio's writings show. See infra, p. lxxix.

ment, by which they sought to make clear that the Poet must be worthy of honour, if he can be shown to be better than the honoured Philosopher or the honoured Historian. So Sidney makes bold to prove that he is the monarch of all sciences[1]; and Puttenham that he is 'above all other artificers scientific or mechanical[2].' We have perhaps lost the perspective of this interminable squabble from the days of Aristotle; but, though we may think lightly of the whole retort, we must at least acknowledge its historical propriety. We have only to look at the authors represented in such collections as the *Artis Penus Historicae*[3] to see how the defenders of 'poor Poetry' were forced, even as a matter of form, to set the balance aright.

It was probably this historical craze which gave point to the old charge that Poets are liars, and compelled the critics' reply. Lodge, who finds the imputation supported 'by no small bird, even Aristotle himself,' and by 'severe Cato,' answers by the aid of his Lactantius[4]. Sidney in his reply is again comparative; 'the poet is the least liar[5],' certainly less so than the Historian, who can 'hardly escape from many lies[6].' The Poet 'never affirmeth[7]': he 'never maketh any circles about your imagination, to conjure you to believe for true what he writes[8].' This is endorsed by Harington, who enlarges on the importance of invention or fiction as one of the main components, and the glory, of Poetry. And after all, as Sidney had said, 'a feigned example hath as much force to teach as a true example[9].' Yet the taunt is ever recurring, not only from the natural Puritan who finds consolation in Socrates's being 'ill brought up to poesy, because he loved the truth[10],' but from others of more generous mind, who are yet strongly prejudiced on some particular point. Thus Nash

---

[1] i. 172.   [2] ii. 3.   [3] 2 vols., Basle, 1579.   [4] i. 73.   [5] i. 184.
[6] Ibid.   [7] i. 185.   [8] Ibid.   [9] i. 169.   [10] i. 342.

is seldom more angry than when he is speaking of mediaeval Romance as ' that forgotten legendary licence of lying[1].'

That poets are wanton is of course one of the main topics of the Gosson-Lodge controversy[2], and is fully met by Sidney[3], Nash[4], and Harington[5], who readily admit the danger when Cupido is lawlessly crept in. Gosson's plea that Poetry makes men effeminate directly inspires Sidney's memorable countercuff that it, above all things, is the companion of camps[6]. Harington, with Ariosto as his illustration to hand, shows that there may be even literary *decorum* in ' the persons of those that speak lasciviously,' that ' obscenousness ' may be altogether a matter of good or bad interpretation of the poems, and that the Puritans who so disregard the context convict themselves of the failing of the chaste wife of Brutus[7]. The hackneyed statement that Plato banished poets, so that youth might not be corrupted, is easily answered by several of the writers[8].

To the third, that the study of poetry is a waste of time and a pleasure to fools, Sidney and Harington reply with some word-chopping and sarcasm, which, though not a convincing reply to a Precisian, is reasonably sufficient. Sidney ends the controversy curtly—' but I still and utterly deny that there is sprung out of earth a more fruitful knowledge[9]'; and Harington concludes his answer by expressing the doubt whether the charge be worth the answering[10]. Puttenham, who is firmly convinced of the dignity of Poesy and approves all manner of toys, even ' pillars ' and ' fuzies,' has of course no doubt of the silliness of the proposition.

The pleas for Poetry in the general are supplemented by others dealing with special forms or subjects, or with

---

[1] i. 323.　　[2] i. 73, &c.　　[3] i. 183, 186.　　[4] i. 332.　　[5] ii. 209.
[6] i. 188.　　[7] ii. 209.　　[8] Cf. infra, lxxii, lxxix.　　[9] i. 184.　　[10] ii. 208.

topics arising from the consideration of them. The chief
interest of these more particular discussions lies, as we
shall see, in their critical intention. The essayists, un-
hampered by the necessity of answering a vaguely expressed
attack on the whole art, condescend to the more detailed
examination of one or other form ; and in these separate
studies they give us the positive side of Elizabethan
criticism. It is thus in the special analyses of the dramatic
forms, or heroic poetry, or the art of translation, that they,
to our eyes, not only best express the character of the
onslaught of the poet-whippers, but lay the foundations of
later speculation on literary principles. In the drama, for
example, which is the chief area of conflict, it is a minor
matter to learn how they met Gosson's pronouncement
that morality is impossible in the play-house, or the
quasi-literary absurdity that the plays of Buchanan or the
Christus ascribed to Nazianzen were written 'dialoguewise' for the closet. On the other hand, it is clear that
the purpose of the essayists in the detailed treatment of
certain portions was less in the interest of critical theory
than in support of their side in the controversy with
the poet-haters. For they argued that the excellence
possible in each and all, whether tragedy, comedy, heroic
poetry, pastoral, elegy, satire, epigram, or anagram, had
a cumulative value in proving the excellence of Poetry
itself. Sidney, Webbe, and the others distinctly imply
that the poet is not merely the monarch of all the arts,
but that his empire is wide and self-sufficing. Poetry,
says Webbe, 'is not debarred from any matter which
may be expressed by pen or speech [1].' The consuming
sense of the dignity and compass of the art is the
most striking characteristic of its most eloquent defenders, who seldom, if ever, forget to refer to these
things, even when they bury themselves in professional

[1] i. 249. Cf. Chapman, *Epist.* to *First XII Books of Homer*, ll. 118–19.

problems of technique. Though their large assurance
sometimes led them into critical blind-alleys, as in their
confusion of the functions of verse and prose, it supplied
the staying power to these beginnings in criticism, and
moreover was thoroughly appropriate to the circumstances. Nor was their superior manner of debate, and
an occasional irritation at their opponents, less appropriate
to the occasion. In feeling with Harington that the whole
matter was but the Sophister's praise of Hercules [1], they
intimated an intellectual confidence which promised well
for an English doctrine of taste.

IV. THE CLASSICAL PURPOSE.

The apologetic character of the essays is, however, of
less importance to the present purpose. It is at most
only of historical interest, as a clue to the cause of the
remarkable attention to a great literary problem. Their
true value lies in the evidence which they give of an
incipient, and to some extent unconscious, effort towards
an appreciation of the principles of literature, and towards a systematic investigation of the capabilities of
the craft of English.

Proof of the conviction of the critics that their house
must be put in order need not be sought in their classi-
fication of literary types and forms. The favourite
groupings by style, as in Ascham [2], Sidney [3], Webbe [4], or
Puttenham [5], by subject, most elaborately in Meres's
Comparative Discourse, or by prosodic forms, are little
else than the accentuation of a mediaeval fashion which is
observed in the earlier Renaissance stages of all European
literatures. We find the first positive evidence of the
awakening criticism in the dissatisfaction with certain

---

[1] ii. 194.   [2] i. 23-6.   [3] i. 175.   [4] i. 249.   [5] ii. 155.

existing conditions and in the acknowledgement that English is in transition.

The persistency of contemporary reference to this chaos and to the necessity of some immediate interference is perhaps the most striking feature of these early efforts. They are the topic of every writer, and they supply the *motif* for reform, however much the ultimate purpose of each critic may differ. The vocabulary of denunciation has the Elizabethan fullness. Ascham laments the 'fond books,' the 'lewd and rude rhymes,' sold in every shop[1]. 'Good God,' says Stanyhurst, 'what a fry of *wooden rythmours* doth swarm in stationers' shops[2]': and Webbe thinks sadly of the 'infinite fardels of printed pamphlets wherewith this country is pestered[3].' 'E. K.' anathematizes 'the rakehelly rout of ragged rhymers[4],' and Sidney, who mourns that 'an over-faint quietness should seem to strew the house for poets[5],' candidly admits, 'I that, before ever I durst aspire unto the dignity, am admitted into the company of the paper-blurrers, do find the very true cause of our wanting estimation in wanting desert; taking upon us to be poets in despite of Pallas[6].' It is a world of 'rude smatterers[7],' 'brainless bussards[8],' 'pottical, poetical heads,' who rhyme 'in commendation of Copper noses or Bottle Ale[9]'; and full enough of fooleries, without these 'new-new writers, the loadstones of the press, wonderfully beholden to the Ass[10].' 'Such is this golden age wherein we live,' quoth Nash, who elsewhere bids the poets put out their rush-candles[11], 'and so replenished with golden asses of all sorts, that, if learning had lost itself in a grove of genealogies, we need do no more but set an old goose over half a dozen pottle pots (which are as it were

---

[1] i. 2, 4, 31.   [2] i. 141.   [3] i. 226.   [4] i. 131.
[5] i. 194.   [6] i. 195.   [7] i. 229.   [8] i. 322.
[9] i. 246.   [10] ii. 231, 238.   [11] ii. 225.

the eggs of invention) and we shall have such a breed of books within a little while after, as will fill all the world with the wild fowl of good wits[1].' Nor does the verse lag behind the prose in hunting down the abuse : witness Jonson in his *Every Man in his Humour*[2], as in his *Discoveries*; or Daniel in his *Musophilus*[3], and in his dedication to the Countess of Pembroke, who is to pre-serve the Muses from ' these hideous beasts Oblivion and Barbarism[4].' So fly the words : yet the censors claim that they are not severe. When Webbe has recorded the 'pottical, poetical' gibe, he amiably quotes 'E.K.'s censure, because he would not be 'too broad' with them in his own speech[5]. Though it may be suspected that this long-drawn denunciation is directed chiefly against the vulgar crowd of Martinist and Eldertonian pamphlets, it will be found, on closer examination, that such an assumption is too narrow.

Their explanation of this barbarism and their sugges-tion for its cure are not less clearly stated. ' Marry,' says Sidney, ' they that delight in Poesy itself should seek to know what they do, and how they do. . . . A Poet no industry can make, if his own genius be not carried unto it. . . . Yet confess I always that as the fertilest ground must be manured, so must the highest flying wit have a Daedalus to guide him. That Daedalus, they say, both in this and in other, hath three wings to bear itself up into the air of due commendation : that is, Art, Imitation, and Exercise. But these, neither arti-ficial rules nor imitative patterns, we much cumber our-selves withal[6].' Classicists like Harvey plead for the bringing of our language ' into Art[7],' and protest that ' right artificiality is not mad-brained, or ridiculous, or absurd, or blasphemous, or monstrous[8].' Webbe is con-

---

[1] i. 227.   [2] ii. 388.   [3] Ed. Grosart, i. ll. 227, 239, 446-9.
[4] Ibid. i. p. 53.   [5] i. 246.   [6] i. 195.   [7] i. 102.   [8] ii. 234.

vinced that cure is possible, and that reformation can come only when English literature is freed from the 'cankered enmity of curious custom[1].' With Puttenham Poetry must be 'corrected and reformed by discreet judgments,' and with no less cunning and curiosity than Greek and Latin. To disallow this improvement in the most ancient of arts is but to admit that Adam and Eve's aprons were the gayest garments, and the shepherd's tent the best housing[2]. Poetry, he believes, may be an Art in our vulgar, and that very methodical and commendable : indeed, the whole aim of the author of the *Arte of English Poesie* is to bring order into the literary chaos, and to show, in Nash's words, 'what an obloquy these impudent incipients in Arts are unto Art[3].' In the 'rabblement' of English the critics see a cause why Poetry is in disrepute, and why their general defence, which they feel to be somewhat of a supererogation, is justified. But they do not rest there. Their confidence that all will yet be well with English Poetry, the immediate recognition by all groups of critics of the first signs of revival in contemporary work—a recognition which has proved to be historically just,—their enthusiasm in experiment, and their general good sense in the discussion of its results, show that the Matter of English Literature was now acknowledged to be a subject for profitable reflection. The very seriousness with which they approach the problem, and their own never-ending protests that the Essays are too haphazard and unworthy of the occasion, are symptoms of vital importance.

It is not too much to say that the intention is strongly *classical*. When ' E. K.' in his eulogy of Spenser takes upon himself to tell how the New Poet differs from most English writers, he points out that his work is 'well grounded, finely framed, and strongly trussed up together[4].' This

[1] i. 228.   [2] ii. 24.   [3] i. 334.   [4] i. 131.

is somewhat inconsistent with the accepted judgement on the author of the *Faerie Queene* (though it must be remembered that it is with the *Shepheards Calender* that the critics are chiefly concerned), but the rightness or wrongness of it is of less importance than the fact that they looked for these qualities as an explanation of superiority. In other words, what was disorder in mediaeval and contemporary literature is in Spenser changed to order. Poetry, they believe, cannot be good, unless it show the discipline of Art. This admitted, it was the function of criticism to teach that discipline, to tell lovers of poetry 'what they do, and how they do.'

Ascham appears to be the first in English to give definite expression to this doctrine in the notable passage on Εὐφυής [1], which supplied the *motif* and title to Lyly's work, and through that, as well as directly, left its mark on Elizabethan literature. The idea is of course not original [2], but the credit for its more complete expression and its introduction to English letters is undoubtedly Ascham's [3]. It must be noted that the proposition is not exclusively literary, or rather that its literary application is but part of a more comprehensive conception. For literature is to be 'well-grown,' to show the just proportions of art in subject, technique, and intention, just as the human body and the body politic are to express the ideal harmony of line and plan. The larger notion runs throughout the Essays, from Ascham's own reflections on the rude writing of men who are themselves rude [4] and his reminiscences of Cheke's conversations [5] to Puttenham's defence of his inclusion in his *Arte of Poesie* [6] of the question of decencies in general conduct.

The acknowledgement of the necessity of discipline, implied in this classical argument, gives a point of contact

---

[1] i. 1–2. [2] See infra, lxxii; i. 349. [3] See note to i. 349. [4] i. 6–7.
[5] i. 40–1. [6] See the opening sentence of chap. xxiv, ii. 181.

between the critics and their Puritan adversaries. But they approach from quite opposite directions, and their agreement is, after all, merely accidental. It is more important to note that in the acceptance of this principle we find the explanation of the strong dislike of mediaeval literature and Italian fashions, two of the most remarkable of the *idées fixes* of the Elizabethans[1]. Other causes, as we have seen, contributed to the unpopularity of the Romances : they were 'bold bawdry,' they were the amusement of abbey-lubbers, they were jingles of rhymes; but they were also the disordered product of a disordered literary age. They had no decency in proportions, no coherence of episodes. The Italian, if he could not be charged with barbarousness, was, apart from being a danger to English morals, an extravagant in his literary motives and literary forms, as he was in his dress and social habits. And the Italianate Englishman, whether a mere adventurer or an enthusiast for Italian tales and sonnets, if not always a *diavolo incarnato*, was at least bad company. It is quite clear that beyond the growing national feeling against foreign affectations in public and private life—which must have had its effect in the determination of literary taste—there was the more purely critical dislike of the licence and curiosity of Italian romanticism. The combination of these impressions, that the Middle Ages were discredited because they were barbarous and Gothic, and that the contemporary inflow of Italianate habits and ideas was no less disorderly and dangerous, supplemented by the full confidence in the sufficiency and possibilities of English, forced the critics to some immediate consideration of the cure, especially as they found ready to hand, in Renaissance literature, an apparently perfect rule of health.

It may be premised that the first endeavours towards

[1] See supra, xvi, xvii.

reform would be concerned with technical details rather than with general principles. Criticism could not begin otherwise, and a criticism which was to a great extent derived was at first attracted to the nicer points of the canon. Yet despite the attention to the things of vocabulary and prosody, it is possible to unravel the general principles which are threaded through these miscellanies, and thereafter to show how one or other of these minor problems relates itself to a larger critical purpose.

The saving quality of this incipient classicism, for so let us call it, is that it is not extreme. There is much good sense, even in the most partisan discussions on the reformation of English prosody, and in the most ample borrowings from the rules of the Italian critics. Not only is the whole matter tentative, as the historical eye cannot fail to see, but it is acknowledged to be so by the essayists themselves. They have a genuine conviction of their inefficiency, and though they play with dogma, which in the immediate future became the creed of a militant criticism, they seldom forget that they cannot claim to be more than experimenters. 'God help us,' says Harvey to Spenser, after recitation of a set of 'pawlting bungrely' verses, 'you and I are wisely employed (are we not?) when our pen and ink, and time and wit, and all runneth away in this goodly yonkerly vein : as if the world had nothing else for us to do, or we were born to be the only Nonproficients and Nihilagents of the world[1].' So far as the critics are minded to expound the classical reform of English, they are content to prove its necessity rather than to be dictatorial in defining a new body of laws. 'And that is enough for me,' says Puttenham, 'seeking but to fashion an art, and not to finish it : which time only and custom have authority to do[2].' The moderation of the Elizabethan view is the more remarkable, since it was

[1] i. 116.   [2] ii. 130.

held that the time had come to English when she must prove that she can match the greatness of Greece and Rome, and not less clearly admitted that in these rivals were to be found the alpha and omega of literary perfection.

The classical quality of Elizabethan criticism is disclosed in its main theses that English literature must improve itself by attention to suitable models, and that the most absolute matters for consideration are restraint and symmetry. The necessity of studying and imitating the masterpieces begins with Ascham's plea in his *Scholemaster*. His memorable account of a conversation with Cheke[1] defines the character of the new discipline. The ' ancients ' offer ' experience,' which cannot but be useful to a youthful vernacular: but there is to be no blind imitation of them, and certainly no superficial copy of what is after all but mannerism. Writing is not to be 'more Art than nature and more labour than Art[2],' for a writer's uncontented care to write better than he can is as hateful as disorder. This qualification is but the general expression of that dislike of unnatural effort which they found grown to such enormity in the archaic, inkhorn, and over-sea affectations of the age[3]. Imitation must be reasonable[4]; it is a training of the judgement, for writers must not be common porters and carriers[5]; there is in this doctrine no shackling of the wit, no hindering of the course of a man's good nature[6]. Rome herself had her 'unmeasurable confluence of scribblers[7].' In all this there is good sense, and it was well for the future that Cheke and Ascham, who gave the password to their contemporaries, had put it so. Harvey, though he knows the value of a 'good pattern' to the Poet[8], shows not less clearly than they do that the adaptation of Method must

[1] i. 40, &c.   [2] i. 40.   [3] See infra, lv et seq.   [4] i. 9-10.
[5] i. 19.   [6] i. 10.   [7] ii. 363.   [8] i. 109.

proceed with a lively knowledge of its propriety to the case in hand, and that the vitality of the model, and not its mere *corpus*, must be transferred to the canvas. 'He must not dream of perfection that improveth not the perfectest Art with the most perfect industry[1].' 'Perfect use worketh masteries . . . : singular practice [is] the only singular and admirable workman of the world[2].' There is no mistaking the deep purpose of this classical appeal : it is at bottom that English may draw upon the life and spirit of the great things of antiquity, not that she should become the ape of Greece and Rome, simply because she is heartily sick of her present confusion. When Chapman sees in Homer a means to the absolute redress of all the unmanly degeneracies of his age, he is thinking only of the direct vigour and free soul of the old poet which will cure the fantasies of a transposed and Italianate England[3]. And though Campion rather spoiled by bad logic his excellent aphorism that the world is made by symmetry and proportion[4], his error was confined to the technical details of prosody. The critics had convinced themselves that symmetry and proportion must be the corner-stones of the new edifice : they saw how Greece and Rome had builded. So far they were wise : but they were wiser in refusing to be mere copyists.

The essayists are explicit on this point. Indeed, there is nothing which is so often and so strenuously urged throughout these pages than their repugnance to a rigid classical canon. They are suspicious of 'ram's-horn rules of direction[5],' of a 'rabble of scholastical precepts[6],' of 'strict and regular forms[7],' of the cumber of 'artificial rules and imitative patterns[8].' Even in the narrower problem of the reformed versifying we find Harvey disclaiming any intention to lay down a general Art[9]: and

---

[1] ii. 237.   [2] ii. 236.   [3] ii. 302-3.   [4] ii. 329.   [5] i. 336.
[6] ii. 176.   [7] ii. 393.   [8] i. 195.   [9] i. 103, 122.

Stanyhurst[1] and King James VI[2] are against a final judgement. Daniel, who perhaps reaches deepest to the philosophical bases of criticism, enters a general caveat against arrogance, and draws attention to the 'unnecessary intrications' which confound the understanding—'as if Art were ordained to afflict Nature[3].' So open-minded is this defender of rhyme against the attacks by one of its happiest exponents, that he can admit that it should be used with great moderation. He sees that the tyranny of licence may be as great as the tyranny of a code[4].

If the main interest of this criticism is that it is classical, whether as a preliminary symptom of later academic theory or as an instrument for the reform of contemporary literature, we must note that, taken in its most general bearings, this criticism is as yet quite unprejudiced. In other words, we should have had no reason to assume, had we been ignorant of later history, that the forces of classicism were destined to become paramount. On the other hand, our knowledge of later developments makes it clear that we have in these propositions the true awakening of the classical spirit in English literature. And it is only when we have searched these beginnings and the work of the neglected successors of these essayists in the first half of the seventeenth century that we find ourselves in a position to interpret aright Johnson's dictum that Dryden is the Father of English Criticism. Then, and then only, do we know how much Dryden and his age drew from later continental sources through French channels, and how much from earlier English critical tradition, however or whenever his Elizabethan masters had been themselves inspired[5].

Though the classical quality of these Essays is sug-

---

[1] i. 144.   [2] i. 210.   [3] ii. 365.
[4] See infra, 'Romantic Qualities,' p. lx et seq.
[5] It is probably more than a coincidence that makes the questions of

gested rather than carefully defined, it is none the less
true that, even in their brief compass, some progression
in its application may be observed. Jonson's criticism
is not Sidney's, nor is it Ascham's : and the difference
between these must be expressed in terms of a greater
or less classical intention. Jonson marks the close of
the first stage ; but the full statement of his position
is outside the scope of these volumes, and more fitly
belongs to Jacobean and Caroline criticism, to which it
is the natural introduction.

While therefore the leading propositions of Elizabethan
criticism are classical only in a general sense, there are
certain special problems in which, through the heat of
controversy or the narrow area of argument, the classical
character is thrown into stronger relief. These discussions have a value of their own, for though their relation
to fundamental principles was not readily, if at all, recognized, and though some, such as the question of the
hexameter, could not but be of passing interest, they represent the laboratory experience of independent workers
in a young science.

V. The Special Problems.

1. *Decorum.*

One of the most persistent topics is the adjustment of
the classical notion of *Decorum* to English style. It
recurs in the discussion of almost every 'kind,' but chiefly
of the dramatic forms. In its most general acceptation it
is identical with what has been understood by proportion,
'decency,' the truly euphuistic, or, as Puttenham puts

'Barbarism,' 'Monosyllables,' and 'Prosody' interesting to Dryden in
his *Discourse concerning the Original and Progress of Satire,* his *Dedication
of the Aeneis,* and his Preface to *Albion and Albanius* ; and, later, to
Shaftesbury in his *Advice to an Author.*

it excellently in his chapter on this subject [1], 'the good grace of everything in his kind.' 'We in our vulgar,' he says, 'call it by a scholastical term *decency*; our own Saxon English term is *seemliness*. . . .: we call it also *comeliness*, for (so runs Puttenham's philology) the delight it bringeth coming towards us, and to that purpose may be called *pleasant approach* [2].' In an earlier chapter he points out the necessity of style being fashioned to the matter, so that '*decorum* and good proportion' be kept in every respect [3]. This notion appears in nearly all the Essays. Ascham shows its importance in his scheme of perfect imitation of classical authors [4]; Gascoigne sees its breach in the mingling of merry jests in serious matter [5]; 'E. K.' notes its due observance in the construction and details of the *Shepheards Calender* [6], as Stanyhurst does in the *Aeneid* [7]; and Puttenham fails to find it in parts of Stanyhurst's translation [8]. It is intended in King James's plea for *vocabula artis* [9]. The term is of course not understood in the modern restricted sense. Harington defends the naughty passages in Ariosto at the expense of Virgil, and shows that there may be *decorum* 'in the persons of those that speak lasciviously [10].' All are but re-expressing the Horatian maxims, either directly or through media such as Fabricius's *Catholica*, which Webbe has translated [11].

As a problem of dramatic style it assumes greater importance, and is the common element in the varied discussions on the character and *differentia* of tragedy and comedy, on the mixed tragi-comedy, on the doctrine of the Unities, on the development of the notion of the Humours. The main charge against contemporary stage-craft, in the few places where the critics refer to the

---

[1] ii. 173, et seq.   [2] ii. 174.   [3] i. 155.   [4] i. 23.   [5] i. 48.
[6] i. 128.   [7] i. 137.   [8] ii. 178.   [9] i. 218.
[10] ii. 215.   [11] i. 290, &c.

romantic drama, is its lack of *decorum* in one or more
ways; and the attempts at positive criticism of the
English examples of the classical type are concerned
with the exposition of their observance or neglect of
'true decency.' Robert Wilmot exactly expresses the
critical attitude in the Address prefixed to *Tancred and
Gismund* (1591), where he warns his Gismund not to
'straggle in her plumes abroad, but to contain herself
within the walls of your house; so I am sure she shall
be safe from the tragedian tyrants of our time.' Gascoigne, who for *decorum's* sake divided his *Discourse of
Promos and Cassandra* into two comedies[1], shows how the
Englishman in his play-making is 'out of order'; Sidney
follows suit[2]; and Jonson condemns these 'ill customs of
the age[3],' as he does later its 'scenical strutting and
furious vociferation[4].'

The criticism of the mixed kinds of Drama is the effect
of a double set of influences—classical example, enforced
by the definitions of the Renaissance commentators, and
distrust of the contemporary Romantic Drama in England.
The domination of the former is first indicated by Ascham,
who bases his judgement of the excellence of plays on the
'precepts' of Aristotle and Horace and the examples of
Euripides, Sophocles, and Seneca[5]; but it receives its
fuller acknowledgement from Sidney, who may be said
to be the first to enuntiate the formulae of Elizabethan
dramatic criticism. He and his contemporaries, excepting Ascham, are in their views on tragedy more
exclusively Aristotelian and Senecan: for comedy their
models are Plautus and Terence or the Terentian
Scholia. The hard-and-fast distinction between tragedy
and comedy, which is a Renaissance tradition, appears

[1] i. 58.   [2] i. 199.
[3] ii. 389. For other references, see notes to this and the preceding
passages.   [4] *Discoveries*, lxv, '*Ingeniorum Discrimina.*'   [5] i. 23.

in the definitions given in Webbe and Puttenham, and is
suggested in Sidney. It is probably unnecessary here to
restate these well-known differences, especially as the
texts are quite explicit [1], but it is important to note that
the rigidity of these canons, as incorporated in the English
ars poetica, was one of the main causes of the not less
rigid censure of English dramatic practice. The objections which came most naturally to the classicists were
that English was not careful in its differentiation of kinds,
that it mixed the tragic and comic purposes, that it neglected the propriety of the characters and the relationship of each with its neighbours, and that it was careless
of the so-called Unities in the development of the plot.
It is interesting to observe that this criticism is to
some extent an academic anticipation of what became
later a practical problem to English dramatists in the
Comedy of Humours, and in the Rules of the Dramatic
Unities. Indeed, all the later classical manner, as all
this Elizabethan criticism, was based on a more or less
acute appreciation of the virtues of *decorum*. Sidney is
somewhat inconsistent in his argument against mixed
kinds, for he says in one passage that 'if severed they
be good, the conjunction cannot be hurtful [2]'; but it is
easy to see from his later utterances, despite a certain
romantic predisposition, hinted rather than expressed, that
his sense of literary decency is jarred by the matching of
hornpipes and funerals, and by the intrusion of the clownish element in the so-called tragi-comedy. There is a
suspicion in his case that it is less a reasoned objection
against the combination of the different elements than
a courtly dislike of the vulgar buffoon *per se* and of
the vulgar associations of the contemporary stage. He

---

[1] See Spingarn, *Lit. Crit.*, pp. 283-90; H. Symmes, *Les Débuts de la Critique Dramatique*, &c., Paris, 1903, passim; and infra, i. pp. 391-2, 398-400, &c.   [2] i. 174.

more readily disapproves these forms because they do not appear to be countenanced in the statelier drama and more learned criticism to which he is of necessity attracted. In his pronouncement on the Unities, the neglect of which is his chief fault with the well-esteemed *Gorboduc*, he formulates a doctrine which, though disregarded by the Elizabethan Romantic Drama, passed into English criticism, and is always present, in a more or less definite way, in the later history of that criticism. The fruit of the doctrine which required *decorum* in character came early in the Humorous Comedy of Ben Jonson, and lingered for a time in the seventeenth century[1]. It too, though discredited by later playwrights, has never lost its influence in later criticism, even outside the more strictly classical eighteenth century.

In the other literary forms Elizabethan criticism finds small opportunity: but in so far as it defines or ventures on commentary it is essentially classical. Thus in the references to Heroic Poetry, such as are given by Sidney, Webbe, Puttenham, Harington, and Campion, there is the restatement, at second or third hand, and probably without knowledge of the source, that it is 'the most accomplished kind of Poetry,' i.e. στασιμώτατον καὶ ὀγκωδέστατον[2]. But Harington goes further and makes the first contact between English criticism and Aristotle on this topic. He is not content in his panegyric of Ariosto with the expected comparison with Virgil, in which Ariosto would have had the better of the Roman, but he meets those who 'reduce all heroical poems unto the method of Homer and certain precepts of Aristotle' by showing how Ariosto fulfils every requirement. With regard to the latter he is quite certain. 'As for Aristotle's rules, I take it he hath followed them very strictly[3]': and he proceeds to prove this by Ariosto's

---

[1] See note, ii. p. 462.
[2] See notes, ii. pp. 43 (l. 21), 338 (l. 2).   [3] ii. 216.

attention to three things, the historical basis, the credibility of the narrative, and the περιπέτεια[1]. Yet the main interest of Heroic Poetry to these defenders of Poetry is that it offers a standing refutation of the charge of wantonness, for 'of all kind of poesy the heroical is least infected therewith[2].' It at least satisfied the broader claims of *decorum*. It was left to a later period of English criticism, to Dryden and his age, to feel the professional classical influence of Le Bossu, Rapin, and the French specialists in epical theory. The comments on the Pastoral, Elegy, Lyric, Satire, Epigram, and other kinds are slight, and are, especially in Sidney's *Apologie* and the more formal *artes poeticae* of Webbe and Puttenham, a mere echo of Latin and neo-Latin opinion. When Webbe gives his list, he appears to be not less concerned to illustrate his view that 'Poetry is not debarred from any matter which may be expressed by pen or speech[3]' than to discuss the differences of the kinds.

It is, however, in the discussions of problems of even more detailed and technical interest that the real force of the classical influence is felt. These arguments are concerned with two main topics, the reconstruction of English Prosody—the 'reform of English versifying,' as the pioneers of the Areopagus called it, and the purification of English from archaism, inkhornism, and over-sea affectation.

2. *Prosody.*

No subject obtrudes itself more than Prosody. Even in the Essays which are not intended to be exclusively interested in it, there are continual references and digressions to some part of it, and in especial to the establishment of the so-called Hexameter. This matter is indeed an obsession of the Elizabethan mind; and in it we find the most positive evidence of a classicizing purpose. It

[1] ii. 216.   [2] ii. 209.   [3] Supra, p. xxx and note.

is confessed that here, if anywhere, something must be done by way of reform, and it is as readily taken for granted by the greater number of the writers that something can be done. Their grievances were more patent. To them the older verse, Chaucer's excepted, was poor enough, and the Eldertonian doggerel plentiful enough: and the revel of even the better poets in Italian stanzas was the despair of the least censorious. The cure was at hand, though the measure of its success on the continent was not considered in the hurry to stay the spasms of ingenuity[1] and restore English to prosodic *decorum*. Not the least remarkable feature of this special controversy, and of the poets' experimental interest in it, is its brief life, which begins and ends within the limits of these volumes. When Daniel struck his blow the craze was at the point of death, for Campion, who incited Daniel, was a belated theorist; and the curious preface to the *First Booke of the Preservation of King Henry the VII*[2] is the enthusiasm of a monomaniac out of touch with the times. The effects of the discussion continued to be felt, and may be seen in later experiments in better though not less inappropriate hexameters, down to our own day: but the problem over which the Elizabethans fought so well must be considered, both in its intention and in its specific terms, as a strictly Elizabethan matter—an episode in critical development which derives its meaning from Elizabethan conditions.

The proposition of the classicists resolved itself into three parts: that the metrical chaos was due largely to the use of rhyme; that the accentual structure of the line ·was monotonous and should be changed for quantitative variety; and that a uniform orthography and a rule of pronunciation was necessary. They are mixed up in the different arguments of the classicists. Not a few of the writers make the discrediting of rhyme a necessary

[1] Cf. i. 224, 225.   [2] See i. pp. 377-8.

preliminary to their reform of the measures. Harvey sees the honour of the hexameter in being the 'high controller of rhymes[1].' It is not impossible that the philological confusion of rhyme and rhythm, as shown in Puttenham[2] and others, may have put some of those who honoured the hexameter in a false position towards the function of rhyme.

Ascham, in repeating Cheke's opinion, set the fashion of abuse, and he also to a great extent prescribed the terms to his successors. To them the 'rude beggarly rhyming' was a foreign thing, and the heritage of the Goths and Huns; and English poets in following it rather than the 'true versifying' of the Greeks had eaten acorns with swine, when they might have freely eaten wheaten bread amongst men[3]. There can be no doubt that much of the dislike of rhyme had been nourished by the rhyming Latin verses of the mediaeval church. Webbe[4] and Puttenham[5] say as much, and the latter, though he is by no means an opponent, recognizes the impropriety of this Gothic intrusion in Latin poetry. Moreover, as such lines were generally the 'idle invention of monastical men[6],' they were less commendable to the Renaissance temper. To a man of Harvey's turn of mind there could be no allowance, but he is less severe in his attack on rhyme than on the loose rhythm of the line; and this gives some point to Nash's taunt that he was clapped in the Fleet for a rhymer[7]. The details of the arguments for and against rhyme do not concern us in this place: all that can be said against it will be found in Campion's Essay, and all for it, and in the best possible manner, in Daniel's reply. Not a few cast side glances of reproof at rhyme, as if it were responsible for the mischief in metre; but the historical writers, and especially Puttenham, are inclined in its

[1] ii. 230.   [2] ii. 81.   [3] i. 30.   [4] i. 240.   [5] ii. 11–15.
[6] ii. 14.   [7] ii. 241.

favour. The most curious fact in the whole controversy is Spenser's and Campion's rôles as anti-rhymers. Fortunately in both cases theory was divorced from their general practice; and it is possible to make too much of Spenser's college gossip with Harvey[1], for he appears to be but half-hearted in his critical interest in their burlesque toys. Campion's attitude is, as Daniel himself hints, difficult to understand, though it is the extremeness of his special pleading rather than his demand for prosodic revision that is unintelligible. Later criticism has been seldom more superficial than when it has condemned these critical experiments as foolishness. Their value is not to be measured by the metrical illustrations which accompanied them, perhaps between jest and earnest[2]. Daniel's judgement set the matter at rest for a while: when rhyme again involves the critics, in the seventeenth century, the problem is restricted to its usefulness in one literary form. To the historical student the controversy has another and all-important interest of which the Elizabethans were quite unconscious. It does not appear to have been suggested to any one of them that in their efforts to be rid of the jingle of English metres they were working for the recognition of blank verse, and were in reality justifying it on the side of theory. They are not at fault because they had not the gift of prophecy, nor because they lacked insight in connecting their plans with the beginnings of that later triumph of English. Yet so far were they out that they did not understand Surrey's 'strange metre.' Not only did they fail to perceive how different it was from the metre of such a piece as Gascoigne's *Steele Glas*; but the stumbling Webbe thought it was written in *hexametrum epicum*[3].

The plea for the 'new versifying' shows the classical influence in a more constructive way. It follows naturally

---

[1] See i. 380 (note).   [2] i. 245.   [3] i. 283.

on the attack on rhyme, for by the law of compensation it was necessary to find some new rhythm within the line to make good the loss : and the absence of unrhymed verse, or the ignorance of the possibilities of Surrey's example, made the transition to out-and-out classicism not only probable but quite reasonable.   The first symptoms of the 'hexameter fury[1]' appear in Ascham[2], who, while admitting that the dactyl is difficult to manage in English on account of the monosyllabic richness of the language, thinks that the *carmen iambicum* may be naturalized[3]. But the impetus to the movement came from the Areopagus, of which we have a vague account in the Spenser-Harvey correspondence[4].   The inspirer of these deliberations, 'gorbellied' Archdeacon Drant, is a mere shadow to us.   It·is doubtful whether his famous 'rules' were committed to writing, and whether it was not certain of his experiments, like Thomas Watson's, rather than any critical argument, which had fired Harvey to be a reformer and had created an interest in the circle of Spenser, Sidney, and Dyer.   The earlier efforts of Ascham, Watson, and Blenerhasset (in his *Complaint of Cadwallader[5]*), are accentual hexameters, as not a few of the later examples are ; but the difference which the Areopagites, excepting Harvey, endeavoured to establish was that English verse should be quantitative.   Between Drant's system (in so far as we know it) and Harvey's there is a serious disagreement.   The first is an uncompromising imitation of classical usage, which accepts the rule of 'position' and gives absolute values to monosyllables and word-endings.   When accentuation and long quantity coincide, as they frequently do, the agreement is treated

[1] i. 315.

[2] The first known examples are his (see *Toxophilus*) : and he is the first to give the oft-quoted lines by Thomas Watson.

[3] i. 30—1.   [4] i. 87 et seq.

[5] In the *Mirror for Magistrates*.

as an accident. Harvey, on the other hand, sees
that what appears to be an accident in the system is
really an insidious proof that it cannot reckon without
accent. 'I dare swear,' he says to Spenser, '. . . that it
is not either Position, or Diphthong, or Diastole, or any
like grammar-school device that doth or can indeed
either make long or short, or increase, or diminish the
number of syllables, but only the common allowed and
received Prosody, taken up by a universal consent of
all, and continued by a general use and custom of all.
Wherein nevertheless I grant, after long advice and
diligent observation of particulars, a certain uniform
analogy and concordance being in process of time espied
out, sometime this, sometime that, hath been noted by
good wits in their analyses to fall out generally alike,
and as a man would say, regularly, in all or most
words : as Position, Diphthong, and the like : *not as first
and essential causes of this or that effect* (here lieth the
point), *but as secondary and accidental signs of this or
that quality*[1].' Harvey, therefore, though an hexametrist[2],
and the traditional standard-bearer of the faction, does not
hesitate to make certain qualifications. His conception
of the importance of accent, which was left to Puttenham
and others to develop, shows that he would be no party
to the mere 'dranting' of verses. What he appears to
have fully recognized, and this is the sum of his reform, is that something should be done to extend the
possibilities of English verse, and that the hints towards
effecting that lay to hand in classical practice : and, having
committed himself to the party which loved not rhyme,
he saw the necessity of compensating the loss by a re-
arrangement and elaboration of the rhythm. It is perhaps

---

[1] i. 120-1.
[2] See note on Nash's epithet and Harvey's acceptance of it (ii. 230,
239).

not remarkable that he and the extremer critics who
were so blind to the meaning of Surrey's experiment
did not observe that they entirely failed in practice to
secure rhythm in their hexameters, except in those places
where accent agreed with quantity. Harvey did not see
that his acute criticism of Drant's verses was perhaps not
less valid against his own. Yet, despite this limitation, he
was the truer classicist, in that he adapted rather than
adopted direct. He shows this in his subsidiary plea for
a uniform orthography, by which he hoped to exorcise the
spirits of confusion which had undone English Prosody.

Harvey's argument proved of greater force. Stanyhurst
shows his agreement in the deliberate attempt to define
orthography, and in his protest against being too 'stiffly
tied to the ordinances of the Latins[1],' though it may
be said he went somewhat further than some of the
Priscianists in his devotion to quantity[2]. Sidney reveals
but a courteous interest in the topic, and, notwithstanding
the use of quantity in his early verses in the *Arcadia*, is
not partisan in his *Apologie*. There he holds the balance
fairly, speaks kindly of both, and even shows how admir-
ably suited English is for rhyme[3]. Of Webbe, who has not
even the merit of respectable scholarship, little need be said
beyond this, that he is 'fully and certainly persuaded'
that had English submitted early to the rigid discipline of
classical quantity, it would by his time have enjoyed a
reputation with the best[4]. So fast does this Procrustes
stand for 'position' that he would that words and syllables
which do not suit 'be a little wrested[5].' He is sadly
out in his interpretation of Surrey's 'strange metre,' and
his own experiments are not in his favour. We can

---

[1] i. 141.
[2] See the paper by Mr. R. B. McKerrow in *Mod. Lang. Quart.* (v. 6)
for Stanyhurst's treatment of the accentual values of the last two feet.
[3] i. 204-5.   [4] i. 278.   [5] i. 282.

only guess that Fraunce, perhaps the most active prac-
titioner of the new versification, was on the same side,
for he has left no record of critical opinion. Yet the
domination of accent, or rather its coincidence, in his
so-called hexameters, shows that he was no Dranter:
and his heresy of 'rhythming' or rhyming [1] hexameters
must have disturbed the archdeacon. Harvey's triumph
came with Puttenham, who, while recognizing the usefulness of Latin models, is all for accent [2]. He explains his
attitude with a pretty condescension to young poets and
others who delight in novelty, and refers to the problem
that he 'may not seem by ignorance or oversight to
omit any point of subtlety.' He points out the essential
antipathies between Classical and English prosody [3], and
feels that if anything must be done it must be in the
English way of compromise. His general plan amounts
to the substitution of accent for quantity. Some minor
allowances which he offers as a sacrifice to 'position' are
the only blemishes in a thoroughly common-sense judgement. At the close of the discussion he frankly states
that he thinks them 'but vain and superstitious observations, nothing at all furthering the pleasant melody of
our English metre,' and so will say no more of them,
rather wishing 'the continuance of our old manner of
poesy [4].' Though the experiments continued, the next
critical opinion is Campion's on the eve of the dissolution
of the whole craze. He is of course chiefly concerned
with rhyme; and he holds that the classical rhythms
have been attempted with 'passing pitiful success.' He
thinks that accent must be diligently observed, 'for
chiefly by the accent in any language the true value of
the syllables is to be measured [5]'; but 'position' must be

---

[1] Not necessarily 'rhyming' in the modern sense, but showing *some*
likeness in the last syllables.   [2] ii. 117 et seq.   [3] ii. 122.
[4] ii. 134.   [5] ii. 351.

a rule [1], and we must take our syllables as we speak them, not as we write them, because our English orthography differs from our common pronunciation [2]. As far as rhythm is concerned he is hardly at variance with Puttenham; indeed, as Daniel points out, he admits that his feet are but the old English 'apparelled in foreign titles [3].' If he is aiming at anything tangible it is at equality in the reading length of the lines, and his rules to this end assume the propriety of syllabic equivalence [4]. As our period closes, the scheme in both its extremer and more elastic forms is already discredited by the critics, as it had been neglected by the great body of poets. The discussion had gradually resolved itself to the conclusion that

> 'Sweet Poesy
> Will not be clad in her supremacy
> With those strange garments (Rome's hexameters),
> As she is English; but in right prefers
> Our native robes (put on with skilful hands—
> English heroics) to those antic garlands [5].'

So the poet. And so the satirist, who wrote :—

> 'Manhood and garboils shall be chaunt "with changed feet,
> And head-strong dactyls making music meet [6]."'

And so, too, the philosopher, when the matter was ended : 'Illud reprehendendum, quod quidam antiquitatis nimium studiosi linguas modernas ad mensuras antiquas (heroïcas, elegiacas, sapphicas, etc.) traducere conati sunt ; quas ipsarum linguarum fabrica respuit, nec minus aures exhorrent. In huiusmodi rebus sensus iudicium artis praeceptis praeponendum . . . Neque vero ars est, sed artis abusus, cum illa naturam non perficiat sed pervertat [7].'

We must not, however, fail to observe that this criticism

---

[1] ii. 352.   [2] Ibid.   [3] ii. 350, 377.   [4] See MᶜKerrow, u.s., p. 12.
[5] Chapman, *The Shadow of Night* (*Hymnus in Cynthiam*, ll. 86–91).
[6] Hall, i. vi.   [7] Bacon, *De Dign. & Augm. Scient.* vi. i.

of rhyme and rhythm is touched by the shyness which characterizes all the critical work of the age. If Drant did seek to establish a tyranny, he has been badly served by history. Harvey, whom posterity would make god-father to every pedantry, and in this matter to the most ridiculous of codes, is careful to disclaim any 'general certainty[1].' 'Credit me,' he says, 'I dare give no pre-cepts nor set down any certain general art[2].' Stany-hurst tells us that his preface was written to explain his own verses, not to publish a 'directory' to the learned[3]. Puttenham gently persuades to discipline by showing the discredit of a rhymer 'that will be tied to no rules at all[4],' and, after showing the danger of inventing a new prosody and the folly of thinking that it will please every-body, proceeds to his account, only that the subject may be 'pleasantly scanned upon[5].' If the details of this con-troversy are less important to us than the general prin-ciple for which the writers strove, that general principle is in its turn of subsidiary interest in the history of criti-cism to the temper in which it was presented and handled. And here as elsewhere the Elizabethan critics showed something of the true classical spirit, not less in the manner of their argument than in their predisposition to certain lines of thought.

3. *Diction.*

The plans for the reform of the vocabulary of English poetry deal with three varieties of excess, archaism, inkhornism, and over-sea language ; that is, with the affectation of antique forms, latinized terms of Humanist study, and foreign, especially Italian, words and phrases. They may be conveniently grouped together in this place, as the critical problem involved is, despite obvious differences, fundamentally the same in all. Here, again, the

---

[1] i. 122.   [2] i. 102.   [3] i. 147.   [4] ii. 79.   [5] ii. 124.

intention is classical—a desire to restrain the curiosity
and eclecticism which had shown such scant respect
to the 'sufficiency' of English. In a sense the disease
itself was classical in origin—an attempt to bring order
and to add ornament in the transitional and dialectal
confusion of the language by borrowing from more fully
developed literatures; to do for English what the Bur-
gundian *Rhétoriqueurs* had done, with less reason, for
French. But excess was inevitable, and the English 'de-
spumation of the Latial verbocination' and the craze for
antiquity required correction. So it fell out that while
English at one stage sought to imitate the more learned
and rhetorical style of Latin and the greater vernaculars,
in the next she felt that she had but substituted one disorder for another, and that she must return to simplicity.
The first conviction of the English poet was that he must
write better than he had done; the later, that he had an
uncontented care to write better than he could [1].

The discussion of Diction [2] was due to several causes,
and was not primarily literary. The growing feeling of
nationality, which was stimulated by the dislike of Italian
influences, had already found voice in literature, and had
urged writers like the author of *Toxophilus*, for purely
patriotic reasons, to write English matters in the English
tongue for Englishmen [3]. On this there naturally followed
a defence of the mother-speech, to prove its sufficiency
as well as its right to be heard. Some of the more deliberate vindications appear to have been prompted by
continental examples, as Carew's was by Henri Estienne's [4]; or to have been suggested by the argument of
continental purists, as Harvey's was by Bembo's teaching. But the defence was not complete until there had
been a critical inquiry into the possible reasons for the
delay or undoing of the vernacular triumph. These the

[1] i. 40.   [2] Cf. Sidney, i. 201.   [3] *Toxophilus (Dedication).*   [4] ii. 444.

critics found in the outworn, outlandish, and pedantic licence of their age. The protest had been made before the appearance of the *Scholemaster*. Wilson, in the first pages of his *Arte of Rhetorique*, had reminded his reader how the philosopher Favorinus had served a youth for using words too old and strange. Cheke had told Thomas Hoby that English by ever borrowing would fain keep her house as bankrupt [1]. Ascham, despite his enthusiasm for Latin as an instrument of culture, is with them in pointing out that English must not ape foreign fashions, old or new. Mulcaster, too, loves Rome, but London better : ' I favour Italy, but England more ; I honour the Latin, but I worship the English.' And he adds : ' If we must cleave to the eldest and not the best, we should be eating acorns and wearing old Adam's pelts. But why not all in English ? I do not think that any language, be it whatsoever, is better able to utter all arguments either with more pith or greater plainness than our English tongue is [2].' Puttenham in his shrewd chapter on language [3] argues that nothing is to be added or changed in a national speech ' but by extraordinary occasions, by little and little ' ; and he gives warning of the evils which have come from preachers, schoolmasters, secretaries, merchants, and travellers [4]. To Daniel these affectations of antiquity and novelty are a deformity next to the folly of the reformed versifying [5]. Nash notes the fault of this ' overracked absonism [6].' But no one sees it more clearly than Jonson in his *Poetaster* [7]. His counsel of ' fair abstinence ' is the sum of the classicists' purpose, fittingly delivered by the greatest of their company.

It would be wrong to interpret this critical propaganda as the mere backwash of Humanism. Far from being a tired reaction after the enthusiasm of the past century, it

---

[1] i. 357. [2] *First Part of the Elementarie* (1582). [3] ii. 149.
[4] Ibid. 151, 159. [5] ii. 384. [6] ii. 242. [7] ii. 397.

was the intelligent application of the principles of classicism to the disorders which had come upon English from
different quarters.   There was, in the first place, the glut
of translations which, though they did inestimable good
to the literature and language, if only by way of exercise,
showed many serious symptoms of excess.   The 'trade of
glose or translations [1]' was so enlarged, that the charge of
insular ignorance which Hoby had brought against his
countrymen had lost its meaning.   Now Nash could wish
nothing worse to those who 'feed on nought but the crumbs
that fall from the translators' trencher' than that they be
left to the mercy of their mother-tongue [2].   To such
a pass had it come that Harington and others thought it
necessary to defend the craft of the translator.   There
was, in the second place, the remarkable interest in
Chaucer and in the pseudo-Chaucerian pieces of the
fifteenth century, of which the more aureate examples
were greedily gorged in the general hunger.   They were
at least English, and so far would escape the censure
directed against foreign influences.   Nash saw the danger
of this insidious argument, and in brave language maintained that Chaucer, had he lived, would have been
scandalized by these 'balductums'; and, further, in a brief
historical argument, that there was then no reason that
English, 'when she hath recovered her state,' should
be compelled to 'wear the robes of adversity and jet
it in her old rags [3].'   Later, Drayton showed that the
enthusiasm must be for Chaucer's genius, not for the
assumed perfection of his form :—

> 'As much as then
> The English language could express to men
> He made it do [4].'

And in the third place, there was the effect, also native

---

[1] i. 315.   [2] i. 308.   [3] ii. 242-3.   [4] *Epistle to Henry Reynolds.*

in process, of the artificial style of Euphuism. This was as alien in the eyes of the more reasonable purists as the most foreign, inkhornish, or antique affectation. Sidney, taking his metaphor from the Italianate folly, calls it a transformed and awry thing. Lyly, though he deserved, and received, full allowance for his aid in the betterment of English style, must take his share of blame with the imitators of 'his ridiculous tricks[1].' English had outgrown the youthful fervour when *Euphues* was *ipse ille*[2].

Definite as this criticism is in its exposure of the causes of disorder, and in its conviction of the 'equipollence' and individuality of English[3], it too is tempered by that fine discretion which Horace exhorted the poet to observe[4]. The writers who are most sensible of the dangers of eclecticism are just those who admit that English must be a borrower. But the poet must borrow as the translators do, or should do, by making his adornments appear natural and fitting to the tongue which receives them[5]. Gascoigne enters a caveat against strange words, but admits, as Ronsard had done, that in some places they may 'draw attentive reading[6].' Spenser's panegyrist naturally, and yet with stated reasons, is sure that ancient solemn words are a great ornament[7]. Though Sidney disapproves of the 'dictionary' method[8], he understands the proposition that English is a mingled language[9]. Chapman in defence of his translation craves Englishmen to accept his variety of new words as a compromise between 'discountryed affection' and the nakedness of ordinary table-talk[10]. And Daniel denounces foreign words not because they are altogether

[1] Drayton, *Epistle to Henry Reynolds.*   [2] ii. 243.
[3] See, in addition, i. 138, 142, 159, &c.; ii. 122, &c., 285, 297, 300, &c.   And cf. Fletcher's *Licia* and Daniel's *Cleopatra.*
[4] Cf. i. 300.   [5] Cf. ii. 296.   [6] i. 53.   [7] i. 129.   [8] i. 202.
[9] Ibid. 204.   [10] ii. 305.

bad, but because they are established free-denizens 'without a Parliament, without consent or allowance [1].' It was Peele's praise of Harington (the 'well-lettered and discreet') that he had

> ' So purely naturalized
> Strange words and made them all free-denizens [2].'

So that here again, as in the discussion on Prosody, we have not only in the direct attack but also in the tone and terms of the reformers the true expression of the classical temper.

VI. THE ROMANTIC QUALITIES.

It is not inconsistent with what has been said about the marked classical tendency in Elizabethan criticism to find hints of a contrary movement in the direction of romantic taste. In the first place, it is fair to assume that however much criticism was indifferent to the fervours of the age—by which that age has commended itself to posterity—it could not altogether escape the influence of the popular manner. And, in the second place, we are reminded that the two apparently opposite moods of Classicism and Romanticism are always found co-existing in the greatest periods and greatest writers. Indeed, if we look for a too strong antithesis, and certainly if we expect exclusiveness for the one or the other, the distinction must entirely fail as a critical instrument. It is not necessary to defend the paradox of the classicism of Shakespeare, or of the romanticism of Virgil; or to show in cases of minor importance that the 'placing' of an author or of his period may be difficult and inconclusive, and indeed that the choice of the epithet largely depends on the point of view of the critic. We have illustration of this in these essays. The persistent plea of Harvey and others that

[1] ii. 384.   [2] *Ad Maecenatem Prologus*, 1593.

custom, common usage, or 'natural instinct' must rule in
the shaping of style, is in one sense the romantic claim
for freedom from the tyranny of the canon, in another
an admission that the writer, far from enjoying individual
liberty, is conditioned by practice, which is not less
exacting than classical convention. Daniel's hearty
counsel that the world is to be suffered 'to enjoy that
which it knows and what it likes[1]' may quite reasonably be accepted by the classicists, or prove irksome
to the romanticists. Experience, another of Harvey's
favourites, commends itself to his party, because it hits
at tradition and deals with things known to, or felt by, the
poet. Experience, say the opponents, especially perfected
experience, gives the 'Ancients' and the Great Patterns
their claim upon the obedience of their successors. To
the first, it makes the individual writer and creates the
living pages of literature; to the others, it is the sum
of the past, discovered of old, and handed on by the
'classics' as the unsurpassed, perhaps unsurpassable,
expression of the wisdom of life and beauty of art. When
Harington, in his critique on Ariosto, answers certain
objections with the striking words, 'Methinks it is a sufficient defence to say Ariosto doth it[2],' what appears so
modern and aesthetic in its tone is after all but the masked
admiration of the classicist for another Homer or Virgil.
And so our signposts may be Knights or Saracens,
according as we look upon them; for much may be said
on both sides.

The unwillingness to have rigid rules, whether in the
choice of subject, in language, or in prosody, has been
already noted. The caution against interference with existing habit, against drawing Poetry by the ears[3], is not only
Sidney's and Daniel's, but the commonplace of this collection of essays. The dictum, too, that Poetry has no limita-

---

[1] ii. 363.   [2] ii. 217.   [3] i. 195.

tions, which is urged hardly less frequently, is on the side of eclecticism, though the critics may not have quite realized the fact. So much freedom is allowed to the writer that he is advised not to 'compose of seen subjects[1],' but to rely on his own invention. In a sense, this unwillingness is an effect of the classical restraint and discretion, a transference of method from literary practice to criticism *per se*, though it is in time lost when critics have made up their minds as to what is orthodoxy, and how it is to be enforced. Or it may be to some extent due to timidity or confusion in interpreting the relationship of the classical canon to English use and wont. But if there be little or no evidence of romantic bias in the call for discretion, it is otherwise when the critics condescend to discuss the reasons. Thus Puttenham says, 'Since the actions of man with their circumstances be infinite, and the world likewise replenished with many judgements, it may be a question who shall have the determination of such controversy as may arise whether this or that action or speech be decent or indecent[2].' And Daniel, who in many places speaks strongly against arrogance in judging the positive though varying virtues of 'this manifold creature man[3],' advances a step further when he admits that he dare not take upon himself to dictate to his fellows, because he holds a fixed view and thinks it right; for 'indeed there is no right in these things that are continually in a wandering motion, carried with the violence of uncertain likings, being but only the time that gives them their power[4].' Here there is no truce with either the stricter discipline, or with the good-mannered discretion of the classicist.

Daniel's remark foreshadows the modern conception of historical process in literature. There is no hint of it in the generality of Elizabethan writings, which tacitly

[1] i. 48, 220.   [2] ii. 175.   [3] ii. 367.   [4] ii. 383.

accept the restricted Mediaeval tradition or substitute for
it the not less exclusive views of the Renaissance.   There
is nothing more remarkable in the Elizabethans than their
neglect of the earlier literary conditions in England, as
bearing on the problems which interested them so much.
It was indeed more than neglect, for the reformers, and
those who had hopes of a great English revival, made it
a preliminary to their argument to abuse the lack-learning
times, and on every occasion to scoff at the Amadises and
Arthurs.   Sidney, in notable exception to Ascham and his
friends, shows a genuine, though reserved, appreciation
of Romance, but he does not make any effort to justify
his catholicity.   And Puttenham, who in one place appears
to think kindly of the old stuff[1], is neither acute nor consistent, and is perhaps thinking most of his own historical
ditty.   There is a hint of the later attitude in Blenerhasset's
Epistle in the Second Part of the *Mirror for Magistrates*,
where he excuses his style by pointing out that those
whose falls he has described lived not 'of late time,'
and that he had not thought it decent 'that the men
of the old world should speak with so garnished a style,
as they of the latter time[2].'   We have here the superior
manner of Renaissance criticism, but there is also the
confession that ages differ, and that each has its own
mode.   And the importance of this allowance is not
diminished, although his attitude may be reasonably explained as the application of the classical doctrine of
decorum in the representation of different times as in
that of different characters.   In Daniel, however, the expression of the modern idea is, for the first time in
English, unequivocal.   His apology for the Middle Ages
and his demurrer to the infallibility of Latin are a direct
retort to the classicists.   As different conceptions of
wisdom throughout the world are but one, 'apparelled

[1] ii. 44 ; contrast ii. 15. 87, 166.   [2] Haslewood, i. 349.

according to the fashion of every nation [1],' so the tastes
of different ages but express 'that perpetual revolution
which we see to be in all things that never remain
the same [2].' He speaks of this continuity as 'the law of
time [3],' and sees in its process the passing of all things—
including Campion's craze against rhyme. What matters
it, when this 'will make all that for which we now contend
Nothing'? There is more in this than in Puttenham's
commonplace that all old things soon wax stale [4]; it
is, as it were, the exaltation of fate and the refutation of
finality in Art. The practical application therefore is, to
the artist, that he shall take such opportunity as comes by
mood rather than by convention; and to the critic, that he
shall not arrogantly find perfection in one phase of artistic
experience. Daniel is but further expounding this larger
doctrine when he brings home the difficulty of finding the
true perspective of an age which shall stand the test when
'after-times shall make a quest of inquiry [5].' If it be
claimed for this historical sense, which is the flower of
Elizabethan criticism, that it is but the perception of a
larger unity, and the extension of the old bounds, and
is therefore nothing more nor less than a transcendent
classicism, we must bear in mind that it shows the building
up of the whole by its parts, not the illustration of that
unity by certain forms and works. The Renaissance
allowed little to the individual except in his relationship to the general principle which it had accepted; here
criticism accepted the individual works on their own merits,
and thereafter based its conception of unity and continuity
on the evidence of their essential qualities. Daniel's essay,
even considered in the narrowest sense of re-establishing
the literary credit of the Middle Ages, was an important
document on the side of romanticism.

The Renaissance individualism which stimulated this

---

[1] ii. 372.   [2] ii. 384.   [3] Ibid.   [4] ii. 166.   [5] ii. 380.

sense by giving to each age, or literary kind, or writer, the consideration which it accorded to each *man*, shows other immediate effects in the critical work of the time. And these further illustrate the coincidence of classical and romantic purpose, to which reference has already been made. For the plea, as expressed by Puttenham, that criticism shall give 'special regard to all circumstances of the person, place, time, cause, and purpose [1],' or by Chapman, that 'the whole drift, weight, and height' of a poet's works shall be set before the 'apprehensive eyes of his judge [2],' is a classical conception, at base but the familiar *decorum* ; and it is here applied to criticism *per se*, as it was later, and with fuller meaning, by Dryden, Pope, and Johnson. But it also meant the recognition of individual workmanship, and the giving of fair treatment even to inferior writers [3]. In other words, it broke with the Renaissance habit of judging works only as part of a system or as examples of a certain kind.

There could be as yet but little aesthetic criticism in the modern acceptation of the term; but there are hints of it in the claim by the critics for a freer expression of their personal liking. Puttenham speaks of his 'singular opinion [4],' and admits that it may be disputed. Chapman says that his chief pleasure of his labours is in his own profit, and that he does not tremble before the feverish censure of a 'young prejudicate or castigatory brain [5].' Daniel's 'own ease' is his guide in certain questions. Yet he and the others admit that though such are their own conclusions, they may not be commendable to others. 'I must not out of mine own daintiness condemn this kind of writing, which peradventure to another may seem most delightful [6].' This then is more than unwillingness to accept the authority of a

---

[1] ii. 161.   [2] ii. 299.   [3] ii. 282.   [4] ii. 126.
[5] ii. 306.   [6] ii. 382.

body of rules: it grants the reasonableness of individual criticism, and by allowing that criticism may be based on impression, whether fixed or tentative, hits at the heart of convention. Jonson, as a classicist, saw the danger of this unloosing in the insidious working of the pathetic fallacy[1]; but the tendency made for critical sympathy, and was not without good influence in the strictest age of classical orthodoxy.

VII. The Critical Temper.

In this period, in which Criticism first claims, or is preparing to claim, the right to be recognized as a 'kind' in English letters, the method, tone, and craftsmanship of the critic are hardly less important than the general principles by which he is guided. It might not be too much to say that it is by reason of these qualities that this *olla* of treatise, preface, and letter deserves the name of criticism in the accepted sense. For it is clear that such general questions as the origin of poetry, or its defence, or the respective advantages of a classical or romantic theory of Art, may remain entirely academic, and may neither help nor harm the critic in his efforts to interpret individual genius or record his impressions of a literary group. The additional interest of these essays, therefore, is that in them we have the first hints in English of the Critical Temper.

The evidence of this is scattered; and there are many passages and points of views which on analysis must lose their apparent claims to novelty in this respect. This is especially true of the judgements on Classical and Renaissance writers. With perhaps the exception of Cheke's ingenious explanation of Sallust's style[2], or Chapman's assault on Scaliger[3], nothing is said in appreciation of the gods of the Old and the New Rome which had not been

---

[1] ii. 396.　　　[2] i. 40.　　　[3] ii. 301.

said before, or might have been said. The historical sketches of classical literature by Sidney, or Webbe, or Puttenham, or even Jonson, are but shreds of Horatian tradition or patchwork of Renaissance commentary. In their references to the later material, down even to their own time, the critics wield the weapons and give the cries of the Aristotelian and Ciceronian wars of the previous century. Harvey's panegyric on Petrarch is but a heap of epithetic scrap-iron ; Harington's special pleading for Ariosto at the expense of Virgil discloses little more than the wisdom of Renaissance commonplace.

When we come to their treatment of contemporaries, there are signs of vitality, though they are occasional, and appear in a phrase here and there rather than in the complete argument. It may not be difficult to see that at times the purpose and method of these references to writers of their day have been suggested by such Renaissance models as Scaliger or Lilius Gyraldus, or have been devised as the appropriate retort to the Puritan attack ; yet their frequency is a new and noteworthy feature. Jonson, himself a ready censurer and gossip on fellow-authors, drew attention, a few years later, to these ' running judgements upon poetry and poets[1].' That they were in the main preposterous, as Jonson holds, does not lessen the historical importance of the activity of such early experiment. It may be said that the heat of controversy which gave the critics their opportunity, did not at the same time give them a keener judicial faculty. Their praise and blame, their descriptions and groupings, appear in the false relief which is familiar in the argument of the special pleader. They cite and quote to prove or illustrate some definite thesis ; less frequently do they attempt to give an independent appreciation. Thus there is a certain historical value in the lucubrations of Lodge on

---

[1] *Discoveries*, lxiii, ' *Censura de Poetis.*'

Gosson, Stanyhurst on Phaer, Harvey on Nash, or Nash on Kyd, which may or may not be negligible in a later critical estimate of Gosson, Phaer, Nash, or Kyd. Occasionally, as in the uniform correctness of their judgement of Spenser, they have anticipated the verdict of posterity ; but it is no disrespect to either the intelligence or humanity of any of them to say that their opinion might have been different had Spenser been less a free and uncontentious person.

Two of the more striking features of their work they owed to humanistic culture ; the one of method, the other of manner : and their chief claim to originality is shown in the way which they modified these. The former, the Comparative Method, was a choice of necessity ; but it was the surest beginning. At first an author is good or bad according as he stands comparison with some accepted pattern ; English is a noble and self-sufficing language because it is as rich and subtle as other honoured vernaculars ; English prosody is at fault because it does not carry the Latin measures. This is but the humanistic pitting of the one against the other, without due consideration of the fairness of the encounter, or indeed of the necessity of their fighting at all. The habit was doubtless confirmed by the anthological craze of the age, and by the prevalence of the Euphuistic mood, by which accidental or far-fetched similitudes and antipathies had acquired a false importance. The extreme is found in Meres's fantastic catalogue ; there is much that appears meaningless in the more scholarly Harvey, and perhaps not less in Nash and others. But it is not difficult to see that, by some, comparison is less and less used as an instrument for shaping forth a prejudice, and more as an exercise for widening the literary horizon. Daniel, at the close, hits at the narrow scholastic method when he says : ' It is our weakness that makes us mistake or misconceive in these delineations of men the true figure of their worth. And our passion and belief is so apt to lead us beyond truth, that unless we try them by the just compass of humanity, and as they were men, we shall cast their figures in the air, when we should make their models upon earth [1].' He argues that differences between nations and individuals are of fashion rather than of degree, and that in the 'collation of writers' men rather weigh the accidents than the positive merit [2]. This is but another expression of the romantic argument for toleration; and evidence of its more direct application to critical method.

A like tendency is recognizable in the change in the tone of Elizabethan criticism. The earlier critics are not less humanist in their manner of censure than they are in their erudition. They have a fine genius for denunciation and personality, which would do credit to the noisiest of the Ciceronians. In their statement of general principles they are tolerably meek, but they show small measure of ' decency' when an opponent is to be damned. Yet scholars' quarrels have always been lively; and it is perhaps no accident, though it is not a primary cause, that as scholarship decreases in Elizabethan criticism a gentler habit begins to rule. There is of course no lack of biting speeches in the later writers, but these are to be treated on their individual merits, and as idiosyncrasies of the authors. Thus Nash's ' declamatory vein ' is Nash's own : much more so than Harvey's is his own natural rudeness, unaffected by his pedantic training and recreation. Yet it would be too fine and unprofitable a discussion to distinguish between these kinds of ' flyting.' There is poor sport for the modern in this cockpit of abuse. We feel a change when we pass from Ascham to Sidney, or from Harvey to Daniel. How much of the difference is directly due to Sidney it might be difficult to say, but it

[1] ii. 371.   [2] ii. 380.

is at least reasonable to assume that his reputation and his literary tone had some effect, else the multitudinous references to the ' Sidnaean showers of sweet discourse [1] ' have no meaning. The fact that he and Puttenham and Harington and others are courtiers—by profession, let us say—could not fail to ameliorate the harshness of the mere scholar or the Martinist, though it was on the other hand a barrier to their critical appreciation of the great work of the Bohemians. Yet mere courtliness will not explain the enthusiasm, the generous wisdom, and, above all, the absolute temper of his *Apologie*, or account for its influence on contemporaries. Nor can it have been altogether a personal quality, for in the Italian sources, from which Sidney and the others drew not a little, already something of the old harshness had been lost.

It is to be observed that this change, both in the outlook and manner of English criticism, is first associated with those whose sympathies are on the romantic side, and especially with Sidney and Daniel, the most striking exponents of that turn in taste. It is they who establish the claim of English criticism as a separate literary kind, as an instrument of power outside the craft of rhetoricians and scholars. For though it was for classical ends that this criticism was first turned to account, and though it was later by classical hands made perfect, it was by the genius of those who were least trammelled by classical tradition that it first found its cunning. There are many passages in Sidney, and more than enough in Daniel, of inspired knowledge, happy suggestion, and generous common sense, to show how far the best of the Elizabethans had wandered from the old ways, and how very near they could come to some of the best of their later successors. And in other places, in essays of less sustained power, as in Puttenham's definition of style [2], or

---

[1] Crashaw, *Wishes*.   [2] ii. 153.

Chapman's defence of Homer's 'ascential muse[1],' or in Harvey's spasms of phrase, there is no lack of critical intelligence, which more than balances all the dreary pages of the 'most threatening slashers[2]' and pedants.

VIII. The Sources.

There remains the question of origins: how much of Elizabethan criticism expresses a general tendency or deals with matters which are as English as they are Italian or French, and how much is directly drawn from foreign sources. It is of course impossible to measure the latter with accuracy, and it is easy to err in over-estimating its extent. Yet it is not the less true that Elizabethan criticism, especially on its theoretical side, shows, and to some extent admits, a considerable assimilation of argument and illustration from without. Whatever may be said of the original qualities of these essays, it is clear that their authors, like certain wits described by Jonson, usurped freely from others; but it must be put to their credit that, unlike these, they did not protest against all reading, or make a 'false vendition of their own naturals[3].' The notes will show how handsomely some of them borrowed.

We shall confine ourselves here to a general statement of that indebtedness, and in attempting to estimate its extent we shall assume that the essayists drew from one or more of three main sources, (1) from Classical canon, either directly or through the medium of the mediaeval recensions of Plato, Aristotle, Horace, and others, (2) from Italian and French criticism, Latin and vernacular, of the sixteenth century, and (3) from English writers before 1570 and from contemporaries.

It is hardly necessary to remark on the persistence of

---

[1] ii. 301.   [2] ii. 252.   [3] *Discoveries*, lxv. § 8.

classical tradition in criticism, at all stages of its history, whether in the theory of poetry or in the regulation of poetic form. The chief guides had been Plato, Aristotle, and Horace, or what passed for them at the hands of the grammarians. Of these, Plato is of least account. There is nothing in Elizabethan criticism corresponding to the influence exerted by the Platonic philosophy in the works of contemporary poets and thinkers. The all-important notion of εὐφυής is an adaptation to literature from philosophy, and, though Platonic in origin, was most probably known to the Renaissance writers and the Elizabethans through later works, such as Plutarch's *Moralia*[1]. The direct references to Plato (and their directness is sometimes disputable) are almost without exception to the passage dealing with the expulsion of poets from the commonwealth : and in these the critics more often discuss the plain question of Plato's intention[2] than his general views on the fable and the relation of poetry to philosophy, by which he appeared to conclude against the poets[3]. Though the critics strain to prove that Plato was no enemy to poetry, they show that they bear him some grudge. Sidney is careful to say that he reverences him as a philosopher[4]; and Puttenham, on his first page, challenges the 'Platonists with their Ideas[5].' Webbe's references to the Platonic explanation of rhythm[6] are unimportant. It is perhaps possible, with the aid of the Italians, to find some threads of Plato's doctrine in the Elizabethan application of the arguments in favour of the philosopher to the defence of the poet ; or in the assumption that the Platonic theory of beauty can be extended as a justification of poetry. There is certainly something

[1] See i. 349.
[2] e.g. Lodge, i. 67 ; Sidney, i. 184, and especially 190-2 ; Nash, i. 328; Hoby, i. 341; Harington, ii. 204. See infra, p. lxxix.
[3] e.g. Sidney, i. 152 ; Harington, ii. 203.
[4] i. 190.   [5] ii. 3.   [6] i. 231, 248.

Platonic in Sidney's conception of the golden world of art beyond the brazen world of nature[1]. But it would be pushing the historical method too far to explain such positions as direct borrowings, even from the Renaissance Platonists. And it would be not less extreme to connect the romantic feeling for freedom in the exercise of the imagination with any special system or dictum. If these things were originally Plato's, Plato had been absorbed in European thought; and the impulses, though first expressed by him, were, in every valid sense, each thinker's own.

With Aristotle, and especially with Horace, the case is otherwise. As formalists they more readily commended themselves to a young criticism which was concerned before everything with practical matters of form. Ascham puts it on record, that he, Cheke, and Watson, the author of *Absolon*, 'had many pleasant talks together in comparing the precepts of Aristotle and Horace *de Arte Poetica* with the examples of Euripides, Sophocles, and Seneca[2].' The passage has the additional interest of containing, as far as we know, the first allusion in English to the *Poetics*[3]. Hitherto all the Aristotelian borrowings had been from the philosophical works, the *Politics*, and the *Rhetoric*; and, indeed, for some time to come the tradition of the scholastic discipline was paramount in English letters, or at least the writers show by their allusions to the *Politics*, *Ethics*[4], and *Analytics* greater intimacy with these works. Of the ten or twelve passages in these essays which are based on the *Poetics*, only a few imply any knowledge of the text or discuss its doctrine; and nearly all of them are to be found in Sidney's *Apologie*, in which the *Poetics*

[1] i. 156.   [2] i. 23.

[3] The recovery of the *Poetics* in Italy, France, and England inaugurated the critical reputation of Aristotle, just at the time when his long-established authority in philosophy was on the decline.

[4] e.g. Sidney, i. 161, 20 (note).

takes its place in the list of literary testimonies in favour
of poetry [1]. They refer to the commonplace on μίμησις [2],
to the comparison of poetry with history [3], to the Unity
of Time [4], and to τὸ γελοῖον [5]. But there is a suspicion
even in these that Sidney had reached Aristotelian theory
in a roundabout way—a suspicion which is confirmed by
other vague and unauthenticated references [6], and is but
slightly removed by his recommendation in his correspondence that Aristotle should be studied in the original [7].
The passage on the ' Unity of Time,' for example, derives
its importance from its relationship to recent Italian views
rather than to the original [8]. Of the other writers, Harington, who owes so much to Sidney, merely alludes to
μίμησις [9], and to the fable [10], though he elsewhere speaks
approvingly of 'Aristotle and the best censurers of Poetry [11].'
Webbe's allusions are accidental, and as valueless as his
references to Plato [12]. Puttenham refers to Aristotle thrice,
but does not seem to have known the *Poetics* ; and Daniel
makes mention at second-hand of some Latin account of
Aristotle's views on rhythm [13]. There are but few traces
of other Greek critics in the Essays. Demetrius Pha-
lereus and Dionysius of Halicarnassus are known to
Ascham, and possibly to Puttenham, whose strangely
mixed list of points of ' good utterance ' would appear to
be based upon them, though perhaps indirectly [14]. From
Longinus little or nothing has been borrowed.

The vitality of Horatian tradition in late classical and
mediaeval times, and especially throughout the Renais-

---

[1] i. 192.   [2] i. 158, 173.   [3] i. 167.
[4] i. 197.   [5] i. 200.   [6] e.g. i. 206.   See note.
[7] Ed. Pears, pp. 28, 195, 208.

[8] See note to i. 398. Yet Sidney has the credit, however much he
may have drawn from Scaliger and others, of infusing the Aristotelian
elements into English criticism, especially on the dramatic side.

[9] ii. 200.   [10] ii. 203.   [11] ii. 216.   [12] i. 231, 236, 248.
[13] ii. 360.   [14] See note to ii. p. 162, l. 4, &c.

sance, is one of the most remarkable facts of literary history. An essentially derivative criticism such as the Elizabethan could not but draw freely from this storehouse ; and it did so from the first, before it had acquired anything from Aristotle, directly or indirectly. The Horatian notion of the original function of the poet as the legislator and *vates* commended itself to the English mind, and would have done so hardly less easily had there been no predisposing cause in mediaeval and Renaissance habit. Horace, too, in his body of general rules, met the taste and practical needs of the defenders of poetry ; Aristotle, in a sense a new acquaintance, offered theory and canon for the drama, which was but one of their interests, and not the most important. The debt to Horace is certainly greater than would appear at the first estimate, for much that stands to the credit of Aristotle and others is really his, or is at least Horatian. The *Ars Poetica* had usurped the place of mentor, not only to many who would write poetry, but to all who would write about it. Though the direct references in these essays to it or its author are not frequent, and though Webbe's inclusion in his *Discourse* of a complete translation of Fabricius's *vademecum*[1] is an exceptional proof of enthusiasm by one of the least scholarly of the critics, there is no lack of borrowing of Horatian doctrine and rule, not to speak of innumerable tags of quotation in Latin. But the matter need not be laboured further ; and the many references in the Notes may be accepted as evidence.

The critical influence of Cicero and Quintilian was, as might be expected, confined almost exclusively to rhetorical matters. When it is found outside these, it is merely illustrative or analogical ; that is, it occasionally applies arguments in favour of poetry which were familiar in the Rhetorics. This is, however, more noticeable in the Italians,

---

[1] i. 290-301.

as in Minturno [1], than in the Elizabethans who are indebted to them. Cicero's sole claim on English, as a critic and not as the educational demi-god of the Ciceronians, is based on an error; for the credit of the definition of comedy given by Lodge [2] and others belongs to Donatus. Quintilian has some share in the genesis of the doctrine of imitation upheld by Ascham. The latter was directly inspired by Sturm [3], and by Cheke, too, we may be certain; and they, with Melanchthon and others, had well digested the chapter on imitation in the *Institutes* [4]. Though Ascham criticizes Quintilian, and even qualifies Sturm's view, which he thinks is 'far best of all [5],' he helps us to trace the genealogy of the argument. Yet Quintilian's influence was never active, then or later. The frequent quotations and allusions in the *Discoveries* prove nothing more than that the rhetorician was one of Jonson's favourites.

Plautus, Terence, and Seneca are referred to merely as models of dramatic form. Aelius Donatus, the scholiast of the second, was too well known, even to schoolboys, to escape being pilfered from by some. His characterization of comedy was a commonplace, though nobody gave him the credit of its authorship. Lodge evidently knew his tract [6], and it is plausible that not a little of what passes for older dramatic theory and history in these essays is not more ancient [7]. Plutarch, whose *Moralia* was not less popular than his *Lives*, stands sponsor for

---

[1] For example: 'Nam, ut id quoque de oratore ad poetam, ex M. Tullio in hunc locum, quemadmodum et alia non pauca transferamus, hic noster Heroicus, quem . . .,' &c. (*De Poeta*, p. 105). Cf. the application of the Platonic eulogy of the philosopher to the poet, supra.

[2] i. 81, 1, and note.   [3] i. 9.   [4] X. ii.   [5] i. 13.

[6] See notes to i. 68, 25, and 80, 7.

[7] We may go even further, though with less truth here than in the next century, and say that not a little which comes originally from Donatus was known only through Scaliger.

Simonides' metaphor of the speaking picture[1], but for little else.

Virgil is used but sparingly as a critical aid, though there is ample proof in the quotations and references that mediaeval Maronism was still a living faith, now disciplined by Humanism. When he is alluded to, it is to point a comparison with some later author; or his verses are treated as practical models by the reformers of English measures. The comparative passages, somewhat in the Macrobian vein, are of no critical value, except when Harington turns the balance in favour of Ariosto, and Chapman in favour of Homer; and there the critical interest lies, not in what they say in behalf of their literary gods, but in the one's daring so bravely for Ariosto, and in the other's trouncing Scaliger so roundly.

These classical authorities, and, we may add, the 'classics' of early patristic literature[2] are the general quarries where every man who would build his house found his stone. So far the borrowing is inevitable, and its extent cannot be satisfactorily determined. The difficulty is perhaps not less when we endeavour to estimate the debt to immediate predecessors and contemporaries. There the detective of plagiarism must carry himself with the greatest circumspection, even though it be clear that the borrowings have a more individual character and deal with narrower issues, instead of being the consensus of long-established opinion. At the same time it must be kept in mind that not a few of these appropriations, of which the writers make full confession, are of value only as indicating the personal liking, or perhaps the recent reading of the critic, and have little or no bearing on the general critical process. For example, it is easy to exaggerate the importance of Harvey's lists and

---

[1] See i. 386.   [2] Supra, xv.

interesting allusions as evidence of the debt of the Elizabethans to Italian literature ; perhaps even to overestimate
the influence of that literature on Harvey himself.

The difficulty lies in tracing the original owners of the
contents of these 'packets of pilferies,' not in proving that
they are stolen goods. Whatever objections may be taken
to the detailed evidence advanced by enthusiasts for the
Italian origin of Elizabethan criticism, there can be no
doubt as to the validity of the general contention. Its
truth will be apparent to every one who reads, more or
less carefully, the series of critical essays between Giraldi
Cintio's *Discorsi* (1554) and Castelvetro's version of
Aristotle's *Poetics* (1570). The identities and parallelisms
recorded in the notes to this collection may be taken as
merely illustrative ; they are not an adequate estimate
of the evidence in some cases. If their cumulative
strength does not bring conviction, let us admit that the
proofs have been indifferently marshalled, or but partially
stated ; or, as we incline to believe, that they are of a
kind that must be judged by general impression rather
than by painful statistics. It would be an easy matter
for the historical critic were all plagiarists, and especially
Elizabethan plagiarists, to disclose where and how they
borrowed. Yet, even if we neglect the occasional clues
which the essays themselves afford, it would be difficult to
escape the impression that they had been written with an
intimate knowledge of Italian criticism.

It may be at times a question how much of the borrowing from Italian sources is taken direct from Boccaccio's
De Genealogia Deorum or from the sixteenth-century
critics who were undoubtedly inspired by that work. Its
great popularity throughout Europe, especially between
1500 and 1600, must have established a critical tradition ;
and it is plausible to find in it, in the fourteenth and
fifteenth books, the originals of some of the propositions

which were in vogue in the later Renaissance. Thus, to give but one or two illustrations, we have an anticipation of the Agrippan argument and its answer in the chapter 'Poetas non esse mendaces,' in a second beginning 'Porro zelantes hi suasores criminum Poetas affirmant,' and in another, entitled 'Philosophorum simias minime Poetas esse[1].' So, too, the comparison of the Poet with the Historiographer[2], and the interpretation of Plato's much quoted dictum about the danger of Poetry[3], at once connect themselves with passages in Sidney's *Apologie*[4]. The assumption that Sidney not merely knew but used the book comes in one place as near as possible to proved fact[5]. Yet in whatever way future research may adjust the claims of Boccaccio and of his successors, the Elizabethan debt to Renaissance Italy will remain undisputed.

The period between Cintio and Castelvetro is but a portion of a full century of critical activity in Italy, which begins with Vida's *De Arte Poetica* (1527), but it contains nearly all the material which was used by the Elizabethans. Important as Vida was to Renaissance criticism generally, as the high-priest of *decorum*, the upholder of the Horatian canon, and the panegyrist of classical culture, he appears to have had no influence in England at this stage[6]. He is neither named nor quoted. It may be that the extremeness of his view did not readily attract the more moderate English mind, as it did Du Bellay and

---

[1] Bk. xiv. chaps. xiii, xv, xvii (Basle edition of Hervagius, 1532, pp. 369 et seqq.).

[2] ib. p. 371.   [3] ib. p. 381.   [4] Infra, i. p. 191.

[5] See note to i. p. 206, ll. 6–7. References like that to Robert of Sicily (ed. u. s., p. 385) may be the sources of some of the Elizabethan allusions.

[6] In the late seventeenth century, and especially in the eighteenth, Vida's 'honour'd brow' is reverently crowned with the 'critic's ivy.' (Cf. Pope, *Essay on Criticism*, 704.)

Vauquelin in France[1]; it is probable that he was forgotten in the crush of immediate interests. Minturno and
Scaliger barely preceded the earlier Elizabethans, and
were, with certain others, apart from any intrinsic value
or reputation, the writers who would most naturally come
under the notice of Englishmen who knew Italy and her
literature. This chronological fact, and another not less
important, that the general defence of poetry, which was
the first pressing problem of English criticism, was the
main topic with these Italians, compel us to assume that
some interconnexion was not merely possible, but almost
inevitable. It is a question whether the Elizabethans
would have been attracted by Italian criticism had their
needs not been so happily met by the Italian discussion of the general principles. The other matters dealt
with in the complex body of Italian criticism could have
had but little interest for them. Its unbounded confidence in Italian and supercilious neglect of other literatures, its business in ordering the minutiae of Italian
vocabulary and grammar, its over-elaboration of strict
classical canon were more or less outside the English
purpose. The only exception might be found in
metrical theory, which would interest the English hexa-
metrists. Yet Daniel's reference to Tolomei's treatise[2]
(1539) does not imply more than that he had heard of it,
and knew its drift. Ascham is interested in Tomitano[3],
not as a prosodist, but as a critic of the Aristotelian
logic. The various allusions to Italian prosody[4] have
but a secondary importance, and are merely illustrative

---

[1] It is possible that the accepted view that Vida exercised a strong
influence on the continent, especially in the sixteenth and seventeenth
centuries, is an exaggeration. At least it is difficult to prove it. For
beyond the testimony of Scaliger, inspired by a common enthusiasm for
Virgil, there is little of sincere discipleship.

[2] *Versi e Regole della Nuova Poesia.*   [3] i. 21, and note.

[4] As in Puttenham, ii. 73, 90, 91, 92, &c.

of the Italianate practice of contemporary English verse.
Ascham's mention of Pigna [1], though interesting evidence
of an Englishman's knowledge of one of the most original
of sixteenth-century critics, is provokingly disappointing
by its narrow concern in the Italian's views on Horace's
'golden' Epistle, Aristotle's *Rhetoric*, and the plays of
Sophocles. If any one wandered beyond the limits which
we have chosen, it is Sidney, in his reference to Cristofero
Landino [2], and perhaps in his echoes of Daniello. But the
latter [3] are merely conjectural.

After all, the more important question is not whether
Italian influence can be found in English criticism, but
why it is not more active. There were strong predisposing causes to borrow other things than an academic
defence of Poetry. Italy had for some time supplied the
models to English letters, as it had to art and music. We
know what the pastoral owed to Tasso and Guarini, or
satire to Alamanni, or the epic to Ariosto; how much
Wyatt, Surrey, Sidney, and Spenser owed in the structure of their verse; how much, in fact, of the *form* of
Elizabethan literature was defined by Italian practice.
For great as is the debt to the *matter* of Italian literature,
it is small and accidental compared with the debt to its
rules and artistic habit. The poets 'tasted the sweet
and stately *measures and style* of the Italian Poesy [4]': the
courtly ordered themselves by the etiquette of Della Casa,
Castiglione, and Guazzo [5]. The entire Italianate controversy resolves itself into a discussion of *ways* and *manner*.
Further, English by its translating fury had established
the custom of going to Italy for everything, even for learn-

---

[1] See i. 349.   [2] i. 206, and note.
[3] i. 151, 13, note; i. 164, 11-13, note.   [4] ii. 62.
[5] Note, too, that the epithetic habit of the Elizabethans, including the
critics, was most generally Italian : e. g. Harvey's 'Petrarchize,' and his
calling of Nash the 'English Aretine.' Spenser to others is the 'English Petrarch.'

ing, which it might have had direct through native scholarship. How reasonable, therefore, to assume that when
the Elizabethans turned their attention to criticism they
should look first to the literature from which they had
drawn their formal experience, and in which the principles
of the art of writing had already been fully discussed. And
it might not be less reasonable to assume that the rise and
activity of critical writing in Italy not merely defined the
content of English criticism, but was the immediate cause
of its appearance at this time. When the essayists show
an acquaintance with even the lesser-known Italian poets
and prose-writers, and refer to books like Celiano's which
had just been published[1], it is unlikely that they passed
by the critics. There was, of course, greater temptation
to be silent when plagiarizing from the latter than when
praising or damning a Tuscan poet.

This relationship to Italian may be traced in several
ways. There is, in the first place, the more specific
indebtedness to individual authors, either expressly admitted by the essayists or reasonably certain to the reader
who makes the comparison. This evidence[2] is drawn
mainly from Minturno and Scaliger, but not entirely.
Thus Daniel's statement about *Remensi*, which has disturbed his editors and tempted them to an absurd correction, is Giraldi Cintio's, and is fixed down by Daniel's
parenthesis 'as some Italians hold[3].' Sidney's explanation of the function of comedy is strangely like Trissino's[4],
as is his comparison of poetry with ethics and law like
Varchi's[5]; and there is a temptation to think that he knew
Castelvetro's opinion when he enlarged on verse's 'being

[1] i. 428.
[2] The citations on the following pages are, as stated above, merely illustrative. The index will help the reader to further references in the Notes.
[3] ii. 360, note.   [4] See note to i. 176, 30.
[5] See note to i. 163, 29; and Spingarn, *Lit. Crit.*, p. 51.

but an ornament and no cause of Poetry[1],' and that he may have been helped by that critic to his extension of the notion of the Dramatic Unities[2]. Such points are of minor importance by themselves, but they strengthen the general impression that the Elizabethan critics, and especially Sidney, were in one way or another conversant with the work of their Italian contemporaries.

In the case of Minturno and Scaliger the claim might be urged on the side of general theory alone, by the terms of the defence of poetry, the view as to its origin, and the history of its development. Minturno is not named by any of the essayists : Scaliger is frequently cited by them, and at least four times by Sidney. The contrast may be explained by the fact that Minturno was almost exclusively a critic[3], known to critics by two works, while Scaliger had already a European reputation, based on a long series of treatises, of which the *Poetice* was but a part. It was easier to draw silently from Minturno than from imperial Scaliger, a name to be conjured with even in the *Pueriles* of the schools.

Minturno's earlier work *De Poeta* (1559)[4] shows nearly all the points of contact. Harington may have his *Arte Poetica* (1564)[5] in mind when he refers to the opinion of

---

[1] See note to i. 159, 35.   [2] i. 398.

[3] He wrote verses in Latin and Italian. He is the author of *L'amore innamorato* (1559).

[4] ANTONII | SEBASTIANI MINTVRNI | DE POETA, AD HE-CTOREM | PIGNATELLVM, VIBONEN-|SIVM DVCEM, | LIBRI SEX | .. | VENETIIS, ANN. MDLIX.   4to. pp. v + 567.

[5] L'ARTE POETICA | DEL SIG. ANTONIO | MINTVRNO, | NELLA QVALE SI CONTENGONO | *i precetti Heroici, Tragici, Comici, Saty*|*r-ici, e d'ogni altra Poesia :* | CON LA DOTTRINA DE' SONETTI, CANZO-|*ni, & ogni sorte di Rime Thoscane, doue s'insegna il mo-*|*do, che tenne il Petrarca nelle sue opere.* | *Et si dichiara a' suoi luoghi tutto quel, che da Aristotele, Horatio,* | *& altri auttori Greci, e Latini è stato scritto per* | *ammaestramento di Poeti.* | CON LE POSTILLE DEL DOTTOR VAL-VASSORI, ... || *Per Gio. Andrea Valuassori del* M.D.LXIIII.   4to. x + 48 (Contents and Index) + 453 + 2 (unnumbered).

'Aristotle and the best censurers of Poesy' on the 'period' of the Epic [1]. There is less doubt about Sidney's connexion with the *De Poeta*. Almost all the references are to be found in the *Apologie*, and there in the first instance; for, as we shall see, Sidney was in turn freely copied by his English contemporaries. Yet his disciple Harington, who had stronger Italian interests than any, must have known it at first hand, if only because of the very guilty passage on 'Peripeteia' and 'Agnition [2].' The traces of Minturno are more obvious in the earlier portion of Sidney's essay, where indeed they should occur, as the portion is concerned with general doctrine and allows less opportunity for original and English matter. Of these may be mentioned the terms of his plea for the antiquity of poetry [3], and for its being found in all nations [4]; the order of the illustrative details in the passage on the works of Nature as the principal object of art [5]; the view that the poet feigns notable images of virtues and vices [6]; the criticism of the 'thorny argument' of the philosopher [7], which, though found in Daniello, probably takes its true place with the subsequent passage comparing the poet with the philosopher [8]. These and the important reference to 'Admiration [9]' are seven: the Notes will supply as many more; and others may be discoverable. It is open to any one to dispute Sidney's debt in each case, but we cannot escape the lesson of the whole body, even if they are only possibilities. A dozen possible indications of borrowing constitute the best of circumstantial evidence.

The case for Scaliger [10] is still more clear, partly be-

---

[1] See note to ii. 216, 17–18.   [2] Note to ii. 216, 18, &c.

[3] i. 151, 22. See the notes to this passage and the following for the references to Minturno's text.

[4] i. 153, 12.   [5] i. 155, 34, &c.   [6] i. 160, 13–16.

[7] i. 164, 12–13.   [8] i. 164, 25, &c.   [9] See note, i. 392.

[10] IVLII CAESARIS | SCALIGERI, VIRI | CLARISSIMI, |

cause the writers have on not a few occasions admitted
their knowledge of his treatise. It is not difficult, for
example, to see that Sidney's dramatic theory, though
Aristotelian, is derived through the medium of Scaliger,
and that his illustrations[1] and his ' lists ' are reminiscent
of the *Poetice*. Passages such as that on the poet as
maker[2], on imitation[3], on the three several kinds[4], and
on the very end of poetry[5], give point to the direct
reference in Sidney's peroration[6]. He is, by his own
admission, brought to the question of the necessity of
verse to poetry by a passage in Scaliger[7]. Webbe may
be echoing Scaliger when he points to the *Iliad* and
Odyssey as fixing the distinction of the dramatic kinds[8],
though the idea was widely diffused[9], and may have been
borrowed from Donatus. Puttenham, who had lived abroad
and refers to Italian and French matters in his *Arte*, is
distinctly Scaligerian in his general notion of poetry and
the function of the poet, and comes perilously near direct
copying in details of the more rhetorical kind ; e. g. in
his treatment of the ' figured ' verses[10], and perhaps in
his definition of *Energia* and *Enargia*[11]. Harington
refers to Scaliger's Maronism[12], a topic which gives
Chapman an opportunity for vigorous denunciation. Yet
in the latter's epithets and taunts there is something more

POETICES LIBRI SEPTEM : || I. *Historicus*. II. *Hyle*. III. *Idea*.
IV. *Parasceve*. V. *Criticus*. VI. *Hypercri-ticus*. VII. *Epinomis*. | *Ad
Sylvium Filium*. || *Apud Ioannem Crispinum* | M.D.LXI. Fol., 364 pp.
double columns + 36 pp. of Index (triple columns). The second edition
appeared in 1581 ('*Apud Petrum Santandreanum*'). The fifth, which is
now the most easily procurable, was issued in 1617 ('*In Bibliopolio Com-
meliano*').

[1] e. g. Theagines and Cariclea, i. 160, 8, note.
[2] i. 155, 26. See the notes to this passage and the others for the
references to Scaliger's text.
[3] i. 158, 5, &c.   [4] i. 158, 9.   [5] i. 197, 3.   [6] i. 206, 9-11.
[7] i. 182.   [8] i. 249. See note to i. 248, 26, &c.   [9] Cf. Puttenham.
[10] ii. 95 ; ch. xiii, note.   [11] ii. 148, 9-12, note.   [12] ii. 210, 11.

than angry froth : 'Thou soule-blind Scaliger, that neuer hadst anything *but place, time, and termes* to paint thy proficiencie in learning[1].'

The relationship may, however, be illustrated in other ways than by chapter and page in specified authors. There are certain common topics, and metaphors and phrases, and methods, which, though they cannot be ascribed to any one, were first formulated in Italian, or at least came from it to English criticism. The evergreen antithesis of the soldier and scholar[2] is an Italian commonplace, which is used to some purpose in Sidney's plea for poetry as the companion of the camps. The notion of the speaking picture, though as old as Simonides, was discovered by English critics in Renaissance Italy. So too was the culinary metaphor by which poetry is a dainty dish of divers ingredients ; and so the nursery figure of coated pills, and rhubarb and candy, which do so much for the allegorical part of the argument. And the bee which distilled honey and the spider which sucked poison, for the benefit of controversialists on the goodness or badness of poetry, were creatures of the South. We may reasonably suspect that Sidney's metaphor of the ulcer[3] discovers a trace of that Italian tradition which expresses the original medical sense of κάθαρσις. Minturno clearly leans to this view[4], though he is, with the majority of his countrymen, as with Milton in English[5], medical rather than surgical. Again, in regard to the form and literary manner, apart from the material of the essays, there are salient likenesses which are best explained by some sort of kinship. The conception of the treatise, whether 'art' or 'apology,' its ordonnance, its restriction to poetry, its

---

[1] ii. 301. [2] See note, i. 395. [3] i. 177. [4] *De Poeta*, especially p. 64.
[5] *Preface* to *Samson Agonistes*. See Mr. Bywater's article on ' Milton and the Aristotelian Definition of Tragedy' in the *Journal of Philology*, xxvii. 54 (1900), pp. 267-75.

monotony in title, give these essays a familiar look to the reader who knows the Italian predecessors, and is yet willing to make full allowance for the English quality of such a writer as Sidney. Of the mere cataloguing manner, shown at its best, or worst, in the *Palladis Tamia*, it is reasonable, and certainly generous, to think of the models supplied by Lilius Gyraldus and others. And as for the 'trade of glose,' which Nash saw to be as painfully enlarged as that of translation, it is not fantastical to find some clue in the well-strewn *postilli* and *sposizioni* of the Italian critics and poets [1]—even if we had not had 'E. K.'s frank statement that the manner then seemed 'strange and rare in our tongue [2].'

The 'filcheries' from French criticism are unimportant and would appear to be confined to the contemporary prefaces of Du Bellay and Ronsard [3]. The earlier dissertations from Deschamps to Sibilet, had they been known, would have given little to the theorists of Poetry, and would have been useless to English prosodists. Interesting as it is to find the old lines of argument on the antiquity of poetry in Sibilet [4], Pelletier [5], Fauchet [6], or De Laudun [7]; or Sidney's comparison of the poet with the orator in Pelletier [8], or his views on poets' being more than rhymers in Sibilet [9]; or to read the general defence of French against 'outlandish' and 'inkhorn' dangers such as beset English; or to be reminded in Fauchet [10] of Ascham's

---

[1] Self-commentators, like Watson in his 'Εκατομπαθία, had many patterns in the Italian poets, from the author of the *Vita Nuova* onwards.
[2] i. 132.   [3] See the bibliographical notes, i. 404.
[4] Thomas Sibilet, *Art Poetique François* (1548), I. 1.
[5] Jacques Pelletier, *L'Art Poëtique* (1555), I.
[6] Claude Fauchet, *Recueil de l'Origine de le Langue et Poesie Françoise, ryme et romans*, 1581 (*Œuvres*, 1610, p. 545).
[7] Pierre de Laudun, *L'Art Poetique François* (1598), I.
[8] u s.   [9] u. s., II. 2.   [10] u. s., pp. 548⁰, 549.

account of the origin of rhyme, or in Jean de la Taille[1] of Sidney's advance in the conception of the Dramatic Unities—nothing but parallelism can be proved, or is likely. This is perhaps remarkable, when we consider how much of French literature was known to the Elizabethans, and how even these essays show some knowledge of French authors. On the other hand, it need not be pointed out that though this fact makes French criticism of small account for our present purpose, that criticism is of the greatest importance to the comparative study of critical development. For a spontaneous parallelism in idea in two literatures may give a better clue to first principles than a parallelism which is merely, or largely, derivative. So it would appear that though the French Arts of Poetry are not very helpful in explaining the genealogy of English doctrine, their interpretative value in the study of Renaissance theory in England is not inferior to that of the Italian models. And, it may be added, this would appear to be the true lesson of the French analogies in later periods and in other 'kinds,' where direct influence, though stronger than here, has without doubt been exaggerated.

The French influence showed itself in borrowings of words, as noted by 'E. K.'[2] and Puttenham[3]—quaffings of the 'cup of Frenchman's Helicon' as the *Returne from Parnassus* has it[4]—and in certain plagiarisms of conceits and verse-forms from the literature of the *Pléiade*[5]; or it acted in the more general way of suggesting a topic, as is shown in Carew's acknowledgements to Henri Estienne[6]. The technical concern of Du Bellay and Ronsard in matters of poetic diction and metre per-

---

[1] *De l'Art de la Tragedie*, the preface to *Paul le Furieux* (1572).
[2] i. 130.   [3] ii. 171.   [4] ii. 402.
[5] See Mr. Bullen's note in *Lyrics from Elizabethan Dramatists*, 1891, p. 288.   [6] ii. 285, note.

force restricted their effect to a small part of English criticism. Indeed, if any critical debts or parallelisms are to be found we must look for them in metrical essays of the type of Gascoigne's and King James's. An agreement such as appears between Sidney[1] and Ronsard is reached independently, and most probably from Scaliger or other Italian sources.

The hard characterization of the poet by Gascoigne, and especially by James[2], is in marked contrast with the Italian view, and is strongly reminiscent of Du Bellay and Ronsard. The former is named by James in his tract, when he explains his reasons for undertaking an Art of Scots Poetry, and excuses himself for repeating second-hand observations. His seventh chapter[3], on the difference between the attitude of the translator and of the poet, may be part of his debt. Puttenham's theft from the *Defense*[4], though not of critical importance, shows at least that he was familiar with its text. The suggestions of indebtedness to Ronsard are perhaps more numerous. These may be found in the remarks on invention[5], on the musical value of the caesura[6], and on the use of 'comparisons[7].' Puttenham's reference to the metre of twelve syllables, which 'the Frenchman calleth a verse *Alexandrine*[8],' may well have come from Ronsard's chapter, 'Des vers Alexandrins' in the *Abrége*.

Great as is the debt of Elizabethan literature to Spain[9], it would appear that criticism owes nothing. Occasional references, such as Ascham's to Gonçalvo Perez's translation of Homer[10], or Puttenham's to Vargas[11], or

---

[1] i. 182, 17–18, note.   [2] See i. 211, 19–32, note.
[3] i. 221. See the notes to this and the other passages for the references to Du Bellay and Ronsard.   [4] See ii. 417.   [5] i. 47, &c.
[6] i. 54, 216.   [7] i. 219, 9 and perhaps 18.   [8] [11] ii. 75.
[9] Cf. e. g. ii. p. 440.   [10] i. 32.   [11] ii. 18.

Puttenham's and Harvey's to Guevara[1], show but a more or less direct knowledge of certain Spanish books. It could not well be otherwise, for Spanish criticism, if we exclude the older rhetorical treatises, does not begin before the close of the century, in Rengifo (1592) and Alonzo Lopez (1596); and these do not appear to have been known in England. Even the excusable suspicion that something of the Spanish dramatic heresies of the mixture of kinds and of indifference to the Unities may have affected English criticism, and perhaps Sidney himself, is dispelled when we find that the earlier Spanish examples were not yet available. All that is allowed to us is to speculate on the change of attitude which might have taken place in English dramatic criticism had chronology been other than it was.

The tale of indebtedness is not complete until we know how much the Elizabethans borrowed from each other. That it can be proved that they plagiarized may strengthen the contention that they would not be less inclined to draw from such foreign writers as were accessible ; but at the same time it compels us to guard against overestimating the extent of that draught. For it is clear that not a few of the statements, which are obviously non-English in origin, are taken from English writers who had already made them their own. We are helped to this in some places by the greater frankness of the borrowers (partly due to the growing pride in the sufficiency of English letters), and in others by the forced confession of the texts.

We have an interesting side-light on this literary habit in the frequent efforts to apportion what is, in Puttenham's words, 'as borrowed, and what as of our own peculiar[2].' It is one of 'E. K.'s commendations of Spenser that he follows the 'footing' of many poets, 'yet so as few, but

---

[1] Haslewood, p. 176; Arber, p. 220; ii. 276.   [2] ii. 26.

they be well scented, can trace him out[1].' The Sidney of
the *Apologie* can protest, as the poet lover of Stella,

> ' Some doe I heare of Poets fury tell,
> But God wot, wot not what they meane by it:
> And this I sweare by blackest brooke of hell,
> I am no Pickepurse of an others wit[2].'

Nash resents the charge that he has borrowed from
Greene, or Tarlton, or Lyly: 'the vein which I have . . .
is of my own begetting, and calls no man father in
England but myself[3].' As things went, each critic, like
each poet, might well suspect his neighbour. Harington's
preface takes a different place when we discover how
inadequately his acknowledgement to Sidney covers his
debt to the *Apologie*. Meres, obviously a dullard to the
most casual reader, discloses an editorial cunning which
does him credit, and indeed makes his *Comparative Discourse* not the least important of these documents. For by
having no mind of his own, and only a plodding interest
in the whims of others, he has given us a digest of contemporary history and opinion which is of positive value.

Not a little comes to these essayists from writers of the
earlier part of the century: notably from the different
editions of Wilson's *Arte of Rhetorique* (1553) and his
Rule of Reason, conteinyng the Art of Logique (1551),
and from Sir Thomas Elyot's *Governour* (1531)[4]. Yet
the relationship is one of general agreement rather than
of literal copying. We can see, for example, in Wilson's
view that 'eloquence itself came not up first by the art,
but the art rather was gathered upon eloquence[5]' something of his successors' dislike of a critical tyranny.
Of their own number, Ascham and Sidney are the
favourite quarries. Ascham's 'dead advertisement and

---

[1] i. 132.   [2] *Astrophel and Stella*, lxxiv. 5-8.   [3] ii. 243.
[4] e. g. i. 360, 388, 413. No influence from Coxe's earlier work on
Rhetoric (*c.* 1530) is recognizable.   [5] Fol. 3.

persuasion,' as Harvey calls it[1], in behalf of artificial
verses, is kindly remembered by the reformers. Stanyhurst cites the 'golden pamphlet entitled *The Scholemaster*' on this point[2]; and Webbe repeats its views on
the barbarous origin of rhyming[3], and incorporates at
least one passage *verbatim*[4]. Nash refers his reader to its
excellent censures on Greek and Latin authors[5]. The
debt to Sidney is greater—a fact the more striking
when we remember that the *Apologie* remained in MS.
till 1595. He is known to everybody, and cited by nearly
all, but never so greedily as by his admirer Harington[6].
Puttenham, however, is not far behind[7]. And Harington
is in turn indebted to Puttenham[8]; as James VI and
Webbe are to Gascoigne[9]. But we cannot thread this
labyrinth. The Notes will supply clues to what each
author has taken from his contemporaries. There is some
recompense in this discounting of the originality of these
essayists. It may minimize their individual value, but it at
least shows that a critical interest had arisen, and that by
it not only many, but the best of them, had been attracted.
The activity discloses, as it were, a rude concerted plan
for the recognition of the Art of Criticism as a separate
branch of English literature. It matters not how much
was copied, or how much was inappropriate to English
needs, if we acknowledge the vitality of the Elizabethan
endeavour which lies behind old argument and metaphor,
and see in these registers the genuine beginnings of
a literary 'kind' in England, and the first hints of the
true temper of English criticism.

[1] i. 101.   [2] i. 137.   [3] i. 240.   [4] i. 267.   [5] i. 337.
[6] ii. 196, and notes from p. 422 onwards.   [7] e.g. ii. 408, 410, &c.
[8] ii. 196, &c.   [9] i. 414, &c.; and see the notes to James VI's *Schort
Treatise*, i. 403 et seq.

ROGER ASCHAM

(From *The Scholemaster*)

1570

[THE First Book of *The Scholemaster* (London, John Daye: 1570) deals with 'the bringyng up of youth,' and is only incidentally concerned with matters of literary interest; but it supplies hints of certain topics which are discussed more fully elsewhere. Ascham defines the Platonic εὐφυής, the first of the seven 'trewe notes of a good witte'; he interpolates a recommendation of the new 'versifying,' on which he promises to speak 'more at large hereafter'; and, in the well-known passage on the evil influence of Italian travel and Italian books (especially in English translation), he shows his sympathy with the Puritanical principles of Gosson and the anti-stage pamphleteers. In introducing the seven 'trewe notes' he says:

'And bicause I write English, and to Englishemen, I will plainlie declare in Englishe both what thies wordes of *Plato* meane, and how aptlie they be linked and how orderlie they folow one an other.'

He then proceeds:

'Εὐφυής is he that is apte by goodnes of witte, and appliable by readines of will, to learning, hauing all other qualities of the minde and partes of the bodie, that must an other day serue learning, not trobled, mangled, and halfed, but sounde, whole, full, and hable to do their office: as, a tong, not stamering, or ouer hardlie drawing forth wordes, but plaine, and redie to deliuer the meaning of the minde; a voice, not softe, weake, piping, womannishe, but audible, stronge, and manlike; a countenance, not werishe and crabbed, but faire and cumlie; a personage, not wretched and deformed, but taule and

'goodlie: for surelie a cumlie countenance, with a goodlie
stature, geueth credit to learning, and authoritie to the
person; otherwise, commonlie, either open contempte or
priuie disfauour doth hurte, or hinder, both person and
learning. And euen as a faire stone requireth to be sette
in the finest gold with the best workmanshyp, or else it
leseth moch of the Grace and price, euen so excellencye
in learning, and namely Diuinitie, ioyned with a cumlie
personage, is a meruelous Iewell in the world. And how
can a cumlie bodie be better employed than to serue the
fairest exercise of Goddes greatest gifte, and that is learning?
But commonlie the fairest bodies ar bestowed on the foulest
purposes. I would it were not so, and with examples herein
I will not medle: yet I wishe that those shold both mynde
it and medle with it, which haue most occasion to looke to
it, as good and wise fathers shold do, and greatest authoritie
to amend it, as good and wise magistrates ought to do.
And yet I will not let openlie to lament the vnfortunate
case of learning herein.

'For, if a father haue foure sonnes, three faire and well
formed both mynde and bodie, the fourth wretched, lame,
and deformed, his choice shalbe to put the worst to learning,
as one good enoughe to becum a scholer. I haue spent the
most parte of my life in the Vniuersitie, and therfore I can
beare good witnes that many fathers commonlie do thus;
wherof I haue hard many wise, learned, and as good men
as euer I knew make great and oft complainte: a good
horseman will choise no soch colte, neither for his own
nor yet for his masters sadle.'

Further over, Ascham enlarges on the moral weakness of
Italianate Englishmen, and concludes:

'These be the inchantementes of *Circes*, brought out of
Italie, to marre mens maners in England; much by example of ill life, but more by preceptes of fonde bookes,
of late translated out of *Italian* into English, sold in
euery shop in London, commended by honest titles the
soner to corrupt honest maners, dedicated ouer boldlie
to vertuous and honorable personages the easielier to
begile simple and innocent wittes. It is pitie that those
which haue authoritie and charge to allow and dissalow

'bookes to be printed be no more circumspect herein than they are. Ten Sermons at Paules Crosse do not so moch good for mouyng men to trewe doctrine as one of those bookes do harme with inticing men to ill liuing. Yea, I say farder, those bookes tend not so moch to corrupt honest liuing as they do to subuert trewe Religion. Mo Papistes be made by your mery bookes of *Italie* than by your earnest bookes of *Louain*. And bicause our great Phisicians do winke at the matter, and make no counte of this sore, I, though not admitted one of their felowshyp, yet hauyng bene many yeares a prentice to Gods trewe Religion, and trust to continewe a poore iorney man therein all dayes of my life, for the dewtie I owe, and loue I beare, both to trewe doctrine and honest liuing, though I haue no authoritie to amend the sore my selfe, yet I will declare my good will to discouer the sore to others.

' S. Paul saith that sectes and ill opinions be the workes of the flesh and frutes of sinne : this is spoken no more trewlie for the doctrine than sensiblie for the reason. And why? For ill doinges breed ill thinkinges. And of corrupted maners spryng peruerted iudgementes. And how? There be in man two speciall thinges : Mans will, mans mynde. Where will inclineth to goodnes, the mynde is bent to troth : Where will is caried from goodnes to vanitie, the mynde is sone drawne from troth to false opinion. And so the readiest way to entangle the mynde with false doctrine is first to intice the will to wanton liuyng. Therfore, when the busie and open Papistes abroad could not, by their contentious bookes, turne men in England fast enough from troth and right iudgement in doctrine, than the sutle and secrete Papistes at home procured bawdie bookes to be translated out of the *Italian* tonge, whereby ouer many yong willes and wittes allured to wantonnes do now boldly contemne all seuere bookes that sounde to honestie and godlines. In our forefathers tyme, whan Papistrie, as a standyng poole, couered and ouerflowed all England, fewe bookes were read in our tong, sauyng certaine bookes of Cheualrie, as they sayd, for pastime and pleasure, which, as some say, were made in Monasteries, by idle Monkes or wanton Chanons: as 'one for example, *Morte Arthure*; the whole pleasure of which booke standeth in two speciall poyntes, in open mans slaughter and bold bawdrye: In which booke those be counted the noblest Knightes that do kill most men without any quarell, and commit fowlest aduoulteres by sutlest shiftes; as Sir *Launcelote*, with the wife of king *Arthure*, his master: Syr *Tristram*, with the wife of kyng *Marke*, his vncle: Syr *Lamerocke*, with the wife of king *Lote*, that was his own aunte. This is good stuffe for wise men to laughe at, or honest men to take pleasure at. Yet I know when Gods Bible was banished the Court, and *Morte Arthure* receiued into the Princes chamber. What toyes the dayly readyng of such a booke may worke in the will of a yong ientleman, or a yong mayde, that liueth welthelie and idlelie, wise men can iudge, and honest men do pitie. And yet ten *Morte Arthures* do not the tenth part so much harme as one of these bookes made in *Italie* and translated in England. They open, not fond and common wayes to vice, but such subtle, cunnyng, new, and diuerse shiftes, to cary yong willes to vanitie, and yong wittes to mischief, to teach old bawdes new schole poyntes, as the simple head of an English man is not hable to inuent, nor neuer was hard of in England before, yea when Papistrie ouerflowed all. Suffer these bookes to be read, and they shall soone displace all bookes of godly learnyng. For they, carying the will to vanitie and marryng good maners, shall easily corrupt the mynde with ill opinions and false iudgement in doctrine; first to thinke ill of all trewe Religion, and at last to thinke nothyng of God hym selfe, one speciall pointe that is to be learned in *Italie* and *Italian* bookes. And that which is most to be lamented, and therfore more nedefull to be looked to, there be moe of these vngratious bookes set out in Printe within these fewe monethes than haue bene sene in England many score yeare before. And bicause our English men made *Italians* can not hurt but certaine persons, and in certaine places, therfore these *Italian* bookes are made English, to bryng mischief enough openly and boldly to all states, great and meane, yong and old, euery where.'

The Second Book, 'teachyng the ready way to the Latin tong,' begins with some general remarks on the practical value of 'double translation,' and then proceeds to discuss the 'six wayes appointed by the best learned men for the learning of tonges and encreace of eloquence,' viz. *Translatio linguarum*, *Paraphrasis*, *Metaphrasis*, *Epitome*, *Imitatio*, *Declamatio*. The more important matter for our present purpose is found in the fifth and concluding section[1] (fol. 45 v° to the end), which is here printed from the copy in the Bodleian Library (Malone, 645).]

IMITATIO

*I*MITATION is a facultie to expresse liuelie and perfitelie that example which ye go about to folow. And of it selfe it is large and wide: for all the workes of nature in a maner be examples for arte to folow.

5   But to our purpose: all languages, both learned and mother tonges, be gotten, and gotten onelie by *Imitation*. For as ye vse to heare, so ye learne to speake: if ye heare no other, ye speake not your selfe: and whome ye onelie heare, of them ye onelie learne.

10   And therefore, if ye would speake as the best and wisest do, ye must be conuersant where the best and wisest are: but if yow be borne or brought vp in a rude contrie, ye shall not chose but speake rudelie: the rudest man of all knoweth this to be trewe.

15   Yet neuerthelesse, the rudenes of common and mother tonges is no bar for wise speaking. For in the rudest contrie, and most barbarous mother language, many be found [that] can speake verie wiselie: but in the Greeke and Latin tong, the two onelie learned tonges, which be
20 kept not in common taulke but in priuate bookes, we finde always wisdome and eloquence, good matter and good vtterance, neuer or seldom asonder. For all soch Authors as be fullest of good matter and right iudgement in

---

[1] Ascham omits the sixth section. It was perhaps never written. See the Notes for his account of his original scheme.

doctrine be likewise alwayes most proper in wordes, most apte in sentence, most plaine and pure in vttering the same.

And, contrariwise, in those two tonges, all writers, either in Religion or any sect of Philosophie, who so euer be 5 founde fonde in iudgement of matter, be commonlie found as rude in vttering their mynde. For Stoickes, Anabaptistes, and Friers, with Epicures, Libertines, and Monkes, being most like in learning and life, are no fonder and pernicious in their opinions than they be rude and barbarous in their 10 writinges. They be not wise therefore that say, 'What care I for a mans wordes and vtterance, if his matter and reasons be good.' Soch men say so, not so moch of ignorance, as eyther of some singular pride in themselues or some speciall malice or other, or for some priuate and 15 parciall matter, either in Religion or other kinde of learn-ing. For good and choice meates be no more requisite for helthie bodies than proper and apte wordes be for good matters, and also plaine and sensible vtterance for the best and depest reasons : in which two pointes standeth 20 perfite eloquence, one of the fairest and rarest giftes that God doth geue to man.

Ye know not what hurt ye do to learning, that care not for wordes but for matter, and so make a deuorse betwixt the tong and the hart. For marke all aiges : looke vpon 25 the whole course of both the Greeke and Latin tonge, and ye shall surelie finde that, whan apte and good wordes began to be neglected, and properties of those two tonges to be confounded, than also began ill deedes to spring, strange maners to oppresse good orders, newe and fond 30 opinions to striue with olde and trewe doctrine, first in Philosophie and after in Religion, right iudgement of all thinges to be peruerted, and so vertue with learning is contemned, and studie left of : of ill thoughtes cummeth peruerse iudgement, of ill deedes springeth lewde taulke. 35

Which fower misorders, as they mar mans life, so destroy
they good learning withall.

But behold the goodnesse of Gods prouidence for learning: all olde authors and sectes of Philosophy, which were
5 fondest in opinion and rudest in vtterance, as Stoickes
and Epicures, first contemned of wise men and after forgotten of all men, be so consumed by tymes, as they be
now not onelie out of vse but also out of memorie of man :
which thing, I surelie thinke, will shortlie chance to the
10 whole doctrine and all the bookes of phantasticall Anabaptistes and Friers, and of the beastlie Libertines and
Monkes.

Againe, behold on the other side how Gods wisdome
‘hath wrought, that of *Academici* and *Peripatetici*, those
15 that were wisest in iudgement of matters and purest in
vttering their myndes, the first and chiefest that wrote
most and best in either tong, as *Plato* and *Aristotle* in
Greeke, *Tullie* in Latin, be so either wholie or sufficiently
left vnto vs, as I neuer knew yet scholer that gaue him-
20 selfe to like, and loue, and folowe chieflie those three
Authors, but he proued both learned, wise, and also an
honest man, if he ioyned with all the trewe doctrine of
Gods holie Bible, without the which the other three be
but fine edge tooles in a fole or mad mans hand.

25 But to returne to *Imitation* agayne : There be three
kindes of it in matters of learning.

The whole doctrine of Comedies and Tragedies is a
perfite *imitation*, or faire liuelie painted picture of the life
of euerie degree of man. Of this *Imitation* writeth *Plato*
30 at large in 3. *de Rep.*, but it doth not moch belong at this
time to our purpose.

The second kind of *Imitation* is to folow for learning
of tonges and sciences the best authors. Here riseth,
emonges proude and enuious wittes, a great controuersie,
35 whether one or many are to be folowed: and, if one, who

is that one; *Seneca* or *Cicero*; *Salust* or *Cæsar*; and so forth in Greeke and Latin.

The third kinde of *Imitation* belongeth to the second: as, when you be determined whether ye will folow one or mo, to know perfitlie, and which way to folow, that one; 5 in what place; by what meane and order; by what tooles and instrumentes ye shall do it; by what skill and iudgement ye shall trewelie discerne whether ye folow rightlie or no.

This *Imitatio* is *dissimilis materiei similis tractatio*; and, 10 also, *similis materiei dissimilis tractatio*, as *Virgill* folowed *Homer*: but the Argument to the one was *Vlysses*, to the other *Æneas*. *Tullie* persecuted *Antonie* with the same wepons of eloquence that *Demosthenes* vsed before against *Philippe*. 15

Horace foloweth *Pindar*, but either of them his owne Argument and Person; as the one, *Hiero* king of *Sicilie*, the other, *Augustus* the Emperor: and yet both for like respectes, that is, for their coragious stoutnes in warre and iust gouernment in peace. 20

One of the best examples for right *Imitation* we lacke, and that is *Menander*, whom our *Terence* (as the matter required), in like argument, in the same Persons, with equall eloquence, foote by foote did folow.

Som peeces remaine, like broken Iewelles, whereby 25 men may rightlie esteme and iustlie lament the losse of the whole.

Erasmus, the ornament of learning in our tyme, doth wish that som man of learning and diligence would take the like paines in *Demosthenes* and *Tullie* that *Macrobius* 30 hath done in *Homer* and *Virgill*, that is, to write out and ioyne together where the one doth imitate the other. *Erasmus* wishe is good, but surelie it is not good enough: for *Macrobius* gatherings for the *Æneados* out of *Homer*, and *Eobanus Hessus* more diligent gatherings for the 35

Bucolikes out of *Theocritus*, as they be not fullie taken out
of the whole heape, as they should be, but euen as though
they had not sought for them of purpose but fownd them
scatered here and there by chance in their way, euen so,
5 onelie to point out and nakedlie to ioyne togither their
sentences, with no farder declaring the maner and way
how the one doth folow the other, were but a colde helpe
to the encrease of learning.

But if a man would take his paine also, whan he hath
10 layd two places of *Homer* and *Virgill* or of *Demosthenes*
and *Tullie* togither, to teach plainlie withall, after this sort :

1. *Tullie* reteyneth thus moch of the matter, thies sentences, thies wordes :

2. This and that he leaueth out, which he doth wittelie
15 to this end and purpose.

3. This he addeth here.

4. This he diminisheth there.

5. This he ordereth thus, with placing that here, not
there.

20 6. This he altereth and changeth, either in propertie of
wordes, in forme of sentence, in substance of the matter,
or in one or other conuenient circumstance of the authors
present purpose.

In thies fewe rude English wordes are wrapt vp all
25 the necessarie tooles and instrumentes, where with
trewe *Imitation* is rightlie wrought withall in any tonge.
Which tooles, I openlie confesse, be not of myne owne
forging, but partlie left vnto me by the cunningest
Master, and one of the worthiest Ientlemen that euer
30 England bred, Syr *Iohn Cheke*, partelie borowed by me
out of the shoppe of the dearest frende I haue out of
England, *Io. St.* And therefore I am the bolder to borow
of him, and here to leaue them to other, and namelie to
my Children : which tooles, if it please God that an other
35 day they may be able to vse rightlie, as I do wish and

daylie pray they may do, I shal be more glad than if
I were able to leaue them a great quantitie of land.

This foresaide order and doctrine of *Imitation* would
bring forth more learning, and breed vp trewer iudgement, than any other exercise that can be vsed, but not for 5
yong beginners, bicause they shall not be able to consider
dulie therof. And, trewelie, it may be a shame to good
studentes, who, hauing so faire examples to follow, as
Plato and *Tullie*, do not vse so wise wayes in folowing
them for the obteyning of wisdome and learning as rude 10
ignorant Artificers do for gayning a small commoditie.
For surelie the meanest painter vseth more witte, better
arte, greater diligence, in hys shoppe, in folowing the
Picture of any meane mans face, than commonlie the best
studentes do, euen in the vniuersitie, for the atteining of 15
learning it selfe.

Some ignorant, vnlearned, and idle student, or some
busie looker vpon this litle poore booke, that hath neither
will to do good him selfe, nor skill to iudge right of others,
but can lustelie contemne, by pride and ignorance, all 20
painfull diligence and right order in study, will perchance
say that I am to precise, to curious, in marking and
piteling thus about the imitation of others ; and that the
olde worthie Authors did neuer busie their heades and
wittes in folowyng so preciselie, either the matter what 25
other men wrote, or els the maner how other men wrote.
They will say it were a plaine slauerie, and iniurie to,
to shakkle and tye a good witte, and hinder the course of
a mans good nature, with such bondes of seruitude, in
folowyng other.   30

Except soch men thinke them selues wiser then *Cicero*
for teaching of eloquence, they must be content to turne
a new leafe.

The best booke that euer *Tullie* wrote, by all mens
iudgement, and by his owne testimonie to, in wrytyng 35

wherof he employed most care, studie, learnyng, and
iudgement, is his booke *de Orat. ad Q. F.* Now let vs see
what he did for the matter, and also for the maner of
writing therof. For the whole booke consisteth in these
5 two pointes onelie : In good matter, and good handling of
the matter. And first, for the matter, it is whole *Aristotles*,
what so euer *Antonie* in the second and *Crassus* in the
third doth teach. Trust not me, but beleue *Tullie* him
selfe, who writeth so, first, in that goodlie long Epistle *ad*
10 *P. Lentulum*, and after in diuerse places *ad Atticum.* And
in the verie booke it selfe Tullie will not haue it hidden,
but both *Catulus* and *Crassus* do oft and pleasantly lay that
stelth to *Antonius* charge. Now, for the handling of the
matter, was *Tullie* so precise and curious rather to follow
15 an other mans Paterne than to inuent some newe shape
him selfe, namelie in that booke, wherein he purposed to
leaue to posteritie the glorie of his witte ? yea forsoth, that
he did. And this is not my gessing and gathering, nor
onelie performed by *Tullie* in verie deed, but vttered also
20 by *Tullie* in plaine wordes : to teach other men thereby
what they should do in taking like matter in hand.

And that which is especially to be marked, *Tullie* doth
vtter plainlie his conceit and purpose therein, by the
mouth of the wisest man in all that companie : for sayth
25 *Scaeuola* him selfe, *Cur non imitamur, Crasse, Socratem
illum, qui est in Phaedro Platonis ? etc.*

And furder to vnderstand that *Tullie* did not *obiter* and
bichance, but purposelie and mindfullie, bend him selfe to
a precise and curious Imitation of *Plato*, concernyng the
30 shape and forme of those bookes, marke, I pray you, how
curious *Tullie* is to vtter his purpose and doyng therein,
writing thus to *Atticus.*

*Quod in his Oratoriis libris, quos tantopere laudas, per-
sonam desideras Scaeuolae, non eam temere dimoui : sed
35 feci idem, quod in πολιτείᾳ deus ille noster Plato, cum in*

Piraeeum Socrates venisset ad Cephalum locupletem et festi-
uum senem, quoad primus ille sermo haberetur, adest in
disputando senex : deinde, cum ipse quoque commodissime
locutus esset, ad rem diuinam dicit se velle discedere, neque
postea reuertitur. Credo Platonem vix putasse satis con- 5
sonum fore, si hominem id aetatis in tam longo sermone
diutius retinuisset. Multo ego satius hoc mihi cauendum
putaui in Scaeuola, qui et aetate et valetudine erat ea qua [esse]
meministi, et his honoribus, vt vix satis decorum videretur,
eum plures dies esse in Crassi Tusculano. Et erat primi 10
libri sermo non alienus a Scaeuolae studiis : reliqui libri
τεχνολογίαν *habent, vt scis. Huic ioculatoriae disputationi*
senem illum, vt noras, interesse sane nolui.

If *Cicero* had not opened him selfe and declared hys
owne thought and doynges herein, men that be idle, and 15
ignorant, and enuious of other mens diligence and well
doinges, would haue sworne that *Tullie* had neuer mynded
any soch thing, but that of a precise curiositie we fayne
and forge and father soch thinges of *Tullie* as he neuer
ment in deed. I write this not for nought ; for I haue 20
heard some both well learned and otherwayes verie wise,
that by their lustie misliking of soch diligence haue drawen
back the forwardnes of verie good wittes. But euen as
such men them selues do sometymes stumble vpon doyng
well by chance and benefite of good witte, so would I haue 25
our scholer alwayes able to do well by order of learnyng
and right skill of iudgement.

Concernyng *Imitation* many learned men haue written,
with moch diuersitie for the matter, and therfore with
great contrarietie and some stomacke amongest them 30
selues. I haue read as many as I could get diligentlie,
and what I thinke of euerie one of them I will freelie say
my mynde. With which freedome I trust good men
will beare, bicause it shall tend to neither spitefull nor
harmefull controuersie. 35

In *Tullie*, it is well touched, shortlie taught, not fullie declared by *Ant.* in 2. *de Orat.* : and afterward in *Orat. ad Brutum*, for the liking and misliking of *Isocrates* : and the contrarie iudgement of *Tullie* agaynst *Caluus*, *Brutus*, and
5 *Calidius, de genere dicendi Attico et Asiatico.*

Dionis. Halic. περὶ μιμήσεως I feare is lost : which Author, next *Aristotle, Plato,* and *Tullie,* of all other that write of eloquence, by the iudgement of them that be best learned, deserueth the next prayse and place.
10 *Quintilian* writeth of it, shortly and coldlie for the matter, yet hotelie and spitefullie enough agaynst the Imitation of *Tullie.*

Erasmus, beyng more occupied in spying other mens faultes than declaryng his owne aduise, is mistaken of
15 many, to the great hurt of studie, for his authoritie sake. For he writeth rightlie, rightlie vnderstanded : he and *Longolius* onelie differing in this, that the one seemeth to giue ouermoch, the other ouer litle, to him whom they both best loued and chiefly allowed of all other.
20 *Budæus* in his Commentaries roughlie and obscurelie, after his kinde of writyng : and for the matter, caryed somewhat out of the way in ouermuch misliking the Imitation of *Tullie.*

Phil. Melancthon learnedlie and trewlie.
25 *Camerarius* largely with a learned iudgement, but somewhat confusedly, and with ouer rough a stile.

Sambucus largely, with a right iudgement but somewhat a crooked stile.

Other haue written also, as *Cortesius* to *Politian,* and
30 that verie well : *Bembus ad Picum* a great deale better : but *Ioan. Sturmius, de Nobilitate literata et de Amissa dicendi ratione,* farre best of all, in myne opinion, that euer tooke this matter in hand. For all the rest declare chiefly this point, whether one, or many, or all are to be followed :
35 but *Sturmius* onelie hath most learnedlie declared who is

to be followed, what is to be followed, and, the best point of all, by what way and order trew Imitation is rightlie to be exercised. And although *Sturmius* herein doth farre passe all other, yet hath he not so fullie and perfitelie done it as I do wishe he had, and as I know he could. 5 For though he hath done it perfitelie for precept, yet hath he not done it perfitelie enough for example : which he did, neither for lacke of skill, nor by negligence, but of purpose, contented with one or two examples, bicause he was mynded in those two bookes to write of it both 10 shortlie, and also had to touch other matters.

Barthol. Riccius Ferrariensis also hath written learnedlie, diligentlie, and verie largelie of this matter, euen as hee did before verie well *de Apparatu linguae Lat.* He writeth the better in myne opinion, bicause his whole doctrine, 15 iudgement, and order semeth to be borowed out of *Io. Stur.* bookes. He addeth also examples, the best kinde of teaching : wherein he doth well, but not well enough : in deede, he committeth no faulte, but yet deserueth small praise. He is content with the meane, and followeth not 20 the best : as a man that would feede vpon Acornes, whan he may eate as good cheape the finest wheat bread. He teacheth, for example, where and how two or three late *Italian* Poetes do follow *Virgil*; and how *Virgil* him selfe in the storie of *Dido* doth wholie imitate *Catullus* in the 25 like matter of *Ariadna* : Wherein I like better his diligence and order of teaching than his iudgement in choice of examples for *Imitation.* But, if he had done thus, if he had declared where and how, how oft and how many wayes, *Virgil* doth folow *Homer*, as for example the 30 comming of *Vlysses* to *Alcynous* and *Calypso*, with the comming of *Æneas* to *Cartage* and *Dido* ; Likewise the games, running, wrestling, and shoting, that *Achilles* maketh in *Homer*, with the selfe same games that *Æneas* maketh in *Virgil*; The harnesse of *Achilles*, with the harnesse of 35

Æneas, and the maner of making of them both by *Vulcane*;
The notable combate betwixt *Achilles* and *Hector*, with as
notable a combate betwixt *Æneas* and *Turnus*; The going
downe to hell of *Vlysses* in *Homer*, with the going downe
5 to hell of *Æneas* in *Virgil*; and other places infinite mo,
as similitudes, narrations, messages, discriptions of persons, places, battels, tempestes, shipwrackes, and common
places for diuerse purposes, which be as precisely taken
out of *Homer* as euer did Painter in London follow the
10 picture of any faire personage; And when thies places
had bene gathered together by this way of diligence, than
to haue conferred them together by this order of teaching,
as diligently to marke what is kept and vsed in either
author, in wordes, in sentences, in matter, what is added,
15 what is left out, what ordered otherwise, either *praeponendo*,
interponendo, or *postponendo*, and what is altered for any
respect, in word, phrase, sentence, figure, reason, argument, or by any way of circumstance : If *Riccius* had done
this, he had not onely bene well liked for his diligence in
20 teaching, but also iustlie commended for his right iudgement in right choice of examples for the best *Imitation*.

Riccius also for *Imitation* of prose declareth where and
how *Longolius* doth folow *Tullie*; but, as for *Longolius*,
I would not haue him the patern of our *Imitation*. In
25 deede, in *Longolius* shoppe be proper and faire shewing
colers, but as for shape, figure, and naturall cumlines, by
the iudgement of best iudging artificers he is rather
allowed as one to be borne withall than especially
commended as one chieflie to be folowed.

30 If *Riccius* had taken for his examples where *Tullie* him
selfe foloweth either *Plato* or *Demosthenes*, he had shot
than at the right marke. But to excuse *Riccius* somwhat,
though I can not fullie defend him, it may be sayd his
purpose was to teach onelie the Latin tong; when thys
35 way that I do wish, to ioyne *Virgil* with *Homer*, to read

Tullie with *Demosthenes* and *Plato*, requireth a cunning
and perfite Master in both the tonges. It is my wish in
deede, and that by good reason: For who so euer will
write well of any matter must labor to expresse that that
is perfite, and not to stay and content himselfe with the 5
meane: yea, I say farder, though it be not vnposible, yet
it is verie rare, and meruelous hard, to proue excellent in
the Latin tong for him that is not also well seene in the
Greeke tong. *Tullie* him selfe, most excellent of nature,
most diligent in labor, brought vp from his cradle in that 10
place and in that tyme where and whan the Latin tong
most florished naturallie in euery mans mouth, yet was
not his owne tong able it selfe to make him so cunning in
his owne tong, as he was in deede, but the knowledge and
Imitation of the Greeke tong withall.   15

This he confesseth himselfe; this he vttereth in many
places, as those can tell best that vse to read him most.

Therefore thou that shotest at perfection in the Latin
tong think not thy selfe wiser than *Tullie* was, in choice
of the way that leadeth rightlie to the same: thinke not 20
thy witte better than *Tullies* was, as though that may serue
thee that was not sufficient for him. For euen as a hauke
flieth not hie with one wing, euen so a man reacheth not
to excellency with one tong.

I haue bene a looker on in the Cokpit of learning thies 25
many yeares: And one Cock onelie haue I knowne,
which with one wing, euen at this day, doth passe all
other, in myne opinion, that euer I saw in any pitte in
England, though they had two winges. Yet neuerthelesse,
to flie well with one wing, to runne fast with one leg, be 30
rather rare Maistreis moch to be merueled at than sure
examples safelie to be folowed. A Bushop that now
liueth, a good man, whose iudgement in Religion I better
like than his opinion in perfitnes in other learning, said
once vnto me: 'We haue no nede now of the Greeke tong, 35

when all thinges be translated into Latin.' But the good
man vnderstood not that euen the best translation is, for
mere necessitie, but an euill imped wing to flie withall,
or a heuie stompe leg of wood to go withall: soch, the
5 hier they flie, the sooner they falter and faill: the faster
they runne, the ofter they stumble, and sorer they fall.
Soch as will nedes so flie, may flie at a Pye and catch
a Dawe: And soch runners, as commonlie they shoue
and sholder to stand formost, yet in the end they cum
10 behind others and deserue but the hopshakles, if the
Masters of the game be right iudgers.

Therefore, in perusing thus so many diuerse bookes
for *Imitation*, it came into my head that a verie profitable
booke might be made *de Imitatione*, after an other sort
15 than euer yet was attempted of that matter, conteyning
a certaine fewe fitte preceptes, vnto the which should be
gathered and applied plentie of examples, out of the
choisest authors of both the tonges. This worke would
stand rather in good diligence for the gathering, and right
20 iudgement for the apte applying of those examples, than
any great learning or vtterance at all.

The doing thereof would be more pleasant than painfull,
and would bring also moch proffet to all that should read
it, and great praise to him [that] would take it in hand,
25 with iust desert of thankes.

Erasmus, giuyng him selfe to read ouer all Authors,
Greke and *Latin*, seemeth to haue prescribed to him selfe
this order of readyng, that is, to note out by the way
three speciall pointes, All Adagies, all similitudes, and all
30 wittie sayinges of most notable personages: And so, by
one labour, he left to posteritie three notable bookes, and
namelie two, his *Chiliades*, *Apophthegmata*, and *Similia*.
Likewise, if a good student would bend him selfe to read
diligently ouer Tullie, and with him also at the same tyme
35 as diligently *Plato* and *Xenophon* with his bookes of

Philosophie, *Isocrates* and *Demosthenes* with his orations, and *Aristotle* with his Rhetorickes, which fiue of all other be those whom *Tullie* best loued and specially followed, and would marke diligently in *Tullie* where he doth *exprimere* or *effingere* (which be the verie proper wordes 5 of Imitation) either *copiam Platonis* or *venustatem Xenophontis, suauitatem Isocratis,* or *vim Demosthenis, propriam et puram subtilitatem Aristotelis,* and not onelie write out the places diligentlie, and lay them together orderlie, but also to conferre them with skilfull iudgement by those 10 few rules which I haue expressed now twise before: if that diligence were taken, if that order were vsed, what perfite knowledge of both the tonges, what readie and pithie vtterance in all matters, what right and deepe iudgement in all kinde of learnyng would follow, is scarse 15 credible to be beleued.

These bookes be not many, nor long, nor rude in speach, nor meane in matter, but, next the Maiestie of Gods holie word, most worthie for a man, the louer of learning and honestie, to spend his life in. Yea, I haue 20 heard worthie *M. Cheke* many tymes say: I would haue a good student passe and iorney through all Authors both *Greke* and *Latin*; but he that will dwell in these few bookes onelie, first in Gods holie Bible, and than ioyne with it *Tullie* in *Latin, Plato, Aristotle, Xenophon, Iso-* 25 *crates,* and *Demosthenes* in *Greke,* must nedes proue an excellent man.

Some men alreadie in our dayes haue put to their helping handes to this worke of Imitation : As *Perionius, Henr. Stephanus in dictionario Ciceroniano,* and *P. Victorius* 30 most praiseworthelie of all, in that his learned worke conteyning xxv. bookes *de varia lectione* : in which bookes be ioyned diligentlie together the best Authors of both the tonges where one doth seeme to imitate an other.

But all these, with *Macrobius, Hessus,* and other, be no 35

more but common porters, caryers, and bringers of matter
and stuffe togither. They order nothing. They lay before
you what is done : they do not teach you how it is done.
They busie not them selues with forme of buildyng. They
5 do not declare, this stuffe is thus framed by *Demosthenes*,
and thus and thus by *Tullie*, and so likewise in *Xenophon*,
Plato, and *Isocrates*, and *Aristotle*. For ioyning *Virgil*
with *Homer* I haue sufficientlie declared before.

The like diligence I would wish to be´ taken in *Pindar*
10 and *Horace*, an equall match for all respectes.

In Tragedies (the goodliest Argument of all, and, for the
vse either of a learned preacher or a Ciuill Ientleman,
more profitable than *Homer, Pindar, Virgill,* and *Horace*,
yea comparable in myne opinion with the doctrine of
15 *Aristotle, Plato,* and *Xenophon*), the *Grecians Sophocles*
and *Euripides* far ouer match our *Seneca* in Latin, namely
in Οἰκονομίᾳ *et Decoro*, although *Senacaes* elocution and verse
be verie commendable for his tyme. And for the matters
of *Hercules, Thebes, Hippolytus,* and *Troie*, his Imitation is
20 to be gathered into the same booke, and to be tryed by the
same touchstone, as is spoken before.

In histories, and namelie in *Liuie*, the like diligence of
Imitation could bring excellent learning, and breede stayde
iudgement, in taking any like matter in hand. Onely
25 *Liuie* were a sufficient taske for one mans studie, to
compare him, first with his fellow for all respectes, *Dion.
Halicarnassaeus* ; who both liued in one tyme, tooke both
one historie in hande to write, deserued both like prayse
of learnynge and eloquence : Than with *Polybius* that wise
30 writer, whom *Liuie* professeth to follow ; and, if he would
denie it, yet it is plaine that the best part of the thyrd
Decade in *Liuie* is in a maner translated out of the
thyrd and rest of *Polibius* : Lastlie with *Thucydides*, to
whose Imitation *Liuie* is curiouslie bent, as may well
35 appeare by that one Oration of those of *Campania*, asking

aide of the *Romanes* agaynst the *Samnites*, which is wholie
taken, Sentence, Reason, Argument, and order, out of
the Oration of *Corcyra*, asking like aide of the *Athenienses*
against them of *Corinth*.   If some diligent student would
take paynes to compare them togither, he should easelie 5
perceiue that I do say trew.   A booke thus wholie filled
with examples of Imitation, first out of *Tullie*, compared
with *Plato*, *Xenophon*, *Isocrates*, *Demosthenes*, and *Aristotle*,
than out of *Virgil* and *Horace*, with *Homer* and *Pindar*,
next out of *Seneca*, with *Sophocles* and *Euripides*, lastlie 10
out of *Liuie*, with *Thucydides*, *Polibius*, and *Halicarnassaeus*,
gathered with good diligence, and compared with right
order, as I haue expressed before, were an other maner
of worke for all kinde of learning, and namely for eloquence, than be those cold gatheringes of *Macrobius*, *Hessus*, 15
Perionius, *Stephanus*, and *Victorius*, which may be vsed,
as I sayd before, in this case, as porters and caryers,
deseruing like prayse, as soch men do wages ; but onely
Sturmius is he, out of whom the trew suruey and whole
workemanship is speciallie to be learned.   20

I trust this my writyng shall giue some good student
occasion to take some peece in hand of this worke of
Imitation.   And as I had rather haue any do it than
my selfe, yet surelie my selfe rather than none at all.
And by Gods grace, if God do lend me life, with health, 25
free laysure, and libertie, with good likyng and a merie
heart I will turne the best part of my studie and tyme
to toyle in one or other peece of this worke of Imitation.

This diligence to gather examples, to giue light and
vnderstandyng to good preceptes, is no new inuention, 30
but speciallie vsed of the best Authors and oldest writers.
For *Aristotle* him selfe (as *Diog. Laertius* declareth), when
he had written that goodlie booke of the *Topickes*, did
gather out of stories and Orators so many examples as
filled xv. bookes, onelie to expresse the rules of his 35

Topickes. These were the Commentaries that *Aristotle*
thought fit for hys *Topickes*: And therfore to speake as
I thinke, I neuer saw yet any Commentarie vpon *Aristotles*
Logicke, either in *Greke* or *Latin,* that euer I lyked,
5 bicause they be rather spent in declaryng scholepoynt
rules than in gathering fit examples for vse and vtterance,
either by pen or talke. For preceptes in all Authors,
and namelie in *Aristotle*, without applying vnto them the
Imitation of examples, be hard, drie, and cold, and ther-
10 fore barrayn, vnfruitfull, and vnpleasant. But *Aristotle*,
namelie in his *Topickes* and *Elenches*, should be not onelie
fruitfull but also pleasant to, if examples out of *Plato*
and other good Authors were diligentlie gathered and
aptlie applied vnto his most perfit preceptes there. And
15 it is notable that my frende *Sturmius* writeth herein, that
there is no precept in *Aristotles Topickes* wherof plentie
of examples be not manifest in *Platos* workes. And I
heare say, that an excellent learned man, *Tomitanus* in
Italie, hath expressed euerie fallacion in *Aristotle* with
20 diuerse examples out of *Plato.* Would to God I might
once see some worthie student of *Aristotle* and *Plato* in
Cambrige, that would ioyne in one booke the preceptes
of the one with the examples of the other. For such
a labor were one speciall peece of that worke of Imita-
25 tion, which I do wishe were gathered together in one
Volume.

Cambrige, at my first comming thither, but not at my
going away, committed this fault in reading the preceptes
of *Aristotle* without the examples of other Authors: But
30 herein, in my time, thies men of worthie memorie,
M. Redman, M. Cheke, M. Smith, M. Haddon, M. Watson,
put so to their helping handes, as that vniuersitie, and
all studentes there, as long as learning shall last, shall
be bounde vnto them, if that trade in studie be trewlie
35 folowed which those men left behinde them there. . . . .

Now to returne to that Question, whether one, a few, many, or all are to be followed, my aunswere shalbe short : All, for him that is desirous to know all : yea, the worst of all, as Questionistes, and all the barbarous nation of scholemen, helpe for one or other consideration : 5 But in euerie separate kinde of learnyng, and studie by it selfe, ye must follow choselie a few, and chieflie some one, and that namelie in our schole of eloquence, either for penne or talke. And as in port[r]aicture and paintyng wise men chose not that workman that can onelie make 10 a faire hand, or a well facioned legge, but soch one as can furnish vp fullie all the fetures of the whole body of a man, woman, and child, and with all is able to, by good skill, to giue to euerie one of these three, in their proper kinde, the right forme, the trew figure, the naturall color, 15 that is fit and dew to the dignitie of a man, to the bewtie of a woman, to the sweetnes of a yong babe ; euen like-wise do we seeke soch one in our schole to folow, who is able alwayes, in all matters, to teach plainlie, to delite pleasantlie, and to cary away by force of wise talke, all 20 that shall heare or read him, and is so excellent in deed as witte is able or wishe can hope to attaine vnto : And this not onelie to serue in the *Latin* or *Greke* tong, but also in our own English language. But yet, bicause the prouidence of God hath left vnto vs in no other tong, saue 25 onelie in the *Greke* ᛁd *Latin* tong, the trew preceptes and perfite examples of eloquence, therefore must we seeke in the Authors onelie of those two tonges the trewe Paterne of Eloquence, if in any other mother tongue we looke to attaine either to perfit vtterance of it our selues 30 or skilfull iudgement of it in others.

And now to know what Author doth medle onelie with some one peece and member of eloquence, and who doth perfitelie make vp the whole bodie, I will declare, as I can call to remembrance the goodlie talke that I haue had 35 oftentymes of the trew difference of Authors with that Ientleman of worthie memorie, my dearest frend, and teacher of all the litle poore learning I haue, Syr *Iohn Cheke.*

5   The trew difference of Authors is best knowne *per diuersa genera dicendi* that euerie one vsed.   And therfore here I will deuide *genus dicendi,* not into these three, *Tenue, mediocre, et grande,* but as the matter of euerie Author requireth, as

10

$$in \ Genus \left\{ \begin{array}{l} Poeticum, \\ Historicum, \\ Philosophicum, \\ Oratorium. \end{array} \right.$$

These differre one from an other in choice of wordes, 15 in framyng of Sentences, in handling of Argumentes, and vse of right forme, figure, and number, proper and fitte for euerie matter ; and euerie one of these is diuerse also in it selfe, as the first,

20

$$Poeticum, \ in \left\{ \begin{array}{l} Comicum, \\ Tragicum, \\ Epicum, \\ Melicum. \end{array} \right.$$

And here, who soeuer hath bene diligent to read aduisedlie ouer *Terence, Seneca, Virgil, Horace,* or els 25 *Aristophanes, Sophocles, Homer,* and *Pindar,* and shall diligently marke the difference they vse, in proprietie of wordes, in forme of sentence, in handlyng of their matter, he shall easelie perceiue what is fitte and *decorum* in euerie one, to the trew vse of perfite Imitation.   Whan 30 *M. Watson* in S. Iohns College at Cambrige wrote his excellent Tragedie of *Absalon, M. Cheke,* he, and I, for that part of trew Imitation, had many pleasant talkes togither, in comparing the preceptes of *Aristotle* and *Horace de Arte Poetica* with the examples of *Euripides,*

Sophocles, and *Seneca*. Few men, in writyng of Tragedies in our dayes, haue shot at this marke. Some in *England*, moe in *France*, *Germanie*, and *Italie* also, haue written Tragedies in our tyme : of the which not one I am sure is able to abyde the trew touch of *Aristotles* preceptes and 5 *Euripides* examples, saue onely two that euer I saw, *M. Watsons Absalon* and *Georgius Buckananus Iephthe*. One man in Cambrige, well liked of many, but best liked of him selfe, was many tymes bold and busie to bryng matters vpon stages, which he called Tragedies. In one, 10 wherby he looked to wynne his spurres, and whereat many ignorant felowes fast clapped their handes, he began the *Protasis* with *Trochoeiis Octonariis* : which kinde of verse, as it is but seldome and rare in Tragedies, so it is neuer vsed, saue onelie *in Epitasi* : whan the Tragedie is hiest 15 and hotest, and full of greatest troubles. I remember ful well what *M. Watson* merelie sayd vnto me of his blindnesse and boldnes in that behalfe, although otherwise there passed much frendship betwene them. *M. Watson* had an other maner care of perfection, with a feare and re- 20 uerence of the iudgement of the best learned : Who to this day would neuer suffer yet his *Absalon* to go abroad, and that onelie bicause, *in locis paribus*, *Anapestus* is twise or thrise vsed in stede of *Iambus* : A smal faulte, and such one as perchance would neuer be marked, no neither in 25 *Italie* nor *France*. This I write, not so much to note the first, or praise the last, as to leaue in memorie of writing, for good example to posteritie, what perfection, in any tyme, was most diligentlie sought for in like maner, in all kinde of learnyng, in that most worthie College of 30 S. Iohns in Cambrige.

Historicum, in $\begin{cases} Diaria, \\ Annales, \\ Commentarios, \\ Iustam\ Historiam. \end{cases}$

35

For what proprietie in wordes, simplicitie in sentences, plainnesse and light, is cumelie for these kindes, *Cæsar* and *Liuie*, for the two last, are perfite examples of Imitation : And for the two first the old paternes be lost, and as for some that be present and of late tyme, they be fitter to be read once for some pleasure than oft to be perused for any good Imitation of them.

Philosophicum, in	*Sermonem,* as *Officia* *Cic. et Eth. Arist.* *Contentionem,* as the Dialoges of *Plato, Xenophon,* and *Cicero* :

Of which kinde of learnyng, and right Imitation therof, *Carolus Sigonius* hath written of late, both learnedlie and eloquentlie : but best of all my frende *Ioan. Sturmius* in hys Commentaries vpon *Gorgias Platonis,* which booke I haue in writyng, and is not yet set out in Print.

Oratorium, in	*Humile,* *Mediocre,* *Sublime.*

Examples of these three, in the *Greke* tong, be plentifull and perfite, as *Lycias, Isocrates,* and *Demosthenes* : and all three in onelie *Demosthenes,* in diuerse orations, as *contra Olimpiodorum, in Leptinem, et pro Ctesiphonte.* And trew it is that *Hermogenes* writeth of *Demosthenes* that all formes of Eloquence be perfite in him. In *Ciceroes* Orations *Medium et sublime* be most excellentlie handled, but *Humile* in his Orations is seldome sene. Yet neuerthelesse in other bookes, as in some part of his Offices, and specially *in Partitionibus,* he is comparable *in hoc humili et disciplinabili genere,* euen with the best that euer wrote in *Greke.* But of *Cicero* more fullie in fitter place. And thus the trew difference of stiles, in euerie Author

and euerie kinde of learnyng, may easelie be knowne by
this diuision:

$$in\ Genus \begin{cases} Poeticum, \\ Historicum, \\ Philosophicum, \\ Oratorium. \end{cases}$$

5

Which I thought in this place to touch onelie, not to
prosecute at large, bicause, God willyng, in the *Latin* tong,
I will fullie handle it in my booke *de Imitatione*.

Now, to touch more particularlie which of those Authors, 10
that be now most commonlie in mens handes, will some
affourd you some peece of Eloquence, and what maner a
peece of eloquence, and what is to be liked and folowed,
and what to be misliked and eschewed in them, and how
some agayne will furnish you fully withall, rightly, and 15
wisely considered, somwhat I will write as I haue heard
Syr *Iohn Cheke* many tymes say.

The Latin tong, concerning any part of purenesse of it,
from the spring to the decay of the same, did not endure
moch longer than is the life of a well aged man, scarse 20
one hundred yeares from the tyme of the last *Scipio*
Africanus and *Laelius* to the Empire of *Augustus*. And
it is notable that *Vellius Paterculus* writeth of *Tullie*, how
that the perfection of eloquence did so remayne onelie in
him and in his time, as before him were few which might 25
moch delight a man, or after him any worthy admiration,
but soch as *Tullie* might haue seene, and such as might
haue seene *Tullie*. And good cause why: for no perfection
is durable. Encrease hath a time, and decay likewise,
but all perfit ripenesse remaineth but a moment: as is 30
plainly seen in fruits, plummes, and cherries, but more
sensibly in flowers, as Roses and such like; and yet as
trewlie in all greater matters. For what naturallie can
go no hier must naturallie yeld and stoupe againe.

Of this short tyme of any purenesse of the Latin tong, 35

for the first fortie yéare of it, and all the tyme before, we haue no peece of learning left, saue *Plautus* and *Terence*, with a litle rude vnperfit pamflet of the elder *Cato*. And as for *Plautus*, except the scholemaster be
5 able to make wise and ware choice, first in proprietie of wordes, than in framing of phrases and sentences, and chieflie in choice of honestie of matter, your scholer were better to play then learne all that is in him. But surelie, if iudgement for the tong, and direction for the maners, be
10 wisely ioyned with the diligent reading of *Plautus*, than trewlie *Plautus* for that purenesse of the Latin tong in Rome, whan Rome did most florish in well doing, and so thereby in well speaking also, is soch a plentifull store-ho[u]se for common eloquence, in meane matters, and all
15 priuate mens affaires, as the Latin tong, for that respect, hath not the like agayne. Whan I remember the worthy tyme of Rome wherein *Plautus* did liue, I must nedes honor the talke of that tyme which we see *Plautus* doth vse.

20 *Terence* is also a storehouse of the same tong, for an other tyme, following soone after; and although he be not so full and plentiful as *Plautus* is, for multitude of matters and diuersitie of wordes, yet his wordes be chosen so purelie, placed so orderly, and all his stuffe
25 so neetlie packed vp and wittely compassed in euerie place, as, by all wise mens iudgement, he is counted the cunninger workeman, and to haue his shop, for the rowme that is in it, more finely appointed and trimlier ordered than *Plautus* is.

30 Three thinges chiefly, both in *Plautus* and *Terence*, are to be specially considered : The matter, the vtterance, the words, the meter. The matter in both is altogether within the compasse of the meanest mens maners, and doth not stretch to any thing of any great weight at all, but
35 standeth chiefly in vtteryng the thoughtes and conditions

of hard fathers, foolish mothers, vnthrifty yong men, craftie seruantes, sotle bawdes, and wilie harlots, and so is moch spent in finding out fine fetches and packing vp pelting matters, soch as in London commonlie cum to the hearing of the Masters of Bridewell.   Here is base stuffe for that 5 scholer that should becum hereafter either a good minister in Religion or a Ciuill Ientleman in seruice of his Prince and contrie (except the preacher do know soch matters to confute them), whan ignorance surelie in all soch thinges were better for a Ciuill Ientleman than knowledge.   And 10 thus, for matter, both *Plautus* and *Terence* be like meane painters, that worke by halfes, and be cunning onelie in making the worst part of the picture, as if one were skilfull in painting the bodie of a naked person from the nauell downward, but nothing else.   15

For word and speach *Plautus* is more plentifull, and *Terence* more pure and proper: And for one respect *Terence* is to be embraced aboue all that euer wrote in hys kinde of argument : Bicause it is well known by good recorde of learning, and that by *Ciceroes* owne witnes, that some 20 Comedies bearyng *Terence* name were written by worthy *Scipio* and wise *Laelius*, and namely *Heauton* and *Adelphi*. And therefore, as oft as I reade those Comedies, so oft doth sound in myne eare the pure fine talke of Rome, which was vsed by the floure of the worthiest nobilitie that euer 25 Rome bred.   Let the wisest man, and best learned that liueth, read aduisedlie ouer the first scene of *Heauton* and the first scene of *Adelphi*, and let him consideratlie iudge whether it is the talke of the seruile stranger borne, or rather euen that milde eloquent wise speach which *Cicero* 30 in *Brutus* doth so liuely expresse in *Laelius*.   And yet, neuerthelesse, in all this good proprietie of wordes and purenesse of phrases which be in *Terence*, ye must not follow him alwayes in placing of them, bicause for the meter sake some wordes in him somtyme be driuen 35

awrie, which require a straighter placing in plaine prose,
if ye will forme, as I would ye should do, your speach and
writing to that excellent perfitnesse which was onely in
Tullie, or onelie in *Tullies* tyme.

5   The meter and verse of *Plautus* and *Terence* be verie
meane, and not to be followed : which is not their reproch,
but the fault of the tyme wherein they wrote, whan no
kinde of Poetrie in the Latin tong was brought to perfection, as doth well appeare in the fragmentes of *Ennius*,
10 *Cecilius*, and others, and euidentlie in *Plautus* and *Terence*,
if thies in Latin be compared with right skil with *Homer*,
Euripides, *Aristophanes*, and other in Greeke of like sort.
Cicero him selfe doth complaine of this vnperfitnes, but
more plainly *Quintilian*, saying, *in Comoedia maxime claudi-*
15 *camus, et vix leuem consequimur vmbram* : and most earnestly
of all *Horace in Arte Poetica*, which he doth namely *propter
carmen Iambicum*, and referreth all good studentes herein
to the Imitation of the Greeke tong, saying,

                  Exemplaria Graeca
20   *nocturna versate manu, versate diurna.*

   This matter maketh me gladly remember my sweete
tyme spent at Cambrige, and the pleasant talke which
I had oft with *M. Cheke* and *M. Watson* of this fault, not
onely in the olde Latin Poets, but also in our new English
25 Rymers at this day. They wished as *Virgil* and *Horace*
were not wedded to follow the faultes of former fathers
(a shrewd mariage in greater matters) but by right *Imitation*
of the perfit Grecians had brought Poetrie to perfitnesse
also in the Latin tong, that we Englishmen likewise would
30 acknowledge and vnderstand rightfully our rude beggerly
ryming, brought first into Italie by *Gothes* and *Hunnes*,
whan all good verses and all good learning to were
destroyd by them, and after caryed into France and
Germanie, and at last receyued into England by men of

excellent wit in deede, but of small learning and lesse
iudgement in that behalfe.

But now, when men know the difference, and haue the
examples, both of the best and of the worst, surelie to
follow rather the *Gothes* in Ryming than the *Greekes* in 5
trew versifiyng were euen to eate ackornes with swyne,
when we may freely eate wheate bread emonges men.
In deede, *Chauser, Th. Norton* of Bristow, my L. of Surrey,
M. Wiat, Th. Phaer, and other Ientlemen, in translating
Ouide, Palingenius, and *Seneca,* haue gonne as farre to 10
their great praise as the copie they followed could cary
them ; but, if soch good wittes and forward diligence had
bene directed to follow the best examples, and not haue
bene caryed by tyme and custome to content themselues
with that barbarous and rude Ryming, emonges their other 15
worthy praises, which they haue iustly deserued, this had
not bene the least, to be counted emonges men of learning
and skill more like vnto the Grecians than vnto the
Gothians in handling of their verse.

In deed, our English tong, hauing in vse chiefly wordes 20
of one syllable which commonly be long, doth not well
receiue the nature of *Carmen Heroicum,* bicause *dactylus,*
the aptest foote for that verse, conteining one long and two
short, is seldom therefore found in English ; and doth also
rather stumble than stand vpon *Monasyllabis.   Quintilian,* 25
in hys learned Chapiter *de Compositione,* geueth this lesson
de Monasyllabis before me ; and in the same place doth
iustlie inuey against all Ryming ; that if there be any who
be angrie with me for misliking of Ryming may be angry
for company to with *Quintilian* also for the same thing. 30
And yet *Quintilian* had not so iust cause to mislike of it
than as men haue at this day.

And although *Carmen Exametrum* doth rather trotte
and hoble than runne smothly in our English tong, yet
I am sure our English tong will receiue *carmen Iambicum* 35

as naturallie as either *Greke* or *Latin.* But for ignorance men can not like, and for idlenes men will not labor, to cum to any perfitenes at all. For, as the worthie Poetes in *Athens* and *Rome* were more carefull to satisfie the iudgement of one learned than rashe in pleasing the humor of a rude multitude, euen so if men in England now had the like reuerend regard to learning, skill, and iudgement, and durst not presume to write except they came with the like learnyng, and also did vse like diligence in searchyng out not onelie iust measure in euerie meter, as euerie ignorant person may easely do, but also trew quantitie in euery foote and sillable, as onelie the learned shalbe able to do, and as the *Grekes* and *Romanes* were wont to do, surelie than rash ignorant heads, which now can easely recken vp fourten sillabes, and easelie stumble on euery Ryme, either durst not, for lacke of such learnyng, or els would not, in auoyding such labor, be so busie as euerie where they be ; and shoppes in London should not be so full of lewd and rude rymes, as commonlie they are. But now the ripest of tong be readiest to write : And many dayly in setting out bookes and balettes make great shew of blossomes and buddes, in whom is neither roote of learning nor frute of wisedome at all. Some that make *Chaucer* in English and *Petrarch* in Italian their Gods in verses, and yet be not able to make trew difference, what is a fault and what is a iust prayse in those two worthie wittes, will moch mislike this my writyng. But such men be euen like followers of *Chaucer* and *Petrarke,* as one here in England did folow Syr *Tho. More,* who, being most vnlike vnto him in wit and learnyng, neuertheles in wearing his gowne awrye vpon the one shoulder, as Syr *Tho. More* was wont to do, would nedes be counted lyke vnto him.

This mislikyng of Ryming beginneth not now of any newfangle singularitie, but hath bene long misliked of

many, and that of men of greatest learnyng and deepest
iudgement. And soch that defend it do so, either for
lacke of knowledge what is best, or els of verie enuie that
any should performe that in learnyng, whereunto they, as
I sayd before, either for ignorance can not, or for idlenes 5
will not, labor to attaine vnto.

And you that prayse this Ryming, bicause ye neither
haue reason why to like it nor can shew learning to
defend it, yet I will helpe you with the authoritie of the
oldest and learnedst tyme. In *Grece*, whan Poetrie was 10
euen as the hiest pitch of perfitnes, one *Simmias Rhodius*
of a certaine singularitie wrote a booke in ryming *Greke*
verses, naming it ᾠόν, conteyning the fable how *Iupiter*
in likenes of a swan gat that egge vpon *Leda*, whereof
came *Castor*, *Pollux*, and faire [*H*]*elena*. This booke was 15
so liked that it had few to read it, but none to folow
it : But was presentlie contemned : and, sone after, both
Author and booke so forgotten by men, and consumed
by tyme, as scarse the name of either is kept in memorie
of learnyng. And the like folie was neuer folowed of any 20
many hondred yeares after, vntill the *Hunnes* and *Gothians*
and other barbarous nations of ignorance and rude
singularitie did reuiue the same folie agayne.

The noble Lord *Th*. Earle of Surrey, first of all English
men in translating the fourth booke of *Virgill*, and *Gonsaluo* 25
Periz, that excellent learned man, and Secretarie to kyng
Philip of *Spaine*, in translating the *Vlisses* of *Homer* out
of *Greke* into *Spanish*, haue both, by good iudgement,
auoyded the fault of Ryming, yet neither of them hath
fullie hit[t]e perfite and trew versifying. In deede, they 30
obserue iust number, and euen feete : but here is the
fault, that their feete be feete without ioyntes, that is to
say, not distinct by trew quantitie of sillabes : And so
soch feete be but numme feete, and be euen as vnfitte
for a verse to turne and runne roundly withall as feete 35

of brasse or wood be vnweeldie to go well withall. And
as a foote of wood is a plaine shew of a manifest maime,
euen so feete in our English versifing without quantitie
and ioyntes be sure signes that the verse is either borne
5 deformed, vnnaturall, and lame, and so verie vnseemlie
to looke vpon, except to men that be gogle eyed them
selues.

The spying of this fault now is not the curiositie of
English eyes, but euen the good iudgement also of the
10 best that write in these dayes in *Italie* : and namelie of
that worthie *Senese Felice Figliucci,* who, writyng vpon
Aristotles Ethickes so excellentlie in *Italian,* as neuer did
yet any one in myne opinion either in *Greke* or *Latin,*
amongest other thynges doth most earnestlie inuey agaynst
15 the rude ryming of verses in that tong : And whan soeuer
he expresseth *Aristotles* preceptes with any example out
of *Homer* or *Euripides,* he translateth them, not after the
Rymes of *Petrarke,* but into soch kinde of perfite verse,
with like feete and quantitie of sillabes, as he found them
20 before in the *Greke* tonge ; exhortyng earnestlie all the
Italian nation to leaue of their rude barbariousnesse in
ryming, and folow diligently the excellent *Greke* and *Latin*
examples in trew versifiyng.

And you that be able to vnderstand no more then ye
25 finde in the *Italian* tong, and neuer went farder than the
schole of *Petrarke* and *Ariostus* abroad, or els of *Chaucer*
at home, though you haue pleasure to wander blindlie
still in your foule wrong way, enuie not others that seeke,
as wise men haue done before them, the fairest and
30 rightest way ; or els, beside the iust reproch of malice,
wisemen shall trewlie iudge that you do so, as I haue
sayd and say yet agayne vnto you, bicause either for
idlenes ye will not, or for ignorance ye can not, cum by no
better your selfe.

35 And therfore, euen as *Virgill* and *Horace* deserue most

worthie prayse, that they, spying the vnperfitnes in *Ennius*
and *Plautus*, by trew Imitation of *Homer* and *Euripides*
brought Poetrie to the same perfitnes in *Latin* as it was
in *Greke*, euen so those that by the same way would
benefite their tong and contrey deserue rather thankes 5
than disprayse in that behalfe.

And I reioyce that euen poore England preuented *Italie*,
first in spying out, than in seekyng to amend this fault in
learnyng.

And here for my pleasure I purpose a litle by the way 10
to play and sporte with my Master *Tully*; from whom
commonlie I am neuer wont to dissent. He him selfe,
for this point of learnyng, in his verses doth halt a litle,
by his leaue. He could not denie it, if he were aliue,
nor those defend hym now that loue him · best. This fault 15
I lay to his charge : bicause once it pleased him, though
somwhat merelie, yet oueruncurteslie, to rayle vpon poore
England, obiecting both extreme beggerie and mere bar-
bariousnes vnto it, writyng thus vnto his frend *Atticus* :
There is not one scruple of siluer in that whole Isle, 20
or any one that knoweth either learnyng or letter.

But now, master *Cicero*, blessed be God and his sonne
Iesus Christ, whom you neuer knew, except it were as it
pleased him to lighten you by some shadow, as couertlie
in one place ye confesse saying, *Veritatis tantum vmbram* 25
consectamur, as your Master *Plato* did before you : blessed
be God, I say, that sixten hundred yeare after you were
dead and gone it may trewly be sayd, that for siluer there
is more cumlie plate in one Citie of England than is in
foure of the proudest Cities in all *Italie*, and take *Rome* 30
for one of them. And for learnyng, beside the knowledge
of all learned tongs and liberall sciences, euen your owne
bookes, *Cicero*, be as well read, and your excellent eloquence is as well liked and loued, and as trewlie folowed,
in England at this day, as it is now, or euer was, sence 35

your owne tyme in any place of *Italie*, either at *Arpinum*, where ye were borne, or els at *Rome*, where ye were brought vp. And a litle to brag with you, *Cicero*, where you your selfe, by your leaue, halted in some point of learnyng in your owne tong, many in England at this day go streight vp, both in trewe skill and right doing therein.

This I write, not to reprehend *Tullie*, whom aboue all other I like and loue best, but to excuse *Terence*, because in his tyme, and a good while after, Poetrie was neuer perfited in *Latin*, vntill by trew *Imitation* of the Grecians it was at length brought to perfection : And also thereby to exhorte the goodlie wittes of England, which, apte by nature and willing by desire, geue them selues to Poetrie, that they, rightly vnderstanding the barbarous bringing in of Rymes, would labor, as *Virgil* and *Horace* did in Latin, to make perfit also this point of learning in our English tong.

And thus much for *Plautus* and *Terence*, for matter, tong, and meter, what is to be followed, and what to be exchewed in them.

After *Plautus* and *Terence* no writing remayneth vntill *Tullies* tyme, except a fewe short fragmentes of *L. Crassus* excellent wit, here and there recited of *Cicero* for example sake, whereby the louers of learnyng may the more lament the losse of soch a worthie witte.

And although the Latin tong did faire blome and blossome in *L. Crassus* and *M. Antonius*, yet in *Tullies* tyme onely, and in *Tullie* himselfe chieflie, was the Latin tong fullie ripe and growne to the hiest pitch of all perfection.

And yet in the same tyme it began to fade and stoupe, as *Tullie* him selfe, in *Brutus de Claris Oratoribus*, with weeping wordes doth witnesse.

And bicause emongs them of that tyme there was some difference, good reason is that of them of that tyme should

D 2

be made right choice also. And yet let the best *Ciceronian* in Italie read *Tullies* familiar epistles aduisedly ouer, and I beleue he shall finde small difference for the Latin tong, either in propriety of wordes or framing of the stile, betwixt *Tullie* and those that write vnto him: As *Ser.* 5 *Sulpitius, A. Cecinna, M. Cael[i]us, M. et D. Bruti, A. Pollio, L. Plancus,* and diuerse other. Read the epistles of *L. Plancus* in *x. Lib.,* and for an assay that Epistle namely to the *Coss.* and whole *Senate,* the eight Epistle in number; and what could be eyther more eloquentlie or more 1 wiselie written, yea by *Tullie* himselfe, a man may iustly doubt. Thies men and *Tullie* liued all in one tyme, were like in authoritie, not vnlike in learning and studie, which might be iust causes of this their equalitie in writing: And yet surely they neyther were in deed, not yet were 1 counted in mens opinions, equall with *Tullie* in that facultie. And how is the difference hid in his Epistles? verelie, as the cunning of an expert Seaman in a faire calme fresh Ryuer doth litle differ from the doing of a meaner work-man therein, euen so, in the short cut of a priuate letter, 2 where matter is common, wordes easie, and order not moch diuerse, small shew of difference can appeare. But where *Tullie* doth set vp his saile of eloquence, in some broad deep Argument, caried with full tyde and winde of his witte and learnyng, all other may rather stand and 2 looke after him than hope to ouertake him, what course so euer he hold, either in faire or foule. Foure men onely, whan the Latin tong was full ripe, be left vnto vs, who in that tyme did florish, and did leaue to posteritie the fruite of their witte and learning: *Varro, Salust, Caesar,* 3 and *Cicero.* Whan I say these foure onely, I am not ignorant that euen in the same tyme most excellent Poetes, deseruing well of the Latin tong, as *Lucretius, Catullus, Virgill,* and *Horace,* did write, but bicause in this litle booke I purpose to teach a yong scholer to go, not to 3

daunce, to speake, not to sing (whan Poetes in deed,
namelie *Epici* and *Lyrici*, as these be, are fine dauncers
and trime singers): but *Oratores* and *Historici* be those
cumlie goers, and faire and wise speakers, of whom
5 I wishe my scholer to wayte vpon first, and after in
good order and dew tyme to be brought forth to the
singing and dauncing schole: And for this consideration
do I name these foure to be the onelie writers of that
tyme.

VARRO.

10 *Varro*, in his bookes *de lingua Latina et Analogia*, as
these be left mangled and patched vnto vs, doth not enter
there in to any great depth of eloquence, but as one caried
in a small low vessell him selfe verie nie the common shore,
15 not much vnlike the fisher men of Rye and Hering men
of Yarmouth, who deserue, by common mens opinion,
small commendacion for any cunning sailing at all, yet
neuertheles in those bookes of *Varro* good and necessarie
stuffe, for that meane kinde of Argument, be verie well and
20 learnedlie gathered togither.

His bookes of Husbandrie are moch to be regarded
and diligentlie to be read, not onelie for the proprietie,
but also for the plentie of good wordes, in all contrey and
husbandmens affaires: which can not be had by so good
25 authoritie out of any other Author, either of so good
a tyme, or of so great learnyng, as out of *Varro*. And
yet, bicause he was fourscore yeare old whan he wrote
those bookes, the forme of his style there compared with
Tullies writyng is but euen the talke of a spent old man:
30 whose wordes commonlie fall out of his mouth, though
verie wiselie, yet hardly and cold[l]ie, and more heauelie
also than some eares can well beare, except onelie for age

and authorities sake. And, perchance, in a rude contrey argument, of purpose and iudgement he rather vsed the speach of the contrey than talke of the Citie.

And so, for matter sake, his wordes sometyme be somewhat rude, and, by the imitation of the elder *Cato*, old and out of vse : And beyng depe stept in age, by negligence some wordes do so scape and fall from him in those bookes, as be not worth the taking vp by him that is carefull to speak or write trew Latin, as that sentence in him, *Romani in pace a rusticis alebantur, et in bello ab his tuebantur.* A good student must be therfore carefull and diligent to read with iudgement ouer euen those Authors which did write in the most perfite tyme : and let him not be affrayd to trie them, both in proprietie of wordes and forme of style, by the touch stone of *Caesar* and *Cicero*, whose puritie was neuer soiled, no not by the sentence of those that loued them worst.

All louers of learnyng may sore lament the losse of those bookes of *Varro* which he wrote in his yong and lustie yeares with good leysure and great learnyng of all partes of Philosophie : of the goodliest argumentes perteyning both to the common wealth and priuate life of man, as *de Ratione studii et educandis liberis*, which booke is oft recited and moch praysed in the fragmentes of *Nonius*, euen for authoritie sake. He wrote most diligentlie and largelie also the whole historie of the state of *Rome*; the mysteries of their whole Religion ; their lawes, customes, and gouernement in peace ; their maners, and whole discipline in warre. And this is not my gessing, as one in deed that neuer saw those bookes, but euen the verie iudgement and playne testimonie of *Tullie* him selfe, who knew and read those bookes, in these wordes :— *Tu aetatem patriae: tu descriptiones temporum: tu sacrorum, tu sacerdotum iura: tu domesticam, tu bellicam disciplinam: tu sedem regionum, locorum ; tu omnium diuinarum hu-*

manarumque rerum nomina, genera, officia, causas aperuisti,
etc.

But this great losse of *Varro* is a litle recompensed by
the happy comming of *Dionysius Halicarnassaeus* to *Rome*
5 in *Augustus* dayes : who, getting the possession of *Varros*
librarie, out of that treasure house of learning did leaue
vnto vs some frute of *Varros* witte and diligence ; I meane
his goodlie bookes *de Antiquitatibus Romanorum.* *Varro*
was so estemed for his excellent learnyng, as *Tullie* him
10 selfe had a reuerence to his iudgement in all doutes of
learnyng. And *Antonius Triumuir*, his enemie, and of
a contrarie faction, who had power to kill and bannish
whom he listed, whan *Varros* name amongest others was
brought in a schedule vnto him to be noted to death, he
15 tooke his penne and wrote his warrant of sauegard with
these most goodlie wordes, *Viuat Varro, vir doctissimus.*
In later tyme, no man knew better, nor liked and loued
more *Varros* learnyng than did S. *Augustine*, as they
do well vnderstand that haue diligentlie read ouer his
20 learned bookes *de Ciuitate Dei*: Where he hath this
most notable sentence : 'Whan I see how much *Varro*
wrote, I meruell much that euer he had any leasure to
read ; and, whan I perceiue how many thinges he read,
I meruell more that euer he had any leasure to write,'
25 etc.

And, surelie, if *Varros* bookes had remained to posteritie,
as by Gods prouidence the most part of *Tullies* did, than
trewlie the *Latin* tong might haue made good comparison
with the *Greke*.

30   SALUSTE.

Salust is a wise and worthy writer ; but he requireth
a learned Reader, and a right considerer of him. My
dearest frend, and best master that euer I had or heard in

learning, Syr *I. Cheke*, soch a man as, if I should liue to see
England breed the like againe, I feare I should liue ouer
long, did once giue me a lesson for *Salust*, which, as
I shall neuer forget my selfe, so is it worthy to be remembred of all those that would cum to perfite iudgement 5
of the Latin tong. He said that *Salust* was not verie fitte
for yong men to learne out of him the puritie of the Latin
tong, because he was not the purest in proprietie of
wordes, nor choisest in aptnes of phrases, nor the best
in framing of sentences; and therefore is his writing, 10
sayd he, neyther plaine for the matter, nor sensible for
mens vnderstanding. 'And what is the cause thereof, Syr?'
quoth I. ' Verilie,' said he, ' bicause in *Salust* writing is
more Arte than nature, and more labor than Arte : and
in his labor also to moch toyle, as it were, with an vncon- 15
tented care to write better than he could, a fault common
to very many men. And therefore he doth not expresse
the matter liuely and naturally with common speach, as ye
see *Xenophon* doth in Greeke ; but it is caried and driuen
forth artificiallie, after to learned a sorte, as *Thucydides* 20
doth in his orations.' 'And how cummeth it to passe,' sayd
I, 'that *Caesar* and *Ciceroes* talke is so naturall and plaine,
and *Salust* writing so artificiall and darke, whan all they
three liued in one tyme?' 'I will freelie tell you my
fansie herein,' said he : ' surely *Caesar* and *Cicero*, beside 25
a singular prerogatiue of naturall eloquence geuen vnto
them by God, both two, by vse of life, were daylie orators
emonges the common people and greatest councellers in
the Senate house, and therefore gaue themselues to vse soch
speach as the meanest should well vnderstand and the 30
wisest best allow, folowing carefullie that good councell
of *Aristotle, loquendum vt multi, sapiendum vt pauci*. *Salust*
was no soch man, neyther for will to goodnes nor skill
by learning ; but, ill geuen by nature, and made worse by
bringing vp, spent the most part of his yougth very misor- 35

derly in ryot and lechery, in the company of soch, who, neuer geuing theyr mynde to honest doyng, could neuer inure their tong to wise speaking; but at last cummyng to better yeares, and bying witte at the dearest hand, that
5 is by long experience of the hurt and shame that commeth of mischeif, moued by the councell of them that were wise, and caried by the example of soch as were good, first fell to honestie of life, and after to the loue of studie and learning; and so became so new a man that *Caesar*,
10 being dictator, made him Pretor in *Numidia*, where he, absent from his contrie and not inured with the common talke of Rome, but shut vp in his studie and bent wholy to reading, did write the storie of the Romanes. And for the better accomplishing of the same, he red *Cato* and
15 *Piso* in Latin for gathering of matter and troth, and *Thucydides* in Greeke for the order of his storie and furnishing of his style. *Cato* (as his tyme required) had more troth for the matter than eloquence for the style. And so *Salust*, by gathering troth out of *Cato*, smelleth
20 moch of the roughnes of his style: euen as a man that eateth garlike for helth shall cary away with him the sauor of it also, whether he will or not. And yet the vse of old wordes is not the greatest cause of *Salustes* rough-nes and darknesse: There be in *Salust* some old wordes
25 in deed as *patrare bellum, ductare exercitum*, well noted by *Quintilian*, and verie much misliked of him; and *sup-plicium* for *supplicatio*, a word smellyng of an older store than the other two so misliked by *Quint.* And yet is that word also in *Varro*, speaking of Oxen thus, *boues ad*
30 *victimas faciunt, atque ad Deorum supplicia*: and a few old wordes mo. Read *Saluste* and *Tullie* aduisedly together, and in wordes ye shall finde small difference; yea *Salust* is more geuen to new wordes than to olde, though som olde writers say the contrarie: as *Claritudo* for *Gloria*,
35 *exacte* for *perfecte, Facundia* for *eloquentia.* Thies two

last wordes *exacte* and *facundia*, now in euery mans mouth,
be neuer (as I do remember) vsed of *Tullie*, and therefore
I thinke they be not good: For surely *Tullie* speaking
euery where so moch of the matter of eloquence would not
so precisely haue absteyned from the word *Facundia* 5
if it had bene good, that is proper for the tong, and
common for mens vse. I could be long in reciting many
soch like, both olde and new wordes in *Salust*, but in very
dede neyther oldnes nor newnesse of wordes maketh the
greatest difference betwixt *Salust* and *Tullie*, but first 10
strange phrases made of good Latin wordes but framed
after the Greeke tonge, which be neyther choisly borowed
of them, nor properly vsed by him; than a hard composition and crooked framing of his wordes and sentences,
as a man would say, English talke placed and framed 15
outlandish like. As for example first in phrases, *nimius
et animus* be two vsed wordes, yet *homo nimius animi* is
an vnused phrase. *Vulgus, et amat, et fieri,* be as common
and well known wordes as may be in the Latin tong, yet
id quod vulgo amat fieri, for *solet fieri,* is but a strange and 20
Grekysh kind of writing. *Ingens et vires* be proper wordes,
yet *vir ingens virium* is an vnproper kinde of speaking; and
so be likewise *aeger consilii, promptissimus belli, territus
animi,* and many soch like phrases in *Salust,* borowed, as
I sayd, not choisly out of Greeke, and vsed therefore 25
vnproperlie in Latin. Againe, in whole sentences, where
the matter is good, the wordes proper and plaine, yet
the sense is hard and darke, and namely in his prefaces
and oration[s], wherein he vsed most labor, which fault
is likewise in *Thucydides* in Greeke, of whom *Salust* hath 30
taken the greatest part of his darkenesse. For *Thucydides*
likewise wrote his storie, not at home in Grece, but abrode
in Italie, and therefore smelleth of a certaine outlandish
kinde of talke, strange to them of *Athens*, and diuerse
from their writing that liued in Athens and Grece, and 35

wrote the same tyme that *Thucydides* did, as *Lysias*,
Xenophon, *Plato*, and *Isocrates*, the purest and playnest
writers that euer wrote in any tong, and best examples for
any man to follow whether he write Latin, Italian, French,
5 or English. *Thucydides* also semeth in his writing not
so much benefited by nature as holpen by Arte, and
caried forth by desire, studie, labor, toyle, and ouer great
curiositie ; who spent xxvii. yeares in writing his eight
bookes of his history. *Salust* likewise wrote out of his
10 contrie, and followed the faultes of *Thuc.* to moch ; and
boroweth of him som kinde of writing which the Latin
tong can not well beare, as *Casus nominatiuus* in diuerse
places *absolute positus*, as in that place of *Iugurth*, speaking *de Leptitanis, Itaque ab imperatore facile quae petebant*
15 *adepti, missae sunt eo cohortes Ligurum quatuor.* This
thing in participles, vsed so oft in *Thucyd.* and other
Greeke authors to, may better be borne with all, but
Salust vseth the same more strangelie and boldlie, as in
thies wordes, *Multis sibi quisque imperium petentibus.* I
20 beleue the best Grammarien in England can scarse giue
a good reule why *quisque*, the nominatiue case, without
any verbe, is so thrust vp amongest so many oblique
cases.' Some man perchance will smile, and laugh to
scorne this my writyng, and call it idle curiositie thus to
25 busie my selfe in pickling about these small pointes of
Grammer, not fitte for my age, place, and calling to trifle
in : I trust that man, be he neuer so great in authoritie,
neuer so wise and learned, either by other mens iudgement or his owne opinion, will yet thinke that he is not
30 greater in England than *Tullie* was at *Rome*, not yet wiser
nor better learned than *Tullie* was him selfe, who, at
the pitch of three score yeares, in the middes of the broyle
betwixt *Caesar* and *Pompeie*, whan he knew not whither to
send wife and children, which way to go, where to hide
35 him selfe, yet, in an earnest letter, amongest his earnest

councelles for those heuie tymes concerning both the
common state of his contrey and his owne priuate great
affaires, he was neither vnmyndfull nor ashamed to reason
at large, and learne gladlie of *Atticus*, a lesse point of
Grammer than these be, noted of me in *Salust*, as whether 5
he should write *ad Piraeea, in Piraeea,* or *in Piraeeum,* or
Piraeeum, sine praepositione : And in those heuie tymes he
was so carefull to know this small point of Grammer
that he addeth these wordes, *Si hoc mihi ζήτημα persolueris,
magna me molestia liberaris.* If *Tullie,* at that age, in that 10
authoritie, in that care for his contrey, in that ieoperdie
for him selfe and extreme necessitie of hys dearest
frendes, beyng also the Prince of Eloquence hym selfe,
was not ashamed to descend to these low pointes of
Grammer, in his owne naturall tong, what should scholers 15
do, yea what should any man do, if he do thinke well
doyng better than ill doyng : And had rather be perfite
than meane, sure than doutefull, to be what he should be
in deed, not seeme what he is not in opinion. He that
maketh perfitnes in the *Latin* tong his marke must cume 20
to it by choice and certaine knowledge, not stumble vpon
it by chance and doubtfull ignorance. And the right
steppes to reach vnto it be these, linked thus orderlie
together, aptnes of nature, loue of learnyng, diligence in
right order, constancie with pleasant moderation, and 25
alwayes to learne of them that be best ; and so shall you
iudge as they that be wisest. And these be those reules
which worthie Master *Cheke* dyd impart vnto me concernyng *Salust* and the right iudgement of the *Latin*
tong. 30

CAESAR.

Caesar, for that litle of him that is left vnto vs, is
like the halfe face of a *Venus,* the other part of the head

beyng hidden, the bodie and the rest of the members
vnbegon, yet so excellentlie done by *Apelles*, as all men
may stand still to mase and muse vpon it, and no man
step forth with any hope to performe the like.

5   His seuen bookes *de bello Gallico* and three *de bello
ciuili* be written so wiselie for the matter, so eloquentlie
for the tong, that neither his greatest enemies could euer
finde the least note of parcialitie in him (a meruelous
wisdome of a man, namely writyng of his owne doynges),
10 nor yet the best iudegers of the *Latin* tong, nor the
most enuious lookers vpon other mens writynges, can
say any other but all things be most perfitelie done
by him.

Brutus, Caluus, and *Calidius,* who found fault with
15 *Tullies* fulnes in woordes and matter, and that rightlie,
for *Tullie* did both confesse it and mend it, yet in *Caesar*
they neither did, nor could, finde the like or any other
fault.

And therfore thus iustlie I may conclude of *Caesar,*
20 that where, in all other, the best that euer wrote, in any
tyme, or in any tong, in *Greke* or *Latin* (I except neither
Plato, Demosthenes, nor *Tullie*), some fault is iustlie noted,
in *Caesar* onelie could neuer yet fault be found.

Yet neuertheles, for all this perfite excellencie in him,
25 yet it is but in one member of eloquence, and that but of
one side neither, whan we must looke for that example
to folow, which hath a perfite head, a whole bodie, forward
and backward, armes and legges and all.

GEORGE GASCOIGNE

(*Certayne Notes of Instruction*)

1575[1]

[Gascoigne's *Certayne Notes of Instruction* first appeared in the quarto edition of *The Posies of George Gascoigne, Esquire, corrected, perfected, and augmented by the Author*, London (Feb.) 1575, and was reprinted in the *Whole Woorkes* (1587). The text is taken from the copy of the *Posies* in the Bodleian Library (Malone, 792), which is freely annotated in the handwriting of Gabriel Harvey (see notes *passim*). The *Notes* occupy five leaves, in black-letter (sig. Tij—Uij).]

CERTAYNE NOTES OF INSTRUCTION CONCERNING THE MAKING OF VERSE OR RYME IN ENGLISH, WRITTEN AT THE REQUEST OF MASTER *EDOUARDO DONATI.*

SIgnor Edouardo, since promise is debt, and you (by the lawe of friendship) do burden me with a promise that I shoulde lende you instructions towards the making of English verse or ryme, I will assaye to discharge the same, though not so perfectly as I would, yet as readily as I may: and therwithall I pray you consider that *Quot*

[1] In 1573 Richard Willes published (*a*) *Poematum Liber* (London, Tottell), and (*b*) *In suorum Poemat. librum Ricardi Willeii Scholia* (London, Tottell), a separate issue, though also contained in (*a*). The second book, which is dedicated to the Warden and Scholars of Wykeham's College at Winchester, is divided into (1) *De Re Poetica Disputatio* (Aj—Cj), and (2) *Scholia* (Cj v°—E iiij). It is prefaced by an *Epistola* (three leaves) and by two pages of introduction to the *Disputatio* praising Wykeham's domicile (the school) and exalting the study of poetry. ' Erunt igitur nostrae disputationis partes tres.

homines, tot Sententiae, especially in Poetrie, wherein (neuerthelesse) I dare not challenge any degree, and yet will I at your request aduenture to set downe my simple skill in such simple manner as I haue vsed, referring the
5 same hereafter to the correction of the *Laureate*. And you shall haue it in these few poynts followyng.

The first and most necessarie poynt that euer I founde meete to be considered in making of a delectable poeme is this, to grounde it upon some fine inuention. For it is
10 not inough to roll in pleasant woordes, nor yet to thunder in *Rym, Ram, Ruff* by letter (quoth my master *Chaucer*), nor yet to abounde in apt vocables or epythetes, vnlesse the Inuention haue in it also *aliquid salis*. By this *aliquid salis* I meane some good and fine deuise, shewing the
15 quicke capacitie of a writer : and where I say some *good and fine inuention* I meane that I would haue it both fine and good. For many inuentions are so superfine that they are *Vix good*. And, againe, many Inuentions are good, and yet not finely handled. And for a general for-

Primo commentarium de Poeticae natura atque ortu, de Poeticae significatione, diversisque Poetarum generibus, de origine metri atque usu carminum diversis ex auctoribus colligam ': and he goes on to explain his plan. He has three theses, viz. (1) *Poeticam esse praestantiorem caeteris artibus* (four pages) ; (2) *Poeticen artem esse fructuosam* (one and a half pages); and (3) *Poeticen esse iucundissimam*, with a sub-section, *Quae obiici contra Poeticam solent, illa modo erunt diluenda*, containing *calumnia* and *resp*[*onsiones*] (about six leaves). The *Scholia* explain and expound various words, figures, and tech-nical matters used in poetry (about a page to each), such as *Donat atque dedicat* (being the first title), *Quincunx, Ara, Gladius, Paruum ovum, Pyrum, Pastoricia fistula, Alae, Cantuariensis ecclesiae insignia, Pyramis inversa, Securis, Cento, Rhapsodia*, &c. Willes is not tempted to refer to contemporary English verse, or to any of the problems of versification. The volume concludes with a poem on the life of William of Wykeham and a number of distichs on the Wardens of the School, and with a 'didascalorum elenchus.' [From the copy preserved in the Bodleian Library (Wood, 105).]

warning : what Theame soeuer you do take in hande, if
you do handle it but *tanquam in oratione perpetua*, and
neuer studie for some depth of deuise in the Inuention,
and some figures also in the handlyng thereof, it will
appeare to the skilfull Reader but a tale of a tubbe. To 5
deliuer vnto you generall examples it were almoste vnpossible, sithence the occasions of Inuentions are (as it were)
infinite ; neuerthelesse, take in worth mine opinion, and
perceyue my furder meanyng in these few poynts. If
I should vndertake to wryte in prayse of a gentlewoman, 10
I would neither praise hir christal eye, nor hir cherrie
lippe, etc. For these things are *trita et obuia*. But I would
either finde some supernaturall cause wherby my penne
might walke in the superlatiue degree, or els I would
vndertake to aunswere for any imperfection that shee 15
hath, and therevpon rayse the prayse of hir commendacion. Likewise, if I should disclose my pretence in
loue, I would eyther make a strange discourse of some
intollerable passion, or finde occasion to pleade by the
example of some historie, or discouer my disquiet in 20
shadowes *per Allegoriam*, or vse the couertest meane that
I could to auoyde the vncomely customes of common
writers. Thus much I aduenture to deliuer vnto you
(my freend) vpon the rule of Inuention, which of all other
rules is most to be marked, and hardest to be prescribed 25
in certayne and infallible rules ; neuerthelesse, to conclude
therein, I would haue you stand most vpon the excellencie
of your Inuention, and sticke not to studie deepely for
some fine deuise. For, that beyng founde, pleasant woordes
will follow well inough and fast inough. 30

2. Your Inuention being once deuised, take heede that
neither pleasure of rime nor varietie of deuise do carie
you from it : for as to vse obscure and darke phrases in
a pleasant Sonet is nothing delectable, so to entermingle
merie iests in a serious matter is an *Indecorum*. 35

3. I will next aduise you that you hold the iust measure wherwith you begin your verse. I will not denie but this may seeme a preposterous ordre; but, bycause I couet rather to satisfie you particularly than to vndertake a
5 generall tradition, I wil not somuch stand vpon the manner as the matter of my precepts. I say then, remember to holde the same measure wherwith you begin, whether it be in a verse of sixe syllables, eight, ten, twelue, etc.: and though this precept might seeme ridiculous vnto you, since
10 euery yong scholler can conceiue that he ought to continue in the same measure wherwith he beginneth, yet do I see and read many mens Poems now adayes, whiche beginning with the measure of xij. in the first line, and xiiij. in the second (which is the common kinde of verse), they wil yet
15 (by that time they haue passed ouer a few verses) fal into xiiij. and fourtene, *et sic de similibus*, the which is either forgetfulnes or carelesnes.

4. And in your verses remembre to place euery worde in his natural *Emphasis* or sound, that is to say, in such
20 wise, and with such length or shortnesse, eleuation or depression of sillables, as it is commonly pronounced or vsed. To expresse the same we haue three maner of accents, *grauis, leuis, et circumflexa*, the whiche I would english thus, the long accent, the short accent, and that
25 whiche is indifferent: the graue accent is marked by this caracte \, the light accent is noted thus /, and the circum-flexe or indifferent is thus signified ⌒: the graue accent is drawen out or eleuate, and maketh that sillable long wherevpon it is placed; the light accent is depressed or
30 snatched vp, and maketh that sillable short vpon the which it lighteth; the circumflexe accent is indifferent, sometimes short, sometimes long, sometimes depressed and some-times eleuate. For example of th' emphasis or natural sound of words, this word *Treasure* hath the graue accent
35 vpon the first sillable; whereas if it shoulde be written in

this sorte *Treasúre,* nowe were the second sillable long, and that were cleane contrarie to the common vse wherwith it is pronounced. For furder explanation hereof, note you that commonly now a dayes in English rimes (for I dare not cal them English verses) we vse none other 5 order but a foote of two sillables, wherof the first is depressed or made short, and the second is eleuate or made long; and that sound or scanning continueth throughout the verse. We haue vsed in times past other kindes of Meeters, as for example this following : 10

No wight in this world, that wealth can attayne,
Vnlesse he beleue, that all is but vayne.

Also our father *Chaucer* hath vsed the same libertie in feete and measures that the Latinists do vse : and who so euer do peruse and well consider his workes, he shall 15 finde that although his lines are not alwayes of one selfe same number of Syllables, yet, beyng redde by one that hath vnderstanding, the longest verse, and that which hath most Syllables in it, will fall (to the eare) correspondent vnto that whiche hath fewest sillables in it : and like 20 wise that whiche hath in it fewest syllables shalbe founde yet to consist of woordes that haue such naturall sounde, as may seeme equall in length to a verse which hath many moe sillables of lighter accentes. And surely I can lament that wee are fallen into suche a playne and simple manner 25 of wryting, that there is none other foote vsed but one ; wherby our Poemes may iustly be called Rithmes, and cannot by any right challenge the name of a Verse. But, since it is so, let vs take the forde as we finde it, and lette me set downe vnto you suche rules or precepts that euen 30 in this playne foote of two syllables you wreste no woorde from his natural and vsuall sounde. I do not meane hereby that you may vse none other wordes but of twoo sillables,

for therein you may vse discretion according to occasion
of matter, but my meaning is, that all the wordes in your
verse be so placed as the first sillable may sound short or
be depressed, the second long or eleuate, the third shorte,
5 the fourth long, the fifth shorte, etc. For example of my
meaning in this point marke these two verses:

I vnderstand your meanying by your eye.
Your meaning I vnderstand by your eye.

In these two verses there seemeth no difference at all,
10 since the one hath the very selfe same woordes that the
other hath, and yet the latter verse is neyther true nor
pleasant, and the first verse may passe the musters. The
fault of the latter verse is that this worde *vnderstand* is
therein so placed as the graue accent falleth upon *der*,
15 and therby maketh *der* in this worde *vnderstand* to be
eleuated; which is contrarie to the naturall or vsual pronunciation, for we say *vnderstánd*, and not *vnderstand*.

5. Here by the way I thinke it not amisse to forewarne
you that you thrust as few wordes of many sillables into
20 your verse as may be: and herevnto I might alledge many
reasons. First, the most aunciant English wordes are of one
silable, so that the more monasyllables that you vse the
truer Englishman you shall seeme, and the lesse you shall
smell of the Inkehorne: Also wordes of many syllables
25 do cloye a verse and make it vnpleasant, whereas woordes
of one syllable will more easily fall to be shorte or long as
occasion requireth, or wilbe adapted to become circumflexe
or of an indifferent sounde.

6. I would exhorte you also to beware of rime without
30 reason: my meaning is hereby that your rime leade you
not from your firste Inuention, for many wryters, when
they haue layed the platforme of their inuention, are yet

drawen sometimes (by ryme) to forget it or at least to alter
it, as when they cannot readily finde out a worde whiche
maye rime to the first (and yet continue their determinate
Inuention) they do then eyther botche it vp with a worde
that will ryme (howe small reason soeuer it carie with it), 5
or els they alter their first worde and so percase decline
or trouble their former Inuention : But do you alwayes
hold your first determined Inuention, and do rather searche
the bottome of your braynes for apte wordes than chaunge
good reason for rumbling rime.   1

7. To help you a little with ryme (which is also a plaine
yong schollers lesson), worke thus : when you haue set
downe your first verse, take the last worde thereof and
coumpt ouer all the wordes of the selfe same sounde by
order of the Alphabete : As, for example, the laste woorde 1
of your firste line is *care*, to ryme therwith you haue *bare*,
clare, *dare*, *fare*, *gare*, *hare*, and *share*, *mare*, *snare*, *rare*,
stare, and *ware*, *&c.* Of all these take that which best may
serue your purpose, carying reason with rime : and if none
of them will serue so, then alter the laste worde of your 2
former verse, but yet do not willingly alter the meanyng
of your Inuention.

8. You may vse the same Figures or Tropes in verse
which are vsed in prose, and in my iudgement they serue
more aptly and haue greater grace in verse than they haue 2
in prose : but yet therein remember this old adage, *Ne quid
nimis*, as many wryters which do not know the vse of any
other figure than that whiche is expressed in repeticion of
sundrie wordes beginning all with one letter, the whiche
(beyng modestly vsed) lendeth good grace to a verse, but 3
they do so hunte a letter to death that they make it
Crambe, and *Crambe bis positum mors est* : therfor *Ne
quid nimis.*

9. Also, asmuche as may be, eschew straunge words, or
obsoleta et inusitata, vnlesse the Theame do giue iust occa- 3

sion : marie, in some places a straunge worde doth drawe attentiue reading, but yet I woulde haue you therein to vse discretion.

10. And asmuch as you may, frame your stile to *per-*
5 *spicuity* and to be sensible, for the haughty obscure verse doth not much delight, and the verse that is to easie is like a tale of a rosted horse ; but let your Poeme be such as may both delight and draw attentiue readyng, and there-withal may deliuer such matter as be worth the marking.

10 11. You shall do very well to vse your verse after thenglishe phrase, and not after the maner of other languages. The Latinists do commonly set the adiectiue after the Substantiue : As, for example, *Femina pulchra,* *aedes altae, &c.* ; but if we should say in English a woman
15 fayre, a house high, etc. it would haue but small grace, for we say a good man, and not a man good, etc. And yet I will not altogether forbidde it you, for in some places it may be borne, but not so hardly as some vse it which wryte thus :
20   *Now let vs go to Temple ours.*
     I will go visit mother myne &c.

Surely I smile at the simplicitie of such deuisers which might aswell haue sayde it in playne Englishe phrase, and yet haue better pleased all eares, than they satisfie
25 their owne fancies by suche *superfinesse.* Therefore euen as I haue aduised you to place all wordes in their naturall or most common and vsuall pronunciation, so would I wishe you to frame all sentences in their mother phrase and proper *Idióma* ; and yet sometimes (as I haue sayd before)
30 the contrarie may be borne, but that is rather where rime enforceth, or *per licentiam Poëticam,* than it is otherwise lawfull or commendable.

12. This poeticall licence is a shrewde fellow, and couereth many faults in a verse ; it maketh wordes longer,
35 shorter, of mo sillables, of fewer, newer, older, truer,

falser ; and, to conclude, it turkeneth all things at pleasure,
for example, *ydone* for *done, adowne* for *downe, orecome* for
ouercome, tane for *taken, power* for *powre, heauen* for *heaun,
thewes* for good partes or good qualities, and a numbre of
other, whiche were but tedious and needelesse to rehearse, 5
since your owne iudgement and readyng will soone make
you espie such aduauntages.

13. There are also certayne pauses or restes in a verse,
whiche may be called *Ceasures,* whereof I woulde be
lothe to stande long, since it is at discretion of the wryter, 10
and they haue bene first deuised (as should seeme) by the
Musicians : but yet thus much I will aduenture to wryte,
that in mine opinion in a verse of eight sillables the pause
will stand best in the middest ; in a verse of tenne it will
best be placed at the ende of the first foure sillables ; in 15
a verse of twelue, in the midst ; in verses of twelue in the
firste and fouretene in the seconde wee place the pause
commonly in the midst of the first, and at the ende of the
first eight sillables in the second. In Rithme royall it is
at the wryters discretion, and forceth not where the pause 20
be vntill the ende of the line.

14. And here, bycause I haue named Rithme royall,
I will tell you also mine opinion aswell of that as of the
names which other rymes haue commonly borne hereto-
fore. Rythme royall is a verse of tenne sillables ; and 25
seuen such verses make a staffe, whereof the first and thirde
lines do aunswer (acrosse) in like terminations and rime,
the second, fourth, and fifth do likewise answere eche
other in terminations, and the two last do combine and
shut vp the Sentence : this hath bene called Rithme 30
royall, and surely it is a royall kinde of verse, seruing
best for graue discourses. There is also another kinde,
called Ballade, and thereof are sundrie sortes : for a man
may write ballade in a staffe of six lines, euery line conteyning eighte or sixe sillables, whereof the firste and 35

third, second and fourth do rime acrosse, and the fifth
and sixth do rime togither in conclusion. You may write
also your ballad of tenne sillables, rimyng as before is
declared ; but these two were wont to be most commonly
5 vsed in ballade, which propre name was (I thinke) deriued
of this worde in Italian *Ballare*, whiche signifieth to
daunce. And in deed those kinds of rimes serue beste
for daunces or light matters. Then haue you also a rond-
lette, the which doth alwayes end with one self same
10 foote or repeticion, and was thereof (in my iudgement)
called a rondelet. This may consist of such measure as
best liketh the wryter. Then haue you Sonnets : some
thinke that all Poemes (being short) may be called Sonets,
as in deede it is a diminutiue worde deriued of *Sonare*, but
15 yet I can beste allowe to call those Sonnets whiche are of
fouretene lynes, euery line conteyning tenne syllables.
The firste twelue do ryme in staues of foure lines by
crosse meetre, and the last two ryming togither do conclude the whole. There are Dyzaynes, and Syxaines,
20 which are of ten lines, and of sixe lines, commonly vsed
by the French, which some English writers do also terme
by the name of Sonettes. Then is there an old kinde
of Rithme called Ver layes, deriued (as I haue redde) of
this worde *Verd*, whiche betokeneth Greene, and *Laye*,
25 which betokeneth a Song, as if you would say greene
Songes : but I muste tell you by the way that I neuer
redde any verse which I saw by aucthoritie called *Verlay*
but one, and that was a long discourse in verses of tenne
sillables, whereof the foure first did ryme acrosse, and the
30 fifth did aunswere to the firste and thirde, breaking off
there, and so going on to another termination. Of this
I could shewe example of imitation in mine own verses
written to the right honorable the Lord *Grey* of *Wilton*
upon my iourney into *Holland*, etc. There are also
35 certaine Poemes deuised of tenne syllables, whereof the

first aunswereth in termination with the fourth, and the
second and thirde answere eche other: these are more
vsed by other nations than by vs, neyther can I tell
readily what name to giue them. And the commonest
sort of verse which we vse now adayes (*viz.* the long verse 5
of twelue and fourtene sillables) I know not certainly
howe to name it, vnlesse I should say that it doth consist of Poulters measure, which giueth xii. for one
dozen and xiiij. for another. But let this suffise (if it be
not to much) for the sundrie sortes of verses which we vse 10
now adayes.

15. In all these sortes of verses, when soeuer you vndertake to write, auoyde prolixitie and tediousnesse, and euer,
as neare as you can, do finish the sentence and meaning
at the end of euery staffe where you wright staues, and 15
at the end of euery two lines where you write by cooples
or poulters measure: for I see many writers which draw
their sentences in length, and make an ende at latter
Lammas: for, commonly, before they end, the Reader hath
forgotten where he begon. But do you (if you wil follow 20
my aduise) eschue prolixitie and knit vp your sentences as
compendiously as you may, since breuitie (so that it be not
drowned in obscuritie) is most commendable.

16. I had forgotten a notable kinde of ryme, called
ryding rime, and that is suche as our Mayster and Father 25
Chaucer vsed in his Canterburie tales, and in diuers other
delectable and light enterprises; but, though it come to my
remembrance somewhat out of order, it shall not yet come
altogether out of time, for I will nowe tell you a conceipt
whiche I had before forgotten to wryte: you may see (by 30
the way) that I holde a preposterous order in my traditions
but, as I sayde before, I wryte moued by good wil, and not
to shewe my skill. Then to returne too my matter, as this
riding rime serueth most aptly to wryte a merie tale, so
Rythme royall is fittest for a graue discourse. Ballades 35

are beste of matters of loue, and rondlettes moste apt for
the beating or handlyng of an adage or common prouerbe :
Sonets serue aswell in matters of loue as of discourse :
Dizaynes and Sixaines for shorte Fantazies : Verlayes
5 for an effectual proposition, although by the name you
might otherwise iudge of Verlayes ; and the long verse
of twelue and fouretene sillables, although it be now adayes
vsed in all Theames, yet in my iudgement it would serue
best for Psalmes and Himpnes.

10   I woulde stande longer in these traditions, were it not
that I doubt mine owne ignoraunce ; but, as I sayde before,
I know that I write to my freende, and, affying my selfe
therevpon, I make an ende.

GEORGE WHETSTONE

(*THE DEDICATION TO PROMOS AND CASSANDRA*)

1578

[The text of the *Dedication* to *The right excellent and famous
Historye of Promos and Cassandra*, 1578, is printed from
the copy in the British Museum (C 34. e. 42).]

TO HIS WORSHIPFVLL FRIENDE AND KINSEMAN, *WILLIAM FLEETEWOODE ESQUIER, RECORDER OF LONDON.*

SYR, (desirous to acquite your tryed frendships with
some token of good will) of late I perused diuers 5
of my vnperfect workes, fully minded to bestowe on you
the trauell of some of my forepassed time. But (resolued
to accompanye the aduenturous Captaine Syr *Humfrey
Gylbert* in his honorable voiadge) I found my leysure too
littel to correct the errors in my sayd workes. So that 10
(inforced) I lefte them disparsed amonge my learned
freendes, at theyr leasure to polish, if I faild to returne :
spoyling (by this meanes) my studdy of his necessarye
furnyture. Amonge other vnregarded papers I fownde
this Discource of *Promos* and *Cassandra* ; which for the 15
rarenesse (and the needeful knowledge) of the necessary
matter contained therein (to make the actions appeare
more liuely) I deuided the whole history into two Commedies, for that, *Decorum* vsed, it would not be conuayed
in one. The effects of both are good and bad : vertue 20
intermyxt with vice, vnlawfull desyres (yf it were posible)
queancht with chaste denyals : al needeful actions (I

thinke) for publike vewe. For by the rewarde of the
good the good are encouraged in wel doinge : and with
the scowrge of the lewde the lewde are feared from euill
attempts : mainetayning this my oppinion with *Platoes*
5 auctority. *Nawghtinesse commes of the corruption of nature,
and not by readinge or hearinge the liues of the good or lewde
(for such publication is necessarye), but goodnesse (sayth he)
is beawtifyed by either action.* And to these endes *Menander,
Plautus,* and *Terence,* them selues many yeares since in-
10 tombed, (by their Commedies) in honour liue at this daye.
The auncient *Romanes* heald these showes of suche prise
that they not onely allowde the publike exercise of them,
but the graue Senators themselues countenaunced the
Actors with their presence : who from these trifles wonne
15 morallytye, as the Bee suckes honny from weedes. But
the aduised deuises of auncient Poets, disc[r]edited with
tryfels of yonge, vnaduised, and rashe witted wryters, hath
brought this commendable exercise in mislike. For at
this daye the *Italian* is so lasciuious in his commedies that
20 honest hearers are greeued at his actions : the *Frenchman*
and *Spaniarde* folowes the *Italians* humor : the *Germaine*
is too holye, for he presentes on euerye common Stage
what Preachers should pronounce in Pulpets. The *Englishman* in this quallitie is most vaine, indiscreete, and
25 out of order : he fyrst groundes his worke on impossi-
bilities ; then in three howers ronnes he throwe the
worlde, marryes, gets Children, makes Children men,
men to conquer kingdomes, murder Monsters, and bringeth
Gods from Heauen, and fetcheth Diuels from Hel. And
30 (that which is worst) their ground is not so vnperfect as
their workinge indiscreete : not waying, so the people
laugh, though they laugh them (for theyr follyes) to scorne.
Manye tymes (to make mirthe) they make a Clowne companion with a Kinge ; in theyr graue Counsels they allow
35 the aduise of fooles ; yea, they vse one order of speach for

all persons : a grose *Indecorum*, for a Crowe wyll yll counterfet the Nightingale's sweete voice ; euen so affected speeche doth misbecome a Clowne.   For, to worke a Com-medie   kindly,   graue   olde men   should   instruct,   yonge men should showe the imperfections of youth, Strumpets 5 should be lasciuious, Boyes vnhappy, and Clownes should   speake   disorderlye :   entermingling   all   these actions in such sorte as the graue matter may instruct and the pleasant delight ;   for without this chaunge the attention would be small, and the likinge lesse.   10

But leaue I this rehearsall of the vse and abuse of Commedies, least that I checke that in others which I cannot amend in my selfe.   But this I am assured, what actions so ever passeth in this History, either merry or morneful, graue or lasciuious, the conclusion showes the 15 confusion of Vice and the cherising of Vertue.   And sythe the end tends to this good, although the worke (because of euel handlinge) be vnworthy your learned Censure, allowe (I beseeche you) of my good wyll, vntyl leasure serues me to perfect some labour of more worthe.   No more, but 20 that almightye God be your protector, and. preserue me from dainger in this voiadge, the xxix of July, 1578.

Your Kinsman to vse,

GEORGE WHETSTONE.

THOMAS LODGE

(*DEFENCE OF POETRY*)

1579

[Of Lodge's ' Defence of Poetry, Music, and Stage Plays,'
written in reply to Stephen Gosson's *Schoole of Abuse*, only
two copies are known, one being in the Bodleian, the other
in the Britwell Collection. Neither copy has a title-page.
The book was issued privately in 1579, and was with-
drawn immediately. It was reprinted by the Shakespeare
Society in 1853. The present version, which has been
transcribed from the Bodleian copy (Malone, Add. 896),
restores a few words and spellings which had been mistaken in the reprint. The text is very corrupt, and in some
places defies emendation. Many of the errors seem to be
due to the printer's ignorance of MS. contractions. In the
original there are only two paragraph-breaks.

The accompanying table gives the earlier contributions to
the anti-stage controversy.

1577. John Northbrooke enters his *Treatise wherein
Dicing, Dauncing, vaine Playes or Enterluds, with other
idle Pastimes, &c., commonly vsed on the Sabaoth Day,
are reproued by the Authoritie of the Word of God and
auntient Writers* (ed. Collier, Shakes. Soc., 1843).

1579. *The Schoole of Abuse. Conteining a plesaunt in-
vectiue against Poets, Pipers, Plaiers, Jesters and such
like Catterpillers of a Commonwelth; setting vp the
Flagge of Defiance to their mischieuous exercise, and
ouerthrowing their Bulwarkes, by Prophane Writers,
Naturall reason, and common Experience. . . . By
Stephan Gosson. Stud. Oxon.* Dedicated to Sir Philip
Sidney (See Spenser's letter, 16th Oct., *infra*, p. 89)
The pamphlet has been reprinted in Somers's *Collec-
tion* (1810, iii. 552), by the Shakespeare Society (ed.
Collier), and by Mr. Arber in his *English Reprints*
(New Issue, 1895).

1579. *Straunge News out of Affrick.* A Defence of the
stage, of which nothing is known except the account
given by Gosson in his *Ephemerides* (see Arber's
edit. *u. s.* pp. 62–3).

1579. *A Short Apologie of the Schoole of Abuse, against Poets,
Pipers, Players, and their Excusers,* by Gosson. Added
to his *Ephemerides of Phialo.* The *Apologie* is dedicated to Sir Philip Sidney. Reprinted by Arber,
u. s. pp. 64–75.

Towards the close Gosson writes : ' It is tolde mee
that they haue got one in London to write
certaine *Honest excuses,* for so they tearme it, to
their dishonest abuses which I reuealed . . . .
How he frames his excuses, I know not yet, because it is doone in hudder mudder. Trueth can
neuer be Falsehods Visarde, which maketh him
maske without a torch, and keepe his papers very
secret.' It is doubtful whether this passage, and
especially the allusion to secrecy, refers to the next
work.

1579. Lodge's *Defence* (here reprinted).

1579. *The Play of Playes,* an unknown ' Defence,' described
by Gosson in the Fourth ' Action ' of his *Playes
Confuted.*

1580. Henry Denham enters his tract, *A Second and
Third Blast of Retreat from Plays and Theatres.*

1581. *A Treatise of Daunses, wherein it is showed, that they
are as it were accessories and dependants (or things
annexed) to whoredom* : *where also by the way is touched
and proved, that Playes are ioyned and knit together in
a ranck or rowe with them* (see Chatsworth Library
Catalogue, vol. iv. p. 49).

? 1582. *Playes confuted in five Actions* &c., by Gosson, in
answer to Lodge's *Defence* and the *Play of Playes.*
Dedicated to Sir Francis Walsingham. (Reprinted by
Mr. W. C. Hazlitt in the Roxburghe Library, 1868.)

1581–3. Sidney writing his *Apologie* or *Defence.* Published in 1595 (see p. 148).

1583. *The Anatomie of Abuses*, by Philip Stubbes. (Reprinted by the New Shaks. Soc. 1877, ed. F. J. Furnivall.)

1584. *A Touchstone for the Time*, by George Whetstone. (Added to *A Mirour for Magestrates of Cyties*.)

1587. *A Mirrour of Monsters*, by William Rankins.

} All anti-stage.

There is but little material of literary interest in these controversial works (excluding Sidney's *Apologie* or *Defence*); they are almost exclusively devoted to partisan discussion of the social influence of the playhouse. Gosson's essays have not been reprinted here, for though he is the best known and the most active of the Puritan pamphleteers, and though he prompted Lodge to write his rhetorical answer and may have inspired Sidney's essay, he but rarely ventures to touch on the art or theory of poetry and the drama. The more important passages in his works are printed in the notes to Lodge and others, by way of illustration and commentary. Lodge's *Defence*, even in the portion here printed, is almost as uncritical as Gosson's attack, but it has a superior historical importance in defining a special trend in the later development of Elizabethan criticism.]

PROTOGENES can know Apelles by his line though he se him not, and wise men can consider by the Penn of aucthoritie of the writer thoughe they know him not. The Rubie is discerned by his pale rednes; and
5 who hath not hard that the Lyon is knowne by hys clawes? Though Æsopes craftie crowe be neuer so deftlye decked, yet is his double dealing esely desiphered: & though men neuer so perfectly pollish there wrytings with others sentences, yet the simple truth wil discouer the shadow of
10 ther follies: and bestowing euery fether in the bodye of the right M. tourne out the naked dissembler into his

owen cote, as a spectacle of follye to all those which can rightlye Iudge what imperfections be.

There came to my hands lately a litle (woulde God a wittye) pamphelet, baring a fayre face as though it were the scoole of abuse ; but, being by me aduisedly wayed, 5 I fynd it the oftscome of imperfections, the writer fuller of wordes then iudgement, the matter certainely as ridiculus as serius. Assuredly his mother witte wrought this wonder, the child to disprayse his father, the dogg to byte his mayster for his dainty morcell : but I se (with Seneca) that 10 the wrong is to be suffered, since he disprayseth, who by costome hath left to speake well. But I meane to be short, and teach the Maister what he knoweth not, partly that he may se his own follie, and partly that I may discharge my promise,—both binde me : therefore I would 15 wish the good scholmayster to ouer looke his abuses againe with me, so shall he see an ocean of inormities which begin in his first prinsiple in the disprayse of poetry. And first let me familiarly consider with this find faulte what the learned haue always esteemed of poetrie. 20 Seneca, thoughe a stoike, would haue a poeticall sonne, and, amongst the auncientest, Homer was no les accompted then *Humanus deus.* What made Alexander, I pray you, esteme of him so much ? why allotted he for his works so curious a closset ? was ther no fitter vnderprop for his 25 pillow then a simple pamphelet ? in all Darius cofers was there no iewell so costly ? Forsoth, my thinks, these two (the one the father of Philosophers, the other the cheftaine of chiualrie) were both deceiued if all were as a GossoN would wish them ; yf poets paynt naughte but 30 palterie toyes in vearse, their studies tended to foolishnesse, and in all their indeuors they did naught els but *agendo nihil agere.* Lord, howe Virgil's poore gnatt pricketh him, and how Ouid's fley byteth him ! he can beare no bourde, he hath raysed vp a new sect of serius 35

stoikes, that can abide naught but their owen shadowe,
and alow nothing worthye but what they conceaue. Did
you neuer reade (my ouer wittie frend) that vnder the persons of beastes many abuses were dissiphered? haue you
5 not reason to waye that whatsoeuer ether Virgil did write
of his gnatt or Ouid of his fley was all couertly to declare
abuse? but you are *homo literatus*, a man of the letter,
little sauoring of learning; your giddy brain made you
leaue your thrift, and your abuses in London some part of
10 your honestie. You say that Poets are subtil; if so, you
haue learned that poynt of them; you can well glose on
a trifeling text. But you haue dronke perhaps of Lethe;
your gramer learning is out of your head; you forget your
Accidence; you remember not that vnder the person of
15 Æneas in Virgil the practice of a dilligent captaine is
discribed, vnder the shadow of byrds, beastes, and trees
the follies of the world were disiphered; you know not
that the creation is signified in the Image of Prometheus,
the fall of pryde in the person of Narcissus; these are toyes,
20 because they sauor of wisedome which you want. Marke
what Campanus sayth: *Mira fabularum vanitas, sed quae si
introspiciantur videri possunt non vanae.* The vanitie of
tales is wonderful; yet if we aduisedly looke into them they
wil seme and proue wise. How wonderful are the pithie
25 poemes of Cato? the curious comedies of Plautus? how
brauely discouereth Terence our imperfection in his Eunuch?
how neatly dissiphereth he Dauus? how pleasauntly paynt-
eth he out Gnatho? whom if we shoulde seeke in our
dayes, I suppose he would not be farr from your parson.
30 But I see you would seeme to be that which you are
not, and, as the prouerb sayth, *Nodum in [s]cirpo quaerere.*
Poetes, you say, vse coullors to couer their inco[n]-
u[en]iences, and wittie sentences to burnish their bawdery;
and you diuinite to couer your knauerye. But tell mee
35 truth, Gosson, speakest thou as thou thinkest? what

coulers findest thou in a Poete not to be admitted? are
his speeches vnperfect? sauor they of inscience? I think,
if thou hast any shame, thou canst not but like and approue them: are their gods displesant vnto thee? doth
Saturne in his maiesty moue thee? doth Iuno with her 5
riches displease thee? doth Minerua with her weapon
discomfort thee? doth Apollo with his harping harme
thee?—thou mayst say nothing les then harme thee,
because they are not, and, I thinke so to, because thou
knowest them not. For wot thou that in the person of 10
Saturne our decaying yeares are signified; in the picture
of angry Iuno our affections are dissiphered; in the person of Minerua is our vnderstanding signified, both in
respect of warre as policie. When they faine that Pallas
was begotten of the braine of Iupiter, their meaning is 15
none other but that al wisedome (as the learned say) is
from aboue, and commeth from the father of Lights: in
the portrature of Apollo all knowledge is denotated. So
that, what so they wrot, it was to this purpose, in the way
of pleasure to draw men to wisedome: for, seing the world 20
in those daies was vnperfect, yt was necessary that they
like good Phisitions should so frame their potions that
they might be appliable to the quesie stomaks of their
werish patients. But our studientes by your meanes haue
made shipwrack of theyr labors; our schoolemaisters haue 25
so offended that by your iudgement they shall *subire
poenam capitis* for teaching poetry; the vniuersitie is litle
beholding to you,—al their practices in teaching are friuolus.
Witt hath wrought that in you, that yeares and studie
neuer setled in the heads of our sagest doctors. No 30
meruel though you disprayse poetrye, when you know not
what it meanes.

   Erasmus will make that the path waye to knowledge
which you dysprayse; and no meane fathers vouchsafe in
their seriouse questiones of deuinitie to inserte poeticall 35

sensures. I think, if we shal wel ouerloke the philosophers, we shal find their iudgements not halfe perfect.
Poetes, you saye, fayle in their fables, Philosophers in the
verye secrets of Nature. Though Plato could wish the
5 expulsion of Poetes from his well publiques, which he
might doe with reason, yet the wisest had not all that
same opinion : it had bene better for him to haue sercht
more narowly what the soule was, for his definition was
verye friuolus, when he would make it naught els but
10 *Substantiam intellectu predictam.* If you say that Poetes
did labour about nothing, tell me (I besech you) what
wonders wroughte those your dunce Doctors in ther
reasons *de ente, et non ente,* in theyr definition of no
force, and les witt? how sweate they, power soules, in
15 makinge more things then cold be? that I may vse your
owne phrase, did not they spende one candle by seeking
another? Democritus, Epicurus, with ther scholler Metro-
dorus, how labored they in finding out more worlds
then one? Your Plato in midst of his presisnes wrought
20 that absurdite that neuer may be redd in Poets, to make
a yearthly creature to beare the person of the creator, and
a corruptible substance an incomprehensible God! for,
determining of the principall causes of all thinges, a made
them naughte els but an Idea, which if it be conferred
25 wyth the truth, his sentence will sauour of Inscience.
But I speake for Poetes; I answeare your abuse; therefore
I will disproue or disprayse naught, but wish you with
the wise Plato to disprayse that thing you offend not in.
Seneca sayth that the studdie of Poets is to make children
30 ready to the vnderstanding of wisdom, and that our
aunciens did teache *artes Eleutherias, i. liberales,* because
the instructed children by the instrument of knowledg in
time became *homines liberi, i. Philosophye.* It may be that
in reding of poetry it happened to you as it is with the
35 Oyster, for she in her swimming receiueth no ayre, and

you in your reding lesse instruction. It is reported that
the shepe of Euboia want ther gale, and on the contrarye
side that the beastes of Naxus have *distentum fel.* Men
hope that scollers should have witt, brought vpp in the
Vniuersite ; but your sweet selfe, with the cattell of 5
Euboia, since you left your College, haue lost your learning. You disprayse Maximus Tirius pollicey, and that
thinge that he wrott to manifest learned Poets mening
you atribute to follye. O holy hedded man ! why may
not Iuno resemble the ayre ? why not Alexander valour ? 10
why not Vlisses pollice ? Will you have all for your
owne tothe ? must men write that you maye know theyr
meaning ? as though your wytt were to wrest all things ?
Alas ! simple Irus, begg at knowledge gate awhile ; thou
haste not wonne the mastery of learning. Weane thy 15
selfe to wisdome, and vse thy tallant in zeale, not for
enuie ; abuse not thy knowledge in dispraysing that which
is pereles. I shold blush from a Player to become an
enuiouse Preacher, if thou hadst zeale to preach ; if for
Sions sake thou coldst not holde thy tongue, thy true 20
dealing were prayse worthy, thy reuolting woulde counsell me to reuerence thee. Pittie weare it that Poetrye
should be displaced ; full little could we want Buchanan's
workes, and Boetius comfortes may not be banished.
What made Erasmus labor in Euripides tragedies ? Did 25
he indeuour by painting them out of Greeke into Latine
to manifest sinne vnto vs ? or to confirme vs in goodness ?
Labor (I pray thee) in Pamphelets more prayse worthy :
thou haste not saued a Senator, therefore not worthye
a Lawrell wreth ; thou hast not (in disprouing poetry) re- 30
proued an abuse, and therfore not worthy commendation.

Seneca sayth that *Magna vitae pars elabitur male agen-*
tibus, maxima nihil agentibus, tota aliud agentibus. The
most of our life (sayd he) is spent ether in doing euill, or
nothing, or that wee should not ; and I would wish you 35

weare exempted from this sensure.   Geue eare but a little
more what may be said for poetrie, for I must be briefe ;
you haue made so greate matter that I may not stay on
one thing to long, lest I leaue another vntouched.   And
5 first, whereas you say that Tullie, in his yeres of more
iudgement, despised Poetes, harke (I pray you) what he
worketh for them in his Oration *pro Archia poeta* : but
before you heare him, least you fayle in the incounter,
I would wysh you to followe the aduise of the dasterdlye
10 Ichneumon of Ægipt, who, when shee beholdeth the Aspis
her enemye to drawe nighe, calleth her fellowes together,
bismering herselfe with claye, agaynst the byting and
stroke of the serpent : arme your selfe, call your witts
together : want not your wepons, lest your imperfect
15 iudgement be rewardede with Midas eares.   You had
neede play the night burd now, for you[r] day Owl hath
misconned his parte, and for 'to who' now a dayes he cryes
'foole you' : which hath brought such a sort of wondering
birds about your eares, as I feare me will chatter you out
20 of your Iuey bush.   The worlde shames to see you, or els
you are afrayde to shew your selfe.   You thought poetrye
should want a patron (I think) when you fyrste published
this inuectiue, but yet you fynd al to many, euen *preter
expectationem* ; yea, though it can speake for its selfe, yet
25 her patron Tullie now shall tell her tale. *Haec studia*
(sayth he) *adolescentiam alunt, senectutem oblectant, secundas
res ornant, aduersis perfugium ac solatium praebent, delectant domi, non impediunt foris, pernoctant nobiscum, pere-
grinantur, rusticantur.*   Then will you dispraise that
30 which all men commend ? you looke only vpon the refuse
of the abuse, nether respecting the importance of the
matter nor the weigh[t]e of the wryter.   Solon can fayne
himselfe madde, to further the Athenians.   Chaucer in
pleasant vein can rebuke sin vncontrold ; and, though he
35 be lauish in the letter, his sence is serious. ·Who in

Rome lamented not Roscius death ? and canst thou suck
no plesure out of thy M. Claudian's writings ?   Hark
what Cellarius a learned father attributeth to it ; *Acuit
memoriam* (saith he), it profiteth the memory.   Yea and
Tully atributeth it for prais to Archias that vpon any 5
theame he cold versify extempory.   Who liketh not of the
promptnes of Ouid ? who not vnworthely cold bost of
himself thus, *Quicquid conabar dicere versus erat.*   Who
then doothe not wonder at poetry ? who thinketh not that
it procedeth from aboue ? what made the Chians and 10
Colophonians fal to such controuersy ?   Why seke the
Smirnians to recouer from the Salaminians the prais of
Homer ?   Al wold haue him to be of ther city : I hope
not for harme, but because of his knowledge.   Themistocles desireth to be acquainted with those who could 15
best discipher his praises.   Euen Marius himselfe, tho
neuer so cruel, accompted of Plotinus poems.   What
made Aphricanus esteme Ennius ?   Why did Alexander
giue prais to Achilles, but for the prayses which he found
written of him by Homer ?   Why estemed Pompie so 20
muche of Theophanes Mitiletus ? or Brutus so greatlye
the wrytinges of Accius ?   Fuluius was so great a fauorer
of Poetry, that, after the Aetolian warres, he attributed to
the Muses those spoiles that belonged to Mars.   In all
the Romaine conquest, hardest thou euer of a slayne 25
Poete ? nay rather the Emperours honored them, beautified them with benefites, and decked their sanctuaries
with sacrifice.   Pindarus colledg is not fit for spoil of
Alexander ouercome ; nether feareth poetry the perse-
cutors sword.   What made Austin so much affectate that 30
heauenly fury ? not folly, for, if I must needes speake,
illud non ausim affirmare, his zeale was in setting vp of
the house of God, not in affectate eloquence ; he wrot not,
he accompted not, he honnored not so much that (famous
poetry) whyche we prayse, without cause, for, if it be true 35

that Horace reporteth in his booke *de Arte Poetica,* all the
answeares of the Oracles weare in verse. Among the precise Iewes you shall find Poetes ; and for more maiestie
Sibilla will prophesie in verse. Beroaldus can witnes
5 with me that Dauid was a poet, and that his vayne was in
imitating (as S. Ierom witnesseth) Horace, Flaccus, and
Pindarus ; somtimes his verse runneth in an Iambus foote,
anone he hath recourse to a Saphic vaine, and *aliquando
semipede ingreditur.* Ask Iosephus, and he wil tel you
10 that Esay, Iob, and Salomon voutsafed poetical practises,
for (if Origen and he fault not) theyre verse was Hexameter and pentameter. Enquire of Cassiodorus, he will
say that all the beginning of Poetrye proceeded from the
Scripture. Paulinus, tho the Byshop of Nolanum, yet
15 voutsafe[th] the name of a Poet ; and Ambrose, tho he
be a patriarke in Mediolanum, loueth versifing. Beda
shameth not the science that shamelesse GOSSON misliketh. Reade ouer Lactantius, his proofe is by poetry ;
and Paul voutsafeth to ouerlooke Epimenides : let the
20 Apostle preach at Athens, he disdaineth not of Aratus
authorite. It is a pretye sentence, yet not so prety as
pithy, *Poeta nascitur, Orator fit* : as who should say,
Poetrye commeth from aboue, from a heauenly seate of
a glorious God, vnto an excellent creature man ; an
25 Orator is but made by exercise. For, if we examine well
what befell Ennius amonge the Romans, and Hesiodus
among his contrimen the Grecians, howe they came by
theyr knowledge, whence they receued their heauenly
furye, the first will tell vs that, sleping on the Mount of
30 Parnassus, he dreamed that he received the soule of
Homer into him, after the which he became a Poete ; the
next will assure you that it commeth not by labor,
nether that night watchings bringeth it, but that we must
haue it thence whence he fetched it, which was (he saith)
35 from a well of the Muses which Persius calleth Caballinus,

a draught whereof drewe him to his perfection; so of a shephard he becam an eloquent Poet. Wel then you see that it commeth not by exercise of play making, nether insertion of gawds, but from nature, and from aboue: and I hope that Aristotle hath sufficiently taught you that 5 *Natura nihil fecit frustra.* Persius was made a poete *Diuino furore percitus*; and whereas the poets were sayde to call for the Muses helpe, ther mening was no other, as Iodocus Badius reporteth, but to call for heauenly inspiration from aboue to direct theyr endeuors. Nether were 10 it good for you to sette light by the name of a Poet, since the offspring from whence he commeth is so heauenly. Sibilla in her answers to Æneas against hir will, as the poet telleth vs, was possessed with thys fury; ye[a], wey consideratly but of the writing of poets, and you shal se 15 that when ther matter is most heauenly their stile is most loftye, a strange token of the wonderfull efficacy of the same. I would make a long discourse vnto you of Platoes 4 furies, but I leue them: it pitieth me to bring a rodd of your owne making to beate you wythal. 20

But, mithinks, while you heare thys, I see you swallowe down your owne spittle for reuenge, where (God wot) my wryting sauoreth not of enuye. In this case I could wyshe you fare farre otherwyse from your foe; yf you please, I wyll become your frende, and see what a potion or re- 25 ceypt I can frame fytt for your diet. And herein I will proue myselfe a practiser; before I purdge you, you shall take a preparatiue to disburden your heuay hedde of those grose follis you haue conceued: but the receipt is bitter, therfore I would wysh you first to tasten your mouth with 30 the Sugar of perseuerance: for ther is a cold collop that must downe your throate, yet such a one as shall chaunge your complection quit. I wyll haue you therfore to tast first of the cold riuer Phricus, in Thracia, which, as Aristotle reporteth, changeth blacke into white, or of Scaman- 35

dar, which maketh gray yalow, that is of an enuious man
a wel minded person, reprehending of zeale that wherein
he hath sinned by folly; and so being prepard, thy pur-
gation wyll worke more easy, thy vnderstandinge wyll be
5 more perfit, thou shalt blush at thy abuse, and reclaime
thy selfe by force of argument; so wilt thou proue a clene
recouered patient, and I a perfecte practiser in framing so
good a potion. This broughte to passe, I with thee wil
seeke out some abuse in poetry, which I wil seeke for to
10 disproue by reason, first pronounced by no smal birde, euen
Aristotle himselfe. *Poetae* (sayth he) *multa mentiuntur*;
and to further his opinion seuer Cato putteth in his censure, *Admiranda canunt, sed non credenda, Poetae*. These
were sore blemishes, if obiected rightly; and heare you
15 may say the streme runnes a wronge; but, if it be so, by
you[r] leue, I wyll bring him shortly in his right chanel.
My answere shall not be my owne, but a learned father
shall tell my tale; if you wil know his name, men call
him Lactantius, who, in hys booke *de diuinis institutionibus*,
20 reesoneth thus. I suppose (sayth he) Poets are full of
credit, and yet it is requisite for those that wil vnderstand
them to be admonished that among them not onely the
name but the matter beareth a show of that it is not; for
if, sayth he, we examine the Scriptures litterallye, nothing
25 will seeme more falls, and, if we way Poetes wordes and
not ther meaning, our learning in them wilbe very mene.
You see nowe that your Catoes iudgement is of no force,
and that all your obiections you make agaynst Poetrye be
of no valor; yet, lest you should be altogether discoraged,
30 I wyll helpe you forwarde a little more. It pities me to
consider the weaknes of your cause; I wyll therfore make
your strongest reason more strong, and, after I have builded
it vp, destroy it agayn. Poets you confesse are eloquent,
but you reproue them in their wantonnesse : they write of
35 no wisedom ; you may say their tales are friuolus, they

prophane holy thinges, they seeke nothing to the perfection of our soules, theyr practise is in other things of lesse force. To this obiection I answer no otherwise then Horace doeth in his booke *de Arte Poetica*, where he wryteth thus.

5

> *Siluestres homines sacer interpresque deorum*
> *Caedibus et victu foedo deterruit Orpheus:*
> *Dictus ob hoc lenire tigres, rabidosque leones:*
> *Dictus et Amphion, Thebanae conditor vrbis,*
> *Saxa mouere sono testudinis, et prece blanda*
> *Ducere quo vellet: fuit haec sapientia quondam,*
> *Publica priuatis secernere, sacra profanis;*
> *Concubitu prohibere vago; dare iura maritis;*
> *Oppida moliri; leges incidere ligno.*

10

The holy spokesman of the Gods,
Wich heaue[n]ly Orpheus hight,
Did driue the sauage men from wods,
And made them liue aright;
And therefore is sayd the Tygers fierce
And Lyons full of myght
To ouercome: Amphion, he
Was sayd of Theabs the founder,
Who by his force of Lute did cause
The stones to part a sonder,
And by his speach them did derect,
Where he would haue them staye.
This wisedome this was it of olde
All strife for to allay;
To giue to euery man his owne;
To make the Gods be knowne;
To driue each lecher from the bed
That neuer was his owne;
To teach the law of mariage;
The way to build a towne;
For to engraue these lawes in woods—
This was these mens renowne.

15

20

25

30

35

I cannot leaue Tirtheus pollicy vntouched, who by force
of his pen could incite men to the defence of theyr countrye. If you require of the Oracle of Apollo what successe
you shal haue, *respondet bellicoso numine.*

5　Lo now you see your obiections [and] my answers; you
behold or may perceiue manifestlye that Poetes were the
first raysors of cities, prescribers of good lawes, mayn-
tayners of religion, disturbors of the wicked, aduancers
of the wel disposed, inuentors of laws, and lastly the
10 very fot-paths to knowledge and vnderstanding; ye[a], if
we shold beleue Hierome, he will make Plato's exiles
honest men, and his pestiferous poets good preachers, for
he accounteth Orpheus, Museus, and Linus Christians;
therefore Virgil (in his 6 boke of Æneiados, wher he
15 lernedly describeth the iourny of Æneas to Elis[i]um)
asserteneth vs that, among them that were ther for the
zeale they beare toward their country, ther wer found
Quique pii Vates, et Phoebo digna loqu[u]ti : but I must answer al obiections, I must fil euery nooke. I must arme
20 myself now, for here is the greatest bob I can gather out
of your booke, forsoth Ouid's abuses, in descrybing
whereof you labour very vehementlye, terming him letcher,
and in his person dispraise all poems : but shall on[e]
man's follye destroye a vniuersal commodity ? what gift,
25 what perfit knowledg hath ther bin among the professors
of which ther hath not bin a bad on[e]; the Angels haue
sinned in heauen, Adam and Eue in earthly paradise,
emong the holy Apostles vngratious Iudas. I reson not
that al poets are holy, but I affirme that poetry is a
30 heauenly gift, a perfit gift, then which I know not greater
plesure. And surely, if I may speak my mind, I think we
shal find but few Poets, if it were exactly wayd, what they
oughte to be : your Muscouian straungers, your Scithian
monsters wonderful, by one Eurus brought vpon one
35 stage in ships made of Sheepe skins, wyll not proue you

a poet, nether your life alow you to bee of that learning. If you had wisely wayed the abuse of poetry, if you had reprehended the foolish fantasies of our Poets *nomine non re* which they bring forth on stage, my self wold haue liked of you and allowed your labor. But I perceiue nowe 5 that all red colloured stones are not Rubies, nether is euery one Alexander that hath a scare in his cheke; al lame men are not Vulcans, nor hooke nosed men Ciceroes, nether each professor a poet. I abhore those poets that sauor of ribaldry: I will with the zealous admit the ex- 10 pullcion of such enormities: poetry is dispraised not for the folly that is in it, but for the abuse whiche manye ill Wryters couller by it. Beleeue mee the magestrats may take aduise (as I knowe wisely can) to roote out those odde rymes which runnes in euery rascales mouth, sauor- 15 ing of rybaldry. Those foolishe ballets that are admitted make poets good and godly practises to be refused. I like not of a wicked Nero that wyll expell Lucan, yet admit I of a zealous gouernour that wil seke to take away the abuse of poetry. I like not of an angrye Augustus which 20 wyll banishe Ouid for enuy. I loue a wise Senator, which in wisedome wyll correct him, and with aduise burne his follyes: vnhappy were we, yf like poore Scaurus we shoulde find [a] Tiberius that wyll put vs to death for a tragedy making; but most blessed were we, if we might find a 25 iudge that seuerely would amende the abuses of Tragedies. But I leaue the reformation thereof to more wyser than myselfe, and retourne to GOSSON, whom I wyshe to be fully perswaded in this cause; and therefore I will tell hym a prety story, which Iustin wryteth in the prayse of 30 poetrye. The Lacedemonians, when they had loste many men in diuers incountryes with theyr enemyes, soughte to the Oracles of Apollo requiring how they myght recouer theyr losses. It was answered, that they mighte ouercome if so be that they could get an Athenian gouernor: Where- 35

upon they sent Orators vnto the Athenians, humbly re-
questing them that they woulde appoynt them out one of
theyr best captaynes. The Athenians, owinge them old
malice, sent them in steede of a *soldado vechio* a scholar
5 of the Muses, in steede of a worthy warrior a poore poet,
for a couragious Themistocles a silly Tirthetus, a man of
great eloquence and singuler wytte, yet was he but a lame
lymde captaine, more fit for the coche then the field. The
Lacedemonians, trusting the Oracle, receued the champion,
10 and, fearing the gouernment of a stranger, made him ther
Citizen; which once don, and he obteining the Dukdome,
he assended the theater, and ther very learnedly wyshing
them to forget theyr folly and to thinke on victory, they,
being acuate by his eloquence, waging battail, won the
15 fielde.

Lo now you see that the framing of common welthes,
and defence therof, proceedeth from poets, how dare you
therfore open your mouth against them? how can you
disprayse the preseruer of a countrye? You compare
20 Homer to Methecus, cookes to Poetes, you shame your
selfe in your vnreuerent similituds, you may see your
follyes; *verbum sapienti sat.* Where as Homer was an
ancient poet, you disalow him, and accompte of those of
lesser iudgement. Strabo calleth poetry *primam sapien-*
25 *tiam.* Cicero, in his firste of hys Tusculans, attributeth
the inuencion of philosophy to poets. God keepe vs from
a Plato that should expel such men: pittie were it that
the memory of these valiant victours should be hidden,
which haue dyed in the behalfe of ther countryes. Miser-
30 able were our state yf we wanted those worthy volumes of
Poetry: could the learned beare the losse of Homer? or
our younglings the wrytings of Mantuan? or you your
volumes of Historyes? Belieue me, yf you had wanted
your Mysteries of nature, and your stately storyes, your
35 booke would haue scarce bene fedde wyth matter. If

therefore you will deale in things of wisdome, correct the
abuse, honor the science, renewe your schoole ; crye out
ouer Hierusalem wyth the prophet the woe that he pronounced ; wish the teacher to reforme hys lyfe, that his
weake scholler may proue the wyser ; cry out against vn- 5
saciable desyre in rich men ; tel the house of Iacob theyr
iniquities ; lament with the Apostle the want of laborers in
the Lords vineyards ; cry out on those dume doggs that
will not barke ; wyll the mightye that they ouer mayster
not the poore ; and put downe the beggars prowde heart 10
by thy perswasions.   Thunder oute wyth the Prophete
Micha the mesage of the Lord, and wyth him desyre
the Iudges to heare thee, the Prynces of Iacob to hearken
to thee, and those of the house of Israell to vnderstande ;
then tell them that they abhorre iudgement, and preuent 15
equitie, that they iudge for rewardes, and that theyr priests
teach for hyre, and the prophets thereof prophesie for
money, and yet that they saye the Lorde is wyth them,
and that no euil can befall them ; breath out the sweete
promises to the good, the cursses to the badde, tell them 20
that a peace muste needes haue a warre, and that God
can rayse vp another Zenacharib ; shew them that Sala-
mons kingdome was but for a season, and that aduersitie
cometh ere we espye it.   These be the songes of Sion,
these be those rebukes which you oughte to add to abuses ; 25
recouer the body, for it is sore ; the appe[n]dices thereof
will easely be reformed, if that we ar at a staye.

[*Lodge proceeds to discuss Gosson's Second Abuse—
Music,* 'which you vnaduisedly terme Pyping.'   Homer
commended it.   'Looke vppon the harmonie of the 30
Heauens? hange they not by Musike?'   Dauid sang
and praised the Lord with the harp: and the testimony
of the Greek philosophers is in fauour of its vse.   'But
as I like Musik, so admit I not of thos that depraue
the same: your Pipers are so odius to mee as yourselfe ; 35

nether alowe I your harpinge merye beggars, although
I knewe you my self a professed play maker and a paltry
actor.']

Well, I leaue this poynt til I know further of your
5 mynde ; mean while I must talke a little wyth you about
the ·thyrd abuse, for the cater cosens of Pypers, theyr
names (as you terme them), be Players, and I thinke as
you doe, for your experience is sufficient to enforme me ;
but here I must loke about me, *quacunque te t[et]igeris vlcus*
10 *est* : here is a task that requireth a long treatis, and what
my opinion is of Players ye now shall plainly perceue.
I must now search my wits; I see this shall passe throughe
many seuere sensors handling ; I must aduise me what
I write, and write that I would wysh. I way wel the
15 seriousnes of the cause, and regarde very much the
iudges of my endeuor, whom, if I could, I would perswade
that I woulde not nourish abuse, nether mayntaine that
which should be an vniversall discomoditye. I hope they
wil not iudge before they read, nether condemne without
20 occasion. The wisest wil alwais carry t[w]o eares, in that
they are to diserne two indifferent causes. I meane
not to hold you in suspenc[e] (seuere Iudges) : if you
gredely expect my verdit, brefely this it is.

Demost[he]nes thoughte not that Phillip shoulde ouer-
25 come when he reproued hym, nether feared Cicero
Anthonies force when in the Senate hee rebuked hym.
To the ignorant ech thinge that is vnknowne semes vnprofitable, but a wise man can forsee and prayse by proofe.
Pythagoras could spy oute in women's eyes two kind of
30 teares, the one of grefe, the other of disceit ; and those
of iudgement can from the same flower suck honey with
the bee, from whence the Spyder (I mean the ignorant)
take their poison. Men that haue knowledge what
comedies and tragedis be wil comend them, but it is
35 sufferable in the folish to reproue that they know not,

becaus ther mouthes will hardly be stopped. Firste therfore, if it be not tedious to GOSSON to harken to the lerned, the reder shal perceiue the antiquity of play-making, the inuentors of comedies, and therewithall the vse and comoditye of them. So that in the end I hope 5 my labor shall be liked, and the learned wil soner con-ceue his folly. For tragedies and comedies, Donate the gramarian sayth, they wer inuented by lerned fathers of the old time to no other purpose but to yeelde prayse vnto God for a happy haruest or plentiful yeere. And 10 that thys is trewe the name of Tragedye doth importe, for, if you consider whence it came, you shall perceiue (as Iodocus Badius reporteth) that it drewe his original of *Tragos, Hircus, et Ode, Cantus* (so called), for that the actors thereof had in rewarde for theyr labour a gotes 15 skynne fylled wyth wyne. You see then that the fyrste matter of Tragedies was to giue thankes and prayses to God, and a gratefull prayer of the countrymen for a happye haruest, and this I hope was not discommendable. I knowe you will iudge i[t] farthest from abuse. But to 20 wade farther, thys fourme of inuention being found out, as the dayes wherein it was vsed did decay, and the world grew to more perfection, so the witt of the younger sorte became more riper, for they leauing this fourme inuented an other, in the which they altered the nature but not the 25 name ; for, for sonnets in prayse of the gods, they did set forth the sower fortune of many exiles, the miserable fal of haples princes, the reuinous decay of many countryes ; yet not content with this, they presented the liues of Satyers, so that they might wiselye, vnder the abuse 30 of that name, discouer the follies of many theyr folish fellow citesens. And those monsters were then as our parasites are now adayes : suche as with pleasure repre-hended abuse. As for Commedies, because they bear a more plesanter vain, I will leaue the other to speake 35

of them. Tulley defines them thus : *Comedia* (saith he)
is *imitatio vitae, speculum consuetudinis, et imago veritatis ;*
and it is sayde to be termed of *Comai* (emongste the
Greekes), which signifieth *Pagos,* and *Ode, Cantus ;* for
5 that they were exercised in the fielde, they had they[r]
beginning with tragedies, but their matter was more
plessaunt, for they were suche as did réprehend, yet
quodam lepore. These first very rudly were inuented by
Susarion Bullus and Magnes, t[w]o auncient poets, yet
10 so that they were meruelous profitable to the reclamynge
of abuse ; whereupon Eupolis with Cratinus and Aristophanes began to write, and with ther eloquenter vaine
and perfection of stil dyd more seuerely speak agaynst
the abuses then they : which Horace himselfe witnesseth.
15 For, sayth he, ther was no abuse but these men reprehended it ; a thefe was loth to be seene [at] one [of] there
spectacle[s], a coward was neuer present at theyr assemblies,
a backbiter abhord that company ; and I my selfe could
not haue blamed you (Gosson) for exempting yourselfe
20 from this theater ; of troth I shoulde have lykt your
pollicy. These therefore, these wer they that kept men
in awe, these restrayned the vnbridled cominaltie ; wher-
upon Horace wisely sayeth,

Oderunt peccare boni, virtutis amore :
25 *Oderunt peccare mali, formidine poenae.*

The good did hate al sinne for vertues loue :
The bad for feare of shame did sin remoue.

Yea, would God our realme could light vppon a Lucilius ;
then should the wicked bee poynted out from the good ;
30 a harlot woulde seeke no harbor at stage plais, lest she
shold here her owne name growe in question, and the discourse of her honesty cause her to bee hated of the godly.
As for you, I am sure of this one thing, he would paint you
in your players ornaments, for they best becam you. But

as these sharpe corrections were disanulde in Rome when
they grewe to more licenciousnes, so I fear me if we shold
practise it in our dayes the same intertainmente would
followe. But in ill reformed Rome what comedies now?
A poet's wit can correct, yet not offend. Philemon will 5
mitigate the corrections of sinne by reprouing them
couertly in shadowes. Menander dare not offend the
Senate openly, yet wants he not a parasite to touch them
priuely. Terence wyl not report the abuse of harlots
vnder there proper stile, but he can finely girde them 10
vnder the person of Thais. Hee dare not openly tell the
Rich of theyr couetousnesse and seuerity towards their
children, but he can controle them vnder the person of
Durus Demeas. He must not shew the abuse of noble
yong gentilmen vnder theyr owne title, but he wyll warne 15
them in the person of Pamphilus. Wil you learne to
knowe a parasite? Looke vpon his Dauus. Wyl you
seke the abuse of courtly flatterers? Behold Gnato. And
if we had some Satericall Poetes nowe a dayes to penn our
commedies, that might be admitted of zeale to discypher 20
the abuses of the worlde in the person of notorious
offenders, I knowe we should wisely ryd our assemblyes
of many of your brotherhod.

But, because you may haue a full scope to reprehende,
I will ryp vp a rablement of play makers, whose wright- 25
inges I would wishe you ouerlooke, and seeke out theyr
abuses. Can you mislike of Cecilius? or dispise Plinius?
or amend Neuius? or find fault with Licinius? Wherein
offended Atilius? I am sure you can not but wonder at
Terence? Wil it please you to like of Turpilius? or 30
alow of Trabea? You muste needs make much of Ennius;
for ouerloke al thes and you shal find ther volums ful of
wit if you examin them; so that, if you had no other
masters, you might deserue to be a doctor, wher now you
are but a folishe scholemaister: but I wyll deale wyth 35

you very freendlye, I wil resolue eueri doubt that you
find; those instrumentes which you mislike in playes grow
of auncient custome, for, when Roscius was an Actor, be
sure that as with his tears he moued affections, so the
5 Musitian in the Theater before the entrance did morne-
fully record it in melody (as Seruius reporteth). The
actors in Rome had also gay clothing, and euery mans
aparel was apliable to his part and person. The old men
in white, the rich men in purple, the parasite disguisedly,
10 the yong men in gorgeous coulours, ther wanted no deuise
nor good iudgement of the comedy, where I suppose our
players both drew ther plaies and fourme of garments.
As for the appointed dayes wherin comedies wer showen,
I reede that the Romaynes appoynted them on the festiual
15 dayes; in such reputation were they had at that time.
Also Iodocus Badius will assertain you that the actors for
shewing pleasure receued some profite. But let me apply
those dayes to ours, their actors to our players, their
autors to ours. Surely we want not a Roscius, nether
20 ar ther great scarsity of Terence's profession, but yet our
men dare not nowe a dayes presume so much as the old
Poets might, and therfore they apply ther writing to the
peoples vain; wheras, if in the beginning they had ruled,
we should now adaies have found smal spectacles of folly.
25 But (of truth) I must confes with Aristotle that men are
greatly delighted with imitation, and that it were good to
bring those things on stage that were altogether tending
to vertue: all this I admit and hartely wysh, but you say
vnlesse the thinge be taken away the vice will continue.
30 Nay, I say if the style were changed the practise would
profit, and sure I thinke our theaters fit that Ennius,
seeing our wanton Glicerium, may rebuke her. If our
poetes will nowe become seuere, and for prophane things
write of vertue, you I hope shoulde see a reformed state
35 in those thinges; which I feare me yf they were not, the

idle hedded commones would worke more mischiefe. I wish
as zealously as the best that all abuse of playinge weare
abolished; but for the thing, the antiquitie causeth me to
allow it, so it be vsed as it should be.   I cannot allow the
prophaning of the Sabaoth.   I praise your reprehension 5
in that; you did well in discommending the abuse, and
surely I wysh that that folly wer disclaymed; it is not to
be admitted, it maks those sinne, whiche perhaps, if it
were not, would have binne present at a good sermon.
It is in the Magistrate to take away that order, and 10
appoynt it otherwyse.   But sure it were pittie to abolish
that which hath so great vertue in it, because it is abused.
The Germanes, when the vse of preaching was forbidden
them, what helpe had they I pray you?   Forsoth the
learned were fayne couertly in comedies to declare abuses, 15
and by playing to incite the people to vertues, when they
might heare no preaching.   Those were lamentable dayes
you will say, and so thinke I; but was not this, I pray you,
a good help in reforming the decaying Gospel?   You see
then how comedies (my seuere iudges) are requesit both 20
for ther antiquity and for ther commoditye, for the dignity
of the wrighters, and the pleasure of the hearers.   But,
after your discrediting of playmaking, you salue vppon the
sore somewhat, and among many wise workes there be
some that fitte your vaine : the practice of parasites is one, 25
which I meruel it likes you so well, since it bites you so
sore.   But sure in that I like your iudgement, and for the
rest to I approue your wit, but for the pigg of your owne
sow (as you terme it) assuredly I must discommend your
verdit.   Tell me, GOSSON, was all your owne you wrote 30
there ?   did you borow nothing of your neyghbours ?   Out
of what booke patched you out Cicero's Oration ?   Whence
fet you Catilin's Inuectiue.   Thys is one thing, *alienam olet
lucernam, non tuam ;* so that your helper may wisely reply
vpon you with Virgil— 35

Hos ego versiculos feci: tulit alter honores.

I made these verses, other bear[s] the name.

Beleue me I should preferr Wilson's : Shorte and sweete,
if I were iudge, a peece surely worthy prayse, the practice
5 of a good scholler; would the wiser would ouerlooke that,
they may perhaps cull some wisedome out of a player's
toye.   Well, as it is wisedome to commend where the
cause requireth, so it is a poynt of folly to praise without
deserte.   You dislike players very much, theyr dealings
10 be not for your commodity; whom if I myghte aduise,
they should learne thys of Iuuenal.

Viuendum est recte, cum propter plurima, tum his
Praecipue causis, vt linguas mancipiorum
Contemnas.   Nam lingua mali pars pessima serui.

15   We ought to leade our liues aright,
        For many causes moue.
        Especially for this same cause,
        Wisedom doth vs behoue
        That we may set at nought those blames
20   Which seruants to vs lay;
        For why, the tongue of euel slaue
        Is worst, as wisemen euer say.

Methinks I heare some of them verifiing these verses vpon
you; if it be so that I hear them, I will concele it: as for
25 the statute of apparrell and the abuses therof, I see it
manifestly broken, and, if I should seeke for example, you
cannot but offend my eyes.   For, if you examine the
statuts exactly, a simple cote should be fitted to your
backe, we sholde bereue you of your brauerye, and examine
30 your auncestry, and by profession, in respect of that
statute, we should find you cater cosens with a, (but
hush) you know my meaning: I must for pitie fauor your
credit, in that you weare once a scholler.

[*Lodge then refers briefly to Gosson's attack on* 'Carders, Dicers, Fencers, Bowlers, Daunsers, and Tomblers,' *and closes his* Defence *with these words—*]

And because I think my selfe to haue sufficiently answered that I supposed, I conclude wyth this: God preserue our peaceable Princes, and confound her enemies: God enlarge her wisedom, that like Saba she may seeke after a Salomon: God confounde the imaginations of her enemies, and perfit his graces in her, that the daies of her rule may be continued in the bonds of peace, that the house of the chosen Isralites may be maynteyned in happinesse: lastly, I frendly bid GOSSON farwell, wyshinge him to temper his penn with more discretion.

EDMUND SPENSER

AND

GABRIEL HARVEY

(*Letters on Reformed Versifying, &c.*)

1579–80

[Letters I and II, dated 5 [? 16] Oct. and 23 Oct. 1579 re-
spectively, were printed at London in 1580 by H. Bynneman, 'dwelling in Thames streate, neere unto Baynardes
Castell,' and entitled *Two other | very commendable Letters | of
the same mens writing : | both touching the foresaid | Artificiall
Versifying, and cer|tain other Particulars || More lately de-
liuered vnto the | Printer.* The later letters, III and IV,
dated April 1580, were printed earlier in the same year
by the same printer, and, with a third (placed second
in the book-order), constituted the *Three Proper | and wittie
familiar Letters : | lately passed betweene two V-|niuersitie men :
touching the Earth-|quake in Aprill last, and our | English
refourmed Versifying. || With a Preface of a well willer to
them both.* The second letter in the earlier publication,
which is omitted here, contains Gabriel Harvey's reflections on the recent earthquake. The text has·been copied
from the rare volume in the British Museum, C 40. d. 16,
pp. 51 and 61 (I and II), and pp. 1 and 31 (III and IV).
The concluding extracts, which have a direct bearing on
this correspondence, are from the Letter-Book of Gabriel
Harvey (1573–1580) B. M. Sloane 93.]

[I]

TO THE WORSHIPFULL HIS VERY SINGULAR GOOD FRIEND, MAISTER G. H., FELLOW OF TRINITIE HALL IN CAMBRIDGE.

5 GOOD Master G., I perceiue by your most curteous
and frendly Letters your good will to be no lesse
in deed than I alwayes esteemed. In recompence wherof,

think, I beseech you, that I wil spare neither speech nor
wryting, nor aught else, whensoeuer and wheresoeuer
occasion shal be offred me: yea, I will not stay till it be
offred, but will seeke it in al that possibly I may.   And
that you may perceiue how much your Counsel in al 5
things preuaileth with me, and how altogither I am ruled
and ouerruled thereby, I am nowe determined to alter
mine owne former purpose, and to subscribe to your
aduizement, being notwithstanding resolued stil to abide
your farther resolution.   My principal doubts are these. 10
First, I was minded for a while to haue intermitted the
vttering of my writings, leaste, by ouermuch cloying their
noble eares, I should gather a contempt of my self, or
else seeme rather for gaine and commoditie to doe it, for
some sweetnesse that I haue already tasted.   Then also 15
me seemeth the work too base for his excellent Lordship,
being made in Honour of a priuate Personage vnknowne,
which of some ylwillers might be vpbraided not to be
so worthie as you knowe she is: or the matter not so
weightie that it should be offred to so weightie a Person- 20
age: or the like.   The selfe former Title stil liketh me
well ynough, and your fine Addition no lesse.   If these
and the like doubtes maye be of importaunce in your
seeming to frustrate any parte of your aduice, I beeseeche
you, without the leaste selfe loue of your own purpose, 25
councell me for the beste: and the rather doe it faithfullye
and carefully, for that in all things I attribute so muche
to your iudgement, that I am euer more content to anni-
hilate mine owne determinations in respecte thereof.   And
indeede for your selfe to, it fitteth with you now to call 30
your wits and senses togither (which are alwaies at call),
when occasion is so fairely offered of Estimation and
Preferment.   For, whiles the yron is hote, it is good
striking; and minds of Nobles varie as their Estates.
Verum ne quid durius.   35

I pray you bethinke you well hereof, good Maister G.,
and forthwith write me those two or three special points
and caueats for the nonce, *De quibus in superioribus illis
mellitissimis longissimisque Litteris tuis.* Your desire to
5 heare of my late beeing with hir Maiestie muste dye in
it selfe. As for the twoo worthy Gentlemen, Master
SIDNEY and Master DYER, they haue me, I thanke them,
in some vse of familiarity: of whom, and to whome, what
speache passeth for youre credite and estimation, I leaue
10 your selfe to conceiue, hauing alwayes so well conceiued
of my vnfained affection and zeale towardes you. And
nowe they haue proclaimed in their ἀρείῳ πάγῳ a generall
surceasing and silence of balde Rymers, and also of the
verie beste to: in steade whereof, they haue, by autho[ri]tie
15 of their whole Senate, prescribed certaine Lawes and
rules of Quantities of English sillables for English Verse,
hauing had thereof already greate practise, and drawen
mee to their faction. Newe Bookes I heare of none, but
only of one, that writing a certaine Booke, called THE
20 SCHOOLE OF ABUSE, and dedicating it to Maister SIDNEY,
was for hys labor scorned, if at leaste it be in the goodnesse of that nature to scorne. Suche follie is it not to
regarde aforehande the inclination and qualitie of him
to whome wee dedicate oure Bookes. Suche mighte
25 I happily incurre, entituling my SLOMBER and the other
Pamphlets vnto his honor. I meant them rather to
MAISTER DYER. But I am, of late, more in loue wyth
my Englishe Versifying than with Ryming; whyche
I should haue done long since, if I would then haue
30 followed your councell. *Sed te solum iam tum suspicabar
cum Aschamo sapere: nunc Aulam video egregios alere
Poëtas Anglicos.* Maister E. K. hartily desireth to be
commended vnto your Worshippe: of whome what
accompte he maketh youre selfe shall hereafter perceiue,
35 by hys paynefull and dutifull Verses of your selfe.

Thus much was written at Westminster yesternight; but comming this morning, beeyng the sixteenth of October, to Mystresse *Kerkes*, to haue it deliuered to the Carrier, I receyued youre letter, sente me the laste weeke; whereby I perceiue you otherwhiles continue 5 your old exercise of Versifying in English : whych glorie I had now thought shoulde haue bene onely ours heere at London and the Court.

Truste me, your Verses I like passingly well, and enuye your hidden paines in this kinde, or rather maligne and 10 grudge at your selfe that would not once imparte so muche to me.   But once or twice you make a breache in Maister Drants Rules : *quod tamen condonabimus tanto Poëtae tuaeque ipsius maximae in his rebus autoritati.* You shall see when we meete in London (whiche, when it 15 shall be, certifye vs) howe fast I haue followed after you in that Course : beware leaste in time I ouertake you. *Veruntamen te solum sequar (vt saepenumero sum professus), nunquam sane assequar dum viuam.*   And nowe requite I you with the like, not with the verye beste, but with 20 the verye shortest, namely with a fewe *Iambickes* : I dare warrant they be precisely perfect for the feete (as you can easily iudge) and varie not one inch from the Rule. I will imparte yours to Maister Sidney and Maister Dyer at my nexte going to the Courte.   I praye you 25 keepe mine close to your selfe, or your verie entire friendes, Maister Preston, Maister Still, and the reste.

Iambicum Trimetrum.

Vnhappie Verse, the witnesse of my vnhappie state,
　Make thy selfe fluttring wings of thy fast flying   30
　　Thought, and fly forth vnto my Loue, whersoeuer
　　she be :
Whether lying reastlesse in heauy bedde, or else
　Sitting so cheerelesse at the cheerfull boorde, or else

Playing alone carelesse on hir heauenlie Virginals.
 If in Bed, tell hir that my eyes can take no reste;
    If at Boorde, tell hir that my mouth can eate no
       meate;
5 If at hir Virginals, tel hir I can heare no mirth.
 Asked why? say, Waking Loue suffereth no sleepe;
    Say that raging Loue dothe appall the weakè
       stomacke;
    Say that lamenting Loue marreth the Musicall.
10 Tell hir that hir pleasures were wonte to lull me
       asleepe;
    Tell hir that hir beautie was wonte to feede mine
       eyes;
    Tell hir that hir sweete Tongue was wonte to make
15   me mirth.
 Nowe doe I nightly waste, wanting my kindely reste;
    Nowe do I dayly starue, wanting my liuely foode;
    Nowe do I alwayes dye, wanting thy timely mirth.
 And if I waste, who will bewaile my heauy chaunce?
20   And if I starue, who will record my cursed end?
    And if I dye, who will saye, *this was Immerito*?

I thought once agayne here to haue made an ende, with
a heartie *Vale* of the best fashion; but loe an ylfauoured
myschaunce. My last farewell, whereof I made great
25 accompt, and muche maruelled you shoulde make no
mention thereof, I am nowe tolde (in the Diuels name)
was thorough one mans negligence quite forgotten, but
shoulde nowe vndoubtedly haue beene sent, whether
I hadde come or no. Seing it can now be no otherwise,
30 I pray you take all togither, wyth all their faultes: and
nowe I hope you will vouchsafe mee an answeare of the
largest size, or else I tell you true you shall bee verye
deepe in my debte, notwythstandyng thys other sweete
but shorte letter, and fine but fewe Verses. But I woulde

rather I might yet see youre owne good selfe, and receiue
a Reciprocall farewell from your owne sweete mouth.

Ad Ornatissimum virum, multis iamdiu nominibus cla-
rissimum, G. H. IMMERITO *sui mox in Gallias nauigaturi*
εὐτυχεῖν.   5

[*Here follow* 114 *lines of Latin verse.*]

I was minded also to haue sent you some English
verses, or Rymes, for a farewell; but, by my Troth,
I haue no spare time in the world to thinke on such
Toyes, that you knowe will demaund a freer head than 10
mine is presently.   I beseeche you by all your Curtesies
and Graces let me be answered ere I goe: which will be,
(I hope, I feare, I thinke) the next weeke, if I can be
dispatched of my Lorde.   I goe thither, as sent by him,
and maintained most what of him: and there am to employ 15
my time, my body, my minde, to his Honours seruice.
Thus, with many superhartie Commendations and Recommendations to your selfe and all my friendes with you,
I ende my last farewell, not thinking any more to write
vnto you before I goe; and withall committing to your 20
faithfull Credence the eternall Memorie of our euerlasting
friendship, the inuiolable Memorie of our vnspotted friend-
shippe, the sacred Memorie of our vowed friendship,
which I beseech you Continue with vsuall writings, as
you may; and of all things let me heare some Newes from 25
you, as gentle M. SIDNEY, I thanke his good Worship,
hath required of me, and so promised to doe againe.   *Qui*
monet, vt facias, quod iam facis; you knowe the rest.   You
may alwayes send them most safely to me by MISTRESSE
KERKE, and by none other.   So once againe, and yet 30
once more, farewell most hartily, mine owne good
MASTER H. and loue me, as I loue you, and thinke vpon
poore IMMERITO, as he thinketh vppon you.

Leycester House.   This 5 [? 16] of *October* 1579.

Per mare, per terras, Viuus mortuusque, Tuus Immerito. 35

[II]

TO MY VERIE FRIENDE
M. IMMERITO.

Liberalissimo Signor Immerito, in good soothe my poore
Storehouse will presently affourd me nothing, either to
5 recompence or counteruaile your gentle Masterships long,
large, lauish, Luxurious, Laxatiue Letters withall (now,
a Gods name, when did I euer in my life hunt the Letter
before? but, belike, theres no remedie; I must needes
be euen with you once in my dayes), but only, forsoothe,
10 a fewe Millions of Recommendations and a running
Coppie of the Verses enclosed. Which Verses (*extra
iocum*) are so well done in Latin by two Doctors, and
so well Translated into English by one odde Gentleman,
and generally so well allowed of all that chaunced to haue
15 the perusing of them, that, trust mee, G. H. was at the
first hardly intreated to shame himselfe, and, truely, now
blusheth to see the first Letters of his name stande so
neere their Names, as of necessitie they must. You know
the *Greeke* prouerb, πορφύρα περὶ πορφύραν διακριτέα, and
20 many colours (as in a manner euery thing else), that
seuerally by themselues seeme reasonably good and
freshe ynough, beyng compared and ouermatched wyth
their betters are maruellously disgraced, and, as it were,
dashed quite oute of Countenaunce. I am at this instant
25 very busilye and hotly employed in certaine greate and
serious affayres: whereof, notwithstanding (for all youre
vowed and long experimented secrecie), you are not like
to heare a worde more at the moste, till I my selfe see
a World more at the leaste. And, therefore, for this once
30 I beseech you (notwithstanding your greate expectation of
I knowe not what Volumes for an aunsweare) content your
good selfe with these Presentes (pardon me, I came lately

out of a Scriueners shop) and, in lieu of many gentle
Farewels and goodly Godbewyes at your departure,
gyue me once againe leaue to playe the Counsaylour
a while, if it be but to iustifie your liberall Mastershippes,
Nostri Cato maxime saecli: and I coniure you by the 5
Contents of the Verses and Rymes enclosed, and by al
the good and bad Spirites that attende vpon the Authors
themselues, immediatly vpon the contemplation thereof
to abandon all other fooleries, and honour Vertue, the
onely immortall and suruiuing Accident amongst so manye 10
mortall and euer-perishing Substaunces.   As I strongly
presume, so good a Texte, so clearkly handeled by three
so famous Doctours, as olde MAISTER WYTHIPOLE and
the other two bee, may easily and will fully perswade you,
howsoeuer you tush at the fourths vnsutable Paraphrase. 15
But a worde or two to your large, lauishe, laxatiue
Letters, and then for thys time *Adieu*.   Of my credite,
youre doubtes are not so redoubted as youre selfe ouer
suspiciously imagine; as I purpose shortely to aduize you
more at large.   Your hotte yron is so hotte that it 20
striketh mee to the hearte; I dare not come neare to
strike it.   The Tyde tarryeth no manne, but manye a good
manne is fayne to tarry the Tyde.   And I knowe some,
whyche coulde be content to bee theyr own Caruers, that
are gladde to thanke other for theyr courtesie.   But 25
Beggars, they saye, must be no choosers.

Your new-founded ἄρειον πάγον I honoure more than you
will or can suppose, and make greater accompte of the
twoo worthy Gentlemenne than of two hundreth *Dionisii
Areopagitae*, or the verye notablest Senatours that euer 30
Athens dydde affourde of that number.

Your Englishe *Trimetra* I like better than perhappes
you will easily beleeue, and am to requite them wyth
better, or worse, at more conuenient leysure.   Marry, you
must pardon me, I finde not your warrant so sufficiently 35

good and substauntiall in Lawe that it can persuade me
they are all so precisely perfect for the feete, as your
selfe ouer-partially weene and ouer-confidently auouche :
especiallye the thirde, whyche hathe a foote more than
a Lowce (a wonderous deformitie in a righte and pure
SENARIE), and the sixte, whiche is also in the same
Predicament, vnlesse happly one of the feete be sawed
off wyth a payre of SYNCOPES : and then shoulde the
Orthographie haue testified so muche : and, in steade
of *Heauēnlĭ Virgĭnăls*, you should haue written *Heaūnlĭ
Virgnăls*, and *Virgnăls* againe in the ninth, and should
haue made a Curtoll of *Immĕrĭtō* in the laste : being all
notwithstandyng vsuall, and tollerable ynoughe, in a mixte
and licentious IAMBICKE : and of two euilles better (no
doubte) the fyrste than the laste, a thyrde superfluous
sillable than a dull SPONDEE. Then me thinketh you
haue in my fancie somwhat too many SPONDEES beside :
and whereas TROCHEE sometyme presumeth in the firste
place, as namely in the second Verse, *Make thy*, whyche
thy by youre Maistershippes owne authoritie muste needes
be shorte, I shall be faine to supplye the office of the
Arte Memoratiue, and putte you in minde of a pretty
Fable in ABSTEMIO the Italian, implying thus much, or
rather thus little, in effect.

A certaine lame man, beyng inuited to a solempne
Nuptiall Feaste, made no more adoe, but sate me hym
roundlye downe foremoste at the hyghest ende of the Table.
The Master of the feast, suddainly spying his presumption,
and hansomely remoouing him from thence, placed me
this haulting Gentleman belowe at the nether end of the
bourd ; alledging for his defence the common verse
Sedes nulla datur praeterquam sexta Trochaeo, and
pleasantly alluding to this foote, which, standing vppon
two syllables, the one long, the other short (much like,
of a like, his guestes feete), is alwayes thrust downe to the

last place in a true Hexameter, and quite thrust out of
doores in a pure and iust SENARIE. Nowe, Syr, what
thinke you I began to thinke with my selfe, when I began
to reade your warrant first, so boldly and venterously
set downe in so formall and autentique wordes as these, 5
PRECISELY PERFIT, AND NOT AN INCH FROM THE RULE?
Ah Syrrha, and Iesu Lord, thought I, haue we at the
last gotten one, of whom his olde friendes and Companions
may iustly glory *In eo solum peccat, quod nihil peccat,*
and that is yet more exacte and precise in his English 10
Comicall Iambickes than euer M. WATSON himselfe
was in his Latin Tragicall Iambickes, of whom M. *Ascham*
reporteth that he would neuer to this day suffer his famous
Absolon to come abrode, onely because *Anapaestus in locis
paribus* is twice or thrice vsed in steade of *Iambus*? A 15
small fault, ywisse, and such a one, in M. ASCHAMS owne
opinion, as perchaunce would neuer haue beene espyed,
no neither in *Italy* nor in *Fraunce*. But when I came to
the curious scanning and fingering of euery foote and
syllable: So here, quoth I, M. WATSONS *Anapaestus* for 20
all the worlde: A good horse, that trippeth not once in
a iourney: and M. IMMERITO doth but as M. WATSON,
and in a manner all other *Iambici* haue done before him:
marry, he might haue spared his preface, or, at the least,
that same restrictiue and streightlaced terme PRECISELY, 25
and all had been well enough: and I assure you, of my
selfe, I beleeue, no peece of a fault marked at all. But
this is the Effect of warrantes, and perhappes the Errour
may rather proceede of his Master M. DRANTES Rule
than of himselfe. Howsoeuer it is, the matter is not 30
great, and I alwayes was, and will euer continue, of this
Opinion, *Pauca multis condonanda vitia Virtutibus,*
especially these being no *Vitia* neither, in a common
and licencious IAMBICKE. *Verum ista obiter, non quidem
contradicendi animo aut etiam corrigendi mihi crede: sed* 35

nostro illo Academico, pristinoque more ratiocinandi. And, to saye trueth, partely too to requite your gentle courtesie in beginning to me, and noting I knowe not what breache in your gorbellyed Maisters Rules : which Rules go for
5 good, I perceiue, and keepe a Rule, where there be no better in presence. My selfe neither sawe them, nor heard of them before, and therefore will neither praise them, nor dispraise them nowe ; but, vppon the suruiewe of them and farther conference (both which I desire), you
10 shall soone heare one mans opinion too or fro. Your selfe remember I was wonte to haue some preiudice of the man ; and I still remaine a fauourer of his deserued and iust commendation. Marry in these poyntes, you knowe, PARTIALITIE in no case may haue a foote : and
15 you remember mine olde Stoicall exclamation, FIE ON CHILDISH AFFECTION, IN THE DIS-COURSING AND DECIDING OF SCHOOLE MATTERS. This I say, because you charge me with an vnknowne authoritie, which, for aught I know yet, may as wel be either vnsufficient or faultie as other-
20 wisè ; and I dare more than halfe promise (I dare not saye warrant) you shall alwayes in these kinde of con-trouersies finde me nighe hande answerable in mine owne defence. *Reliqua omnia quae de hac supersunt Anglicorum versuum ratione in aliud tempus reseruabimus otiosum*
25 *magis.* Youre Latine farewell is a goodly braue yonkerly peece of work, and, Goddilge yee, I am alwayes maruellously beholding vnto you for your bountifull Titles : I hope by that time I haue been resident a yeare or twoo in ITALY I shall be better qualifyed in this kind, and more able to
30 requite your lauishe and magnificent liberalitie that way.
`. . .` TRINITIE HALL, stil in my Gallerie, 23 Octob. 1579. In haste.

Yours, as you knowe,

G. H.

[III]

TO MY LONG APPROOUED AND SINGULAR
GOOD FRENDE, MASTER G. H.

Good Master H.   I doubt not but you haue some great
important matter in hande, which al this while restraineth
youre Penne and wonted readinesse in prouoking me vnto
that wherein your selfe nowe faulte.   If there bee any
such thing in hatching, I pray you hartily lette vs knowe 5
before al the worlde see it.   But if happly you dwell
altogither in Iustinians Courte, and giue your selfe to
be deuoured of secreate Studies, as of all likelyhood you
doe, yet at least imparte some your olde or newe, Latine
or Englishe, Eloquent and Gallant Poesies to vs, from 10
whose eyes, you saye, you keepe in a manner nothing
hidden.   Little newes is here stirred : but that olde greate
matter still depending.   His Honoure neuer better.   I
thinke the Earthquake was also there wyth you (which
I would gladly learne) as it was here with vs, ouerthrow- 15
ing diuers old buildings and peeces of Churches.   Sure
verye straunge to be hearde of in these Countries, and
yet I heare some saye (I knowe not howe truely) that
they haue knowne the like before in their dayes. *Sed
quid vobis videtur magnis Philosophis ?*   I like your late 20
English Hexameters so exceedingly well that I also
enure my Penne sometime in that kind : whyche I fynd
indeede, as I haue heard you often defende in worde,
neither so harde, nor so harshe, that it will easily and
fairely yeelde it selfe to oure Moother tongue.   For the 25
onely or chiefest hardnesse, whych seemeth, is in the
Accente ; whyche sometime gapeth, and, as it were, yawneth
ilfauouredly, comming shorte of that it should, and sometime exceeding the measure of the Number, as in Carpenter the middle sillable, being vsed shorte in speache, 30

when it shall be read long in Verse, seemeth like a lame
Gosling that draweth one legge after hir: and Heauen,
beeing vsed shorte as one sillable, when it is in Verse
stretched out with a *Diastole*, is like a lame Dogge that
5 holdes vp one legge. But it is to be wonne with Custome,
and rough words must be subdued with Vse. For why,
a Gods name, may not we, as else the Greekes, haue the
kingdome of oure owne Language, and measure our Accentes by the sounde, reseruing the Quantitie to the
10 Verse? Loe, here I let you see my olde vse of toying
in Rymes turned into your artificial straightnesse of
Verse by this Tetrasticon. I beseech you tell me your
fancie without parcialitie.

See yee the blindefoulded pretie God, that feathered
Archer,
15 Of Louers Miseries which maketh his bloodie Game?
Wote ye why his Moother with a Veale hath coouered
his Face?
Trust me, least he my Looue happely chaunce to
beholde.

Seeme they comparable to those two, which I translated
you *ex tempore* in bed, the last time we lay togither in
20 Westminster?

That which I eate did I ioy, and that which I greedily
gorged.
As for those many goodly matters leaft I for others.

I would hartily wish you would either send me the Rules
and Precepts of Arte, which you obserue in Quantities,
25 or else followe mine, that M. Philip Sidney gaue me,
being the very same which M. Drant deuised, but enlarged
with M. Sidneys own iudgement, and augmented with my
Obseruations, that we might both accorde and agree in
one, leaste we ouerthrowe one an other and be ouerthrown

of the rest. Truste me, you will hardly beleeue what greate good liking and estimation Maister Dyer had of youre Satyricall Verses, and I, since the viewe thereof, hauing before of my selfe had speciall liking of Englishe Versifying, am euen nowe aboute to giue you some token, 5 and howe well therein I am able to doe : for, to tell you trueth, I minde shortely at conuenient leysure to sette forth a Booke in this kinde, whyche I entitle *Epithalamion Thamesis*, whyche Booke I dare vndertake wil be very profitable for the knowledge and rare for the Inuention 10 and manner of handling. For in setting forth the marriage of the Thames I shewe his first beginning and offspring, and all the Countrey that he passeth thorough, and also describe all the Riuers throughout Englande whyche came to this Wedding, and their righte names, and right 15 passage, &c. A worke, beleeue me, of much labour, wherein notwithstanding Master *Holinshed* hath muche furthered and aduantaged me, who therein hath bestowed singular paines in searching oute their firste heades and sources, and also in tracing and dogging oute all their 20 course til they fall into the Sea.

> *O Tite, siquid ego,*
> *Ecquid erit pretii?*

But of that more hereafter. ·Nowe, my *Dreames* and *Dying Pellicane* being fully finished (as I partelye signi- 25 fied in my laste Letters) and presentlye to bee imprinted, I wil in hande forthwith with my *Faery Queene*, whyche I praye you hartily send me with al expedition ; and your frendly Letters and long expected Iudgement wythal, whyche let not be shorte, but in all pointes suche as you 30 ordinarilye vse and I extraordinarily desire. *Multum vale. Westminster, Quarto Nonas Aprilis* 1580. *Sed, amabo te, meum Corculum tibi se ex animo commendat plurimum : iam diu mirata, te nihil ad literas suas responsi dedisse.*

Vide quaeso, ne id tibi Capitale sit : Mihi certe quidem erit,
neque tibi hercle impune, vt opinor, iterum vale, et quam
voles saepe.

Yours alwayes to commaunde,

IMMERITO.

5

[IV]

A GALLANT FAMILIAR LETTER, CONTAINING AN
   ANSWERE TO THAT OF M. IMMERITO, WITH
   SUNDRY PROPER EXAMPLES AND SOME PRE-
   CEPTS OF OUR ENGLISH REFORMED VERSI-
10   FYING.

To my very friend M. *Immerito.*

   Signor Immerito, to passe ouer youre needelesse complaint, wyth the residue of your preamble (for of your
EARTHQUAKE I presuppose you haue ere this receyued
15 my goodly discourse), and withall to let my late Englishe
Hexametres goe as lightlye as they came, I cannot
choose but thanke and honour the good Aungell (whether
it were Gabriell or some other) that put so good a motion
into the heads of those two excellent Gentlemen MR.
20 SIDNEY and M. DYER, the two very Diamondes of hir
Maiesties Courte for many speciall and rare qualities,
as to helpe forwarde our new famous enterprise for the
Exchanging of Barbarous and Balductum Rymes with
Artificiall Verses, the one being in manner of pure and
25 fine Goulde, the other but counterfet and base ylfauoured
Copper. I doubt not but their liuelie example and Practise wil preuaile a thousand times more in short space
than the dead Aduertizement and persuasion of M. ASCHAM

to the same Effecte, whose SCHOLEMAISTER, notwithstanding, I reuerence in respect of so learned a Motiue.
I would gladly be acquainted with M. DRANTS Prosodye,
and I beseeche you commende me to good M. SIDNEYS
iudgement, and gentle M. IMMERITOS Obseruations.   I 5
hope your nexte Letters, which I daily expect, wil bring
me in farther familiaritie and acquaintance with al three.
Mine owne Rules and Precepts of Arte I beleeue wil fal
out not greatly repugnant, though peraduenture somewhat
different : and yet I am not so resolute but I can be 10
content to reserue the Coppying out and publishing
thereof vntil I haue a little better consulted with my
pillowe, and taken some farther aduize of MADAME
SPERIENZA.   In the meane, take this for a general
Caueat, and say I haue reuealed one great mysterie 15
vnto you : I am of Opinion there is no one more regular
and iustifiable direction, eyther for the assured and infallible Certaintie of our English Artificiall Prosodye
particularly, or generally to bring our Language into
Arte and to frame a Grammer or Rhetorike thereof, 20
than first of all vniuersally to agree vpon ONE AND THE
SAME ORTOGRAPHIE, in all pointes conformable and pro-
portionate to our COMMON NATURAL PROSODYE.   Whether
SIR THOMAS SMITHES in that respect be the most perfit,
as surely it must needes be very good ; or else some 25
other of profounder Learning and longer Experience
than SIR THOMAS was, shewing by necessarie demonstration wherin he is defectiue, wil vndertake shortely to
supplie his wantes and make him more absolute ; my
selfe dare not hope to hoppe after him, til I see something 30
or other, too or fro, publickely and autenticly established,
as it were by a generall Counsel or acte of Parliament :
and then peraduenture, standing vppon firmer grounde,
for Companie sake, I may aduenture to do as other do.
Interim, credit me, I dare geue no Preceptes, nor set 35

downe any CERTAINE GENERAL ARTE; and yet see my
boldenesse. I am not greatly squaimishe of my PAR-
TICULAR EXAMPLES, whereas he that can but reasonably
skil of the one wil giue easily a shreude gesse at the
5 other, considering that the one fetcheth his original and
offspring from the other. In which respecte, to say troth,
WE BEGINNERS haue the start and aduantage of our Followers, who are to frame and conforme both their Examples and Precepts according to that President which they
10 haue of vs: as no doubt Homer or some other in *Greeke*,
and ENNIUS or I know not who else in *Latine*, did preiudice and ouerrule those that followeth them, as well for
the quantities of syllables as number of feete, and the
like: their onely Examples going for current payment,
15 and standing in steade of Lawes and Rules with the posteritie. In so much that it seemed a sufficient warrant
(as still it doth in our Common Grammer Schooles) to
make τι in τιμή and υ in *Vnus* long, because the one hath
τιμὴ δ᾽ ἐκ διός ἐστί and the other *Vnus homo nobis,* and so
20 consequently in the rest. But to let this by-disputation
passe, which is already so throughly discoursed and can-
uassed of the best Philosophers, and namely ARISTOTLE,
that poynt vs, as it were with the forefinger, to the very
FOUNTAINES AND HEAD SPRINGES of Artes and Artificiall
25 preceptes, in the ANALITIQUES and METAPHYSIKES: most
excellently set downe in these FOURE GOLDEN TERMES,
the famoussest Termes to speake of in all LOGIQUE and
PHILOSOPHIE, ἐμπειρία, ἰστορία, αἴσθησις, ἐπαγωγή.

Shall I nowe by the way sende you a IANUARIE GIFT
30 in APRILL, and, as it were, shewe you a CHRISTMAS
GAMBOWLDE after EASTER? Were the manner so very
fine, as the matter is very good, I durst presume of an
other kinde of *Plaudite* and GRAMERCIE than now I will:
but, being as it is, I beseeche you set parcialitie aside, and
35 tell me your maisterships fancie.

A New yeeres Gift to my old friend Maister
George Bilchaunger : in commendation of three
most precious Accidentes, *Vertue*, *Fame*, and
Wealth : and finally of the fourth, *a good*
Tongue. 5

Vertue sendeth a man to *Renowne*; *Fame* lendeth
   Aboundaunce;
Fame with Aboundaunce maketh a man thrise blessed
   and happie;
So the Rewarde of Famous Vertue makes many
   wealthy,
And the Regard of Wealthie Vertue makes many
   blessed :
O blessed Vertue, blessed Fame, blessed Aboundaunce, 10
O that I had you three, with the losse of thirtie
   Comencementes.
Nowe farewell *Mistresse*, whom lately I loued aboue all.
These be my three bonny lasses, these be my three
   bonny Ladyes;
Not the like *Trinitie* againe, saue onely the Trinitie
   aboue all :
Worship and Honour first to the one and then to 15
   the other.
A thousand good leaues be for euer graunted *Agrippa*,
For squibbing and declayming against many fruitlesse
Artes and Craftes, deuisde by the *Diuls and Sprites*
   for a torment
And for a plague to the world : as both *Pandora*,
   Prometheus,
And that cursed *good bad Tree* can testifie at all times : 20
Meere Gewegawes and Bables, in comparison of these,
Toyes to mock Apes and Woodcockes, in comparison
   of these,
Iugling castes and knicknackes, in comparison of these.

Yet behinde there is one thing, worth a prayer at all
tymes,.

A good Tongue in a mans Head, *A good Tongue* in
a woomans.

And what so precious matter and foode for a good
Tongue

As blessed Vertue, blessed Fame, blessed Aboundaunce.

5   L'Enuoy.

Maruell not that I meane to send these Verses at
Euensong,

On *Neweyeeres* Euen, and Oldyeeres End, as a
Memento:

Trust me, I know not a richer Iewell, newish or oldish,

Than blessed Vertue, blessed Fame, blessed Aboundaunce.

10   O blessed Vertue, blessed Fame, blessed Aboundaunce,
O that you had these three, with the losse of *Fortie
Valetes.*

> *He that wisheth you may liue to see a hundreth
> Good Newe yeares, euery one happier and merrier
> than other.*

15   Now to requite your Blindfolded pretie God (wherin
by the way I woulde gladly learne why *Thĕ* in the first,
Yĕ in the first and thirde, *Hĕ* and *My* in the last, being
shorte, Mē alone should be made longer in the very
same). Imagin me to come into a goodly Kentishe *Garden*
20 of your old Lords, or some other Noble man, and, spying
a florishing Bay Tree there, to demaunde *ex tempore* as
followeth. Thinke vppon Petrarches

> *Arbor vittoriosa, trionfale,
> Onor d'Imperadori e di Poeti,*

25 and perhappes it will aduance the wynges of your Imagination a degree higher: at the least if any thing can be

added to the loftinesse of his conceite, who[m] gentle Mistresse *Rosalinde* once reported to haue all the Intelligences at commaundement, and an other time christened her *Segnior Pegaso.*

ENCOMIUM LAURI. 5

What might I call this Tree? *A Laurell*? O bonny
    Laurell:
Needes to thy bowes will I bow this knee, and vayle
    my bonetto.
Who, but thou, the renowne of Prince and Princely
    Poeta?
Th' one for Crowne, for Garland th' other thanketh
    Apollo.
Thrice happy *Daphne*, that turned was to the *Bay* 10
    Tree,
Whom such seruauntes serue, as challenge seruice of
    all men.
Who chiefe Lorde, and King of Kings, but th' *Emperour* only?
And *Poet* of right stampe ouerawith th' *Emperour*
    himselfe.
Who but knowes *Aretyne*, was he not halfe Prince
    to the Princes?
And many a one there liues, as nobly minded at all 15
    poyntes.
Now farewell *Bay Tree*, very Queene, and Goddesse
    of all trees,
Ritchest perle to the Crowne, and fayrest Floure to
    the Garland!
Faine wod I craue, might I so presume, some farther
    aquaintaunce;
O that I might? but I may not: woe to my destinie
    therefore.

Trust me, not one more loyall seruaunt longes to thy
Personage.

But what says *Daphne*? *Non omni dormio*, worse
lucke.

Yet Farewell, Farewell, the Reward of those that I
honour :

Glory to *Garden* : Glory to *Muses* : Glory to *Vertue*.

5
 Partim Ioui et Palladi,
 Partim Apollini et Musis.

But seeing I must needes beuray my store, and set open
my shoppe wyndowes, nowe I pray thee, and coniure thee
by all thy amorous Regardes and Exorcismes of Loue,
10 call a Parliament of thy Sensible and Intelligible powers
together, and tell me, in Tom Trothes earnest, what *Il
fecondo & famoso Poeta* MESTER IMMERITO sayth to
this bolde Satyri[c]all Libell, lately deuised at the instaunce
of a certayne worshipfull Hartefordshyre Gentleman of
15 myne olde acquayntaunce *in Gratiam quorundam Illustrium* Anglofrancitalorum, *hic et ubique apud nos volitan-
tium. Agedum vero, nosti homines, tanquam tuam ipsius
cutem.*

SPECULUM TUSCANISMI.

Since *Galateo* came in and *Tuscanisme* gan vsurpe,
20 Vanitie aboue all, Villanie next her, Statelynes Em-
presse ;

No man but Minion, Stowte Lowte, Plaine swayne,
quoth a Lording :

No wordes but valorous, no workes but woomanish onely.

For life Magnificoes, not a beck but glorious in shew,

In deede most friuolous, not a looke but Tuscanish
alwayes :

25 His *cringing side necke, Eyes glauncing, Fisnamie
smirking,*

With *forefinger kisse*, and braue *embrace to the foote-
    warde*:

Largebelled Kodpeas'd Dublet, vnkodpeased halfe hose,

Straite to the dock, like a shirte, and close to the
    britch, like a diueling,

A little Apish Hatte, cowched fast to the pate, like an
    Oyster,

French Camarick Ruffes, deepe with a witnesse,
    starched to the purpose ;   5

Euery one A per se A ; his termes and braueries in
    Print,

Delicate in speach, queynte in araye, conceited in all
    poyntes :

In Courtly guyles a passing singular odde man ;

For Gallantes a braue Myrrour, a Primerose of
    Honour ;

A Diamond for nonce, a fellowe perelesse in England. 10

Not the like *Discourser* for Tongue and head to be
    found out,

Not the like *resolute Man* for great and serious
    affayres,

Not the like *Lynx* to spie out secretes and priuities
    of States,

Eyed like to *Argus*, *Earde* like to *Midas*, *Nosd* like
    to *Naso*,

Winged like to *Mercury*, fittst of a Thousand for to 15
    be employde :

This, nay more than this, doth practise of *Italy* in one
    yeare.

None doe I name, but some doe I know, that a peece
    of a tweluemonth

Hath so perfited, outly and inly, both body, both soule,

That none for sense, and senses, halfe matchable with
    them.

A *Vulturs smelling, Apes tasting, sight* of an *Eagle*, 20

A *spiders touching, Hartes hearing, might* of a *Lyon,*
Compoundes of wisedome, witte, prowes, bountie, be-
    hauiour,
All gallant Vertues, all qualities of body and soule :
O thrice tenne hundreth times blessed and happy,
5 Blessed and happy *Trauaile, Trauailer* most blessed
    and happy.

> *Penatibus Hetruscis laribusque nostris*
> *Inquilinis.*

Tell me, in good sooth, doth it not too euidently appeare
that this English Poet wanted but A GOOD PATTERNE before
10 his eyes, as it might be some delicate and choyce elegant
Poesie of good M. SIDNEY or M. DYERS (ouer very CASTOR
and POLLUX for such and many greater matters) when this
trimme geere was in hatching : Much like some GENTLE-
WOOMEN I coulde name in England, who by all Phisick and
15 Physiognomie too might as well haue brought forth all
goodly faire children, as they haue now some ylfauored
and deformed, had they, at the tyme of their CONCEPTION,
had in sight the amiable and gallant beautifull Pictures of
ADONIS, CUPIDO, GANYMEDES, or the like, which no doubt
20 would haue wrought such deepe impression in their
fantasies and imaginations, as their children, and perhappes their Childrens children too, myght haue thanked
them for as long as they shall haue Tongues in their
heades.
25 But myne owne leysure fayleth me, and, to say troth,
I am lately become a maruellous great straunger at myne
olde MISTRESSE POETRIES, being newly entertayned and
dayly employed in our Emperour IUSTINIANS SERUICE
(sauing that I haue alreadie addressed a certaine pleasur-
30 able, and Morall, Politique; Naturall, mixte deuise to his
most Honourable Lordshippe in the same kynde, wherevnto my next Letter, if you please mee well, may per-

chaunce make you priuie): marrie nowe, if it lyke you in
the meane while, for varietie sake, to see howe I taske
a young Brother of myne (whom of playne IOHN our
ITALIAN Maister hath Cristened his *Picciolo Giouannibat-*
tista), Lo here (and God will) a peece of hollydayes 5
exercise. In the morning I gaue him this THEAME out of
OUID to translate, and varie after his best fashion.

> *Dum fueris felix, multos numerabis amicos;*
> *Tempora si fuerint nubila, solus eris.*
> *Aspicis, vt veniant ad candida tecta columbae?*　　　10
> *Accipiat nullas sordida turris aues.*

His translation, or rather Paraphrase, before dinner was
first this:

1.

Whilst your Bearnes are fatte, whilst Cofers stuff'd
with aboundaunce,
Freendes will abound: If bearne waxe bare, then 15
adieu sir a Goddes name.
See ye the Dooues? they breede, and feede in gor-
geous Houses:
Scarce one Dooue doth loue to remaine in ruinous
Houses.

And then forsooth this, to make proofe of his facultie
in Pentameters too, affecting a certain *Rithmus* withall:

2.

Whilst your Ritches abound, your friends will play the 20
Placeboes;
If your wealth doe decay, friend, like a feend, will away.
Dooues light and delight in goodly fairetyled houses:
If your House be but olde, Dooue to remoue be ye
bolde.

And the last and largest of all, this :

3.

If so be goods encrease, then dayly encreaseth a goods
friend.

If so be goods decrease, then straite decreaseth a
goods friend.

Then G[o]od night goods friend, who seldome prooueth
a good friend.

5 Giue me the goods, and giue me the good friend ; take
ye the goods friend.

Douehouse and Louehouse in writing differ a letter ;

In deede scarcely so much, so resembleth an other an
other.

Tyle me the Doouehouse trimly, and gallant : where
the like storehouse ?

Tyle me the Doouehouse ; leaue it vnhansome : where
the like poorehouse ?

10 Looke to the Louehouse ; where the resort is, there
is a gaye showe :

Gynne port and mony fayle, straight sports and Companie faileth.

Beleeue me I am not to be charged with aboue one or
two of the Verses, and a foure or fiue wordes in the rest.
His afternoones THEAME was borrowed out of him, whom
15 one in your Coate, they say, is as much beholding vnto as
any Planet or Starre in Heauen is vnto the Sunne, and
is quoted, as your self best remember, in the Close of your
October.

> *Giunto Alessandro a[l]la famosa tomba*
20 > *Del fero Achille, sospirando disse,*
> *O fortunato, che si chiara tromba*
> *Trouasti.*

Within an houre, or there aboutes, he brought me these

foure lustie Hexameters, altered since not past in a worde
or two.

Noble *Alexander*, when he came to the tombe of
    Achilles,
Sighing spake with a bigge voyce : O thrice blessed
    Achilles,
That such a Trump, so great, so loude, so glorious 5
    hast found,
As the renowned and surprizing *Archpoet Homer*.

Vppon the viewe whereof : Ah my Syrrha, quoth I, here
is a gallant exercise for you in deede : we haue had
a little prettie triall of you[r] LATIN and ITALIAN Translation : Let me see now, I pray, what you can doo in your 10
owne TONGUE. And with that, reaching a certaine famous
Booke, called the newe SHEPHARDES CALENDER, I turned
to WILLYES and THOMALINS EMBLEMES, in MARCHE, and
bad him make them eyther better or worse in English
verse. I gaue him an other howres respite ; but, before 15
I looked for him, he suddainely rushed vpon me, and gaue
me his deuise, thus formally set downe in a faire peece of
Paper.

1. Thomalins Embleme.

Of Honny and of Gaule in Loue there is store :   20
The Honny is much, but the Gaule is more.

2. Willyes Embleme.

To be wize, and eke to Loue,
Is graunted scarce to God aboue.

3. Both combined in one.   25

Loue is a thing more fell, than full of Gaule, than of
    Honny.
And to be wize, and Loue, is a worke for a God, or
    a Goddes peere.

With a small voluntarie Supplement of his owne, on
the other side, in commendation of hir most gratious and
thrice excellent Maiestie :

> Not the like *Virgin* againe, in Asia, or Afric, or
>   Europe,
> 5 For Royall Vertues, for Maiestie, Bountie, Behauiour.
>   *Raptim, vti vides.*

In both not passing a worde or two corrected by mee.
Something more I haue of his, partly that very day begun,
and partly continued since : but yet not so perfitly finished
that I dare committe the viewe and examination thereof
10 to MESSER IMMERITOES Censure, whom after those same
two incomparable and myraculous GEMINI, *omni exceptione
maiores,* I recount and chaulk vppe in the Catalogue of
our very principall Englishe ARISTARCHI.   Howbeit, I am
nigh halfe perswaded that in tyme (*siquidem vltima primis
15 respondeant*) for length, bredth, and depth it will not come
far behinde your *Epithalamion Thamesis* : the rather, hauing so fayre a president and patterne before his Eyes as
I warrant him, and he presumeth, to haue of that : both
MASTER COLLINSHEAD and M. HOLLI[N]SHEAD too being
20 togither therein.   But euer and euer, me thinkes, your
great CATOES, *Ecquid erit pretii,* and our little CATOES,
Res age quae prosunt, make suche a buzzing and ringing in
my head, that I haue little ioy to animate and encourage
either you or him to goe forward, vnlesse ye might make
25 account of some certaine ordinarie wages, at the leastwise
haue your meate and drinke for your dayes workes.   As
for my selfe, howsoeuer I haue toyed and trifled hereto-
fore, I am nowe taught, and I trust I shall shortly learne
(no remedie, I must of meere necessitie giue you ouer in
30 the playne fielde) to employ my trauayle and tyme wholly,
or chiefely, on those studies and practizes that carrie, as
they saye, meate in their mouth, hauing euermore their

eye vppon the Title *De pane lucrando*, and their hand
vpon their halfpenny. For, I pray now, what saith
M. Cuddie, *alias* you know who, in the tenth Æglogue of
the foresaid famous new Calender :

> Piers, I haue piped erst so long with payne,   5
> That all myne oten reedes been rent and wore,
> And my poore Muse hath spent hir spared store,
> Yet little good hath got, and much lesse gayne.
> Such pleasaunce makes the Grashopper so poore,
> And ligge so layde, when winter doth her strayne.   10
> The Dapper Ditties, that I woont deuize
> To feede youthes fancie, and the flocking fry,
> Delighten much: what I the bett for-thy?
> They han the pleasure, I a sclender prize.
> I beate the bushe, the birdes to them doe flye.   15
> What good thereof to Cuddy can arise?

But Master Collin Cloute is not euery body, and
albeit his olde Companions, Master Cuddy and Master
Hobbinoll, be as little beholding to their Mistresse
Poetrie as euer you wist; yet he, peraduenture, by the
meanes of hir speciall fauour and some personall priui-
ledge, may happely liue by Dying Pellicanes, and pur-
chase great landes and Lordshippes with the money
which his Calendar and Dreames haue, and will,
affourde him. *Extra iocum*, I like your Dreames passingly well: and the rather, bicause they sauour of that
singular extraordinarie veine and inuention whiche I
euer fancied moste, and in a manner admired onelye, in
Lucian, Petrarche, Aretine, Pasquill, and all the
most delicate and fine conceited Grecians and Italians
(for the Romanes to speake of are but vèrye Ciphars in
this kinde): whose chiefest endeuour and drifte was
to haue nothing vulgare, but in some respecte or other,
and especially in liuely Hyperbolicall Amplifications,

rare, queint, and odde in euery pointe, and, as a man
woulde saye, a degree or two at the leaste aboue the
reach and compasse of a common Schollers capacitie.
In which respecte notwithstanding, as well for the sin-
5 gularitie of the manner as the Diuinitie of the matter,
I hearde once a Diuine preferre SAINT JOHNS REUE-
LATION before al the veriest MÆTAPHYSICALL VISIONS
and iollyest conceited DREAMES or EXTASIES that euer
were deuised by one or other, howe admirable or super-
10 excellent soeuer they seemed otherwise to the worlde.
And truely I am so confirmed in this opinion, that when
I bethinke me of the verie notablest and moste wonderful Propheticall or Poeticall Vision that euer I read or
hearde, me seemeth the proportion is so vnequall, that
15 there hardly appeareth anye semblaunce of Comparison :
no more in a manner (specially for Poets) than doth betweene the incomprehensible Wisedome of God and the
sensible Wit of Man.   But what needeth this digression
betweene you and me : I dare saye you wyll holde your
20 selfe reasonably wel satisfied if youre DREAMES be but as
well esteemed of in Englande as PETRARCHES VISIONS be in
Italy : whiche I assure you is the very worst I wish you.
But see how I haue the Arte MEMORATIUE at commaundement.   In good faith I had once again nigh forgotten
25 your FAERIE QUEENE : howbeit, by good chaunce, I haue
nowe sent hir home at the laste, neither in better nor
worse case than I founde hir.   And must you of necessitie haue my Iudgement of hir in deede : To be plaine,
I am voyde of all iudgement, if your NINE COMŒDIES,
30 wherunto, in imitation of HERODOTUS, you giue the names
of the *Nine Muses* (and in one mans fansie not vn-
worthily), come not neerer ARIOSTOES COMŒDIES, eyther
for the finenesse of plausible Elocution or the rarenesse of
Poetical Inuention, than that the ELUISH QUEENE doth to
35 his ORLANDO FURIOSO, which, notwithstanding, you wil

needes seeme to emulate, and hope to ouergo, as you
flatly professed your self in one of your last Letters.
Besides, that you know it hath bene the vsual practise of
the most exquisite and odde wittes in all nations, and
specially in *Italie*, rather to shewe and aduaunce them- 5
selues that way than any other : as, namely, those three
notorious dyscoursing heads, BIBIENA, MACHIAUEL, and
ARETINE did (to let BEMBO and ARIOSTO passe) with the
great admiration and wonderment of the whole countrey :
being in deede reputed matchable in all points, both for 10
conceyt of Witte and eloquent decyphering of matters,
either with ARISTOPHANES and MENANDER in Greek or
with PLAUTUS and TERENCE in Latin, or with any other,
in any other tong. But I wil not stand greatly with you
in your owne matters. If so be the FAERYE QUEENE be 15
fairer in your eie than the NINE MUSES, and HOBGOBLIN
runne away with the Garland from APOLLO, Marke what
I saye, and yet I will not say that I thought ; but there
an End for this once, and fare you well, till God or some
good Aungell putte you in a better minde. 20

And yet, bicause you charge me somewhat suspitiouslye
with an olde promise to deliuer you of that iealousie,
I am so farre from hyding mine owne matters from you,
that loe I muste needes be reuealing my friendes secreates,
now an honest Countrey Gentleman, sometimes a Scholler : 25
At whose request I bestowed this pawlting bungrely
Rime vpon him, to present his Maistresse withall. The
parties shall bee namelesse, sauing that the Gentle-
womans true, or counterfaite, Christen name must necessarily be bewrayed. 30

[*Here follow forty-two lines of burlesque verse,* 'To my
good Mistresse *Anne,* the very lyfe of my lyfe, and onely
beloued Mystresse.]

God helpe vs, you and I are wisely employed (are wee
not ?) when our Pen and Inke, and Time and Wit, and all 35

runneth away in this goodly yonkerly veine : as if the
world had nothing else for vs to do, or we were borne
to be the only NONPROFICIENTS and NIHILAGENTS of the
world. *Cuiusmodi tu nugis, atque nanis, nisi vna mecum*
5 *(qui solemni quodam iureiurando atque voto obstringor,*
relicto isto amoris Poculo, iuris Poculum primo quoque tem-
pore exhaurire) iam tandem aliquando valedicas, (quod tamen
vnum tibi, credo, τῶν ἀδυνάτων videbitur): *nihil dicam amplius* :
Valeas.   E meo municipio.   Nono Calendas Maias.

10   But hoe I pray you, gentle sirra, a word with you more.
In good sooth, and by the faith I beare to the Muses, you
shal neuer haue my subscription or consent (though you
should charge me wyth the authoritie of fiue hundreth
Maister DRANTS) to make your *Carpēnter,* our *Carpĕnter,*
15 an inche longer or bigger than God and his Englishe
people haue made him. Is there no other Pollicie to pull
downe Ryming and set vppe Versifying but you must
needes correcte *Magnificat* : and againste all order of Lawe,
and in despite of Custome, forcibly vsurpe and tyrannize
20 vppon a quiet companye of wordes that so farre beyonde
the memorie of man haue so peaceably enioyed their
seueral Priuiledges and Liberties, without any disturb-
ance or the leaste controlement ? What ? ˙ Is HORACES
Ars Poetica so quite out of our Englishe Poets head that
25 he muste haue his Remembrancer to pull hym by the
sleeue, and put him in mind of *Penes vsum,* and *ius,* and
norma loquendi ? Indeed I remember who was wont
in a certaine brauerie to call our M. VALANGER Noble
M. VALANGER.   Else neuer heard I any that durst pre-
30 sume so much ouer the Englishe (excepting a fewe suche
stammerers as haue not the masterie of their owne
Tongues) as to alter the Quantitie of any one sillable, otherwise than oure common speache and generall receyued
Custome woulde beare them oute. Woulde not I laughe,
35 thinke you, to heare MESTER IMMERITO come in baldely

with his *Maiēstie, Royāltie, Honēstie, Scīences, Facŭlties,
Excēllent, Tauērnour, Manfŭlly, Faithfŭlly,* and a thousande
the like, in steade of *Maiĕstie, Royăltie, Honĕstie,* and so
forth : And trowe you anye coulde forbeare the byting of
his lippe or smyling in his Sleeue, if a iolly fellowe and 5
greate Clarke (as it mighte be youre selfe) reading a fewe
Verses vnto him, for his owne credit and commendation,
should nowe and then tell him of *bargaīneth, follōwing,
harrōwing, thoroŭghly,* or the like, in steade of *bargaĭneth,
follŏwing, harrŏwing,* and the reste : Or will Segnior Im- 10
merito, bycause, may happe, he hathe a fat-bellyed Archdeacon on his side, take vppon him to controll Maister
Doctor Watson for his *All Trauaīlers,* in a Verse so highly
extolled of Master Ascham ? or Maister Ascham himselfe,
for abusing Homer and corrupting our Tongue, in that 15
he saith,

> *Quite throŭghe a Doore flĕwe a shafte with a brasse
>   head?*

Nay, haue we not somtime, by your leaue, both the
Position of the firste and Dipthong of the seconde con- 20
curring in one and the same sillable, which neuerthelesse
is commonly and ought necessarily to be pronounced
short ?   I haue nowe small time to bethink me of many
examples.   But what say you to the second in *Mer-
chaŭndise*? to the third in *Couenaŭnteth*? and to the 25
fourth in *Appurtenaŭnces*?   Durst you aduenture to make
any of them long, either in Prose or in Verse ?   I assure
you I knowe who dareth not, and *suddaĭnly* feareth the
displeasure of all true Englishemen if he should.   Say you
suddaīnly, if you like ; by my *certaĭnly* and *certaĭnty* I wil 30
not.   You may perceiue by the *Premisses* (which very
worde I woulde haue you note by the waye to) the Latine
is no rule for vs : or imagine aforehande (bycause you are
like to proue a great Purchaser, and leaue suche store of
money and possessions behinde you) your *Execŭtors* wil 35

deale *fraudulently* or *violently* with your *succĕssour* (whiche
in a maner is euery mans case), and it will fall oute
a resolute pointe : the third in *Execūtores, fraudulenter,
violenter,* and the seconde in *Succēssor,* being long in the
5 one and shorte in the other, as in seauen hundreth
more, suche as *discĭple, recīted, excīled* : *tenĕment, orătour,
laudĭble,* and a number of their fellowes are long in
English, short in Latine, long in Latine, short in English.
Howbeit, in my fancy such words as *violently, diligently,
10 magnificently, indifferently* seeme in a manner reasonably
indifferent, and tollerable either waye ; neither woulde
I greatly stande with him that translated the Verse

Cur mittis violas ? vt me violentius vras ?

WHY SEND YOU VIOLETS ? TO BURNE MY POORE HART
15   VIOLĒNTLY.

Marry so, that being left common for verse, they are to
be pronounced shorte in Prose, after the maner of the
Latines, in suche wordes as these, *Cathedra, Volucres,
mediocres, Celebres.*

20 And thus farre of your *Carpĕnter* and his fellowes,
wherin we are to be moderated and ouerruled by the
vsuall and common receiued sounde, and not to deuise
any counterfaite fantasticall Accent of oure owne, as manye,
otherwise not vnlearned, haue corruptely and ridiculouslye
25 done in the Greeke.

Nowe for your *Heauen, Seauen, Eleauen,* or the like,
I am likewise of the same opinion, as generally in all
words else : we are not to goe a little farther, either for
the PROSODY or the ORTHOGRAPHY (and therefore your
30 Imaginarie DIASTOLE nothing worthe) then we are licenced
and authorized by the ordinarie vse, and custome, and
proprietie, and Idiome, and, as it were, Maiestie of our
speach : which I accounte the only infallible and soueraigne
Rule of all Rules. And therefore, hauing respecte there-
35 unto, and reputing it Petty Treason to reuolt therefro, dare

hardly eyther in the PROSODIE, or in the ORTHOGRAPHY either, allowe them two sillables in steade of one, but woulde as well in Writing as in Speaking haue them vsed as *Monosyllaba*, thus : *heavn, seavn, a leavn*, as Maister ASCHAM in his TOXOPHILUS doth YRNE, commonly 5 written Yron :

> *Vp to the pap his string did he pull, his shafte to the harde yrne :*

especially the difference so manifestly appearing by the Pronunciation betweene these two, *a leavn a clocke* and 10 *a leaven of Dowe*, whyche *lea-ven* admitteth the DIASTOLE you speake of.   But see what absurdities thys yl fauoured ORTHOGRAPHYE, or rather PSEUDOGRAPHY, hathe in-gendred, and howe one errour still breedeth and begetteth an other.   Haue wee not *Mooneth* for *Moonthe, sithence* 15 for *since, whilest* for *whilste, phantasie* for *phansie, euen* for *evn, Diuel* for *Divl, God hys wrath* for *Goddes wrath*, and a thousande of the same stampe, wherein the corrupte ORTHOGRAPHY in the moste hathe beene the sole, or principall, cause of corrupte PROSODYE in ouer many ?   20

Marry, I confesse some wordes we haue indeede, as for example *fayer*, either for *beautifull* or for a *Marte, ayer*, bothe *pro aere* and *pro haerede*, for we say not *Heire* but plaine *Aire* for him to (or else SCOGGINS AIER were a poore iest), whiche are commonly and maye indifferently be vsed 25 eyther wayes.   For you shal as well and as ordinarily heare *fayer* as *faire*, and *Aier* as *Aire*, and bothe alike, not onely of diuers and sundrye persons but often of the very same, otherwhiles vsing the one, otherwhiles the other : and so *died* or *dyde, spied* or *spide, tryed* or *tride,* 30 *fyer* or *fyre, myer* or *myre*, wyth an infinyte companye of the same sorte, sometime *Monosyllaba*, sometime *Poly-syllaba*.

To conclude both pointes in one, I dare sweare priuately to your selfe, and will defende publiquely againste any, it is 35

neither Heresie nor Paradox to sette downe and stande
vppon this assertion (notwithstanding all the Preiudices
and Presumptions to the contrarie, if they were tenne
times as manye moe) that it is not either Position, or
5 Dipthong, or Diastole, or anye like Grammer Schoole
Deuice that doeth or can indeede either make long or
short, or encrease, or diminish the number of Sillables,
but onely the common allowed and receiued PROSODYE,
taken vp by an vniuersall consent of all, and continued by
10 a generall vse and Custome of all. Wherein neuerthelesse I grant, after long aduise and diligent obseruation
of particulars, a certain Vniform Analogie and Concordance being in processe of time espyed out, sometime
this, sometime that, hath been noted by good wits in their
15 ANALYSES to fall out generally alyke, and, as a man woulde
saye, regularly, in all or moste wordes: as Position,
Dipthong, and the like: not as firste and essentiall causes
of this or that effecte (here lyeth the point), but as Secun-
darie and Accidentall Signes of this or that Qualitie.
20 It is the vulgare and naturall Mother PROSODYE that
alone worketh the feate, as the onely supreame Foundresse
and Reformer of Position, Dipthong, Orthographie, or
whatsoeuer else: whose Affirmatiues are nothing worth,
if she once conclude the Negatiue: and whose *secundae*
25 *intentiones* muste haue their whole allowance and warrante
from hir *primae*. And therefore, in shorte, this is the verie
shorte and the long: Position neither maketh shorte nor
long in oure Tongue, but so farre as we can get hir good
leaue. Peraduenture, vppon the diligent suruewe and
30 examination of Particulars, some the like Analogie and
Vniformity might be founde oute in some other respecte,
that shoulde as vniuersally and Canonically holde amongst
vs as Position doeth with the Latines and Greekes. I
saye peraduenture, bycause, hauing not yet made anye
35 speciall obseruation, I dare not precisely affirme any

generall certaintie : albeit I presume, so good and sensible
a Tongue as our is, beeyng wythall so like itselfe as it is,
cannot but haue something equipollent and counteruaile-
able to the beste Tongues in some one such kinde of
conformitie or other.   And this forsooth is all the Artificial 5
Rules and Precepts you are like to borrowe of one man at
this time.

Sed amabo te, ad Corculi tui delicatissimas Literas, prope-
diem, qua potero, accuratissime: tot interim illam exquisi-
tissimis salutibus, atque salutationibus impertiens, quot habet 10
in Capitulo, capillos semiaureos, semiargenteos, semigemmeos.
Quid quaeris ?   Per tuam Venerem altera Rosalindula est:
eamque non alter, sed idem ille, (tua, vt ante, bona cum
gratia) copiose amat Hobbinolus.   O mea Domina Immerito,
mea bellissima Collina Clouta, multo plus plurimum salue, 15
atque vale.

You knowe my ordinarie Postscripte : you may com-
municate as much or as little as you list of these Patcheries
and fragments with the two Gentlemen : but there a straw,
and you loue me : not with any else, friend or foe, or other : 20
vnlesse haply you haue a special desire to imparte some
parte hereof to my good friend *M. Daniel Rogers,* whose
curtesies are also registred in my Marble booke.   You
know my meaning.

Nosti manum et stylum.   25

G.

FROM HARVEY'S 'LETTER-BOOK.'

WHAT thoughe Italy, Spayne, and Fraunce, rauisshed
with a certayne glorious and ambitious desier (your gal-
lantshipp would peraduenture terme it zeale and deuotion)
5 to sett oute and aduaunce ther owne languages aboue the
very Greake and Lattin, if it were possible, and standinge
altogither vppon termes of honour and exquisite formes of
speaches, karriinge a certayne braue magnificent grace
and maiestye with them, do so highly and honorablely
10 esteeme of ther countrye poets, reposing on greate parte
of their souraigne glory and reputation abroade in the
worlde in the famous writings of their nobblist wittes?
What though you and a thousand such nurrishe a stronge
imagination amongst yourselues that Alexander, Scipio,
15 Cæsar, and most of ower honorablist and worthyest captaynes had neuer bene that they were but for pore blinde
Homer? What thoughe it hath vniversally bene the
practisse of the floorishingist States and most politique
commonwelthes, from whence we borrowe our substan-
20 tiallist and most materiall præceptes and examples of
wise and considerate gouernement, to make the very most
of ther vulgare tunges, and togither with there seignioryes
and dominions by all meanes possible to amplifye and
enlarge them, deuisinge all ordinarye and extraordinarye
25 helpes, both for the polisshinge and refininge of them
at home, and alsoe for the spreddinge and dispersinge
of them abroade? What though Il Magnifico Segnior
Beniuolo hath notid this amongst his politique Discourses and matters of state and gouernemente, that the
30 most couragious and valorous minds have euermore
bene where was most furniture of eloquence, and greatist
stoare of notable orators and famous Poets? What,
a goddes name, passe we what was dun in ruinous

Athens or decayid Roome a thousand or twoe thousande
yeares agoe? Doist thou not ouersensibely perceiue that
the markett goith far otherwise in Inglande, wherein
nothinge is reputid so contemptible, and so baselye and
vilelye accountid of, as whatsoeuer is taken for Inglishe, 5
whether it be handsum fasshions in apparell, or seemely
and honorable in behauiour, or choise wordes and phrases
in speache, or anye notable thinge else in effecte that
sauorith of our owne cuntrye and is not ether merely or
mixtely outlandishe? Is it not cleerer then the sonne at 10
noonedayes that oure most excellent Inglish treatises,
were they neuer so eloquentlye contriued in prose, or
curiously deuised in meeter, haue euer to this daye, and
shall euer hereafter, be sibb to arithmetericians or
Marchantes cownters, which nowe and then stande for 15
hundreds and thowsands, by and bye for odd halfpens or
farthinges, and otherwhiles for very nihils? Hath your
monsieurshipp so soone forgottin our long Westminster
conference the verie last Ester terme touchinge certayne
odd peculiar qualities, appropriate in a manner to Inglishe 20
heddes, and esspeciallye that same worthy and notorious
βριταννικὴν ζηλοτυπίαν that Erasmus prettily playeth withall
in a certayne gallant and braue politique epistle of his,
written purposely to an Inglish gentleman, a courtier, to
instructe him howe he mighte temporize and courte it 25
best here in Inglande? Is not this the principall fundation
and grande maxime of our cuntry Pollicy, not to be ouer
hasty in occupying a mans talent, but to be very chary
and circumspect in opening himselfe and reuealinge his
giftes vnto others? Is it not on of the highest pointes of 30
our Inglish experiencid wisdum, and, as a man would
saye, the very profoundist mystery of our most deepe and
stayd hedds, to haue euery on in continuall ielouzye lest
he sitt ouer neere there schirtes or haue familiar insighte
in ther commendable and discommendable qualityes? 35

Doth not silence couer and conceale many a want, and is
it not both an easier and far surer way to maynetayne and
nurrish the opinion of a mans excellency by noddinge
and countenauncinge oute the matter ether with tunge
5 or penne withoute thessame discoursing vagaries after a
certayne solemne manner then by speakinge or writinge
to purchisse creddit : Esspecially in Inglishe where Inglishe is contemnid, or in meeter where meeter goith
a begginge ? And canst thou tell me nowe, or doist
10 thou at the last begin to imagin with thyselfe what
a wonderfull and exceeding displeasure thou and thy
Prynter have wroughte me, and howe peremptorily ye
have preiudishd my good name for euer in thrustinge me
thus on the stage to make tryall of my extemporall faculty,
15 and to play Wylsons or Tarletons parte ? I suppose thou
wilt go nighe hande shortelye to sende my lorde Vawsis
or my lord Ritches Players or sum other freshe starteupp
comedanties vnto me for sum newe deuised interlude,
or sum maltconceiuid comedye fitt for the Theater or sum
20 other paintid stage, whereat thou and thy liuely copesmates
in London maye lawghe ther mouthes and bellyes full for
pence or twoepence apeece : by cause peraduenture thou
imaginest Vnico Aretino and the pleasurable Cardinall
Bibiena that way esspecially attraynid to be so singularly
25 famous. And then perhappes not longe after vppon newe
occasion (an God will) I must be M. Churchyards and
M. Eldertons successours tooe, and finally cronycled for
on of the most notorious ballat makers and Christmas
carollers in the tyme of Her Maiestyes reigne. *Extra*
30 *iocum,* In good troothe, and by the fayth of a most
faythfull frende, I feare me exceedinglye thou haste
alreddy hazardid that that will fall owte to your
greatist . . .

In the nexte seate to thes hexameters, adonickes, and

iambicks I sett those that stand vppon the number, not in meter, sutch as my lorde of Surrey is sayde first to haue putt forthe in prynte, and my lorde Buckhurste and M. Norton in the Tragedye of Gorboduc, M. Gascoygnes Steele Glasse, an vncertayne autor in certayne cantions 5 agaynst the wylde Irishe, and namelye Mack Morrice, an inuectiue agaynst Simmias Rhodius, a folishe idle phantasticall poett that first deuised this odd riminge with many other triflinge and childishe toyes to make verses, that shoulde in proportion represente the form and figure of 10 an egg, an ape, a winge, and sutche ridiculous and madd gugawes and crockchettes, and of late foolishely reuiuid by sum, otherwise not vnlernid, as Pierius, Scaliger, Crispin, and the rest of that crue. Nothinge so absurde and fruteles but beinge once taken vpp shall haue sume imitatoures. 15 The like veyne of those that hunte the letter; and I heard one Mr. Willes, a greate trauelour, very well lernid, and nowe of riper yeares and sownder iudgment, that hath vsid them himselfe, call them meere fooleryes, vices taken vpp for virtues, apish deuices, friuolous boyishe grammer schole 20 trickes.

And heare will I take occasion to shewe you a peece of a letter that I lately receyuid from the Courte written by a frende of mine, that, since a certayn chaunce befallen vnto him, a secrett not to be reuealid, calleth himself 25 Immerito.

'The twoe worthy gentlemen, Mr. Sidney and Mr. Dyer, haue me, I thanke them, in sum vse of familiarytye; of whome and to whome what speache passith for your creddite and estimation, I leaue yourselfe to conceyue, hauinge 30 allwayes so well conceyuid of my vnfainid affection and good will towardes yow. And nowe they haue proclaymid in there ἀρείῳ πάγῳ.'

[This Epistle, addressed by 'E. K.' to Gabriel Harvey in commendation of Spenser's *Shepheards Calender*, is reprinted
from the first edition of the *Calender*, issued by Hugh
Singleton of Creed Lane near Ludgate, towards the close
of 1579.]

TO THE MOST EXCELLENT AND LEARNED, BOTH
ORATOR AND POETE, MAYSTER GABRIELL
HARVEY, HIS VERIE SPECIAL AND SINGULAR
GOOD FREND E. K. COMMENDETH THE GOOD
5 LYKING OF THIS HIS LABOUR, AND THE
PATRONAGE OF THE NEW POETE.

UNCOVTHE, vnkiste, sayde the old famous Poete
Chaucer: whom, for his excellencie and wonderfull
skil in making, his scholler Lidgate, a worthy scholler
10 of so excellent a maister, calleth the Loadestarre of our
Language, and whom our Colin Clout in his Æglogue
calleth Tityrus the God of shepheards, comparing hym
to the worthines of the Roman Tityrus, Virgile.   Which
prouerbe, myne owne good friend Ma. Haruey, as in that
15 good old Poete it serued well Pandares purpose for the
bolstering of his baudy brocage, so very well taketh place
in this our new Poete, who for that he is vncouthe (as said
Chaucer) is vnkist, and vnknown to most men is regarded
but of few.   But I dout not, so soone as his name shall
20 come into the knowledg of men, and his worthines be
sounded in the tromp of fame, but that he shall be not
onely kiste, but also beloued of all, embraced of the most,

and wondred at of the best. No lesse, I thinke, deserueth
his wittinesse in deuising, his pithinesse in vttering, his
complaints of loue so louely, his discourses of pleasure so
pleasantly, his pastoral rudenesse, his morall wisenesse,
his dewe obseruing of Decorum euerye where, in per- 5
sonages, in seasons, in matter, in speach; and generally,
in al seemely simplycitie of handeling his matter and
framing his words : the which, of many thinges which in
him be straunge, I know will seeme the straungest, the
words them selues being so auncient, the knitting of them 10
so short and intricate, and the whole Periode and compasse of speache so delightsome for the roundnesse, and
so graue for the straungenesse. And firste of the wordes
to speake, I graunt they be something hard, and of most
men vnused, yet both English, and also vsed of most 15
excellent Authors and most famous Poetes. In whom,
whenas this our Poet hath bene much traueiled and
throughly redd, how could it be (as that worthy Oratour
sayde) but that walking in the sonne, although for other
cause he walked, yet needes he mought be sunburnt; and, 20
hauing the sound of those auncient Poetes still ringing in
his eares, he mought needes, in singing, hit out some of
theyr tunes. But whether he vseth them by such casualtye
and custome, or of set purpose and choyse, as thinking
them fittest for such rusticall rudenesse of shepheards, 25
eyther for that theyr rough sounde would make his rymes
more ragged and rustical, or els because such olde and obsolete wordes are most vsed of country folke, sure I think,
and think I think not amisse, that they bring great grace,
and, as one would say, auctoritie to the verse. For albe, 30
amongst many other faultes, it specially be obiected of
Valla against Liuie, and of other against Saluste, that with
ouer much studie they affect antiquitie, as coueting thereby
credence and honor of elder yeeres, yet I am of opinion,
and eke the best learned are of the lyke, that those auncient 35

solemne wordes are a great ornament, both in the one
and in the other ; the one labouring to set forth in hys
worke an eternall image of antiquitie, and the other carefully discoursing matters of grauitie and importaunce.
5 For, if my memory faile not, Tullie, in that booke wherein
he endeuoureth to set forth the paterne of a perfect
Oratour, sayth that ofttimes an auncient worde maketh
the style seeme graue, and as it were reuerend, no otherwise then we honour and reuerence gray heares, for a cer-
10 tein religious regard which we haue of old age. Yet
nether euery where must old words be stuffed in, nor the
common Dialecte and maner of speaking so corrupted
therby, that, as in old buildings, it seme disorderly and
ruinous. But all as in most exquisite pictures they vse
15 to blaze and portraict not onely the daintie lineaments of
beautye, but also rounde about it to shadow the rude
thickets and craggy clifts, that, by the basenesse of such
parts, more excellency may accrew to the principall ; for
oftimes we fynde ourselues, I knowe not how, singularly
20 delighted with the shewe of such naturall rudenesse, and
take great pleasure in that disorderly order. Euen so doe
those rough and harsh termes enlumine, and make more
clearly to appeare, the brightnesse of braue and glorious
words. So oftentimes a dischorde in Musick maketh a
25 comely concordaunce : so great delight tooke the worthy
Poete Alceus to behold a blemish in the ioynt of a wel
shaped body. But if any will rashly blame such his purpose in choyse of old and vnwonted words, him may
I more iustly blame and condemne, or of witlesse headi-
30 nesse in iudging or of heedelesse hardinesse in con-
demning ; for, not marking the compasse of hys bent, he
wil iudge of the length of his cast : for in my opinion
it is one special prayse of many whych are dew to this
Poete, that he hath laboured to restore, as to theyr
35 rightfull heritage, such good and naturall English words

as haue ben long time out of vse and almost cleane dis-
herited.   Which is the onely cause that our Mother
tonge, which truely of it self is both ful enough for
prose and stately enough for verse, hath long time ben
counted most bare and barrein of both.   Which default 5
when as some endeuoured to salue and recure, they
patched up the holes with peces and rags of other languages, borrowing here of the French, there of the Italian,
every where of the Latine ; not weighing how il those
tongues accorde with themselues, but much worse with 10
ours : So now they haue made our English tongue a
gallimaufray or hodgepodge of al other speches.   Other
some, no[t] so wel sene in the English tonge as perhaps in
other languages, if they happen to here an olde word,
albeit very naturall and significant, crye out streightway 15
that we speak no English, but gibbrish, or rather such as
in old time Euanders mother spake : whose first shame is,
that they are not ashamed, in their own mother tonge,
straungers to be counted and alienes.   The second shame,
no lesse then the first, that what so they vnderstand not 20
they streight way deeme to be sencelesse and not at al to
be vnderstode.   Much like to the Mole in Æsopes fable,
that, being blynd her selfe, would in no wise be perswaded
that any beast could see.   The last, more shameful then
both, that of their owne country and natural speach, which 25
together with their Nources milk they sucked, they haue
so base regard and bastard iudgement, that they will not
onely themselues not labor to garnish and beautifie it, but
also repine that of other it shold be embellished.   Like to
the dogge in the maunger, that him selfe can eate no hay, and 30
yet barketh at the hungry bullock that so faine would feede :
whose currish kind, though it cannot be kept from barking,
yet I conne them thanke that they refrain from byting.

Now, for the knitting of sentences, whych they call the
ioynts and members therof, and for al the compasse of 35

the speach, it is round without roughnesse, and learned
wythout hardnes, such indeede as may be perceiued of
the leaste, vnderstoode of the moste, but iudged onely
of the learned.   For what in most English wryters vseth
5 to be loose, and as it were vngyrt, in this Authour is well
grounded, finely framed, and strongly trussed up together.
In regard wherof, I scorne and spue out the rakehellye
route of our ragged rymers (for so themselues vse to hunt
the letter) which without learning boste, without iudge-
10 ment iangle, without reason rage and fome, as if some
instinct of Poeticall spirite had newly rauished them aboue
the meanenesse of commen capacitie.   And being in the
middest of all theyr brauery, sodenly, eyther for want of
matter or of ryme, or hauing forgotten theyr former con-
15 ceipt, they seeme to be so pained and traueiled in theyr
remembrance, as it were a woman in childebirth, or as
that same Pythia when the traunce came vpon her : *Os
rabidum fera corda domans*, &c.

Nethelesse, let them a Gods name feede on theyr owne
20 folly, so they seeke not to darken the beames of others
glory.   As for Colin, vnder whose person the Authour selfe
is shadowed, how furre he is from such vaunted titles and
glorious showes, both him selfe sheweth, where he sayth,

Of Muses, Hobbin[ol], I conne no skill,
25 and
Enough is me to paint out my vnrest, &c :

And also appeareth by the basenesse of the name,
wherein it semeth he chose rather to vnfold great matter
of argument couertly then, professing it, not suffice thereto
30 accordingly.   Which moued him rather in Æglogues then
other wise to write, doubting perhaps his habilitie, which
he little needed, or mynding to furnish our tongue with
this kinde wherein it faulteth ; or following the example
of the best and most auncient Poetes, which deuised
35 this kind of wryting, being both so base for the matter

K 2

and homely for the manner, at the first to trye theyr
habilities, and, as young birdes that be newly crept out
of the nest, by little first to proue theyr tender wyngs
before they make a greater flyght. So flew Theocritus,
as you may perceiue he was all ready full fledged. So 5
flew Virgile, as not yet well feeling his winges. So flew
Mantuane, as not being full somd. So Petrarque. So
Boccace. So Marot, Sanazarus, and also diuers other
excellent both Italian and French Poetes, whose foting
this Author euery where followeth; yet so as few, but 10
they be wel sented, can trace him out. So finally flyeth
this our new Poete as a birde whose principals be scarce
growen out, but yet as [one] that in time shall be hable to
keepe wing with the best.

Now, as touching the generall dryft and purpose of his 15
Æglogues, I mind not to say much, him selfe labouring
to conceale it. Onely this appeareth, that his vnstayed
yougth had long wandred in the common Labyrinth of
Loue, in which time to mitigate and allay the heate of his
passion, or els to warne (as he sayth) the young shepheards, 20
.f. his equalls and companions, of his vnfortunate folly, he
compiled these xij Æglogues, which, for that they be proportioned to the state of the xij monethes, he termeth the
SHEPHEARDS CALENDAR, applying an olde name to a new
worke. Hereunto haue I added a certain Glosse or scho- 25
lion, for thexposition of old wordes and harder phrases;
which maner of glosing and commenting, well I wote, wil
seeme straunge and rare in our tongue : yet, for so much
as I knew many excellent and proper deuises, both in
wordes and matter, would passe in the speedy course of 30
reading, either as vnknowen or as not marked, and that
in this kind, as in other, we might be equal to the learned
of other nations, I thought good to take the paines vpon
me, the rather for that by meanes of some familiar ac-
quaintaunce I was made priuie to his counsell and secret 35

meaning in them, as also in sundry other works of his, which albeit I know he nothing so much hateth as to promulgate, yet thus much haue I aduentured vpon his frendship, him selfe being for long time furre estraunged, hoping
5 that this will the rather occasion him to put forth diuers other excellent works of his which slepe in silence, as his *Dreames*, his *Legendes*, his *Court of Cupide*, and sondry others, whose commendations to set out were verye vaine, the thinges though worthy of many yet being knowen to
10 few. These my present paynes, if to any they be pleasurable or profitable, be you iudge, mine own good Maister Haruey, to whom I haue, both in respect of your worthinesse generally and otherwyse vpon some particular and special considerations, voued this my labour and the may-
15 denhead of this our commen frends Poetrie ; himselfe hauing already in the beginning dedicated it to the Noble and worthy Gentleman, the right worshipfull Ma. Phi. Sidney, a special fauourer and maintainer of all kind of learning. Whose cause, I pray you, Sir, yf Enuie shall stur vp
20 any wrongful accusasion, defend with your mighty Rhetorick and other your rare gifts of learning, as you can, and shield with your good wil, as you ought, against the malice and outrage of so many enemies, as I know wilbe set on fire with the sparks of his kindled glory. And thus recom-
25 mending the Author vnto you, as vnto his most special good frend, and my selfe vnto you both, as one making singuler account of two so very good and so choise frends, I bid you both most hartely farwel, and commit you and your most commendable studies to the tuicion of the greatest.

30   Your owne assuredly to be commaunded,

                         E. K.

Post scr.

NOW I trust, M. Haruey, that vpon sight of your speciall frends and fellow Poets doings, or els for enuie of so many vnworthy Quidams which catch at the garlond which to you alone is dewe, you will be perswaded to pluck out of the hateful darknesse those so many excellent English poemes of yours which lye hid, and bring them forth to eternall light. Trust me, you doe both 5 them great wrong, in depriuing them of the desired sonne, and also your selfe, in smoothering your deserued prayses, and all men generally, in withholding from them so diuine pleasures, which they might conceiue of your gallant English verses, as they haue already doen of your 10 Latine Poemes, which, in my opinion, both for inuention and Elocution are very delicate and superexcellent. And thus againe I take my leaue of my good Mayster Haruey: from my lodging at London thys 10. of Aprill, 1579.

RICHARD STANYHURST

(*FROM THE TRANSLATION OF THE* AENEID)

1582

[The Dedication and the Preface ('Too thee Learned Reader') are prefixed to *Thee First Fou|re Bookes of Vir-|gil his Aeneis |transla|ted in too English Heroical Verse . . . || Imprinted at Leiden in Holland by John Pates | Anno M.D.LXXXII.*

The following extracts are taken from the copy which was formerly in the Ashburnham Library, and is now in the British Museum. The only other known copy is preserved in the library at Britwell Court, Burnham, Bucks. The second (or 1583) edition, which is now hardly less rare, was a London reprint by Henry Bynneman, the printer of the Spenser and Harvey Letters (ante, p. 87). As the difference between these editions is entirely orthographical, it appeared, prima facie, to be desirable to take the London text, partly because it is more 'modern,' and partly because the earlier is accessible in Mr. Arber's excellent reprint (1880). Bynneman's text, on the other hand, was reprinted by James Maidment in 1836 in a private issue of fifty copies. But a collation of the British Museum text of 1582 with that of 1583, in the copy presented to the library of the University of Edinburgh in 1628 by the poet William Drummond, has made it clear that the former is the better. For though Pates speaks, in his Note 'To thee Cvrteovs Reader,' of 'thee noooueltye of imprinting English in theese partes, and thee absence of the author from perusing soom proofes,' his text is more consistent with Stanyhurst's rules, and seems, as far as the prefatory matter is concerned, to have been revised by the author. Bynneman, who is somewhat impatient of the 'newe Ortographie vsed in the booke (whether with the writers mind or the Printers fault, I know not)', sets himself to cut out most of the double 'e's and 'o's and

other eccentricities of the text; but he retains Stanyhurst's
account of these special forms.   His rendering is therefore
a botch, neither illustrating his author's theory nor con-
forming to contemporary English usage.   Stanyhurst's
orthography, like that of the *Ormulum*, must be considered
as a necessary part of the writer's prosodic theory.

The Dedication is dated 'From Leiden in Holland, thee
last of Iune 1582.']

TOO THEE RIGHT HONOVRABLE MY VERIE LOOVING BROOTHER THEE LORD BARON OF DVNSANYE.

WHAT deepe and rare poynctes of hydden secrets
Virgil hath sealde vp in his twelue bookes of
Æneis may easelye appeere too such reaching wyts as
bend theyre endewours too thee vnfolding thereof, not
onlye by gnibling vpon thee outward ryne of a supposed
historie, but also by groaping thee pyth that is shrind
vp wythin thee barck and bodye of so exquisit and singular
a discourse.   For where as thee chiefe prayse of a wryter
consisteth in thee enterlacing of pleasure wyth profit,
oure author hath so wiselye alayed thee one wyth thee
oother as thee shallow reader may bee delighted wyth
a smooth tale, and thee diuing searcher may bee aduantaged
by sowning a pretiouse treatise.   And certes this pre-
heminencye of writing is chieflye (yf wee respect oure
old latin Poëtes) too bee affurded too *Virgil* in this wurck,
and too *Ouid* in his *Metamorphosis*.   As for *Ennius, Horace,
Iuuenal, Persius,* and thee rablement of such cheate Poëtes,
theyre dooinges are, for fauoure of antiquitye, rather
to be pacientlye allowed then highlye regarded.   Such
leauinges as wee haue of *Ennius* his ragged verses are
nothing current, but sauoure soomwhat nappy of thee
spigget, as one that was neauer accustomed too strike
vp thee drum, and too crye, in blazing martial exploytes,

'alarme,' but when hee were haulfe tipsye, as *Horace* recordeth. Thee oother three, ouer this that theyre Verses in camfering wise run harshe and rough, perfourme nothing in matter but biting quippes, taunting Darcklye certeyn
5 men of state that liued in theyre age, beesprinckling theyre *inuectiues* with soom moral preceptes aunswerable too thee capacitye of eurie weake brayne. But oure *Virgil*, not content wyth such meigre stuffe, dooth laboure, in telling as yt were a *Cantorburye tale*, too ferret owt thee
10 secretes of *Nature*, with woordes so fitlye coucht, wyth verses so smoothlye slyckte, with sentences so featlye orderd, with orations so neatlie burnisht, with similitudes so aptly applyed, with eeche *decorum* so duely obserued, as in truth hee hath in right purchased too hym self thee
15 name of a surpassing poët, thee fame of an od oratoure, and thee admiration of a profound philosopher. Hauing therefore (mi good lord) taken vpon mee too execute soom part of mayster *Askam* his wyl, who, in his goulden pamphlet intituled *thee Schoolemayster*, dooth wish thee
20 Vniuersitie students too applie theyre wittes in bewtifying oure English language with heroical verses, I heeld no *Latinist* so fit, too geeue thee onset on, as *Virgil*, who, for his peerelesse style and machlesse stuffe, dooth beare thee prick and price among al thee Roman Poëts. How beyt,
25 I haue heere haulf a guesh that two sortes of carpers wyl seeme too spurne at this myne entreprise ; thee one vtterlie ignorant, thee oother meanelye letterd. Thee ignorant wyl imagin that thee passage was nothing craggye, in as much as M. *Phaere* hath broken thee ice before mee:
30 Thee meaner clarcks wyl suppose my trauail in theese heroical verses too carrye no great difficultie, in that yt lay in my choise too make what word I would short or long, hauing no English writer beefore mee in this kind of poëtrye with whose squire I should leauel my syllables.
35 Too shape therefor an answer too thee first, I say they

are altogeather in a wrong box : considering that such
woordes as fit M. *Phaer* may bee very vnapt for mee,
which they would confesse, yf theyre skil were, so much
as spare, in theese verses. Further more, I stand so
nicelie on my pantofles that way, as yf I could, yeet I
would not renne on thee skore with M. *Phaer* or ennie
oother, by borrowing his termes in so copious and fluent
a language as oure English tongue is. And in good
sooth althogh thee gentleman hath translated *Virgil* in too
English rythme with such surpassing excellencie, as a verie
few (in my conceit) for pyckt and loftie wordes can burd
hym, none, I am wel assured, ouergoe hym : yeet hee hath
rather dubled then defalckt oght of my paines, by reason
that, in conferring his translation with myne, I was forced
too weede owt from my verses such choise woordes as
were forestald by him, vnlesse they were so feeling as
oothers could not countreuaile theyre signification : In
which case yt were no reason too sequester my pen from
theyre acquaintance, considering that, as M. *Phaer* was
not thee first founder, so hee may not bee accoumpted
thee only owner of such termes. Truely I am so far from
embeazling his trauailes, as that for thee honoure of thee
English I durst vndertake too renne ouer theese bookes
agayne, and too geeue theym a new liuerie in such different
wise, as they should not iet with M. *Phaer* his badges,
ne yeet bee clad with this apparaile, wherewith at this
present they coom furth atyred. Which I speake not of
vanitie, too enhaunce my coonning, but of meere veritie,
too aduaunce thee riches of oure speeche. More ouer
in soom poinctes of greatest price, where thee matter, as
yt were, doth bleede, I was mooued too shun M. *Phaer*
his enterpretation, and clinge more neere too thee meaning of myne authoure, in slising thee husk and cracking
thee shel, too bestow thee kernel vpon thee wyttye and
enquisitiue reader.

*[Stanyhurst then proceeds to discuss some points of differ-
ence between his version and Phaer's.]*

Now too coom too theym that guesh my trauaile too be
easye by reason of thee libertye I had in English woordes
5 (for as I can not deuine vpon such bookes that happlye
rouke in studentes mewes, so I trust I offer no man iniurie
yf I assume too my selfe thee maydenhed of al wurcks
that hath beene beefore this tyme in print, too my know-
legde, diuulged in this kind of verse), I wil not greatly
10 wrangle with theym therein : yeet this much they are too
consider, that as thee first applying of a woord may ease
mee in thee first place, so perhaps, when I am occasioned
too vse thee selfe same woord els where, I may bee as
much hyndered as at thee beginning I was furthred. For
15 example : In thee first verse of *Virgil* I mak *season* long ;
in an oother place yt woul[d] steede mee percase more
yf I made yt short, and yeet I am now tyed too vse yt
as long. So that the aduantage that way is not verie
great. But as for thee general facilitiee, this much I dare
20 warrant yoong beginners, that when they shal haue soom
firme footing in this kind of Poetrie, which by a litle
payneful exercise may bee purchast, they shal find as
easye a veyne in thee English as in thee Latin verses,
yee, and much more easye than in the *English rythmes.*
25 Touching myne owne trial, this much I wil discoouer.
Thee three first bokes I translated by startes, as my
leasure and pleasure would serue mee. In thee fourth
booke I did task my self, and persued thee matter soomwhat hoatlie. M. *Phaer* tooke too thee making of that
30 booke fifteene dayes. I hudled vp myne in ten. Wherein
I coouet no prayse, but rather doe craue pardon. Fore
lyke as forelittring biches whelp blynd puppies, so I may
bee perhaps entwighted of more haste then good speede,
as *Syr Thomas More* in lyke case gybeth at one that made
35 vaunt of certeyn pild verses clowted vp *extrumpere.*

Hos quid te scripsisse mones ex tempore versus ?
  Nam liber hoc loquitur, te reticente, tuus.

But too leaue that too thee veredict of oothers (wherein
I craue thee good lyking of thee curteouse, and skorne
thee controlment of thee currish, as those that vsuallie 5
reprehend moste, and yeet can amend leaste), thee ods
beetweene *verses* and *rythme* is verye great. For, in thee
one, euerye *foote*, euerye *word*, euerye *syllable*, yea euerye
letter is too bee obserued : in thee oother, thee last *woord*
is onlye too bee heeded : As is very liuelye exprest by 10
thee *lawyer* in empaneling a iurye.

Johannes Doa :	*Iohannes Den :*	*Johannes Hye :*
Richardus Roa :	*Willielmus Fen :*	*Thomas Pye :*
Iohannes Myles :	*Willielmus Neile :*	*Richardus Leake :*
Thomas Giles :	*Iohannes Sneile :*	*Johannes Peake.*

15

Happlye such curious *makers* as youre lordship is wyl
accompt this but *rythme dogrel*; but wee may suite yt
wyth a more ciuil woord, by terming yt *rythme peale meale*—
yt rowles so roundlye in thee hyrer his eares. And are
there not diuerse skauingers of draftye poëtrye in this 20
oure age, that bast theyre papers wyth smearie larde
sauoring al too geather of thee frying pan ? What *Tom
Towly* is so simple that wyl not attempt too bee a *rith-
moure ?* Yf your Lordship stand in doubt thereof, what
thinck you of thee *thick skyn* that made this for a *fare wel* 25
for his *mystresse* vpon his departure from *Abingtowne ?*

  Abingtowne, Abingtowne, God bee wyth thee :
  For thou haste a steeple lyke a dagger sheathe.

And an oother in thee prayse, not of a steeple, but of
a dagger.   30

  When al is goane but thee black scabbard,
  Wel fare thee haft wyth thee duggeon dagger.

Thee therd (for I wyl present your lordship with a leshe) in thee commendacion of bacon.

> *Hee is not a king that weareth satten,*
> *But hee is a king that eateth bacon.*

Haue not theese men made a fayre speake? If they had put in *Mightye Ioue*, and *Gods* in thee plural number, and *Venus* wyth *Cupide thee blynd Boy*, al had beene in thee nick, thee rythme had beene of a right stamp. For a few such stiches boch vp oure newe fashion makers: Prouyded not wythstanding alwayes that *Artaxerxes*, al be yt hee bee spurgalde, beeing so much gallopt, bee placed in thee dedicatorye epistle receauing a cuppe of water of a swayne, or elles al is not wurth a beane. Good God, what a frye of such *wooden rythmours* dooth swarme in stacioners shops, who neauer enstructed in any grammar schoole, not atayning too thee paringes of thee Latin or Greeke tongue, yeet lyke blynd bayards rush on forward, fostring theyre vayne conceites wyth such ouerweening silly follyes, as they reck not too bee condemned of thee learned for ignorant, so they bee commended of thee ignorant for learned. Thee reddyest way therefore too flap theese droanes from thee sweete senting hiues of *Poëtrye* is for thee learned too applye theym selues wholye (yf they be delighted wyth that veyne) too thee true making of verses in such wise as thee *Greekes* and *Latins*, thee fathers of knowledge, haue doone, and too leaue too theese doltish coystrels theyre rude rythming and balducktoom ballads. . . .

TOO THEE LEARNED READER.

In thee obseruation of quantitees of syllables, soom happlye wyl bee so stieflie tyed too thee ordinaunces of thee Latins, as what shal seeme too swarue from theyre

maximes they wyl not stick too skore vp for errours. In
which resolution such curious *Priscianistes* dooe attribute
greater prerogatiue too thee Latin tongue than reason
wyl affurd, and lesse libertye too oure language than
nature may permit.   For in as much as thee Latins haue 5
not beene authors of theese verses, but traced in thee
steps of thee Greekes, why should we with thee stringes
of thee Latin rules cramp oure tongue more than the
Latins doe fetter theyre speeche, as yt were wyth thee
chaynes of thee Greeke preceptes.   Also that nature wyl 10
not permit vs too fashion oure wordes in al poinctes
correspondent too thee Latinistes, may easely appeere
in suche termes as we borrow of theym.   For exemple:
The first of *Breuiter* is short, thee first of *briefly* wyth
vs must bee long.   Lykewise, *sonans* is short, yeet 15
sowning in English must bee long, and much more yf
yt were *Sounding*, as thee ignorant generaly, but falslye,
dooe wryte; nay, that where at I woonder more, thee
learned trip theyre pennes at this stoane, in so much as
M. *Phaer* in thee verye first verse of Virgil mistaketh thee 20
woorde.   Yeet *sound* and *sowne* differ as much in English
as *solidus* and *sonus* in Latin.   Also in thee midest of
a woord wee differ soomtymes from the Romans.   As in
Latin wee pronounce *Orâtor, Audîtor, Magîster* long: in
English, *Orătoure, Audĭtoure, Magĭstrat* short.   Lykewise 25
wee pronounce *Præpăro, compăro* short in Latin, and
prepâred and *compâred* long in English.   Agayne thee
infallibelist rule that thee Latins haue for thee quantitye
of middle syllables is this. *Penultima acuta producitur,
vt virtûtis; penultima grauata corripitur, vt sanguĭnis.* 30
Honoure in English is short, as wyth thee Latins; yeet
dishonour must bee long by thee formoure maxime: which
is contrary too an oother ground of thee Latins, whereby
they prescribe that thee *primatiue* and *deriuatiue*, thee
simple and *compound,* bee of one quantitye.   But that rule 35

of al oothers must be abandoned from thee English, oother
wise al woordes in effcct should bee abridged. *Moother*
I make long; yeet *graundmother* must bee short. *Buckler*
is long; yeet *swashbuckler* is short. And albeyt that
woord bee long by *position*, yeet doubtlesse thee natural
dialect of English wyl not allow of that rule in middle
syllables, but yt must bee of force with vs excepted, where
thee natural pronuntiation wyl so haue yt. For ootherwise wee should bannish a number of good and necessarye
wordes from oure verses; as *M. Gabriel Haruye* (yf I
mystake not thee gentleman his name) hath verye wel
obserued in one of his familiar letters: where hee layeth
downe diuerse wordes straying from thee Latin preceptes,
as *Maiestye, Royaltye, Honestie, &c.* And soothly, too my
seeming, yf thee coniunction *And* were made common
in English, yt were not amisse, although yt bee long by
position: For thee Romans are greatly aduantaged by
theyre woordes *Et, Que, Quoque, Atque*: which were they
disioincted from thee Latin poëtrie, many good verses
would bee rauelde and dismembred that now cary a good
grace among theym, hauing theyre ioynctes knit with
theese copulatiue sinnewes. But too rip vp further thee
peculiar propretye of oure English, let vs listen too *Tullye*
his iudgement, wherein thogh hee seeme verie peremptorie,
yeet, with his fauoure, hee misheth thee cushen. Thus
in his booke intituled *Orator*, hee writeth, *Ipsa natura,
quasi modularetur hominum orationem, in omni verbo posuit
acutam vocem, nec vna plus, nec a postrema syllaba citra
tertiam.* In this saying Tullye obserueth three poinctes.
First, that by course of *Nature* euerye woord hath an
accent: next, one only: lastlye, that thee sayde *accent*
must be on thee last syllable, as *propè*, or on thee last
saluing one, as *Virtûtis*, or, at thee furthest, on thee therd
syllable, as *Omnîpotens*. Yeet this rule taketh no such
infallible effect with vs, althogh *Tully* maketh yt natural,

who by thee skyl of thee Greek and Latin dyd ayme at
oother languages too hym vnknowen, and therefor is too
bee borne wythal. As, *Peremtorie* is a woord of foure
syllables, and yeet thee *accent* is on thee first. So
Sêcundarie, *ôrdinarie*, *Mâtrimonie*, *Pâtrimonie*, *Plânetarie*, 5
imperatiue, *Côsmographie*, *ôrtography*, with many lyke.
For althogh thee ignorant pronounce *Impêratiue*, *Cosmô-
graphie*, *Ortôgraphy*, geeuing the *accent* too thee therd
syllable, yeet that is not thee true English pronuntiation.
Now put case thee cantel of thee Latin verse *Sapiens* 10
dominabitur astris were thus Englished, *Planetary woorck-
inges thee wismans vertue represseth*, albeyt thee middle
of *planeta* bee long with thee Romans, yeet I would not
make yt scrupulus too shorten yt in English, by reason
thee natural pronountiation would haue yt so. For thee 15
final eende of a verse is to please thee eare, which must
needes bee thee vmpyre of thee woord, and according too
that weight oure syllables must bee poysed. Wherefor
syth thee *poëtes* theymselues aduouch, *Tu nihil inuita facies
dicesue Minerua*, That nothing may bee doone or spoaken 20
agaynst nature, and that *Art* is also bound too shape yt
self by al imitation too *Nature*, wee must request theese
grammatical Precisians, that as euery countrye hath his
peculiar law, so they permit euerye language too vse
his particular loare. For my part I purpose not too beat 25
on euerye childish tittle that concerneth *Prosodia*, neither
dooe I vndertake too chalck owt any lines or rules too
oothers, but too lay downe too thee reader his view thee
course I tooke in this my trauaile. Such woordes as
proceede from thee Latin, and bee not altred by oure 30
English, in theym I obserue thee quantitie of thee Latin.
As *Honest*, *Honor*: a few I excepted, as thee first of
apeered, *auenture*, *aproched* I make short, althogh they
are long in Latin, as *Appareo*, *Aduenio*, *Appropinquo*:
for which, and percase a few such woordes, I must craue 35

pardon of thee curteous reader. For ootherwise yt were lyke ynough that soom *grammatical pullet,* hacht in *Dispater* his sachel, would stand clocking aganyst mee, as thogh hee had found an horse nest, in laying that downe for
5 a falt that perhaps I dooe knowe better then hee. Yeet in theese *diriuations* of termes I would not bee doomde by euerye reaching herrault, that in roaming wise wyl attempt too fetche thee petit degree of woordes, I know not from what auncetoure. As I make thee first of *Riuer*
10 short, a Wrangler may imagin yt should bee long, by reason of *Riuus,* of which yt seemeth too bee deriued. And yeet forsooth *riuus* is but a *brooke,* and not a *riuer.* Likewyse soom English woordes may bee read in soom places long, in soom short, as *skyeward, seaward, searowme.*
15 Thee difference thereof groweth beecause they are but compound woordes that may bee with good sense sunderd: and thee last of *Sea* and *skye* beeing common breedeth that diuersitie. Also thee self same woord may varye beecause of thee signification. Thee first of *Felon* for
20 a *theefe* I make long, but when yt signifieth thee disease, so named, I hold yt better too make yt short. Agayne a woord that is short beeing deuided may bee long in an oother place contracted. As thee first of *Leaues,* yf you deuide yt in two syllables, I make short; yf you
25 contract yt too one syllabe, I make yt long. So thee first in *Crauing* is long, and thee therd person of thee verb, too wyt, *Craues,* may seeme short, where the next woord following beginneth with a vocal, yet yt is long by contrac-tion: and so diuerse lyke woordes are too bee taken.
30 And truely such nice obseruations that *Grammarians* dooe prescribe are not by thee choysest poëtes alwayes so pre-ciselye put in execution: as in this oure authour I haue by thee way marckt. In thee fore front of thee first booke hee maketh thee first of *Lauin[i]um* long. In thee
35 same booke hee vseth yt for short. Likewise dooth he

varie thee first of *Sichæus*. So in thee therd booke thee
midest of *Cyclopes* soomtyme is made long, soomtyme
short. And in the same booke the coniunction *Que* is
long, as

Liminaque laurusque Dei ; *totusque moueri* :   5

And in thee fourth :

    Cretesque Dryopesque fremunt, pictique Agathyrsi :

Also thee first of *Italia* is long : yeet in thee therd book
Italus is short, as

Has autem terras, Italique hanc littoris oram.   10

Touching the *termination* of syllables, I made a *prosodia*
too my selfe squaring soomwhat from thee Latin : in this
wise.

A. *finita communia.* B. D. T. *breuia* : yeet theese
woordes that eende lyke dipthonges are common : as 15
mouth, south, &c. C. common. E. common : yf yt bee
short, I wryte yt vsualy with a single E, as *the, me* ; yf
long with two, as *thee, mee* ; althogh I would not wish
thee quantitie of syllables too depend so much vpon thee
gaze of thee eye as thee censure of thee eare. F. *breuia.* 20
G. *breuia* : soomtyme long by *position* where D may bee
enterserted, as *passage* is short, but yf you make yt long,
passadge with D would bee written ; albeyt, as I sayd
right now, thee eare, not ortographie, must decyde thee
quantitye as neere as is possible. I. common. K. 25
common. L. *breuia, præter Hebræa, vt Michaël, Gabriel.*
N. *Breuia* ; yeet woordes eending in dipthongwise would
bee common, as *playne, fayne, swayne.* O. common,
præter ô longum. P. *Breuia.* R. *Breuia*, except
woordes eending lyke dipthonges that may bee common, 30
as *youre, oure, houre, soure, succour, &c.* As and Es
common. Is *breuia.* Os common. Vs *breuia.* V.
common. As for M. yt is either long by *position*, or els

clipt, yf thee next woord begyn with a vocal, as *fame*,
name: for albeyt E bee thee last letter, that must not
salue M from accurtation, beecause in thee eare M is
thee last letter, and E dooth noght els but leng[t]hen and
5 mollifye thee pronountiation.   As for I. Y. W., in as much
as they are moungrels, soomtyme consonantes, soomtyme
vocals, where they further I dooe not reiect theym,
where they hinder I doe not greatlye weigh theym: As
thee middle of *folowing* I make short, notwythstanding
10 thee W, and lykwise the first of *power*: But where
a consonant immediatly followeth the W, I make yt
alwayes long, as *fowling*.

This much I thoght good too acquaynt thee gentle
reader wythal, rather too discoouer wyth what priuat
15 preceptes I haue embayed my verses then too publish
a *directorye* too thee learned, who in theyre trauayls
may franckly vse theyre owne discretion wythowt my
direction.

SIR PHILIP SIDNEY

(*An Apologie for Poetrie*)

c. 1583 (printed 1595)

[Two editions of Sidney's famous essay (written c. 1583) appeared in 1595—(a) *The | Defence of | Poesie. | By Sir Philip Sidney, | Knight || London. | Printed for William Ponsonby. |* 1595, and (b) *An | Apologie | for Poetrie. | Written by the right noble, vertu-|ous, and learned, Sir Phillip | Sidney, Knight. || Odi profanum vulgus, et arceo. || At London, | Printed for Henry Olney, and are to be sold at | his shop in Paules Church-yard, at the signe | of the George, neere to Cheap-gate. | Anno 1595.* Ponsonby's edition, which is extant in the unique copy in the collection of Mr. F. Locker, seems, from the evidence of the Stationers' Register[1], to have been the earlier of the two. It is the basis of the later texts from the folio of 1598, where the essay appears as an addition to the *Arcadia*. It has been reprinted by Dr. Ewald Flügel in his *Sir Philip Sidney's Astrophel and Stella und Defence of Poesie*, Halle 1889. Yet Olney's text is more carefully printed than Ponsonby's and his successors'. It was last reprinted by Mr. Arber in his *English Reprints* and by Mr. Shuckburgh in the *Pitt Press Series*. The present text has been taken from the copy of Olney's edition presented to the library of the University of Edinburgh by the poet William Drummond. The important differences between it and Mr. Locker's copy of Ponsonby's edition (ed. Flügel) are pointed out in the Notes.

It will be seen that there is bibliographical justification for either title—*Defence* or *Apologie*. The popularity of the later editions, founded on Ponsonby's, gave greater vogue to the former. Sidney himself speaks of his effort

[1] See Notes.

as a 'pittiful defence of poore Poetry': and the term was frequently employed by contemporary critics in their pamphlet feuds. But the title *Apologie*, of the 1595 edition, was perhaps not less common among Sidney's friends and successors, for we find Harington so styling the Essay in his *Briefe Apologie of Poetrie* (q. v.), which was printed four years before the first edition of Sidney's work. So also William Vaughan (q. v.).

The Essay is preceded in Olney's edition by four sonnets ' written by Henrie Constable to Sir Phillip Sidney's soule,' and by the following note 'To the Reader':—

'The stormie Winter (deere Chyldren of the Muses), which hath so long held backe the glorious Sunshine of diuine Poesie, is heere by the sacred pen-breathing words of diuine Sir *Phillip Sidney* not onely chased from our fame-inuiting Clyme, but vtterly for euer banisht eternitie: then graciously regreet the perpetuall spring of euer-growing inuention, and like kinde Babes, either enabled by wit or power, help to support me poore Midwife, whose daring aduenture hath deliuered from Obliuions wombe this euer-to-be-admired wits miracle. Those great ones who in themselues haue interr'd this blessed innocent wil with *Aesculapius* condemne me as a detractor from their Deities: those who Prophet-like haue but heard presage of his coming wil (if they wil doe wel) not onely defend but praise mee as the first publique bewrayer of Poesies *Messias*. Those who neither haue seene, thereby to interre, nor heard, by which they might be inflamed with desire to see, let them (of duty) plead to be my Champions, sith both theyr sight and hearing by mine incurring blame is reasoned. Excellent Poesie (so created by this Apologie), be thou my Defendresse; and if any wound mee, let thy beautie (my soules Adamant) recure mee; if anie commend mine endeuored hardiment, to them commend thy most diuinest fury as a winged incouragement; so shalt thou haue deuoted to thee, and to them obliged,

Henry Olney.]

AN APOLOGIE FOR POETRIE.

WHEN the right vertuous *Edward Wotton* and I were at the Emperors Court together, wee gaue our selues to learne horsemanship of *Iohn Pietro Pugliano*, one that with great commendation had the place of an 5 Esquire in his stable. And hee, according to the fertilnes of the Italian wit, did not onely afoord vs the demonstration of his practise, but sought to enrich our mindes with the contemplations therein which hee thought most precious. But with none I remember mine eares were at any time 10 more loden, then when (either angred with slowe paiment, or mooued with our learner-like admiration) he exercised his speech in the prayse of his facultie. Hee sayd, Souldiours were the noblest estate of mankinde, and horsemen the noblest of Souldiours. Hee sayde they 15 were the Maisters of warre, and ornaments of peace; speedy goers, and strong abiders; triumphers both in Camps and Courts. Nay, to so vnbeleeued a poynt hee proceeded, as that no earthly thing bred such wonder to a Prince as to be a good horseman. Skill of gouernment 20 was but a Pedanteria in comparison. Then would hee adde certaine prayses, by telling what a peerlesse beast a horse was; the onely seruiceable Courtier without flattery, the beast of most beutie, faithfulnes, courage, and such more, that if I had not beene a peece of a Logician before I came 25 to him, I think he would haue perswaded mee to haue wished my selfe a horse. But thus much at least with his no fewe words hee draue into me, that selfe-loue is better then any guilding to make that seeme gorgious wherein our selues are parties. Wherein, if *Pugliano* his strong 30 affection and weake arguments will not satisfie you, I wil giue you a neerer example of my selfe, who (I knowe not by what mischance) in these my not old yeres and idelest times, hauing slipt into the title of a Poet, am prouoked

to say somthing vnto you in the defence of that my vn-
elected vocation, which if I handle with more good will
then good reasons, beare with me, sith the scholler is to
be pardoned that foloweth the steppes of his Maister.
5 And yet I must say that as I haue iust cause to make
a pittiful defence of poore Poetry, which from almost the
highest estimation of learning is fallen to be the laughing-
stocke of children; so haue I need to bring some more
auaileable proofes : sith the former is by no man barred of
10 his deserued credite, the silly latter hath had euen the
names of Philosophers vsed to the defacing of it, with
great danger of ciuill war among the Muses. And first,
truly to al them that professing learning inueigh against
Poetry, may iustly be obiected, that they goe very neer to
15 vngratfulnes, to seek to deface that which, in the noblest
nations and languages that are knowne, hath been the first
light-giuer to ignorance, and first Nurse, whose milk by
little and little enabled them to feed afterwards of tougher
knowledges : and will they now play the Hedghog that,
20 being receiued into the den, draue out his host ? or rather
the Vipers, that with theyr birth kill their Parents ? Let
learned Greece in any of her manifold Sciences be able
to shew me one booke before *Musœus, Homer,* and
Hesiodus, all three nothing els but Poets. Nay, let any
25 historie be brought that can say any Writers were there
before them, if they were not men of the same skil, as
Orpheus, Linus, and some other are named : who, hauing
beene the first of that Country that made pens deliuerers
of their knowledge to their posterity, may iustly chalenge
30 to bee called their Fathers in learning : for not only in
time they had this priority (although in it self antiquity
be venerable) but went before them, as causes to drawe
with their charming sweetnes the wild vntamed wits to
an admiration of knowledge. So as *Amphion* was sayde
35 to moue stones with his Poetrie to build Thebes; and

Orpheus to be listened to by beastes, indeed stony and beastly people. So among the Romans were *Liuius, Andronicus,* and *Ennius.* So in the Italian language the first that made it aspire to be a Treasure-house of Science were the Poets *Dante, Boccace,* and *Petrarch.* So in our 5 English were *Gower* and *Chawcer.*

After whom, encouraged and delighted with theyr excellent fore-going, others haue followed, to beautifie our mother tongue, as wel in the same kinde as in other Arts. This did so notably shewe it selfe, that the Phylosophers 10 of Greece durst not a long time appeare to the worlde but vnder the masks of Poets. So *Thales, Empedocles,* and *Parmenides* sange their naturall Phylosophie in verses : so did *Pythagoras* and *Phocilides* their morrall counsells : so did *Tirteus* in war matters, and *Solon* in matters of 15 policie : or rather, they, beeing Poets, dyd exercise their delightful vaine in those points of highest knowledge, which before them lay hid to the world. For that wise *Solon* was directly a Poet it is manifest, hauing written in verse the notable fable of the Atlantick Iland, which 20 was continued by *Plato.*

And truely, euen *Plato,* whosoeuer well considereth, shall find that in the body of his work, though the inside and strength were Philosophy, the skinne as it were and beautie depended most of Poetrie : for all standeth vpon 25 Dialogues, wherein he faineth many honest Burgesses of Athens to speake of such matters, that, if they had been sette on the racke, they would neuer haue confessed them. Besides, his poetical describing the circumstances of their meetings, as the well ordering of a banquet, the delicacie 30 of a walke, with enterlacing meere tales, as *Giges* Ring, and others, which who knoweth not to be flowers of Poetrie did neuer walke into *Apollos* Garden.

And euen Historiographers (although theyr lippes sounde of things doone, and veritie be written in theyr 35

fore-heads) haue been glad to borrow both fashion and
perchance weight of Poets. So *Herodotus* entituled his
Historie by the name of the nine Muses: and both he
and all the rest that followed him either stole or vsurped
5 of Poetrie their passionate describing of passions, the
many particularities of battailes, which no man could
affirme, or, if that be denied me, long Orations put in the
mouthes of great Kings and Captaines, which it is certaine
they neuer pronounced. So that, truely, neyther Phylo-
10 sopher nor Historiographer coulde at the first haue entred
into the gates of populer iudgements, if they had not taken
a great pasport of Poetry, which in all Nations at this
day, wher learning florisheth not, is plaine to be seene: in
all which they haue some feeling of Poetry. In Turky,
15 besides their lawe-giuing Diuines, they haue no other
Writers but Poets. In our neighbour Countrey Ireland,
where truelie learning goeth very bare, yet are theyr
Poets held in a deuoute reuerence. Euen among the
most barbarous and simple Indians where no writing is,
20 yet haue they their Poets, who make and sing songs, which
they call *Areytos*, both of theyr Auncestors deedes and
praises of theyr Gods: a sufficient probabilitie that if
euer learning come among them, it must be by hauing
theyr hard dull wits softned and sharpened with the
25 sweete delights of Poetrie. For vntill they find a pleasure
in the exercises of the minde, great promises of much
knowledge will little perswade them that knowe not the
fruites of knowledge. In Wales, the true remnant of the
auncient Brittons, as there are good authorities to shewe
30 the long time they had Poets, which they called *Bardes*,
so thorough all the conquests of Romaines, Saxons,
Danes, and Normans, some of whom did seeke to ruine
all memory of learning from among them, yet doo their
Poets, euen to this day, last; so as it is not more notable
35 in soone beginning then in long continuing. But since

the Authors of most of our Sciences were the Romans, and before them the Greekes, let vs a little stand vppon their authorities, but euen so farre as to see what names they haue giuen vnto this now scorned skill.

Among the Romans a Poet was called *Vates*, which is as much as a Diuiner, Fore-seer, or Prophet, as by his conioyned wordes *Vaticinium* and *Vaticinari* is manifest: so heauenly a title did that excellent people bestow vpon this hart-rauishing knowledge. And so farre were they carried into the admiration thereof, that they thought in the chaunceable hitting vppon any such verses great fore-tokens of their following fortunes were placed. Where-upon grew the worde of *Sortes Virgilianae*, when, by suddaine opening *Virgils* booke, they lighted vpon any verse of hys making: whereof the histories of the Emperors liues are full; as of *Albinus*, the Gouernour of our Iland, who in his childehoode mette with this verse,

Arma amens capio nec sat rationis in armis;

and in his age performed it: which although it were a very vaine and godles superstition, as also it was to think that spirits were commaunded by such verses— whereupon this word charmes, deriued of *Carmina*, com-meth—so yet serueth it to shew the great reuerence those wits were helde in. And altogether not without ground, since both the Oracles of *Delphos* and *Sibillas* prophecies were wholy deliuered in verses. For that same exquisite obseruing of number and measure in words, and that high flying liberty of conceit proper to the Poet, did seeme to haue some dyuine force in it.

And may not I presume a little further, to shew the reasonablenes of this worde *Vates*? And say that the holy *Dauids* Psalmes are a diuine Poem? If I doo, I shall not do it without the testimonie of great learned men, both auncient and moderne: but euen the name

Psalmes will speake ˊfor mee, which, being interpreted, is
nothing but songes. Then that it is fully written in meeter,
as all learned Hebricians agree, although the rules be not
yet fully found. Lastly and principally, his handeling his
5 prophecy, which is meerely poetical. For what els is the
awaking his musicall instruments ; the often and free
changing of persons ; his notable *Prosopopeias*, when he
maketh you, as it were, see God comming in his Maiestie ;
his telling of the Beastes ioyfulnes, and hills leaping, but
10 a heauenlie poesie, wherein almost hee sheweth himselfe
a passionate louer of that vnspeakable and euerlasting
beautie to be seene by the eyes of the minde, onely
cleered by fayth ? But truely nowe hauing named him,
I feare mee I seeme to prophane that holy name, applying
15 it to Poetrie, which is among vs throwne downe to so
ridiculous an estimation : but they that with quiet iudgements will looke a little deeper into it, shall finde the end
and working of it such, as beeing rightly applyed, deserueth
not to bee scourged out of the Church of God.
20 But now, let vs see how the Greekes named it, and
howe they deemed of it. The Greekes called him a Poet,
which name hath, as the most excellent, gone thorough
other Languages. It commeth of this word *Poiein*, which
is to make : wherein I know not, whether by lucke or
25 wisedome, wee Englishmen haue mette with the Greekes
in calling him a maker : which name, how high and
incomparable a title it is, I had rather were knowne by
marking the scope of other Sciences then by my partiall
allegation.
30 There is no Arte deliuered to mankinde that hath not
the workes of Nature for his principall obiect, without
which they could not consist, and on which they so
depend, as they become Actors and Players, as it were, of
what Nature will haue set foorth. So doth the Astronomer
35 looke vpon the starres, and, by that he seeth, setteth downe

what order Nature hath taken therein. So doe the Geometrician and Arithmetician in their diuerse sorts of quantities. So doth the Musitian in times tel you which by nature agree, which not. The naturall Philosopher thereon hath his name, and the Morrall Philosopher standeth vpon the naturall vertues, vices, and passions of man ; and 'followe Nature' (saith hee) 'therein, and thou shalt not erre.' The Lawyer sayth what men haue determined. The Historian what men haue done. The Grammarian speaketh onely of the rules of speech ; and the Rethorician and Logitian, considering what in Nature will soonest proue and perswade, thereon giue artificial rules, which still are compassed within the circle of a question, according to the proposed matter. The Phisition waigheth the nature of a mans bodie, and the nature of things helpeful or hurtefull vnto it. And the Metaphisick, though it be in the seconde and abstract notions, and therefore be counted supernaturall, yet doth hee indeede builde vpon the depth of Nature. Onely the Poet, disdayning to be tied to any such subiection, lifted vp with the vigor of his owne inuention, dooth growe in effect another nature, in making things either better then Nature bringeth forth, or, quite a newe, formes such as neuer were in Nature, as the *Heroes, Demigods, Cyclops, Chimeras, Furies,* and such like : so as hee goeth hand in hand with Nature, not inclosed within the narrow warrant of her guifts, but freely ranging onely within the Zodiack of his owne wit.

Nature neuer set forth the earth in so rich tapistry as diuers Poets haue done, neither with plesant riuers, fruitful trees, sweet smelling flowers, nor whatsoeuer els may make the too much loued earth more louely. Her world is brasen, the Poets only deliuer a golden. But let those things alone and goe to man, for whom as the other things are, so it seemeth in him her vtter-

most cunning is imployed, and knowe whether shee haue brought foorth so true a louer as *Theagines*, so constant a friende as *Pilades*, so valiant a man as *Orlando*, so right a Prince as *Xenophons Cyrus*, so excellent a man euery
5 way as *Virgils Aeneas*: neither let this be iestingly conceiued, because the works of the one be essentiall, the other, in imitation or fiction; for any vnderstanding knoweth the skil of the Artificer standeth in that *Idea* or fore-conceite of the work, and not in the work it selfe.
10 And that the Poet hath that *Idea* is manifest, by deliuering them forth in such excellencie as hee hath imagined them. Which deliuering forth also is not wholie imaginatiue, as we are wont to say by them that build Castles in the ayre: but so farre substantially it worketh, not onely to
15 make a *Cyrus*, which had been but a particuler excellencie, as Nature might haue done, but to bestow a *Cyrus* vpon the worlde, to make many *Cyrus's*, if they wil learne aright why and how that Maker made him.

Neyther let it be deemed too sawcie a comparison to
20 ballance the highest poynt of mans wit with the efficacie of Nature: but rather giue right honor to the heauenly Maker of that maker, who, hauing made man to his owne likenes, set him beyond and ouer all the workes of that second nature, which in nothing hee sheweth so much
25 as in Poetrie, when with the force of a diuine breath he bringeth things forth far surpassing her dooings, with no small argument to the incredulous of that first accursed fall of *Adam*: sith our erected wit maketh vs know what perfection is, and yet our infected will keepeth vs from
30 reaching vnto it. But these arguments wil by fewe be vnderstood, and by fewer granted. Thus much (I hope) will be giuen me, that the Greekes with some probabilitie of reason gaue him the name aboue all names of learning. Now let vs goe to a more ordinary opening of him, that
35 the trueth may be more palpable: and so I hope, though

we get not so vnmatched a praise as the Etimologie of his names wil grant, yet his very description, which no man will denie, shall not iustly be barred from a principall commendation.

Poesie therefore is an arte of imitation, for so *Aristotle* termeth it in his word *Mimesis*, that is to say, a representing, counterfetting, or figuring foorth : to speake metaphorically, a speaking picture : with this end, to teach and delight. Of this haue beene three seuerall kindes.

The chiefe both in antiquitie and excellencie were they that did imitate the inconceiuable excellencies of GOD. Such were *Dauid* in his Psalmes, *Salomon* in his song of Songs, in his Ecclesiastes, and Prouerbs, *Moses* and *Debora* in theyr Hymnes, and the writer of *Iob* ; which, beside other, the learned *Emanuell Tremelius* and *Franciscus Iunius* doe entitle the poeticall part of the Scripture. Against these none will speake that hath the holie Ghost in due holy reuerence. In this kinde, though in a full wrong diuinitie, were *Orpheus, Amphion, Homer* in his hymnes, and many other, both Greekes and Romaines: and this Poesie must be vsed, by whosoeuer will follow S. *Iames* his counsell, in singing Psalmes when they are merry : and I knowe is vsed with the fruite of comfort by some, when, in sorrowfull pangs of their death-bringing sinnes, they find the consolation of the neuer-leauing goodnesse.

The second kinde is of them that deale with matters Philosophicall ; eyther morrall, as *Tirteus, Phocilides*, and *Cato* ; or naturall, as *Lucretius* and *Virgils Georgicks* ; or Astronomicall, as *Manilius* and *Pontanus* ; or historical, as *Lucan* : which who mislike, the faulte is in their iudgements quite out of taste, and not in the sweet foode of sweetly vttered knowledge.

But because thys second sorte is wrapped within the folde of the proposed subiect, and takes not the course of his owne inuention, whether they properly be Poets or no let Gramarians dispute: and goe to the thyrd, indeed right Poets, of whom chiefly this question ariseth; betwixt whom and these second is such a kinde of difference as betwixt the meaner sort of Painters (who counterfet onely such faces as are sette before them) and the more excellent, who, hauing no law but wit, bestow that in cullours vpon you which is fittest for the eye to see: as the constant though lamenting looke of *Lucrecia*, when she punished in her selfe an others fault; wherein he painteth not *Lucrecia* whom he neuer sawe, but painteth the outwarde beauty of such a vertue. For these third be they which most properly do imitate to teach and delight, and to imitate borrow nothing of what is, hath been, or shall be: but range, onely rayned with learned discretion, into the diuine consideration of what may be, and should be. These bee they that, as the first and most noble sorte, may iustly bee termed *Vates*, so these are waited on in the excellen[te]st languages and best vnderstandings, with the fore described name of Poets: for these indeede doo meerely make to imitate, and imitate both to delight and teach, and delight to moue men to take that goodnes in hande, which without delight they would flye as from a stranger; and teach, to make them know that goodnes whereunto they are mooued, which being the noblest scope to which euer any learning was directed, yet want there not idle tongues to barke at them.

These be subdiuided into sundry more speciall denominations. The most notable bee the *Heroick, Lirick, Tragick, Comick, Satirick, Iambick, Elegiack, Pastorall,* and certaine others, some of these being termed according to the matter they deale with, some by the sorts of verses they liked best to write in, for indeede the greatest part of Poets haue apparelled their poeticall inuentions in that numbrous kinde of writing which is called verse: indeed but apparelled, verse being but an ornament and no cause

to Poetry, sith there haue beene many most excellent
Poets that neuer versified, and now swarme many versifiers that neede neuer aunswere to the name of Poets.
For *Xenophon*, who did imitate so excellently as to giue
vs *effigiem iusti imperii*, the portraiture of a iust Empire 5
vnder the name of *Cyrus* (as *Cicero* sayth of him), made
therein an absolute heroicall Poem ; so did *Heliodorus*
in his sugred inuention of that picture of loue in *Theagines*
and *Cariclea* ; and yet both these writ in Prose : which
I speak to shew that it is not riming and versing that 10
maketh a Poet, no more then a long gowne maketh an
Aduocate, who though he pleaded in armor should be
an Aduocate and no Souldier. But it is that fayning
notable images of vertues, vices, or what els, with that
delightfull teaching, which must be the right describing 15
note to know a Poet by : although indeed the Senate of
Poets hath chosen verse as their fittest rayment, meaning, as in matter they passed all in all, so in maner
to goe beyond them : not speaking (table talke fashion
or like men in a dreame) words as they chanceably fall 20
from the mouth, but peyzing each sillable of each worde
by iust proportion according to the dignitie of the
subiect.

Nowe therefore it shall not bee amisse first to waigh
this latter sort of Poetrie by his works, and then by his 25
partes ; and if in neyther of these Anatomies hee be
condemnable, I hope wee shall obtaine a more fauourable
sentence. This purifing of wit, this enritching of memory,
enabling of iudgment, and enlarging of conceyt, which
commonly we call learning, vnder what name soeuer it 30
com forth, or to what immediat end soeuer it be directed,
the final end is to lead and draw vs to as high a perfection
as our degenerate soules, made worse by theyr clayey
lodgings, can be capable of. This, according to the inclination of the man, bred many formed impressions. For some 35

that thought this felicity principally to be gotten by knowledge, and no knowledge to be so high and heauenly
as acquaintance with the starres, gaue themselues to
Astronomie; others, perswading themselues to be *Demi-*
5 *gods* if they knewe the causes of things, became naturall
and supernaturall Philosophers; some an admirable delight
drew to Musicke; and some the certainty of demonstration to the Mathematickes: But all, one and other,
hauing this scope—to knowe, and by knowledge to lift vp
10 the mind from the dungeon of the body to the enioying
his owne diuine essence. But when by the ballance of
experience it was found that the Astronomer looking
to the starres might fall into a ditch, that the enquiring
Philosopher might be blinde in himselfe, and the Mathe-
15 matician might draw foorth a straight line with a crooked
hart; then loe, did proofe, the ouer ruler of opinions, make
manifest that all these are but seruing Sciences, which as
they haue each a priuate end in themselues, so yet are
they all directed to the highest end of the mistres Know-
20 ledge, by the Greekes called *Arkitecktonike*, which stands,
(as I thinke) in the knowledge of a mans selfe, in the
Ethicke and politick consideration, with the end of well
dooing and not of well knowing onely; euen as the
Sadlers next end is to make a good saddle, but his
25 farther end to serue a nobler facultie, which is horsemanship; so the horsemans to souldiery, and the Souldier not
onely to haue the skill, but to performe the practise of
a Souldier: so that, the ending end of all earthly learning
being vertuous action, those skilles that most serue to
30 bring forth that haue a most iust title to bee Princes ouer
all the rest. Wherein if wee can shewe the Poets noblenes,
by setting him before his other Competitors, among whom
as principall challengers step forth the morrall Philosophers, whom, me thinketh, I see comming towards mee
35 with a sullen grauity, as though they could not abide vice

by day light, rudely clothed for to witnes outwardly their
contempt of outward things, with bookes in their hands
agaynst glory, whereto they sette theyr names, sophisti-
cally speaking against subtility, and angry with any man
in whom they see the foule fault of anger : these men 5
casting larges as they goe of Definitions, Diuisions, and
Distinctions, with a scornefull interogatiue doe soberly
aske whether it bee possible to finde any path so ready
to leade a man to vertue as that which teacheth what
vertue is ? and teacheth it not onely by deliuering forth 10
his very being, his causes, and effects ; but also by making
known his enemie vice, which must be destroyed, and his
combersome seruant Passion, which must be maistered ;
by shewing the generalities that contayneth it, and the
specialities that are deriued from it ; lastly, by playne 15
setting downe, how it extendeth it selfe out of the limits
of a mans own little world to the gouernment of families,
and maintayning of publique societies.

The Historian scarcely giueth leysure to the Moralist
to say so much, but that he, loden with old Mouse-eaten 20
records, authorising himselfe (for the most part) vpon other
histories, whose greatest authorities are built vpon the
notable foundation of Heare-say, hauing much a-doe to
accord differing Writers and to pick trueth out of
partiality, better acquainted with a thousande yeeres 25
a goe then with the present age, and yet better knowing
how this world goeth then how his owne wit runneth,
curious for antiquities and inquisitiue of nouelties, a
wonder to young folkes and a tyrant in table talke,
denieth, in a great chafe, that any man for teaching of 30
vertue, and vertuous actions, is comparable to him.   I am
*Lux vitae, Temporum magistra, Vita memoriae, Nuncia
vetustatis, &c.*

'The Phylosopher' (sayth hee) 'teacheth a disputatiue
vertue, but I doe an actiue : his vertue is excellent in 35

the dangerlesse Academie of *Plato*, but mine sheweth
foorth her honorable face in the battailes of *Marathon,
Pharsalia, Poitiers,* and *Agincourt.* Hee teacheth vertue
by certaine abstract considerations, but I onely bid you
5 follow the footing of them that haue gone before you.
Olde-aged experience goeth beyond the fine-witted Phylosopher, but I giue the experience of many ages. Lastly,
if he make the Song-booke, I put the learners hande to
the Lute : and if hee be the guide, I am the light.'
10 Then woulde hee alledge you innumerable examples,
conferring storie by storie, how much the wisest Senatours
and Princes haue beene directed by the credite of history,
as *Brutus, Alphonsus* of *Aragon,* and who not, if need
bee ? At length the long lyne of theyr disputation maketh
15 a poynt in thys, that the one giueth the precept, and the
other the example.

Nowe, whom shall wee finde (sith the question standeth
for the highest forme in the Schoole of learning) to bee
Moderator ? Trulie, as mee seemeth, the Poet ; and if not
20 a Moderator, euen the man that ought to carrie the title
from them both, and much more from all other seruing
Sciences. Therefore compare we the Poet with the
Historian, and with the Morrall Phylosopher, and, if
hee goe beyond them both, no other humaine skill can
25 match him. For as for the Diuine, with all reuerence it
is euer to be excepted, not only for hauing his scope
as far beyonde any of these as eternitie exceedeth a
moment, but euen for passing each of these in themselues.
And for the Lawyer, though *Ius* bee the Daughter of
30 Iustice, and Iustice the chiefe of Vertues, yet because hee
seeketh to make men good rather *Formidine poenae* then
Virtutis amore, or, to say righter, dooth not indeuour to
make men good, but that their euill hurt not others,
hauing no care, so hee be a good Cittizen, how bad
35 a man he be : Therefore, as our wickednesse maketh

him necessarie, and necessitie maketh him honorable, so is hee not in the deepest trueth to stande in rancke with these who all indeuour to take naughtines away, and plant goodnesse euen in the secretest cabinet of our soules. And these foure are all that any way deale in 5 that consideration of mens manners, which beeing the supreme knowledge, they that best breed it deserue the best commendation.

The Philosopher therfore and the Historian are they which would win the gole, the one by precept, the other 10 by example. But both not hauing both, doe both halte. For the Philosopher, setting downe with thorny argument the bare rule, is so hard of vtterance, and so mistie to bee conceiued, that one that hath no other guide but him shall wade in him till hee be olde before he shall finde sufficient 15 cause to bee honest: for his knowledge standeth so vpon the abstract and generall, that happie is that man who may vnderstande him, and more happie that can applye what hee dooth vnderstand. On the other side, the Historian, wanting the precept, is so tyed, not to what 20 shoulde bee but to what is, to the particuler truth of things and not to the general reason of things, that hys example draweth no necessary consequence, and therefore a lesse fruitfull doctrine.

Nowe dooth the peerelesse Poet performe both: for 25 whatsoeuer the Philosopher sayth shoulde be doone, hee giueth a perfect picture of it in some one, by whom hee presupposeth it was doone. So as hee coupleth the generall notion with the particuler example. A perfect picture I say, for hee yeeldeth to the powers of the minde 30 an image of that whereof the Philosopher bestoweth but a woordish description: which dooth neyther strike, pierce, nor possesse the sight of the soule so much as that other dooth.

For as in outward things, to a man that had neuer 35

seene an Elephant or a Rinoceros, who should tell him
most exquisitely all theyr shapes, cullour, bignesse, and
perticular markes, or of a gorgeous Pallace the Archi-
tecture, with declaring the full beauties, might well make
5 the hearer able to repeate, as it were by rote, all hee had
heard, yet should neuer satisfie his inward conceits with
being witnes to it selfe of a true liuely knowledge : but the
same man, as soone as hee might see those beasts well
painted, or the house wel in moddel, should straightwaies
10 grow, without need of any description, to a iudicial comprehending of them : so no doubt the Philosopher with his
learned definition, bee it of vertue, vices, matters of
publick policie or priuat gouerment, replenisheth the
memory with many infallible grounds of wisdom, which,
15 notwithstanding, lye darke before the imaginatiue and
iudging powre, if they bee not illuminated or figured
foorth by the speaking picture of Poesie.

Tullie taketh much paynes, and many times not without
poeticall helpes, to make vs knowe the force loue of our
20 Countrey hath in vs. Let vs but heare old *Anchises*
speaking in the middest of Troyes flames, or see *Vlisses*
in the fulnes of all *Calipso's* delights bewayle his absence
from barraine and beggerly *Ithaca*. Anger, the *Stoicks*
say, was a short madnes : let but *Sophocles* bring you
25 *Aiax* on a stage, killing and whipping Sheepe and Oxen,
thinking them the Army of Greeks, with theyr Chiefe-
taines *Agamemnon* and *Menelaus*, and tell mee if you
haue not a more familiar insight into anger then finding
in the Schoolemen his *Genus* and difference. See whether
30 wisdome and temperance in *Vlisses* and *Diomedes*, valure
in *Achilles*, friendship in *Nisus* and *Eurialus*, euen to an
ignoraunt man carry not an apparent shyning : and, contrarily, the remorse of conscience in *Oedipus*, the soone
repenting pride of *Agamemnon*, the selfe-deuouring crueltie
35 in his Father *Atreus*, the violence of ambition in the two

Theban brothers, the sowre-sweetnes of reuenge in *Medœa*, and, to fall lower, the *Terentian Gnato* and our *Chaucers Pandar* so exprest that we nowe vse their names to signifie their trades : and finally, all vertues, vices, and passions so in their own naturall seates layd to the viewe, 5 that wee seeme not to heare of them, but cleerely to see through them.   But euen in the most excellent determination of goodnes, what Philosophers counsell can so redily direct a Prince, as the fayned *Cyrus* in *Xenophon*? or a vertuous man in all fortunes, as *Aeneas* in *Virgill*? 10 or a whole Common-wealth, as the way of Sir *Thomas Moores Eutopia*?   I say the way, because where Sir *Thomas Moore* erred, it was the fault of the man and not of the Poet, for that way of patterning a Commonwealth was most absolute, though hee perchaunce hath 15 not so absolutely perfourmed it : for the question is, whether the fayned image of Poesie or the regular instruction of Philosophy hath the more force in teaching : wherein if the Philosophers haue more rightly shewed themselues Philosophers then the Poets haue obtained 20 to the high top of their profession, as in truth,

Mediocribus esse poetis,
Non Di, non homines, non concessere Columnae,

it is, I say againe, not the fault of the Art, but that by fewe men that Arte can bee accomplished.   Certainly, 25 euen our Sauiour Christ could as well haue giuen the morrall common places of vncharitablenes and humblenes as the diuine narration of *Diues* and *Lazarus*; or of disobedience and mercy, as that heauenly discourse of the lost Child and the gratious Father; but that hys 30 through-searching wisdom knewe the estate of *Diues* burning in hell, and of *Lazarus* being in *Abrahams* bosome, would more constantly (as it were) inhabit both the memory and iudgment.   Truly, for my selfe, mee

seemes I see before my eyes the lost Childes disdainefull prodigality, turned to enuie a Swines dinner: which by the learned Diuines are thought not historicall acts, but instructing Parables. For conclusion, I say the Philo-
5 sopher teacheth, but he teacheth obscurely, so as · the learned onely can vnderstande him, that is to say, he teacheth them that are already taught; but the Poet is the foode for the tenderest stomacks, the Poet is indeed the right Popular Philosopher, whereof *Esops* tales giue
10 good proofe: whose pretty Allegories, stealing vnder the formall tales of Beastes, make many, more beastly then Beasts, begin to heare the sound of vertue from these dumbe speakers.

But now may it be alledged that if this imagining of
15 matters be so fitte for the imagination, then must the Historian needs surpasse, who bringeth you images of true matters, such as indeede were doone, and not such as fantastically or falsely may be suggested to haue been doone. Truely, *Aristotle* himselfe, in his discourse of
20 Poesie, plainely determineth this question, saying that Poetry is *Philosophoteron* and *Spoudaioteron*, that is to say, it is more Philosophicall and more studiously serious then history. His reason is, because Poesie dealeth with *Katholou*, that is to say, with the vniuersall
25 consideration; and the history with *Kathekaston*, the per-ticuler: 'nowe,' sayth he, 'the vniuersall wayes what is fit to bee sayd or done, eyther in likelihood or necessity, (which the Poesie considereth in his imposed names), and the perticuler onely marks whether *Alcibiades* did, or
30 suffered, this or that.' Thus farre *Aristotle*: which reason of his (as all his) is most full of reason. For indeed, if the question were whether it were better to haue a per-ticular acte truly or falsly set down, there is no doubt which is to be chosen, no more then whether you had
35 rather haue *Vespasians* picture right as hee was, or at

the Painters pleasure nothing resembling. But if the
question be for your owne vse and learning, whether it
be better to haue it set downe as it should be, or as it
was, then certainely is more doctrinable the fained *Cirus*
in *Xenophon* then the true *Cyrus* in *Iustine*, and the 5
fayned *Aeneas* in *Virgil* then the right *Aeneas* in *Dares
Phrigius*. As to a Lady that desired to fashion her
countenance to the best grace, a Painter should more
benefite her to portraite a most sweet face, wryting
Canidia vpon it, then to paynt *Canidia* as she was, who, 10
Horace sweareth, was foule and ill fauoured.

If the Poet doe his part a-right, he will shew you in
Tantalus, *Atreus*, and such like, nothing that is not to
be shunned; in *Cyrus*, *Aeneas*, *Vlisses*, each thing to
be followed; where the Historian, bound to tell things 15
as things were, cannot be liberall (without hee will be
poeticall) of a perfect patterne, but, as in *Alexander* or
Scipio himselfe, shew dooings, some to be liked, some
to be misliked. And then how will you discerne what
to followe but by your owne discretion, which you had 20
without reading *Quintus Curtius*? And whereas a man
may say, though in vniuersall consideration of doctrine
the Poet preuaileth, yet that the historie, in his saying
such a thing was doone, doth warrant a man more in that
hee shall follow, the aunswere is manifest, that if hee 25
stande vpon that was—as if hee should argue, because it
rayned yesterday, therefore it shoulde rayne to day—then
indeede it hath some aduantage to a grose conceite; but
if he know an example onlie informes a coniectured likelihood, and so goe by reason, the Poet dooth so farre 30
exceede him, as hee is to frame his example to that which
is most reasonable, be it in warlike, politick, or priuate
matters, where the Historian in his bare *Was* hath
many times that which wee call fortune to ouer-rule
the best wisedome. Manie times he must tell euents 35

whereof he can yeelde no cause : or, if hee doe, it must
be poeticall.

For that a fayned example hath asmuch force to teach
as a true example (for as for to mooue, it is cleere, sith
5 the fayned may bee tuned to the highest key of passion),
let vs take one example wherein a Poet and a Historian
doe concur. *Herodotus* and *Iustine* do both testifie that
Zopirus, King *Darius* faithfull seruaunt, seeing his Maister
long resisted by the rebellious *Babilonians*, fayned him-
10 selfe in extreame disgrace of his King : for verifying of
which, he caused his own nose and eares to be cut off :
and so flying to the *Babylonians*, was receiued, and for
his knowne valour so far credited, that hee did finde
meanes to deliuer them ouer to *Darius*. Much like
15 matter doth *Liuie* record of *Tarquinius* and his sonne.
Xenophon excellently faineth such another stratageme,
performed by *Abradates* in *Cyrus* behalfe. Now would
I fayne know, if occasion bee presented vnto you to
serue your Prince by such an honest dissimulation, why
20 you doe not as well learne it of *Xenophons* fiction as
of the others verity : and truely so much the better, as
you shall saue your nose by the bargaine ; for *Abradates*
did not counterfet so far. So then the best of the Historian is subiect to the Poet ; for whatsoeuer action, or
25 faction, whatsoeuer counsell, pollicy, or warre stratagem
the Historian is bound to recite, that may the Poet (if
he list) with his imitation make his own ; beautifying it
both for further teaching, and more delighting, as it
pleaseth him : hauing all, from *Dante* his heauen to hys
30 hell, vnder the authoritie of his penne. Which if I be
asked what Poets haue done so, as I might well name
some, yet say I, and say againe, I speak of the Arte, and
not of the Artificer.

Nowe, to that which commonly is attributed to the prayse
35 of histories, in respect of the notable learning is gotten by

marking the successe, as though therein a man should see vertue exalted and vice punished.   Truely that commendation is peculiar to Poetrie, and farre of from History.   For indeede Poetrie euer setteth vertue so out in her best cullours, making Fortune her wel-wayting hand-mayd, that 5 one must needs be enamored of her.   Well may you see *Vlisses* in a storme, and in other hard plights ; but they are but exercises of patience and magnanimitie, to make them shine the more in the neere-following prosperitie. And of the contrarie part, if euill men come to the stage, 1 they euer goe out (as the Tragedie Writer answered to one that misliked the shew of such persons) so manacled as they little animate folkes to followe them.   But the Historian, beeing captiued to the trueth of a foolish world, is many times a terror from well dooing, and an incourage- 1 ment to vnbrideled wickednes.

For see wee not valiant *Milciades* rot in his fetters ? The iust *Phocion* and the accomplished *Socrates* put to death like Traytors ? The cruell *Seuerus* liue prosperously? The excellent *Seuerus* miserably murthered ?   *Sylla* and 2 *Marius* dying in theyr beddes ?   *Pompey* and *Cicero* slaine then when they would haue thought exile a happinesse ? See wee not vertuous *Cato* driuen to kyll himselfe ? and rebell *Cæsar* so aduaunced that his name yet, after 1600 yeares, lasteth in the highest honor ?   And marke but euen 2 *Cæsars* own words of the fore-named *Sylla* (who in that onely did honestly, to put downe his dishonest tyrannie), *Literas nesciuit*, as if want of learning caused him to doe well.   Hee meant it not by Poetrie, which, not content with earthly plagues, deuiseth new punishments in hel for 3 Tyrants : nor yet by Philosophie, which teacheth *Occidendos esse*; but no doubt by skill in Historie, for that indeede can affoord your *Cipselus, Periander, Phalaris, Dionisius*, and I know not how many more of the same kennell, that speede well enough in theyr abhominable 3

vniustice or vsurpation. I conclude, therefore, that hee
excelleth Historie, not onely in furnishing the minde with
knowledge, but in setting it forward to that which deserueth to be called and accounted good: which setting
5 forward, and moouing to well dooing, indeed setteth the
Lawrell crowne vpon the Poet as victorious, not onely
of the Historian, but ouer the Phylosopher, howsoeuer
in teaching it may bee questionable.

For suppose it be granted (that which I suppose with
10 great reason may be denied) that the Philosopher, in
respect of his methodical proceeding, doth teach more
perfectly then the Poet, yet do I thinke that no man is
so much *Philophilosophos* as to compare the Philosopher,
in moouing, with the Poet.

15 And that moouing is of a higher degree then teaching,
it may by this appeare, that it is wel nigh the cause and
the effect of teaching. For who will be taught, if hee bee
not mooued with desire to be taught? and what so much
good doth that teaching bring forth (I speak still of morrall
20 doctrine) as that it mooueth one to doe that which it dooth
teach? for, as *Aristotle* sayth, it is not *Gnosis* but *Praxis*
must be the fruit. And howe *Praxis* cannot be, without
being mooued to practise, it is no hard matter to consider.

25 The Philosopher sheweth you the way, hee informeth
you of the particularities, as well of the tediousnes of the
way, as of the pleasant lodging you shall haue when your
iourney is ended, as of the many by-turnings that may
diuert you from your way. But this is to no man but to
30 him that will read him, and read him with attentiue studious
painfulnes. Which constant desire, whosoeuer hath in
him, hath already past halfe the hardnes of the way, and
therefore is beholding to the Philosopher but for the other
halfe. Nay truely, learned men haue learnedly thought
35 that, where once reason hath so much ouer-mastred passion

as that the minde hath a free desire to doe well, the inward
light each minde hath in it selfe is as good as a Philosophers booke ; seeing in nature we know it is wel to doe
well, and what is well and what is euill, although not in
the words of Arte which Philosophers bestowe vpon vs. 5
For out of naturall conceit the Philosophers drew it ; but
to be moued to doe that which we know, or to be mooued
with desire to knowe, *Hoc opus, hic labor est.*

Nowe therein of all Sciences (I speak still of humane,
and according to the humaine conceits) is our Poet the 10
Monarch.   For he dooth not only show the way, but
giueth so sweete a prospect into the way, as will intice
any man to enter into it.   Nay, he dooth, as if your
iourney should lye through a fayre Vineyard, at the first
giue you a cluster of Grapes, that, full of that taste, you 15
may long to passe further.   He beginneth not with obscure
definitions, which must blur the margent with interpretations, and load the memory with doubtfulnesse ; but hee
commeth to you with words sent in delightfull proportion, either accompanied with, or prepared for, the well 20
inchaunting skill of Musicke ; and with a tale forsooth he
commeth vnto you, with a tale which holdeth children
from play, and old men from the chimney corner.   And,
pretending no more, doth intende the winning of the mind
from wickednesse to vertue : euen as the childe is often 25
brought to take most wholsom things by hiding them in
such other as haue a pleasant tast : which, if one should
beginne to tell them the nature of *Aloes* or *Rubarb* they
shoulde receiue, woulde sooner take their Phisicke at their
eares then at their mouth.   So is it in men (most of which 30
are childish in the best things, till they bee cradled in their
graues) : glad they will be to heare the tales of *Hercules,*
Achilles, Cyrus, and *Aeneas* ; and, hearing them, must needs
heare the right description of wisdom, valure, and iustice ;
which, if they had been barely, that is to say Philo- 35

sophically, set out, they would sweare they bee brought to
schoole againe.

That imitation, wherof Poetry is, hath the most con-
ueniency to Nature of all other, in somuch that, as
Aristotle sayth, those things which in themselues are
horrible, as cruell battailes, vnnaturall Monsters, are
made in poeticall imitation delightfull. Truely, I haue
knowen men, that euen with reading *Amadis de Gaule*
(which God knoweth wanteth much of a perfect Poesie)
haue found their harts mooued to the exercise of courtesie, liberalitie, and especially courage. Who readeth
Aeneas carrying olde *Anchises* on his back, that wisheth
not it were his fortune to perfourme so excellent an
acte? Whom doe not the words of *Turnus* mooue?
(the tale of *Turnus* hauing planted his image in the
imagination)

> *Fugientem haec terra videbit?*
> *Vsque adeone mori miserum est?*

Where the Philosophers, as they scorne to delight, so
must they bee content little to mooue, sauing wrangling
whether Vertue bee the chiefe or the onely good, whether
the contemplatiue or the actiue life doe excell: which *Plato*
and *Boetius* well knew, and therefore made Mistres Philosophy very often borrow the masking rayment of Poesie.
For euen those harde harted euill men who thinke vertue
a schoole name, and knowe no other good but *indulgere
genio*, and therefore despise the austere admonitions of
the Philosopher, and feele not the inward reason they
stand vpon, yet will be content to be delighted, which is
al the good felow Poet seemeth to promise; and so steale
to see the forme of goodnes (which seene they cannot but
loue) ere themselues be aware, as if they tooke a medicine
of Cherries. Infinite proofes of the strange effects of this
poeticall inuention might be alledged; onely two shall

serue, which are so often remembred, as I thinke all men knowe them.

The one of *Menenius Agrippa*, who, when the whole people of Rome had resolutely deuided themselues from the Senate, with apparant shew of vtter ruine, though hee were (for that time) an excellent Oratour, came not among them vpon trust of figuratiue speeches or cunning insinuations; and much lesse with farre fet *Maximes* of Phylosophie, which (especially if they were *Platonick*) they must haue learned Geometrie before they could well haue conceiued; but forsooth he behaues himselfe like a homely and familiar Poet. Hee telleth them a tale, that there was a time when all the parts of the body made a mutinous conspiracie against the belly, which they thought deuoured the fruits of each others labour : they concluded they would let so vnprofitable a spender starue. In the end, to be short, (for the tale is notorious, and as notorious that it was a tale) with punishing the belly they plagued themselues. This applied by him wrought such effect in the people, as I neuer read that euer words brought forth but then so suddaine and so good an alteration; for vpon reasonable conditions a perfect reconcilement ensued. The other is of *Nathan* the Prophet, who when the holie *Dauid* had so far forsaken God as to confirme adulterie with murther, when hee was to doe the tenderest office of a friende, in laying his owne shame before his eyes, sent by God to call againe so chosen a seruant, how doth he it but by telling of a man whose beloued Lambe was vngratefullie taken from his bosome? the applycation most diuinely true, but the discourse it selfe fayned; which made *Dauid* (I speake of the second and instrumentall cause) as in a glasse to see his own filthines, as that heauenly Psalme of mercie wel testifieth.

By these, therefore, examples and reasons, I think it may be manifest that the Poet, with that same hand of

delight, doth draw the mind more effectually then any
other Arte dooth : and so a conclusion not vnfitlie ensueth,
that as vertue is the most excellent resting place for all
worldlie learning to make his end of, so Poetrie, beeing
the most familiar to teach it, and most princelie to moue
towards it, in the most excellent work is the most excellent
workman.   But I am content not onely to decipher him
by his workes (although works in commendation or disprayse must euer holde an high authority), but more
narrowly will examine his parts : so that (as in a man)
though al together may carry a presence ful of maiestie
and beautie, perchance in some one defectious peece we
may find a blemish.   Now in his parts, kindes, or *Species*
(as you list to terme them), it is to be noted that some
Poesies haue coupled together two or three kindes, as
Tragicall and Comicall, wher-vpon is risen the Tragicomicall.   Some in the like manner haue mingled Prose
and Verse, as *Sanazzar* and *Boetius*.   Some haue mingled
matters Heroicall and Pastorall.   But that commeth all to
one in this question, for, if seuered they be good, the
coniunction cannot be hurtfull.   Therefore perchaunce
forgetting some, and leauing some as needlesse to be
remembred, it shall not be amisse in a worde to cite the
speciall kindes, to see what faults may be found in the
right vse of them.

Is it then the Pastorall Poem which is misliked ? (for
perchance, where the hedge is lowest they will soonest
leape ouer).   Is the poore pype disdained, which sometime
out of *Melibeus* mouth can shewe the miserie of people
vnder hard Lords or rauening Souldiours ? and again,
by *Titirus*, what blessednes is deriued to them that lye
lowest from the goodnesse of them that sit highest ?
sometimes, vnder the prettie tales of Wolues and Sheepe,
can include the whole considerations of wrong dooing
and patience ; sometimes shew that contention for trifles

can get but a trifling victorie. Where perchaunce a man may see that euen *Alexander* and *Darius*, when they straue who should be Cocke of thys worlds dunghill, the benefit they got was that the after-liuers may say,

Haec memini et victum frustra contendere Thirsin: 5
Ex illo Coridon, Coridon est tempore nobis.

Or is it the lamenting Elegiack, which in a kinde hart would mooue rather pitty then blame, who bewailes with the great Philosopher *Heraclitus* the weakenes of man-kind and the wretchednes of the world: who surely is 10 to be praysed, either for compassionate accompanying iust causes of lamentation, or for rightly paynting out how weake be the passions of wofulnesse? Is it the bitter but wholsome Iambick, which rubs the galled minde, in making shame the trumpet of villanie with 15 bolde and open crying out against naughtines? Or the Satirick, who

Omne vafer vitium ridenti tangit amico?

who sportingly neuer leaueth vntill hee make a man laugh at folly, and, at length ashamed, to laugh at him- 20 selfe; which he cannot auoyd, without auoyding the follie; who, while

circum praecordia ludit,

giueth vs to feele how many head-aches a passionate life bringeth vs to—how, when all is done, 25

Est Vlubris, animus si nos non deficit aequus?

No, perchance it is the Comick, whom naughtie Play-makers and Stage-keepers haue iustly made odious. To the argument of abuse I will answer after. Onely thus much now is to be said, that the Comedy is an imitation 30 of the common errors of our life, which he representeth in the most ridiculous and scornefull sort that may be;

so as it is impossible that any beholder can be content to be such a one.

Now, as in Geometry the oblique must bee knowne as wel as the right, and in Arithmetick the odde as well as the euen, so in the actions of our life who seeth not the filthines of euil wanteth a great foile to perceiue the beauty of vertue. This doth the Comedy handle so in our priuate and domestical matters, as with hearing it we get as it were an experience, what is to be looked for of a nigardly *Demea*, of a crafty *Dauus*, of a flattering *Gnato*, of a vaine glorious *Thraso*, and not onely to know what effects are to be expected, but to know who be such, by the signifying badge giuen them by the Comedian. And little reason hath any man to say that men learne euill by seeing it so set out : sith, as I sayd before, there is no man liuing but, by the force trueth hath in nature, no sooner seeth these men play their parts, but wisheth them in *Pistrinum* : although perchance the sack of his owne faults lye so behinde hys back that he seeth not himselfe daunce the same measure ; whereto yet nothing can more open his eyes then to finde his own actions contemptibly set forth. So that the right vse of Comedy will (I thinke) by no body be blamed, and much lesse of the high and excellent Tragedy, that openeth the greatest wounds, and sheweth forth the Vlcers that are couered with Tissue ; that maketh Kinges feare to be Tyrants, and Tyrants manifest their tirannicall humors ; that, with sturring the affects of admiration and commiseration, teacheth the vncertainety of this world, and vpon how weake foundations guilden roofes are builded ; that maketh vs knowe,

> *Qui sceptra saeuus duro imperio regit,*
> *Timet timentes, metus in auctorem redit.*

But how much it can mooue, *Plutarch* yeeldeth a notable

testimonie of the abhominable Tyrant *Alexander Pheraeus*; from whose eyes a Tragedy, wel made and represented, drewe aboundance of teares, who, without all pitty, had murthered infinite nombers, and some of his owne blood. So as he, that was not ashamed to make matters for 5 Tragedies, yet coulde not resist the sweet violence of a Tragedie.   And if it wrought no further good in him, it was that he, in despight of himselfe, withdrewe himselfe from harkening to that which might mollifie his hardened heart.   10

But it is not the Tragedy they doe mislike : For it were too absurd to cast out so excellent a representation of whatsoeuer is most worthy to be learned.   Is it the Liricke that most displeaseth, who with his tuned Lyre, and wel accorded voyce, giueth praise, the reward of vertue, 15 to vertuous acts? who giues morrall precepts, and naturall Problemes, who sometimes rayseth vp his voice to the height of the heauens, in singing the laudes of the immortall God.   Certainly I must confesse my own barbarousnes : I neuer heard the olde song of *Percy* and *Duglas* that 20 I found not my heart mooued more then with a Trumpet; and yet is it sung but by some blinde Crouder, with no rougher voyce then rude stile ; which being so euill apparrelled in the dust and cobwebbes of that vnciuill age, what would it worke trymmed in the gorgeous eloquence 25 of *Pindar*?   In *Hungary* I haue seene it the manner at all Feasts, and other such meetings, to haue songes of their Auncestours valour ; which that right Souldier-like Nation thinck the chiefest kindlers of braue courage.   The incomparable *Lacedemonians* did not only carry that kinde 30 of Musicke euer with them to the field, but euen at home, as such songs were made, so were they all content to bee the singers of them, when the lusty men were to tell what they dyd, the olde men what they had done, and the young men what they wold doe.   And where a man may 35 say that *Pindar* many times prayseth highly victories of small moment, matters rather of sport then vertue; as it may be aunswered, it was the fault of the Poet, and not of the Poetry; so indeede the chiefe fault was in the 5 tyme and custome of the Greekes, who set those toyes at so high a price that *Phillip* of *Macedon* reckoned a horse-race wonne at *Olimpus* among hys three fearefull felicities. But as the vnimitable *Pindar* often did, so is that kinde most capable and most fit to awake the 10 thoughts from the sleep of idlenes, to imbrace honorable enterprises.

There rests the Heroicall, whose very name (I thinke) should daunt all back-biters; for by what conceit can a tongue be directed to speake euill of that which draweth 15 with it no lesse Champions then *Achilles, Cyrus, Aeneas, Turnus, Tideus,* and *Rinaldo?* who doth not onely teach and moue to a truth, but teacheth and mooueth to the most high and excellent truth; who maketh magnanimity and iustice shine throughout all misty fearefulnes 20 and foggy desires; who, if the saying of *Plato* and *Tullie* bee true, that who could see Vertue would be wonderfully rauished with the loue of her beauty: this man sets her out to make her more louely in her holyday apparell, to the eye of any that will daine not to disdaine 25 vntill they vnderstand. But if any thing be already sayd in the defence of sweete Poetry, all concurreth to the maintaining the Heroicall, which is not onely a kinde, but the best and most accomplished kinde of Poetry. For as the image of each action styrreth and instructeth 30 the mind, so the loftie image of such Worthies most inflameth the mind with desire to be worthy, and informes with counsel how to be worthy. Only let *Aeneas* be worne in the tablet of your memory; how he gouerneth himselfe in the ruine of his Country; in the preseruing 35 his old Father, and carrying away his religious ceremonies; in obeying the Gods commandement to leaue *Dido*, though not onely all passionate kindenes, but euen the humane consideration of vertuous gratefulnes, would haue craued other of him; how in storms, howe in sports, howe in warre, howe in peace, how a fugitiue, 5 how victorious, how besiedged, how besiedging, howe to strangers, howe to allyes, how to enemies, howe to his owne; lastly, how in his inward selfe, and how in his outward gouernment; and I thinke, in a minde not preiudiced with a preiudicating humor, hee will be found 10 in excellencie fruitefull, yea, euen as *Horace* sayth,

Melius Chrisippo et Crantore.

But truely I imagine it falleth out with these Poet-whyppers, as with some good women, who often are sicke, but in fayth they cannot tel where. So the name of 15 Poetrie is odious to them, but neither his cause nor effects, neither the sum that containes him nor the particularities descending from him, giue any fast handle to their carping disprayse.

Sith then Poetrie is of all humane learning the most 20 auncient and of most fatherly antiquitie, as from whence other learnings haue taken theyr beginnings; sith it is so vniuersall that no learned Nation dooth despise it, nor no barbarous Nation is without it; sith both Roman and Greek gaue diuine names vnto it, the one of pro- 25 phecying, the other of making; and that indeede that name of making is fit for him, considering that where as other Arts retaine themselues within their subiect, and receiue, as it were, their beeing from it, the Poet onely bringeth his owne stuffe, and dooth not learne a conceite 30 out of a matter, but maketh matter for a conceite; Sith neither his description nor his ende contayneth any euill, the thing described cannot be euill; Sith his effects be so good as to teach goodnes and to delight the learners;

Sith therein (namely in morrall doctrine, the chiefe of all
knowledges) hee dooth not onely farre passe the Historian, but, for instructing, is well nigh comparable to the
Philosopher, and, for mouing, leaues him behind him;
5 Sith the holy scripture (wherein there is no vncleannes)
hath whole parts in it poeticall, and that euen our
Sauiour Christ vouchsafed to vse the flowers of it; Sith
all his kindes are not onlie in their vnited formes but
in their seuered dissections fully commendable: I think
10 (and think I thinke rightly) the Lawrell crowne appointed
for tryumphing Captaines doth worthilie (of al other
learnings) honor the Poets tryumph. But because wee
haue eares aswell as tongues, and that the lightest reasons
that may be will seeme to weigh greatly, if nothing be
15 put in the counter-ballance, let vs heare, and aswell as
wee can ponder, what obiections may bee made against
this Arte, which may be worthy eyther of yeelding or
answering.

First, truely I note not onely in these *Mysomousoi*,
20 Poet-haters, but in all that kinde of people who seek
a prayse by dispraysing others, that they doe prodigally
spend a great many wandering wordes in quips and
scoffes, carping and taunting at each thing, which, by
styrring the Spleene, may stay the braine from a through
25 beholding the worthines of the subiect.

Those kinde of obiections, as they are full of very idle
easines, sith there is nothing of so sacred a maiestie but
that an itching tongue may rubbe it selfe vpon it, so
deserue they no other answer, but, in steed of laughing
30 at the iest, to laugh at the iester. Wee know a playing
wit can prayse the discretion of an Asse, the comfortable-
nes of being in debt, and the iolly commoditie of beeing
sick of the plague. So of the contrary side, if we will
turne *Ouids* verse,

35   *Vt lateat virtus proximitate mali,*

that good lye hid in neerenesse of the euill, *Agrippa* will
be as merry in shewing the vanitie of Science as *Erasmus*
was in commending of follie.   Neyther shall any man or
matter escape some touch of these smyling raylers.   But
for *Erasmus* and *Agrippa*, they had another foundation 5
then the superficiall part would promise.   Mary, these
other pleasant Fault-finders, who wil correct the Verbe
before they vnderstande the Noune, and confute others
knowledge before they confirme theyr owne, I would
haue them onely remember that scoffing commeth not of 10
wisedom.   So as the best title in true English they gette
with their merriments is to be called good fooles, for so
haue our graue Fore-fathers euer termed that humorous
kinde of iesters.   But that which gyueth greatest• scope
to their scorning humors is ryming and versing.   It is 15
already sayde (and, as I think, trulie sayde) it is not
ryming and versing that maketh Poesie.   One may bee
a Poet without versing, and a versifyer without Poetry.
But yet presuppose it were inseparable (as indeede it
seemeth *Scaliger* iudgeth) truelie it were an inseparable 20
commendation.   For if *Oratio* next to *Ratio*, Speech next
to Reason, bee the greatest gyft bestowed vpon mortalitie,
that can not be praiselesse which dooth most pollish that
blessing of speech, which considers each word, not only
(as a man may say) by his forcible qualitie but by his best 25
measured quantitie, carrying euen in themselues a Harmonie (without, perchaunce, Number, Measure, Order,
Proportion be in our time growne odious).   But lay a side
the iust prayse it hath, by beeing the onely fit speech for
Musick (Musick I say, the most diuine striker of the 30
sences), thus much is vndoubtedly true, that if reading
bee foolish without remembring, memorie being the onely
treasurer of knowled[g]e, those words which are fittest for
memory are likewise most conuenient for knowledge.
   Now, that Verse farre exceedeth Prose in the knitting 35

vp of the memory, the reason is manifest; the words
(besides theyr delight, which hath a great affinitie to
memory) beeing so set as one word cannot be lost but
the whole worke failes: which accuseth it selfe, calleth
5 the remembrance backe to it selfe, and so most strongly
confirmeth it; besides, one word so, as it were, begetting
another, as, be it in ryme or measured verse, by the
former a man shall haue a neere gesse to the follower:
lastly, euen they that haue taught the Art of memory
10 haue shewed nothing so apt for it as a certaine roome
deuided into many places well and throughly knowne.
Now, that hath the verse in effect perfectly, euery word
hauing his naturall seate, which seate must needes make
the words remembred. But what needeth more in a thing
15 so knowne to all men? who is it that euer was a scholler
that doth not carry away some verses of *Virgill*, *Horace*,
or *Cato*, which in his youth he learned, and euen to his
old age serue him for howrely lessons? But the fitnes it
hath for memory is notably proued by all deliuery of Arts:
20 wherein for the most part, from Grammer to Logick,
Mathematick, Phisick, and the rest, the rules chiefely
necessary to bee borne away are compiled in verses. So
that, verse being in it selfe sweete and orderly, and beeing
best for memory, the onely handle of knowledge, it must
25 be in iest that any man can speake against it.

Nowe then goe wee to the most important imputations
laid to the poore Poets: for ought I can yet learne, they
are these. First, that there beeing many other more
fruitefull knowledges, a man might better spend his tyme
30 in them then in this. Secondly, that it is the mother of
lyes. Thirdly, that it is the Nurse of abuse, infecting
vs with many pestilent desires; with a Syrens sweetnes,
drawing the mind to the Serpents tayle of sinfull fancy.
And heerein, especially, Comedies giue the largest field to
35 erre, as *Chaucer* sayth: howe both in other Nations and in

ours, before Poets did soften vs, we were full of courage, giuen to martiall exercises, the pillers of manlyke liberty, and not lulled a sleepe in shady idlenes with Poets pastimes. And lastly, and chiefely, they cry out with an open mouth, as if they out shot *Robin Hood*, that *Plato* banished them out of hys Common-wealth. Truely, this is much, if there be much truth in it. First to the first: that a man might better spend his tyme is a reason indeede: but it doth (as they say) but *Petere principium*: for if it be, as I affirme, that no learning is so good as that which teacheth and mooueth to vertue, and that none can both teach and moue thereto so much as Poetry, then is the conclusion manifest that Incke and Paper cannot be to a more profitable purpose employed. And certainly, though a man should graunt their first assumption, it should followe (me thinkes) very vnwillingly, that good is not good because better is better. But I still and vtterly denye that there is sprong out of earth a more fruitefull knowledge. To the second therefore, that they should be the principall lyars, I aunswere paradoxically, but, truely, I thinke truely, that of all Writers vnder the sunne the Poet is the least lier, and, though he would, as a Poet can scarcely be a lyer. The Astronomer, with his cosen the Geometrician, can hardly escape, when they take vpon them to measure the height of the starres. How often, thinke you, doe the Phisitians lye, when they auer things good for sicknesses, which afterwards send *Charon* a great nomber of soules drownd in a potion before they come to his Ferry? And no lesse of the rest, which take vpon them to affirme. Now, for the Poet, he nothing affirmes, and therefore neuer lyeth. For, as I take it, to lye is to affirme that to be true which is false. So as the other Artists, and especially the Historian, affirming many things, can, in the cloudy knowledge of mankinde, hardly escape from many lyes.

But the Poet (as I sayd before) neuer affirmeth. The Poet neuer maketh any circles about your imagination, to coniure you to beleeue for true what he writes. Hee citeth not authorities of other Histories, but euen for hys entry calleth the sweete Muses to inspire into him a good inuention; in troth, not labouring to tell you what is, or is not, but what should or should not be: and therefore, though he recount things not true, yet because hee telleth them not for true, he lyeth not, without we will say that *Nathan* lyed in his speech, before alledged, to *Dauid*. Which as a wicked man durst scarce say, so think I none so simple would say that *Esope* lyed in the tales of his beasts: for who thinks that *Esope* writ it for actually true were well worthy to haue his name cronicled among the beastes hee writeth of. What childe is there that, comming to a Play, and seeing *Thebes* written in great Letters vpon an olde doore, doth beleeue that it is *Thebes*? If then a man can ariue, at that childs age, to know that the Poets persons and dooings are but pictures what should be, and not stories what haue beene, they will neuer giue the lye to things not affirmatiuely but allegorically and figuratiuelie written. And therefore, as in Historie, looking for trueth, they goe away full fraught with falshood, so in Poesie, looking for fiction, they shal vse the narration but as an imaginatiue groundplot of a profitable inuention.

But heereto is replyed, that the Poets gyue names to men they write of, which argueth a conceite of an actuall truth, and so, not being true, prooues a falshood. And doth the Lawyer lye then, when vnder the names of *Iohn a stile* and *Iohn a noakes* hee puts his case? But that is easily answered. Theyr naming of men is but to make theyr picture the more liuely, and not to builde any historie; paynting men, they cannot leaue men namelesse. We see we cannot play at Chesse but that wee must giue names to our Chesse-men; and yet, mee thinks, hee were a very partiall Champion of truth that would say we lyed for giuing a peece of wood the reuerend title of a Bishop. The Poet nameth *Cyrus* or *Aeneas* no other way then to shewe what men of theyr fames, fortunes, and estates should doe.

Their third is, how much it abuseth mens wit, trayning it to wanton sinfulnes and lustfull loue: for indeed that is the principall, if not the onely abuse I can heare alledged. They say the Comedies rather teach then reprehend amorous conceits. They say the Lirick is larded with passionate Sonnets: The Elegiack weepes the want of his mistresse: And that euen to the Heroical *Cupid* hath ambitiously climed. Alas, Loue, I would thou couldest as well defende thy selfe as thou canst offende others. I would those, on whom thou doost attend, could eyther put thee away, or yeelde good reason why they keepe thee. But grant loue of beautie to be a beastlie fault (although it be very hard, sith onely man, and no beast, hath that gyft to discerne beauty). Grant that louely name of Loue to deserue all hatefull reproches (although euen some of my Maisters the Phylosophers spent a good deale of theyr Lamp-oyle in setting foorth the excellencie of it). Grant, I say, what soeuer they wil haue granted; that not onely loue, but lust, but vanitie, but (if they list) scurrilitie, possesseth many leaues of the Poets bookes: yet thinke I, when this is granted, they will finde theyr sentence may with good manners put the last words foremost, and not say that Poetrie abuseth mans wit, but that mans wit abuseth Poetrie.

For I will not denie but that mans wit may make Poesie (which should be *Eikastike*, which some learned haue defined, figuring foorth good things) to be *Phantastike*: which doth, contrariwise, infect the fancie with vnworthy obiects. As the Painter, that shoulde giue to

the eye eyther some éxcellent perspectiue, or some fine
picture, fit for building or fortification, or contayning in
it some notable example, as *Abraham* sacrificing his
Sonne *Isaack, Iudith* killing *Holofernes, Dauid* fighting
5 with *Goliah,* may leaue those, and please an ill-pleased
eye with wanton shewes of better hidden matters. But
what, shall the abuse of a thing make the right vse
odious? Nay truely, though I yeeld that Poesie may
not onely be abused, but that beeing abused, by the
10 reason of his sweete charming force, it can doe more
hurt then any other Armie of words, yet shall it be so
far from concluding that the abuse should giue reproch
to the abused, that contrariwise it is a good reason, that
whatsoeuer, being abused, dooth most harme, beeing
15 rightly vsed (and vpon the right vse each thing con-
ceiueth his title), doth most good.

Doe wee not see the skill of Phisick (the best rampire
to our often-assaulted bodies) beeing abused, teach poyson,
the most violent destroyer? Dooth not knowledge of
20 Law, whose end is to euen and right all things being
abused, grow the crooked fosterer of horrible iniuries?
Doth not (to goe to the highest) Gods word abused breed
heresie? and his Name abused become blasphemie?
Truely, a needle cannot doe much hurt, and as truely
25 (with leaue of Ladies be it spoken) it cannot doe much
good. With a sword thou maist kill thy Father, and
with a sword thou maist defende thy Prince and Country.
So that, as in their calling Poets the Fathers of lyes they
say nothing, so in this theyr argument of abuse they
30 prooue the commendation.

They alledge heere-with, that before Poets beganne to
be in price our Nation hath set their harts delight vpon
action, and not vpon imagination: rather doing things
worthy to bee written, then writing things fitte to be done.
35 What that before tyme wás, I thinke scarcely *Sphinx*

can tell: Sith no memory is so auncient that hath the
precedence of Poetrie. And certaine it is that, in our
plainest homelines, yet neuer was the *Albion* Nation
without Poetrie. Mary, thys argument, though it bee
leaueld against Poetrie, yet is it indeed a chaine-shot
against all learning, or bookishnes, as they commonly
tearme it. Of such minde were certaine *Gothes*, of whom
it is written that, hauing in the spoile of a famous Citie
taken a fayre librarie, one hangman (bee like fitte to
execute the fruites of their wits), who had murthered a
great number of bodies, would haue set fire on it: 'no,'
sayde another very grauely, 'take heede what you doe,
for whyle they are busie about these toyes, wee shall
with more leysure conquer their Countries.'

This indeede is the ordinary doctrine of ignorance, and
many wordes sometymes I haue heard spent in it: but
because this reason is generally against all learning, aswell
as Poetrie, or rather, all learning but Poetry; because
it were too large a digression to handle, or at least to
superfluous (sith it is manifest that all gouernment of
action is to be gotten by knowledg, and knowledge best
by gathering many knowledges, which is reading), I onely,
with *Horace*, to him that is of that opinion,

Iubeo stultum esse libenter:

for as for Poetrie it selfe, it is the freest from thys obiection. For Poetrie is the companion of the Campes.

I dare vndertake, *Orlando Furioso*, or honest King
Arthur, will neuer displease a Souldier: but the quiddity
of *Ens* and *Prima materia* will hardely agree with a
Corslet: and therefore, as I said in the beginning, euen
Turks and Tartares are delighted with Poets. *Homer*,
a Greek, florished before Greece florished. And if to
a slight coniecture a coniecture may be opposed, truly
it may seeme, that as by him their learned men tooke

almost their first light of knowledge, so their actiue men
receiued their first motions of courage.   Onlie *Alexanders*
example may serue, who by *Plutarch* is accounted of such
vertue, that Fortune was not his guide but his foote-
stoole : whose acts speake for him, though *Plutarch* did
not ; indeede the Phœnix of warlike Princes.   This
Alexander left his Schoolemaister, liuing *Aristotle*, behinde him, but tooke deade *Homer* with him : he put
the Philosopher *Calisthenes* to death for his seeming
philosophicall, indeed mutinous, stubburnnes ; but the
chiefe thing he euer was heard to wish for was that
Homer had been aliue.   He well found he receiued more
brauerie of minde bye the patterne of *Achilles* then by
hearing the definition of Fortitude : and therefore, if *Cato*
misliked *Fuluius* for carying *Ennius* with him to the
fielde, it may be aunswered that, if *Cato* misliked it, the
noble *Fuluius* liked it, or els he had not doone it : for it
was not the excellent *Cato Vticensis* (whose authority
I would much more haue reuerenced), but it was the
former, in truth a bitter punisher of faults, but else
a man that had neuer wel sacrificed to the Graces.   Hee
misliked and cryed out vpon all Greeke learning, and yet,
being 80 yeeres olde, began to learne it ; be-like fearing
that *Pluto* vnderstood not Latine.   Indeede, the Romaine
lawes allowed no person to be carried to the warres but
hee that was in the Souldiers role : and therefore, though
Cato misliked his vnmustered person, hee misliked not his
worke.   And if hee had, *Scipio Nasica*, iudged by common
consent the best Romaine, loued him.   Both the other
Scipio Brothers, who had by their vertues no lesse sur-
names then of *Asia* and *Affrick*, so loued him that they
caused his body to be buried in their Sepulcher.   So as
Cato his authoritie being but against his person, and that
aunswered with so farre greater then himselfe, is heerein
of no validitie.

But now indeede my burthen is great; now *Plato* his name is layde vpon mee, whom, I must confesse, of all Philosophers I haue euer esteemed most worthy of reuerence, and with great reason, sith of all Philosophers he is the most poeticall. Yet if he will defile 5 the Fountaine out of which his flowing streames haue proceeded, let vs boldly examine with what reasons hee did it. First truly, a man might maliciously obiect that *Plato*, being a Philosopher, was a naturall enemie of Poets : for indeede, after the Philosophers had picked out 10 of the sweete misteries of Poetrie the right discerning true points of knowledge, they forthwith, putting it in method, and making a Schoole-arte of that which the Poets did onely teach by a diuine delightfulnes, beginning to spurne at their guides, like vngratefull Prentises, were 15 not content to set vp shops for themselues, but sought by all meanes to discredit their Maisters. Which by the force of delight beeing barred them, the lesse they could ouerthrow them, the more they hated them. For indeede, they found for *Homer* seauen Cities stroue who should 20 haue him for their Citizen ; where many Citties banished Philosophers as not fitte members to liue among them. For onely repeating certaine of *Euripides* verses, many *Athenians* had their lyues saued of the *Siracusians* ; when the *Athenians* themselues thought many Philosophers 25 vnwoorthie to liue. Certaine Poets, as *Simonides* and *Pindarus*, had so preuailed with *Hiero* the first, that of a Tirant they made him a iust King, where *Plato* could do so little with *Dionisius*, that he himselfe of a Philosopher was made a slaue. But who should doe thus, I confesse, 30 should requite the obiections made against Poets with like cauillation against Philosophers, as likewise one should doe that should bid one read *Phædrus* or *Symposium* in *Plato*, or the discourse of loue in *Plutarch*, and see whether any Poet doe authorize abhominable filthines, as they doe. 35

Againe, a man might aske out of what Common-wealth *Plato* did banish them? insooth, thence where he himselfe alloweth communitie of women. So as belike this banish-ment grewe not for effeminate wantonnes, sith little should poeticall Sonnets be hurtfull when a man might haue what woman he listed. But I honor philosophicall instructions, and blesse the wits which bred them: so as they be not abused, which is likewise stretched to Poetrie.

S. *Paule* himselfe, who (yet for the credite of Poets) alledgeth twise two Poets, and one of them by the name of a Prophet, setteth a watch-word vpon Philosophy, in-deede vpon the abuse. So dooth *Plato* vpon the abuse, not vpon Poëtrie. *Plato* found fault that the Poets of his time filled the worlde with wrong opinions of the Gods, making light tales of that vnspotted essence; and, there-fore, would not haue the youth depraued with such opinions. Heerin may much be said: let this suffice: the Poets did not induce such opinions, but dyd imitate those opinions already induced. For all the Greek stories can well testifie that the very religion of that time stoode vpon many, and many-fashioned, Gods, not taught so by the Poets, but followed according to their nature of imitation. Who list may reade in *Plutarch* the discourses of *Isis* and *Osiris*, of the cause why Oracles ceased, of the diuine prouidence, and see whether the Theologie of that nation stood not vpon such dreames which the Poets indeed supersticiously obserued, and truly (sith they had not the light of Christ) did much better in it then the Philosophers, who, shaking off superstition, brought in Atheisme. *Plato* therefore (whose authoritie I had much rather iustly conster then vniustly resist) meant not in general of Poets, in those words of which *Iulius Scaliger* saith, *Qua authoritate barbari quidam atque hispidi abuti velint ad Poetas e republica exigendos*; but only meant to driue out those wrong opinions of the Deitie (whereof now, without further law, Christianity hath taken away all the hurtful beliefe), perchance (as he thought) norished by the then esteemed Poets. And a man need goe no further then to *Plato* himselfe to know his meaning: who, in his Dialogue called *Ion*, giueth high and rightly diuine commendation to Poetrie. So as *Plato*, banishing the abuse, not the thing, not banishing it, but giuing due honor vnto it, shall be our Patron and not our aduersarie. For indeed I had much rather (sith truly I may doe it) shew theyr mistaking of *Plato* (vnder whose Lyons skin they would make an Asse-like braying against Poesie) then goe about to ouerthrow his authority, whom the wiser a man is the more iust cause he shall find to haue in admiration; especially sith he attributeth vnto Poesie more then my selfe doe, namely, to be a very inspiring of a diuine force, farre aboue mans wit, as in the afore-named Dialogue is apparant.

Of the other side, who wold shew the honors haue been by the best sort of iudgements granted them, a whole Sea of examples woulde present themselues: *Alexanders*, *Cæsars*, *Scipios*, al fauorers of Poets; *Lelius*, called the Romane *Socrates*, him selfe a Poet, so as part of *Heauton-timorumenos* in *Terence* was supposed to be made by him. And euen the Greek *Socrates*, whom *Apollo* confirmed to be the onely wise man, is sayde to haue spent part of his old tyme in putting *Esops* fables into verses. And therefore, full euill should it become his scholler *Plato* to put such words in his Maisters mouth against Poets. But what need more? *Aristotie* writes the Arte of Poesie: and why, if it should not be written? *Plutarch* teacheth the vse to be gathered of them, and how, if they should not be read? And who reades *Plutarchs* eyther historie or philosophy shall finde hee trymmeth both theyr garments with gards of Poesie. But I list not to

defend Poesie with the helpe of her vnderling Historio-
graphy. Let it suffise that it is a fit soyle for prayse to
dwell vpon ; and what dispraise may set vpon it, is eyther
easily ouer-come, or transformed into iust commendation.
5 So that, sith the excellencies of it may be so easily and
so iustly confirmed, and the low-creeping obiections so
soone troden downe ; it not being an Art of lyes, but of
true doctrine ; not of effeminatenes, but of notable stirring
of courage ; not of abusing mans witte, but of strengthning
10 mans wit ; not banished, but honored by *Plato* ; let vs
rather plant more Laurels for to engarland our Poets
heads (which honor of beeing laureat, as besides them
onely tryumphant Captaines weare, is a sufficient authority
to shewe the price they ought to be had in) then suffer the
15 ill-fauouring breath of such wrong-speakers once to blowe
vpon the cleere springs of Poesie.

But sith I haue runne so long a careere in this matter,
me thinks, before I giue my penne a fulle stop, it shalbe
but a little more lost time to inquire why England (the
20 Mother of excellent mindes) should bee growne so hard
a step-mother to Poets, who certainly in wit ought to
passe all other ; sith all onely proceedeth from their wit,
being indeede makers of themselues, not takers of others.
How can I but exclaime,

25   *Musa mihi causas memora, quo numine laeso.*

Sweete Poesie, that hath aunciently had Kings, Emperors,
Senators, great Captaines, such as, besides a thousand
others, *Dauid, Adrian, Sophocles, Germanicus,* not onely
to fauour Poets, but to be Poets. And of our neerer
30 times can present for her Patrons a *Robert,* king of Sicil,
the great king *Francis* of France, King *Iames* of Scotland.
Such Cardinals as *Bembus* and *Bibiena.* Such famous
Preachers and Teachers as *Beza* and *Melancthon.* So
learned Philosophers as *Fracastorius* and *Scaliger.* So

great Orators as *Pontanus* and *Muretus*. So piercing
wits as *George Buchanan*. So graue Counsellors as, besides many, but before all, that *Hospitall* of Fraunce,
then whom (I thinke) that Realme neuer brought forth
a more accomplished iudgement, more firmely builded 5
vpon vertue. I say these, with numbers of others, not
onely to read others Poesies, but to Poetise for others
reading. That Poesie, thus embraced in all other places,
should onely finde in our time a hard welcome in
England, I thinke the very earth lamenteth it, and ther- 10
fore decketh our Soyle with fewer Laurels then it was
accustomed. For heertofore Poets haue in England also
florished; and, which is to be noted, euen in those times
when the trumpet of *Mars* did sounde loudest. And now
that an ouer-faint quietnes should seeme to strew the 15
house for Poets, they are almost in as good reputation
as the *Mountibancks* at *Venice*. Truly euen that, as of
the one side it giueth great praise to Poesie, which like
Venus (but to better purpose) hath rather be troubled in
the net with *Mars* then enioy the homelie quiet of *Vulcan*; 20
so serues it for a peece of a reason why they are lesse
gratefull to idle England, which nowe can scarce endure
the payne of a pen. Vpon this necessarily followeth, that
base men with seruile wits vndertake it: who think it
inough if they can be rewarded of the Printer. And so 25
as *Epaminondas* is sayd, with the honor of his vertue, to
haue made an office, by his exercising it, which before
was contemptible, to become highly respected; so these,
no more but setting their names to it, by their owne dis-
gracefulnes disgrace the most gracefull Poesie. For now, 30
as if all the Muses were gotte with childe, to bring foorth
bastard Poets, without any commission they doe poste
ouer the banckes of *Helicon*, tyll they make the readers
more weary then Post-horses; while, in the mean tyme, they,

Queis meliore luto finxit praecordia Titan, 35

are better content to suppresse the out-flowing of their wit, then by publishing them to bee accounted Knights of the same order. But I that, before euer I durst aspire vnto the dignitie, am admitted into the company of the
5 Paper-blurrers, doe finde the very true cause of our wanting estimation is want of desert; taking vpon vs to be Poets in despight of *Pallas*. Nowe, wherein we want desert were a thanke-worthy labour to expresse: but if I knew, I should haue mended my selfe. But
10 I, as I neuer desired the title, so haue I neglected the meanes to come by it. Onely, ouer-mastred by some thoughts, I yeelded an inckie tribute vnto them. Mary, they that delight in Poesie it selfe should seeke to knowe what they doe, and how they doe; and, especially, looke
15 themselues in an vnflattering Glasse of reason, if they bee inclinable vnto it. For Poesie must not be drawne by the eares; it must bee gently led, or rather it must lead. Which was partly the cause that made the auncient-learned affirme it was a diuine gift, and no
20 humaine skill: sith all other knowledges lie ready for any that hath strength of witte: A Poet no industrie can make, if his owne *Genius* bee not carried vnto it: and therefore is it an old Prouerbe, *Orator fit, Poeta nascitur.* Yet confesse I alwayes that as the firtilest ground must
25 bee manured, so must the highest flying wit haue a *Dedalus* to guide him. That *Dedalus*, they say, both in this and in other, hath three wings to beare it selfe vp into the ayre of due commendation: that is, Arte, Imitation, and Exercise. But these, neyther artificiall rules
30 nor imitatiue patternes, we much cumber our selues withall. Exercise indeede wee doe, but that very fore-backwardly: for where we should exercise to know, wee exercise as hauing knowne: and so is oure braine deliuered of much matter which neuer was begotten by knowledge.
35 For, there being two principal parts, matter to be expressed

by wordes and words to expresse the matter, in neyther wee vse Arte or Imitation rightly. Our matter is *Quodlibet* indeed, though wrongly perfourming *Ouids* verse

Quicquid conabar dicere versus erat:

neuer marshalling it into an assured rancke, that almost 5 the readers cannot tell where to finde themselues.

Chaucer, vndoubtedly, did excellently in hys *Troylus* and *Cresseid*; of whom, truly, I know not whether to meruaile more, either that he in that mistie time could see so clearly, or that wee in this cleare age walke so 10 stumblingly after him. Yet had he great wants, fitte to be forgiuen in so reuerent antiquity. I account the *Mirrour of Magistrates* meetely furnished of beautiful parts; and in the Earle of Surries *Liricks* many things tasting of a noble birth, and worthy of a noble minde. 15 The *Sheapheards Kalender* hath much Poetrie in his Eglogues: indeede worthy the reading, if I be not deceiued. That same framing of his stile to an old rustick language I dare not alowe, sith neyther *Theocritus* in Greeke, *Virgill* in Latine, nor *Sanazar* in Italian did 20 affect it. Besides thesè, doe I not remember to haue seene but fewe (to speake boldely) printed, that haue poeticall sinnewes in them: for proofe whereof, let but most of the verses bee put in Prose, and then aske the meaning; and it will be found that one verse did but 25 beget another, without ordering at the first what should be at the last; which becomes a confused masse of words, with a tingling sound of ryme, barely accompanied with reason.

Our Tragedies and Comedies (not without cause cried 30 out against), obseruing rules neyther of honest ciuilitie nor of skilfull Poetrie, excepting *Gorboduck* (againe, I say, of those that I haue seene), which notwithstanding, as it is full of stately speeches and well sounding Phrases,

clyming to the height of *Seneca* his stile, and as full of
notable moralitie, which it doth most delightfully teach,
and so obtayne the very end of Poesie, yet in troth it
is very defectious in the circumstaunces, which greeueth
5 mee, because it might not remaine as an exact model of
all Tragedies. For it is faulty both in place and time,
the two necessary companions of all corporall actions.
For where the stage should alwaies represent but one
place, and the vttermost time presupposed in it should
10 be, both by *Aristotles* precept and common reason, but
one day, there is both many dayes, and many places,
inartificially imagined. But if it be so in *Gorboduck*, how
much more in al the rest? where you shal haue *Asia*
of the one side, and *Affrick* of the other, and so many
15 other vnder-kingdoms, that the Player, when he commeth
in, must euer begin with telling where he is, or els
the tale wil not be conceiued. Now ye shal haue three
Ladies walke to gather flowers, and then we must beleeue the stage to be a Garden. By and by, we heare
20 newes of shipwracke in the same place, and then wee
are to blame if we accept it not for a Rock. Vpon
the backe of that, comes out a hidious Monster, with
fire and smoke, and then the miserable beholders are
bounde to take it for a Caue. While in the meantime
25 two Armies flye in, represented with foure swords and
bucklers, and then what harde heart will not receiue it
for a pitched fielde? Now, of time they are much more
liberall, for ordinary it is that two young Princes fall in
loue. After many trauerces, she is got with childe,
30 deliuered of a faire boy; he is lost, groweth a man, falls
in loue, and is ready to get another child; and all this in
two hours space: which how absurd it is in sence euen
sence may imagine, and Arte hath taught, and all auncient
examples iustified, and, at this day, the ordinary Players
35 in Italie wil not erre in. Yet wil some bring in an

example of *Eunuchus* in *Terence*, that containeth matter
of two dayes, yet far short of twenty yeeres.   True it is,
and so was it to be playd in two daies, and so fitted to the
time it set forth.   And though *Plautus* hath in one place
done amisse, let vs hit with him, and not misse with him. 5
But they wil say, how then shal we set forth a story,
which containeth both many places and many times?
And doe they not knowe that a Tragedie is tied to the
lawes of Poesie, and not of Historie? not bound to follow
the storie, but, hauing liberty, either to faine a quite newe 10
matter, or to frame the history to the most tragicall
conueniencie.   Againe, many things may be told which
cannot be shewed, if they knowe the difference betwixt
reporting and representing.   As, for example, I may
speake (though I am heere) of *Peru*, and in speech 15
digresse from that to the description of *Calicut*; but in
action I cannot represent it without *Pacolets* horse: and
so was the manner the Auncients tooke, by some *Nuncius*,
to recount thinges done in former time or other place.
Lastly, if they wil represent an history, they must not (as 20
Horace saith) beginne *Ab ouo*, but they must come to
the principall poynt of that one action which they wil
represent.   By example this wil be best expressed.   I haue
a story of young *Polidorus*, deliuered for safeties sake,
with great riches, by his Father *Priamus* to *Polimnestor*, 25
king of *Thrace*, in the Troyan war time.   Hee after some
yeeres, hearing the ouer-throwe of *Priamus*, for to make
the treasure his owne, murthereth the child; the body of
the child is taken vp by *Hecuba*; shee the same day findeth
a slight to bee reuenged most cruelly of the Tyrant: where 30
nowe would one of our Tragedy writers begin, but with
the deliuery of the childe?   Then should he sayle ouer
into *Thrace*, and so spend I know not how many yeeres,
and trauaile numbers of places.   But where dooth *Euripides*?
Euen with the finding of the body, leauing the rest to be 35

tolde by the spirit of *Polidorus*. This need no further to
be inlarged; the dullest wit may conceiue it.

But besides these grosse absurdities, how all theyr
Playes be neither right Tragedies, nor right Comedies;
5 mingling Kings and Clownes, not because the matter so
carrieth it, but thrust in Clownes by head and shoulders, to
play a part in maiesticall matters, with neither decencie nor
discretion: So as neither the admiration and commiseration,
nor the right sportfulnes, is by their mungrell Tragy-
10 comedie obtained. I know *Apuleius* did some-what so,
but that is a thing recounted with space of time, not represented in one moment: and I knowe the Auncients haue
one or two examples of Tragy-comedies, as *Plautus* hath
Amphitrio. But, if we marke them well, we shall find,
15 that they neuer, or very daintily, match Horn-pypes and
Funeralls. So falleth it out that, hauing indeed no right
Comedy, in that comicall part of our Tragedy we haue
nothing but scurrility, vnwoorthy of any chast eares, or
some extreame shew of doltishnes, indeed fit to lift vp
20 a loude laughter, and nothing els: where the whole tract
of a Comedy shoulde be full of delight, as the Tragedy
shoulde be still maintained in a well raised admiration.
But our Comedians thinke there is no delight without
laughter; which is very wrong, for though laughter may
25 come with delight, yet commeth it not of delight, as
though delight should be the cause of laughter; but well
may one thing breed both together: nay, rather in themselues they haue, as it were, a kind of contrarietie: for
delight we scarcely doe but in things that haue a con-
30 ueniencie to our selues or to the generall nature: laughter
almost euer commeth of things most disproportioned to our
selues and nature. Delight hath a ioy in it, either perma-
nent or present. Laughter hath onely a scornful tickling.
For example, we are rauished with delight to see a faire
35 woman, and yet are far from being moued to laughter.

We laugh at deformed creatures, wherein certainely we cannot delight. We delight in good chaunces, we laugh at mischaunces; we delight to heare the happines of our friends, or Country, at which he were worthy to be laughed at that would laugh; wee shall, contrarily, laugh sometimes to finde a matter quite mistaken and goe downe the hill agaynst the byas, in the mouth of some such men, as for the respect of them one shalbe hartely sorry, yet he cannot chuse but laugh; and so is rather pained then delighted with laughter. Yet deny I not but that they may goe well together; for as in *Alexanders* picture well set out wee delight without laughter, and in twenty mad Anticks we laugh without delight, so in *Hercules*, painted with his great beard and furious countenance, in womans attire, spinning at *Omphales* commaundem∍nt, it breedeth both delight and laughter. For the representing of so strange a power in loue procureth delight: and the scornefulnes of the action stirreth laughter. But I speake to this purpose, that all the end of the comicall part bee not vpon such scornefull matters as stirreth laughter onely, but, mixt with it, that delightful teaching which is the end of Poesie. And the great fault euen in that point of laughter, and forbidden plainely by *Aristotle*, is that they styrre laughter in sinfull things, which are rather execrable then ridiculous: or in miserable, which are rather to be pittied then scorned. For what is it to make folkes gape at a wretched Begger, or a beggerly Clowne? or, against lawe of hospitality, to iest at straungers, because they speake not English so well as wee doe? what do we learne? sith it is certaine

Nil habet infelix paupertas durius in se,
Quam quod ridiculos homines facit.

But rather a busy louing Courtier, a hartles threatening *Thraso*, a selfe-wise-seeming schoolemaster, a awry-trans-

formed Traueller : These if wee sawe walke in stage
names, which wee play naturally, therein were delightfull
laughter, and teaching delightfulnes : as in the other,
the Tragedies of *Buchanan* doe iustly bring forth a diuine
5 admiration. But I haue lauished out too many wordes
of this play matter. I doe it because as they are excel-
ling parts of Poesie, so is there none so much vsed in
England, and none can be more pittifully abused. Which
like an vnmannerly Daughter, shewing a bad education,
10 causeth her mother Poesies honesty to bee called in
question.

Other sorts of Poetry almost haue we none, but that
Lyricall kind of Songs and Sonnets : which, Lord, if he
gaue vs so good mindes, how well it might be imployed,
15 and with howe heauenly fruite, both priuate and publique,
in singing the prayses of the immortall beauty, the
immortall goodnes of that God who gyueth vs hands to
write and wits to conceiue ; of which we might well want
words, but neuer matter ; of which we could turne our
20 eies to nothing, but we should euer haue new budding
occasions. But truely many of such writings as come
vnder the banner of vnresistable loue, if I were a Mistres,
would neuer perswade mee they were in loue ; so coldely
they apply fiery speeches, as men that had rather red
25 Louers writings, and so caught vp certaine swelling
phrases, which hang together like a man which once
tolde mee the winde was at North West, and by South,
because he would be sure to name windes enowe,—then
that in truth they feele those passions, which easily (as
30 I think) may be bewrayed by that same forciblenes, or
Energia (as the Greekes cal it), of the writer. But let
this bee a sufficient though short note, that wee misse the
right vse of the materiall point of Poesie.

Now, for the out-side of it, which is words, or (as
35 I may tearme it) *Diction*, it is euen well worse. So is

that honny-flowing Matron Eloquence apparelled, or
rather disguised, in a Curtizan-like painted affectation :
one time with so farre fette words, they may seeme Monsters, but must seeme straungers to any poore English
man ; another tyme, with coursing of a Letter, as if 5
they were bound to followe the method of a Dictionary ;
an other tyme, with figures and flowers, extreamelie
winter-starued.   But I would this fault were only peculier
to Versifiers, and had not as large possession among
Prose-printers, and (which is to be meruailed) among 10
many Schollers, and (which is to be pittied) among
some Preachers.   Truly I could wish, if at least I might
be so bold to wish in a thing beyond the reach of my
capacity, the diligent imitators of *Tullie* and *Demosthenes*
(most worthy to be imitated) did not so much keep 15
Nizolian Paper-bookes of their figures and phrases, as by
attentiue translation (as it were) deuoure them whole,
and make them wholly theirs.   For nowe they cast Sugar
and Spice vpon euery dish that is serued to the table ;
like those Indians, not content to weare eare-rings at 20
the fit and naturall place of the eares, but they will thrust
Iewels through their nose and lippes, because they will
be sure to be fine.   *Tullie*, when he was to driue out
Catiline, as it were with a Thunder-bolt of eloquence,
often vsed that figure of repitition, *Viuit. viuit ? imo in* 25
Senatum venit &c.   Indeed, inflamed with a well-grounded
rage, hee would haue his words (as it were) double out
of his mouth ; and so doe that artificially which we see
men doe in choller naturally.   And wee, hauing noted
the grace of those words, hale them in sometime to a 30
familier Epistle, when it were too much choller to be
chollerick.

Now for similitudes, in certaine printed discourses, I
thinke all Herbarists, all stories of Beasts, Foules, and
Fishes are rifled vp, that they come in multitudes to waite 35

vpon any of our conceits ; which certainly is as absurd a
surfet to the eares as is possible : for the force of a similitude not being to prooue anything to a contrary Disputer
but onely to explane to a willing hearer, when that is done,
5 the rest is a most tedious pratling, rather ouer-swaying
the memory from the purpose whereto they were applyed
then any whit informing the iudgement, already eyther
satisfied, or by similitudes not to be satisfied.   For my
part, I doe not doubt, when *Antonius* and *Crassus*, the
10 great forefathers of *Cicero* in eloquence, the one (as *Cicero*
testifieth of them) pretended not to know Arte, the other
not to set by it, because with a playne sensiblenes they
might win credit of popular eares ; which credit is the
neerest step to perswasion ; which perswasion is the chiefe
15 marke of Oratory ;— I doe not doubt (I say) but that they
vsed these tracks very sparingly, which who doth generally
vse any man may see doth daunce to his owne musick ;
and so be noted by the audience more careful to speake
curiously then to speake truly.

20   Vndoubtedly (at least to my opinion vndoubtedly)
I haue found in diuers smally learned Courtiers a more
sounde stile then in some professors of learning : of which
I can gesse no other cause, but that the Courtier, following
that which by practise hee findeth fittest to nature, therein
25 (though he know it not) doth according to Art, though
not by Art : where the other, vsing Art to shew Art, and
not to hide Art (as in these cases he should doe), flyeth
from nature, and indeede abuseth Art.

But what ? me thinkes I deserue to be pounded for
30 straying from Poetrie to Oratorie : but both haue such
an affinity in this wordish consideration, that I thinke
this digression will make my meaning receiue the fuller
vnderstanding : which is not to take vpon me to teach
Poets howe they should doe, but onely, finding my selfe
35 sick among the rest, to shewe some one or two spots of

the common infection growne among the most part of
Writers : that, acknowledging our selues somewhat awry,
we may bend to the right use both of matter and manner ;
whereto our language gyueth vs great occasion, beeing
indeed capable of any excellent exercising of it.　I know 5
some will say it is a mingled language.　And why not
so much the better, taking the best of both the other ?
Another will say it wanteth Grammer.　Nay truly, it hath
that prayse, that it wanteth not Grammer : for Grammer
it might haue, but it needes it not ; beeing so easie of it 10
selfe, and so voyd of those cumbersome differences of
Cases, Genders, Moodes, and Tenses, which I thinke
was a peece of the Tower of *Babilons* curse, that a man
should be put to schoole to learne his mother-tongue.
But for the vttering sweetly and properly the conceits 15
of the minde, which is the end of speech, that hath it
equally with any other tongue in the world : and is parti-
culerly happy in compositions of two or three words
together, neere the Greeke, far beyond the Latine : which
is one of the greatest beauties can be in a language.　　　20

　　Now, of versifying there are two sorts, the one Auncient,
the other Moderne : the Auncient marked the quantitie
of each silable, and according to that framed his verse ;
the Moderne obseruing onely number (with some regarde
of the accent), the chiefe life of it standeth in that lyke 25
sounding of the words, which wee call Ryme.　Whether
of these be the most excellent, would beare many speeches.
The Auncient (no doubt) more fit for Musick, both words
and tune obseruing quantity, and more fit liuely to expresse
diuers passions, by the low and lofty sounde of the well- 30
weyed silable.　The latter likewise, with hys Ryme,
striketh a certaine musick to the eare : and, in fine, sith
it dooth delight, though by another way, it obtaines the
same purpose : there beeing in eyther sweetnes, and
wanting in neither maiestie.　Truely the English, before 35

any other vulgar language I know, is fit for both sorts :
for, for the Ancient, the Italian is so full of Vowels that
it must euer be cumbred with *Elisions* ; the Dutch so,
of the other side, with Consonants, that they cannot yeeld
5 the sweet slyding fit for a Verse ; the French, in his
whole language, hath not one word that hath his accent
in the last silable, sauing two, called *Antepenultima* ; and
little more hath the Spanish : and, therefore, very grace-
lesly may they vse *Dactiles*. The English is subiect to
10 none of these defects.

  Nowe, for the ryme, though wee doe not obserue
quantity, yet wee obserue the accent very precisely :
which other languages eyther cannot doe or will not
doe so absolutely.   That *Cæsura*, or breathing place
15 in the middest of the verse, neither Italian nor Spanish
haue, the French, and we, neuer almost fayle of.   Lastly,
euen the very ryme it selfe the Italian cannot put in
the last silable, by the French named the Masculine ryme,
but still in the next to the last, which the French call the
20 Female, or the next before that, which the Italians terme
Sdrucciola.   The example of the former is *Buono, Suono*,
of the *Sdrucciola, Femina, Semina*.   The French, of the
other side, hath both the Male, as *Bon, Son*, and the
Female, as *Plaise, Taise*.   But the *Sdrucciola* hee hath
25 not : where the English hath all three, as *Due, True,
Father, Rather, Motion, Potion* ; with much more which
might be sayd, but that I finde already the triflingnes
of this discourse is much too much enlarged.

  So that sith the euer-praise-worthy Poesie is full of
30 vertue-breeding delightfulnes, and voyde of no gyfte that
ought to be in the noble name of learning : sith the blames
laid against it are either false or feeble ; sith the cause why
it is not esteemed in Englande is the fault of Poet-apes,
not Poets ; sith, lastly, our tongue is most fit to honor
35 Poesie, and to bee honored by Poesie ; I coniure you all

that haue had the euill lucke to reade this incke-wasting
toy of mine, euen in the name of the nyne Muses, no
more to scorne the sacred misteries of Poesie, no more
to laugh at the name of Poets, as though they were next
inheritours to Fooles, no more to iest at the reuerent
title of a Rymer; but to beleeue, with *Aristotle*, that they
were the auncient Treasurers of the Græcians Diuinity.
To beleeue, with *Bembus*, that they were first bringers
in of all ciuilitie. To beleeue, with *Scaliger*, that no
Philosophers precepts can sooner make you an honest
man then the reading of *Virgill*. To beleeue, with *Clauserus*, the Translator of *Cornutus*, that it pleased the
heauenly Deitié, by *Hesiod* and *Homer*, vnder the vayle
of fables, to giue vs all knowledge, Logick, Rethorick,
Philosophy, naturall and morall; and *Quid non*? To
beleeue, with me, that there are many misteries contained
in Poetrie, which of purpose were written darkely, least
by prophane wits it should bee abused. To beleeue, with
Landin, that they are so beloued of the Gods that whatsoeuer they write proceeds of a diuine fury. Lastly, to
beleeue themselues, when they tell you they will make
you immortall by their verses.

Thus doing, your name shal florish in the Printers
shoppes; thus doing, you shall bee of kinne to many
a poeticall Preface; thus doing, you shall be most fayre,
most ritch, most wise, most all; you shall dwell vpon
Superlatiues. Thus dooing, though you be *Libertino patre
natus*, you shall suddenly grow *Herculea proles*,

> *Si quid mea carmina possunt.*

Thus doing, your soule shal be placed with *Dantes*
Beatrix, or *Virgils Anchises*. But if (fie of such a but)
you be borne so neere the dull making *Cataphract* of
Nilus that you cannot heare the Plannet-like Musick of
Poetrie, if you haue so earth-creeping a mind that it

cannot lift it selfe vp to looke to the sky of Poetry, or rather, by a certaine rusticall disdaine, will become such a Mome as to be a *Momus* of Poetry; then, though I will not wish vnto you the Asses eares of *Midas*, nor to
5 bee driuen by a Poets verses (as *Bubonax* was) to hang himselfe, nor to be rimed to death, as is sayd to be doone in Ireland; yet thus much curse I must send you, in the behalfe of all Poets, that while you liue, you liue in loue, and neuer get fauour for lacking skill of a *Sonnet*; and
10 when you die, your memory die from the earth for want of an *Epitaph*.

KING JAMES VI

(*ANE SCHORT TREATISE CONTEINING SOME REULIS AND CAUTELIS
TO BE OBSERUIT AND ESCHEWIT IN SCOTTIS POESIE*)

1584

[*Ane schort | Treatise, | conteining some reulis | and cautelis to be
obseruit and | eschewit in Scottis | Poesie*, was issued in the
volume of *The Essayes of a Prentise, in the Diuine Art of
Poesie,* printed at Edinburgh by Thomas Vautroullier in 1584.
The text is taken from the copy which was formerly in the
possession of the poet William Drummond of Hawthornden,
and was presented by him to the Library of the University
of Edinburgh (De. 2. 57). The *Treatise* begins at sig. K.
On the back of the special title-page is printed ' A Qvadrain
of Alexandrin Verse, declaring to qvhome the Authour
hes directit his labour.

> *To ignorants obdurde, quhair wilful errour lyis,*
> *Nor yit to curious folks, quhilks carping dois deiect thee,*
> *Nor yit to learned men, quha thinks thame onelie wyis,*
> *Bot to the docile bairns of knawledge I direct thee.'*

The incorporation in a book of *Elizabethan* texts of a tract
on Scots verse, by a Scottish king, requires no apology,
especially when its relation to earlier Southern work can
be clearly shown (see *Introduction*).

THE PREFACE TO THE READER.

THE cause why (docile Reader) I haue not dedicat this
short treatise to any particular personis (as commounly workis vsis to be) is, that I esteme all thais quha
hes already some beginning of knawledge, with ane earnest ʂ

desyre to atteyne to farther, alyke meit for the reading of this worke, or any vther, quhilk may help thame to the atteining to thair foirsaid desyre. Bot as to this work, quhilk is intitulit *The Reulis and cautelis to be obseruit and* 5 *eschewit in Scottis Poesie*, ye may maruell parauenture quhairfore I sould haue writtin in that mater, sen sa mony learnit men, baith of auld and of late, hes already written thairof in dyuers and sindry languages : I answer that, nochtwithstanding, I haue lykewayis writtin of it, for 10 twa caussis. The ane is : As for them that wrait of auld, lyke as the tyme is changeit sensyne, sa is the ordour of Poesie changeit. For then they obseruit not *Flowing*, nor eschewit not *Ryming in termes*, besydes sindrie vther thingis, quhilk now we obserue and eschew, and dois weil 15 in sa doing : because that now, quhen the warld is waxit auld, we haue all their opinionis in writ, quhilk were learned before our tyme, besydes our awin ingynis, quhair as they then did it onelie be thair awin ingynis, but help of any vther. Thairfore, quhat I speik of Poesie now, I speik of 20 it as being come to mannis age and perfectioun, quhair as then it was bot in the infancie and chyldheid. The vther cause is : That as for thame that hes written in it of late, there hes neuer ane of thame written in our language. For albeit sindrie hes written of it in English, quhilk is 25 lykest to our language, yit we differ from thame in sindrie reulis of Poesie, as ye will find be experience. I haue lykewayis omittit dyuers figures, quhilkis are necessare to be vsit in verse, for twa causis. The ane is, because they are vsit in all languages, and thairfore are spokin of be 30 *Du Bellay*, and sindrie vtheris, quha hes written in this airt. Quhairfore, gif I wrait of them also, it sould seme that I did bot repete that quhilk they haue written, and yit not sa weil as they haue done already. The vther cause is that they are figures of Rhetorique and Dialectique, 35 quhilkis airtis I professe nocht, and thairfore will apply to my selfe the counsale quhilk *Apelles* gaue to the shoomaker, quhen he said to him, seing him find falt with the shankis of the Image of *Venus*, efter that he had found falt with the pantoun, *Ne sutor vltra crepidam.*

I will also wish yow (docile Reidar) that, or ye cummer yow with reiding thir reulis, ye may find in your self sic a beginning of Nature as ye may put in practise in your verse many of thir foirsaidis preceptis, or euer ye sie them as they are heir set doun. For gif Nature be nocht the cheif worker in this airt, Reulis wilbe bot a band to Nature, and will mak yow within short space weary of the haill airt: quhair as, gif Nature be cheif, and bent to it, reulis will be ane help and staff to Nature. I will end heir, lest my preface be langer nor my purpose and haill mater following: wishing yow, docile Reidar, als gude succes and great proffeit by reiding this short treatise as I tuke earnist and willing panis to blok it, as ye sie, for your cause. Fare weill.

I haue insert in the hinder end of this Treatise maist kyndis of versis quhilks are not cuttit or brokin, bot alyke many feit in euerie lyne of the verse, and how they are commounly namit, with my opinioun for quhat subiectis ilk kynde of thir verse is meitest to be vsit.

To knaw the quantitie of your lang or short fete in they lynes, quhilk I haue put in the reule quhilk teachis yow to knaw quhat is *Flowing*, I haue markit the lang fute with this mark —, and abone the heid of the shorte fute I haue put this mark ◡.

SONNET OF THE AVTHOVR

TO THE READER.

SEN for your saik I wryte vpon your airt,
Apollo, Pan, and ye O Musis nyne,
And thou, O Mercure, for to help thy pairt
I do implore, sen thou be thy ingyne,
Nixt efter Pan had found the quhissill, syne
Thou did perfyte that quhilk he bot espyit:
And efter that made Argus for to tyne
(Quha kepit Io) all his windois by it.
Concurre ye Gods, it can not be denyit,
Sen in your airt of Poësie I wryte.
Auld birds to learne by teiching it is tryit:
Sic docens discens, *gif ye help to dyte.*
  Then Reidar sie of nature thou haue pairt,
  Syne laikis thou nocht bot heir to reid the airt.

SONNET DECIFRING

THE PERFYTE POETE.

ANE rype ingyne, ane quick and walkned witt,
With sommair reasons, suddenlie applyit,
For euery purpose vsing reasons fitt,
With skilfulnes, where learning may be spyit,
With pithie wordis, for to expres yow by it
His full intention in his proper leid,
The puritie quhairof weill hes he tryit,
With memorie to keip quhat he dois reid,
With skilfulnes and figuris, quhilks proceid
From Rhetorique, *with euerlasting fame,*
With vthers woundring, preassing with all speid
For to atteine to merite sic a name:
All thir into the perfyte Poëte be.
Goddis, grant I may obteine the Laurell trie.

P 2

THE REVLIS AND CAVTELIS TO BE OB-SERVIT AND ESCHEWIT IN SCOTTIS POESIE.

Chap. I.

First, ye sall keip iust cullouris, quhairof the cautelis are thir.

That ye ryme nocht twyse in ane syllabe. As for exemple, that ye make not *proue* and *reproue* ryme together, nor *houe*, for houeing on hors bak, and *behoue*.

That ye ryme ay to the hinmest lang syllabe (with accent) in the lyne, suppose it be not the hinmest syllabe in the lyne, as *bakbyte yow* and *out flyte yow*. It rymes in *byte* and *flyte*, because of the lenth of the syllabe, and accent being there, and not in *yow*, howbeit it be the hinmest syllabe of ather of the lynis. Or *question* and *digestion* : It rymes in *ques* and *ges*, albeit they be bot the antepenult syllabis, and vther twa behind ilkane of thame.

Ye aucht alwayis to note that, as in thir foirsaidis or the lyke wordis, it rymes in the hinmest lang syllabe in the lyne, althoucht there be vther short syllabis behind it, sa is the hinmest lang syllabe the hinmest fute, suppose there be vther short syllabis behind it, quhilkis are eatin vp in the pronounceing and na wayis comptit as fete.

Ye man be war likewayis (except necessitie compell yow) with *Ryming in Termis*, quhilk is to say, that your first or hinmest word in the lyne exceid not twa or thre syllabis at the maist, vsing thrie als seindill as ye can. The cause quhairfore ye sall not place a lang word first in the lyne is that all lang words hes ane syllabe in them sa verie lang, as the lenth thairof eatis vp in the pronouncing euin the vther syllabes quhilks ar placit lang in the same word, and thairfore spillis the flowing of that lyne. As

for exemple in this word, *Arabia*, the second syllable (*ra*)
is sa lang that it eatis vp in the prononcing (*a*), quhilk is
the hinmest syllabe of the same word. Quhilk (*a*) althocht
it be in a lang place, yit it kythis not sa, because of the
5 great lenth of the preceding syllabe (*ra*). As to the cause
quhy ye sall not put a lang word hinmest in the lyne, it
is because that the lenth of the secound syllabe (*ra*),
eating vp the lenth of the vther lang syllabe (*a*), makis it
to serue bot as a tayle vnto it, together with the short
10 syllabe preceding. And because this tayle nather seruis
for cullour nor fute, as I spak before, it man be thairfore
repetit in the nixt lyne ryming vnto it, as it is set doune
in the first : quhilk makis that ye will scarcely get many
wordis to ryme vnto it, yea nane at all will ye finde to
15 ryme to sindrie vther langer wordis. Thairfore cheifly be
warre of inserting sic lang wordis hinmest in the lyne, for
the cause quhilk I last allegit. Besydis that, nather first
nor last in the lyne, it keipis na *Flowing*. The reulis and
cautelis quhairof are thir, as followis.

20 ## CHAP. II.

FIRST, ye man vnderstand that all syllabis are deuydit
in thrie kindes : That is, some schort, some lang, and
some indifferent. Be indifferent I meane they quhilk are
ather lang or short, according as ye place thame.
25 The forme of placeing syllabes in verse is this. That
your first syllabe in the lyne be short, the second lang,
the thrid short, the fourt lang, the fyft short, the sixt lang,
and sa furth to the end of the lyne. Alwayis tak heid
that the nomber of your fete in euery lyne be euin, and
30 nocht odde : as four, six, aucht, or ten, and not thrie,
fyue, seuin, or nyne, except it be in broken verse, quhilkis
are out of reul and daylie inuentit be dyuers Poetis. Bot
gif ye wald ask me the reulis quhairby to knaw euerie ane
of thir thre foirsaidis kyndis of syllabes, I answer your

eare man be the onely iudge and discerner thairof. And to proue this, I remit to the iudgement of the same, quhilk of thir twa lynis following flowis best,

Into the Sea then Lucifer vpsprang,

In the Sea then Lucifer to vpsprang. 5

I doubt not bot your eare makkis you easilie to persaue that the first lyne flowis weil and the vther nathing at all. The reasoun is because the first lyne keips the reule abone written—to wit, the first fute short, the secound lang, and sa furth, as I shewe before—quhair as the vther is direct contrair to the same. Bot specially tak heid, quhen your lyne is of fourtene, that your *Sectioun* in aucht be a lang monosyllabe, or ellis the hinmest syllabe of a word alwais being lang, as I said before. The cause quhy it man be ane of thir twa is for the Musique, because that quhen your lyne is ather of xiiij or xij fete it wilbe drawin sa lang in the singing, as ye man rest in the middes of it, quhilk is the *Sectioun* : sa as, gif your *Sectioun* be nocht ather a monosyllabe, or ellis the hinmest syllabe of a word, as I said before, bot the first syllabe of a polysyllabe, the Musique sall make yow sa to rest in the middes of that word, as it sall cut the ane half of the word fra the vther, and sa sall mak it seme twa different wordis, that is bot ane. This aucht onely to be obseruit in thir foirsaid lang lynis : for the shortnes of all shorter lynis then thir before mentionat is the cause that the Musique makis na rest in the middes of thame, and thairfore thir obseruationis seruis nocht for thame. Onely tak heid that the *Sectioun* in thame kythe something langer nor any vther feit in that lyne, except the secound and the last, as I haue said before.

Ye man tak heid lykewayis that your langest lynis

exceid nochte fourtene fete, and that your shortest be
nocht within foure.

Remember also to mak a *Sectioun* in the middes of
euery lyne, quhether the lyne be lang or short.   Be
5 *Sectioun* I mean, that gif your lyne be of fourtene fete,
your aucht fute man not only be langer then the seuint, or
vther short fete, but also langer nor any vther lang fete in
the same lyne, except the secound and the hinmest.   Or
gif your lyne be of twelf fete, your *Sectioun* to be in the
10 sext.   Or gif of ten, your *Sectioun* to be in the sext also.
The cause quhy it is not in fyue is because fyue is odde,
and euerie odde fute is short.   Or gif your lyne be of
aucht fete, your *Sectioun* to be in the fourt.   Gif of sex, in
the fourt also.   Gif of four, your *Sectioun* to be in twa.
15 Ye aucht likewise be war with oft composing your haill
lynis of monosyllabis onely (albeit our language haue sa
many as we can nocht weill eschewe it), because the maist
pairt of thame are indifferent, and may be in short or lang
place, as ye like.   Some wordis of dyuers syllabis are
20 likewayis indifferent, as

> *Thairfore, restore.*
>
> *I thairfore, then.*

In the first *thairfore*, (*thair*) is short and (*fore*) is lang ;
in the vther, (*thair*) is lang and (*fore*) is short ; and yit
25 baith flowis alike weill.   Bot thir indifferent wordis, composit of dyuers syllabes, are rare, suppose in monosyllabes
commoun.   The cause then quhy ane haill lyne aucht
nocht to be composit of monosyllabes only is that, they
being for the maist pairt indifferent, nather the secound,
30 hinmest, nor *Sectioun* will be langer nor the other lang
fete in the same lyne.   Thairfore ye man place a word
composit of dyuers syllabes, and not indifferent, ather in
the secound, hinmest, or *Sectioun,* or in all thrie.

Ye man also tak heid that quhen thare fallis any short

syllabis efter the last lang syllabe in the lyne, that ye
repeit thame in the lyne quhilk rymis to the vther, even as
ye set them downe in the first lyne : as for exempill, ye
man not say

> *Then feir nocht* 5
> *Nor heir ocht,*

Bot

> *Then feir nocht*
> *Nor heir nocht,*

repeting the same *nocht* in baith the lynis : because this 10
syllabe *nocht,* nather seruing for cullour nor fute, is bot
a tayle to the lang fute preceding, and thairfore is repetit
lykewayis in the nixt lyne quhilk rymes vnto it euin as
it [is] set doun in the first.

There is also a kynde of indifferent wordis asweill as of 15
syllabis, albeit few in nomber. The nature quhairof is
that gif ye place thame in the begynning of a lyne they
are shorter be a fute nor they are gif ye place thame
hinmest in the lyne, as

> *Sen patience I man haue perforce,*
> *I liue in hope with patience.* 20

Ye se there are bot aucht fete in ather of baith thir lynis
abone written. The cause quhairof is that *patience* in the
first lyne, in respect it is in the beginning thairof, is bot
of twa fete, and in the last lyne of thrie, in respect it is 25
the hinmest word of that lyne. To knaw and discerne
thir kynde of wordis from vtheris, your eare man be the
onely iudge, as of all the vther parts of *Flowing,* the verie
twichestane quhairof is Musique.

I haue teachit yow now shortly the reulis of *Ryming,* 30
Fete, and *Flowing.* There restis yet to teache yow the
wordis, sentences, and phrasis necessair for a Poete to
vse in his verse, quhilk I haue set doun in reulis, as efter
followis.

Chap. III.

First, that in quhatsumeuer ye put in verse, ye put in na wordis ather *metri causa* or yit for filling furth the nomber of the fete, bot that they be all sa necessare as ye sould be constrainit to vse thame in cace ye were speiking the same purpose in prose. And thairfore that your wordis appeare to haue cum out willingly, and by nature, and not to haue bene thrawin out constrainedly, be compulsioun.

That ye eschew to insert in your verse a lang rable of mennis names, or names of tounis, or sik vther names, because it is hard to mak many lang names all placit together to flow weill. Thairfore, quhen that fallis out in your purpose, ye sall ather put bot twa or thrie of thame in euerie lyne, mixing vther wordis amang thame, or ellis specifie bot twa or thre of them at all, saying (*With the laif of that race*), or (*With the rest in thay pairtis*), or sic vther lyke wordis: as for example,

> *Out through his cairt, quhair Eous was eik*
> *With other thre, quhilk Phaëton had drawin.*

Ye sie thair is bot ane name there specifeit, to serue for vther thrie of that sorte.

Ye man also take heid to frame your wordis and sentencis according to the mater: As in Flyting and Inuectiues your wordis to be cuttit short, and hurland ouer heuch. For thais quhilkis are cuttit short, I meane be sic wordis as thir,

> *Iis neir cair,*

for

> *I sall neuer cair,* gif your subiect were of loue, or tragedies. Because in thame your words man be drawin lang, quhilkis in Flyting man be short.

Ye man lykewayis tak heid that ye waill your wordis

according to the purpose: as in ane heich and learnit purpose to vse heich, pithie, and learnit wordis.

Gif your purpose be of loue, to vse commoun language, with some passionate wordis.

Gif your purpose be of tragicall materis, to vse lamentable wordis, with some heich, as rauishit in admiratioun.

Gif your purpose be of landwart effairis, to vse corruptit and vplandis wordis.

And finally, quhatsumeuer be your subiect, to vse *vocabula artis*, quhairby ye may the mair viuelie represent that persoun quhais pairt ye paint out.

This is likewayis neidfull to be vsit in sentences, als weill as in wordis. As gif your subiect be heich and learnit, to vse learnit and infallible reasonis, prouin be necessities.

Gif your subiect be of loue, to vse wilfull reasonis, proceding rather from passioun nor reasoun.

Gif your subiect be of landwart effaris, to vse sklender reasonis, mixt with grosse ignorance, nather keiping forme nor ordour. And sa furth, euer framing your reasonis according to the qualitie of your subiect.

Let all your verse be *Literall*, sa far as may be, quhatsumeuer kynde they be of, bot speciallie *Tumbling* verse for flyting. Be *Literall* I meane that the maist pairt of your lyne sall rynne vpon a letter, as this tumbling lyne rynnis vpon F.

Fetching fude for to feid it fast furth of the Farie.

Ye man obserue that thir *Tumbling* verse flowis not on that fassoun as vtheris dois. For all vtheris keipis the reule quhilk I gaue before, to wit, the first fute short, the secound lang, and sa furth. Quhair as thir hes twa short and ane lang throuch all the lyne, quhen they keip ordour: albeit the maist pairt of thame be out of ordour, and keipis na kynde nor reule of *Flowing*, and for that

cause are callit *Tumbling* verse : except the short lynis
of aucht in the hinder end of the verse, the quhilk flowis
as vther verses dois, as ye will find in the hinder end
of this buke, quhair I giue exemple of sindrie kyndis of
5 versis.

Chap. IIII.

MARK also thrie speciall ornamentis to verse, quhilkis
are *Comparisons, Epithetis*, and *Prouerbis.*

As for *Comparisons*, take heid that they be sa proper for
10 the subiect that nather they be ouer bas, gif your subiect
be heich, for then sould your subiect disgrace your *Comparisoun*, nather your *Comparisoun* be heich quhen your
subiect is basse, for then sall your *Comparisoun* disgrace
your subiect. Bot let sic a mutuall correspondence and
15 similitude be betwix them as it may appeare to be a meit
Comparisoun for sic a subiect, and sa sall they ilkane
decore vther.

As for *Epithetis*, it is to descryue brieflie, *en passant,*
the naturall of euerie thing ye speik of, be adding the
20 proper adiectiue vnto it, quhairof there are twa fassons.
The ane is to descryue it be making a corruptit worde,
composit of twa dyuers simple wordis, as

Apollo gyde-Sunne.

The vther fasson is be *Circumlocution*, as

25 *Apollo, reular of the Sunne.*

I esteme this last fassoun best, because it expressis the
authoris meaning als weill as the vther, and yit makis na
corruptit wordis, as the vther dois.

As for the *Prouerbis*, they man be proper for the sub-
30 iect, to beautifie it, chosen in the same forme as the
Comparisoun.

Chap. V.

It is also meit, for the better decoratioun of the verse, to vse sumtyme the figure of Repetitioun, as

> *Quhylis ioy rang,*
> *Quhylis noy rang. &c.* 5

Ye sie this word *quhylis* is repetit heir. This forme of repetitioun, sometyme vsit, decoris the verse very mekle. Yea, quhen it cummis to purpose, it will be cumly to repete sic a word aucht or nyne tymes in a verse.

Chap. VI. 10

Ye man also be warre with composing ony thing in the same maner as hes bene ower oft. vsit of before. As in speciall, gif ye speik of loue, be warre ye descryue your *Loues* makdome, or her fairnes. And siclyke that ye descryue not the morning and rysing of the Sunne in 15 the Preface of your verse ; for thir thingis are sa oft and dyuerslie writtin vpon be Poëtis already, that gif ye do the lyke it will appeare ye bot imitate, and that it cummis not of your awin *Inuentioun*, quhilk is ane of the cheif properteis of ane Poete. Thairfore, gif your subiect be to 20 prayse your *Loue*, ye sall rather prayse hir vther qualiteis, nor her fairnes or hir shaip ; or ellis ye sall speik some lytill thing of it, and syne say that your wittis are sa smal, and your vtterance sa barren, that ye can not discryue any part of hir worthelie ; remitting alwayis to the Reider to 25 iudge of hir, in respect sho matches, or rather excellis, *Venus,* or any woman, quhome to it sall please yow to compaire her. Bot gif your subiect be sic as ye man speik some thing of the morning or Sunne rysing, tak heid that, quhat name ye giue to the Sunne, the Mone, 30 or vther starris the ane tyme, gif ye happin to wryte thairof another tyme, to change thair names. As gif ye call the Sunne *Titan* at a tyme, to call him *Phœbus* or *Apollo* the vther tyme; and siclyke the Mone, and vther Planettis.

CHAP. VII.

5   Bot sen *Inuention* is ane of the cheif vertewis in a Poete, it is best that ye inuent your awin subiect your self, and not to compose of sene subiectis. Especially translating any thing out of vther language, quhilk doing, ye not onely essay not your awin ingyne of *Inuentioun*, bot be the same
10 meanes ye are bound, as to a staik, to follow that buikis phrasis quhilk ye translate.

Ye man also be war of wryting any thing of materis of commoun weill, or vther sic graue sene subiectis (except Metaphorically, of manifest treuth opinly knawin, yit nocht-
15 withstanding vsing it very seindil), because nocht onely ye essay nocht your awin *Inuentioun*, as I spak before, bot lykewayis they are to graue materis for a Poet to mell in. Bot because ye can not haue the *Inuentioun*, except it come of Nature, I remit it thairvnto, as the cheif cause
20 not onely of *Inuentioun* bot also of all the vther pairtis of Poesie. For airt is onely bot ane help and a remembraunce to Nature, as I shewe yow in the Preface.

CHAP. VIII.

TUICHING THE KYNDIS OF VERSIS MENTIONAT IN THE
25 ### PREFACE.

First, there is ryme quhilk seruis onely for lang historeis, and yit are nocht verse. As for exemple,

> *In Maii when that the blissefull Phœbus bricht,*
> *The lamp of ioy, the heauens gemme of licht,*
30 > *The goldin cairt, and the etheriall King,*
> *With purpour face in Orient dois spring,*

> *Maist angel-lyke ascending in his sphere,*
> *And birds with all thair heauenlie voces cleare*
> *Dois mak a sweit and heauinly harmony,*
> *And fragrant flours dois spring vp lustely:*
> *Into this season, sweitest of delyte,*   5
> *To walk I had a lusty appetyte.*

And sa furth.

¶ For the descriptioun of Heroique actis, Martiall and knichtly faittis of armes, vse this kynde of verse following, callit *Heroicall,* as   10

> *Meik mundane mirrour, myrrie and modest,*
> *Blyth, kynde, and courtes, comelie, clene, and chest,*
> *To all exemple for thy honestie,*
> *As richest rose, or rubie, by the rest,*
> *With gracis graue, and gesture maist digest,*   15
> *Ay to thy honnour alwayis hauing eye,*
> *Were fassons fliemde, they micht be found in the:*
> *Of blissings all, be blyth, thow hes the best ;*
> *With euerie berne belouit for to be.*

¶ For any heich and graue subiectis, specially drawin 20 out of learnit authouris, vse this kynde of verse following, callit *Ballat Royal,* as

> *That nicht he ceist, and went to bed, bot greind*
> *Yit fast for day, and thocht the nicht to lang.*
> *At last Diana doun her head recleind*   25
> *Into the sea.   Then Lucifer vpsprang,*
> *Auroras post, whome sho did send amang*
> *The Ieittie cludds, for to foretell ane hour,*
> *Before sho stay her tears, quhilk Ouide sang*
> *Fell for her loue, quhilk turnit in a flour.*   30

¶ For tragicall materis, complaintis, or testamentis, vse this kynde of verse following, callit *Troilus* verse, as

To thee, Echo, and thow to me agane,
In the desert, amangs the wods and wells,
Quhair destinie hes bound the to remane,
But company, within the firths and fells,
5   *Let vs complein, with wofull youtts and yells,*
A shaft, a shotter, that our harts hes slane :
To thee, Echo, and thow to me agane.

¶ For flyting, or Inuectiues, vse this kynde of verse following, callit *Rouncefallis* or *Tumbling* verse.

10 *In the hinder end of haruest, vpon Alhallow ene,*
Quhen our gude nichtbors rydis (nou gif I reid richt),
Some bucklit on a benwod, and some on a bene,
Ay trottand into troupes fra the twylicht :
Some sadland a sho ape, all grathed into grene :
15 *Some hotcheand on a hemp stalk, hovand on a heicht :*
The king of Fary with the Court of the Elf quene,
With many elrage Incubus, rydand that nicht :
      There ane elf on ane ape ane vnsell begat,
      Besyde a pot baith auld and worne :
20   *This bratshard in ane bus was borne :*
      They fand a monster, on the morne,
      War facit nor a Cat.

¶ For compendious praysing of any bukes, or the authouris thairof, or ony argumentis of vther historeis, 25 quhair sindrie sentences and change of purposis are re-quyrit, vse *Sonet* verse, of fourtene lynis, and ten fete in euery lyne. The exemple quhairof I neid nocht to shaw yow, in respect I haue set doun twa in the beginning of this treatise.

30 ¶ In materis of loue, vse this kynde of verse, quhilk we call *Commoun* verse, as

    Quhais answer made thame nocht sa glaid
    That they sould thus the victors be,

As euen the answer quhilk I haid
Did greatly ioy and confort me :
Quhen lo, this spak Apollo myne,
All that thou seikis, it sall be thyne.

¶ Lyke verse of ten fete, as this foirsaid is of aucht, ye 5
may vse lykewayis in loue materis : as also all kyndis of
cuttit and brokin verse, quhairof new formes are daylie
inuentit according to the Poëtes pleasour, as

Quha wald haue tyrde to heir that tone,
Quhilk birds corroborat ay abone   10
  Throuch schouting of the Larkis !
They sprang sa heich into the skyes,
Quhill Cupide walknis with the cryis
  Of Naturis chapell Clarkis.
Then, leauing all the Heauins aboue,   15
  He lichted on the eard.
Lo ! how that lytill God of loue
  Before me then appeard,
So myld-lyke,
And chyld-lyke,   *With bow thre quarters skant*
So moylie
And coylie,   *He lukit lyke a Sant.*   20

And sa furth.

¶ This onely kynde of brokin verse abonewrittin man
of necessitie, in thir last short fete, as *so moylie and*
coylie, haue bot twa fete and a tayle to ilkane of thame,
as ye sie, to gar the cullour and ryme be in the penult 25
syllabe.

¶ And of thir foirsaidis kyndes of ballatis of haill verse,
and not cuttit or brokin as this last is, gif ye lyke to put
ane owerword till ony of thame, as making the last lyne
of the first verse to be the last lyne of euerie vther verse 30
in that ballat, [will] set weill for loue materis.

Bot besydis thir kyndes of brokin or cuttit verse, quhilks ar inuentit daylie be Poetis, as I shewe before, there are sindrie kyndes of haill verse, with all thair lynis alyke lang, quhilk I haue heir omittit, and tane bot onelie
5 thir few kyndes abone specifeit as the best, quhilk may be applyit to ony kynde of subiect, bot rather to thir quhairof I haue spokin before.

WILLIAM WEBBE

(*A Discourse of English Poetrie*)

1586

[*A Discourse of Eng\lish Poetrie. || Together with the Authors\ iudgment, touching the re-\formation of our Eng-\lish Verse. || By William Webbe | Graduate* was printed at London in 1586 by John Charlewood for Robert Walley (1 vol. 4to). The text is taken from the rare copy in the Bodleian (Malone 708). Webbe dedicated this 'draught of English Poetry' to Edward Suliard, of Flemyngs, in the parish of Runwell, Essex, to whose sons Edward and Thomas he had been tutor. 'I sende it into your sight, not as anie wyttie peece of worke that may delight you, but being a sleight somewhat compyled for recreation in the intermyssions of my daylie businesse (euen thys Summer Eueninges), as a token of that earnest and vn-quenchable desyre I haue to shewe my selfe duetifull and welwylling towardes you[1].']

A PREFACE TO THE NOBLE POETS OF ENGLANDE.

AMONG the innumerable sortes of Englyshe Bookes, and infinite fardles of printed pamphlets, wherewith thys Countrey is pestered, all shoppes stuffed, and euery 5 study furnished, the greatest part I thinke, in any one kinde, are such as are either meere Poeticall, or which tende in some respecte (as either in matter or forme) to

---

[1] Warton informs us that Edward Hake wrote a tract entitled *The Touch-stone of Wittes* (12mo, black letter; London, Edmund Botifaunt, 1588), 'chiefly compiled with some slender additions from William Webbe's *Discourse of English Poetrie*' (*Hist.* iv. 97). He quotes one sentence from it : 'Then haue we the Mirrour of Magistrates lately augmented by my friend mayster Iohn Higgins, and penned by the choysest learned wittes, which, for the stately-proportioned uaine of

Poetry. Of such Bookes therfore, sith I haue beene
one that haue had a desire to reade not the fewest, and
because it is an argument which men of great learning
haue no leysure to handle, or at least hauing to doo with
5 more serious matters doo least regarde, if I write something concerning what I thinke of our English Poets, or
aduenture to sette downe my simple iudgement of English
Poetrie, I trust the learned Poets will giue me leaue, and
vouchsafe my Booke passage, as beeing for the rudenesse
10 thereof no preiudice to their noble studies, but euen (as
my intent is) an *instar cotis* to stirre vppe some other of
meete abilitie to bestowe trauell in this matter : whereby
I thinke wee may not onelie get the meanes, which wee
yet want, to discerne betweene good writers and badde,
15 but perhappes also challenge from the rude multitude of
rusticall Rymers, who will be called Poets, the right
practise and orderly course of true Poetry.

It is to be wondred at of all, and is lamented of manie,
that where as all kinde of good learning haue aspyred
20 to royall dignitie and statelie grace in our English tongue,
being not onelie founded, defended, maintained, and enlarged, but also purged from faultes, weeded of errours,
and pollished from barbarousnes, by men of great
authoritie and iudgement, onelie Poetrie hath founde
25 fewest frends to amende it, those that can reseruing theyr
skyll to themselues, those that cannot running headlong
vppon it, thinking to garnish it with their deuises, but
more corrupting it with fantasticall errours. What shoulde
be the cause that our English speeche, in some of the
30 wysest mens iudgements, hath neuer attained to anie
sufficient ripenes, nay not ful auoided the reproch of

the heroick style and good meetly
proportion of uerse, may challenge
the best of Lydgate, and all our
late rhymers.' This is all we know
of Hake's volume. Warton does
not tell us where he saw the
text. No copy is known to be
preserved.

barbarousnes in Poetry? The rudenes of the Countrey,
or basenesse of wytts; or the course *Dialect* of the
speeche? Experience vtterlie disproueth it to be anie of
these. What then? Surelie the canckred enmitie of
curious custome: which as it neuer was great freend to 5
any good learning, so in this hath it grounded in the most
such a negligent perswasion of an impossibilitie in matching the best, that the finest witts and most diuine heades
haue contented themselues with a base kinde of fingering,
rather debasing theyr faculties in setting forth theyr skyll 10
in the coursest manner, then for breaking custome they
would labour to adorne their Countrey and aduaunce their
style with the highest and most learnedst toppe of true
Poetry. The rudenes or vnaptnesse of our Countrey to
be either none or no hinderaunce, if reformation were 15
made accordinglie, the exquisite excellency in all kindes
of good learning nowe flourishing among vs, inferiour to
none other nation, may sufficiently declare.

That there be as sharpe and quicke wittes in England
as euer were among the peerelesse Grecians or renowmed 20
Romaines, it were a note of no witte at all in me to deny.
And is our speeche so course, or our phrase so harshe,
that Poetry cannot therein finde a vayne whereby it may
appeare like it selfe? Why should we think so basely of
this? rather then of her sister, I meane Rhetoricall 25
Eloquution? which as they were by byrth Twyns, by kinde
the same, by originall of one descent, so no doubt, as
Eloquence hath founde such fauourers in the English
tongue, as she frequenteth not any more gladly, so would
Poetrye, if there were the like welcome and entertainment 30
gyuen her by our English Poets, without question aspyre
to wonderfull perfection, and appeare farre more gorgeous
and delectable among vs. Thus much I am bolde to say
in behalfe of Poetrie, not that I meane to call in question
the reuerend and learned workes of Poetrie written in 35

our tongue by men of rare iudgement and most excellent
Poets, but euen as it were by way of supplication to the
famous and learned Lawreat Masters of Englande, that
they would but consult one halfe howre with their
5 heauenly Muse what credite they might winne to theyr
natiue speeche, what enormities they might wipe out of
English Poetry, what a fitte vaine they might frequent,
wherein to shewe forth their worthie faculties if English
Poetrie were truely reformed, and some perfect platforme
10 or *Prosodia* of versifying were by them ratified and sette
downe, eyther in immitation of Greekes and Latines, or,
where it would skant abyde the touch of theyr Rules, the
like obseruations selected and established by the naturall
affectation of the speeche. Thus much I say, not to per-
15 swade you that are the fauourers of Englishe Poetry, but
to mooue it to you : beeing not the firste that haue thought
vpon this matter, but one that by consent of others haue
taken vpon me to lay it once again in your wayes, if
perhaps you may stumble vppon it, and chance to looke
20 so lowe from your diuine cogitations, when your Muse
mounteth to the starres and ransacketh the Spheres of
heauen : whereby perhaps you may take compassion of
noble Poetry, pittifullie mangled and defaced by rude
smatterers and barbarous immitatours of your worthy
25 studies. If the motion bee worthy your regard, it is
enough to mooue it ; if not, my wordes woulde simply
preuaile in perswading you ; and therefore I rest vppon
thys onely request, that of your courtesies you wyll graunt
passage, vnder your fauourable corrections, for this my
30 simple censure of English Poetry, wherein, if you please to
runne it ouer, you shall knowe breefely myne opinion of
the most part of your accustomed Poets, and particularly,
in his place, the lyttle somewhat which I haue sifted out
of my weake brayne concerning thys reformed versifying.

35   W. W.

A DISCOURSE OF ENGLISHE POETRIE.

INTENDING to write some discourse of English Poetrie,
I thinke it not amysse if I speake something generally of
Poetrie, as, what it is, whence it had the beginning, and
of what estimation it hath alwayes beene and ought to be 5
among al sorts of people. Poetrie, called in Greeke ποετρια
beeing deriued from the Verbe ποιέω, which signifieth in
Latine *facere*, in English to make, may properly be defined the arte of making : which word, as it hath alwaies
beene especially vsed of the best of our English Poets to 10
expresse the very faculty of speaking or wryting Poetically, so doth it in deede containe most fitly the whole
grace and property of the same, the more fullye and
effectually then any other English Verbe. That Poetry is
an Arte (or rather a more excellent thing then can be 15
contayned wythin the compasse of Arte), though I neede
not stande long to prooue, both the witnes of *Horace*, who
wrote *de arte Poetica*, and of *Terence*, who calleth it *Artem
Musicam*, and the very naturall property thereof may
sufficiently declare. The beginning of it, as appeareth by 20
Plato, was of a vertuous and most deuout purpose ; who
witnesseth that by occasion of meeting of a great company
of young men, to solemnize the feasts which were called
Panegeryca, and were wont to be celebrated euery fift
yeere, there they that were most pregnant in wytt, and 25
indued with great gyfts of wysedome and knowledge in
Musicke aboue the rest, did vse commonly to make
goodly verses, measured according to the sweetest notes
of Musicke, containing the prayse of some noble vertue,
or of immortalitie, or of some such thing of greatest 30
estimation : which vnto them seemed so heauenly and
ioyous a thing, that, thinking such men to be inspyrde

with some diuine instinct from heauen, they called them
Vates. So when other among them of the finest wits and
aptest capacities beganne in imitation of these to frame
ditties of lighter matters, and tuning them to the stroake
5 of some of the pleasantest kind of Musicke, then began
there to growe a distinction and great diuersity betweene
makers and makers. Whereby (I take it) beganne thys
difference : that they which handled in the audience of
the people graue and necessary matters were called wise
10 men or eloquent men, which they meant by *Vates*; and
the rest which sange of loue matters, or other lighter
deuises alluring vnto pleasure and delight, were called
Poetæ or makers. Thus it appeareth both Eloquence and
Poetrie to haue had their beginning and originall from
15 these exercises, beeing framed in such sweete measure
of sentences and pleasant harmonie called Ῥυθμός, which
is an apt composition of wordes or clauses, drawing as it
were by force the hearers eares euen whether soeuer
it lysteth, that *Plato* affirmeth therein to be contained
20 γοητεία an inchauntment, as it were to perswade them anie
thing whether they would or no. And heerehence is
sayde that men were first withdrawne from a wylde and
sauadge kinde of life to ciuillity and gentlenes and the
right knowledge of humanity by the force of this measur-
25 able or tunable speaking.

This opinion shall you finde confirmed throughout the
whole workes of *Plato* and *Aristotle* : and that such was
the estimation of this Poetry at those times, that they supposed all wisdome and knowledge to be included mystic-
30 ally in that diuine instinction wherewith they thought
their *Vates* to bee inspyred. Wherevpon, throughout the
noble workes of those most excellent Philosophers before
named, are the authorities of Poets very often alledged.
And *Cicero* in his *Tusculane* questions is of that minde,
35 that a Poet cannot expresse verses aboundantly. suffi-

ciently, and fully, neither his eloquence can flowe pleasauntly, or his wordes sounde well and plenteously, without
celestiall instinction : which Poets themselues doo very
often and gladlie witnes of themselues, as namely *Ouid*
in 6. *Fasto* : *Est deus in nobis ; agitante calescimus illo,* 5
etc. Wherevnto I doubt not equally to adioyne the au-
·thoritye of our late famous English Poet who wrote the
Sheepheards Calender, where, lamenting the decay of Poetry
at these dayes, saith most sweetely to the same :

Then make thee winges of thine aspyring wytt,   10
And, whence thou camest, flye back to heauen apace, etc.

Whose fine poeticall witt and most exquisite learning,
as he shewed aboundantly in that peece of worke, in my
iudgment inferiour to the workes neither of *Theocritus* in
Greeke nor *Virgill* in Latine, whom he narrowly immi- 15
tateth : so I nothing doubt but if his other workes were
common abroade, which are as I thinke in the close
custodie of certaine his freends, we should haue of our
owne Poets whom wee might matche in all respects with
the best. And, among all other his workes whatsoeuer, 20
I would wysh to haue the sight of hys *English Poet*, which
his freend *E. K.* did once promise to publishe, which
whether he performed or not, I knowe not : if he did, my
happe hath not beene so good as yet to see it.

But to returne to the estimation of Poetry. Besides 25
the great and profitable fruites contained in Poetry, for
the instruction of manners and precepts of good life (for
that was cheefly respected in the first age of Poetry), this
is also added to the eternall commendations of that noble
faculty : that Kinges and Princes, great and famous men, 30
did euer encourage, mayntaine, and reward Poets in al
ages, because they were thought onely to haue the whole
power in their handes of making men either immortally
famous for their valiaunt exploytes and vertuous exercises,

or perpetually infamoús for their vicious liues. Where-
vppon it is said of *Achilles* that this onely vantage he
had of *Hector*, that it was his fortune to be extolled and
renowmed by the heauenly verse of *Homer*. And as *Tully*
5 recordeth to be written of *Alexander*, that with natural
teares he wept ouer *Achilles* Tombe, in ioy that he conceiued at the consideration howe it was his happe to be
honoured wyth so diuine a worke as *Homers* was. *Aris-*
totle, a most prudent and learned Philosopher, beeing
10 appointed Schoolemaster to the young Prince *Alexander*,
thought no worke so meete to be reade vnto a King as the
worke of *Homer* : wherein the young Prince, being by
him instructed throughly, found such wonderfull delight
in the same when hee came to maturity, that hee would
15 not onely haue it with him in all his iourneyes, but in his
bedde also vnder his pyllowe, to delight him and teache
him both nights and dayes. The same is reported of
noble *Scipio*, who, finding the two Bookes of *Homer* in the
spoyle of Kyng *Darius*, esteemed them as wonderfull
20 precious Iewelles, making one of them his companion for
the night, the other for the day. And not onely was he
thus affected to that one peece or parte of Poetry, but so
generally he loued the professors thereof, that in his most
serious affayres, and hottest warres against *Numantia* and
25 *Carthage*, he could no whitte be without that olde Poet
Ennius in his company. But to speake of all those noble
and wyse Princes, who bare speciall fauour and countenaunce to Poets, were tedious, and would require a
rehearsall of all such in whose time there grewe any to
30 credite and estimation in that faculty. Thus farre therefore may suffice for the estimation of Poets. Nowe
I thinke most meete to speake somewhat concerning
what hath been the vse of Poetry, and wherin it rightly
consisted, and whereof consequently it obteyned such
35 estimation.

To begin therefore with the first that was first worthelye
memorable in the excellent gyft of Poetrye, the best
wryters agree that it was *Orpheus*, who by the sweete gyft
of his heauenly Poetry withdrew men from raungyng vn-
certainly and wandring brutishly about, and made them 5
gather together and keepe company, make houses, and
keep fellowshippe together, who therefore is reported (as
Horace sayth) to asswage the fiercenesse of Tygers and
mooue the harde Flynts. After him was *Amphion*, who
was the first that caused Citties to bee builded, and men 10
therein to liue decently and orderly according to lawe and
right. Next was *Tyrtœus*, who began to practise warlike
defences, to keepe back enemies and saue themselues
from inuasion of foes. In thys place I thinke were most
conuenient to rehearse that auncient Poet *Pyndarus*; but 15
of the certaine time wherein he flourished I am not very
certaine; but of the place where he continued moste, it
shoulde seeme to be the Citty of *Thebes*, by *Plinie*, who
reporteth that *Alexander* in sacking the same Cittie woulde
not suffer the house wherein he dwelt to be spoyled as all 20
the rest were. After these was *Homer*, who as it were
in one summe comprehended all knowledge, wisedome,
learning, and pollicie that was incident to the capacity of
man. And who so liste to take viewe of hys two Bookes,
one of his *Iliades*, the other his *Odissea*, shall throughly 25
perceiue what the right vse of Poetry is : which indeede
is to mingle profite with pleasure, and so to delight the
Reader with pleasantnes of hys Arte, as in the mean time
his mind may be well instructed with knowledge and wisedome. For so did that worthy Poet frame those his two 30
workes, that in reading the first, that is his *Iliads*, by
declaring and setting forth so liuely the Grecians assembly
against Troy, together with their prowesse and fortitude
against their foes, a Prince shall learne not onely courage
and valiantnesse, but discretion also and pollicie to en- 35

counter with his enemies, yea a perfect forme of wyse consultations with his Captaines and exhortations to the people, with other infinite commodities.

Agayne, in the other part, wherein are described the manifold and daungerous aduentures of *Vlisses*, may a man learne many noble vertues ; and also learne to escape and auoyde the subtyll practises and perrilous entrappinges of naughty persons ; and not onely this, but in what sort also he may deale to knowe and perceiue the affections of those which be neere vnto him, and most familiar with him, the better to put them in trust with his matters of waight and importaunce. Therefore I may boldly sette downe thys to be the truest, auncientest, and best kinde of Poetry, to direct ones endeuour alwayes to that marke, that with delight they may euermore adioyne commoditie to theyr Readers : which because I grounde vpon *Homer*, the Prince of all Poets, therefore haue I alledged the order of his worke, as an authority sufficiently proouing this assertion.

Nowe what other Poets which followed him, and beene of greatest fame, haue doone for the moste parte in their seuerall workes I wyll briefely, and as my slender ability wyll serue me, declare. But, by my leaue, I must content my selfe to speake not of all, but of such as my selfe haue seene and beene best acquainted withall, and those not all nor the moste part of the auncient Grecians, of whom I knowe not how many there were, but these of the Latinists, which are of greatest fame and most obuious among us.

Thus much I can say, that *Aristotle* reporteth none to haue greatly flourished in Greece, at least wyse not left behynd them any notable memoriall, before the time of *Homer*. And *Tully* sayth as much, that there were none wrytt woorth the reading twyce in the Romaine tongue, before the Poet *Ennius*. And surely as the very summe or cheefest essence of Poetry dyd alwayes for the most part consist in delighting the readers or hearers wyth pleasure, so, as the number of Poets increased, they styll inclyned thys way rather then the other, so that most of them had speciall regarde to the pleasantnesse of theyr fine conceytes, whereby they might drawe mens mindes into admi- 5 ration of theyr inuentions, more then they had to the profitte or commoditye that the Readers shoulde reape by their works. And thus, as I suppose, came it to passe among them that, for the most part of them, they would not write one worke contayning some serious matter : but 1 for the same they wold likewise powre foorth as much of some wanton or laciuious inuention. Yet some of the auncientest sort of Grecians, as it seemeth, were not so much disposed to vayne delectation : as *Aristotle* sayth of *Empedocles*, that in hys iudgment he was onley a naturall 1 Philosopher, no Poet at all, nor that he was like vnto *Homer* in any thing but hys meeter or number of feete, that is, that hee wrote in verse. After the time of *Homer* there began the firste Comedy wryters, who compyled theyr workes in a better stile, which continued not long 2 before it was expelled by penalty, for scoffing too broade at mens manners, and the priuie reuengements which the Poets vsed against their ill wyllers. Among these was *Eupolis*, *Cratinus*, and *Aristophanes* ; but afterward the order of thys wryting Comedies was reformed and made 2 more plausible : then wrytte *Plato (Comicus)*, *Menander,* and I knowe not who more.

There be many most profitable workes, of like antiquity, or rather before them, of the Tragedy writers : as of *Euripides* and *Sophocles* ; then was there *Phocilides* and 3 *Theagines*, with many other : which Tragedies had their inuention by one *Thespis*, and were pollished and amended by *Æschilus*. The profitte or discommoditie which aryseth by the vse of these Comedies and Tragedies, which is most, hath beene long in controuersie, and is sore vrged 3

among vs at these dayes: what I thinke of the same,
perhaps I shall breefely declare anon.

Nowe concerning the Poets which wrote in homely
manner, as they pretended, but indeede with great pythe
5 and learned iudgment, such as were the wryters of Sheepe-
heards talke and of husbandly precepts, who were among
the Grecians that excelled, besides *Theocritus* and *Hesiodus*, I know not ; of whom the first, what profitable workes
he left to posterity, besides hys *Idillia* or contentions of
10 Goteheards, tending most to delight and pretty inuentions,
I can not tell. The other, no doubt for his Argument he
tooke in hande, dealt very learnedly and profitably, that is,
in precepts of Husbandry, but yet so as he myxed much
wanton stuffe among the rest.

15 The first wryters of Poetry among the Latines shoulde
seeme to be those which excelled in the framing of Commedies, and that they continued a long time without
any notable memory of other Poets. Among whom the
cheefest that we may see or heare tell of were these :
20 *Ennius, Caecilius, Naeuius, Licinius, Attilius, Turpilius,
Trabea, Luscius, Plautus,* and *Terens.* Of whom these
two last named haue beene euer since theyr time most
famous, and to these dayes are esteemed as greate helpes
and furtheraunces to the obtayning of good Letters. But
25 heere cannot I stay to speake of the most famous, renowmed, and excellent that euer writte among the Latine
Poets, *P. Virgill,* who performed the very same in that
tongue which *Homer* had doone in Greeke, or rather
better, if better might, as *Sex. Propert.* in his *Elegies* gal-
30 lantly recordeth in his praise, *Nescio quid magis nascitur
Iliade.* Vnder the person of *Æneas* he expresseth the valoure
of a worthy Captaine and valiaunt Gouernour, together with
the perrilous aduentures of warre, and polliticke deuises
at all assayes. And as he immitateth *Homer* in that worke,
35 so doth he likewyse followe the very steps of *Theocritus,*

in his most pythy inuentions of his *Æglogues* : and likewyse *Hesiodus* in hys *Georgicks* or bookes of Husbandry,
but yet more grauely, and in a more decent style. But,
notwithstanding hys sage grauity and wonderfull wisedome,
dyd he not altogether restrayne his vayne, but that he 5
would haue a cast at some wanton and skant comely an
Argument, if indeede such trifles as be fathered vppon
him were his owne. There followed after him very many
rare and excellent Poets, wherof the most part writt light
matters, as *Epigrammes* and *Elegies*, with much pleasant 10
dalliance, among whom may be accounted *Propertius, Tibullus, Catullus,* and diuers whom *Ouid* speaketh of in
diuers places of his workes. Then are there two Hystori-
call Poets, no lesse profitable then delightsome to bee read,
Silius and *Lucanus* : the one declaring the valiant prowesse 15
of two noble Captaines, one enemie to the other, that is,
Scipio and *Haniball* ; the other, likewise, the fortitude of
two expert warriours (yet more lamentably then the other,
because these warres were ciuill), *Pompey* and *Cæsar.*
The next in tyme, but (as most men doo account, and so 20
did he himselfe) the second in dignity, we wyll adioyne
Ouid, a most learned and exquisite Poet. The worke of
greatest profitte which he wrote was his Booke of *Metamorphosis*, which though it consisted of fayned Fables for
the most part, and poeticall inuentions, yet beeing moralized 25
according to his meaning, and the trueth of euery tale
beeing discouered, it is a worke of exceeding wysedome
and sounde iudgment. If one lyst in like manner to haue
knowledge and perfect intelligence of those rytes and
ceremonies which were obserued after the Religion of the 30
Heathen, no more profitable worke for that purpose then
his bookes *De fastis*. The rest of his dooinges, though
they tende to the vayne delights of loue and dalliaunce
(except his *Tristibus* wherein he bewayleth hys exile), yet
surely are mixed with much good counsayle and profitable 35

lessons, if they be wisely and narrowly read. After his time I know no worke of any great fame till the time of *Horace*, a Poet not of the smoothest style, but in sharpnesse of wytt inferiour to none, and one to whom all the rest both before his time and since are very much beholding. About the same time *Iuuenall* and *Persius*, then *Martial*, *Seneca*, a most excellent wryter of Tragedies, *Boetius*, *Lucretius*, *Statius*, *Val: Flaccus*, *Manilius*, *Ausonius*, *Claudian*, and many other, whose iust times and seuerall workes to speake of in this place were neither much needefull, nor altogeather tollerable, because I purposed an other argument. Onely I will adde two of later times, yet not farre inferiour to the most of them aforesayde, *Pallengenius* and *Bap. Mantuanus*; and, for a singuler gyft in a sweete Heroicall verse, match with them *Chr. Oclan*, the Authour of our *Anglorum Prœlia*. But nowe, least I stray too farre from my purpose, I wyl come to our English Poets, to whom I would I were able to yeelde theyr deserued commendations: and affoorde them that censure which I know many woulde, which can better if they were nowe to write in my steede.

I know no memorable worke written by any Poet in our English speeche vntill twenty yeeres past: where, although Learning was not generally decayde at any time, especially since the Conquest of King *William* Duke of *Normandy*, as it may appeare by many famous works and learned bookes (though not of this kinde) wrytten by Byshoppes and others, yet surelye that Poetry was in small price among them, it is very manifest, and no great maruayle, for euen that light of Greeke and Latine Poets which they had they much contemned, as appeareth by theyr rude versifying, which of long time was vsed (a barbarous vse it was), wherin they conuerted the naturall property of the sweete Latine verse to be a balde kinde of ryming, thinking nothing to be learnedly written in verse which fell not out in ryme, that is, in wordes whereof the middle worde of eche verse should sound a like with the last, or of two verses the ende of both should fall in the like letters as thus :

    O male viuentes, versus audite sequentes.   5

And thus likewyse :

> *Propter haec et alia dogmata doctorum*
> *Reor esse melius et magis decorum :*
> *Quisque suam habeat, et non proximorum.*

This brutish Poetrie, though it had not the beginning 10 in this Countrey, yet so hath it beene affected heere that the infection thereof would neuer (nor I thinke euer will) be rooted vppe againe : I meane this tynkerly verse which we call ryme. Master *Ascham* sayth that it first began to be followed and maintained among the *Hunnes* and 15 *Gothians* and other barbarous Nations, who, with the decay of all good learning, brought it into *Italy* : from thence it came into *Fraunce*, and so to *Germany* ; at last conueyed into *England*, by men indeede of great wise-dome and learning, but not considerate nor circumspect 20 in that behalfe. But of this I must intreate more heere-after.

Henry the first King of that name in England is won-derfully extolled, in all auncient Recordes of memory, for hys singuler good learning in all kinde of noble studies, 25 in so much as he was named by his surname *Beaucleark*, as much to say as *Fayreclerke* (whereof perhappes came the name of *Fayreclowe*). What knowledge hee attained in the skyll of Poetry, I am not able to say. I report his name for proofe that learning in this Country was not 30 little esteemed of at that rude time, and that like it is, among other studies, a King would not neglect the faculty of Poetry. The first of our English Poets that I haue

heard of was *Iohn Gower*, about the time of king *Rychard*
the seconde, as it should seeme by certayne coniectures
bothe a Knight and questionlesse a singuler well learned
man : whose workes I could wysh they were all whole
5 and perfect among vs, for no doubt they contained very
much deepe knowledge and delight ; which may be gathered
by his freend *Chawcer*, who speaketh of him oftentimes in
diuers places of hys workes. *Chawcer*, who for that excellent fame which hee obtayned in his Poetry was alwayes
10 accounted the God of English Poets (such a tytle for
honours sake hath beene giuen him), was next after if not
equall in time to *Gower*, and hath left many workes, both
for delight and profitable knowledge farre exceeding any
other that as yet euer since hys time directed theyr studies
15 that way. Though the manner of hys stile may seeme
blunte and course to many fine English eares at these
dayes, yet in trueth, if it be equally pondered, and with
good iudgment aduised, and confirmed with the time
wherein he wrote, a man shall perceiue thereby euen a
20 true picture or perfect shape of a right Poet. He by his
delightsome vayne so gulled the eares of men with his
deuises, that, although corruption bare such sway in most
matters that learning and truth might skant bee admitted
to shewe it selfe, yet without controllment myght hee
25 gyrde at the vices and abuses of all states, and gawle
with very sharpe and eger inuentions, which he did so
learnedly and pleasantly that none therefore would call
him into question. For such was his bolde spyrit, that
what enormities he saw in any he would not spare to
30 pay them home, eyther in playne words, or els in some
prety and pleasant couert, that the simplest might espy
him.

Neere in time vnto him was *Lydgate*, a Poet surely for
good proportion of his verse and meetely currant style,
35 as the time affoorded, comparable with *Chawcer*, yet more

occupyed in supersticious and odde matters then was requesite in so good a wytte : which, though he handled them commendably, yet, the matters themselues beeing not so commendable, hys estimation hath beene the lesse. The next of our auncient Poets that I can tell of I sup- 5 pose to be *Pierce Ploughman*, who in hys dooinges is somewhat harshe and obscure, but indeede a very pithy wryter, and. (to hys commendation I speake it) was the first that I haue seene that obserued the quantity of our verse without the curiosity of Ryme. 10

Since these I knowe none other tyll the time of *Skelton*, who writ in the time of Kyng *Henry* the eyght, who as indeede he obtayned the Lawrell Garland, so may I wyth good ryght yeelde him the title of a Poet : hee was doubtles a pleasant conceyted fellowe, and of a very 15 sharpe wytte, exceeding bolde, and would nyppe to the very quicke where he once sette holde. Next hym I thynke I may place master *George Gaskoyne*, as painefull a Souldier in the affayres of hys Prince and Country as he was a wytty Poet in his wryting : whose commenda- 20 tions, because I found in one of better iudgment then my selfe, I wyl sette downe hys wordes, and suppresse myne owne : of hym thus wryteth *E. K.*, vppon the ninth *Æglogue* of the new Poet. ' Master *George Gaskoyne*, a wytty Gen- tleman and the very cheefe of our late rymers, who, and 25 if some partes of learning wanted not (albe it is well knowne he altogether wanted not learning), no doubt would haue attayned to the excellencye of those famous Poets. For gyfts of wytt and naturall promptnes appeare in him aboundantly.' 30

I might next speake of the dyuers workes of the olde Earle of *Surrey*, of the L. *Vaus*, of *Norton* of *Bristow*, *Edwardes*, *Tusser*, *Churchyard*, *Wyl. Hunnis*, *Haiwood*, *Sand*, *Hyll*, *S. Y.*, *M. D.*, and many others ; but to speake of their seuerall gyfts and aboundant skyll shewed forth 35 by them in many pretty and learned workes woulde make my discourse much more tedious.

I may not omitte the deserued commendations of many honourable and noble Lordes and Gentlemen in her 5 Maiesties Courte, which in the rare deuises of Poetry haue beene and yet are most excellent skylfull, among whom the right honourable Earle of *Oxford* may challenge to him selfe the tytle of the most excellent among the rest. I can no longer forget those learned Gentlemen 10 which tooke such profitable paynes in translating the Latine Poets into our English tongue, whose desertes in that behalfe are more then I can vtter. Among these I euer esteemed, and while I lyue in my conceyt I shall account, Master *D. Phaer* without doubt the best: who, 15 as indeede hee had the best peece of Poetry whereon to sette a most gallant verse, so performed he it accordingly, and in such sort, as in my conscience I thinke would scarcely be doone againe, if it were to doo again. Notwithstanding, I speak it but as myne own fancy, not 20 preiudiciall to those that list to thinke otherwyse. Hys worke, whereof I speake, is the englishing of *Æneidos* of *Virgill*, so farre foorth as it pleased God to spare him life, which was to the halfe parte of the tenth Booke, the rest beeing since wyth no lesse commendations finished 25 by that worthy scholler and famous Phisition, Master *Thomas Twyne.*

Equally with him may I well adioyne Master *Arthur Golding*, for hys labour in englishing *Ouids Metamorphosis*, for which Gentleman surely our Country hath for 30 many respects greatly to gyue God thankes : as for him which hath taken infinite paynes without ceasing, trauelleth as yet indefatigably, and is addicted without society by his continuall laboure to profit this nation and speeche in all kind of good learning. The next very well de-35 serueth Master *Barnabe Googe* to be placed, as a painefull furtherer of learning: hys helpe to Poetry, besides hys owne deuises, as the translating of *Pallengenius Zodiac.* *Abraham Flemming*, as in many prety Poesis of hys owne, so in translating hath doone to hys commendations. To whom I would heere adioyne one of hys name, whom I know to haue excelled as well in all kinde of learning as in Poetry most especially, and would appeare so if the dainty morselles and fine poeticall inuentions of hys were as common abroade as I knowe they be among some of hys freendes. I wyl craue leaue of the laudable Authors of *Seneca* in English, of the other partes of *Ouid*, of *Horace*, of *Mantuan*, and diuers other, because I would hasten to ende thys rehearsall, perhappes offensyue to some, whom eyther by forgetfulnes or want of knowledge I must needes ouer passe.

And once againe, I am humbly to desire pardon of the learned company of Gentlemen Schollers and students of the Vniuersities and Innes of Courte, yf I omitte theyr seuerall commendations in this place, which I knowe a great number of them haue worthely deserued, in many rare deuises and singuler inuentions of Poetrie: for neither hath it beene my good happe to haue seene all which I haue hearde of, neyther is my abyding in such place where I can with facility get knowledge of their workes.

One Gentleman notwithstanding among them may I not ouerslyppe, so farre reacheth his fame, and so worthy is he, if hee haue not already, to weare the Lawrell wreathe, Master *George Whetstone*, a man singularly well skyld in this faculty of Poetrie. To him I wyl ioyne *Anthony Munday*, an earnest trauoller in this arte, and in whose name I haue seene very excellent workes, among which, surely, the most exquisite vaine of a witty poeticall heade is shewed in the sweete sobs of Sheepheardes and Nymphes; a worke well worthy to be viewed, and to bee esteemed as very rare Poetrie. With these I may place *Iohn Graunge, Knyght, Wylmott, Darrell, F. C., F. K., G. B.*, and many other, whose names come not nowe to my remembraunce.

5   This place haue I purposely reserued for one, who, if not only, yet in my iudgement principally, deserueth the tytle of the rightest English Poet that euer I read, that is, the Author of the Sheepeheardes Kalender, intituled to the woorthy Gentleman Master *Phillip Sydney*: whether
10 it was Master *Sp.* or what rare Scholler in Pembrooke Hall soeuer, because himself and his freendes, for what respect I knowe not, would not reueale it, I force not greatly to sette downe: sorry I am that I can not find none other with whom I might couple him in this *Cata-*
15 *logue* in his rare gyft of Poetry: although one there is, though nowe long since seriously occupied in **grauer** studies (Master *Gabriell Haruey*), yet as he was once his most special freende and fellow Poet, so because he hath taken such paynes, not onely in his Latin Poetry (for
20 which he enioyed great commendations of the best both in iudgment and dignity in thys Realme), but also to reforme our English verse and to beautify the same with braue deuises, of which I thinke the cheefe lye hidde in hatefull obscurity: therefore wyll I aduenture to sette
25 them together, as two of the rarest witts and learnedst masters of Poetrie in England. Whose worthy and notable styl in this faculty I would wysh, if their high dignities and serious businesses would permit, they would styll graunt to bee a furtheraunce to that reformed kinde
30 of Poetry, which Master *Haruey* did once beginne to ratify: and surely in mine opinion, if hee had chosen some grauer matter, and handled but with halfe that skyll which I knowe he could haue doone, and not powred it foorth at a venture, as a thinge betweene iest and earnest,
35 it had taken greater effect then it did.

As for the other Gentleman, if it would please him or hys freendes to let those excellent *Poemes,* whereof I know he hath plenty, come abroad, as his Dreames, his Legends, his Court of *Cupid,* his English Poet, with other, he shoulde not onely stay the rude pens of my selfe and others, but also satisfye the thirsty desires of many which desire nothing more then to see more of hys rare inuentions. If I ioyne to Master *Haruey* hys two Brethren, I am assured, though they be both busied with great and waighty callinges (the one a godly and learned Diuine, the other a famous and skylfull Phisition), yet if they lysted to sette to their helping handes to Poetry, they would as much beautify and adorne it as any others.

If I let passe the vncountable rabble of ryming Ballet makers and compylers of sencelesse sonets, who be most busy to stuffe euery stall full of grosse deuises and vnlearned Pamphlets, I trust I shall with the best sort be held excused. For though many such can frame an Alehouse song of fiue or sixe score verses, hobbling vppon some tune of a Northen Iygge, or Robyn hoode, or La lubber etc., and perhappes obserue iust number of sillables, eyght in one line, sixe in an other, and there withall an A to make a iercke in the ende : yet if these might be accounted Poets (as it is sayde some of them make meanes to be promoted to the Lawrell) surely we shall shortly haue whole swarmes of Poets : and euery one that can frame a Booke in Ryme, though for want of matter it be but in commendations of Copper noses or Bottle Ale, wyll catch at the Garlande due to Poets ; whose potticall, poeticall (I should say), heades I would wyshe at their worshipfull comencements might in steede of Lawrell be gorgiously garnished with fayre greene Barley, in token of their good affection to our Englishe Malt. One speaketh thus homely of them, with whose words I wyll content my selfe for thys time, because

I woulde not bee too broade wyth them in myne owne speeche.

'In regarde' (he meaneth of the learned framing the newe Poets workes which writt the Sheepheardes Calender) 'I scorne and spue out the rakehelly rout of our ragged Rymers (for so themselues vse to hunt the Letter) which without learning boaste, without iudgment iangle, without reason rage and fume, as if some instinct of poeticall spyrite had newlie rauished them aboue the meanesse of common capacity. And beeing in the midst of all their brauery, suddainly, for want of matter or of Ryme, or hauing forgotten their former conceyt, they seeme to be so payned and trauelled in theyr remembraunce, as it were a woman in Chyldbyrth, or as that same *Pythia* when the traunce came vpon her: *Os rabidum fera corda domans etc.*'

_____

Thus farre foorth haue I aduentured to sette downe parte of my simple iudgement concerning those Poets, with whom for the most part I haue beene acquainted through myne owne reading: which though it may seeme something impertinent to the tytle of my Booke, yet I trust the courteous Readers wyll pardon me, considering that poetry is not of that grounde and antiquity in our English tongue, but that speaking thereof only as it is English would seeme like vnto the drawing of ones pycture without a heade.

Nowe therefore, by your gentle patience, wyll I wyth like breuity make tryall what I can say concerning our Englishe Poetry, first in the matter thereof, then in the forme, that is, the manner of our verse; yet so as I must euermore haue recourse to those times and wryters, whereon the English poetry taketh as it were the discent and proprietye.

English Poetry therefore, beeing considered according

to common custome and auncient vse, is where any
worke is learnedly compiled in measurable speeche, and
framed in wordes contayning number or proportion of
iust syllables, delighting the readers or hearers as well
by the apt and decent framing of wordes in equall resem- 5
blance of quantity, commonly called verse, as by the
skyllfull handling of the matter whereof it is intreated.
I spake somewhat of the beginning of thys measuring of
wordes in iust number, taken out of *Plato* : and indeede
the regarde of true quantity in Letters and syllables 10
seemeth not to haue been much vrged before the time of
Homer in Greece, as *Aristotle* witnesseth.

The matters whereof verses were first made were
eyther exhortations to vertue, dehortations from vices,
or the prayses of some laudable thing. From thence 15
they beganne to vse them in exercises of immitating
some vertuous and wise man at their feastes : where as
some one shoulde be appointed to represent an other
mans person of high estimation, and he sang fine ditties
and wittie sentences, tunably to their Musick notes. Of 20
thys sprang the first kinde of Comedyes, when they
beganne to bring into these exercises more persons then
one, whose speeches were deuised Dyalogue wise, in
aunswering one another. And of such like exercises, or,
as some wyll needes haue it, long before the other, began 25
the first Tragedies, and were so called of τράγος, because
the Actor, when he began to play his part, slewe and
offered a Goate to their Goddesse : but Commedies tooke
their name of κωμάζειν καὶ ᾄδειν, *comessatum ire*, to goe
a feasting, because they vsed to goe in procession with 30
their sport about the Citties and Villages, mingling much
pleasaunt myrth wyth theyr graue Religion, and feasting
cheerefully together wyth as great ioy as might be deuised.
But not long after (as one delight draweth another) they
began to inuent new persons and newe matters for their 35

Comedies, such as the deuisers thought meetest to please the peoples vaine: And from these they beganne to present in shapes of men the natures of vertues and vices, and affections and quallities incident to men, as 5 Iustice, Temperance, Pouerty, Wrathe, Vengeaunce, Sloth, Valiantnes, and such like, as may appeare by the auncient workes of *Aristophanes.* There grewe at last to be a greater diuersitye betweene Tragedy wryters and Comedy wryters, the one expressing onely sorrowfull 10 and lamentable Hystories, bringing in the persons of Gods and Goddesses, Kynges and Queenes, and great states, whose partes were cheefely to expresse most miserable calamities and dreadfull chaunces, which increased worse and worse, tyll they came to the most 15 wofull plight that might be deuised. The Comedies, on the other side, were directed to a contrary ende, which, beginning doubtfully, drewe to some trouble or turmoyle, and by some lucky chaunce alwayes ended to the ioy and appeasement of all parties. Thys distinction grewe, as 20 some holde opinion, by immitation of the workes ot *Homer* ; for out of his *Iliads* the Tragedy wryters founde dreadfull euents, whereon to frame their matters, and the other out of hys *Odyssea* tooke arguments of delight, and pleasant ending after dangerous and troublesome doubtes. 25 So that, though there be many sortes of poeticall wrytings, and Poetry is not debarred from any matter which may be expressed by penne or speeche, yet for the better vnderstanding and breefer method of thys discourse, I may comprehende the same in three sortes, 30 which are Comicall, Tragicall, Historiall. Vnder the first may be contained all such *Epigrammes, Elegies,* and delectable ditties, which Poets haue deuised respecting onely the delight thereof: in the seconde, all dolefull complaynts, lamentable chaunces, and what soeuer is 35 poetically expressed in sorrow and heauines. In the

third we may comprise the reste of all such matters
which is indifferent betweene the other two, [which] doo
commonly occupy the pennes of Poets : such are the
poeticall compyling of Chronicles, the freendly greetings
betweene freendes, and very many sortes besides, which 5
for the better distinction may be referred to one of these
three kindes of Poetry. But once againe, least my discourse runne too farre awry, wyll I buckle my selfe more
neerer to English Poetry : the vse wherof, because it is
nothing different from any other, I thinke best to confirme 10
by the testimony of *Horace*, a man worthy to beare authority in this matter, whose very opinion is this, that the
perfect perfection of poetrie is this, to mingle delight with
profitt in such wyse that a Reader might by his reading
be pertaker of bothe ; which though I touched in the 15
beginning, yet I thought good to alledge in this place, for
more confirmation thereof, some of hys owne wordes. In
his treatise *de arte Poetica*, thus hee sayth :

> *Aut prodesse volunt, aut delectare poetae,*
> *Aut simul et iucunda et idonea dicere vitae.* 20

As much to saie : All Poets desire either by their
works to profitt or delight men, or els to ioyne both
profitable and pleasant lessons together for the instruction of life.

And againe : 25

> *Omne tulit punctum qui miscuit vtile dulci,*
> *Lectorem delectando pariterque monendo.*

That is, He misseth nothing of his marke which ioyneth
profitt with delight, as well delighting his Readers as
profiting them with counsell. And that whole Epistle 30
which hee wryt of his Arte of Poetrie, among all the
parts thereof, runneth cheefelie vppon this, that whether

the argument which the Poet handleth be of thinges
doone or fained inuentions, yet that they should beare such
an Image of trueth that as they delight they may likewise
profitt. For these are his wordes : *Ficta voluptatis causa*
5 *sint proxima veris.* Let thinges that are faigned for pleasures sake haue a neere resemblance of the truth. This
precept may you perceiue to bee most duelie obserued of
Chawcer : for who could with more delight prescribe such
wholsome counsaile and sage aduise, where he seemeth
10 onelie to respect the profitte of his lessons and instructions ? or who coulde with greater wisedome, or more
pithie skill, vnfold such pleasant and delightsome matters
of mirth, as though they respected nothing but the telling
of a merry tale ? So that this is the very grounde of right
15 poetrie, to giue profitable counsaile, yet so as it must be
mingled with delight. For among all the auncient works
of poetrie, though the most of them incline much to that
part of delighting men with pleasant matters of small
importaunce, yet euen in the vainest trifles among them
20 there is not forgotten some profitable counsaile, which
a man may learne, either by flatte precepts which therein
are prescribed, or by loathing such vile vices, the enormities
whereof they largelie discouer. For surelie I am of
this opinion that the wantonest Poets of all, in their
25 most laciuious workes wherein they busied themselues,
sought rather by that meanes to withdraw mens mindes
(especiallie the best natures) from such foule vices
then to allure them to imbrace such beastly follies as they
detected.

30   *Horace,* speaking of the generall dueties of Poets, sayth,
Os tenerum pueri balbumque poeta figurat, and manie more
wordes concerning the profitte to be hadde out of Poets :
which because I haue some of them comprised into an
English translation of that learned and famous knight,
35 Sir *Thomas Elyot,* I wyll set downe his wordes.

The Poet fashioneth by some pleasant meane
The speeche of children stable and vnsure:
Gulling their eares from wordes and thinges vncleane,
Giuing to them precepts that are pure:
Rebuking enuy and wrath if it dure: 5
Thinges well donne he can by example commend:
To needy and sicke he doth also his cure
To recomfort, if ought he can amende.

And manie other like wordes are in that place of *Horace*
to like effect. Therefore poetrie, as it is of it selfe, without 1o
abuse is not onely not vnprofitable to the liues and studies
of menne, but wonderfull commendable and of great excellencie. For nothing can be more acceptable to men, or
rather to be wished, then sweete allurements to vertues
and commodious caueates from vices; of which Poetrie 1s
is exceeding plentifull, powring into gentle witts, not
roughly and tirannicallie, but as it were with a louing
authoritie. Nowe, if the ill and vndecent prouocations,
whereof some vnbridled witts take occasion by the reading of laciuious Poemes, bee obiected—such as are *Ouids* 2o
loue Bookes and *Elegies, Tibullus, Catullus,* and *Martials*
workes, with the Comedies for the most part of *Plautus*
and *Terence*—I thinke it easily aunswered. For though
it may not iustlie be denied that these workes are indeede
very Poetrie, yet that Poetrie in them is not the essentiall 2s
or formall matter or cause of the hurt therein might be
affirmed, and although that reason should come short, yet
this might be sufficient, that the workes themselues doo
not corrupt, but the abuse of the vsers, who, vndamaging
their owne dispositions by reading the discoueries of 3o
vices, resemble foolish folke who, comming into a Garden
without anie choise or circumspection, tread downe the
fairest flowers and wilfullie thrust their fingers among
the nettles.

And surelie to speake what I verelie thinke, this is 35

mine opinion : that one hauing sufficient skyll to reade
and vnderstand those workes, and yet no staie of him
selfe to auoyde inconueniences, which the remembraunce
of vnlawfull things may stirre vppe in his minde, he, in
5 my iudgement, is wholy to bee reputed a laciuious disposed personne, whom the recitall of Sins whether it be
in a good worke or a badde, or vppon what occasion
soeuer, wyll not staie him but prouoke him further vnto
them.   Contrariwise, what good lessons the warie and
10 skylful Readers shall picke out of the very worst of them,
if they list to take anie heede, and reade them not of an
intent to bee made the worse by them, you may see
by these fewe sentences, which the foresayd Sir *Thomas
Elyott* gathered as he sayth at all aduentures, intreating
15 of the like argument.   First, *Plautus* in commendations
of vertue hath such like wordes :

> Verely vertue doth all thinges excell,
> For if liberty, health, liuing, or substaunce,
> Our Country, our parents, and children doo well,
20 > It hapneth by vertue ; she doth all aduaunce ;
> Vertue hath all thinges vnder gouernaunce :
> And in whom of vertue is founde great plenty
> Any thing that is good may neuer be dainty.

Terence, in Eunucho, hath a profitable speeche, in blasing
25 foorth the fashions of harlots before the eyes of young
men.   Thus sayth *Parmeno* :

> In thys thing I tryumphe in myne owne conceite,
> That I haue found for all young men the way,
> Howe they of Harlots shall know the deceite,
30 > Their witts and manners, that thereby they may
> Them perpetuallie hate ; for so much as they
> Out of their owne houses be fresh and delicate,
> Feeding curiously, at home all day
> Lyuing beggerlie in most wretched estate.

And many more wordes of the same matter, but which may be gathered by these fewe.

Ouid, in his most wanton Bookes of loue, and the reme-dies thereof, hath very many pithie and wise sentences, which a heedefull Reader may marke and chose out from 5 the other stuffe. This is one.

Tyme is a medicine if it shall profitt ;
Wine gyuen out of tyme may be annoyaunce.
And man shall irritat vice, if he prohibitt
When time is not meete vnto his vtteraunce. 10
Therfore, if thou yet by counsayle art recuperable,
Fly thou from idlenes and euer be stable.

Martiall, a most dissolute wryter among all other, yet not without many graue and prudent speeches as this, is one worthy to be marked of these fond youthes which in- 15 tangle theyr wytts in raging loue, who, stepping once ouer shoes in theyr fancyes, neuer rest plunging till they be ouer head and eares in their follie.

If thou wylt eschewe bitter aduenture,
And auoyde the annoyance of a pensifull hart, 20
Set in no one person all wholly thy pleasure ;
The lesse maist thou ioy, but the lesse shalt thou smart.

These are but fewe gathered out by happe, yet sufficient to shewe that the wise and circumspect Readers may finde very many profitable lessons dispersed in these workes, 25 neither take any harme by reading such Poemes, but good, if they wil themselues. Neuertheles, I would not be thought to hold opinion that the reading of them is so tollerable, as that there neede no respect to be had in making choyse of readers or hearers : for if they be pro- 30 hibited from the tender and vnconstant wits of children and young mindes, I thinke it not without great reason : neyther am I of that deuillish opinion, of which some

there are, and haue beene, in England, who, hauing charge of youth to instruct them in learning, haue especially made choyse of such vnchildish stuffe to reade vnto young Schollers, as it shoulde seeme of some filthy pur-
5 pose, wylfully to corrupt theyr tender mindes and prepare them the more ready for theyr loathsome dyetts.

For, as it is sayd of that impudent worke of *Luciane*, a man were better to reade none of it then all of it, so thinke I that these workes are rather to be kept alto-
10 gether from children then they should haue free liberty to reade them, before they be meete either of their owne discretion or by heedefull instruction to make choyse of the good from the badde. As for oùr Englishe Poetrie, I know no such perilous peeces (except a fewe balde
15 ditties made ouer the Beere potts, which are nothing lesse then Poetry) which anie man may vse and reade without damage or daunger: which indeede is lesse to be mer-uailed at among vs then among the olde Latines and Greekes, considering that Christianity may be a staie to
20 such illecibrous workes and inuentions as among them (for their Arte sake) myght obtaine passage.

Nowe will I speake somewhat of that princelie part of Poetrie, wherein are displaied the noble actes and valiant exploits of puissaunt Captaines, expert souldiers, wise
25 men, with the famous reportes of auncient times, such as are the Heroycall workes of *Homer* in Greeke and the heauenly verse of *Virgils Æneidos* in Latine: which workes, comprehending as it were the summe and grounde of all Poetrie, are verelie and incomparably the best of
30 all other. To these, though wee haue no English worke aunswerable in respect of the glorious ornaments of gallant handling, yet our auncient Chroniclers and re-porters of our Countrey affayres come most neere them: and no doubt, if such regarde of our English speeche and
35 curious handling of our verse had beene long since thought

vppon, and from time to time been pollished and bettered by men of learning, iudgement, and authority, it would ere this haue matched them in all respects. A manifest example thereof may bee the great good grace and sweete vayne which Eloquence hath attained in our speeche, be- 5 cause it hath had the helpe of such rare and singuler wits, as from time to time myght still adde some amendment to the same. Among whom I thinke there is none that will gainsay but Master *Iohn Lilly* hath deserued moste high commendations, as he which hath stept one steppe further 10 therein then any either before or since he first began the wyttie discourse of his *Euphues.* Whose workes, surely in respecte of his singuler eloquence and braue composi- tion of apt words and sentences, let the learned examine and make tryall thereof thorough all the partes of Retho- 15 ricke, in fitte phrases, in pithy sentences, in gallant tropes, in flowing speeche, in plaine sence, and surely, in my iudgment, I thinke he wyll yeelde him that verdict which *Quintilian* giueth of bothe the best Orators *Demosthenes* and *Tully*, that from the one nothing may be taken away, 20 to the other nothing may be added. But a more neerer example to prooue my former assertion true (I meane the meetnesse of our speeche to receiue the best forme of Poetry) may bee taken by conference of that famous trans- lation of Master D. *Phaer* with the coppie it selfe, who 25 soeuer please with courteous iudgement but a little to compare and marke them both together, and weigh with himselfe whether the English tongue might by little and little be brought to the verye maiesty of a ryght Heroicall verse. First you may marke how *Virgill* always fitteth 30 his matter in hande with wordes agreeable vnto the same affection which he expresseth : as in hys Tragicall ex- clamations, what pathe[ti]call speeches he frameth ? in his comfortable consolations, howe smoothely hys verse runnes ? in his dreadfull battayles and dreery bycker- 35

ments of warres, howe bygge and boystrous his wordes
sound ? and the like notes in all partes of his worke may
be obserued.   Which excellent grace and comely kind of
choyse, if the translatour hath not hitte very neere in our
5 course English phrase, iudge vprightly : wee wyll conferre
some of the places, not picked out for the purpose, but
such as I tooke turning ouer the Booke at randon.
When the Troyans were so tost about in tempestious
wether, caused by *Æolus* at *Iunoes* request, and driuen
10 vpon the coaste of *Affrick* with a very neere scape of their
liues, *Æneas* after hee had gone a land and kylled plenty
of victuals for his company of Souldiours, hee deuided the
same among them, and thus louinglie and sweetely he
comforted them (*Æn. Lib. i*) :

15   *et dictis maerentia pectora mulcet :*
      O socii (neque enim ignari sumus ante malorum),
      O passi grauiora : dabit deus his quoque finem.
      Vos et Scyllaeam rabiem penitusque sonantes
      Accestis scopulos : vos et Cyclopea saxa
20   *Experti.   Reuocate animos, maestumque timorem*
      Mittite.   Forsan et haec olim meminisse iuuabit.
      Per varios casus, per tot discrimina rerum,
      Tendimus in Latium : sedes vbi fata quietas
      Ostendunt.   Illic fas regna resurgere Troiae.
25   *Durate, et vosmet rebus seruate secundis.*
      Talia voce refert : curisque ingentibus aeger
      Spem vultu simulat, premit altum corde dolorem.

Translated thus :

   And then to cheere their heauy harts with these words
          he him bent,
30   O Mates, (quoth he) that many a woe haue bidden and
          borne ere thys,
   Worse haue we seene, and this also shall end when
          Gods wyll is.

Through *Sylla* rage (ye wott) and through the roaring
    rocks we past;

Though *Cyclops* shore was full of feare, yet came we
    through at last.

Plucke vppe your harts, and driue from thence both
    feare and care away;

To thinke on this may pleasure be perhapps another
    day.

By paynes and many a daunger sore, by sundry 5
    chaunce we wend,

To come to *Italy*, where we trust to find our resting
    ende,

And where the destnyes haue decreed *Troyes* King-
    dome eft to ryse.

Be bold and harden now your harts, take ease while
    ease applies.

Thus spake he tho, but in his hart huge cares had
    him opprest;

Dissembling hope with outward eyes, full heauy was 10
    his brest.

Againe, marke the wounding of *Dido* in loue with
Æneas, with howe choyse wordes it is pithily described,
both by the Poet and the translator, in the beginning of
the fourth booke.

> *At regina graui iamdudum saucia cura*   15
> *Vulnus alit venis, et caeco carpitur igni, etc.*

By this time perced satte the Queene so sore with
    loues desire,

Her wound in euery vayne she feedes, she fryes in
    secrete fire.

The manhood of the man full oft, full oft his famous
    lyne

She doth reuolue, and from her thought his face 20
    cannot vntwyne.

His countnaunce deepe she drawes and fixed fast she
    beares in brest
His words also; nor to her carefull hart can come no
    rest.

And in many places of the fourth booke is the same
matter so gallantly prosecuted in sweete wordes, as in
5 mine opinion the coppy it selfe goeth no whit beyond it.
    Compare them likewise in the woefull and lamentable
cryes of the Queene for the departure of *Æneas*, towards
the ende of that Booke.

>   *Terque quaterque manu pectus percussa decorum*
> 10 *Flauentesque abscissa comas, proh Iupiter, ibit*
>   *Hic? ait, et nostris illuserit aduena regnis? etc.*

Three times her hands she bet, and three times strake
    her comely brest,
Her golden hayre she tare and frantiklike with moode
    opprest;
She cryde, O *Iupiter*, O God, quoth she, and shall
    a goe?
15 Indeede? and shall a flowte me thus within my king-
    dome so?
Shall not mine Armies out, and all my people them
    pursue?
Shall they not spoyle their shyps and burne them vp
    with vengance due?
Out people, out vppon them, follow fast with fires and
    flames,
Set sayles aloft, make out with oares, in ships, in
    boates, in frames.
20 What speake I? or where am I? what furies me doo
    thus inchaunt?
O *Dydo*, wofull wretch, now destnyes fell thy head
    dooth haunt.

And a little after preparing to kyll her owne selfe:

> But *Dydo* quaking fierce with frantike moode and
>   griesly hewe,
> With trembling spotted cheekes, her huge attempting[s]
>   to persue,
> Besides her selfe for rage, and towards death with
>   visage wanne,
> Her eyes about she rolde; as redde as blood they 5
>   looked than.

At last ready to fall vppon *Æneas* sworde:

> O happy (welaway) and ouer happy had I beene,
> If neuer Troian shyps (ahlas) my Country shore had
>   seené.
> Thus sayd, she wryde her head.   And vnreuenged
>   must we die?
> And let vs boldly die (quoth shee); thus, thus to death 10
>   I ply.

Nowe likewise for the braue warlike phrase and bygge
sounding kynd of thundring speeche, in the hotte skyr-
myshes of battels, you may confer them in any of the
last fiue Bookes: for examples sake, thys is one about
the ninth Booke.   1

> *It clamor totis per propugnacula muris:*
> *Intendunt acris arcus, amentaque torquent.*
> *Sternitur omne solum telis: tum scuta cauaeque*
> *Dant sonitum flictu galeae: pugna aspera surgit, etc.*

> A clamarous noyse vpmounts on fortresse tops and 2
>   bulwarks towres;
> They strike, they bend their bowes, they whirle from
>   strings sharp shoting showres.
> All streetes with tooles are strowed, than helmets,
>   skulles, with battrings marrd;
> And shieldes dishyuering cracke, vpriseth roughnesse
>   byckring hard.

Looke how the tempest storme when wind out wrast-
   ling blowes at south,
Raine ratling beates the grownde, or clowdes of haile
   from Winters mouth
Downe dashyng headlong driues, when God from
   skyes with griesly steuen
His watry showres outwrings, and whirlwind clowdes
   downe breakes from heauen.

5 And so foorth much more of the like effect.

Onely one comparison more will I desire you to marke
at your leysures, which may serue for all the rest, that is,
the description of Fame, as it is in the 4. booke, towardes
the end, of which it followeth thus.

10 *Monstrum horrendum ingens, cui quot sunt corpore plumae*
   Tot vigiles oculi, etc.

   Monster gastly great, for euery plume her carkasse beares
   Like number learing eyes she hath, like number harkning
      eares,
   Like number tongues and mouthes she wagges, a won-
      drous thing to speake ;
15 At midnight foorth shee flyes, and vnder shade her sound
      dooth squeake.
   All night she wakes, nor slumber sweete doth take nor
      neuer sleepes ;
   By dayes on houses tops shee sits, or gates of Townes
      she keepes.
   On watching Towres she clymbes, and Citties great she
      makes agast :
   Both trueth and falshood forth she telles, and lyes abroade
      doth cast.

20 But what neede I to repeate any more places ?   There
is not one Booke among the twelue which wyll not yeelde
you most excellent pleasure in conferring the translation

with the Coppie, and marking the gallant grace which our Englishe speeche affoordeth. And in trueth the like comparisons may you choose out through the whole translations of the *Metamorphosis* by Master *Golding*, who (considering both their Coppyes) hath equally deserued commendations for the beautifying of the English speeche. It would be tedious to stay to rehearse any places out of him nowe : let the other suffice to prooue that the English tongue lacketh neyther variety nor currantnesse of phrase for any matter.

———

I will nowe speake a little of an other kinde of poetical writing, which might notwithstanding for the variablenesse of the argument therein vsually handled bee comprehended in those kindes before declared : that is, the compyling *Eglogues*, as much to say as Goteheardes tales, because they bee commonly Dialogues or speeches framed or supposed betweene Sheepeheardes, Neteheardes, Goteheardes, or such like simple men; in which kind of writing many haue obtained as immortall prayse and commendation as in any other.

The cheefest of these is *Theocritus* in Greeke ; next him, and almost the very same, is *Virgill* in Latin. After *Virgyl* in like sort writ *Titus Calphurnius* and *Baptista Mantuan*, wyth many other both in Latine and other languages very learnedlye. Although the matter they take in hand seemeth commonlie in appearaunce rude and homely, as the vsuall talke of simple clownes, yet doo they indeede vtter in the same much pleasaunt and profitable delight. For vnder these personnes, as it were in a cloake of simplicitie, they would eyther sette foorth the prayses of theyr freendes, without the note of flattery, or enueigh grieuously against abuses, without any token of bytternesse.

Somwhat like vnto these works are many peeces of

Chawcer, but yet not altogether so poeticall. But nowe yet at the last hath England hatched vppe one Poet of this sorte, in my conscience comparable with the best in any respect : euen Master *Sp:*, Author of the *Sheepeheardes* 5 *Calender*, whose trauell in that peece of English Poetrie I thinke verely is so commendable, as none of equall iudgment can yeelde him lesse prayse for hys excellent skyll and skylfull excellency shewed foorth in the same then they would to eyther *Theocritus* or *Virgill*, whom in 10 mine opinion, if the coursenes of our speeche (I meane the course of custome which he woulde not infringe) had beene no more let vnto him then theyr pure natiue tongues were vnto them, he would haue (if it might be) surpassed them. What one thing is there in them so worthy admi-15 ration whereunto we may not adioyne some thing of his of equall desert ? Take *Virgil* and make some little com-parison betweene them, and iudge as ye shall see cause.

Virgill hath a gallant report of *Augustus* couertly com-prysed in the first *Æglogue* ; the like is in him of her 20 Maiestie, vnder the name of *Eliza*. *Virgill* maketh a braue coloured complaint of vnstedfast freendshyppe in the person of *Corydon* ; the lyke is him in his 5 *Æglogue*. Agayne, behold the pretty Pastorall contentions of *Virgill* in the third *Æglogue* ; of him in the eight *Eglogue*. 25 Finally, either in comparison with them, or respect of hys owne great learning, he may well were the Garlande, and steppe before the best of all English Poets that I haue seene or hearde ; for I thinke no lesse 'deserueth' (thus sayth *E. K.* in hys commendations) 'hys wittinesse in 30 deuising, his pithinesse in vttering, his complaintes of loue so louely, his discourses of pleasure so pleasantly, his Pastrall rudenes, his Morrall wysenesse, his due obseruing of *decorum* euery where, in personages, in season[s], in matter, in speeche, and generally in all seemely 35 simplicity of handling hys matter and framing hys wordes.'

The occasion of his worke is a warning to other young
men, who, being intangled in loue and youthful vanities,
may learne to looke to themselues in time, and to auoyde
inconueniences which may breede if they be not in time
preuented. Many good Morrall lessons are therein con- 5
tained, as the reuerence which young men owe to the aged,
in the second *Eglogue* : the caueate or warning to beware
a subtill professor of freendshippe, in the fift *Eglogue* : the
commendation of good Pastors, and shame and disprayse
of idle and ambitious Goteheardes, in the seauenth : the 10
loose and retchlesse lyuing of Popish Prelates, in the
ninth : the learned and sweete complaynt of the contempt
of learning vnder the name of Poetry, in the tenth. There
is also much matter vttered somewhat couertly, especially
the abuses of some whom he would not be too playne 15
withall : in which, though it be not apparent to euery one
what hys speciall meaning was, yet so skilfully is it
handled, as any man may take much delight at hys
learned conueyance, and picke out much good sence in
the most obscurest of it. Hys notable prayse deserued in 20
euery parcell of that worke, because I cannot expresse as
I woulde and as it should, I wyll cease to speake any
more of, the rather because I neuer hearde as yet any that
hath reade it, which hath not with much admiration commended it. One only thing therein haue I hearde some 25
curious heades call in question, *viz*: the motion of some vnsauery loue, such as in the sixt *Eglogue* he seemeth to
deale withall, which (say they) is skant allowable to English
eares, and might well haue beene left for the Italian
defenders of loathsome beastlines, of whom perhappes 30
he learned it : to thys obiection I haue often aunswered
(and I thinke truely) that theyr nyce opinion ouer shooteth
the Poets meaning, who though hee in that as in other
thinges immitateth the auncient Poets, yet doth not
meane, no more did they before hym, any disordered 35

loue, or the filthy lust of the deuillish *Pederastice* taken
in the worse sence, but rather to shewe howe the dissolute
life of young men, intangled in loue of women, doo neglect
the freendshyp and league with their olde freendes and
5 familiers. Why (say they) yet he shold gyue no occasion
of suspition, nor offer to the viewe of Christians any
token of such filthinesse, howe good soeuer hys meaning
were : wherevnto I oppose the simple conceyte they haue
of matters which concerne learning or wytt, wylling them
10 to gyue Poets leaue to vse theyr vayne as they see good :
it is their foolysh construction, not hys wryting that is
blameable. Wee must prescrybe to no wryters (much
lesse to Poets) in what sorte they should vtter theyr con-
ceyts. But thys wyll be better discussed by some I hope
15 of better abillity.

One other sorte of Poeticall wryters remayneth yet to
bee remembred, that is, The precepts of Husbandry,
learnedly compiled in Heroycall verse. Such were the
workes of *Hesiodus* in Greeke, and *Virgils Georgickes* in
20 Latine. What memorable worke hath beene handled in
immitation of these by any English Poet I know not (saue
onely one worke of M. *Tusser,* a peece surely of great wytt
and experience, and wythal very prettilye handled). And
I thinke the cause why our Poets haue not trauayled in that
25 behalfe is, especially, for that there haue beene alwayes
plenty of other wryters that haue handled the same argument very largely. Among whom Master *Barnabe Googe,*
in translating and enlarging the most profitable worke of
Heresbachius, hath deserued much commendation, as well
30 for hys faythfull compyling and learned increasing the
noble worke as for hys wytty translation of a good part
of the *Georgickes* of *Virgill* into English verse.

Among all the translations which hath beene my fortune to see, I could neuer yet finde that worke of the
35 *Georgicks* wholly performed. I remember once Abraham

Flemming in his conuersion of the *Eglogues* promised to translate and publishe it ; whether he dyd or not I knowe not, but as yet I heard not of it. I my selfe wott well I bestowed some time in it two or three yeeres since, turning it to that same English verse which other such 5 workes were in, though it were rudely : howe beit, I did it onely for mine owne vse, and vppon certayne respectes towardes a Gentleman mine especiall freende, to whom I was desirous to shewe some token of duetifull good wyll, and not minding it should goe farre abroade, considering 10 howe slenderly I ranne it ouer : yet, since then, hath one gott it in keeping, who, as it is told me, eyther hath or wyll vnaduisedly publishe it : which iniury though he meanes to doo me in myrth, yet I hope he wyll make me some suffycient recompence, or els I shall goe neere to 15 watch hym the like or a worse turne.

But concerning the matter of our Englysh wryters lett thys suffice : nowe shall ye heare my simple skyl in what I am able to say concerning the forme and manner of our Englyshe verse. 20

The most vsuall and frequented kind of our English Poetry hath alwayes runne vpon and to this day is obserued in such equall number of syllables and likenes of wordes that in all places one verse either immediatly, or by mutuall interposition, may be aunswerable to an other both 25 in proportion of length and ending of lynes in the same Letters. Which rude kinde of verse, though (as I touched before) it rather discrediteth our speeche, as borrowed from the *Barbarians*, then furnisheth the same with any comely ornament, yet beeing so ingraffed by custome, and 30 frequented by the most parte, I may not vtterly dissalowe it, least I should seeme to call in question the iudgement of all our famous wryters, which haue wonne eternall prayse by theyr memorable workes compyled in that verse. 35

For my part, therefore, I can be content to esteeme it as a thing the perfection whereof is very commendable, yet so as wyth others I could wysh it were by men of learning and ability bettered, and made more artificiall, according to the woorthines of our speeche..

The falling out of verses together in one like sounde is commonly called, in English, Ryme, taken from the Greeke worde 'Ρυθμός, which surely in my iudgment is verye abusiuelye applyed to such a sence: and by thys the vnworthinesse of the thing may well appeare, in that wanting a proper name wherby to be called, it borroweth a word farre exceeding the dignitye of it, and not appropriate to so rude or base a thing. For Ryme is properly the iust proportion of a clause or sentence, whether it be in prose or meeter, aptly comprised together : wherof there is both an naturall and an artificiall composition, in any manner or kynde of speeche, eyther French, Italian, Spanish, or English, and is propper not onely to Poets, but also to Readers, Oratours, Pleaders, or any which are to pronounce or speake any thing in publike audience.

The first begynning of Ryme (as we nowe terme it), though it be somewhat auncient, yet nothing famous. In Greece (they say) one *Symias Rhodius*, because he would be singuler in somthing, wryt poetically of the Fable, contayning howe *Iupiter* beeing in shape of a Swanne begatte the Egge on Leda, wherof came Castor, Pollux, and Helena, whereof euery verse ended in thys Ryme, and was called therefore ᾠόν; but thys foolyshe attempt was so contemned and dispysed that the people would neither admitte the Author nor Booke any place in memory of learning. Since that it was not hearde of till the time the *Hunnes* and *Gothians* renued it agayne, and brought it into Italie. But howsoeuer or wheresoeuer it beganne, certayne it is that in our Englishe tongue it beareth as good grace, or rather better, then in any other ; and is a faculty whereby many may and doo deserue great prayse and commendation, though our speeche be capable of a farre more learned manner of versifying, as I wyl partly declare heereafter.

There be three speciall notes necessary to be obserued in the framing of our accustomed English Ryme. The first is, that one meeter or verse be aunswerable to an other, in equall number of feete or syllables, or proportionable to the tune whereby it is to be reade or measured. The seconde, to place the words in such sorte as none of them be wrested contrary to the naturall inclination or affecta- tion of the same, or more truely the true quantity thereof. The thyrd, to make them fall together mutually in Ryme, that is, in wordes of like sounde, but so as the wordes be not disordered for the Rymes sake, nor the sence hindered. These be the most pryncipall obseruations which I thinke requisite in an English verse : for as for the other ornaments which belong thereto, they be more properly belonging to the seuerall gyfts of skylfull Poets then common notes to be prescribed by me : but somewhat perhaps I shall haue occasion to speake heereafter.

Of the kyndes of English verses which differ in number of syllables there are almost infinite, which euery way alter according to hys fancy, or to the measure of that meeter wherein it pleaseth hym to frame hys ditty. Of the best and most frequented I wyll rehearse some. The longest verse in length which I haue seene vsed in English consisteth of sixteene syllables, eache two verses ryming together, thus,

Wher vertue wants and vice abounds, there wealth is
    but a bayted hooke
To make men swallow down their bane, before on danger
    deepe they looke.

Thys kynde is not very much vsed at length thus, but is commonly deuided, eche verse into two, whereof eche shal

containe eyght syllables, and ryme crosse wyse, the first
to the thyrd, and the second to the fourth, in this manner,

> Great wealth is but a bayted hooke,
> Where vertue wants, and vice aboundes :
> Which men deuoure before they looke,
> So them in daungers deepe it drownes.

An other kynd next in length to thys is where eche
verse hath fourteene syllables, which is the most accustomed of all other, and especially vsed of all the trans-
latours of the Latine Poets, for the most part thus,

> My mind with furye fierce inflamde of late, I know not
> howe,
> Doth burne Parnassus hyll to see, adorned wyth, Lawrell
> bowe.

Which may likewyse, and so it often is deuyded, eche
verse into two, the first hauing eyght sillables, the second
sixe, wherof the two sixes shall alwayes ryme, and sometimes the eyghtes, sometimes not, according to the wyll of
the maker.

> My minde with furye fierce inflamde
> Of late, I knowe not howe,
> Doth burne *Pernassus* hyll to see,
> Adornd wyth Lawrell bowe.

There are nowe wythin this compasse as many sortes
of verses as may be deuised differences of numbers :
wherof some consist of equall proportions, some of long
and short together, some of many rymes in one staffe (as
they call it), some of crosse ryme, some of counter ryme,
some ryming wyth one worde farre distant from another,
some ryming euery thyrd or fourth word, and so likewyse
all manner of dytties applyable to euery tune that may be
sung or sayd, distinct from prose or continued speeche.
To auoyde therefore tediousnesse and confusion, I wyll

repeate onely the different sortes of verses out of the *Sheepeheardes Calender*, which may well serue to beare authoritie in thys matter.

There are in that worke twelue or thirteene sundry sorts of verses which differ eyther in length or ryme, of des- tinction of the staues ; but of them which differ in length or number of sillables, not past sixe or seauen. The first of them is of tenne sillables, or rather fiue feete in one verse, thus,

> A Sheepheards boy (no better doo him call),
> When Winters wastfull spight was almost spent.

Thys verse he vseth commonly in hys sweete com- playntes and mornefull ditties, as very agreeable to such affections.

The second sort hath naturally but nine syllables, and is a more rough or clownish manner of verse, vsed most commonly of him if you mark him in hys satyricall repre- hensions and his Sheepeheardes homelyest talke, such as the second *Æglogue* is.

> Ah for pitty! wyll rancke Winters rage
> These bytter blasts neuer gynne to asswage?

The number of nine sillables in thys verse is very often altered, and so it may without any disgrace to the same, especially where the speeche should be most clownish and simple, which is much obserued of hym.

The third kynd is a pretty rounde verse, running currantly together, commonly seauen sillables or some- time eyght in one verse, as many in the next, both ryming together : euery two hauing one the like verse after them, but of rounder wordes, and two of them likewyse ryming mutually. That verse expresseth, notably, light and youth- full talke, such as is the thyrde *Æglogue* betweene two Sheepheardes boys concerning loue.

> *Thomalin*, why sitten we so,
> As weren ouerwent with woe
> Vpon so fayre a morrowe?
> The ioyous time now nigheth fast,
> 5   That wyll allay this bitter blast
> And slake the Winter sorrow.

The fourth sort containeth in eche staffe manie vnequall verses, but most sweetelie falling together, which the Poet calleth the tune of the waters fall. Therein is his song in 10 prayse of *Eliza*.

> Ye daintie Nymphes, which in this blessed brooke
>   doo bathe your brest,
> Forsake your watrie bowres, and hether looke,
>   at my request.
> 15 And eke yee Virgins that on *Parnass* dwell,
> Whence floweth *Helicon*, the learned Well,
>   helpe me to blaze
>   her woorthy praise,
> That in her sex doth all excell. etc.

20   The fift is a deuided verse of twelue sillables into two verses, whereof I spake before, and seemeth most meete for the handling of a Morrall matter, such as is the praise of good Pastors, and the dispraise of ill, in the seauenth *Æglogue*.
25   The sixt kinde is called a round, beeing mutuallie sung betweene two : one singeth one verse, the other the next ; eche rymeth with himselfe.

> Per. It fell vppon a holie eue,
> Wyl. Hey ho holliday!
> 30 Per. When holie fathers wont to shrieue ;
> Wyl. Thus ginneth our Rondelay. etc.

The seauenth sorte is a verie tragicall mournefull measure,

wherein he bewayleth the death of some freend vnder the person of *Dydo*.

Vp then *Melpomene*! the mournfulst Muse of nyne,
   such cause of mourning neuer hadst afore:
Vp griesly ghostes! and vp my mournfull ryme!   5
   matter of myrth now shalt thou haue no more.
      Dydo, my deere, alas! is dead,
      Dead, and lyeth wrapt in leade:
        O heauie hearse!
Let streaming teares be powred out in store: 10
        O carefull vearse!

These sortes of verses for breuities sake haue I chosen foorth of him, whereby I shall auoide the tedious rehearsall of all the kindes which are vsed : which I thinke would haue beene vnpossible, seeing they may be altered to as 15 manie formes as the Poets please : neither is there anie tune or stroke which may be sung or plaide on instruments, which hath not some poetical ditties framed according to the numbers thereof, some to Rogero, some to Trenchmore, to downe right Squire, to Galliardes, to Pauines, 20 to Iygges, to Brawles, to all manner of tunes which euerie Fidler knowes better then my selfe, and therefore I will let them passe.

Againe, the diuersities of the staues (which are the number of verses contained with the diuisions or partitions 25 of a ditty) doo often times make great differences in these verses. As when one staffe containeth but two verses, or (if they bee deuided) foure ; the first or the first couple hauing twelue sillables, the other fourteene, which versifyers call Powlters measure, because so they talle their 30 wares by dozens. Also, when one staffe hath manie verses, whereof eche one rimeth to the next, or mutuallie crosse, or distant by three, or by foure, or ended contrarye to the beginning, and a hundred sortes, whereof to shewe

seuerall examples would bee too troublesome. Nowe for
the second point.

The naturall course of most English verses seemeth to
run vppon the olde Iambicke stroake, and I may well
5 thinke by all likelihoode it had the beginning thereof. For
if you marke the right quantitie of our vsuall verses, ye
shall perceiue them to containe in sound the very propertie
of Iambick feete, as thus,

I that my slender oaten pipe in verse was wont to sounde.

10 For transpose anie of those feete in pronouncing, and
make short either the two, foure, sixe, eight, tenne,
twelue sillable, and it will (doo what you can) fall out
very absurdly.

Againe, though our wordes can not well bee forced to
15 abyde the touch of *Position* and other rules of *Prosodia*,
yet is there such a naturall force or quantity in eche
worde, that it will not abide anie place but one, without
some foule disgrace: as for example try anie verse, as
thys,

20 Of shapes transformde to bodies strange I purpose to intreate.

Make the first sillable long, or the third, or the fift, and
so foorth, or, contrariwise, make the other sillables to
admitte the shortnesse of one of them places, and see
what a wonderfull defacing it wil be to the wordes, as
25 thus,

Of strange bodies transformd to shapes purpose I to intreate.

So that this is one especiall thing to be taken heede of
in making a good English verse, that by displacing no
worde bee wrested against his naturall propriety, where-
30 vnto you shal perceyue eche worde to be affected, and
may easilie discerne it in wordes of two sillables or aboue,
though some there be of indifferencie, that wyll stand in

any place. Againe, in chouching the whole sentence, the like regarde is to be had that wee exceede not too boldly in placing the verbe out of his order and too farre behinde the nowne : which the necessitie of Ryme may oftentimes vrge. For though it be tollerable in a verse to sette wordes so extraordinarily as other speeche will not admitt, yet heede is to be taken least by too much affecting that manner we make both the verse vnpleasant and the sence obscure. And sure it is a wonder to see the folly of manie in this respect, that vse not onely too much of thys ouerthwart placing, or rather displacing of wordes, in theyr Poemes and verses, but also in theyr prose or continued writings; where they thinke to rolle most smoothlie and flow most eloquently, there by this means come foorth theyr sentences dragging at one anothers tayle as they were tyde together with poynts, where often you shall tarrie (scratching your heade) a good space before you shall heare hys principall verbe or speciall word, leaste hys singing grace, which in his sentence is contained, should be lesse and his speeche seeme nothing poeticall.

The thyrd obseruation is the Ryme or like ending of verses, which, though it is of least importance, yet hath won such credite among vs that of all other it is most regarded of the greatest part of Readers. And surely, as I am perswaded, the regarde of wryters to this hath beene the greatest decay of that good order of versifying which might ere this haue beene established in our speeche. In my iudgment, if there be any ornament in the same, it is rather to be attributed to the plentifull fulnesse of our speeche, which can affoorde ryming words sufficient for the handling of any matter, then to the thing it selfe for any beautifying it bringeth to a worke, which might bee adorned with farre more excellent collours then ryming is. Notwithstanding I cannot but yeelde vnto it (as custome

requireth) the deserued prayses, especially where it is
with good iudgement ordered. And I thinke them right
worthy of admiration for their readines and plenty of wytt
and capacity, who can with facility intreate at large and, as
5 we call it, *extempore*, in good and sencible ryme, vppon some
vnacquainted matter.

The ready skyll of framing anie thing in verse, besides
the naturall promptnesse which many haue therevnto,
is much helped by Arte, and exercise of the memory:
10 for, as I remember, I reade once among *Gaskoynes*
workes a little instruction to versifying, where is prescribed, as I thinke, thys course of learning to versifye
in Ryme.

When ye haue one verse well setled and decently
15 ordered, which you may dispose at your pleasure, to ende
it with what word you wyll, then, what soeuer the word
is, you may speedilie runne ouer the other wordes which
are aunswerable therevnto (for more readines through all
the letters Alphabetically), whereof you may choose that
20 which wyll best fitte the sence of your matter in that place:
as for example, if your last worde ende in Booke, you may
straightwayes in your minde runne them ouer thus, Brooke,
Cooke, crooke, hooke, looke, nooke, pooke, rooke, forsooke,
tooke, awooke, etc. Nowe it is twenty to one but alwayes
25 one of these shall iumpe with your former worde and matter
in good sence. If not, then alter the first.

And indeede I thinke that, next to the Arte of memory,
thys is the readyest way to attaine to the faculty of ryming
well Extempore, especially if it be helped with thus much
30 paynes. Gather together all manner of wordes, especially
Monasillables, and place them Alphabetically in some note,
and either haue them meetely perfectly by hart (which is
no verye laboursome matter) or but looke them diligently
ouer at some time, practising to ryme indifferent often,
35 whereby I am perswaded it wil soone be learned, so as

the party haue withall any reasonable gyft of knowledge and learning, whereby hee want not bothe matter and wordes altogether.

What the other circumstaunces of Ryming are, as what wordes may tollerably be placed in Ryme, and what not; what words doo best become a Ryme, and what not; how many sortes of Ryme there is; and such like; I wyll not stay nowe to intreate. There be many more obseruations and notes to be prescribed to the exacte knowledge of versifying, which I trust wilbe better and larger laide forth by others, to whom I deferre manie considerations in this treatise, hoping that some of greater skill will shortlie handle this matter in better sorte.

Nowe the sundry kindes of rare deuises and pretty inuentions which come from the fine poeticall vaine of manie in strange and vnacustomed manner, if I could report them, it were worthie my trauell : such are the turning of verses, the infolding of wordes, the fine repititions, the clarklie conueying of contraries, and manie such like. Whereof though I coulde sette downe manie, yet because I want bothe manie and the best kindes of them, I will ouerpasse, onelie pointing you to one or two which may suffice for example.

Looke vppon the rufull song of *Colin* sung by *Cuddie* in the *Sheepheardes Calender*, where you shall see a singuler rare deuise of a dittie framed vpon these six wordes *Woe, sounde, cryes, part, sleep, augment,* which are most prettilie turned and wounde vppe mutually together, expressing wonderfully the dolefulnesse of the song. A deuise not much vnlike vnto the same is vsed by some who, taking the last wordes of a certaine number of verses as it were by the rebound of an *Echo,* shall make them fall out in some prettie sence.

Of this sorte there are some deuised by *Iohn Graunge,* [of] which, because they be not long, I wyll rehearse one.

If feare oppresse, howe then may hope me shielde?
Denyall sayes, vayne hope hath pleased well;
But as such hope thou wouldest not be thine,
So would I not the like to rule my hart.
For, if thou louest, it bidds thee graunt forthwith;
Which is the ioy whereof I liue in hope.

Here if you take the last worde of euerie verse, and place them orderlie together, you shall haue this sentence: *Shielde well thyne hart with hope.* But of these *Echoes* I knowe indeede verie daintie peeces of worke, among some of the finest Poets this day in London, who for the rarenesse of them keepe them priuelie to themselues and wil not let them come abroad.

A like inuention to the last rehearsed, or rather a better, haue I seene often practised in framing a whole dittie to the Letters of ones name, or to the wordes of some two or three verses, which is very witty: as for example, this is one of *W. Hunnis,* which for the shortnes I rather chusde then some that are better.

If thou desire to liue in quiet rest,
Gyue eare and see, but say the best.

These two verses are nowe, as it were, resolued into dyuers other, euery two wordes or sillables being the beginning of an other like verse, in this sort.

If thou   delight in quietnes of life,
Desire   to shunne from brawles, debate, and strife,
To liue   in loue with GOD, with freend and foe,
In rest   shalt sleepe when other cannot so.

Gyue eare   to all, yet doo not all beleeue,
And see   the end and then thy sentence gyue:
But say   For trueth of happy liues assignde
The best   hath he that quiet is in minde.

Thus are there infinite sortes of fine conueiances (as they may be termed) to be vsed, and are much frequented by versifyers, as well in composition of their verse as the wittines of their matter : which all I will referre to the consideration of euerie pleasant headded Poet in their proper gifts ; onelie I sett downe these fewe sortes of their formes of versifying, which may stand in steede to declare what manie others may be deuised in like sorte.

But nowe to proceede to the reformed kind of English verse, which manie haue before this attempted to put in practise and to establish for an accustomed right among English Poets, you shall heare in like manner my simple iudgment concerning the same.

I am fully and certainlie perswaded that if the true kind of versifying in immitation of Greekes and Latines had beene practised in the English tongue, and put in vre from time to tyme by our Poets, who might haue continually beene mending and pollyshing the same, euery one according to their seuerall giftes, it would long ere this haue aspyred to as full perfection as in anie other tongue whatsoeuer. For why may I not thinke so of our English, seeing that among the Romaines a long time, yea euen till the dayes of *Tully*, they esteemed not the Latine Poetrie almost worth any thing in respecte of the Greeke, as appeareth in the Oration *pro Archia Poeta* ; yet afterwardes it increased in credite more and more, and that in short space, so that in *Virgilles* time wherein were they not comparable with the Greekes ? So likewise now it seemeth not currant for an English verse to runne vpon true quantity and those feete which the Latines vse, because it is straunge, and the other barbarous custome, beeing within compasse of euery base witt, hath worne it out of credite or estimation. But if our wryters, beeing of learning and iudgment, would rather infringe thys curious custome then omitte the occasion of inlarging the credite

of their natiue speeche, and theyr owne prayses, by practising that commendable kind of wryting in true verse, then
no doubt, as in other partes of learning, so in Poetry
shoulde not stoupe to the best of them all in all maner
5 of ornament and comlinesse. But some obiect that our
wordes are nothing resemblaunt in nature to theirs, and
therefore not possible to bee framed with any good grace
after their vse : but cannot we then, as well as the Latines
did, alter the cannon of the rule according to the quality
10 of our worde, and where our wordes and theyrs wyll agree,
there to iumpe with them, where they will not agree, there
to establish a rule of our owne to be directed by ?   Likewise, for the tenor of the verse, might we not (as *Horace*
dyd in the Latine) alter their proportions to what sortes
15 we listed, and to what we sawe wold best become the
nature of the thing handled or the quallity of the words ?
Surely it is to be thought that if any one, of sound iudgment and learning, shoulde putt foorth some famous worke,
contayning dyuers formes of true verses, fitting the
20 measures according to the matter, it would of it selfe
be a sufficient authority, without any prescription of rules,
to the most part of Poets for them to follow and by
custome to ratify.   For sure it is that the rules and
principles of Poetry were not precisely followed and
25 obserued of the first beginners and wryters of Poetry,
but were selected and gathered seuerally out of theyr
workes for the direction and behoofe of their followers.
And indeede, he that shall with heedefull iudgment make
tryall of the English wordes shall not finde them so grosse
30 or vnapt but that they wyll become any one of the most
accustomed sortes of Latine or Greeke verses meetely, and
run thereon somewhat currantly.
    I my selfe, with simple skyll, I confesse, and farre vnable
iudgment, haue ventured on a fewe, which notwithstanding
35 the rudenes of them may serue to shewe what better might

bee brought into our speeche, if those which are of meete abilitye woulde bestowe some trauell and endeuour thereuppon. But before I sette them downe, I wyll speake somewhat of such obseruations as I could gather necessary to the knowledge of these kinde of verses, least I should 5 seeme to runne vpon them rashly, without regarde either of example or authority.

The speciall poyntes of a true verse are the due obseruations of the feete and place of the feete.

The foote of a verse is a measure of two sillables, or of 10 three, distinguished by time which is eyther long or short. A foote of two sillables is eyther simple or mixt, that is, of like time or of diuers. A simple foote of two sillables is likewise twofolde, eyther of two long sillables, called *Spondæus*, as − − *goodnesse*, or of two short, called 15 *Pyrrichius*, as ∪ ∪ *hyther*. A myxt foote of 2 sillables is eyther of one short and one long, called *Iambus*, as ∪ − *dying*, or of one long and one short, called *Choreus*, as − ∪ *gladly*. A foote of 3 sillables in like sorte is either simple or myxt. The simple is eyther *Molossus*, that is 20 of three long, as − − − *forgiuenes*, or *Tribrachys*, that is of 3 short, as ∪ ∪ ∪ *merylie*. The mixt is of 6 diuers sortes, 1. *Dactylus*, of one long and two short, as − ∪ ∪ *happily*; 2. *Anapæstus*, of two shorte and one long, as ∪ ∪ − *t[r]auelers*; 3. *Bacchius*, of one short and two long, as 25 ∪ − − *remembrers*; 4. *Palimbachius*, of two long and one short, as − − ∪ *accorded*; 5. *Creticus*, of a long, a short, and a long, [as] − ∪ − *daungerous*; 6. *Amphibrachus*, of a short, a long, and a short, as ∪ − ∪ *reioyced*.

Many more deuisions of feete are vsed by some, but 30 these doo more artificially comprehende all quantities necessary to the skanning of any verse, according to *Tallæus* in hys Rethorique. The place of the feete is the disposing of them in theyr propper roomes, whereby may be discerned the difference of eche verse which is 35

the right numbring of the same. Now as for the quantity
of our wordes, therein lyeth great difficultye, and the
cheefest matter in this faculty. For in truth there being
such diuersity betwixt our words and the Latine, it cannot
5 stande indeede with great reason that they shoulde frame,
wee beeing onelie directed by such rules as serue for
onely Latine words; yet notwithstanding one may well
perceiue by these fewe that these kinde of verses would
well become the speeche, if so bee there were such Rules
10 prescribed as woulde admitt the placing of our aptest and
fullest wordes together. For indeede, excepting a fewe
of our *Monasyllables*, which naturally shoulde most of them
be long, we haue almost none that wyll stande fitlie in
a short foote: and therfore, if some exception were made
15 against the precise obseruation of *Position* and certaine
other of the rules, then might we haue as great plenty
and choyse of good woordes to furnish and sette foorth
a verse as in any other tongue.

Likewise, if there were some derection in such wordes
20 as fall not within the compasse of Greeke or Latine rules,
it were a great helpe, and therefore I had great misse in
these few which I made. Such as is the last sillable in
these wordes, *able*, *noble*, or *possible*, and such like: againe
for the nature and force of our *W*, of our *th*, of our *oo*, and
25 *ee*, of our wordes which admytte an *e* in the ende after
one or two Consonantes, and many other. I for my part,
though (I must needes confesse) many faultes escaped me
in these fewe, yet tooke I as good heede as I coulde, and
in trueth did rather alwaies omitt the best wordes and such
30 as would naturally become the speech best then I wolde
committe any thing which shoulde notoriously impugne
the Latine rules, which herein I had onely for my direction. Indeede most of our *Monasyllables* I am forced to
make short, to supply the want of many short wordes
35 requisite in these verses. The Participle *A*, being but

the English article adioyned to Nownes, I alwayes make
short, both alone and in composition, and likewise the
wordes of one sillable ending in *E*, as *the*, when it is an
article, *he*, *she*, *ye*, etc. *We* I thinke should needes be
alwayes long because we pronounce continually *VVe*. 5
I, beeing alone standing for the Pronowne *Ego*, in my
iudgment might well be vsed common; but because I neuer
sawe it vsed but short I so obserued it. Words ending
in *y* I make short without doubt, sauing that I haue marked
in others one difference which they vse in the same, that 10
is to make it short in the ende ◡ of an Aduerb, as *gladly*,
and long in the ende — of an Adiectiue, as *goodly*: but the
reason is, as I take it, because the Adiectiue is or should be
most commonly written thus, *goodlie*. *O*, beeing an Aduerbe,
is naturally long: in the ende of wordes, both *Monasyllables* 15
and other, I thinke it may be vsed common. The first of
Pollisyllables I directed according to the nature of the
worde, as I thought most aunswerable to Latine examples,
sauing that somewhere I am constrayned to straine curtesy
with the preposition of a worde compounded or such like, 20
which breaketh no great square, as in *defence* or *depart*,
etc. The myddle sillables, which are not very many, come
for the most part vnder the precinct of *Position*, whereof
some of them will not possibly abide the touch, and therfore must needes be a little wrested: such are commonly 25
the Aduerbs of three sillables, as *mournfully*, *spyghtfully*,
and such like words, deriued of this Adiectiue *full*: and
therfore if there be great occasion to vse them, they
must be reformed by detracting onely (*l*) and then they
stand meetely currant, as *mournfuly*. The last sillables 30
I wholly directed so neere as I could to the touch of
common rules.

The most famous verse of all the rest is called *Hexametrum Epicum*, which consisteth of sixe feete, wherof
the first foure are indifferently either *Spondæi* or *Dactyli*, 35

the fift is euermore a *dactyl*, and the sixt a *Spondœ*, as
thus,

    Tyterus happily thou liest tumbling vnder a beetchtree.

    Thys kinde of verse I haue onely seene to be practised
5 in our English speeche; and indeede wyll stand somewhat more orderlye therein then any of the other kindes,
vntill we haue some tolleration of wordes made by
speciall rule. The first that attempted to practise thys
verse in English should seeme to be the Earle of *Surry*,
10 who translated some part of *Virgill* into verse indeede, but
without regard of true quantity of sillables. There is one
famous *Distichon*, which is common in the mouthes of all
men, that was made by one Master *Watson*, fellowe of
S. *Iohns* Colledge in Cambrydge, about 40. yeeres past,
15 which for the sweetnes and gallantnes therof in all
respects doth mat[c]h and surpasse the Latine coppy of
Horace, which he made out of *Homers* wordes, *qui mores
hominum etc.*

All trauellers doo gladlie report great praise to Vlisses,

20 *For that he knewe manie mens maners, and saw many citties.*

    Which two verses, if they be examined throughout, all
the rules and obseruations of the best versifying shall bee
founde to attaine the very perfection of them all. There
be two other not much inferiour to these, which I found in
25 the Glosse of *E. K.* vppon the fift *Æglogue* of the newe
Poet: which Tully translated out of Greeke into Latine,
Haec habui quae edi etc.

    All that I eate did I ioy and all that I greedilie gorged.

    As for those manie goodlie matters left I for others.

30 Which though they wyll not abide the touch of *Synalœpha*
in one or two places, yet perhappes some English rule,

which might wyth good reason be established, would make them currant enough, and auoyde that inconuenience which is very obuious in our wordes. The great company of famous verses of thys sort which Master *Haruey* made is not vnknowne to any, and are to be viewed at all times. 5 I for my part, so farre as those examples would leade me, and mine owne small skyll affoorde me, haue blundered vppon these fewe, whereinto I haue translated the two first Æglogues of Virgil, because I thought no matter of mine owne inuention nor any other of antiquitye more 10 fitte for tryal of thys thyng, before there were some more speciall direction which might leade to a lesse troublesome manner of wryting.

[*Then follow Webbe's versions of the first and second Eclogues, of which the opening verses are—* 15

𝕸elibaeus.   𝕿ityrus.

Tityrus, happilie thou lyste tumbling vnder a beech tree,
All in a fine oate pipe these sweete songs lustilie chaunting:
We, poore soules, goe to wracke, and from these coastes be remooued,
And fro our pastures sweete: thou Tityr, at ease in a shade plott, 20
Makst thicke groues to resound with songes of braue Amarillis.

𝕿ityrus.

O Melibaeus, he was no man but a God who releeude me:
Euer he shalbe my God: from this same Sheepcot his alters
Neuer a tender Lambe shall want, with blood to bedew them. 25
This good gift did he giue, to my steeres thus freelie to wander,
And to my selfe (thou seest) on pipe to resound what I listed.]

I durst not enterpryse to goe any further with this rude translation, beeing for the respects aforesayd a trouble-some and vnpleasant peece of labour: And therefore these 30 shall suffice till further occasion shall serue to imploy some profitable paynes in this behalfe.

The next verse in dignity to the *Hexameters* is the *Carmen Elegiacum,* which consisteth of foure feete and two od sillables, viz: the two first feete, eyther *Dactyli* or *Spondæi* indifferent, the one long sillable, next two
5 *Dactyli* and an other long sillable − − − ◡ ◡ − − ◡ ◡ − ◡ ◡ − : some doo measure it in this sorte (and more truely yet not so readily to all) accounting first two indifferently either *Dactyli* or *Spondæi,* then one *Spondæ* and two *Anapæsti.* But it commeth all to one reckoning. Thys
10 verse is always vnseperably adioyned vnto the Hexameter, and serueth especially to the handling of loue and dalliances, whereof it taketh the name. It will not frame altogether so currantlye in our English as the other, because the shortnesse of the seconde *Penthimimer* will
15 hardly be framed to fall together in good sence after the Latine rules. I haue not seene very many of them made by any, and therefore one or two for example sake shall be sufficient.

This *Distichon* out of *Ouid,*

20   *Ingenium quondam fuerat pretiosius auro ;*
         At nunc barbaria grandis habere nihil.

may thus be translated,
Learning once was thought to be better then any gold was ;
Now he that hath not wealth is but a barbarian.

25 And thys,

         Omnia sunt hominum tenui pendentia filo :
         Et subito casu quae valuere ruunt.

Tis but a slender thread, which all mens states do depend on :
And most goodly thinges quickly doo fall to decay.

30   As for the verses *Phalaecium* and *Iambicum,* I haue not as yet made any tryall in them : but the *Sapphic* I assure you, in my iudgment, wyl doo very pretty, if the

wants which I speake were once supplied.   For tryall of which I haue turned the new Poets sweete song of *Eliza* into such homely *Sapphick* as I coulde.

Thys verse consisteth of these fiue feete, one *Chore*, one *spondæ*, one *dactyl*, and two *Choreis*, with this addition, 5 that after euery third verse be sette one *Adonium* verse, which consisteth of a *dactyl* and a *spondæ*.   It is more troublesome and tedious to frame in our speeche by reason they runne without difference, euery verse being a like in quantity throughout, yet in my iudgement standeth 10 meetely well in the same.   I pray looke the Coppy which I haue translated in the fourth *Æglogue* of the *Sheep-heardes Calender*—the song of *Colins* making which *Hob-binoll* singeth in prayse of the Queenes maiesty vnder the name of *Eliza*.   15

> Ye dainty Nymphes, that in this blessed brooke
> doo bathe your brest,
> Forsake your watry bowres, and hether looke,
> at my request.
> And onely you Virgins that on *Parnass* dwell, 20
> Whence floweth *Helicon*, the learned well,
> helpe me to blase
> her worthy praise,
> That in her sex doth all excell.
>
> Of fayre *Eliza* be your siluer song, 25
> that blessed wight :
> The flowre of Virgins, may she flourish long
> in princely plight.
> For she is *Syrinx* daughter without spott,
> Which *Pan*, the Sheepheards God, on her begot : 30
> so sprang her grace
> of heauenly race,
> No mortall blemish may her blott.
>
> See where she sittes, etc.

The *Saphick* Verse.

```
− ∪ − − − ∪ ∪ − ∪ − − −
− ∪ − − − ∪ ∪ − ∪ − − −
− ∪ − − − ∪ ∪ − ∪ − − −
              − ∪ ∪ − −
```

5

O ye Nymphes most fine, who resort to this brooke,
For to bathe there your pretty breasts at all times,
Leaue the watrish bowres, hyther and to me come
                      at my request nowe.

10 And ye Virgins trymme, who resort to *Parnass,*
Whence the learned well *Helicon* beginneth,
Helpe to blase her worthy deserts, that all els
                      mounteth aboue farre.

Nowe the siluer songes of *Eliza* sing yee,
15 Princely wight, whose peere not among the virgins
Can be found : that long she may remaine among vs,
                      now let vs all pray.

For *Syrinx* daughter she is, of her begotten
Of the great God *Pan*; thus of heauen aryseth
20 All her exlent race ; any mortall harde happe
                      cannot aproche her.

See, she sittes most seemely in a grassy greene plott,
Clothed in weedes meete for a princely mayden,
Boste with Ermines white, in a goodly scarlett
25   brauely beseeming.

Decked is that crowne that vpon her head standes
With the red Rose and many Daffadillies ;
Bayes, the Primrose, and violetts be sette by : how
                      ioyfull a sight ist.

30 Say, behold did ye euer her Angelike face,
Like to *Phœbe* fayre ? or her heauenly hauour,
And the princelike grace that in her remaineth,
                      haue yee the like seene ?

Medled ist red rose with a white together,
Which in either cheeke do depeinct a trymme cheere ;
Her maiestie and eye to behold so comely, her
               like who remembreth ?

Phœbus once peept foorth with a goodly guilt hewe,   5
For to gaze ; but when he sawe the bright beames
Spread abroade fro' her face with a glorious grace,
               it did amaze him.

When another sunne he behelde belowe heere,
Blusht he red for shame, nor againe he durst looke :   10
Would he durst bright beames of his owne with hers match,
               for to be vanquisht.

Shew thy selfe now, *Cynthia*, with thy cleere rayes,
And behold her : neuer abasht be thou so :
When she spreades those beames of her heauenly beauty, 15
    how
               thou art in a dump dasht ?

But I will take heede that I match not her grace
With the *Laton* seede ; *Niobe* that once did,
Nowe she doth therefore in a stone repent ; to all
               other a warning.   20

Pan he may well boaste that he did begit her,
Such a noble wight; to *Syrinx* is it ioy
That she found such lott with a bellibone trym
               for to be loaden.

When my younglinges first to the dammes doo bleat out, 25
Shall a milke white Lambe to my Lady be offred :
For my Goddesse shee is, yea I my selfe her Heardgrome,
               though but a rude Clowne.

Vnto that place *Caliope* dooth high her,
Where my Goddesse shines : to the same the Muses 30
After her, with sweete Violines about them
               cheerefully tracing.

Is not it Bay braunche that aloft in handes they haue,
Eune to giue them sure to my Lady *Eliza* :
O so sweete they play—and to the same doo sing too :
  heaunly to heare ist.

5 See, the Graces trym to the stroake doo foote it,
Deftly dauncing, and meriment doo make them,
Sing to the instruments to reioyce the more, but
  wants not a fourth grace ?

Then the daunce wyll be eune, to my Lady therefore
10 Shalbe geune that place, for a grace she shall be
For to fill that place, that among them in heaune she
  may be receiued.

Thys beuy of bright Nymphes, whether ist goe they now,
Raunged all thus fine in a rowe together ?
15 They be Ladies all i' the Lake behight soe ;
  they thether all goe.

One, that is there chiefe that among the rest goes,
Called is *Chloris* ; of Olyues she bears a
Goodly Crownett, meete for a Prince that in peace
20 euer abideth.

All ye Sheepheardes maides that about the greene dwell,
Speede ye there to her grace ; but among ye take heede
All be Virgins pure that aproche to deck her,
  duetie requireth.

25 When ye shall present ye before her in place,
See ye not your selues doo demeane too rudely :
Bynd the fillets, and to be fine the waste gyrt
  fast with a tawdryne.

Bring the Pinckes, therewith many Gelliflowers sweete,
30 And the Cullambynes : let vs haue the Wynesops,
With the Cornation that among the loue laddes
  wontes to be worne much.

Daffadowndillies all a long the ground strowe,
And the Cowslyppe with a prety paunce let heere lye;
Kyngcuppe, and Lillies so beloude of all men,
                    And the deluce flowre.

One verse there remaineth vntranslated as yet, with 5
some other of this sorte, which I meant to haue finished,
but by reason of some let which I had, I am constrained
to defer to some other time, when I hope to gratify the
Readers with more and better verses of this sort; for in
trueth I am perswaded a little paine taking might furnish 1
our speeche with as much pleasaunt delight in this kinde
of verse as any other whatsoeuer.

Heere followe the Cannons or generall cautions of
Poetry, prescribed by Horace, first gathered by *Georgius
Fabricius Chemnicensis* : which I thought good to annex to 1
thys Treatise, as very necessary obseruations to be marked
of all Poets.

IN HIS EPISTLE *AD PISONES DE ARTE POETICA.*

First, let the inuention be meete for the matter, not 2
differing, or straunge, or monstrous. For a womans head,
a horse necke, the bodie of a dyuers coloured Byrd, and
many members of sundry creatures compact together,
whose legges ending like a Fyshes tayle, this in a picture
is a wonderful deformitie ; but if there be such diuersitye 2
in the frame of a speeche, what can be more vncomely or
ilfauoured ?

2. The ornaments or colours must not bee too many,
nor rashly aduentured on ; neither must they be vsed
euery where and thrust into euery place.   3
3. The proprietie of speeche must bee duely obserued

that wayghty and great matters be not spoken slenderly or matters of length too briefly: for it belongeth much both to the comlinesse and nature of a matter that in big matters there be lykewise vsed boysterous wordes.

5   4. In Poeticall descriptions the speeche must not exceede all credite, nor any thing fainedlie brought in against all course of nature.

    5. The disposing of the worke must be such that there be no offence committed, as it were by too exquisite dilli-
10 gence : for many thinges may be oft committed, and some thing by too curious handling be made offenciue. Neyther is it in one part to be well furnished, and in another to be neglected. Which is prooued by example of a Caruer, who expressed very artificially the heade and vpper part of
15 a body, but the rest hee could not make an ende of. Againe, it is prooued thus, that a body should not be in other partes beautifull, and yet bee deformed in the crooked nose; for all the members in a well shapen bodie must be aunswerable, sound, and well proportioned.

20   6. He that taketh in hande to write any thing must first take heede that he be sufficient for the same: for often vnwary fooles through their rashnes are ouertooke with great want of ability.

    7. The ornament of a worke consisteth in wordes, and
25 in the manner of the wordes; [they] are either simple or mixt, newe or olde, propper or translated. In them all good iudgment must be vsed and ready wytt. The chiefest grace is in the most frequented wordes, for the same reason holdeth in wordes as doth in coynes, that the most
30 vsed and tried are best esteemed.

    8. The kinde of verse is to be considered and aptly applied to the argument, in what measure is most meete for euery sort. The most vsuall kindes are foure, the *Heroic, Elegiac, Iambick,* and *Lyric.*

35   9. One must vse one kynde of speeche alike in all

wrytings.   Sometime the *Lyric* ryseth aloft, sometime the
comicall.   To the Tragicall wryters belong properly the
bygge and boysterous wordes.   Examples must be inter-
placed, according fitly to the time and place.

10. Regarde is to be had of affections : one thing becom-
meth pleasant persons, an other sadde, an other wrathfull,
an other gentle, which must all be heedefully respected.
Three thinges therefore are requisite in verses, beauty,
sweetnes, and the affection.   *Theophrastus* sayth that
this beauty or delectablenesse is a deceyt, and Aristotle
called it τυραννίδα ὀλιγοχρόνιον, a momentany tyrany.   Sweetnesse retayneth a Reader ; affection moueth him.

11. Euery person must be fitted accordingly, and the
speeche well ordered : wherein are to be considered the
dignity, age, sex, fortune, condition, place, Country, &c.
of eche person.

12. The personnes are eyther to be fayned by the Poets
them selues, or borrowed of others.   If he borrow them,
then must hee obserue τὸ ὅμοιον, that is, that he folow that
Author exactly whom he purposeth to immitate and where-
out he bringeth his examples.   But if he fayne newe personnes, then must he keepe his τὸ ὁμαλόν, that is equallie :
so bringing them in eche place, that it be alwayes agreeable,
and the last like vnto the first, and not make one person
nowe a bolde boaster, and the same straightwaies a wise
warie man, for that is passing absurd.   Againe, euery one
must obserue τὸ ἁρμοστόν, which is interpreted *conuenientiam*, fitnesse : as it is meete and agreeable euery where
a man to be stoute, a woman fearefull, a seruant crafty,
a young man gentle.

13. Matters which are common may be handled by a
Poet as they may be thought propper to himselfe alone.
All matters of themselues are open to be intreated of by
any man : but if a thing be handled of some one in such
sort as he thereby obtaine great prayse, he maketh it his

owne or propper to himselfe; as many did write of the
Troiane war, but yet *Homer* made matter which was
common to all propper to himselfe.

14. Where many thinges are to be taken out of auncienter
tongues, as the Latines tooke much out of the Greekes,
the wordes are not so preciselie to be followed but that
they bee altered according to the iudgment and will of the
Immitator; which precept is borrowed of Tully, *Non verbum verbo necesse est reddere.*

15. The beginning must not be foolishly handled, that
is, straungly or too long.

16. The proposition or narration let it not be far fetched
or vnlikely, and in the same forget not the differences of
ages and persons.

17. In a Comedie it is [not] needfull to exhibite all the
actions openlie, as such as are cruell, vnhonest, or ougly;
but such thinges may better bee declared by some meete
and handsome wordes, after what sorte they are supposed
to bee doone.

18. If a Commedye haue more Actes then fiue, it is
tedious; if fewer, it is not sufficient.

It fytteth not to bring in the personnes of Gods but in
verie great matters. *Cicero* sayth, when the Tragedy
wryters cannot bring theyr matters to good passe, they
runne to God. Let not more personnes speake together
then foure, for auoyding confusion.

The *Chori* must be well garnished and sette foorth:
wherein eyther menne are admonished, or reprehended,
or counsayled vnto vertue. Such matter must bee chosen
for the *Chorus* as may bee meete and agreeable to that
which is in hand. As for instruments and singing, they
are Reliques of olde simplicitye. For the Musicke com-
monlye vsed at Theaters and the licenciousnesse of theyr
songes, which together wyth theyr wealth increased among
the Romaines, is hurtfull to discipline and good manners.

19. In a *Satyr* the clownish company and rurall Gods are brought in to temperate the Heauinesse of Tragedies wyth some myrth and pastyme. In iesting it must be obserued that it bee not lacyuious, or Rybaldlike, or slaunderous; which precept holdeth generallie in all sortes of 5 wrytynges.

In a *Satyr* greate heede is to be taken of the place, of the day, and of the personnes: as of *Bacchus, Silenus,* or the *Satyres.* Againe of the vnmeetnesse or inconuenience of the matter, and of the wordes that they be 10 fitted according to the persons: of *Decorum,* that he which represented some noble personage in the Tragedie bee not some busy foole in the *Satyr*: finallie of the hearers, least they bee offended by myxing filthy matters with iestes, wanton toyes wyth vnhonest, or noysome with 15 merry thinges.

20. The feete are to be applied propper to euery kinde of verse, and therin a Poet must not vse too much licence or boldnes. The auncient writers in *Iambick* verses vsed at first pure *Iambicks*: Afterwards *Spondæus* was admitted 20 into *Locos impares,* but at last such was the licentious custome, that they woulde both *Spondæus* where they listed, and other feete without regarde.

21. In compyling of verses great care and circumspection must be vsed. 25

Those verses which be made Extempore are of no great estimation: those which are vnartificiall are vtterly repelled as too foolish. Though many doo lightlie regard our verses, yet ought the Carelesnesse of the hearers to bee no cause in vs of errour and negligence. Who 30 desireth to make any thing worthy to be heard of learned eares, let hym reade Greeke Authors heedefullie and continually.

22. Artes haue their increasinges euen as other things, beeing naturall: so haue Tragedies, which were first rudely 35

inuented by *Thespis*, at last were much adorned by *Æschylus*: at the first they were practised in Villages of the Countrey, afterwardes brought to stages in great Citties.

23. Some Artes doo increase; some doo decay by a certayne naturall course. The olde manner of Commedies decayde by reason of slaundering which therein they vsed against many, for which there was a penaltie appointed, least their bitternes should proceede to farre: In place of which, among the Latines, came the *Satyres*.

The auncient Authors of Comedies were *Eupolis, Cratinus*, and *Aristophanes*; of the middle sorte *Plato Comicus*; of the last kinde *Menander*, which continued and was accounted the most famous.

24. A Poet should not content himselfe onely with others inuentions, but himselfe also by the example of old wryters sholde bring something of his owne industry which may bee laudable. So did they which writte among the Latines the Comedies called *Togatae*, whose arguments were taken from the Greekes, and the other which wrytt the *Pretextatae*, whereof the arguments were Latine.

25. Heedefulnesse and good composition maketh a perfecte verse, and that which is not so may be reprehended. The faculty of a good witte exceedeth Arte.

26. A Poet, that he may be perfect, hath neede to haue knowledge of that part of Philosophy which informeth the life to good manners. The other which pertaineth to naturall thinges is lesse plausible, hath fewer ornaments, and is not so profitable.

27. A Poet to the knowledge of Philosophie shoulde also adde greater experience, that he may know the fashions of men and dispositions of people. Thys profit is gott by trauelling, that whatsoeuer he wryteth he may so expresse and order it that hys narration may be formable.

28. The ende of Poetry is to wryte pleasant thinges, and profitable. Pleasant it is which delighteth by beeing not

too long or vneasy to be kept in memory, and which is somewhat likelie and not altogether forged. Profitable it is which styrreth vppe the mindes to learning and wisedome.

29. Certaine escapes are to be pardoned in some Poets, specially in great workes. A faulte may bee committed either in respect of hys propper Arte or in some other Arte: that a Poet shoulde erre in precepts of hys owne arte is a shamefull thing; to committe a faulte in another Arte is to be born withal: as in *Virgil*, who fayneth that *Æneas* comming into *Affrica* slew with hys darte certaine Stagges, whereas indeede *Affrica* hath in it none of those beastes. Such errours doo happen eyther by vnheedefulnes, when one escapeth them by negligence; or by the common fragility of man, because none there is which can know all thinges. Therefore this last kinde of errour is not to be stucke vppon.

30. A good Poet should haue respect to thys, how to retaine hys Reader or hearer. In a picture some thing delighteth beeing sette farre of, something neerer, but a Poet should delight in all places as well in sunne as shaddowe.

31. In a Poet is no meane to be admitted, which, if hee bee not [t]he [best] of all, is the worst of all.

32. A Poeme if it runne not sweetely and smoothly is odious; which is proued by a *simile* of the two senses, hearing and tasting, as in sweete and pleasaunt meates. And the Poem must bee of that sorte, that for the sweetenesse of it may bee acceptable and continue like it selfe vnto the ende, least it wearye or driue away a Reader.

33. He that would wryte any thing worthy the posteritye, let him not enterprise any thing wherevnto his nature is not agreeable. *Mercury* is not made of wood (as they say), neyther doth *Minerua* fauour all studies in euery one. In all Artes nature is the best helpe, and

learned men vse commonly to say that *A Poet is as well borne as made a Poet.*

34. Let no man esteeme himselfe so learned but that he may submytte hys wrytinges to the iudgments of 5 others, and correct and thoroughly amend the same himselfe.

35. The profitte of Poetry sprang thus, for that the auncient wyse men set downe the best things that pertained to mans life, manners, or felicity, and, examining 10 and proouing the same by long experience of time, when they were aged they published them in wrytinges. The vse of Poetry, what it was at the first, is manifest by the examples of the moste learned men: as of *Orpheus,* who first builded houses; of *Amphion,* who made Citties; of 15 *Tyrtœus,* who first made warre; of *Homer,* who wryt most wysely.

36. In an artificiall Poet three thinges are requisite, nature, Arte, and dilligence.

37. A wryter must learne of the learned, and he must 20 not sticke to confesse when he erreth; that the worse he may learne to auoyde, and knowe howe to follow the better.

The confession of an errour betoken[eth] a noble and a gentle minde. *Celsus* and *Quintillian* doo report of *Hippo-* 25 *crates* that, least he should deceiue his posterity, he confessed certayne errours, as it well became an excellent minded man and one of great credite. For (as sayth *Celsus*) light witts, because they haue nothing, wyll haue nothing taken from them.

30 38. In making choise of such freendes as should tell vs the trueth and correct our wrytinges, heedefull iudgment must bee vsed; least eyther we choose vnskylfull folke, or flatterers, or dissemblers. The vnskilfull know not how to iudge; flatterers feare to offende; dissemblers in not 35 praysing doo seeme to commende.

39. Let no man deceiue himselfe, or suffer himselfe to be deceiued, but take some graue learned man to be iudge of his dooing, and let him according to hys counsayle change and put out what hee thinketh good.

40. He which will not flatter and is of ability to iudge, let him endeuour to nothing so much as to the correction of that which is wrytten, and that let be doone with earnest and exquisite iudgment. He which dooth not thus, but offendeth wilfully in breaking his credite too rashly, may be counted for a madde, furious, and franticke foole.

41. The faultes commonly in verses are seauen, as either they be destitute of Arte, of facility, or ornament, or els they be superfluous, obscure, ambicious, or neede-lesse.

OUT OF THE EPISTLES *AD MAECENATEM, AUGUSTUM, ET FLORUM.*

42. An immitation should not be too seruile or super-stitious, as though one durst not varry one iotte from the example : neyther should it be so sencelesse or vnskilfull as to immitate thinges which are absurde and not to be followed.

43. One should not altogether treade in the steppes of others, but sometime he may enter into such wayes as haue not beene haunted or vsed of others. *Horace* borrowed the *Iambick* verse of *Archilocus*, expressing fully his numbers and elegantly, but his vnseemely wordes and pratling tauntes hee moste wyselye shunned.

44. In our verses we should not gape after the phrases of the simpler sorte, but striue to haue our writings allowable in the iudgments of learned menne.

45. The common peoples iudgments of Poets is seldome true, and therefore not to be sought after. The vulgar sort in *Rome* iudged *Pacuuius* to be very learned ; *Accius*

to bee a graue wryter; that *Affranius* followed *Menander*, *Plautus Epicharmus*; that *Terence* excelled in Arte, *Caecilius* in grauity : but the learned sorte were not of this opinion. There is extant in *Macrobius* (I knowe not 5 whether *Angellius*) the like verdite concerning them which wryt *Epigrammes* : That *Catullus* and *Caluus* wrytt fewe thinges that were good, *Naeuius* obscure, *Hortensius* vncomely, *Cynna* vnpleasant, and *Mummius* rough.

46. The olde wryters are so farre to be commended 10 as nothing be taken from the newe : neyther may we thinke but that the way lyeth open styll to others to attaine to as great matters. Full well sayd *Sidonius* to *Eucherius*, 'I reuerence the olde wryters, yet not so as though I lesse esteemed the vertues and desertes of the wryters 15 in this age.'

47. Newnes is gratefull if it be learned : for certaine it is Artes are not bothe begunne and perfected at once, but are increased by time and studie ; which notwithstanding, when they are at the full perfection, doo debate and 20 decrease againe.

Cic. de orat. There is nothing in the world which bursteth out all at once and commeth to light all wholly together.

48. No man should dare to practise an Arte that is 25 daungerous, especially before he haue learned the same perfectly ; so doo guyders of Shyppes, so doo Phisitions, but so did not manie Romaine Poets (yea so doo not too many English wryters) who in a certaine corragious heate gaped after glory by wryting verses, but fewe of them 30 obtayned it.

49. A Poet should be no lesse skylfull in dealing with the affectes of the mynde then a tumbler or a Iuggler shoulde bee ready in his Arte. And with such pyth shoulde he sette foorth hys matters that a Reader 35 shoulde seeme not onely to heare the thing, but to see

and be present at the dooing thereof. Which faculty *Fabius* calleth ὑποτύπωσιν, and *Aristotle* πρὸ ὀμμάτων θέσιν ἢ ποίησιν.

50. Poets are either such as desire to be liked of on stages, as Commedie and Tragedie wryters, or such as 5 woulde bee regestered in Libraries. Those on stages haue speciall respect to the motions of the minde, that they may stirre bothe the eyes and eares of their beholders. But the other, which seeke to please priuately with[in] the walles, take good aduisement in their workes, that 10 they may satisfy the exact iudgments of learned men in their studies.

51. A Poet shoùlde not bee too importunate, as to offende in vnseasonable speeches ; or vngentle, as to con-temne the admonitions of others ; or ambicious, as to thinke 15 too well of his owne dooinges ; or too wayward, as to thinke reward enough cannot be gyuen him for his deserte ; or, finally, too proude, as to desyre to be honoured aboue measure.

52. The emendations of Poemes be very necessary, that 20 in the obscure poyntes many thinges may be enlightned, in the baser partes many thinges may be throughly garnished. Hee may take away and put out all vnpropper and vnseemely words ; he may with discretion immitate the auncient wryters ; he may abridge thinges that are 25 too lofty, mittigate thynges that are too rough, and may vse all remedies of speeche throughout the whole worke. The thinges which are scarce seemely he may amende by Arte and methode.

53. Let a Poet first take vppon him as though he were 30 to play but an Actors part, as he may bee esteemed like one which wryteth without regarde ; neyther let him so pollish his works but that euery one for the basenesse thereof may think to make as good. Hee may likewyse exercise the part of gesturer, as though he seemed to 35

meddle in rude and common matters, and yet not so deale
in them, as it were for variety sake, nor as though he had
laboured them thoroughly, but tryfled with them, nor as
though he had sweat for them, but practised a little. For
5 so to hyde ones cunning, that nothing should seeme to bee
laborsome or exquisite, when, notwithstanding, euery part
is pollished with care and studie, is a speciall gyft which
Aristotle calleth κρύψιν.

54. It is [not] onely a poynt of wysedome to vse many
10 and choyse elegant wordes, but to vnderstand also and to
set foorth thinges which pertaine to the happy ende of
mans life. Whereuppon the Poet *Horace* calleth the Arte
poeticall, without the knowledge of learning and philosophy,
a *prating vanity*. Therfore a good and allowable Poet
15 must be adorned with wordes, plentious in sentences, and,
if not equall to an Orator, yet very neere him, and a special
louer of learned men.

EPILOGUS.

This small trauell (courteous Reader) I desire thee take
20 in good worth: which I haue compyled, not as an exquisite censure concerning this matter, but (as thou mayst
well perceiue, and in trueth to that onely ende) that it
might be an occasion to haue the same throughly and
with greater discretion taken in hande and laboured by
25 some other of greater abilitie: of whom I knowe there be
manie among the famous Poets in London, who, bothe for
learning and leysure, may handle this Argument far more
pythilie then my selfe. Which if any of them wyll vouchsafe to doo, I trust wee shall haue Englishe Poetry at
30 a higher price in short space: and the rabble of balde
Rymes shall be turned to famous workes, comparable
(I suppose) with the best workes of Poetry in other tongues.

In the meane time, if my poore skill can sette the same any thing forwarde, I wyll not cease to practise the same towardes the framing of some apt English *Prosodia*, styll hoping and hartelie wishing to enioy first the bene-fitte of some others iudgment, whose authority may beare greater credite, and whose learning can better performe it.

ABRAHAM FRAUNCE

(*The Arcadian Rhetorike*)

1588

[Abraham Fraunce issued, in 1588, from the press of Thomas Orwin, *The Arcadian Rhetorike:* | *Or* | *The Præcepts of Rhetorike made plaine | by examples, Greeke, Latin, English, Ita\lian, French, Spanish, out of* || *Homers Ilias, and Odissea, | Virgils Æglogs, Georgikes, and Æneis | Sir Philip Sydneis Arcadiæ, Songs, and Sonets, | Torquato Tassoes Gosfredo, Aminta, Torrismondo, | Salust his Judith, and both his Se-maines, | Boscan and Garcilassoes Sonets and Æglogs.* || Only one copy is preserved, that in the Bodleian (Malone 514). Sheet B 1–8 (eight leaves) is missing. A MS. note on the fly-leaf states that the tract was entered on the Stationers' Books by T. Gubbyn and J. Newman on June 11, 1588.

A summary and a few extracts are here given in place of the complete text, which consists almost entirely of quotations from the authors named above. The rhetorical plan of the book is less elaborate than that of the contemporary *Arte of Englishe Poesie* (q. v. vol. ii. p. 1). The volume is dedicated ' To the Right excellent and most honorable Ladie, the Ladie Marie, Countesse of Pembroke,' in words which are printed thus [1] :

' Voi, pia nympha, tuum quem tolse, la morte, Philippum.
AEdentem llenas cœlesti melle palabras.
Italicum lumen, flowre of Fraunce, splendor Iberus,
Italicus Tasso, French Salust, Boscan Iberus,

---

[1] The lines are reprinted here exactly as they are in the original.

Τῆς Ρωμης Ρωμη Virgil, τῆς Ελλαδος Ελλας,
Greekis. Ἡomer, tanto læti iunguntur ἑταιρῷ.

Your Honors most affectionate

ABRAHAM FRAUNCE.'

The first book contains thirty-six chapters, and extends
to Sig. H 6. The second book begins on H 6 v⁰, and has
but six chapters.

Bk. I. chap. 1 defines ' What Rhetorike is,' as two parts,
'Eloqution & Pronuntiation.' ' Eloqution is the first part
of Rhetorike, concerning the ordering & trimming of
speach. It hath also two parts, Congruitie and Brauerie.'
Congruitie includes 'grammaticall rules'—which Fraunce
omits. ' Brauerie of speech consisteth in tropes or turn-
ings : and in figures or fashionings. A trope or turning
is when a word is turned,' &c. . . . ' So much of the
general proprieties of tropes : now to the divers kindes
thereof.'

Chap. 2 to chap. 5 treat of the Metonymia of the subject
and adjunct, &c.; chap. 6 of Ironia. Then comes the
break in the text, which resumes in the midst of chap. 14,
on feet and poetical dimensions, and the different sorts of
verse, with examples. Chap. 15 is on the dimension for
Orators ; chap. 16, of Epizeuxis ; chap. 17, of Anadiplosis ;
chap. 18, of Climax ; chap. 19, of Anaphora ; chap. 20,
of Epistrophe ; chap. 21, of Symploce ; chap. 22, of
Epanalepsis ; chap. 23, of Epanodos ; chap. 24, of Paro-
nomasia ; chap. 25, of Polyptoton (a long chapter) ; chap. 26,
of Figures of Sentences ; chap. 27, of Exclamation (with
many classified examples) ; chap. 28, of Epanorthosis ;
chap. 29, of Aposiopesis ; chap. 30, of Apostrophe ; chap.
31, of Prosopopoia ; chap. 32, of Addubitation ; chap. 33,
of Communication ; chap. 34, of Præoccupation ; chap. 35,
of Sufferance ; chap. 36, of Graunting. The Second Book
consists of these chapters :—chap. 1, ' of utterance or pronunciation '; chap. 2, ' of the application of the voyce to
severall affections '; chap. 3, ' of action or gesture of the
whole bodie '; chap. 4, ' of the gesture of the head, eyes,
lipps, &c.'; chap. 5, ' of the gesture of the arme, hand,

fingers, &c.; chap. 6, Of the gesture of other parts of the bodie.

Chap. 19, 'Of Anaphora,' may be quoted as an average example of Fraunce's method:—

'Chap. 19. *Of Anaphora.*

Thus much of the continued repetition of the same word in one or diuers sentences; now followeth the severed repetition of the same sound, and that either in the same place, or in divers. In the same place, either simple or conioined. Simple, *Anaphora* and *Epistrophe.* Anaphora, a bringing back of the same sound, is when the same sound is iterated in the beginning of the sentence.'

Then follow quotations from Homer (*Iliad* I), Virgil (*Georg.* IV, *Eclog.* I, *Aen.* III), Sir Philip Sidney, Tasso, Du Bartas (four passages from the *Semaines*), Boscan, and Garcilasso.

In the volume there are three quotations from Spenser's works: (*a*) fol. C 4, to illustrate mixed iambics and spondees, the lines beginning, 'Vnhappie verse, the witnes of my vnhappie state (see Spenser's letter to Harvey, *ante*, p. 90): (*b*) fol. D 7, vᵒ, where the author, after giving some illustrations of *Polyptoton*, says, 'Before I leaue of to talk of these figures of woords, I will here confusedlie insert a number of conceited verses, sith all their grace and delicacie proceedeth from the figures afore-named. Theocritus hath expressed the forme of an egge and an alter in verse; so hath Willy represented the figure of a swoard, and an old Abbot the image of the crosse, in verie laboured and intangled verses: but let them passe, and come we to such as are more plausible;' and, among several examples, he quotes, 'Ye wastfull woods, beare witnesse of my woe,' &c. (*Sheph. Cal., August*): and (*c*), fol. E 3, in further illustration of 'conceipted kindes of verses,' he quotes Spenser, 'in his Fairie Queene, 2 booke, cant. 4'—

'Wrath, iealousie, griefe, loue, doo thus expell,' &c.

to the end of the stanza. The last quotation has the special

interest of having been made before the publication of
the *Faerie Queene*, and of being probably the first lines of
the poem to appear in print. The MS. was already in
circulation among Spenser's intimate friends, and the poet
made no secret of it even in more general society (see
Ludovick Bryskett's introduction to his *Discourse of Civill
Life*, 1606, but written before 1589).]

THOMAS NASH

(I. Preface to Greene's *Menaphon* ;
II. From *The Anatomie of Absurditie*)

1589

I.

[The Preface *To the Gentlemen Students of both Universities* is
prefixed to Robert Greene's *Menaphon: Camillas alarum
to slumbering Euphues in his melancholie Cell at Silexedra,*
London, printed by T. O. for Sampson Clarke, 1589.
The text is printed from the copy in the British Museum,
which is deficient at the end, from the words 'ere long to
their juggling (p. 319, l. 35).' The lost portion is supplied
from the copy of the edition of 1610, also in the British
Museum.]

TO THE GENTLEMEN STUDENTS OF
BOTH VNIUERSITIES.

CVRTEOVS and wise, whose iudgements (not entangled
with enuie) enlarge the deserts of the Learned by
5 your liberall censures, vouchsafe to welcome your scholler-
like Shepheard with such Vniuersitie entertainement as
either the nature of your bountie or the custome of your
common ciuilitie may affoord. To you he appeales that
knew him *ab extrema pueritia,* whose *placet* he accounts the
10 *plaudite* of his paines; thinking his daie labour was not
altogether lauisht *sine linea,* if there be anie thing of all in
it that doth *olere atticum* in your estimate. I am not
ignorant how eloquent our gowned age is growen of late,
so that euerie mœchanicall mate abhorres the english he

was borne too, and plucks with a solemne periphrasis his *vt vales* from the inkhorne: which I impute not so much to the perfection of arts as to the seruile imitation of vain-glorious tragœdians, who contend not so seriouslie to excell in action as to embowell the clowdes in a speach of comparison; thinking themselues more than initiated in poets immortalitie if they but once get *Boreas* by the beard, and the heauenlie bull by the deaw-lap. But herein I cannot so fully bequeath them to follie, as their idiote art-masters, that intrude themselues to our eares as the alcumists of eloquence, who (mounted on the stage of arrogance) think to outbraue better pens with the swelling bumbast of a bragging blanke verse. Indeed, it may be the ingrafted ouerflow of some kilcow conceipt, that ouer-cloieth their imagination with a more than drunken resolu-tion, beeing not extemporall in the inuention of anie other meanes to vent their manhood, commits the digestion of their cholerick incumbrances to the spacious volubilitie of a drumming decasillabon. Mongst this kinde of men that repose eternitie in the mouth of a player, I can but ingrosse some deepe read Grammarians, who, hauing no more learning in their scull than will serue to take vp a com-moditie, nor Arte in their brain than was nourished in a seruing mans idlenesse, will take vpon them to be the ironicall censors of all, when God and Poetrie doth know they are the simplest of all.

To leaue these to the mercie of their mother tongue, that feed on nought but the crummes that fal from the translators trencher, I come (sweet friend) to thy *Arcadian Menaphon*, whose attire, though not so statelie, yet comelie, dooth entitle thee aboue all other to that *temperatum dicendi genus* which *Tullie* in his *Orator* tearmeth true eloquence. Let other men (as they please) praise the mountaine that in seauen yeares brings foorth a mouse, or the Italianate pen that of a packet of pilfries affoordeth

the presse a pamphlet or two in an age, and then in disguised arraie vaunts *Ouids* and *Plutarchs* plumes as their
owne ; but giue me the man whose extemporall vaine in
anie humor will excell our greatest Art-masters deliberate
thoughts, whose inuention, quicker than his eye, will
challenge the proudest Rethoritian to the contention of
like perfection with like expedition. What is he amongst
Students so simple that cannot bring forth (*tandem aliquando*) some or other thing singular, sleeping betwixt
euerie sentence ? Was it not *Maros* xij. years toyle that
so famed his xij. *Æneidos ?* Or *Peter Ramus* xvj. yeares
paines that so praised his pettie Logique ? Howe is it,
then, our drowping wits should so wonder at an exquisite
line that was his masters day labour ? Indeede, I must
needes say the descending yeares from the Philosophers
Athens haue not been supplied with such present Orators
as were able in anie English vaine to be eloquent of their
owne, but either they must borrow inuention of *Ariosto*
and his Countreymen, take vp choyce of words by ex-
change in *Tullies Tusculane* and the Latine Historiographers store-houses, similitudes, nay whole sheetes and
tractacts *verbatim*, from the plentie of *Plutarch* and *Plinie*,
and, to conclude, their whole methode of writing from the
libertie of Comical fictions that haue succeeded to our
Rethoritians by a second imitation : so that well may the
Adage, *Nil dictum quod non dictum prius*, bee the most
iudiciall estimate of our latter Writers.

But the hunger of our vnsatiate humorists, beeing such
as it is, readie to swallowe all draffe without indifference,
that insinuates it selfe to their senses vnder the name of
delight, imployes oft times manie thred bare witts to
emptie their inuention of their Apish deuices, and talke
most superficiallie of Pollicie, as those that neuer ware
gowne in the Vniuersitie ; wherein they reuiue the olde
saide Adage, *Sus Mineruam*, & cause the wiser to quippe

them with *Asinus ad Lyram*. Would Gentlemen & riper
iudgements admit my motion of moderation in a matter of
follie, I wold perswade them to phisicke their faculties of
seeing & hearing, as the *Sabæans* doo their dulled senses
with smelling; who (as *Strabo* reporteth), ouer-cloyed with 5
such odoriferous sauours as the naturall encrease of their
Countrey (Balsamum, Amomum, with Myrrhe and Franken-
cense) sends foorth, refresh their nosthrills with the vn-
sauorie sent of the pitchie slime that *Euphrates* casts vp,
and the contagious fumes of Goates beardes burnt; so 10
woulde I haue them, beeing surfetted vnawares with the
sweete satietie of eloquence which the lauish of our
copious Language maie procure, to vse the remedie of
contraries, and recreate their rebated witts not, as they
did, with the senting of slyme or Goates beardes burnt, 15
but with the ouer-seeing of that *sublime dicendi genus*,
which walkes abroad for wast paper in each seruing mans
pocket, and the otherwhile perusing of our Gothamists
barbarisme; so shoulde the opposite comparison of *Puritie*
expell the infection of absurditie, and their ouer-rackte 20
Rhethorique bee the Ironicall recreation of the Reader.
But so farre discrepant is the idle vsage of our vnexperienst
punies from this prescription, that a tale of Ihon a Brain-
fords will and the vnluckie furmentie wilbe as soon inter-
teined into their libraries as the best poeme that euer 25
Tasso eternisht: which, being the effect of an vndescerning
iudgement, makes drosse as valuable as gold, and losse as
welcome as gaine, the Glowworme mentioned in *Æsops*
fables, namelie the apes follie, to be mistaken for fire,
when, as God wot, poore soules, they haue nought but their 30
toyle for their heate, their paines for their sweate, and (to
bring it to our english prouerbe) their labour for their
trauaile. Wherin I can but resemble them to the Panther,
who is so greedie of mens excrements that, if they be
hangd vp in a vessell higher than his reach, he sooner 35

killeth himselfe with the ouer-stretching of his windlesse
bodie than he wil cease from his intended enterprise. Oft
haue I obserued what I now set downe ; a secular wit, that
hath liued all daies of his life by what doo you lacke, to
5 bee more iudiciall in matters of conceit than our quadrant
crepundios that spit *ergo* in the mouth of euerie one they
meete : yet those & these are so affectionate to dogged
detracting, as the most poysonous *Pasquil* anie durtie
mouthed *Martin* or *Momus* euer composed is gathered vp
10 with greedinesse before it fall to the ground, and bought
at the deerest, though they smell of the friplers lauander
halfe a yeere after : for I know not how the minde of the
meanest is fedde with this follie, that they impute singularitie to him that slanders priuelie, and count it a great
15 peece of arte in an inkhorne man, in anie tapsterlie tearmes
whatsoeuer, to oppose his superiours to enuie. I will not
denie but in scholler-like matters of controuersie a quicker
stile may passe as commendable, and that a quippe to an
asse is as good as a goad to an oxe ; but when an irregular
20 idiot, that was vp to the eares in diuinitie before euer he
met with *probabile* in the Vniuersitie, shall leaue *pro &*
contra before he can scarcely pronounce it, and come to
correct Common weales, that neuer heard of the name of
Magistrate before he came to *Cambridge*, it is no meruaile
25 if euery alehouse vaunt the table of the world turned
vpside down ; since the childe beats his father, & the asse
whippes his master. But least I might seeme with these
night crowes *Nimis curiosus in aliena republica*, I'le turne
backe to my first text, of studies of delight, and talke a
30 little in friendship with a few of our triuiall translators.

It is a common practise now a daies amongst a sort of
shifting companions, that runne through euery arte and
thriue by none, to leaue the trade of *Nouerint*, whereto they
were borne, and busie themselues with the indeuors of Art,
35 that could scarcelie latinize their necke-verse if they should

haue neede; yet English *Seneca* read by candle light
yeeldes manie good sentences, as *Bloud is a begger*, and
so foorth; and, if you intreate him faire in a frostie morning,
he will affoord you whole *Hamlets*, I should say handfulls
of tragical speaches. But O griefe! *tempus edax rerum*, 5
what's that will last alwaies? The sea exhaled by droppes
will in continuance be drie, and *Seneca* let bloud line by
line and page by page at length must needes die to our
stage: which makes his famisht followers to imitate the
Kidde in *Æsop*, who, enamored with the Foxes newfangles, 10
forsooke all hopes of life to leape into a new occupation,
and these men, renowncing all possibilities of credit or
estimation, to intermeddle with Italian translations: wherein
how poorelie they haue plodded (as those that are neither
prouenzall men nor are able to distinguish of Articles), let 15
all indifferent Gentlemen that haue trauailed in that tongue
discerne by their twopenie pamphlets: & no meruaile
though their home-born mediocritie be such in this matter,
for what can be hoped of those that thrust *Elisium* into
hell, and haue not learned, so long as they haue liued in 20
the spheares, the iust measure of the Horizon without an
hexameter. Sufficeth them to bodge vp a blanke verse
with ifs and ands, & other while for recreation after their
candle stuffe, hauing starched their beardes most curiouslie,
to make a peripateticall path into the inner parts of the 25
Citie, & spend two or three howers in turning ouer French
Doudie, where they attract more infection in one minute
than they can do eloquence all dayes of their life by
conuersing with anie Authors of like argument.

But least in this declamatorie vaine I should condemne all 30
& commend none, I will propound to your learned imitation
those men of import that haue laboured with credit in this
laudable kinde of Translation. In the forefront of whom
I cannot but place that aged Father *Erasmus*, that inuested
most of our Greeke Writers in the roabes of the auncient 35

Romaines; in whose traces *Philip Melancthon, Sadolet, Plantine,* and manie other reuerent Germaines insisting haue reedified the ruines of our decayed Libraries, and merueilouslie inriched the Latine tongue with the expence
5 of their toyle. Not long after, their emulation beeing transported into *England,* euerie priuate Scholler, *William Turner* and who not, beganne to vaunt their smattering of Latine in English Impressions. But amongst others in that Age, Sir *Thomas Eliots* elegance did seuer it selfe
10 from all equalls, although Sir *Thomas Moore* with his Comicall wit at that instant was not altogether idle : yet was not Knowledge fullie confirmed in hir Monarchie amongst vs till that most famous and fortunate Nurse of all learning, Saint *Iohns* in *Cambridge,* that at that time was
15 as an Vniuersitie within it selfe—shining so farre aboue all other Houses, Halls, and Hospitalls whatsoeuer, that no Colledge in the Towne was able to compare with the tythe of her Students; hauing (as I haue hearde graue men of credite report) more candles light in it euerie
20 Winter Morning before fowre of the clocke than the fowre of clocke bell gaue stroakes—till Shee (I saie), as a pitty- ing Mother, put too her helping hande, and sent from her fruitefull wombe sufficient Schollers, both to support her owne weale as also to supplie all other inferiour founda-
25 tions defects, and namelie that royall erection of *Trinitie Colledge,* which the Vniuersitie Orator, in an Epistle to the Duke of *Somerset,* aptlie tearmed *Colona diducta* from the Suburbes of *Saint Iohns :* In which extraordinarie con- ception, *vno partu in rempublicam prodiere* the Exchequer
30 of eloquence Sir *Iohn Cheeke,* a man of men, supernaturally traded in al tongues, Sir *John Mason,* Doctor *Watson, Redman, Aschame, Grindall, Leuer, Pilkington,* all which haue, either by their priuate readings or publique workes, repurged the errors of Arts expelde from their puritie,
35 and set before our eyes a more perfect Methode of Studie.

But howe ill their preceptes haue prospered with our
idle Age, that leaue the fountaines of sciences, to follow the
riuers of Knowledge, their ouer-fraught Studies with trifling
Compendiaries maie testifie: for I knowe not howe it
comes to passe by the doating practise of our Diuinitie 5
dunces, that striue to make their Pupills pulpet men before
they are reconciled to *Priscian,* but those yeares which
shoulde bee employed in *Aristotle* are expired in Epitomes;
and well too they maye haue so much Catechisme vacation
to rake vp a little refuse Philosophie.   And heere could 10
I enter into a large fielde of inuectiue against our abiect
abbreuiations of Artes, were it not growen to a newe
fashion amongst our Nation to vaunt the pride of contrac-
tion in euerie manuarie action: in so much, that the *Pater
noster,* which was woont to fill a sheete of paper, is written 15
in the compasse of a pennie; whereupon one merelie
affirmed that prouerb to be deriued, *No pennie, no pater
noster;* which their nice curtailing puts me in mind of the
custome of the *Scythians,* who, if they be at any time dis-
tressed with famin, take in their girdles shorter & swaddle 20
themselues streighter, to the intent, no *vacuum* beeing left
in their intrayles, hunger should not so much tirannize
ouer their stomacks; euen so these men, opprest with a
greater penurie of Art, do pound their capacitie in barren
Compendiums, and bound their base humors in the 25
beggerly straites of a hungry Analysis, least, longing after
that *infinitum* which the pouertie of their conceit cannot
compasse, they sooner yeeld vp their youth to destinie
than their heart to vnderstanding.   How is it, then, such
bungling practitioners in principles shuld euer profite the 30
Common wealth by their negligent paines, who haue no
more cunning in Logique or Dialogue Latine than apper-
tains to the literall construction of either: neuerthelesse,
it is daily apparant to our domesticall eyes that there is
none so forward to publish their imperfections, either in 35

the trade of glose or translations, as those that are more
vnlearned than ignorance and lesse conceiuing than
infants. Yet dare I not impute absurditie to all of that
societie, though some of them haue set their names to
5 their simplicitie. Who euer my priuate opinion con-
demneth as faultie, Master *Gascoigne* is not to bee abridged
of his deserued esteeme, who first beate the path to that
perfection which our best Poets haue aspired too since his
departure; whereto he did ascend by comparing the Italian
10 with the English, as *Tullie* did *Græca cum Latinis*. Neither
was Master *Turberuile* the worst of his time, although in
translating he attributed too much to the necessitie of rime.
And, in this page of praise, I cannot omit aged *Arthur
Golding*, for his industrious toile in Englishing *Ouids
15 Metamorphosis*, besides manie other exquisite editions of
Diuinitie, turned by him out of the French tongue into
our own. Master *Phaer* likewise is not to be forgot in
regard of his famous *Virgil*, whose heauenly verse had it
not bin blemisht by his hautie thoghts, *England* might haue
20 long insulted in his wit, and *corrigat qui potest* haue been
subscribed to his workes. But fortune, the Mistres of
change, with a pitying compassion respecting Master
Stanihursts praise, would that *Phaer* shoulde fall that hee
might rise, whose heroicall Poetrie, infired, I should say
25 inspired, with an hexameter furie, recalled to life whateuer
hissed barbarisme hath bin buried this hundred yeare,
and reuiued by his ragged quill such carterlie varietie as
no hodge plowman in a countrie but would haue held as
the extremitie of clownerie; a patterne whereof I will
propounde to your iudgements, as neere as I can, being
parte of one of his descriptions of a tempest, which is thus:

*Then did he make heauens vault to rebounde, with rounce
   robble hobble
Of ruffe raffe roaring, with thwick thwack thurlery bouncing.*

Which strange language of the firmament, neuer subiect
before to our common phrase, makes vs, that are not vsed
to terminate heauens moueings in the accents of any
voice, esteeme of their triobulare interpreter as of some
Thrasonical huffe snuffe, for so terrible was his stile to all 5
milde eares, as would haue affrighted our peaceable Poets
from intermedling hereafter with that quarrelling kinde of
verse, had not sweete Master *France*, by his excellent
translation of Master *Thomas Watsons* sugred *Amintas*,
animated their dulled spirits to such high witted endeuors. 10
But I knowe not how their ouer timerous cowardise hath
stoode in awe of enuie, that no man since him durst imitate
any of the worste of those Romane wonders in english,
which makes me thinke that either the louers of medocritie
are verie many or that the number of good Poets are very 15
small: and in trueth, Master *Watson* except (whom I
mentioned before), I knowe not almost any of late dayes
that hath shewed himselfe singular in any speciall Latin
Poëm, whose *Amintas* and translated *Antigone* may
march in equipage of honour with any of our ancient 20
Poets. I will not say but wee had a *Haddon* whose pen
would haue challenged the Lawrell from *Homer*, together
with *Carre*, that came as nere him as *Virgil* to *Theocritus*.
But *Tho. Newton* with his *Leyland*, and *Gabriell Haruey*,
with two or three other, is almost all the store that is left 25
vs at this hower. Epitaphers and position Poets haue
wee more than a good many, that swarme like Crowes
to a dead carcas, but flie, like Swallows in the Winter,
from any continuate subiect of witte. The efficient
whereof I imagine to issue from the vpstart discipline 30
of our reformatorie Churchmen, who account wit vanitie,
and poetrie impietie; whose error, although the necessitie
of Philosophie might confute, which lies couched most
closely vnder darke fables profounditie, yet I had rather
referre it as a disputatiue plea to diuines than set it 35

downe as a determinate position, in my vnexperienst
opinion. But how euer their dissentious iudgements
should decree in their afternoone sessions of *an sit*, the
priuat trueth of my discoured Creede in this controuersie
5 is this, that as that beast was thought scarce worthie to
bee sacrifised to the Ægiptian *Epaphus*, who had not
some or other blacke spotte on his skinne, so I deeme
him farre vnworthie of the name of scholler, & so, conse-
quentlie, to sacrifice his endeuors to art, that is not a Poet,
10 either in whole or in a parte. And here, peraduenture,
some desperate quipper will canuaze my proposed comparison *plus vltra*, reconciling the allusion of the blacke
spot to the blacke pot; which makes our Poets vndermeale Muses so mutinous, as euerie stanzo they pen after
15 dinner is full poynted with a stabbe. Which their dagger
drunkennesse, although it might be excused with *Tam
Marti quam Mercurio*, yet will I couer it as well as I may
with that prouerbial *fœcundi calices*, that might wel haue
been doore keeper to the kanne of *Silenus*, when, nodding
20 on his Asse trapt with iuie, hee made his moist nosecloth
the pausing intermedium twixt euerie nappe. Let frugale
scholares and fine fingerd nouices take their drinke by
the ownce and their wine by the halpe-worthes, but it is
for a Poet to examine the pottle pottes and gage the
25 bottome of whole gallons; *qui bene vult* ποιεῖν, *debet ante*
πίνειν. A pot of blew burning ale, with a fierie flaming
tost, is as good as *Pallas* with the nine Muses on *Parnassus* top: without the which, in vaine may they crie,
'O thou, my muse, inspire mee with some pen,' when they
30 want certaine liquid sacrifice to rouze her foorth her
denne. Pardon me, Gentlemen, though somewhat merely
I glaunce at their imoderate follie, who affirme that no
man can write with conceit, except he takes counsell of
the cup: nor would I haue you thinke that *Theonino
35 dente* I arme my stile against all, since I doo knowe the

moderation of many Gentlemen of that studie to be so
farre from infamie as their verse from equalitie : whose
sufficiencie, were it as well seene into, by those of higher
place, as it wanders abroade vnrewarded in the mouthes
of vngratefull monsters, no doubte but the remembrance 5
of *Mæcenas* liberalitie extended to *Maro,* and men of like
qualitie, would haue lefte no memorie to that prouerb of
pouertie, *Si nihil attuleris, ibis Homere foras.* ' Tut,' saies
our English Italians, ' the finest witts our Climate sends
foorth are but drie braind doltes, in comparison of other 10
countries ' : whome if you interrupt with *redde rationem,*
they will tell you of *Petrarche, Tasso, Celiano,* with an
infinite number of others ; to whome if I should oppose
Chaucer, Lidgate, Gower, with such like, that liued vnder
the tirranie of ignorance, I do think their best louers 15
would bee much discontented with the collation of contraries, if I should write ouer al their heads, Haile fellow
well met. One thing I am sure of, that each of these
three haue vaunted their meeters with as much admiration
in English as euer the proudest *Ariosto* did his verse in 20
Italian. What should I come to our court, where the
otherwhile vacations of our grauer Nobilitie are prodigall
of more pompous wit and choyce of words than euer
tragick *Tasso* could attaine too ? But, as for pastorall
Poëmes, I will not make the comparison, least our 25
countrimens credit should bee discountenanst by the
contention, who, although they cannot fare with such
inferior facilitie, yet I knowe would carrie the bucklers
full easilie from all forreine brauers, if their *subiectum
circa quod* should sauor of any thing haughtie : and, should 30
the challenge of deepe conceit be intruded by an forreiner
to bring our english wits to the tutchstone of Arte, I would
preferre diuine Master *Spencer,* the miracle of wit, to
bandie line for line for my life in the honor of *England,*
gainst *Spaine, France, Italie,* and all the worlde. Neither 35

is he the only swallow of our summer (although *Apollo*,
if his *Tripos* were vp again, would pronounce him his
Socrates), but, he being forborne, there are extant about
London many most able men to reuiue Poetrie, though
5 it were executed ten thousand times, as in *Platos*, so in
Puritanes common wealth; as for example *Mathew Roydon, Thomas Atchelow*, and *George Peele*, the first of whome,
as hee hath shewed himselfe singular in the immortall
Epitaph of his beloued *Astrophel*, besides many other
10 most absolute comicke inuentions (made more publique
by euerie mans praise than they can bee by my speache),
so the second hath more than once or twise manifested
his deepe witted schollership in places of credit, and for
the last, thogh not the least of them all, I dare commend
15 him to all that know him as the chiefe supporter of
pleasance nowe liuing, the *Atlas* of Poetrie and *primus
verborum Artifex*, whose first encrease, the Arraigne-
ment of *Paris*, might plead to your opinions his pregnant
dexteritie of wit and manifold varietie of inuention,
20 wherein (*me iudice*) hee goeth a step beyond all that
write. Sundrie other sweete Gentlemen I know, that
haue vaunted their pens in priuate deuices, and trickt
vp a companie of taffata fooles with their feathers, whose
beautie if our Poets had not peecte with the supply of
25 their periwigs, they might haue antickt it vntill this time
vp and downe the countrey with the King of *Fairies*, and
dined euerie daie at the pease porredge ordinarie with
Delphrigus. But *Tolossa* hath forgot that it was sometime
sackt, and beggers that euer they caried their fardles on
30 footback: and in truth no meruaile, when as the deserued
reputation of one *Roscius* is of force to inrich a rabble
of counterfets; yet let subiects for all their insolence
dedicate a *De profundis* euerie morning to the preser-
uation of their *Cæsar*, least their encreasing indignities
35 returne them ere long to their iuggling to mediocrity,

and they bewaile in weeping blankes the wane of their Monarchie.

As Poetrie hath beene honoured in those her forenamed professours, so it hath not beene any whit disparaged by *William Warners* absolute *Albions*. And heere Authoritie hath made a full point: in whose reuerence insisting I cease to expose to your sport the picture of those Pamphleters and Poets, that make a patrimonie of *In speech*, and more than a younger brothers inheritance of their *Abcie*. Reade fauourably, to incourage me in the firstlings of my folly, and perswade your selues I will persecute those idiots and their heires vnto the third generation, that haue made Art bankerout of her orna-ments, and sent Poetry a begging vp and downe the Countrey. It may be my *Anatomie* of *Absurdities* may acquaint you ere long with my skill in surgery, wherein the diseases of Art more merrily discouered may make our maimed Poets put together their blankes vnto the building of an Hospitall.

If you chance to meete it in *Paules*, shaped in a new suite of similitudes, as if, like the eloquent apprentice of *Plutarch*, it were propped at seuen yeares end in double apparell, thinke his master hath fulfilled couenants, and onely cancelled the Indentures of dutie. If I please, I will thinke my ignorance indebted vnto you that applaud it: if not, what rests but that I be excluded from your curtesie, like *Apocrypha* from your Bibles?

How euer, yours euer,

Thomas Nash.

II.

[The following extracts are taken from *The Anatomie of Absurditie . . . Compiled by T. Nashe . . . At London, Printed by I. Charlewood for Thomas Hacket . . . Ann. Dom.* 1589, which may have been written before the Preface to Greene's *Menaphon*. The text is taken from the copy in the Bodleian (Malone 566). The last printed page (from 'me of,' p. 336, l. 32) is missing. It is added in MS., in a careful hand.]

ZEUXES, beeing about to drawe the counterfet of *Iuno*, assembled all the *Agrigentine* Maydes, whom after he pausing had viewed, he chose out fiue of the fayrest, that in their beautie he might imitate what was most
5 excellent: euen so it fareth with mee, who, beeing about to anatomize Absurditie, am vrged to take a view of sundry mens vanitie, a suruey of their follie, a briefe of their barbarisme, to runne through Authors of the absurder sort assembled in the Stacioners shop, sucking
10 and selecting out of these vpstart antiquaries somewhat of their vnsauery duncerie, meaning to note it with a *Nigrum theta*, that each one at the first sight may eschew it as infectious, to shewe it to the world that all men may shunne it. And euen as *Macedon Phillip*, hauing finished
15 his warres, builded a Cittie for the worst sorte of men, which hee called πονηρόπολις, *malorum Ciuitas*, so I, hauing laide aside my grauer studies for a season, determined with my selfe, beeing idle in the Countrey, to beginne in this vacation the foundation of a trifling subiect, which

might shroude in his leaues the abusiue enormities of
these our times. It fareth nowe a daies with vnlearned
Idiots as it doth with she Asses, who bring foorth all
their life long: euen so these brainlesse Bussards are
euery quarter bigge wyth one Pamphlet or other. But 5
as an Egge that is full beeing put into water sinketh to
the bottome, whereas that which is emptie floateth aboue,
so those that are more exquisitly furnished with learning
shroude themselues in obscuritie, whereas they that [are]
voide of all knowledge endeuour continually to publish 10
theyr follie.

Such and the very same are they that obtrude themselues vnto vs as the Authors of eloquence and fountains
of our finer phrases, when as they sette before vs nought
but a confused masse of wordes without matter, a Chaos 15
of sentences without any profitable sence, resembling
drummes, which beeing emptie within sound big without.
Were it that any Morrall of greater moment might be
fished out of their fabulous follie, leauing theyr words
we would cleaue to their meaning, pretermitting their 20
painted shewe we woulde pry into their propounded
sence; but when as lust is the tractate of so many leaues,
and loue passions the lauish dispence of so much paper,
I must needes sende such idle wits to shrift to the vicar
of S. Fooles, who in steede of a worser may be such a 25
Gothamists ghostly Father. Might *Ouids* exile admonish
such Idlebies to betake them to a new trade, the Presse
should be farre better employed; Histories of antiquitie
not halfe so much belyed; Minerals, stones, and herbes
should not haue such cogged natures and names ascribed 30
to them without cause; Englishmen shoulde not be halfe
so much Italianated as they are; finallie, loue woulde
obtaine the name of lust, and vice no longer maske vnder
the visard of vertue.

Are they not ashamed in their prefixed posies to adorne 35

a pretence of profit mixt with pleasure, when as in their bookes there is scarce to be found one precept pertaining to vertue, but whole quires fraught with amorous discourses kindling *Venus* flame in *Vulcans* forge, carrying *Cupid* in
5 tryumph, alluring euen vowed *Vestals* to treade awry, inchaunting chaste mindes and corrupting the continenst? Henceforth, let them alter their posies of profit with inter-mingled pleasure, inserting that of Ouid insteed,

10 *Si quis in hoc artem populo non nouit amandi,*
Me legat, & lecto carmine doctus amet.

So shall the discreet Reader vnderstand the contents by the title, and their purpose by their posie: what els I pray you doe these bable bookemungers endeuor but to repaire the ruinous wals of *Venus* Court, to restore to
15 the worlde that forgotten Legendary licence of lying, to imitate a fresh the fantasticall dreames of those exiled Abbie-lubbers, from whose idle pens proceeded those worne out impressions of the feyned no where acts of Arthur of the rounde table, Arthur of litle Brittaine,
20 Sir Tristram, Hewon of Burdeaux, the Squire of low degree, the foure sons of Amon, with infinite others. It is not of my yeeres nor studie to censure these mens foolerie more theologicallie, but to shew how they to no Commonwealth commoditie tosse ouer their troubled
25 imaginations to haue the praise of the learning which they lack. Many of them to be more amiable with their friends of the Feminine sexe blot many sheetes of paper in the blazing of Womens slender praises, as though in that generation there raigned and alwaies remained such
30 singuler simplicitie that all posterities should be enioyned by duetie to fill and furnish their Temples, nay Townes and streetes, with the shrines of the Saints: Neuer remembring that as there was a loyall *Lucretia*, so there was a light a loue *Lais*, that as there was a modest

Medullina, so there was a mischiuous *Medea,* that as there was a stedfast *Timoclea,* so there was a trayterous *Tarpeya,* that as there was a sober *Sulpitia,* so there was a deceitful *Scylla,* that as there was a chast *Claudia,* so there was a wanton *Clodia.* 5

[*Nash then proceeds to discuss, in no friendly way, the character of woman, and to offer* (*in the words of the subtitle of the pamphlet*) 'a breefe confutation of the slender imputed prayses to feminine perfection.' *He rates the* 'idle heads' *for their* 'prodigall commendation,' *and for* 1 *not consulting their credit* 'in the composition of some other more profitable contrary subiect.']

I leaue these in their follie, and hasten to other mens furie, who make the Presse the dunghill, whether they carry all the muck of their mellancholicke imaginations, 1 pretending, forsooth, to anatomize abuses, and stubbe vp sin by the rootes, when as there waste paper, beeing wel viewed, seemes fraught with naught els saue dogge daies effects ; who, wresting places of Scripture against pride, whoredome, couetousnes, gluttonie, and drunkennesse, 2 extend their inuectiues so farre against the abuse that almost the things remaines not whereof they admitte anie lawfull vse : Speaking of pride, as though they were afraid some body should cut too large peniworthes out of their cloth ; of couetousnes, as though in them that 2 Prouerbe had beene verified, *Nullus ad amissas ibit amicus opes* ; of gluttonie, as though their liuing did lye vppon another mans trencher ; of drunkennesse, as though they had beene brought vppe all the dayes of their life with bread and water : and finally, of whoredome, as though 3 they had beene Eunuckes from theyr cradle, or blind from the howre of their conception. But as the Stage player is nere the happier because hee represents oft times the persons of mightie men, as of Kings & Emperours, so I account such men neuer the holier ;

because they place praise in painting foorth other mens imperfections.

These men resemble Trees, which are wont eftsoones to die if they be fruitfull beyond their wont; euen so they do die in vertue, if they once ouershoote themselues too much wyth inueighing against vice; to be brainsicke in workes, if they be too fruitfull in words. And euen as the Vultures slay nothing themselues, but pray vpon that which of other is slayne, so these men inueigh against no new vice which heeretofore by the censures of the learned hath not beene sharply condemned, but teare that peecemeale wise which long since by ancient wryters was wounded to the death, so that out of their forepassed paines ariseth their Pamphlets, out of theyr volumes theyr inuectiues. Good God, that those that neuer tasted of any thing saue the excrements of Artes, whose threddebare knowledge, beeing bought at the second hand, is spotted, blemished, and defaced through translaters rigorous rude dealing, shoulde preferre their sluttered sutes before other mens glittering gorgious array, should offer them water out of a muddie pit, who haue continually recourse to the Fountaine, or dregs to drink, who haue wine to sell. *At scire tuum nihil est, nisi te scire hoc sciat alter.* Thy knowledge bootes thee not a button, except another knowes that thou hast this knowledge. *Anacharsis* was wont to say that the Athenians vsed money to no other ende but to tell it: euen so these men make no other vse of learning but to shewe it. But as the Panther smelleth sweetelie but onely to brute beastes, which shee draweth vnto her to theyr destruction, not to men in like maner, so these men seeme learned to none but Idiots, whom, with a coloured shew of zeale, they allure vnto them to their illusion, and not to the learned in like sort. I know not howe it delighteth them to put theyr Oare in another mans boate, and their foote in another mans boote, to incurre

that prouerbiall checke, *Ne sutor vltra crepidam,* or that
oratoricall taunt, *Quam quisque norit artem in ea se exerceat* ;
with the Elephant to wade and wallowe in the shallow
water, when they woulde sooner sincke then swym in the
deepe Riuer; to be conuersant in those Authors which 5
they cannot vnderstande but by the translatour their
interpreter; to vaunte reading, when the sum of their
diuinitie consists in twopennie Catichismes : and yet their
ignoraunt zeale wyll presumptuously presse into the Presse,
enquiring most curiouslie into euery corner of the Com- 10
mon wealth, correcting that sinne in others wherwith
they are corrupted themselues. To prescribe rules of
life belongeth not to the ruder sorte ; to condemne those
callings which are approoued by publique authoritie argueth a proude contempt of the Magistrates superiority. 15
Protogenes knew *Apelles* by one lyne, neuer otherwise
seene ; and you may knowe these mens spirit by theyr
speeche, their minds by their medling, their folly by
their phrase. View their workes, and know their vanitie ;
see the Bookes bearing their name, and smile in thy sleeue 20
at their shame. A small ship in a shallow Riuer seemes
a huge thing, but in the sea a very litle vessell ; euen so
each trifling Pamphlet to the simpler sorte a most sub-
stantiall subiect, whereof the wiser lightly account & the
learned laughing contemne. Therefore more earnestly 25
I agrauate their faulte, because their crime is crept into
credit, & their dooinges deemed deuotion, when as
purposelie to some mans despight they bring into act
their cholericke motions.

[*Then, after denouncing hypocritical Malcontents and* 30
those who 'search curiouslie into the secrets of nature'
and publish portents for the superstitious, the pamphlet
proceeds—]

Hence come our babling Ballets, and our new found
Songs & Sonets, which euery rednose Fidler hath at 35

his fingers end, and euery ignorant Ale Knight will breath
foorth ouer the potte, as soone as his braine waxeth hote.
Be it a truth which they would tune, they enterlace it with
a lye or two to make meeter, not regarding veritie so they
5 may make vppe the verse: not vnlike to Homer, who
cared not what he fained so hee might make his Countri-
men famous. But as the straightest things beeing put into
water seeme crooked, so the crediblest trothes if once they
come within compasse of these mens wits seeme tales.
10 Were it that the infamie of their ignoraunce did redound
onlie vppon themselues, I could be content to apply my
speech otherwise then to their *Apuleyan* eares; but sith they
obtaine the name of our English Poets, and thereby make
men thinke more baselie of the wittes of our Countrey,
15 I cannot but turne them out of their counterfet liuerie and
brand them in the foreheade, that all men may know their
falshood. Well may that saying of *Campanus* be applyed
to our English Poets, which hee spake of them in his time:
'They make,' saith he, 'Poetry an occupation; lying is
20 their lyuing, and fables are their mooueables: if thou takest
away trifles, sillie soules, they will famish for hunger.' It
were to be wished that the acts of the ventrous and the
praise of the vertuous were by publique Edict prohibited:
by such mens merry mouthes to be so odiouslie extolde
25 as rather breedes detestation then admiration, lothing then
lyking. What politique Counsailour or valiant Souldier
will ioy or glorie of this, in that some stitcher, Weauer,
spendthrift, or Fidler hath shuffled or slubberd vp a few
ragged Rimes, in the memoriall of the ones prudence or
30 the others prowesse? It makes the learned sort to be
silent, when as they see vnlearned sots so insolent.

These Bussards thinke knowledge a burthen, tapping
it before they haue half tunde it, venting it before they
haue filled it; in whom that saying of the Orator is
35 verified, *Ante ad dicendum quam ad cognoscendum veniunt.*

They come to speake before they come to know. They contemne Arts as vnprofitable, contenting themselues with a little Countrey Grammer knowledge, god wote, thanking God with that abscedarie Priest in Lincolneshire, that he neuer knewe what that Romish popish Latine meant. 5 Verie requisite were it that such blockheads had some *Albadanensis Appollonius* to send them to some other mechanicall Arte, that they might not thus be the staine of Arte. Such kind of Poets were they that *Plato* excluded from his Common wealth and *Augustine* banished *ex* 10 *ciuitate Dei*, which the Romans derided, and the *Lacedæ-monians* scorned, who wold not suffer one of Archilocus bookes to remaine in their Countrey: and amisse it were not, if these which meddle with the Arte they knowe not were bequethed to Bridwell, there to learne a new occupa- 15 tion: for as the Basiliske with his hisse driueth all other Serpents from the place of his aboad, so these rude Rithmours with their iarring verse allienate all mens mindes from delighting in numbers excellence, which they haue so defaced that wee may well exclaime with the Poet 20 *Quantum mutatus ab illo.*

But least I should be mistaken as an enemie to Poetrie, or at least not taken as a friend to that studie, I haue thought good to make them priuie to my mind, by expressing my meaning. I account of Poetrie as of 25 a more hidden & diuine kinde of Philosophy, enwrapped in blinde Fables and darke stories, wherin the principles of more excellent Arts and morrall precepts of manners, illustrated with diuers examples of other Kingdomes and Countries, are contained: for amongst the *Grecians* there 30 were Poets before there were any Philosophers, who em-braced entirely the studie of wisedome, as *Cicero* testifieth in his *Tusculanes*: whereas he saith that, of all sorts of men, Poets are most ancient, who, to the intent they might allure men with a greater longing to learning, haue 35 followed two things, sweetnes of verse and variety of inuention, knowing that delight doth prick men forward to the attaining of knowledge, and that true things are rather admirde if they be included in some wittie fiction, 5 like to Pearles that delight more if they be deeper sette in golde. Wherfore seeing Poetry is the very same with Philosophy, the fables of Poets must of necessitie be fraught with wisdome & knowledge, as framed of those men which haue spent all their time and studies in the 10 one and in the other. For euen as in Vines the Grapes that are fayrest and sweetest are couched vnder the branches that are broadest and biggest, euen so in Poems the thinges that are most profitable are shrouded vnder the Fables that are most obscure : neither is there almost 15 any poeticall fygment wherein there is not some thing comprehended, taken out either of Histories, or out of the Phisicks or Ethicks; wher vpon *Erasmus Roterdamus* very wittilie termes Poetry a daintie dish seasoned with delights of euery kind of discipline. Nowe, whether 20 ryming be Poetry, I referre to the iudgment of the learned ; yea, let the indifferent Reader diuine what deepe misterie can be placed vnder plodding meeter. Who is it that, reading Beuis of Hampton, can forbeare laughing if he marke what scambling shyft he makes to ende his verses 25 a like. I will propound three or foure payre by the way for the Readers recreation.

> The Porter said, by my snout,
> It was Sir Beuis that I let out ;

or this,

30 He smote his sonne on the breast,
That he neuer after spoke with Clark nor Priest ;

or this,

> This almes, by my crowne,
> Gives she for Beuis of South-hamptoune ;

or this,

Some lost a nose, some a lip ;
And the King of Scots hath a ship.

But I let these passe as worne out absurdities, meaning
not at this instant to vrge (as I might) the like instance of 5
Authors of our time, least, in laying foorth their naked-
nesse, I might seeme to haue discouered my mallice,
imitating *Aiax*, who, obiecting more irefully vnto Vlysses
flattery, detected himselfe of follie.

As these men offend in the impudent publishing of 10
witles vanitie, so others ouershoote themselues as much
another waie, in sencelesse stoicall austeritie, accounting
Poetrie impietie and witte follie. It is an old Question,
and it hath beene often propounded, whether it were
better to haue moderate affections, or no affections? The 15
Stoicks said none. The *Peripaticians* answered to haue
temperate affections : and in this respect I am a professed
Peripatician, mixing profit with pleasure, and precepts of
doctrine with delightfull inuention. Yet these men condemne them of lasciuiousnes, vanitie, and curiositie, who 20
vnder fayned Stories include many profitable morrall
precepts, describing the outrage of vnbridled youth hauing
the reine in their owne hands, the fruits of idlenes, the
ofspring of lust, and how auaileable good educations are
vnto vertue. In which their preciser censure they re- 25
semble them that cast away the nutte for mislike of the
shell, & are like to those which loath the fruite for the
leaues, accounting the one sower because the other is
bitter. It may be some dreaming dunce, whose bald
affected eloquence making his function odious, better 30
beseeming a priuie then a pulpit, a misterming Clowne in
a Comedy then a chosen man in the Ministerie, will cry
out that it breedes a scabbe to the conscience to peruse
such Pamphlets, beeing indeed the display of their dun-

cerie, and breeding a mislike of such tedious dolts barbarisme by the view of their rethoricall inuention. Such trifling studies, say they, infect the minde and corrupt the manners, as though the minde were only
5 conuersant in such toies, or shold continuallie stay where the thoughts by chaunce doo stray. The Sunne beames touching the earth remaine still from whence they came; so a wyse mans mind, although sometimes by chance it wandereth here and there, yet it hath recourse in staied
10 yeeres to that it ought. But graunt the matter to be fabulous, is it therfore friuolous? Is there not vnder Fables, euen as vnder the shaddowe of greene and florishing leaues, most pleasant fruite hidden in secrete, and a further meaning closely comprised? Did not
15 *Virgill* vnder the couert of a Fable expresse that diuine misterie which is the subiect of his sixt Eglogue.

Iam noua progenies caelo demittitur alto.

I could send you to *Ouid*, who expresseth the generall Deluge, which was the olde worldes ouerthrowe, in the
20 Fable of *Deucalion* and *Pirrha*: vnder which vndoubtedly it is manifest (although diuers Authors are of contrarie opinion) he meaneth *Noes* floode, in so much as there is a place in *Lucian* in his booke *De Siria Dea*, by the which it appeareth that by *Deucalions* Deluge is vnderstoode,
25 not (as some will) that Enundation, whereby in times past Greece and Italie was ouerflowne and the Ile *Atlanta* destroied, but that vniuersall flood which was in the time of *Noe*. For thus *Lucian* writeth in that place, that it was receiued for a common opinion among the *Grecians* that
30 this generation of men that nowe is hath not been from the beginning, but that it which first was wholy perrished, and this second sort of men which now are be of a newe creation, growing into such a multitude by *Deucalion* and *Pirrhas* meanes. . . .

Hetherto *Lucian* an Heathen Poet. *Plutarch* also recordeth, in his Treatise *De industria animalium*, that a Doue, beeing sent out of *Deucalions* Arke, shewed the waters ceasing. By these proofes it is euident that by *Deucalions* Deluge is vnderstoode *Noes* flood, because the 5 very like thinges are sette downe in *Genesis*, of brute Beastes receiued by Noe into the Arke, and the Doue sent forth by him also. I trust, these probabilities beeing duely pondered, there is no man so distrustful to doubt that deeper diuinitie is included in Poets inuentions, and 10 therefore not to be reiected, as though they were voide of all learning and wisedome.

I woulde not haue any man imagine that in praysing of Poetry I endeuour to approoue *Virgils* vnchast *Priapus*, or *Ouids* obscenitie : I commende their witte, not their 15 wantonnes, their learning, not their lust : yet euen as the Bee out of the bitterest flowers and sharpest thistles gathers honey, so out of the filthiest Fables may profit-able knowledge be sucked and selected. Neuerthelesse, tender youth ought to bee restrained for a time from 20 the reading of such ribauldrie, least, chewing ouer wan-tonlie the eares of this Summer Corne, they be choaked with the haune before they can come at the karnell. Hunters, being readie to goe to their Game, suffer not their dogges to taste or smell of anything by the way, 25 no carrion especially, but reserue them wholy to their approching disport ; euen so youth, beeing ready to vndertake more waightier studies, ought in no case be permitted to looke aside to lasciuious toyes, least the pleasure of the one should breed a loathing of the profit 30 of the other. I would there were not any, as there be many, who in Poets and Historiographers reade no more then serueth to the feeding of their filthy lust, applying those things to the pampering of their priuate *Venus* which were purposely published to the suppressing of 35

that common wandering *Cupid*. These be the Spyders
which sucke poyson out of the hony combe and corruption out of the holiest thinges, herein resembling those
that are troubled with a Feuer, in whome diuers things
5 haue diuers effects, that is to say, of hote things they waxe
cold, of cold things hote; or of Tygers, which by the
sound of melodious Instruments are driuen into madnesse,
by which men are wont to expell melancholie. He that
wil seeke for a Pearle must first learne to know it when
10 he sees it, least he neglect it when hee findes it, or make
a nought worth peeble his Jewell : and they that couet
to picke more precious knowledge out of Poets amorous
Elegies must haue a discerning knowledge before they can
aspire to the perfection of their desired knowledge, least
15 the obtaining of trifles be the repentant end of their
trauell.

Who so snatcheth vp follies too greedilie, making an
occupation of recreation, and delight his day labour, may
happes proue a wittome whiles he fisheth for finer witte,
20 and a Foole while hee findes himselfe laughing pastime
at other mens follies; not vnlike to him who drinking
Wine immoderately, besides that hee many times swal-
lowes downe dregs, at length prooues starke drunke.

There is no extremitie, either in actiue or contemplatiue
25 life, more outragious then the excessiue studies of delight,
wherwith young Students are so besotted that they forsake
sounder Artes to followe smoother eloquence, not vnlike
to him that had rather haue a newe painted boxe, though
there be nothing but a halter in it, then an olde bard
30 hutch with treasure inualuable ; or *Æsops* Cocke, which
parted with a Pearle for a Barlie kurnell.   Euen as a man
is inclined, so his studies are bended ; if to vaineglorie, to
eloquence ; if to profounde knowledge, to *Aristotle* ; if
lasciuious, good in some English deuise of verse ; to con-
35 clude, a passing potman, a passing Poet.

[*Then follows an attack on the* 'abusiue enormities'
practised in the name of knowledge, and a plea for the
'suppression of the rauenous rable' *who discredit learning.* 'There be three things which are wont to slack young
Students endeuour : Negligence, want of Wisedome, & 5
Fortune.' 'Nothing is so great an enemie to a sounde
iudgment as the pride of a peeuish conceit, which causeth
a man both in life and beliefe either to snatch vppe or
hatch newfangles.']

There is no such discredit of Arte as an ignoraunt Arti- 10
ficer,—men of meaner iudgement measuring oft times the
excellencie of the one by the ignoraunce of the other. But
as hee that censureth the dignitie of Poetry by *Cherillus*
paultry paines, the maiestie of Rethorick by the rudenesse
of a stutting *Hortensius*, the subtiltie of Logique by the 15
rayling of *Ramus*, might iudge the one a foole in writing
he knewe not what, the other tipsie by his stammering,
the thirde the sonne of Zantippe by his scolding : so he
that estimats Artes by the insolence of Idiots, who professe that wherein they are Infants, may deeme the 20
Vniuersitie nought but the nurse of follie, and the knowledge of Artes nought but the imitation of the Stage.
This I speake to shew what an obloquie these impudent
incipients in Arts are vnto Art.

Amongst all the ornaments of Artes, Rethorick is to be 25
had in highest reputation, without the which all the rest
are naked, and she onely garnished : yet some there be
who woulde seperate Arts from Eloquence, whose [opinion
we] oppugne, because it abhorres from common experience. Who doth not know that in all tongues taske 30
eloquence is odious if it be affected, and that attention is
altogether wanting where it is reiected ? A man may
baule till his voice be hoarse, exhort with teares till his
tongue ake and his eyes be drie, repeate that hee woulde
perswade til his stalenes dooth secretlie call for a Cloake 35

bagge, and yet moue no more then if he had been all that while mute, if his speech be not seasoned with elo. quence and adorned with elocutions assistance. Nothing is more odious to the Auditor then the artlesse tongue
5 of a tedious dolt, which dulleth the delight of hearing, and slacketh the desire of remembring; and I know not how it comes to passe, but many are so delighted to heare themselues that they are a cumber to the eares of all other, pleasing their Auditors in nothing more then
10 in the pause of a ful point, when as by their humming and hawking respit they haue leisure to gesture the mislike of his rudenes. To the eschewing therefore of the lothing hatred of them that heare them, I would wish them to learne to speake many things in few, neither to speake
15 all things which to theyr purpose they may speake, least those things be lesse profitably spoken which they ought to speake; neither would I haue them ouershoote them-selues with an imitation of breuitie, so that striuing to be very short they should prooue very long, namelie, when
20 as they endeuor to speake many things breefelie. Per-swade one point throughlie rather then teach many things scatteringly; that which we thinke let vs speake, and that which we speake let vs thinke; let our speeche accorde with our life. Endeuour to adde vnto Arte
25 Experience: experience is more profitable voide of arte then arte which hath not experience. Of it selfe arte is vnprofitable without experience, and experience rashe with-out arte. In reading thou must with warie regard learne as wel to discerne thy losse as thy gaine, thy hurt as
30 good, least, being wonne to haue a fauorable like of Poets wanton liues, thou be excited vnto the imitation of their lust. It is very vnseemely that nobler wits shoulde be discredited with baser studies, and those whom high and mightie callings doo expect shold be hindered by the
35 inticements of pleasure and vanitie. Young men are not

so much delighted with solide substances as with painted
shadowes, following rather those thinges which are goodly
to the viewe then profitable to the vse; neither doo they
loue so much those things that are dooing as those things
that are sounding, reioycing more to be strowed with
flowers then nourished with frute. How many be there
that seeke truth, not in truth but in vanitie, and find that
they sought not according to trueth but according to
vanitie, and that, which is most miserable, in the words
of life they toile for the merchandise of death. Hence
commeth it to passe that many make toyes their onelie
studie; storing of trifles, when as they neglect most precious treasures: and, hauing left the Fountaines of truth,
they folow the Riuers of opinions. I can but pittie their
folly, who are so curious in fables and excruciate themselues about impertinent questions, as about *Homers*
Countrey, parentage, and sepulcher, whether *Homer* or
Hesiodus were older, whether *Achilles* or *Patroclus* more
ancient, in what apparrell *Anacharsis* the *Scithian* slept,
whether *Lucan* is to be reckoned amongst the Poets or
Historiographers, in what Moneth in the yere *Virgill*
died, with infinite other, as touching the Letters of the
Hiacinth, the Chestnut tree, the children of *Niobe*, the
trees where *Latona* brought foorth *Diana*, in all which
idle interrogatories they haue left vnto vs not thinges
found, but things to be sought, and peraduenture they
had founde necessary things if they had not sought superfluous thinges.

[*So too in Philosophy there are* 'innumerable such vn-
necessary questions.']

I know the learned wil laugh me to scorne for setting
down such Rams horne rules of direction, and euen nowe
I begin to bethinke me of *Mulcasters Positions*, which
makes my penne heere pause as it were at a full point:
which pause hath changd my opinion, and makes me

rather refer you to Aschame, the antienter of the two: whose prayses seeing Maister Grant hath so gloriously garnished, I will referre you to his workes, and more especially to his Schoolemaster, where he hath most
5 learnedly censured both our Latine and Greeke Authors. As for lighter studies, seeing they are but the exercise of youth to keepe them from idlenes, and the preparation of the minde to more weightie meditations, let vs take heede least, whiles we seeke to make them the furthering helps
10 of our finall profession, they proue not the hindering harmes of our intended vocation, that we dwell not so long in Poetry that wee become Pagans, or that we make not such proceedinges in Aristotle that we prooue proficients in Atheisme. Let not learning, which ought to
15 be the Leuell whereby such as liue ill ought to square theyr crooked waies, be the occasion vnto them of farther corruption who haue already sucked infection, least thair knowledge way them downe into hell, when as the ignorant goe the direct way to heauen.
20 And thus I ende my Anatomie, least I might seeme to haue beene too tedious to the Reader in enlarging a Theame of Absurditie, desiring of the learned pardon, and of Women patience, which may encourage me heereafter to endeuour in some other matter of more moment,
25 as well to be answerable to the expectation of the one as to make amends to the other. In the meane time I bidde them both farewell.

APPENDIX

FROM E. HOBY'S TRANSLATION OF
COIGNET'S *POLITIQUE DISCOURSES*
1586

[The following passage is the thirty-fifth chapter of *Politique*
  Discourses on trueth and lying. *An instruction to Princes to*
  keepe their faith and promise. . . . Translated out of French . . .
  by Sir E. Hoby. *R. Newberrie.* *London* 1586. 4°. (B. M.
  523. g. 13). The original, by Matthieu Coignet, appeared
  in Paris in 1584, with the title *Instruction aux Princes pour*
  garder la Foy promise : contenant un sommaire de la philo-
  sophie Chrestienne et morale . . . en plusieurs discours.]

THAT LYING HATH MADE POETS AND PAINTERS TO BE BLAMED,
AND OF THE GARNISHING OF HOUSES.

PLATO wrote that Poetrie consisted in the cunning inuention
of fables, which are a false narration resembling a true,
and that therein they did often manifest sundrie follies of the
gods ; for this cause he banished and excluded them out of
his common wealth, as men that mingled poyson with honie.
Besides thorough their lying and wanton discourses they corrupt the manners of youth, and diminish that reuerence which
men ought to carrie towards their superiors and the lawes of
God, whom they faine to be replenished with passions & vice.
And the principall ornament of their verses are tales made at
pleasure, & foolish & disorderly subiectes, cleane disguising
the trueth & hystorie, to the end they might be the more delight ;
and for this cause haue they bin thrust out of sundry cities.
Among other, after that *Archilocus* came into *Sparta*, he was
presently thrust out, as soon as they had vnderstood how he
had written in his poemes, that it was better to lose a mans
weopens than his life, & forbad euer after al such deceitful

poesies. Hence grew the common prouerb, that al Poets are
lyers. And it was written of *Socrates*, that hee was yl brought
vp to poesie because he loued the truth. And a man mought
say that this moued *Caligula* to condemne *Virgils & Homers*
books, because of their prophane fables, which S. *Paul* ex- 5
horted *Timothie* to cast away. *Plutarque* telleth of a *Lace-
demonian*, who, when he was demanded what he thought of
the Poet *Tirteus*, answered that he was very good to infect yong
mens wits. And *Hieron* of *Siracusa* condemned *Epicarmus* the
Poet in a great fine, because in his wiues presence he had 10
repeated certaine lasciuious verses. And *Viues* writeth that
Ouid was most iustly sent into banishment, as an instrument
of wantonnesse. He which first inuented the *Iambique* versifying, to byte and quippe, was the first that felt the smart.
And *Archilocus* the Poet fell into confusion through his own 15
detractions, as *Horace* and sundry other haue written; and
Aulus Gellius reporteth that *Orpheus, Homer,* and *Hesiodus* gaue
names & honours to the gods. And *Pithagoras* saide that their
soules hong in hel vpon a tree, still pulled of euery side by
serpents, for their so damnable inuention. And *Domitian* 20
banished *Juvenal*: and Pope *Paull* 2 and *Adrian* 6 held them
as enimies to religion. *Eusebius* in his 8 booke & first Chapter
de Preparatione Euangelica setteth down an example of a Poet,
who, for hauing lewdly applyed a peece of Scripture to a fable,
suddenly lost his naturall sight; and, after that he had done 25
penance, it was restored to him againe. And as touching
Painters, they haue beene greatly misliked of, for representing such fictions & Poetical deceits. For as *Simonides* saide:
Painting is a dumme Poesie, and a Poesie is a speaking painting: & the actions which the Painters set out with visible 30
colours and figures the Poets recken with wordes, as though
they had in deede beene perfourmed. And the end of eche is
but to yeeld pleasure by lying, not esteeming the sequele and
custome, or impression, which hereby giue to the violating of
the lawes and corruption of good manners. For this cause the 35
Prophets called the statuas, images, and wanton pictures, the
teachers of vanitie, of lyes, deceite, & abhomination. And
Lactantius writeth, that a counterfait tooke the name of counter-
faiting, and all deceit (as wee before declared) springeth from
falshood and lying. This was it which mooued S. *John*, in the 40
ende of his first Epistle, to warne men to *keepe themselues from*

images: for an image doeth at their fansie counterfait the bodie of a man dead, but is not able to yeelde the least gaspe of breath. And idolatrie is properly such seruice as is done vnto Idoles. Wee reade howe God especially forbad it in the first
5 table, and how long the *Romanes* and *Persians* liued without any vse thereof: and howe the *Lacedemonians* coulde neuer abyde that an image should stand in their Senate. There hath beene in sundrye councels mention made thereof & S. *Athanasius* more at large discoursed thereof in a sermon he made against
10 Idols: and S. Augustin in his booke *de fide & Simbolo*, and vppon 150 Psalm, & in his eighth book of the citie of God, & *Damascene* in his 4 book & 8 c. The occasion of so free passage giuen to Poets is, for that their fables flyde awaye easily, and cunningly turne them selues to tickel at pleasure, whereas the
15 trueth plainly setteth downe the matter as it is indeede, albeit the euent thereof bee not verie pleasant. *Plato* in like sort compared the disputes in Poetrie to the banquets of the ignorant, who vse Musike in steede of good discourse, and, in his thirde booke of his commonwealth, he forbiddeth Poets
20 or painters to set downe or represent any thinge dishonest or wanton, for feare of corrupting of good manners. And *Aristotle* in his Politiques, the thirde booke and 17 Chapter, would haue all vyle wordes to be banished. And Saint *Paul* to the *Ephesians*, that any vncleannesse, foolish iesting, or talking shoulde bee
25 once named among them. And *Tertullian*, an auncient doctor of the Church, called Poets, and certaine Philosophers, the Patriarches of heretiques. This which I haue spoken of must not be vnderstood of Poesies wherein much trueth and instruction is contained, nor of pictures which represent the actes of
30 holye and vertuous personnages, nor of fables taken out of hystories, whereof, there maye growe some edifying; but onely of that which is lasciuious, and grounded vpon naughtie argument, rendring youth effeminate, and men more giuen to wantonnesse, pleasures, passion, & vayne opinions, then to
35 virtue, cleane turning away the honour that is due vnto God or to good edifying; for according vnto the commaundement of God, Cherubyns were made. The admonition which *Epicletus* gaue to such as were too curious in pictures ought by no meanes to be here forgotten : *Trim not thy house* (saith hee) *with tables*
40 *and pictures, but paint it and guild it with Temperance : the one vainely feedeth the eyes, the other is an eternall ornament which*

cannot be defaced. The same doeth *Plutarque* teache in the life of *Dion*, that more care is to bee taken for the hanging and adorning of the palace of the soule, then of the outwarde. And the same Philosopher did not muche out of the waye warne vs, that wee shoulde take heede that the skirt of our garments 5 shoulde not carrie a stinche of life.

NOTES

NOTES

ASCHAM (pp. 1–45).

THE story of the origin of the *Scholemaster* is told by Ascham in his *Preface to the Reader* (Mayor, pp. xiii–xxiii; Giles, iii. pp. 78–87). The purpose of the book is discussed at great length in a letter addressed by him to his friend Sturm in ? Dec. 1568 (Giles, ii. pp. 174–91). The latter document is chiefly concerned with 'Imitation,' which Ascham appears to have considered the main critical topic of his work. '*Scribis tu de Imitatione, et ego nonnihil cogito de eodem argumento: sed tu absolute, eruditis iam ac viris; ego inchoate, rudibus adhuc et pueris.*' After describing the plan of the book (see note, p. 358), and informing Sturm that he has written in English, he proceeds—

'*In loco de Imitatione longiusculus est* Praeceptor *meus. Fatetur se omnes fere et veteres et recentes, qui de Imitatione scripsere, cupide perlegisse: probare se multos, admirari vero neminem, praeter unum Sturmium. Aliqui certe recte, qui sint imitandi; sed quomodo instituenda sit ipsa imitandi ratio, solus docet Sturmius. Itaque, si cum illa perfectione praeceptorum, quae in* Literata *tua* Nobilitate *et* Amissa dicendi Ratione *plenissime tradita sunt, copiam etiam exemplorum coniunxisses; quid praeterea requirendum esset, non video. Namque, ut in vitae et morum sic in doctrinae et studiorum ratione omni, longe plus possunt exempla quam praecepta. In illarum vero rerum sive arte, sive facultate, quae sola imitatione perfici videntur, praecepta aut nullum aut perexiguum habent locum, quum exempla isthic vel solitaria plane regnant. Pictores, sculptores, scriptores hoc et prudenter intelligunt et perfecte praestant.*

'*Atque ut oratores etiam in horum numero collocem movet nonnulla ratio, iubet quae illa est Quinctiliani auctoritas: qui dicit, Ciceronem (nec Cicero de se hoc ipse tacet) iucunditatem Isocratis, copiam Platonis, vim Demosthenis effinxisse; et effingere, in imitatione necne propriam sedem habeat, omnes vident. Verum enimvero ostendere, et iudicare solum, ubi hoc facit Cicero, mediocris diligentiae, vulgaris et quotidiani est laboris. Hoc Perionius, Victorius, Stephanus, et alii in Cicerone: hoc Macrobius, Hessus, et nuper diligentissime omnium Fulvius Ursinus, in Virgilio: hoc accurate etiam Clemens Alexandrinus, quinto* στρωμάτων *in veteribus Graecis scriptoribus attentavit. Sed hi omnes perinde sunt, ut operarii et baiuli, qui, quum comportent materiam, deesse certe in opere faciundo non possunt,*

*mercedem tamen ipsi perexiguam et laudem quidem non maximam pro-
merentur.* (Cf. supra, p. 19.)

'*Atqui docere perspicue et perfecte, qua ratione Cicero vel Demosthenem
vel Platonem imitatur; singularis, fateor, doctrinae, summi iudicii, et rarae
laudis existit. Sed haec laus adhuc praeceptionis tota propria est. Aliud
volo, plus requiro. Opifex nobis et architectus opus est, qui separata con-
iungere, rudia perpolire, et totum opus construere, artificiosa ratione noverit.
Et illud, mea certe opinione, hoc modo. "Hinc Demosthenis locum, illinc
Ciceronis produci cupio. Tum, digito artificis me primum duci volo ad ea,
quae in utroque sunt aut eadem aut simillima. Deinde, quae sunt in hoc
addita et quo consilio; tum, quae sunt ablata et quo iudicio. Postremo
quae sunt commutata; et quo ac quam vario artificio; sive id in verborum
delectu, sive in sententiarum forma, sive in membrorum circumductione, sive
in argumentorum ratione consistat. Nec uno aut altero exemplo contentus
ero. Numero multa, genera varia, ex Platone, ex Isocrate, ex Demosthene,
et ex Aristotele in libris rhetoricis, exempla expeto.*" (Cf. supra, p. 9.)

'*Patior* Praeceptorem *parcum esse in praeceptorum traditione, modo
liberalem se et largum in exemplorum non solum productione, quod laboris
est et diligentiae, verum etiam tractatione, quod est doctrinae et iudicii,
ostendat.* . . .

'*Equidem amplector unice Ciceronis imitationem: sed eam dico et primam
ordine, et praecipuam dignitate, qua Cicero ipse Graecos; non qua Lactantius
olim, Omphalius nuper, aut qua multo felicius quidam Itali, Galli, Lusi-
tani, et Angli Ciceronem sunt secuti. . . . Non possum probare consilium
Bartholomaei Riccii Ferrariensis, doctissimi licet viri; qui quum sic scripserit
de recta imitandi ratione, ut quum a Sturmio discesseris, caeteris omnibus
mea certe opinione anteponendus sit (praecepta enim eius omnia sunt Stur-
miana, et ex tuis fontibus hausta atque derivata), exempla tamen maluit
Longolii ex Cicerone, quam Longolii ex Platone sibi proponere; et Virgilii
ex Catullo, quam Virgilii ex Homero producere . . .*

'*Si vero optarem ipse fieri alter Cicero (et optare quidem nefas non est),
ut fierem, et qua ratione fierem, quem potius ad consilium mihi adhiberem,
quam ipsum Ciceronem? . . . Ille enim sermo non in Italia natus est,
sed e Graecorum disciplina in Italiam traductus. . . . Unde evenit, ut sola
Ciceronis oratio inter reliquos omnes Romanos, qui illi aetate aut superiores,
aut aequales, aut suppares fuere, non colore solum vernaculo pure tincta, sed
raro et transmarino quodam plene imbuta, tam admirabiliter resplendesceret.*

'*Itaque, quum ipsa lingua Latina, felicissimo suo tempore, in ipsa Roma,
in ipso Cicerone, ad summam perfectionem sine Graeca lingua non pervenit:
cur quisquam in sola Latina quaerit, quod Cicero ipse absque Graeca non
invenit? . . . Sed ait quis, "Recte quidem Cicero; nam ante eum, nemo
fuit praeter Graecos, ad imitationem proponendus. Sed nunc habemus
ipsum Ciceronem, eum quidem, cum universa Graecia, et cum singulo quoque
Graecorum, in ea eloquentiae laude qua maxime quisque floruit, compa-
randum. Cur igitur non Ciceronem solum mihi, variis illis Graecis relictis,
ad imitandum proponerem?*" *Aliquid est, quod dicis. Ipse enim Ciceronem
praecipue imitandum volo; sed tuta via, sed recta ratione, suo ordine, suo
loco. Et rationem meam, cur hoc volo, et quomodo hoc volo, aperte ostendam.
Primum, si optarem ipse alter fieri Cicero (quod ante dixi), qua ratione
potius fierem, quam ea ipsa, qua ipse Cicero factus est Cicero? Hanc viam
certam, cognitam, et expeditam esse, optimus testis est ipse Cicero.* . . .

'*Et haec est illa via, mea certe opinione, qua ad Ciceronis imitationem recta*

*pergendum est. Non, quomodo Riccius ostendit Longolium fecisse (hoc est ut
ipse putat, excellenti ratione; ut ego existimo, valde laudabiliter; ut multi
sentiunt, mediocriter et tolerabiliter; et Erasmus et Paulus Manutius iudicant, inepte, frigide, et pueriliter), sed qua ratione Sturmius Ciceronem
imitandum esse, et praeceptis in* Literata Nobilitate *perfecte docet, et exemplis in* Quinctiana Explicatione *insigniter ostendit. . . .*

'*Sed quorsum tantopere, mi Sturmi, laboramus de imitatione? quum non
desunt, qui docti et prudentes videri volunt, qui imitationem vel nullam esse
putant, vel nihili prorsus aestimant, vel omnem temere permiscent, vel eam
totam, quaecunque sit, cuiuscunque sit, ut servilem et puerilem repudiant.
Sed hi sunt et inertes et imperiti; laborem fugiunt, artem nesciunt. . . .
Artis enim et naturae dissidium faciunt, quicunque casu non delectu, fortuito
non observatione, in literarum studiis versantur. Isti idem sentiunt de
eleganti illa eloquentiae parte, quae in numerorum ratione collocata est;
illam enim aut nullam esse volunt, aut inanem omnem iudicant. Et
aurium sensum cum artificioso et intelligenti animi iudicio nihil commercii
habere existimant.*'

He proceeds to lament the loss of the books of Dionysius of
Halicarnassus, *De imitatione et oratoria et historica*, and to pass
in review Christophorus Longolius, Budaeus, Erasmus, Paulus
Manutius, Petrus Victorius, Jovita Rapicius, author of the *De
Numero Oratorio*, Carolus Sigonius, Giambattista Pigna, and
Angelio Pietro da Barga (Bargaeus). All, except Manutius,
Pigna, and Bargaeus, appear in the English text (see notes);
but of Manutius he says: *Gaudeo* Praeceptorem *meum loqui*
Anglice: *ne, quum tam libere dissentit hac in re a Manutio, tantum
hominem offenderet: tamen Manutium non nominat.* The refer-
ences to Pigna are concerned only with his views on Horace's
Ars Poetica (*aureolum Horatii librum*), Aristotle's *Rhetoric*, and
Quaestiones Sophocleae. Ascham appears to be unaware of
Pigna's more important apology for the methods of Ariosto
in *I Romanzi* (1554), or is perhaps unwilling to dispute with
him on these matters of 'bold bawdrye' (see p. 4). He names
Bargaeus for his *doctissimos commentarios in eruditum illum
Demetrii libellum de Elocutione*.

1. Εὐφυής. Lyly is indebted to this passage for his *Euphues*.
Ascham's definition is built up from classical usage, e.g. Plato,
Aristotle, and especially Plutarch (*Moralia*, ed. Xylander,
p. 81 D), but in its completeness of application has some claim
to originality. Cf. the companion definition in Estienne's
Thesaurus, which appeared in 1572.

2. 20-9. Cf. *Toxophilus*, ed. Giles, ii. p. 150.

3. 36. 'In our forefathers tyme,' &c. Cf. the similar passage

in the Preface to *Toxophilus* ('To all Gentlemen and Yeomen of England'), ed. Giles, ii. pp. 7–8. See Nash, infra, p. 323; Gosson, *Playes Confuted*, Roxb. Libr. p. 172; Jonson, *New Inn*, i. 1. For the argument that Ascham in his attack on Italian books is thinking especially of Painter's *Palace of Pleasure*, see Mr. Jacobs's edition of Painter, i. xix, xxiv.

4. 3. *bold bawdrye*: apparently not Ascham's own phrase. Cf. Sir Thomas Elyot, speaking of those 'that suppose that in the warkes of poetes is contayned nothynge but baudry (suche is their foule worde of reproche) and unprofitable leasinges' (*The Gouernour*, ed. Croft, i. 123).

7. 30. *De Republica*, 393 D.

8. 27. See the *Epistolae*, No. 1708, and the Preface to his 'Demosthenes.'

30. See Macrobius, *Saturnalia*, Bk. V.

35. *Eobanus Hessus*. Helius Eobanus Hessus (1488–1540) here interests Ascham as the editor of Theocritus. Cf. infra, p. 18, l. 35, and p. 20, l. 15. His annotations on the *Bucolics* and *Georgics* were printed in 1529. He had considerable reputation as a poet. 'Potest et terra nostra Germania,' writes Lilius Gyraldus, 'gloriari Helio Eobano Hesso, poeta insigni, cuius complura passim leguntur poemata non in Germania modo, sed et in Italia et Gallia' (*De Poetis*, ed. Wotke, p. 69). His editions of the *Psalms* and his *Medicinae Laus* (*ex Erasmo*) were frequently reprinted. His Life is written by Camerarius.

9. 30. Kindly references to Sir John Cheke (1514–57) are very frequent in Ascham's writings. He had been Ascham's tutor (p. 39, l. 33). See pp. 21 (l. 31), 44 (l. 27 and note).

32. *Io. St.* Ioannes Sturmius. His *De Imitatione Oratoria Libri Tres* was printed at Strassburg in 1574. His *Poeticum primum* [*secundum ... sextum*] *volumen cum lemmatibus* (Strassburg, 1565) was very popular, and his nine-volume edition of Cicero (1557) and the earlier *In partitiones oratorias Ciceronis Dialogi duo* (Strassburg, 1539) gave him an authoritative standing in the Ciceronian controversy. See note to p. 13, l. 31.

10. 23. *piteling*. Cf. *pickling*, infra, p. 43, l. 25. The sense seems to be 'piddling' (cf. ii. p. 248, l. 31), but no other examples of these forms have been recorded.

35. *Ad Atticum*, iv. 13. i.

11. 10. *Ep. ad P. L.* i. 9. 23 ; *Ep. ad Att.* iv. 16. 2 ; *De Orat.* i. 55, ii. 152, 153, 160.

25. *De Orat.* i. 7. 28.

32. *Epist.* iv. 16.

13. 2. *De Orat.* ii. 89, &c.

3. *Orat. ad Brutum*, 40, &c., 172, &c.

4. Cf. infra, p. 45, l. 14. See Cic. *Brut.* passim, also Quint. xii. 1.

10. Quint. x. 2.

16. Especially in his *Dialogus cui titulus Ciceronianus : sive de optimo genere dicendi.* See the Dedication.

17. *Longolius* (Christopher Longueil de Malines) wrote a Commentary on Cicero's *Rhetoric* (1541) and published an edition of the *Letters to Atticus* (1549), which with his own Letters gave him a high contemporary reputation as a Ciceronian. 'Audio Longolium iuvenem Macliniensem,' says Gyraldus, 'inter barbaros natum et altum ita bonas litteras amplecti, ut nisi adversa valetudo obstet, brevi sit Latinae linguae non parum adlaturus ornamenti' (ed. Wotke, p. 42). He edited Quintilian, and published in 1562 the *Libri Elegantiarum* of Lorenzo Valla. See the references in Ascham's letter to Sturm, supra, p. 348, and in Harvey, ii. p. 248, ll. 5, 7.

20. *Budæus* (Guillaume Budé, 1467-1540). Ascham refers to his *Commentarii linguae Graecae* (Paris, 1529) in the First Book (ed. Mayor, p. 6); here, and in his *Letters*, to the Commentaries on Cicero's Letters. His complete works, critical, philosophical (theological), and juridical, were collected by Coelius Secundus Curio (4 vols. fol. Basle, 1557).

24. *Philip Melancthon* (1497-1560) discusses Imitation in his *Elementorum Rhetorices Libri II* (Wittenberg, 1531).

25. *Camerarius* (Joachimus), 1500-74, published several editions of Greek and Latin classics, including Aesop, Cicero, Macrobius, Plautus, and Terence, and a volume *De Imitatione, Comment. in Tullii Tusculan.* His chief historical value lies in his Letters, his *Narratio de H. Eobano Hesso, comprehendens mentionem de compluribus illius aetatis doctis et eruditis viris* (Nuremb. 1553), and his *Life of Melancthon* (Leipzig, 1566).

27. *Io. Sambucus* (*d.* 1584). His book *De Imitatione Cicero-*

niana, Dialogi Tres (Paris, 1561) passed through many editions. An edition of Plautus appeared in 1566, and a commentary on Caesar in 1574. Earlier in the *Scholemaster* (ed. Mayor, p. 127) Ascham refers to his annotated paraphrase of the *Ars Poetica* (Antwerp, 1564). See also note to ii. p. 323, l. 4.

29. *Cortesius* (Paolo Cortese), 1465–1510, Bishop of Urbino, author of a commentary on Peter Lombard and a treatise on the Cardinalate. Cortesius's letter, which Ascham approves, is criticized at considerable length by Erasmus in his *Ciceronianus*. Gabriel Harvey in his *Ciceronianus* (24) takes the other side. The texts are printed in the editions of Politian's Letters. Paolo Cortese must not be confused with another Cortese (Gregorio, originally Giambattista), 1483–1548, also Bishop of Urbino, and of the same family, and author of a volume of Letters (Venice, 1573). Paolo had two brothers, Alessandro, a poet, and Lattanzio, who wrote a commentary on Caesar.

30. *Bembus ad Picum.* This letter on *Imitation* (*De imitatione sermonis*) and another by Pico are printed in the editions of the *Epistolae* of Bembo.

31. *Ioan. Sturmius*, &c. The *De amissa dicendi ratione et quomodo ea recuperanda sit,* his first original work, appeared in 1538. The *Nobilitas litterata* was printed at Strassburg in 1549, and was Englished by 'T. B.' in 1570. See also note to p. 9, l. 32.

14. 12. *Bartholomaeus Riccius Ferrariensis* (Bartolommeo Ricci of Lugo). His *De imitatione libri tres, ad Alfonsum Alestium principem*, &c. (i.e. his pupil, son of Duke Ercole II of Ferrara), was issued from the Aldine press at Venice in 1545. His Latin lexicon, *Apparatus Latinae Locutionis*, had appeared in 1533. He was a friend of Lilius Gyraldus, who refers to him at the beginning of his *De Poetis* (ed. Wotke, pp. 2–3). See the letter to Sturm, supra, p. 348.

21–2. Cf. p. 30, ll. 6–7. *good cheape*, cheaply. Fr. *à bon marché*. Cf. 1 Hen. IV, iii. 3. 51.

Cf. the *Scholemaster*, Bk. I, p. 59 (ed. Mayor), where, speaking of 'the pastimes that be fitte for Courtlie Jentlemen,' he adds, 'But of all kinde of pastimes fitte for a Jentleman, I will, God willing, in fitter place, more at large, declare fullie, in my booke of the Cockpitte.' Ascham's favourite amusement was well known to his literary contemporaries. Cf. Sir Thomas Smith to Haddon (Bordeaux, 6ᵗʰ April, 1565) '*Quid autem agit Aschamus tuus, item ac meus ?* . . . *Credo vero gallos suos ita illum excantasse, ut amicorum suorum prorsum sit oblitus* (*Haddoni Epist.* 307). Fuller, in his *Worthies*, laments that 'in his old age he [Ascham] exchanged [Archery] for a worse pastime, neither so healthfull for his body, nor profitable for his purse, I mean Cock-fighting' (ed. 1662, p. 209).

16. 35. For the *loci* in the wrangle about the merits of Greek and Latin see the excellent note in Mr. Mayor's edition of the *Scholemaster* (1863), pp. 244–8.

17. 26, &c. Cf. *Nizolian Paper-bookes* in Sidney, infra, p. 202, l. 16 (note).

31. *one labour.* See Erasmus, *Adagia*, s. 'Herculei labores.'

32. *namelie*, i. e. 'especially.' Cf. p. 45, l. 9.

Chiliades, Apophthegmata, and *Similia*, i. e. *Adagiorum Chiliades tres* (1508); *Apophthegmatum Opus* (1531), printed, in English, by Grafton, in 1542 ; and *Parabolarum sive Similium liber* (? 1520).

18. 7. *De Orat.* iii. 28.

29. *Perionius* (*Ioachimus*) is best known by his edition of Aristotle (1563) and his *Dialogi de linguae gallicae origine eiusque cum Graeca cognatione* (Paris, 1555). He printed selections from Plato and Livy. Ascham probably refers to his *De optimo genere interpretandi* (Paris, 1540). See Ascham's letter to Sturm, supra, p. 347 ; and Harvey, ii. p. 245, l. 9.

Henr. Stephanus in dictionario Ciceroniano, i. e. Henri Estienne (second of the name) in his *Ciceronianum Lexicon Graecolatinum*, 1557.

P. Victorius . . . de varia lectione. Pietro Vettori (the elder), 1499–1585, printed his *Variarum Lectionum libri XXV* at Florence in 1553. By 1582 it had been expanded to thirty-eight books. His work was mainly editorial (Aristotle, Cicero, Terence, Varro, Sallust, &c.).

35. *Macrobius, Hessus.* Cf. p. 8, ll. 30, 35.

19. 14. Cf. Ascham's letter to Sturm, ed. Giles, ii. p. 189.

20. 32. Mr. Mayor appears to be right in saying 'There is no statement of the kind in Diogenes ' (*Scholemaster*, p. 249).

21. 18. *Tomitanus*, Bernardino Tomitano (1506–76), a physician and scholar of Padua, wrote *Introductiones ad Sophisticos Elenchos*

Aristotelis, but is best known by his vernacular works *Quattro libri della lingua Thoscana* (Venice, 1545), *Ragionamenti della lingua Toscana* (1545), and *Discorso intorno all' eloquenza* (1554).

31. *Redman*, Dr. John (1499–1551), of St. John's College, Cambridge, first Master of Trinity. See p. 313, l. 30.

Cheke. See note to p. 9, l. 30, and p. 44, l. 27.

Smith, Sir Thomas (1513–77), Regius Professor of Civil Law, who with Cheke shared the honour of upholding Classical scholarship at Cambridge: one of 'The two eyes of this University' (Harvey in his *Ciceronianus*, 43)—'duo propugnacula, duo ornamenta eruditionis, literarum, Academiae Angliae' (*Vita Aschami*, 30). See note to p. 102, l. 24.

Haddon, Walter (1516–72).

Watson, Thomas (1513–84), Master of St. John's, Bishop of Lincoln, author of *Absolon* (see p. 23, l. 31, note); not to be confounded with the author of the Ἑκατομπαθία, *or the Passionate Centurie of Love.* See note to p. 316, l. 8, and Index.

23. 3. Cf. ante, p. 21, l. 31, note. See also Ascham's Letters to Cheke, passim.

7. *these three.* Cf. Quintil. xii. 10 (§ 636). See also Scaliger, *Poetice*, iv. chaps. xvi–xxi.

31. *Watson . . . Tragedie of* Absalon, in Latin (ante, p. 21). See other references by Index. He also translated the first book of the *Odyssey* into English verse. See the *Scholemaster*, Bk. I (ed. Mayor, p. 71), where Ascham gives a specimen.

33. Is this the first known reference in English to Aristotle's *Poetics*?

24. 7. The *Iephthes* of George Buchanan (1506–81), written not later than 1554, was printed at the Plantin Press and by the Stephani in 1566, and often later. See Freebairn's edition of the Works, 1715. Cf. Sidney, infra, p. 201, l. 4.

24. 8, &c. Mr. E. K. Chambers thinks this may be John Christopherson, afterwards Bishop of Chichester (see *Mediaeval Stage*, ii. 195, note).

22. The MS. is said to have been at Penshurst in 1860 (see Halliwell, *Dict. of Old English Plays*, p. 2); but Mr. E. K. Chambers points out that it is not recorded in the Hist. MSS. Comm. Report (iii. App. 227), and that it is probably identical with the B.M. Stowe MS. 957 (*Mediaeval Stage*, u. s., ii. 458).

25. 13. *Carolus Sigonius hath written of late.* Carlo Sigonio, also known as (Bernardinus) Lauredanus, 1524–84, printed his *De Dialogo* at Venice in 1561. The *Orationes Septem C. Sigonii* appeared in the previous year (Aldus, Venice), and his *Disputationum patavinarum lib.* [*ii*] at Padua in 1562. He translated Aristotle's *Rhetoric* into Latin. His complete works were edited by Muratori (6 vols., Milan, 1732–7). See ii. p. 246, l. 24.

15. 'Notes of Sturm's lectures, which Ascham procured in London, A. D. 1547 (*Epist.* 14) ; they have not been printed' (Mayor, *Scholemaster*, p. 261).

25. Περὶ ἰδεῶν, i. 1. Sturm's very popular edition of Hermogenes, the rhetorician, was probably the quarry for most of the references to that writer.

26. 23, &c. '*At oratio ac vis forensis, perfectumque prosae eloquentiae decus, ut idem separetur Cato, . . . ita universa sub principe operis sui erupit Tullio, ut delectari ante eum paucissimis, mirari vero neminem possis, nisi aut ab illo visum, aut qui illum viderit.*' Vell. Pat. *Hist. Rom.* i. 17.

27. 30. *Three thinges.* Cf. p. 35, ll. 18–19.

28. 20. Cf. *Epist. ad Att.* vii. 3. 10. Cf. also Quintil. x. 1 (*licet Terentii scripta ad Scipionem Africanum referantur*).

29. 14. Quintil. x. 1 (§ 513).

16. *Ars Poet.* 268–9.

30. *beggerly ryming*, &c. See also bk. i (ed. Arber, p. 73). Cf. the Spenser-Harvey Letters, Webbe, Campion, and Daniel, by Index. Blenerhasset in his *Induction* in the *Mirror for Magistrates* speaks of the 'Gotish kinde of ryming.'

31. Cf. p. 32, l. 21.

30. 6. Cf. ante, p. 14, ll. 21–2.

8. Ascham calls Chaucer 'our English Homer' in *Toxophilus* (Giles, ii. 42), and adds, 'I ever thought his sayings to have as much authority as either Sophocles or Euripides in Greek.'

8. *Thomas Norton of Bristow* ; not to be confounded with Sackville's collaborator. Cf. Webbe (p. 242, l. 32). He wrote in 1477 a poem entitled *The Ordinal, or Manual of Chemical Art.* See the article in the *D. N. B.* : also Warton, ed. 1824, ii. 447.

9. *Thomas Phaer.* See note to p. 137, l. 29, and cf. Gascoigne, Webbe, and Puttenham, by Index.

10. *Palingenius* (*Marcellus*), i.e. Pietro Angelo Manzolli. The *Zodiacus Vitae pulcherrimum opus M. Palingenii Stellati poetae* (? Venice, 1531), of which there are innumerable editions, was translated by B. Googe in 1560 (*First three books*), 1561 (*First six books*), and 1565 (*The Zodiacke of Life* . . .).

20. *wordes of one syllable.* See Index for references in these volumes to the monosyllabic character of English (s. v. Monosyllables). Cf. Dryden, *Discourse concerning Satire* (ed. Scott and Saintsbury, xiii. 121).

26. Quintil. ix. 3 (§ 478).

33. *Carmen Exametrum . . . in our English tong.* Yet Ascham in his *Toxophilus* gives a few examples from his own pen.

31. 5. Probably a reference to the passage in Cicero's *Brutus*, 51.

32. 11. *Simmias Rhodius . . . ᾠόν.* See Webbe and Puttenham, by Index. The title refers only to the *shape* of the verse, and not, as Ascham and his copiers have it, to the subject. Nor is the piece in rhyme.

21. *Hunnes and Gothians.* See p. 29, l. 31.

24. See note to p. 283, l. 9.

25. *Gonsaluo Periz . . . in translating the Vlisses of Homer.* Gonçalo Perez issued his translation in 1553 (*La Vlyxea de Homero . . . traduzida . . . en Romance Castellano*). It was several times reprinted in the sixteenth century. Meres borrows this passage (see vol. ii. p. 314, l. 33). See letter from Ascham to G. Periz, Feb. 20, 1565 (Giles, ii. 108).

33. 11. *Senese Felice Figliucci,* i.e. Felice Figliucci, Sanese (of Sienna), whose volume, *Della filosofia morale* a commentary in Italian on the *Ethics*, appeared at Rome in 1551. He also translated the *Philippics* of Demosthenes (Rome, 1551). See Tiraboschi, vii. 837, 2323. The plea for classical metres was fully advanced earlier by Claudio Tolomei in his *Versi e Regole della Nuova Poesia Toscana*, 1539, and by his friends of the *Accademia della Nuova Poesia.* Daniel notes this (see infra, ii. p. 368, l. 34).

26. And yet the Prologues of Ariosto's *Negromante* and *Cassaria* are in classical form. Earlier examples by Leonardo Dati and others are extant.

34. 20-1. Cic. *Epist. ad Att.* iv. 16 (towards end).

25. '*Sed nos veri iuris, germanaeque iustitiae solidam et expressam effigiem nullam tenemus: umbra et imaginibus utimur: eas ipsas utinam sequeremur! feruntur enim ex optimis naturae et veritatis exemplis.*' *De Officiis*, iii. 17 (§ 69).

36. 18. Cf. the similar metaphor in *Toxophilus* (Giles, ii. 147).

38. 32. *in these wordes.* *Acad. Quaest.* i. 3, § 9.

39. 3. 'Fabricius (*Bibl. Gr.* Harles, iv. 383, note d) has pointed out Ascham's error in confounding the historian with Varro's freedman of the same name (*Epist.* 9), an error common to him with Fras. Philelphus. Dionysius says himself (i. 7) that he came to Rome "in *Augustus* dayes"; but for Ascham's statement respecting Varro's library (here and *Epist.* 9) there seems to be no other ground than his occasional citations from Varro' (Mayor, p. 265).

20. *Civ. Dei*, vi. **2**.

40. 6. See the section '*Qui primi legendi*' in Quintil. ii. 5 (86).

16. Quintil. x. 3 (525). Cf. Saintsbury, *Hist. of Crit.* ii. 151.

29, &c. 'He that will write well in any tongue must follow this counsel of Aristotle, to speak as the common people do, to think as wise men do.' *Toxophilus*, 'To all Gentlemen and Yeomen of England' (Giles, ii. 7).

41. 19, 26. See Quintil. viii. 3 (§§ 391, 393).

33. So Gellius, i. 15. 18 ('*novator verborum*'). Ascham appears to be borrowing from him here. Cf. *exacte* (l. 35), which is not Sallustian.

42. 21. Quintilian (from whom Ascham borrows) gives this example in the section '*Graecanicae figurae*' (ix. 3).

43. 25. *pickling.* See note to p. 10, l. 23.

44. 4 and 9. *Epist. ad Att.* vii. 3.

27. *those reules.* A supplement to these critical remarks is found in Cheke's letter to Thomas Hoby, July 16, 1557 (printed at the end of *The Courtier*, 1561):—'. . . I am of this opinion that our own tung shold be written cleane and pure, vnmixt and vnmangeled with borowing of other tunges, wherein if we take not heed bi tijm, euer borowing and neuer payeng, she shall be fain to keep her house as bankrupt. For then doth our tung naturallie and praisablie vtter her meaning, when she boroweth no conterfeitness of other tunges to attire her self withall, but vseth plainlie her own with such shift, as nature

craft, experiens, and folowing of other excellent doth lead her
vnto: and if she want at ani tijm (as being vnperfight she must),
yet let her borow with suche bashfulnes, that it mai appeer that,
if either the mould of our own tung could serue us to fascion
a woord of our own, or if the old denisoned wordes could
content and ease this neede, we wold not boldly venture of
vnknowen wordes. This I say not for reproof of you, who haue
scarslie and necessarily vsed whear occasion serueth a strange
word so, as it seemeth to grow out of the matter and not to be
sought for ; but for mijn own defens, who might be counted
ouerstraight a deemer of thinges, if I gaue not thys accompt to
you, mi freend and wijs, of mi marring this your handiwork ...'
This passage and the conversation reported by Ascham are
the only critical deliverances by Cheke preserved in the vernacular.

45. 3. *mase and muse.* Cf. Heywood, *Epigrammes*, ' Brought
to this tricker nother muse nor mase' (ed. Spens. Soc., p. 107).

26. *example to follow*, i.e. Cicero (ante, p. 25, l. 32).

The *Scholemaster*, as we have it, is incomplete, and was
probably left unfinished by Ascham, though he had promised to
discuss ' particularlie of everie one' of the six sections named
ante, p. 5. According to the plan which he communicated to
Sturm about Dec. 1568, there were to be eight divisions.
' *Gradus sunt hi; primus, linguarum versio . . . . Sequuntur
reliqui Gradus, Paraphrasis, Metaphrasis, Epitome, Imitatio, Com-
mentatio, Scriptio, et Declamatio*' (Giles, ii. 177).

WILLES (footnote, pp. 46–7).

47. Cf. Harvey, infra, i. p. 126; Fraunce, infra, i. p. 305;
and Puttenham, infra, ii. p. 95 et seq.

GASCOIGNE (pp. 46–57).

[The notes in Gabriel Harvey's hand are here marked (H.):
others, on the same copy, which appear to be in a hand rather
older than Harvey's, are marked (N.). I am indebted to Miss
Toulmin Smith for the collation of the text and for a copy
of these manuscript jottings.]

46. 4. 'Aduertisements, worth the reading & examining' (H.).

47. 7. 'Pregnant & notable points' (H.).

Cf. Ronsard, *Abrégé de l'art poétique françois* (1565), 'Tu auras en premier lieu les conceptions hautes, grandes, belles, et non traînantes à terre. Car le principal poinct est l'invention, laquelle vient tant de la bonne nature, que par la leçon des bons et anciens autheurs,' &c. See the notes to James VI's *Reulis*, infra, p. 210, ll. 5–13, p. 221, ch. vii.

9. *Inuentio salsa. Aliquid lautum, rarum, et singulare* (N.).

11. Prologue to *Persones Tale* (Oxford Chaucer, iv. p. 568: and see note, vol. v. p. 446).

48. 5. *Inventio rara, non vulgaris* (N.). *Contemnenda Musa vulgaris: praesertim in tanta messe exquisitorum Ingeniorum* (H.).

a tale of a tubbe. For early examples of this phrase see Mr. Ward's *Eng. Dram. Lit.* ii. 379, note.

10–12. '*Nota*' (H.): in margin, '*In hoc genere Lucianus excellebat; et post eum plerique Itali: maxime Poetae* (N.)—apparently referring to the words *trita et obuia*.

17, &c. '*Aretinus voluit albis equis praecurrere, et esse Vnicus in suo quodam hyperbolico genere: Petrarcha, Ariostus, Tassus, plus habent et civilis ingenii et heroici animi. Nouissime etiam Sallustius Bartasius, in lingua Gallica, ipse est Homerus diuinus. Nihil unquam tale in Gallia*' (H.).

35. 'A *non sequitur*' (H.). *Indecorum.* See note to p. 59, l. 33.

49. 3 (Top margin) 'The difference of the last verse from the rest in euerie stanza, a grace in the Faerie Queen' (H.).

(Side margin) 'The measure all one thoroughowte' (N.).

7. (Bottom margin) 'His aptest partition had bene into precepts of { Invention. { Elocution. And the seuerall rules of both, to be sorted and marshialled in their proper places. He doth prettily well: but might easely haue don much better, both in the one, and in the other: especially by the direction of Horaces and Aristotles *Ars Poetica*' (H.).

13, 16. xij, xiiij, xiiij. (In margin) 'An errour (if an error) in sum few Eclogues of Sir Philip Sidney' (H.).

19. Over '*emphasis*' H. writes 'Prosodie.' (In the margin)

'The naturall and ordinary Emphasis of euery word, as uiolĕntly : not uiolēntly' (N.). Cp. note to p. 102, l. 23.

34. 'As I haue heard sum straungers, and namely French-men, pronounce it Treasūre, *sed inepte*' (N.).

50. 4–5. Cf. l. 27, and see note to p. 267, ll. 6–15.

6. 'The onlie verse in esse' (H.).

9. 'The reason of menie a good uerse marred in Sir Philip Sidney, M. Spenser, M. Fraunce, and in a manner all owr excellentest poets: in such words as hēauĕn, ĕuĭl, dĭuĕl, and the like ; made dyssyllables, contrarie to their natural pro-nunciation' (H.).

19. *to the eare.* 'So M. Spenser and Sir Philip, for the most part' (H.). 'Our poems only Rymes ; & not verses, Aschami querela (N.) : et mea post illum Reformatio ; post me Sidneius, Spenserus, Francius' (H.).

51. 18, &c. '*Non placet.* A greater grace and Maiesty in longer wordes, so they be current Inglish. Monasyllables ar good to make vpp a hobling and hudling uerse' (N.).

22. Cf. Gascoigne's *Steel Glas* (ed. Arber, p. 77) :—

> 'That *Grammer* grudge not at our english tong,
> Bycause it stands by *Monosyllaba*.'

24. *Inkehorne.* The common Elizabethan phrase 'inkhorn termes' was perhaps established by Wilson in his *Arte of Rhetorique* (1553), though it occurs earlier (see *N. E. D.*). 'Ink-hornism' is frequent in Nash and Harvey (cf. vol. ii. p. 431) and Hall. Florio uses 'inkpot tearmes' in his definition of 'pedantaggine.'

28. 'Sir Philip Sidney and M. Spenser, of mie opinion' (H.).

30–1. '*Idem ante in 2 Regula*' (N.).

52. 10. 'A pithie rule in Sir Philips Apologie for Poetrie. The Inuention must guide & rule the Elocution : *non contra*' (H.).

14, &c. Sidney is thinking of such methods in *Astrophel and Stella*, quoted infra, in note to p. 202, ll. 3–8.

22. (At end of § 7) '*Elocution*' (H.).

23. 'Tropes and figures lende an especiall grace to a uerse' (N.).

26. 'Gallant & fine' (H.).

'Persecuting of our figure too mutely: bald, and childish' (N.).

Ne quid nimis. See ii. p. 161, l. 15.

53. 3. (At end of § 9) 'Spenser hath reuiued *uncouth, whilom, of yore, forthy*' (H.).

4–9. (In margin of § 10) 'The stile sensible and significant; gallant & flowing' (H.).

10–32. (In margin of § 11) 'And yet we use to say, "He is of the *bludd royal*," and not " He is of the roiall bludd ": he is *heier apparant* to the Crowne, and not he is apparant heier to the Crowne: Rime *Roiall*, in regula 13 et 14 (N.), not royal ryme' (H.).

54. 1. *turkeneth*, altereth.   Cf. Gascoigne: 'And for the rest you shall find it now in this second imprinting so turquened and turned, so clensed from all unclenly wordes . . .' (*Posies*, 'Epist. to Reuerend Diuines,' 1575).   This rare word occurs at least twice in Golding's *De Mornay* (1587), pp. 353, 368 (' If they chaunce to stumble vpon some good saying for maners or for the life of man, they turkin it a thousand waies to make it seem good for thir purpose'), and once in Rogers's 39 *Articles* (1607), pref. p. 24.   See Prof. Skeat's article in *Notes and Queries*, 6th Ser. v. 165 (4 Mar. 1882).   The etymology is uncertain.   Such a formation from Fr. *torquer*, L. *torqueo* would be unusual.

3. 'dissyllaba pro monosyllabis' (N.).

7. (End of § 12) 'All theise in Spenser and manie like: but with discretion: & tolerably, though sumtime not greatly commendably' (H.).

12. *Musicians.*   Cf. Ronsard (apropos of masculine and feminine rhymes) in his *Abrégé*.   With him *cesure* is practically elision ('une certaine cesure de la voyelle *e* ').

21. (End of § 13) 'A special note in Sir Philips *Apologie for Poetrie*' (H.).

22. 'The Inglish Pentameter' (H.).

31. 'Ryme Royal still carrieth the credit for a gallant & stately verse ' (H.).

55. 24. Gascoigne is of course out in his etymology.   The older French form *vireli* was falsely associated with *virer* and *lai*.

30. ' Rather better than the royal ' (H.).

34. *Gascoignes voyage into Holland* (1572).

35. 'Sir Philip vseth this kind often: as in Astrophil, Arcadia' (H.).

56. 6. N. writes opposite 'Poulters measure.'

11. (End of § 14) 'Mr. Phaers Virgil in a braue long verse, stately and flowing: the King of owr Inglish metricians' (H.). See note to p. 30, l. 9.

22. (Bottom) '*Gaudent breuitate moderni.* Spenser doth sumtime otherwise, and commendably, as the matter leadeth, the verse floweth, or other circumstance will beare it owt' (H.).

25. Gascoigne, it will be noted, does not give a formal definition of 'riding rime,' as he does in other cases.

33, &c. 'The difference of rymes, according to the difference of the matters subject' (H.).

57. 9. 'Or sum heroical discourse, or statelie argument' (H.).

12. *affying*, trusting, confiding.

WHETSTONE (pp. 58-60).

58. 8. Sir Humphrey Gilbert (? 1539-83) the navigator, stepbrother of Sir Walter Raleigh. Cf. Harvey, ii. 261, 28, &c.

Whetstone's friend Gascoigne had published, in 1576, *A Discourse of a new Passage to Cataia* [Cathay]: *Written by Sir Humfrey Gilbert, Knight.* Gascoigne informs us, in the Preface, that he had interested himself in the matter 'because I vnderstode that M. Fourboiser [i. e. Frobisher] (a kinsman of mine) did pretend to trauaile in the same *Discouerie.*'

15. *Promos and Cassandra* is based on the eighty-fifth novel of Giraldi Cintio's *Hecatommithi*, which Whetstone also translated in his *Heptameron of Ciuill Discourses* (1582). Shakespeare's *Measure for Measure* is founded on Whetstone's play.

59. 15. Cp. p. 79, l. 31 ; p. 332, l. 17, and ii. p. 309, l. 13.

21. *Germaine.* Cf. p. 84, l. 13. Mr. A. W. Ward (*Eng. Dram. Lit.* i. 216, &c.) points out that the objection to the *Germaine* is the same as that brought against English plays by Northbrooke in his *Treatise* (infra, p. 61).

27. Cf. p. 197, l. 29 ; ii. p. 389, l. 22. So Boileau in his *Art Poétique*, iii. 41, apropos of the Spanish drama ; and D'Aubignac

in his *Pratique du Théâtre*, ii. 7, giving a sketch of a play in which the hero is born and 'gets children.'

33. Cf. Sidney, infra, 199. 5. Also Hall, *Satires*, i. 3; and *The Pilgrimage to Parnassus*, v (l. 671, &c.). Whetstone uses *Indecorum* (60. 1) in the specific sense intended by the generality of Renaissance critics. See *Decorum*, by Index.

[In 1584 Whetstone published his *Touchstone for the Time* (see p. 63), in which he allies himself with the anti-stage pamphleteers.]

THOMAS LODGE (pp. 61–86).

62. (Headnote) *Playes Confuted*. Gosson calls Lodge *William* on the title-page and in the text (p. 171).

63. (Headnote) The list may be supplemented by *The French Academie . . . by Peter de la Primaudaye . . . newly translated into English by T*[homas] *B*[owes], London, 1586. 'And I think it wil not be far from the matter, if we say that it is a shameful thing to suffer amongst us, or to loose time that ought to be so precious unto us, in beholding and in hearing plaiers, actors of Interludes and Comedies, who are as pernitious a plague in a common wealth as can be imagined. For nothing marreth more the behavior, simplicitie, and natural goodnes of any people than this, bicause they soone receiue into their soules a liuely impression of that dissolutenes and villanie which they see and heare, when it is ioyned with words, accents, gestures, motions, & actions, wherewith players and iuglers know how to inrich, by all kind of artificiall sleights, the filthiest and most dishonest matters, which commonly they make choice of. And to speek freely in few wordes, we may truely say, that the theatre of players is a school of all unchastnes, uncleannes, whoredom, craft, subtletie, and wickednes (p. 216).'

1. The allusion to Protogenes and Apelles is based upon the story in Pliny, xxxv. 10. See also Carlo Dati's *Vite de' Pittori Antichi*, Florence, 1730 ('Vita di Protogene'). Cf. Nash, infra, p. 326, l. 16.

63. 5. Cf. ii. p. 270, ll. 1–2.

64. 5. Gosson's *Schoole of Abuse* (see p. 61) was entered at

Stationers' Hall on July 22, 1579 (Arber). It was followed on Nov. 7 by his composite volume, *Ephemerides of Phialo* and *A Short Apologie* (see p. 62), in the first portion of which he attacks the *Straunge News out of Affrick* (ib.), and in the second defends the thesis of his *Schoole of Abuse.* Towards the close of the latter he refers to Lodge's counterblast (ib.), and concludes, 'but I stay my handes till I see his booke ; when I haue perusd it I will tell you more.' He fulfils his promise in the *Playes Confuted* (ib.), dealing with Lodge's tract (which 'came not to my handes in one whole yeere after the priuy printing thereof' (p. 169)), and the defence entitled *The Play of Playes* (ib.). Lodge therefore had only the *Schoole of Abuse* before him when he wrote this *Defence.* He returned to the attack later (1584) in his Preface to *An Alarum against Vsurers*, in which he denounces the personalities of the *Playes Confuted.*

23–6. Cf. Sidney, infra, p. 189, ll. 7–8. The persistency of the allusion in Elizabethan literature is jocularly referred to in *The Returne from Parnassus*, Pt. i, Act iv, sc. 1 (1224).

33–4. '*Virgill* sweates in describyng his Gnat: *Ouid* bestirreth him to paint out his Flea : the one shewes his art in the lust of *Dido*, the other his cunning in the inceste of *Myrrha*, and that trumpet of Baudrie, the Craft of Loue' (*Schoole of Abuse*, ed. Arber, p. 19). The pseudo-Ovidian *De Pulice* is often referred to. Cf. Marlowe, *Dr. Faustus*, vi. l. 116.

65. 10. Cf. the *Schoole of Abuse*, passim. The reference is not verbal.

16. Cf. Nash, 331. 12.

21. *Campanus.* Giovannantonio Campano (c. 1429–1477), humanist and poet, pupil of Demetrius Chalcondylas, successively bishop of Crotona and of Teramo. (See Fabricius, *Bibl. med. et inf. Latin.* I. 326 ; Tiraboschi, VI. 1393, &c. ; Gyraldus, *De Poetis*, u. s., p. 19 ; and G. Lesca, *Giovannantonio Campano*, Pontedera, 1892.) His books, other than his volumes of poems, are chiefly editorial. The reference here may be to a popular edition of Aesop in which he collaborated. His complete works appeared at Venice, n. d. (? 1495). See infra, p. 327, l. 17.

31. This common Latin proverb is a favourite with the Elizabethan pamphleteers. Cf. 'nodum in serpo querere' in the *Seruingman's Comfort*, 1598 (Roxb. Libr.).

32. *inco[n]u[en]iences*, improprieties, offences. See Webbe, infra, p. 253. 3 : and p. 294. 9 (with Latin on p. 418). Cf. Genevan Bible (1560) *Numbers, Argt.* 'That either they fall not to such inconueniences, or else return to him quickly by true repentance.' The Shakespeare Soc. edit. proposes 'incontinencies.'

66. 2. *inscience*. Cf. 67. 25. This word had just come into vogue. See *N. E. D.*

14. *as*: perhaps a misprint for ' and,' but not wrong.

18. *Orig.* ' denocated.'

23. *quesie*, unsettled (or easily unsettled), nauseated, squeamish ; of common occurrence in Elizabethan books. Cf. Gosson, u. s., p. 31, and *Playes Confuted* (Roxb. Libr.), p. 168 ; Harvey, infra, ii. p. 231, l. 32 ; Chapman, infra, ii. p. 295, l. 14; *Euphues* (ed. Landmann, p. 20) ; Shakespeare, *M. Ado*, ii. 1. 399 ; Greene, *Friar Bacon*, x. 130.

24. *werish*, here = sick. It is generally applied to food : ' savourless,' *mal savouré* (Palsgrave). Cf. Sc. *wersh*.

67. 4. *Though Plato*, &c. Gosson applies this well-worn argument twice in his *Schoole* (ed. Arber, pp. 20, 21).

5. *well publiques*. Cf. Stanyhurst, ' with a iagged *hystorie* of a ragged Weale publicke' (Epistle in *Description of Ireland*, Arber's 'Stanyhurst,' p. 12).

68. 2. *gale*, gall.

7, &c. *Maximus* [orig. *Maximinus*] *Tirius*, &c. ' Maximus Tyrius taketh vppon him to defend the discipline of these Doctors vnder the name of *Homer*, wresting the rashnes of *Aiax* to valour, the cowardice of *Vlisses* to Policie, the dotage of *Nestor* to graue counsell, and the battaile of *Troy* too the woonderfull conflict of the foure elements ; where *Iuno*, which is counted the ayre, settes in her foote to take vp the strife, and steps boldly betwixt them to part the fray. It is a Pageant woorth the sight, to beholde how he labors with Mountaines to bring foorth Mise.' Gosson, *Schoole of Abuse*, p. 21. Cf. also ib. pp. 29, 40.

14. *Irus*, the proverbial ' poor man,' after the beggar in the house of Ulysses. Cf. ii. p. 45, l. 21.

23. *Buchanan* (p. 24, l. 7, note). Gosson retorts in his *Playes Confuted* that the reference to 'Buchanans booke' is 'an old wormeaten obiection,' and that ' neither Players nor their friends

are able to proue' that it or the 'Playe of Christ' by Nazian-
zenus was performed on the stage. He argues that they were
prepared 'dialoguewise, as Plato and Tullie did their Philosophye, to be reade, not to be played' (pp. 189–197).

24. *Boetius comfortes*, i.e. the *De Consolatione* of Boetius
or Boethius (fl. 525).

25. *Erasmus* 'interpreted' or translated *Hecuba* and *Iphigenia*. Lodge's reference to these, to Buchanan, and to Donatus
(p. 80) suggests the idea that he was familiar with a popular
edition of *Tragœdiæ selectæ* issued by Henri Estienne, printer
to Huldrich Fugger (1567, &c.), which contains the interpretations of *Hecuba* and *Iphigenia* by Erasmus (pp. 5–117), the
tract by Donatus *De Tragœdia et Comœdia* (pp. 118-28), the
interpretations of the *Medea* and *Alcestis* (pp. 129-213), and of
the *Ajax*, *Antigone*, and *Electra* of Sophocles, by Georgius
Rotallerus.

69. 5. 'Tullie accustomed to read them with great diligence
in his youth, but when hee waxed grauer in studie, elder in
yeares, riper in iudgement, hee accompted them the fathers
of lyes, Pipes of vanitie, and Schooles of Abuse [*Tusc.* I. 2],'
Gosson, *Schoole of Abuse*, p. 21.

25. Cicero, *Pro Archia*, xxvi. 7.

70. 3. *Cellarius*. Probably (as suggested by the editor of
the Shakes. Soc. reprint) a printer's error for Cassiodorus (cf.
p. 71, l. 12) : but I have failed to find the passage in the
collected works (Geneva, 1609). He cannot be ' James Cellarius,
editor of Cicero,' as stated in the Index of the Hunterian Club
edition of Lodge's works, for *he*, Jacob Keller, Jesuit, *alias*
' Hercynianus (Fabius),' did not produce his edition of the
Thesaurus Ciceronianus of Nizolius (see p. 202, l. 16, note) till
1613.

8. *Quicquid*, &c. A favourite line. Cf. ii. 323. 17.

16. Gosson had said that Marius ' doubted the abuses of
those Schooles, where Poets were euer the head Maisters'
(*Schoole of Abuse*, p. 23). Lodge's list of examples is in direct
retort to Gosson's list of persons who held poets in no
honour (ib.).

71. 1. Horace, *Ars Poetica*, 403.

4. *Orig.* 'Hiroaldus,' a misprint for Beroaldus, of which

name there were two poets (Filippo Beroaldo). The elder
(1453–1505), humanist and commentator, is here referred to.
See Gyraldus, *De Poetis*, u. s., p. 31.

12. *Cassiodorus* (Magnus Aurelius C., *b.* 468), author of *De
Institutione Divinarum Scripturarum*. See note 70. 3.

14. *Paulinus . . . Byshop of Nolanum.* Saint Paulinus (Meropius Pontius Anicius Paulinus), 353–431. His *Epistolae et
Poema'a* was printed by Badius Ascensius in 1516.

15. *Ambrose . . . in Mediolanum.* St. Ambrose (*b.* 340).

16. Probably a reference to the well-known chapter of
Bæda's *Eccles. Hist.* (iv. 24), 'Quod in monasterio eius fuerit
frater cui donum canendi sit diuinitus concessum'; perhaps
also to Bæda's *Death-Song.*

18. See p. 73, l. 19. Gosson, in his *Apologie* (Arber, p. 70),
quotes Lactantius as a condemner of plays 'without any
manner of exception, thinking them, the better they are
penned or cunninglier handled, the more to be fled.'

19-20. Epimenides of Crete, *Titus* i. 12, from the lost work
' *On Oracles* ': Aratus of Cilicia, *Acts* xvii. 28, from the *Phaenomena* (see Stobaeus, *Eclog.* i. 3. 3). Cf. Sidney, p. 191, l. 10,
and note.

22. *Poeta nascitur*, &c. See note to p. 195, l. 23.

35. The original print reads 'well of the Muses which
Cabelimus calleth Porum,' a strange but explicable travesty of
Lodge's MS. See Persius, *Prol.* i.

72. 9. *Iodocus Badius* (1462-1535), the famous printer, also
a satiric poet: generally known as Iod. Bad. Ascensius, from
Aasche, near Brussels, where he was born.

73. 19. *Lactantius* (Firmianus), *d. c.* 325. See p. 342, and by
Index.

74. 6. *Ars Poetica*, ll. 391-9.

75. 1. Tyrtæus. Ib., l. 402. Cf. infra, p. 77, l. 6, &c.

6. *that Poetes were*: the mediaeval conception of poetry,
adopted by sixteenth-century criticism.

18. *Aen.* vi. 662.

22. See the quotation from Gosson, supra (note to 64. 33-4).
Elsewhere Gosson speaks of Ovid as the 'high martial of
Venus' and the 'amorous scholemaister' (*Schoole*, p. 29). Cf.
also pp. 34-5 (ed. Arber).

33. Gosson is fond of making complimentary allusions to the Scythians throughout his *Schoole*. Cf. 'Poetrie in *Scythia* without vice, as the *Phœnix* in Arabia without a fellow' (sidenote, p. 22). He praises the olden times in England, when there were 'men in valure not yeelding to *Scithia*' (p. 34). See other references by Index.

76. 7. *scare*. The clue to this allusion is to be found in the *Epistle Dedicatorie* to *Euphues*. 'Alexander hauing a Skar in his cheeke helde his finger vpon it that Appelles might not paint it. Appelles painted him with his finger cleauing to his face. "Why," quod Alexander, "I layde my finger on my Skarre, bicause I would not haue thee see it." "Yea," sayd Appelles, "and I drew it there, bicause none els should perceiue it; for if thy finger had bene away, either thy Skarre would haue been seene, or my arte mislyked."' Is this one of Lyly's inventions? There appears to be no record of the scar in the authorities cited by Overbeck in *Die antiken Schriftquellen*.

17–25. '*Tiberius* the Emperour sawe somewhat, when he iudged *Scaurus* to death for writing a Tragidie: *Augustus*, when hee banished *Ouid*: and *Nero* when he charged *Lucan* to put vp his pipes, to stay his penne and write no more' (Gosson, *Schoole*, p. 23).

30, &c. Justinus, *Hist.* iii. 5.

77. 19, &c. 'I may well liken *Homer* to *Mithecus*, and Poets to Cookes: the pleasures of the one winnes the body from labor, and conquereth the sense; the allurement of the other drawes the mind from vertue, and confoundeth wit' (Gosson, *Schoole*, p. 22).

35. Orig. 'ledde.'

78. 30. Gosson himself had said, 'Pythagoras bequeathes them a Clookebagge and condemns them for fooles, that iudge Musicke by sounde and eare. If you will bee good Scholars and profite well in the Arte of Musicke, shutte your Fidels in their cases, and looke vp to heauen: the order of the Spheres, the vnfallible motion of the Planets, the iuste course of the yeere, and varietie of seasons, the concorde of the Elementes and their qualyties, Fyre, Water, Ayre, Earth, Heate, Colde, Moysture, and Drought, concurring togeather

to the constitution of earthly bodies and sustenance of euery creature' (*Schoole*, p. 26). He returns to the subject in *Playes Confuted* (ed. Roxb. Libr., p. 168).

79. 2. Gosson in the *Schoole* refers to *Catilins Conspiracies*, which he dismisses as 'knowen too be a Pig of myne own Sowe' (p. 40), and elsewhere informs us that he had written *The Comedie of Captaine Mario*, and a 'moral,' *Praise at Parting* : but 'since the first printing of my Inuectiue, to this day, I neuer made Playe' (*Playes Confuted*, 'To the Universities, &c.'). He explains his changed attitude thus : ' Now if any man aske me why my selfe haue penned Comedyes in time paste, and inveigh so egerly against them here, let him knowe that *semel insaniuimus omnes* : I haue sinned, and am sorry for my fault : hee runnes farre that neuer turnes ; better late than neuer' (*Schoole*, p. 41).

79. 31. Cf. p. 59, l. 15 ; p. 332. l. 17, and ii. p. 309, l. 13. This passage is in close parallel with Chettle's *Kind-Harts Dreame*, 64.

80. 7. In the opening words of his tract *De Tragœdia* &c. (see note to p. 68, l. 25) : ' *Initium Tragœdiæ & Comœdiæ a rebus diuinis est inchoatum : quibus pro fructibus vota soluentes operabantur antiqui.*'

13. *Iodocus Badius.* Supra, p. 72, l. 9, note.

81. 1. *Tulley defines.* Probably borrowed from Donatus (edit. u. s., p. 123), who is responsible for the ascription of the phrase to Cicero. It is very common, with, and without, reference to its origin ; cf. *Every Man out of his Humour*, iii. 1, and *Hamlet*, iii. 2. 23. It is quoted by Minturno, *De Poeta*, p. 44, Jacques Grévin, *Brief Discours* (1562), and referred to by Cervantes, *Don Quix.* pt. I, ch. xlviii.

Of this passage Gosson says in his *Playes Confuted* : ' Yonge Master Lodge, thinking to iett vpon startoppes, and steale an ynche of his hight by the bare name of Cicero, allegeth from him, that a Play is the Schoolmistresse of life, the lookinge glasse of manners, and the image of trueth. But finding him selfe too weeke in the knees to stand it out, neither alleadging the place where Tullie saith it, nor bringing any reason of his owne to proue it, hee flittes from this to the Etymologie of Plaies, from thence to the inuentors, and so gallops his wisedome out of breath. It seemeth that Master Lodge saw

this in Tullie with other folkes eyes, and not his owne. For
to my remembrance I neuer read it in him, neither doe I
thinke that Master Lodge can shewe it me. [*He then refers
to passages in* Tusc. Orat. *where Cicero* 'misliketh playes'
and to others where 'he is sharpe set against them'.] But because Master Lodge will needes father these wordes vpon
Tullie that neuer spake them, I will first sette downe the
matter, and the persons of both kindes of playes, then rippe
vp every part of this definition, that you may see how this
Gentleman, like the Foxe at the banquet of the Storke, lickes
the outside of the glasse with an empty stomacke, when his
heade will not suffer him to enter in. . . . Master Lodge, finding
some peevish index or gatherer of Tullie to be a sleepe, is
very wel contented to winke for company, and thinking his
worde so currant to goe for payment, woulde gladly persuade
vs vpon Tullies credite that a Play is the Schoolmistres of life.
Wherein I perceive hee is no changeling, for hee disputeth
as soundly, being from the vniversitie and out of exercise, as
hee did when hee was there, and at his booke.' (Roxburghe
Library, ed. Hazlitt, pp. 179-83.)

9. *Susarion Bullus and Magnes,* probably Lodge's printer's
misreading of 'Susario, Myllus, and Magnes.' For an account
of these three early writers of Comedy see Meineke, *Historia
Critica Comicorum Graecorum,* i. pp. 18-35.

11. *Eupolis with Cratinus.* Cf. Webbe, infra, p. 236. See
Meineke, u. s., pp. 104-46, 43-58.

24. Epist. I. xvi. 53, but altered.

82. 5. *Philemon* of Soli, a Greek comic poet, contemporary
with Menander.

7. *Menander,* the Greek comic poet, the model of Terence
(see *Andria,* Prol.).

11, &c. *Thais* in the *Eunuchus; Demeas* (Demea, Δημέας) in
the *Adelphi; Pamphilus* in the *Andria* and *Hecyra; Dauus* 'the
slave' in Terence and Plautus, e. g. in the *Andria* (cf. p. 65,
i. 26) and *Phormio; Gnatho* in the *Eunuchus* (cf. p. 65, l. 28).

27, &c. *Cecilius,* Caecilius Statius, contemporary with
Ennius; *Plinius,* for Livius Andronicus (?); *Neuius,* Cn. Naevius,
epic and dramatic poet; *Licinius,* Licinius Imbrex; *Atilius* (in
original text printed *Actilius*); *Turpilius,* Sextus Turpilius, the

comic poet, and friend of Terence; *Trabea*, the Roman comic poet.

83. 6. *as Seruius reporteth.* Servius Honoratus Maurus, grammarian, best known by his commentary on Virgil.

16. *Iodocus Badius*, supra, p. 72, l. 9, note.

32. *Glicerium.* Glycerium (Γλυκέριον): *Andria*, i. 1. 108.

84. 13. *The Germanes*, supra, p. 59, l. 21, note.

28. 'The last [*Catilins Conspiracies*], because it is knowen too be a Pig of myne owne Sowe, I will speake the lesse of it' (*Schoole*, p. 40). Cf. Harvey's *Letter-Book* (ed. Scott, p. 59), 'And nowe in bestowing uppon myselfe a misshapin illfavorid freshe copy of my precious poems, as it were a pigg of myne owne sowe.' Gosson's unfortunate phrase was not readily forgotten.

85. 1. See the Life of Virgil by Tib. Claudius Donatus. Cf. Puttenham, infra, ii. p. 58.

3. *Wilson*, Robert, the elder (*d.* 1600), comedian and playwright; the fellow of Tarlton, and frequently named with him. See Harvey, infra, i. 125. 15, and Meres, infra, ii. 320. 16, 323. 24. His play of *Catiline* is not extant. It may have been the basis of a play with that title which Henslowe, in his *Diary* (p. 132), tells us was prepared by a Robert Wilson (probably R. W. junior) and Chettle. (See the article on Wilson by Mr. S. Lee in *D. N. B.*)

12. Juvenal, *Sat.* ix. 118.

25. *statute of apparrell.* Cf. *Schoole of Abuse* (p. 39) 'How often hath her Maiestie . . . sette downe the limits of apparell to euery degree, and how soone againe hath the pride of our harts ouerflowen the chanel.'

30, &c. The flout is explained in one of the verses by Barnabe Rich, prefixed to Lodge's later *Alarum against Vsurers* (Shakespeare Society, 1853) :—

'If thus it be, good Lodge, continue still;
  Thou needst not feare Goose sonne, or Gander's hisse,
Whose rude reportes, part from a slaundrous quill,
  Will be determind but in reading this,
  Of whom the wiser sort will thinke amis
To slaunder him whose birth and life is *such
As false report his fame can never tuch.'

See also *Tarlton's Jests*, ed. Halliwell, p. xxi.

SPENSER AND HARVEY (pp. 87–126).

According to Nash, Harvey 'publiquely diuulged these letters,' and Spenser was 'no way priuie to the committing of them to print' (*Foure Letters Confuted* in Grosart's edition of Nash, ii. 231, 233). Cf. also his *Haue with you to Saffron-Walden* (ib. iii. 188).

88. 11, &c. Presumably referring to the *Shepheardes Calender*. Spenser, still hesitating to publish his poem, is doubtful of its welcome by Sidney and the common friends who were received at Penshurst and Leicester House. Cf. p. 112, l. 12 (note).

19. *she.* Cf. p. 106, l. 2.

89. 7. *Master Dyer.* Sir Edward Dyer (*d.* 1607), courtier and poet. See note to p. 94, l. 29. Sidney and Dyer are grouped together in the prefatory verses to Watson's Ἑκατομπαθία—

'Hic quoque seu subeas Sydnaei, siue Dyeri
Scrinia, qua Musis area bina patet.'

12. Orig. ἀρειωπαγῷ. Cf. p. 94, l. 27 (orig. ἄρειονπαγον). Of this *Areopagus* we know little. It was probably an informal society, perhaps unknown by that name except to one or two of its members. 'Academies' were in the air; and it may be that the young writers had Baïf's recent project in mind. It has been suggested that the title was borrowed from 'the Florentine Academy in the time of Lorenzo, which bore the same name' (Einstein, *Ital. Renaissance in England* (1902), p. 357), but it is more probably a direct adaptation from classical history. 'Areopagites' frequently occurs in the ordinary sense.

20. *Schoole of Abuse.* See p. 61, and notes to Lodge's *Defence*, passim.

25. *Slomber* is not known. It may be *A senights slumber*, referred to in the printer's preface to the *Complaints* (1591). See also the *Dreames*, p. 100, l. 24.

32. *Maister E. K.* See p. 127, and note.

90. 3. *Mystresse Kerkes.* See the note on 'E. K.', p. 127.

13. *Maister Drants Rules.* These, if ever committed to writing, are not extant. The references throughout these letters (e. g. pp. 96, 97, 99, 102), and elsewhere, do not preclude the possibility that Drant had merely conveyed his

views to his friends in conversation, and had persuaded them to carry them out in their verse-making.

Thomas Drant (*d.* ? 1578), Archdeacon of Lewes, is known as the author of *A Medicinable Morall*, 1566, and of *Horace his arte of Poetrie, pistles & satyrs Englished*, 1567. In neither is there any critical material. His recognition in later literary history is undoubtedly due to the allusions in these letters (especially Spenser's), and is as undoubtedly in excess of his deserts, even as a contributor to the narrow controversy about the English hexameter.

27. *Maister Preston.* Thomas Preston (1537-98), Master of Trinity Hall, Cambridge, author of *Cambises* (1569).

Maister Still. John Still (? 1543-1608), Bishop of Bath and Wells, and the reputed author, on very doubtful evidence, of *Gammer Gurton's Needle* (1575). See note, ii. p. 443.

91. 21. *Immerito.* Cf. p. 92, l. 4, p. 93, l. 3, &c. Spenser so signs the prefatory verses to his *Shepheardes Calender.*

92. 29. *Mistresse Kerke.* See note to p. 127.

93. 11. *extra iocum,* a favourite phrase of Harvey's. Cf. p. 114.

94. 13. *Maister Wythipole.* Gascoigne entitled a set of verses *Councel giuen to Master Bartholomew Withipoll a little before his latter iourney to Geane, 1572* (*Works*, Roxb. Libr. i. 372). Harvey in his *Letter-Book* introduces these lines (Camden Soc. ed. p. 57)—

> 'But preythe see where Withipolls cum,
> Daniel and Bath both at onse.'

See the verses in Haslewood, ii. 302-3, which associate Harvey with two Wythipolls, father and son.

29. *twoo worthy Gentlemenne.* See pp. 89. ll. 7, 101. 22, 109. 11, 113. 11.

95. 12. *Curtoll,* curtal; here a 'docked' or 'clipped' word.

23. *Abstemio.* Laurentius Abstemius (Lorenzo Abstémio). His *Fabulae nuper compositae* was printed at Venice in 1495, and was often reprinted.

96. 11. *Watson,* ante, p. 354.

29. *Drantes Rule,* supra, p. 90, l. 13, note.

97. 4. *gorbellyed,* corpulent. Here applied to Drant, as again by Harvey on p. 118, l. 11.

26. *Goddilge yee* (= God yield you !).

98. 7. *in Iustinians Courte.* The clue to this is found in a letter in Harvey's *Letter-Book* addressed to Sir Thomas Smith. 'Your wurship mai marvel mutch that to haue absentid mi self thus long time from you, having so great and iust occasion to resort unto you, as I haue had. But suerly, sir, mi lets and hinderances eueri wai haue bene sutch, that I could not possibely do that I purposid fully, and wuld willingly haue dun for mi better proffiting in the ciuil lawe. It were too long a thing to declare them al severally and at larg ; but truly, what for sicknes and priuate busines, I could scars reade ouer thre titles in Justinian before Lent, and euer sins the beginning of Lent, at the instant and importunate request of M. Church, mi verri frend, I haue red the rhetorick lecture in the schooles; so that the prouiding for mi lecture, togither with the reading to mi pupils, the doing of ordinari acts in the howse, and disputing in the schooles, haue made me so unprouidid for Justinian, that, to sai troth, I haue bene ashamid to cum unto you' (Camden Soc. edit. pp. 176–7).

14. *the Earthquake*, April 6, 1580. Thomas Twyne, the translator of the Aeneid, was also prompted to write *A shorte and pithie Discourse* concerning it and earthquakes generally ; and Anthony Munday, too, wrote a *Short Discourse*.

27. Orig. '*pawneth.*'

99. 21–22. These lines, with minor differences, appear in 'E. K.'s gloss on 'May' in the *Shepheardes Calender*. Dr. O. Sommer finds proof in this that 'E. K.' was Spenser himself (*Sh. Cal.* p. 23). But see note on 'E. K.', p. 127. The lines are quoted by Webbe, infra, p. 283.

100. 8. *Epithalamion Thamesis* is unknown. Cf. p. 113, l. 16.

22. Cicero, *De Senect.* i. 1. Generally *praemii*.

24. *my Dreames and Dying Pellicane.* The former is referred to in a postscript to this letter (printed in the 'Globe' *Spenser*, p. 709), and in 'E. K.'s preface (see p. 133, l. 7) ; the latter in the printer's preface to the *Complaints* (1591). Both appear to have been ready for press : but no copies are known. Some have endeavoured to identify the *Dreames* with *Muiopotmos* and the *Visions of Bellay*.

101. 23. *Balductum*, trashy, a favourite word of Harvey's. Cf. Nash, ii. p. 242, l. 26, and Stanyhurst, p. 141, l. 27. Literally a posset or curd, L. Lat. *balducta*.

102. 3. *Drants Prosodye*, supra, p. 372.

13. 'Mistresse Experience.' Cf. Harvey's *Letter-Book*, p. 130, and infra, ii. p. 283, l. 33.

23. *Prosodye*. Harvey appears to use this word, throughout this letter, in the restricted and special sense of the *pronunciation* of a word or syllable (in verse). See note to p. 49, l. 19; and p. 121.

24. *Sir Thomas Smithes* (Orthography): a reference to his *De recta & emendata Linguae Anglicae Scriptione*, Paris, 1568. Harvey had recently written his elegy, *Smithus, vel Musarum lachrymae: pro obitu Thomae Smithi* (1578). See note to p. 21, l. 31.

103. 6-20. Cf. Puttenham, infra, ii. p. 122, l. 34, &c.: and Du Bellay, *Defense*, I. ix.

31. *Gambowlde*, toy, plaything.

104. 21. *Bables*, baubles. Cf. ii. 331. 12.

105. 15. See p. 99, l. 14.

23. Petrarch, Sonnet CCV (225). This is quoted in 'E. K.'s gloss. on 'April' in the *Shepheardes Calender*. Dr. Sommer cites this in support of the theory that 'E. K.' is Spenser. Here, however, it would be as fair to say that 'E. K.' is Gabriel Harvey; and more reasonable to believe that Kirke had heard the lines from Spenser. But see note to p. 127.

106. 2. *Rosalinde*. Cf. p. 88, l. 19, and, more fully, the *Shepheardes Calender*, passim. The name, as 'E. K.' tells us, is an anagram. For an account of editorial guesses on this subject see Mr. Herford's edition of the *Calender*, pp. xvi-xvii. All the solutions assume, quite unnecessarily, that 'Rose' is one of the words, and overlook the choice of such excellent Elizabethan names as Eliza, Delia, Alis. But the matter is of small concern.

107. 19, &c. Harvey's *Letter-Book* (f. 51 b) introduces 'A short poeticall discourse to my gentle masters the readers, conteyning a garden communication or dialogue in Cambridge betwene Master G. H. and his cumpanye at a Midsumer Comencement, togither with certayne delicate sonnetts and epigraumes in Inglish verse of his makinge.' Of the last the verses here printed form a part. (See Camd. Soc. edit. p. 98.) With *Anglofrancitalorum* (l. 16), cf.

'O tymes, O manners, O French, O Italish Inglande'
(ib. p. 97).

Galateo. The *Galateo* (Venice 1558, Milan 1559, Florence 1560) of Giovanni della Casa (1503–56), archbishop of Benevento, shared popular favour with Castiglione's *Courtier*, Guazzo's *Conversations*, and other books of courtesy. It was Englished in 1576, but it was known in a French edition of 1562.

There is an interesting passage in Harvey's *Letter-Book* (pp. 78–9) which describes the reading of his day. 'They have gotten Philbertes Philosopher of the Courte [Englished by G.North, 1575], the Italian Archebysshoppies braue Galateo [u.s.], Castiglioes fine Cortegiano [Eng. by Hoby, 1561], Bengalassoes Ciuil Instructions to his Nephewe Seignor Princisca [? Francesca] Ganzar, Guatzoes new Discourses of curteous behaviour [Eng. by G. Pettie & B. Young, 1586], Jouios and Rassellis Emblemes in Italian, Paradines in Frenche, Plutarche in Frenche, Frontines Stratagemes [Eng. Morysine, 1539], Polyenes Stratagemes, Polonica, Apodemica, Guigiardine [Guicciardini's *Istoria*, Eng. by Fenton, 1579], Philipp de Comines [not Eng. till 1596, by Danett], and I know not how many owtlandishe braveryes besides of the same stampe.'

24. *Tuscanish*: 'Italish' (Letter-Book).

107–8. Harvey's description of the Italianate Englishmen is, according to Nash, directed against the Earl of Oxford, who had just come home from Italy. But see note to ii. 239. 10–12.

108. 5. *with a witnesse*, excessively.

17—109. 5. Not in the Letter-Book text.

109. 11. *ouer very Castor*, &c. See note to p. 94, l. 29.

28. See note, p. 98, l. 7.

110. 3. John Harvey (1564–92). See Index.

8. Ovid, *Tristia*, i. 8. 5.

111. 17. On fol. 43 of the original edition of the *Shepheardes Calender*, again referred to on p. 112, l. 12. The lines are from Petrarch, Sonnet CXXXV (154).

112. 12. Though this allusion to the *Shepheardes Calender* is more obvious than Spenser's own (p. 88), and though both were clear enough to the two friends, it must not be forgotten that the authorship remained a mystery to Spenser's admirers for several years to come. Cf. Webbe, p. 245, and Puttenham, vol. ii. p. 65.

113. 11. *two incomparable*, &c. See note to p. 94, l. 29.

16. *Epithalamion Thamesis.* See supra, p. 100, l. 8.

21. *Ecquid,* &c. See p. 100, l. 23.

114. 3. *alias you know who.* See the gloss to 'October' of the *Shepheardes Calender.* The lines are quoted by Harvey from fol. 40 b of the original edition.

22. *Dying Pellicanes.* See supra, p. 100, l. 24 (note).

25. *Extra iocum.* See p. 93, l. 11, and p. 125, l. 29.

116. 7. *Bibiena* (Bernardo), Cardinal (1470–1560).

8. *Bembo* (Piero), Cardinal (1470–1547). Harvey had been inspired by him in his early lectures at Cambridge (see the *Ciceronianus*).

26. *pawlting,* hesitating or lame : *bungreley,* slovenly (bungling).

117. 10, &c. Harvey's general argument, and his claim, among other things, for a true orthography, is supported by an interesting passage, addressed to the 'Reader' of *The First Booke of the Preservation of King Henry the VII,* written in so-called English hexameters (1599)—printed by Collier in his *Illust. of O. E. Lit.* (1866) II. No. 3, and by Mr. Arber, in his preface to Stanyhurst's *Aeneis.*

'Right honored, worshipfull, and gentell Reader, these Hexameters and Pentameters in Englishe are misliked of many, because they are not yet come to their full perfection, and specially of some that are accounted and knowne to be Doctors and singularly well learned and great Linguistes; but especially of the plaine Rythmer, that scarce knowes the footed quantitie or metricall scanning thereof, muche lesse to reade them with a grace according to the same. But for him, I say thus; *Scientia nullum habet inimicum praeter ignorantem.* Whose bookes are stuft with lines of prose, with a rythme in the end ; which euery fidler or piper can make vpon a theame giuen. Neuerthelesse, I confesse and acknowledge that we haue many excellent and singular good Poets in this our age, as Maister *Spencer,* that was, Maister *Gowlding,* Doctor *Phayer,* Maister *Harrington, Daniell,* and diuers others, whom I reuerence in that kinde of prose-rythme ; wherein *Spencer* (without offence spoken) hath surpassed them all. I would to God they had done so well in trew Hexameters ; for they had then beautified our language. For the *Greekes* and *Latines* did in a manner abolish quite that kinde of rythme-prose: And why should not we doe the like in Englishe? . . . .

For, at the first, Maister *Askam* had much ado to make two or three verses in English: but now euery scholler can make some. What language so hard, harsh, or barbarous, that time and art will not amend? . . . .

This trew kinde of Hexametred and Pentametred verse will bring vnto vs foure commodities. First, it will enrich our speach with good and significant wordes: Secondly, it will bring a delight and pleasure to the skilfull Reader, when he seeth them formally compyled: And, thirdly, it will incourage and learne the good and godly Students that affect Poetry, and are naturally enclyned thereunto, to make the like: Fourthly, it will direct a trew Idioma, and will teach trew Orthography. For as gould surpasseth leade, so the Hexameters surpasse rythme prose.' Yet the author does not 'utterly discommend' this 'prose-rhythme.'

18. *correcte Magnificat.* Cf. Ronsard, *Préface de la Franciade*, 'J'atteste les Muses que je ne suis point ignorant, et ne crie point en langage vulgaire, comme ces nouveaux venus qui veulent corriger le *Magnificat* . . . .' Cf. also Harington, infra, ii. p. 219, and the Epistle to the *Cobler of Canterburie* (1608), in the Appendix to *Tarlton's Jests* (Shakespeare Soc. 1844, p. 107).

26. Horace, *Ars Poet.* 71, 72. Cf. p. 121, l. 10.

118. 11. *Fat-bellyed Archdeacon.* See note to p. 97, l. 4.

17. Ascham, *Toxophilus*, Bk. II (ed. Giles, *Works*, ii. 129). Cf. infra, p. 283. See *Toxophilus*, too, for line quoted on p. 120.

20 (121. 4, 22–33). Cf. Webbe, i. p. 281, l. 15, and note.

120. 24. *Scoggins Aier.* See *The Jests of Scoggin* in Hazlitt's *Old English Jest-Books* (ii. 93).

121. 4. *Position.* Cf. l. 27, p. 281. 15. See Quintil. i. 5, ix. 4.

20. *Prosodye.* See note to p. 102, l. 23.

122. 12. *Rosalindula.* Cf. supra, p. 106, l. 2.

22. *M. Daniel Rogers* (? 1538–91), courtier and diplomatist. He is frequently referred to in the correspondence of Sidney and Languet (ed. Pears, 1845). See also his correspondence with Buchanan (Edin., 1715, vol. ii).

124. 14. *arithmetericians.* Probably a slip for 'arithmet[r]icians.'

124. 22. Erasmus, *Epistolae*, cxlii.

   34. *sitt ∴ . . schirtes.* Cf. note to ii. p. 186, l. 18.

125. 15. *Wylsons or Tarletons.* See supra, p. 85, l. 3, note. Harvey is probably referring to his share of the *Letters*, supra, p. 87, &c.

   18. *comedanties* = 'comediantes,' comedians: probably a press error. Cf. Sidney's *Apology*, p. 199, l. 23, where we have 'comedients' in Ponsonby's text (see p. 148).

   23. *Vnico Aretino.* This is Bernardo Accolti (*d.* 1534) famed as an *improvvisatore.* He is spoken of by Bembo, Harvey's favourite. See Tiraboschi, vi. pp. 1249–52.

   26. *M. Churchyard.* Thomas Churchyard (? 1520–1604), a writer of broadsides. Cf. infra, p. 242, l. 33, note; ii. 280, l. 15.

   27. *M. Elderton.* William Elderton (*d.* ? 1592), ballad writer. See Harvey, ii. 253, l. 5; 273, l. 16, &c.; and cf. 246, ll. 28–34. There are many references to his heavy drinking (e.g. his 'ale crammed nose,' Nash, *Apol. for Pierce Pennilesse*).

126. 2. *Surrey is sayde first,* i.e. in his *Certain Bokes* [II and IV] *of Virgiles Aenœis turned into English meter* (1557). In Day's reprint of the Fourth Book (n. d.) the title describes the translation as *drawn into a strange meter.*

   3. *Buckhurste* [Thomas, Lord Buckhurst] *and M. Norton in . . . Gorboduc* (acted 1561, printed 1565). See Shakespeare Soc. reprint, 1847.

   4. *Gascoygnes Steele Glasse* (1576). See Mr. Arber's reprint.

   5. *cantions,* songs. Cf. *Sheph. Cal.* 'October' (Gloss).

   6. *namelye,* especially.

   13. *Pierius.* Giampetro Valeriano (Pierius Valerianus), *b.* 1477. His *Poemata* appeared at Basle in 1538; his *Amorum lib. V et alia poemata* at Venice in 1549. He was attracted by the subject of symbols, and wrote *Hieroglyphica, siue de sacris Aegyptiorum aliarumque gentium litteris commentariorum lib. LVIII* (Basle, 1556).

   17. *Mr. Willes.* See p. 47, note (col. 2). Harvey's description here is explained by the fact that Willes, after quitting New College, Oxford, travelled in France, Germany, and Italy, graduated at Mainz (1565) and was admitted a Jesuit, thereafter lectured at Perugia and at Trier, and on his return to England, where he abjured Catholicism, was incorporated at

Cambridge. He is probably the co-editor of a *History of Travel in the West and East Indies* (1577) and the author of three papers in Hakluyt's *Collections of Voyages*.

26–33. See p. 89, ll. 6–12.

'E. K.' (pp. 127–34).

The identification of 'E. K.', the author of this 'Epistle Dedicatory' and of the Glosses in the *Shepheardes Calender*, remains a vexed question; but the evidence, such as it is, is in favour of the traditional view that the writer was Edward Kirke or Kerke (1553–1613) of Pembroke Hall, Cambridge. The argument that 'E. K.' is Spenser in masquerade has been fully worked out by Uhlemann in *Jahresbericht No. xiii des K. Kaiser Wilhelms Gymnasium zu Hannover*, 1888, and by O. Sommer in his reprint of the *Shepheardes Calender*, 1890 (pp. 15–25). See Mr. Herford's exhaustive reply to the latter in his edition of the *Sh. Cal.* 1895 (pp. xxii–xxvi), and Mr. Sidney Lee's article in *D. N. B.* This is not the place for further discussion, but it is perhaps excusable to point out that the references to 'Mistresse Kerke' in Spenser's letter (ante, pp. 90, l. 3, and 92, l. 29) have a strong circumstantial value in the argument for a real 'E. K.' They at least show that some one of the name was actually known to Spenser and Harvey; and it may well be that she was the mother of their College contemporary, and had received them as her son's friends at her house in London [1].

127. 7. Chaucer, *Troilus and Criseyde*, i. 809 —
    'Unknowe, unkist, and lost that is un-sought.'
See 'E. K.'s eulogy of Chaucer in his gloss to 'June' of the *Shepheardes Calender*. John Heywood (1562) has two epigrams 'Of kissing,' beginning 'Unknowen vnkist' (Spenser Soc. ed., p. 148).

9. Lydgate, passim: and all the 'Chaucerians,' English and Scottish.

11. *in his Æglogue.* See 'Februarie,' l. 92, and 'E. K.'s gloss.

16. *brocage*, procuracy (by a 'go-between' or 'broker').

---

[1] All were of Pembroke Hall. Spenser was admitted in 1569, and Kirke in 1571. Harvey was elected a Fellow in 1570. His seniority may partly explain his general attitude to Spenser.

128. *32. Valla against Liuie.* See his *Emendationes in Livium de bello Punico*, in the Paris edition of Livy, 1573.

other against Saluste. Cf. *Ascham*, ante, p. 39, &c.

130. 12. *gallimaufray or hodgepodge.* Cf. ii. 253. 12, and note.

131. 7, &c. Quoted by Webbe, infra, p. 247.

132. 7. *full somd*, full fledged.

21. *.f. = scilicet.*

133. 7. *His Dreames, his Legendes, his Court of Cupide.* For the *Dreames*, see note to p. 100, l. 24. The others are also unknown. It has been suggested that they were incorporated in the *Faerie Queene*.

Postscript. Cf. 'E. K.'s gloss to 'September' of *The Shepheardes Calendar*, where he speaks of Gabriel Harvey, 'of whose speciall commendation as well in Poetrye as Rhetorike and other choyce learning we haue lately had a sufficient tryall in diuerse his workes, but specially in his *Musarum Lachrymae* [1578 : see note to p. 102, l. 24], and his late *Gratulation[es] Valdinens[es]* [1578] . . . . Beside other his sundrye most rare and very notable writings, partely vnder vnknown Tytles, and partly vnder counterfayt names, as hys *Tyrannomastix*, his *Ode Natalitia*, his *Rameidos*, and esspecially that parte of *Philomusus*, his diuine *Anticosmopolita*, and diuers other of lyke importance.' See also note to p. 284, l. 4 infra.

STANYHURST (pp. 135–47).

136. *20. cheate Poëtes*, impostors of poets. 'Cheate' (sb.) is used attributively.

137. 3. *in camfering wise.* Unexplained in *N. E. D.*, which quotes Shropshire '*campering*' = mettlesome, high-spirited.

15. *od* = famous, distinguished, rare. Cf. Ascham, *Scholemaster*, ii (ed. Mayor, p. 113), 'For our tyme the odde man to performe all . . . is . . . *Joannes Sturmius*.' See *N. E. D.*, s. v. 'Odd,' ii. 6.

19. See p. 1.

29. *M. Phaere.* Thomas Phaer's translation, which Stanyhurst criticizes, appeared in 1558 (*The Seuen first Bookes of the Eneidos of Virgill*). Two books were added in 1562 (*The nyne fyrst Bookes . . . with so much of the tenth Booke as since his Death* [i. e.

in 1560] *could be found*). The translation of the twelve books was completed by Thomas Twyne in 1573, and republished ten years later with the addition of a version of the thirteenth book (by Maphaeus Vegius).

34. *squire* = square (carpenter's). See Palsgrave.

140. 1. *Mori Epigg.*, p. 261, ed. 1518.

12. *Johannes Doa*, &c. See note to p. 185, l. 30.

20. *draftye*, rubbishy, vile. Cf. vol. ii, pp. 399, l. 11, 400, l. 14, and Hall's *Satires*, v. 2 (ed. Singer, p. 134). *N.E.D.* (q. v.) explains 'draftye' as an early misreading of 'drasty', dreggy.

32. *duggeon dagger*, a dudgeon-hilted dagger. Dudgeon is a hard wood used for handles of knives, &c. Cf. ii. p. 394, l. 16.

141. 27. *balducktoom*. See supra, p. 101, l. 23, note.

142. 2. *Priscianistes*, grammarians (after Priscian).

143. 12. Ante, p. 118, l. 1.

25. *misheth thee cushen*, misseth the cushion, aim, or mark (*Euphues*, ed. Landmann, p. 68). Cf. 'beside the cushion,' 'to put beside the cushion' (to deprive one of place), also common Elizabethan usages. The phrase 'bore with a cushion' is not clear (see ii. p. 271, l. 21, infra).

26. Cicero, *Orator* xviii. 58.

144. 10. *Now put case*, now suppose.

19. Horace, *Ars Poet.* l. 385.

146. 5. *Aen.* iii. 91.

7. *Aen.* iv. 146.

10. *Aen.* iii. 396.

SIDNEY (pp. 148–207).

Headnote—Olney's text has been reprinted also by Mr. E. Rhys in the first volume of his *Literary Pamphlets* (London, 1897). Mr. Albert S. Cook's edition, *The Defense of Poesy, otherwise known as An Apology for Poetry* (Boston, U.S.A., 1890, 1898), contains a modernized text based on both the editions of 1595.

Rodenburg's *Eglentiers Poëtens Borst-weringh*, which appeared in 1619, is in part a paraphrase of the *Apologie* (see Jonckbloet, *Geschiedenis der Nederlandsche Letterkunde*, 1889, iii. p. 200, &c.). Charles Gildon in his *Complete Art of Poetry* (1718) incorporates long passages without acknowledgment (see Dialogue I, pp. 48-74).

150. 1. *Edward Wotton* (1548-1626), afterwards first Baron Wotton. Sir Henry Wotton was his half-brother.

3. *Iohn Pietro Pugliano*, an Equerry of the Emperor Maximilian II, held in high repute as an exponent of knightly exercises on horseback. Sidney shows his enthusiasm for these fashionable accomplishments in an elaborate passage in the *Arcadia* (bk. ii), in *Astrophel and Stella*, Sonnets 41 and 49, and in a letter to his brother Robert, Oct. 18, 1580, in which he recommends the study of Grisone's work on horsemanship (*Correspondence*, ed. Pears, 1845, p. 202). Castiglione, Sidney's model of manners, said that all gentlemen should ride well. Cf. Harvey, ii. p. 263; and see Einstein's *Italian Renaissance in England* (1902), pp. 69-70.

14-18. *Souldiours . . . Camps and Courts*. See note to p. 188, l. 26.

21. *Pedanteria*. The Italian form is significant.

151. 13, &c. Cf. Daniello, *Della Poetica*, pp. 12 and 21.

17. *first Nurse*, &c. Cf. Minturno: 'Io ho sempre stimato . . . la Poesia non pur esser di tutte le scienze reina, ma lor madre anchora; e le Muse non solamente di tutte l'arti eccellenti inuentrici, ma etiandio gouernatrici di tutte le cose.' (*L'Arte Poet.* Preface.) See Harington, infra, ii. p. 194, l. 10.

20. *or rather the Vipers*. Cf. ii. p. 373, l. 11. Perhaps a playful hit at Gosson's *Schoole of Abuse* (ed. Arber, p. 46); but the simile is common, especially in the Euphuistic writers (cf. *Euphues*, ed. Arber, p. 215). It was taken from Pliny (cf. Wilson, *Arte of Rhetorique*, ed. 1553, fol. 69), who may have borrowed it from Herodotus iii. 109.

22. Sidney's plea for the antiquity of poetry and the selection of the names which follow seem to be directly inspired by Minturno's passage, *Poeticae vetustas*, and his list of illustrations on pp. 9, 13, and 15 of the *De Poeta*.

152. 22-5. Cf. Daniello, u.s., p. 22. Cf. p. 190, l. 4.

30-1. Plato, *Symposium* (passim); *Phaedrus*, 230 B; *De Rep.* ii. 359, &c.

34, &c. Cf. Sidney's letter to his brother Robert (Oct. 18, 1580), in which, in speaking of the writing of history, he says:

'This I think in haste, a story is either to be considered as a story, or as a treatise, which, besides that, addeth many things for profit and ornament: as a story, he is nothing but a narration of things done, with the beginnings, causes, and appendances therof . . . and thus much as a very historiographer. Besides this, the historian makes himself a discourser for profit, and an orator, yea a poet, sometimes for ornament. An orator, in making excellent orations, "e re nata," which are to be marked, but marked with the note of rhetorical remembrances: a poet, in painting forth the effects, the motions, the whisperings of the people, which, though in disputation one might say were true, yet who will mark them well shall find them taste of a poetical vein, and in that kind are gallantly to be marked: for though perchance they were not so, yet it is enough they might be so. The last point which tends to teach profit is of a discourser, which name to give to whosoever speaks "non simpliciter de facto, sed de qualitatibus et circumstantiis facti . . ."' Sidney adds: 'This write I to you in great haste, of method without method, but with more leisure and study (if I do not find some book that satisfies), I will venture to write more largely of it unto you.' (*Correspondence*, ed. Pears, 1845, pp. 199–201.)

153. 12. *which in all Nations*, &c. Cf. Minturno: 'Quibus de causis cum ita prodesset, tamquam oblectaret Poësis, nulla unquam profecto natio, nullaque omnino gens fuit, quae non eam libentissime sinu complexuque suo receperit . . . Quod denique genus hominum est tam barbarum, tamque agreste, quod a Poësi fuerit alienum?' (*De Poeta*, Bk. I. p. 9). In the same passage he refers to the Welsh Bards (cf. ll. 28, 30).

21. *Areytos.* Sp. *aréito*, adopted from the West Indians, describing a mixed form of dancing and singing. Puttenham apparently borrows Sidney's reference, infra, ii. 10. 32. For an account of these song-dances see Oviedo, *Hist. Gen. de las Indias*, v. 1 (quoted by A. S. Cook), and Guniston's translation of Jos. de Acosta's *Hist. of the Indies*, ed. Markham, ii. 445 (quoted by Shuckburgh).

154. 5. *a Poet was called Vates*, i. e. in the very earliest and in the post-Virgilian periods. Sidney may be recalling Minturno (though he transposes the premisses): 'Quapropter qui apud

priscos illos veteres essent interpretes Deorum & sacerdotes, qui sapientes, qui eloquentes haberentur, qui recte ac prudenter in publicis rebus versarentur, omnes Poetae dicebantur ' (p. 15) ; but the similarity of phrase suggests that he had Sir Thomas Elyot's words before him : ' in poetes was supposed to be science misticall and inspired, and therefore in Latine they were called *Vates*, which worde signifyeth as moche as prophetes. And therefore Tulli in his Tusculane questyons supposeth that a poete can nat abundantly expresse verses sufficient and complete, or that his eloquence may flowe without labour, wordes wel souninge and plentuouse, without celestiall instruction ' (*Gouernour*, ed. Croft, i. 122). With the last words cf. ll. 26-9. Cf. p. 159, l. 17. Webbe (infra, p. 231) distinguishes between *Vates* and *Poetae*.

16–18. *Albinus*, &c. This anecdote of Albinus is taken from the popular *Sex Scriptores Historiae Augustae* (referred to by Sidney as ' the histories of the Emperors liues '). See the account in Fabricius, *Bibl. Latina*, pp. 546-53. Several Paris editions appeared in Sidney's lifetime.

32, &c. *Dauids Psalmes.* Cf. Lodge, p. 71, l. 5 ; Puttenham, ii. p. 10, l. 3 ; Harington, ii. p. 207, l. 20.

155. 5. *meerely*, wholly.

26. *Maker*, as a technical term, synonymous with ' Poet,' was used more frequently in our northern literature, and especially by the Scottish Chaucerians. Cf. Scaliger's complaint of the lack of the vernacular term in Latin : ' Quod nomen Graeci sapientes vbi commodissime παρὰ τὸ ποιεῖν effinxissent : miror maiores nostros sibi tam iniquos fuisse : vt Factoris vocem, quae illam exprimeret, maluerint oleariorum cancellis circumscribere : eum enim solum qui oleum facit, quum pro consuetudine caste, tum pro significatione stulte appellare licet ' (*Poetice*, I. i). Cf. also Uberto Folieta, *De Similitudine Normae Polybianae* (*Artis Penus Historicae*, 1579, ii. 450*).

Sidney's argument here, and on p. 156, appears to be based on this chapter in Scaliger, especially on the portion immediately preceding the above quotation.

34. *So doth the Astronomer*, &c. The illustrative details in this passage appear to be suggested by Minturno, *De Poeta*, pp. 87-100, where they occur in almost identical order.

157. 2. *Theagines*, in the romance by Heliodorus. See infra, p. 160, l. 10, and note.

3. *Orlando*, in Ariosto's *Orlando Furioso*. Harington's English version did not appear till 1591. See infra, ii. p. 194.

19 &c. Cf. Scaliger, *Poet.* i. 1 'At poeta & naturam alteram & fortunas plures etiam ac demum sese isthoc ipso perinde ac Deum alterum efficit. Nam quae omnium opifex condidit, eorum reliquae scientiae tanquam actores sunt. Poetica vero, quum & speciosius quae sunt, & quae non sunt, eorum speciem ponit: videtur sane res ipsas, non ut aliae, quasi histrio, narrare, sed velut alter deus condere: vnde cum eo commune nomen ipsi non a consensu hominum, sed a naturae prouidentia inditum videatur.' See also Minturno, *De Poeta*, pp. 87, &c.

158. 5–6. *Poesie . . . Mimesis.* Aristotle, *Poetics*, i. 2, &c. It is more probable that Sidney is drawing here, as he does frequently throughout the essay, from Scaliger's *Poetice*. The succeeding words, 'to teach and delight,' are reminiscent of Bk. I. c. i, where, speaking of *Poesis*, Scaliger says: 'Quamobrem tota in imitatione sita fuit. Hic enim finis est medius ad illum vltimum, qui est docendi cum delectatione.' Sidney, like his contemporaries, is Horatian rather than Aristotelian in his co-ordination of the *utile* with the *dulce*. See also note to p. 197, l. 3.

8. *a speaking picture* (cf. p. 165, l. 17), a commonplace of Elizabethan and Renaissance criticism (cf. the verses in Puttenham, iii. ed. Arber, p. 218; E. Hoby, infra, p. 342, l. 29; Daniel's *Musophilus*, 178; Jonson's *Discoveries*, ed. Cunningham, iii. 409), borrowed from Plutarch, *De Aud. Poetis*, 3, who refers to it as an established metaphor. Cf. Horace, *Ars Poet.* 361. Vives, in his account of Comedy, utilizes the figure thus: 'Venit in scenam poesis populo ad spectandum congregato, et ibi sicut pictor tabulam proponit multitudini spectandam, ita poeta imaginem quandam vitae, ut merito Plutarchus de his dixerit, poema esse picturam loquentem, et picturam poema tacens, ita magister est populi, et pictor, et poeta' (*De Causis Corrupt. Artium*, p. 367, ed. 1555). Mambrun in his *De Carmine Epico*, 1652 (pp. 155, 284), mentions it as 'illud Simonidis dictum, quod a Plutarcho lib. de aud. poet. accepimus, ζωγραφίαν, &c. Poesin pictura loquaci et picturam poesi tacita definiri.' (Cf. Jonson, u.s.) Mambrun also says: 'Poesis est vocalis pictura,

quae etiam comparatio Aristoteli familiaris fuit,' which, if not a random association, may perhaps be explained in the light of the passages referred to in Mr. Butcher's *Aristotle's Theory of Poetry*, 3rd ed., p. 187, note. Cf. Scaliger's reference to poetry, 'veluti aurium pictura quadam' (*P.* i. 1). See Mr. Courthope's *Life in Poetry*, &c., p. 172, for an interesting passage on the later influence of the saying of Simonides. The definition of Painting reappears in the ' muda poesia ' of Camoens, *Lus.* vii. 76. Horace's phrase suggested the opening lines of Du Fresnoy's *De Arte Graphica* (1658), which are freely quoted in the eighteenth century. The metaphor is the basis of Lessing's *Laokoon* (see especially the *Preface*). His statement that the ancients were careful to inculcate that each art had its own objects and modes of imitation will not, however, describe the practice of Renaissance writers.

9. *three seuerall kinds*, &c. Sidney's division is as in Scaliger : 'Primum est Theologorum: cuiusmodi Orpheus & Amphion . . . Secundum genus Philosophorum : idque duplex Naturale, quale Empedocles, Nicander, Aratus, Lucretius : Morale secundum suas partes, vt Politicum ab Solone & Tyrtaeo ; Oeconomicum ab Hesiodo ; Commune a Phocilide, Theognide, Pythagora. Tertio loco ponentur ii, de quibus omnibus mox' (*Poetice*, i. 2). It may be compared also with Minturno's parallel division, *De Poeta*, Bk. I. pp. 53–4.

14. *Exodus* xv ; *Deut.* xxxii ; *Judges* v.

15–16. *Emanuell Tremelius* or *Tremellius* (text *Tremilius*) (1510–80), a Jew of Ferrara, converted to Catholic Christianity by Cardinal Pole and Marcantonio Flaminio, and later to Protestantism by Peter Martyr. He devoted himself to Oriental studies and produced a Latin Bible with the collaboration of Franciscus Iunius.

Franciscus Iunius (1545–1602), a French protestant who taught Theology at Neustadt, Heidelberg (where he assisted Tremelius with his translation), and Leyden. Sidney refers to the title-page of the 2nd vol. of their Bible, containing the five ' poetical books.'

23. Perhaps a reference to the translation of the Psalms begun by him, and completed by the Countess of Pembroke.

29. *Cato.* The *Disticha de moribus*, ascribed to a certain

Dionysius Cato. The book, which is referred to by John of Salisbury (*Policraticus*, vii), was frequently printed towards the close of the fifteenth century, and was edited by Erasmus and praised by Luther. See Fabricius, *Bibl. Latina*, pp. 682-5. It was used as a textbook in Elizabethan schools (cf. Drayton, *To Henry Reynolds*; Peele, *Edward I*, ed. Bullen, i. 169).

30. *Pontanus*, J. Jovianus, author of the *Urania* (see ii. p. 315, l. 9, note). Scaliger devotes a considerable portion of Chap. II (*Poetae recentiores*) in the 6th Book of his *Poetice* to a criticism of his work.

159. 5. Cf. Cicero, *Orator* ii. 3.

17. See p. 154, l. 4.

35. *verse being but an ornament*, &c. See p. 182, ll. 17-18 and note, and ll. 19-20, note. Cf. Castelvetro, *Poetica*, pp. 23, &c., 190. For a discussion of this question from the Aristotelian and Sidneian points of view see Mr. Courthope's *Life in Poetry*, pp. 68, &c., and Mr. Butcher's *Aristotle's Theory of Poetry* (3rd edit.), pp. 143, &c.

The contrast between poets and versifiers had been noted by Elyot in the *Gouernour* ('semblably they that make verses, expressynge therby none other lernynge but the craft of versifyeing, be nat of auncient writers named poetes, but onely called versifyers,' ed. Croft, i. 120). Cf. Puttenham, infra, ii. 3. 16-17. The distinction is of course as old as Quintilian.

160. 8. *Theagines and Cariclea*. Supra, p. 157, l. 2. Probably borrowed from Scaliger, who also instances *Theagines and Cariclea* as an epic in prose. See *Poetice*, iii. 95.

13-16. This is in agreement with Minturno's general theory and may even be an echo of his phrases, e. g. 'aut vitia aut virtutes effingunt,' *De Poeta*, p. 27. Cf. also pp. 11 and 35. Mr. Spingarn points out, in support of this contention, that Sidney, like Minturno, makes poets feign images of *virtues and vices*, not merely *actions*, as Aristotle does.

161. 12. Plato, *Theaetetus*, 174. Sidney uses the metaphor again in the 19th Sonnet of *Astrophel and Stella*.

20. *Arkitecktonike* (ἀρχιτεκτονική). Arist. *Eth.* i. 1. 4; with which compare Sidney's ensuing words (ll. 23, &c.).

31. I follow the original text in not making a new paragraph here, though the Philosophers deserve one equally with the

Historians. The following anacoluthon suggests a run-on idea. Ponsonby's text reads: 'wherin if we can shew, the Poet is worthy to haue it before anyother competitors: among whom principall challengers . . .'

162. 2, &c. So Cicero, *Pro Arch.* 11 ; *Tusc.* i. 15.

32. From Cicero, *De Orat.* ii. 9. 36 ' Historia vero testis temporum, lux veritatis, vita memoriae, magistra vitae, nuntia vetustatis . . .'

163. 13. *Alphonsus of Aragon.* Alphonso V of Aragon and I of Sicily (1416–58).

29, &c. For a parallel comparison of poetry with ethics and law in Varchi's *Lezioni* (Florence, 1590), see Spingarn's *Lit. Crit.* pp. 50–1.

31–2. Horace, *Epist.* i. 16. 52–3.

164. 12–13. Cf. Daniello, u.s., p. 19; also Minturno, *De Poeta* 39 (' quae severius asperiusque quam opus fit philosophi disputant').

24. Orig. ' fruitlesse.'

25, &c. Cf. the passage in Minturno, *De Poeta* (I. p. 38), concluding ' Sed tamen docendus erat populus, & ad virtutem informandus, non praeceptis philosophorum, sed exemplis, quae non historici, sed poetae protulissent.' Cf. also Varchi, as above. The continuation of Sidney's argument, on to p. 168, follows Minturno's defence, *De Poeta*, pp. 38–40, both in general drift and in the citation of certain examples. For proof of a direct point of contact, compare Sidney, p. 167, ll. 8–10, with ' Quod autem fabulas illi fingerent eas, quae populo placerent, exprimerentque ; non alia, quam quae populo probarentur ; num adeo philosophi hallucinati ab hominum consuetudine mentis aciem abducebant, vel, ut verius dicam, ita mente capti e statu suo dimouebantur, ut non viderent, nisi esset oratio ad eorum, qui audirent, opinionem accommodanda, nullum esse genus oratorum oportere' (p. 38). And again, ' At enim poeta non ita populo seruit, non ita se vulgo addictum putat, ut praeter id omne, quod probet multitudo, nihil aliud proferre possit' (p. 39). Minturno returns to this on p. 106. See Harington, infra, ii. p. 199, ll. 2–3.

165. 17. Cf. p. 158, l. 8.

24. Orig. ' maddesse.' Hor. *Epist.* i. 2. 62 ' Ira furor brevis est.' Cf. Seneca, *De Ira,* i. 1.

25. Sidney refers to the dramatic situation generally, for the audience did not see the 'killing and whipping.'

166. 2. *Chaucers Pandar*, in *Troilus and Criseyde*.

12. *Eutopia*. Perhaps a misprint, though Mr. Shuckburgh points out that in the prefatory verses to the Latin editions of the *Utopia* there is a punning distinction made between 'Utopia' and 'Eutopia' (ed. *Apologie*, p. 96).

22–4. Horace, *Ars Poet.* ll. 372-3 ('Non homines, non di,' &c.).

26. Cf. Harington, infra, ii. p. 205, l. 35.

167. 9. *Popular*. So Plutarch. See note to p. 164, l. 25, &c.

19-30. See Aristotle's *Poetics*, 9.

31. *full of reason*. Cf. p. 168, l. 32, and p. 197, l. 10. See Mr. Spingarn's section on the growth of Rationalism in Renaissance criticism (*Lit. Crit.* pp. 150, &c., 246, &c.).

168. 11. Horace, *Sat.* i. 8; *Epod.* v.

170. 10–15. Cf. Giraldi Cintio, *Dei Romanzi* (ed. Daelli, i. p. 66).

11. See Plutarch, *De Aud. Poetis*, iv.

17. *Milciades* (Miltiades), the victor at Marathon.

18. See Plutarch's *Life of Phocion*.

19-20. Septimius Severus (193–211) and Alexander Severus (222–35).

28. Suetonius, *Julius Caesar*, 77.

33. *Cipselus, Periander*. Herodotus, v. 92.

Phalaris, tyrant of Agrigentum. Cf. Cicero, *De Off.* ii. 7. 26. See Harington, infra, ii. p. 210, l. 16.

Dionysius, tyrant of Syracuse. Cf. Cicero, *Tusc.* 5. 20.

171. 13. *Philophilosophos* (φιλοφιλόσοφος—Ponsonby's text) : a Renaissance form, perhaps Sidney's own. Cf. *Mysomousoi*, p. 181, l. 19.

14, 15. *moouing*. Cf. Minturno, *De Poeta*, p. 106 ; Varchi, *Lezzioni*, 576.

21. *not Gnosis but Praxis*. Aristotle, *Ethics*, i.

172. 9, &c. Cf. Varchi, passim. (See note to p. 163, l. 29, &c.)

21-3. *with a tale*, &c. Borrowed by Harington, infra, ii. p. 208, ll. 6-8.

25-30. For this common Renaissance simile, see Minturno, *De P.* p. 49, and Daniello, *De P.* p. 19. See also Harington's reference to Plutarch and his quotation from Tasso, *infra*, ii. pp. 198–9, and p. 208, l. 1; Lyly's *Euphues* (Arber, p. 328); and Nash (ed. Grosart, ii. p. 90). It is not probable that Sidney is thinking (as Mr. A. S. Cook suggests) of a passage in the Preface to Part III of the edition of the Bible by Junius and Tremellius (to whom Sidney refers, supra, p. 158). There the figure is the smearing of the mouth of a vessel with honey, as it is in Lucretius, i. 936, &c.—a fact noted by Giulio Guastauino and Scipio Gentili in the 1590 Genoa edition of Tasso, where a parallel is given from Lactantius, *Institutiones*, v. If Sidney be directly indebted to any one, he may be recalling Gosson's *Schoole of Abuse* (ed. Arber, p. 20).

173. 5. *as Aristotle. Poetics*, 4.

17–18. *Aen.* xii. 645–6.

26. Persius, *Sat.* v. 151.

174. 3, &c. *Menenius Agrippa.* Livy, ii. 32. Cf. Shakespeare, *Coriolanus*, i. 1. 94.

8. *farre fet.* A favourite phrase with Sidney. Cf. p. 202, l. 3, and note ; and Puttenham, *infra*, ii. 169, l. 7, &c.

23. *Nathan.* (2 *Sam.* xii.) Cf. p. 185, l. 10. This is borrowed by Harington, infra, ii. p. 205, l. 27.

175. 16, &c. *the Tragicomicall.* Cf. p. 199, ll. 9, 13.

18. In the *Arcadia* and in the *Consolatio*.

176. 5-6. Virgil, *Eclog.* vii. 69–70.

17 and 23. Persius, *Sat.* I. 116–117 :—

> ' Omne vafer vitium ridenti Flaccus amico
> Tangit et admissus circum praecordia ludit.'

26. Horace, *Epist.* i. 11. 30 ' Est Ulubris, animus si te non deficit aequus.'

27. *No, perchance.* A direct reference to the particular attack of the *Schoole of Abuse* and like pamphlets (supra, p. 61 et seq.).

30. *Comedy is an imitation*, &c. Sidney's definition of the function of comedy is analogous to (if not derived from) Trissino's (*Opere*, ii. 127, &c.) and Cicero's (*De Orat.* ii. 58–9), and may be compared with Elyot's statement in the *Gouernour* (1531), ed. Croft, i. 124–5. See also notes to p. 81, l. 1, and ii. p. 389, ll. 35–6. Sidney distinguishes the ' common errors of

our life' and the 'domestical matters' as the special material
for the laughter which is to beget 'admiratio' (see below) in
the breasts of the spectators. The delightfulness of comedy
cannot be found in the greater evils and sorrows which belong
to tragedy: and laughter is an accident and nowise an essential
condition of effective comedy. Cf. Jonson's *Discoveries*, apropos
of Aristotle's views on laughter.

177. 10–11. *Demea*, &c. See supra, p. 370.

18. *Pistrinum*, the 'mill' for troublesome slaves.

24–5. See Introduction, p. lxxxvi.

28. *affects*, feelings. Cf. Sidney's *Arcadia*, p. 351 (ed. 1622).

'Admiration' is used in the technical sense first established
by Minturno, who added it to the Horatian 'instruction' and
'delight' as the third function of Poetry. See *De Poeta*, p. 102:
'Verum, ut quae proposita sunt exponamus, erit Poetae sic
dicere versibus, ut doceat, ut delectet, ut moueat. Qui non
ita dicet, ut haec tria assequi debeat nunquam, mea quidem
sententia, hoc nomine appellabitur'; p. 106, 'Illud autem ne
te praetereat velim, sic poetis esse dicendum, ut siue doceant,
siue oblectent, siue moueant, haec singula statim admiratio
legentis, audientisue consequatur'; and p. 107 (with the margina-
lia). So too Scaliger, *Poetice*, III. xcvi ('sed & docendi &
mouendi & delectandi'). See Mr. Spingarn's exposition of
Minturno's doctrine (*Lit. Crit.* pp. 52–3). Though in some
passages of Elizabethan criticism the term is, as here, con-
joined with 'commiseration' as the equivalent of the Aristotelian 'pity' and 'fear' of tragedy, it defines, in part, the
function of poetry *per se* and in all its kinds. Though 'Admiration' was ultimately raised to the level of Pity and Terror,
its critical place is with 'instruction' and 'delight' in the
general definition of the purpose of Poetry. The narrowing
down comes later, in Corneille, Boileau, and Saint-Évremond,
with whom 'Admiration is a tragic passion.' See the important
letter from Boileau to Ch. Perrault (1700): 'Pouvez-vous nier
que ce ne soit dans Tite-Live ... que M. de Corneille a pris ses
plus beaux traits, a puisé ces grandes idées qui lui ont fait
inventer un nouveau genre de tragédie inconnu à Aristote?
Car c'est sur ce pied, à mon avis, qu'on doit regarder quantité
de ses plus belles pièces de théâtre, où, se mettant au-dessus

des règles de ce philosophe, il n'a point songé, comme les poètes de l'ancienne tragédie, à émouvoir la pitié et la terreur, mais à exciter dans l'âme des spectateurs, par la sublimité des pensées et par la beauté des sentiments, une certaine admiration, dont plusieurs personnes, et les jeunes gens surtout, s'accommodent souvent beaucoup mieux que des véritables passions tragiques.'

32–3. Seneca, *Œdipus*, 705. (Orig. '*authorem.*')

178. 1. Plutarch, *Life of Pelopidas*, 29.

16. *naturall Problemes*, i.e. 'problems' based on, or dealing with, natural history. 'Problem' here and elsewhere is equivalent to 'figure,' 'illustration.' Cf. *Astrophel and Stella*, iii. ll. 6, 10 (ed. Flügel, p. 2).

20. *Percy and Duglas*, a reference to the older version of *Chevy Chase*, or perhaps (as Mr. Child has suggested) to the *Battle of Otterbourne*.

30, &c. See Plutarch's *Lycurgus*, 21.

179. 7. *three fearefull felicities*. Plutarch's *Alexander*, 3.

21. *Plato and Tullie*. See *De Finibus*, ii. 16, and *De Officiis*, i. 5. Cicero refers to Plato in both passages.

28. Cf. Puttenham, infra, ii. p. 43, ll. 21–2, note.

180. 12. Horace, *Epist.* i. 2. 4.

181. 10, 11. See note to p. 188, l. 26.

19. *Mysomousoi*: μυσομουσοι (for μισομουσοι) in Ponsonby's text. Perhaps Sidney's own word. Cf. note to p. 171, l. 13.

35. Ovid, *Ars Amat.* ii. 662, altered of purpose by Sidney:

' Dic habilem, quaecumque brevis ; quae turgida, plenam :
    Et lateat vitium proximitate boni.'

182. 1. Henricus Cornelius Agrippa. See Harington, infra, ii. p. 199, l. 27, &c. Sidney here refers to Agrippa's *De vanitate et incertitudine scientiarum*. The objections against poetry stated on p. 183 are probably inspired by this work, which speaks of *architectrix mendaciorum et cultrix perversorum dogmatum*.

17–18. See p. 159, l. 35. Cf. Ronsard, 'Tous ceux qui escrivent en carmes, tant doctes puissent-ils estre, ne sont pas poëtes. Il y a autant de différence entre un poëte et un versificateur,' &c. (*Préface de la Franciade*).

19–20. Scaliger, *Poetice*, i. 2 'Poetae igitur nomen non a

fingendo, vt putarunt, quia fictis vteretur ; sed initio a faciendo versu dictum est.'

21. *Oratio . . . Ratio*: following Quintilian, ii. 16 (109). Cf. Cicero, *De Officiis*, i. 16. This is a common Renaissance theme. Cf. J. J. Pontanus, *De Sermone*, lib. i (*Opera*, Aldus, 1518, iii. 185 v⁰).

183. 18. '. . . hourely lessons; as *Percontatorem fugito, nam garrulus idem est, Dum tibi quisque placet credula turba sumus.* But the fitnes . . .' (Ponsonby's text). Hor. *Epist.* i. 18, and Ovid, *Rem. Amoris*, 686.

26. Sidney now addresses himself directly to answer Gosson.

35. *erre* (Ponsonby, *eare*) = 'to plough.' Sidney's reference to Chaucer is merely verbal, not as an argument about Comedies. See the passage in *The Knightes Tale*, 28, 'I have, God woot, a large feeld to ere,' which is borrowed from the *Rom. de la Rose*, 21481.

in other Nations, &c. So Gosson's *Schoole of Abuse*, passim.

184. 5. *out shot Robin Hood.* See ii. p. 219, l. 21, note.

5–6. *Plato.* Cf. Gosson and Lodge, supra.

22. Cf. Harington, infra, ii. p. 201, l. 19.

185. 10. *Nathan*, supra, p. 174, l. 23.

30–1. *Iohn a stile and Iohn a noakes* (orig. ' John atte stile,' i.e. John who dwells at the stile, and ' John atten Oke,' i.e. John who dwells at the oak), fictitious names in a legal action. See infra, ii. p. 270, l. 14, and the passage in *The Returne from Parnassus*, pt. II. iv. i. 1537 et seq. Cf. ' John Doe' and ' John Roe' (supra, p. 140); now obsolete in English law, though still retained in American law.

186. 13. Cf. Harington, infra, ii. p. 209, l. 3.

30. ib. ll. 13–14.

32, 33. *Eikastike—Phantastike.* See Plato, *Sophist.* 235-6. Cf. *phantasticall* in Puttenham, infra, ii. p. 19, l. 11.

187. 17. *rampire*, ' rampart,' defence.

35. *before*, previous, earlier.

188. 24. Horace, *Sat.* i. 1. 63 :

    ' Quid facias illi ? iubeas miserum esse, libenter
    Quatenus id facit.'

26. *companion of the Campes* (cf. pp. 150, ll. 14–18, 181, ll. 10–11). So Sidney throughout, both in his life and in his writings. Cf. the more academic Buchanan, esteemed by Sidney, who in the Preface to his *Jephthes*, dedicated to the Maréchal de Brissac, writes 'Absurdam fortasse rem facere quibusdam videbor, qui ad te, hominem ab ineunte aetate militaribus imbutum studiis, & inter arma tubasque semper versatum, munusculum hoc literarium mittam : sed ii fere hoc absurdum existimaturi sunt, qui aut harum rerum inter se consensionem non satis animadvertunt, aut tuum ingenium parum habent perspectum. Neque enim inter rei militaris & literarum studium ea est, quam plerique falso putant, discordia : sed summa potius concordia, et occulta quaedam naturae conspiratio.' This concord is a favourite Renaissance topic. Cf. the controversy between Muzio (*Il Gentiluomo*) and Mora (*Il Cavaliere*) as to whether letters or arms better befit a gentleman ; the sixth dialogue (*Del Paragone dell' Arme & delle Lettere*) of Guazzo's *Dialoghi piaceuoli* ; and N. Breton's *Discourse of a Scholler and a Souldier* (1599), which argues for and against the superiority of 'learning' over 'martiall discipline.' Nash laments, in the Epistle to his *Anatomie of Absurditie*, 'that England afforded many mediocrities, but neuer saw anything more singuler then worthy Sir *Philip Sidney*, of whom it might truely be saide *Arma virumque cano*.' Cf. also Daniel's *Funeral Poem on the Earl of Devonshire*, ll. 120–2 (Grosart, i. 176).

189. 3. Plutarch, *De seu Fortuna seu virtute Alexandri*.

7–8. See note to p. 64, ll. 23–6.

14–16. In answer to Gosson's *Schoole of Abuse*, p. 21.

190. 4. *sith*, &c. Cf. supra, p. 152, l. 22, and note.

9. *naturall enemie of Poets*. Cf. Minturno's passage on the dissension between poets and philosophers, 'Fui quondam inter poeticam et philosophiam non leuis dissensio,' &c. (*De P.* p. 36). See also Plato's *Republic*, x. 607.

33–5. Cf. Scaliger, *Poetice*, i. 2 'Respiciat ipse sese, quot ineptas quot spurcas fabellas inserat: quas Graecanicum scelus olentes sententias identidem inculcet. Certe Symposium & Phaedrum atque alia monstra operae pretium fuerit nunquam legisse.'

191. 10. Cf. supra, p. 71, ll. 19–20, and note. The other

'two' are said to be Cleanthes (*Hymn to Zeus*), also in the *Acts* xvii. 28, and Menander (*Thais*) in 1 Cor. xv. 33. (See Mr. Cook's note, ed. *Apologie*, p. 109.) Ponsonby's text omits the note—'S. Paule himselfe sets a watchword.'

Cf. Lodge, supra, p. 71, ll. 19-20.

31. *conster*, construe.

33. Scaliger, *Poetice*, i. 2. See note to p. 193, l. 34.

192. 5-6. Sidney borrows the reference from Scaliger, u. s.

15-18. Plato, *Ion*, 534 ; elaborated in Minturno, *De Poeta*, passim, especially pp. 67, 74-6. See also later in the *Apologie*, p. 195, ll. 19-20, and Harington's reference, infra, ii. p. 197, ll. 6-7. Cf. too the 'Argument' of 'October' in the *Shepheardes Calender* : 'No arte, but a diuine gift and heauenly instinct not to bee gotten by laboure and learning, but adorned with both ; and poured into the witte by a certaine ἐνθουσιασμός and celestiall inspiration.' Of this, the writer of the Argument continues, 'the author els where discourseth in his book called the English Poete, which booke being lately come to my hands, I mynde also by Gods grace vpon further aduisement to publish.' Spenser's treatise is not extant. (See note to p. 232, l. 21.)

22-4. Cf. Kyd's *Householder's Philosophie* (transl. from Tasso): ed. Boas, p. 267, ll. 37-9.

24. Orig. '*Heautontimorumenon*.'

27. Plato, *Phaedo*, 61.

193. 25. Virgil, *Aen.* i. 12.

28, &c. Hadrian, author of *Animula vagula, blandula*.

30-1. Robert II of Anjou (1309-43); Francis I (1515-47). *King Iames of Scotland* is generally identified with James I, King of Scots (1394-1437), author of the *Kingis Quair*; but Sidney is not likely to have known of James's reputation as a poet, except through Buchanan's *History* which had just been published (1582)[1]. [If this be so, we have a clue to the date of the *Apologie*.] Can he refer to James VI, whose *juvenilia* were collected in 1584 (infra, pp. 208, 404)?

32. *Bembus and Bibiena*, supra, p. 377.

34. *Fracastorius*, Hieronymus (1483-1533), author of the dialogue *Naugerius, siue de Poetica*, and of *Syphilis* and other works in Latin verse. See Scaliger, *Poetice*, vi. 4, u. s.

[1] It is less likely that he knew Major's *De Gestis Scotorum* (1521).

Scaliger, Julius Caesar (1484–1558), named above, p. 191, l. 33, &c. (See the Introduction p. lxxxiv, and Index.) 'Non solum soluta oratione, in qua nonnulla leguntur,' says Gyraldus, 'sed et versu quaedam cecinit, inter quae Elysius (poematis haec inscriptio est), in quo insulam Padi Belvedere Ferrariae ducis eleganti carmine descripsit et omnem fere Estensium genealogiam' (ed. Wotke, p. 84).

194. 1. *Pontanus.* See supra, p. 158, l. 30, note.

Muretus, M. Antonius (1526–85): the *Juvenilia* written at Rome, and the *Hymns* of his old age.

2. *Buchanan*, George. See supra, p. 24, ll. 5–7: infra, p. 201, l. 4.

3. *Hospitall of Fraunce*, Michel de l'Hôpital (1505–73), Chancellor of France.

15. Cf. *Arcadia*, i. (p. 38), where Sidney speaks of men 'disused with a long peace'—significant references by the poet-soldier to the political situation before the coming of the Armada.

17. *Mountibancks.* Cf. Sidney's letter to his brother Robert (*Correspondence*, ed. Pears, 1845, p. 196).

35. Juvenal, xiv.

195. 23. Cf. p. 71, l. 22. The proverb does not appear to be classical, in form at least, and has not as yet been traced further back than the *Lectiones Antiquae* of Coelius Rhodiginus (1450–1525). See Mr. Shuckburgh's note, ed. *Apologie*, p. 144. The genealogy of the more common form *Poeta nascitur, non fit*, is also doubtful, though it may have been suggested by the passage in Florus, *De Qualitate Vitae*, Fragm. viii (quoted by Ben Jonson in his *Discoveries*, ed. Cunningham, iii. p. 420). Cf. Webbe, infra, p. 297, ll. 1–2, and the original Latin of Fabricius in the notes (p. 420).

196. 4. Ovid, *Trist.* iv. 10. 26; printed in the original text, *Quicquid conabor discere versus erit.* A favourite quotation. Cf. Meres, infra, ii. p. 323, l. 17.

13. *Mirrour of [for] Magistrates.* The first edition, with nineteen 'legends' contributed by Baldwin, Ferrers, Phaer, Challoner, and others, appeared in 1559. For the later sixteenth-century issues, see Corser's *Collectanea*, viii. p. 418.

14. *the Earle of Surries Liricks* appeared first in *Tottel's Miscellany* (1557).

16. *The Sheapheards Kalender* was dedicated to Sidney (title-page, and 'To his Booke'). Sidney's criticism may be compared with 'E. K.'s defence, supra.

32. *Gorboduck* (*Tragedie of*), by Thomas Sackville (Lord Buckhurst) and Thomas Norton, 1565 (acted 1561), reprinted [? 1570] with the title, *The Tragidie of Ferrex and Porrex*.

197. 3. *The very end of Poesie*, cf. p. 200, l. 22. See Scaliger, *Poetice*, vii. 2 (p. 831) 'Quamobrem dicendum est Poetae finem esse docere cum delectatione . . . Poetae finem esse docere cum iucunditate': and cf. Giraldi Cintio, u. s. (ed. Daelli), i. 61. See also note to p. 158, ll. 5–6.

6, &c. *in place and time*, &c. This is the earliest known reference in English to the doctrine of 'the Three Unities,' first formulated by Castelvetro in 1570. 'La mutatione tragica non può tirar con esso seco se non vna giornata & vn luogo' (*Poetica*, 1576, p. 534, ll. 20–1). See also ib. pp. 109, 168, &c., and cf. the reference in 1572 by Jean de la Taille in his *Art de la Tragédie*. Sidney drew direct from Castelvetro.

The canon of the Three Unities was a Renaissance development from the single Aristotelian Unity of Action, first by the adoption of the Unity of Time by the Italians Giraldi Cintio, Robortello, Segni, Maggi, Minturno, Scaliger, and Trissino, and later by the addition of the Unity of Place by Castelvetro in Italy, Jean de la Taille in France, and Sidney in England. In Maggi, Scaliger, and Minturno, there is, as Mr. Spingarn has pointed out, a forecast of the third unity which Castelvetro first made absolute. It should be borne in mind that the title 'the three unities' does not occur till well on in the seventeenth century. They had been treated individually, as shown above, and to some extent by Mairet in his Preface to *Silvanire*, ? 1625 (whose attitude is the same as Scaliger's, iv. 97, ed. 1617, p. 334), but it was left to Chapelain to bind them together in a code. Corneille knew nothing of this triple rule when he began to write, nor did Richelieu until he was told of it by Chapelain. It should be added that though Jean de la Taille supplies an interesting hint of the Unity of Place, he exerted no influence in France and was soon forgotten ; and that the later establishment of the canon of the three Unities was directly due to the study of Castelvetro and the Italians. The frequent references

to Castelvetro in Chapelain's correspondence would seem to
narrow down the channel of influence to Chapelain himself,
though he too naively says, in his *Démonstration de la Règle
des vingt-quatre heures* (1630), that he has no defence to offer but
'la pratique des anciens, suiuie d'un consentement vniuersel
par tous les Italiens,' and that he does not remember 'si
Aristote l'a traitté, ou aucun de ses commentateurs.'

For the history of the growth of the theory see Breitinger's
Les unités d'Aristote avant le Cid de Corneille (Geneva, 1879), and
his important correction in the *Revue critique*, December 27,
1879 (pp. 478–80) ; Lintilhac's *De J.-C. Scaligeri Poetice*, Paris,
1887, and his articles in the *Nouvelle Revue*, May 15 and
June 1, 1890 (lxiv. 541); Arnaud's *Études . . . sur les Théories
Dramatiques au XVIIᵉ Siècle* (1887) ; Ebner's *Beitrag zu einer
Geschichte der dramatischen Einheiten in Italien*, Erlangen, 1898 ;
Spingarn's *Literary Criticism in the Renaissance*, pp. 73, 89–101,
206–10 ; Saintsbury's *History of Criticism*, ii. Bks. iv and v,
passim ; Butcher's *Aristotle's Theory of Poetry*, 3rd edit., ch. vii.

It is not pedantic to protest against the popular title, 'The
Unities of Aristotle' (as in M. Breitinger's book, referred to
above), though the 'Dramatic Unities' *were* evolved in the
study of the *Poetics* ; or hypercritical to disclaim M. Lintilhac's
'Unités scaligériennes,' now that Mr. Spingarn has stated
Scaliger's position and established Castelvetro's claim.

10. See note to p. 167, l. 31.

17, &c. Cf. Whetstone, supra, p. 59, ll. 24, &c.; Ben Jonson,
infra, ii. p. 389. Cf. also Shakespeare, Prologue to *Henry V*,
and the passage (parallel even in details) in *Don Quixote*, Pt. i.
ch. xlviii. I am reminded by Mr. Spingarn that Rodenburg
(supra, p. 382) in paraphrasing this passage, in 1619, quotes
Lope de Vega's similar theory (*Arte nuevo de hacer comedias*),
and adds ' 't z'eve ghebruyken oock alle de Poëten in Enghe-
landt' (cited by Jonckbloet, u. s., iii. 201, note). This idea he
probably got from Sidney ; but it is an interesting early foreign
comment on the practice of the Elizabethan dramatists.

35. *some*, &c. Cf. Castelvetro, *Poetica*, p. 109, l. 30 'Per la
qual cosa veggansi Plauto & Terentio, come si possono scusare
di non hauere errato, che in alcune comedie loro hanno fatto
rappresentare l' attione più lunga d' un giorno' : and Scaliger,

Poetice, vi. 3. See also Dryden's reference to Scaliger on the *Heautontimorumenos* (*Essay of Dramatic Poesy, Works*, ed. Scott and Saintsbury, xv. p. 307). Sidney's mention of the *Eunuchus* is a slip. The 'time' of Terence's play was a fruitful topic of discussion by, among others, Muretus, Vossius, Mambrun, d'Aubignac, and Ménage. (See d'Aubignac's *Térence justifié* and *Pratique du Théâtre*.)

198. 17. *Pacolets horse*. See the Romance of *Valentine and Orson* for the story of the magic horse of the dwarf Pacolet. Cf. Rabelais, ii. 24.

21. Horace, *Ars Poet*. 147.

199. 5. *mingling Kings and Clownes*. See Whetstone, supra, p. 58, l. 19 ; p. 59, ll. 33-4 ; p. 60, l. 1, and notes ; and 'E. K.', p. 128, l. 5. Cf. Scaliger, *Poetice*, I. xi (end).

9. *mungrell Tragy-comedie*. Cf. p. 175, l. 16. See the Prologue to *Amphitruo*, 59.

13-14. Cf. Scaliger, 'Festiue (vt solet) Plautus Amphitruonem suam Tragicomoediam appellauit : in qua personarum dignitas atque magnitudo Comoediae humilitati admistae essent' (*Poet*. i. 7, p. 31). See supra, p. 175, l. 16, &c.

200. 22. See note to p. 197, l. 3.

24. Aristotle, *Poetics*, v. 1. On Laughter, cf. Trissino, *Opere*, ii. 127 et seq.

31-2. Juvenal, *Sat*. iii. 152-3.

34. *Thraso*, in the *Eunuchus* of Terence.

awry-transformed Traueller. Cf. Ascham, *Scholemaster* (ed. Mayor, i. p. 74), 'returned out of *Italie* worse transformed.' The sentiment is, of course, an Elizabethan commonplace.

201. 4. *Buchanan*, supra, p. 194.

6-10. *this play matter*. Cf. p. 176, l. 27 (note).

24-25. Cf. Sidney's *Astrophel and Stella*, i. 7-8 ; lxxiv. 8.

31. *Energia* (ἐνέργεια, Arist. *Rhet*. iii. 11. 2, &c. ; Quintil. 401). See note in *N. E. D.*, s. v. 'Energy.' Sidney may be recalling Scaliger's chapter on '*Efficacia*' (*Poetice*, iii. 26), which begins ' Efficaciam Graeci ἐνέργειαν vocant.'

202. 1-2. A retort to Gosson's 'chaste Matrons apparel on common Curtesans' (*Schoole of Abuse*, ed. Arber, p. 20).

3-8. Cf. the identity of phrase in Sidney's fifteenth Sonnet in *Astrophel and Stella* (ed. Flügel, 1899, p. 7) :—

'You that doe search for euery purling spring,
  Which from the rybs of old *Pernassus* flowes,
  And euery flower (not sweete perhaps) which growes
  Neere there about, into your Poems wring.
  You that doe dictionary method bring
  Into your rymes, running in ratling rowes,
  You that old *Petrarchs* long deceased woes
  With new borne sighes and wit disguised sing,
  You take wrong wayes ; those far-fet helps be such
  As doe bewray a want of inward tutch ;
  And sure at length stolne goods doe come to light.
  But if both for your loue & skill you[r] name
  You seeke to nurse at fullest brest of Fame,
  Stella behold, and then begin to write.'

Cf. also the third Sonnet (ib. p. 2).

8–12. Apparently a reference to Gosson, and probably, as
Mr. A. S. Cook suggests, a direct parody of his style.

16. *Nizolian Paper-bookes*, i.e. on the model of the *Thesaurus
Ciceronianus* of Marius Nizolius (1498–? 1576). The style of these
collections of annotations is described by Ascham, supra, p. 17,
ll. 26, &c.

16–18. Mr. A. S. Cook compares Du Bellay, *Defense* (1549),
i. 7 : '[Les Romains] imitant les meilleurs auteurs grecs, se
transformant en eux, les devorant; et, après les avoir bien
digerez, les convertissant en sang et nourriture.' The metaphor
is, however, very common.

25. Cicero, *In Catil.* i. 2, slightly altered.

32. '. . . to be chollericke. How well store of *Similiter
Cadenses* doth sounde with the grauitie of the Pulpit, I woulde
but inuoke Demosthenes soule to tell : who with a rare daintinesse vseth them. Truly they haue made mee thinke of the
Sophister, that with too much subtilitie would proue two Egges
three, and though he might be counted a Sophister, had none
for his labour. So these men bringing in such a kinde of
eloquence, well may they obtaine an opinion of a seeming
finenesse, but perswade few, which should be the ende of
their finenesse, Now for Similitudes . . .' (Ponsonby's text).
See Flügel's edition, p. 107.

34, &c. *all Herbarists*, &c. A gibe at the excesses of Euphuism, and more directly at Gosson's style. Cf. Sidney's third Sonnet in *Astrophel and Stella* :—

> 'Or with straunge similes, inricht each line,
>   Of hearbes or beastes, which *Inde* or *Affricke* hold.'

See i. p. 322, l. 28, note, and ii. p. 269.

203. 10. *as Cicero.* *De Oratore*, ii. 1. 4.

20-2. Ronsard, on the contrary, gives the advice not to affect the style of courts, as courtiers fight more, and better, than they write (ed. Blanchemain, vii. 322).

204. 18. Sidney is fond of this mannerism, especially in his *Arcadia.* Cf. Hall, *Satires*, Bk. vi. 255, &c. (ed. Grosart) :—

> 'He knows the grace of that new elegance
>   Which sweet *Philisides* fetch't of late from *France*,
>   That well beseem'd his high-stil'd *Arcady*,
>   Tho others marre it with much liberty ;
>   In Epithets to ioyne two words in one,
>   Forsooth, for Adiectiues cannot stand alone ;
>   As a great Poet could of *Bacchus* say,
>   That he was *Semele-femori-gena*.'

21. Cf. the Spenser-Harvey Correspondence, passim.

205. 11. *ryme*; here = 'rhythm' (cf. Webbe, infra, p. 267, ll. 13, &c.). Contrast the meaning in ll. 17-18, and cf. Webbe, u. s., ll. 6-7. Cf. also Gascoigne, supra, p. 50, ll. 4-5, 27-8, and p. 52, l. 16. For a kindred Renaissance discussion of these themes cf. Du Bellay, *Defense*, ii. chs. 7 and 8.

For the form *rhythme*=rhyme, see the quotation from the *Preservation of King Henry the VII*, supra, p. 377.

11-12. Cf. Daniel, infra, ii. p. 360, ll. 24-5.

14. *Cæsura*, cf. Gascoigne, supra, p. 54, l. 9, &c.

206. 6. Not in Aristotle ; but probably taken from Boccaccio, *De Geneal. Deorum*, XV. viii (edit. 1532, pp. 392-3), which refers to Aristotle's testimony.

8. *Bembus*, supra, p. 396.

9-11. Scaliger, *Poet*. iii. c. 19 'Nullis profecto Philosophorum praeceptis aut melior aut ciuilior euadere potes quam ex Virgiliana lectione.'

11-12. *Clauserus, the Translator of Cornutus.* Sidney refers to the Preface of the Latin translation, by Conrad Clauser, of the περὶ τῆς τοῦ θεοῦ φύσεως of Annaeus Cornutus.

16–18. Borrowed by Harington, infra, ii. p. 203, ll. 5–10.

19. *Landin* (Cristoforo Landino), 1424–? 1504. The fullest account will be found in the *Specimen Literaturae Florentinae saeculi xv*, by Ang. Bandinio, 2 vols. Florence, 1747. The list of his works is given in ii. p. 179, &c. Sidney probably refers to the *Disputationes Camaldulenses*.

For the doctrine of 'divine fury,' here associated with Landin, see supra, p. 192, ll. 15–18, note.

27. Cf. Horace, *Sat.* i. 6. 6.

29. Virgil, *Aen.* ix. 446.

32–3. This common figure will be found in Cicero's *Somnium Scipionis*, 5. Cf. Overbury, *Characters*, 'A Quack-salver' (ed. Rimbault, p. 141).

207. 3. Will become such a fool as to be a dull critic of poetry.

5. *Bubonax.* 'Sidney is referring to the tale of *Hipponax* (an Iambic poet of Ephesus about B. C. 500), of whom one story was that he satirized the statuary *Bupalus* so bitterly that he hanged himself. By some confusion . . . he has combined the two names' (Shuckburgh, ed. *Apologie*, p. 176). Cf. Hor. *Epod.* vi. 14.

10–11. Cf. *The Pilgrimage to Parnassus*, Act. V (ll. 538–9).

KING JAMES VI (pp. 208–25).

209. 7, &c. James's references to his sources are put darkly. From the writers 'of auld,' whether classical or mediaeval, he could draw little help in his study of Scots prosody; and, as his statement that nothing had been written on the subject in Scots (l. 23) is still valid, the possible originals are narrowed down to English and French. It is difficult to interpret the phrase 'sindrie hes written of it in English' as we do not have, except in one case, any evidence, external or internal, how far the youthful author was then familiar with the criticism of Spenser and his friends and the other tracts printed in this volume, or whether he is referring in a general way to more technical rhetorical works such as Wilson's (cf. ll. 34, 35). The exception is Gascoigne's *Certayne Notes* (supra, pp. 46–57), though

James does not name it. The similar purpose of the two books and the parallelisms noted below seem to prove this, unless it be that in some places James, like Gascoigne (see note to p. 47, l. 7), has drawn direct from the French. He mentions Du Bellay (l. 30); and the 'sindrie others' may reasonably include Ronsard (see note to l. 30).

It has been surmised that the material of the volume of *Essayes of a Prentise in the Divine Art of Poesie*, in which this tract appears, was selected from the school-exercises which James had done when he was Buchanan's pupil at Stirling. It may be that his effort towards an *Ars Poetica* was directly inspired by his master's *De Prosodia* and his annotations on Vives (*Opera*, Edin. 1715, vol. ii).

12. *Flowing*, i.e. rhythm. Cf. p. 210, l. 26; p. 216, l. 28; p. 218, l. 34.

13. *Ryming in termes*: defined on p. 212, l. 25.

30. *Du Bellay.* See *La Defense et Illustration de la langue françoise* (1st edit. 1549), the *Epistre au Lecteur* prefixed to *L'Olive* (1st edit. 1549), the shorter poems *Discours au Roy sur la Poësie* and *Le Poëte courtisan* (added to *L'Olive*), and the *Epistre* to *Vers traduits* (1552).

See also Ronsard, *Préface de la Franciade* and *Abrégé de l'Art poétique françois* (1565).

210. 1–4. Cf. Thomas Randolphe's letter to Buchanan (Mar. 15, 1579): 'No lesse famous then *Apelles* Table was, & as voyde of Comptrollment as his Worke was, howe curiouse soeuer the Souter would seme to be' (Buchanan, *Opera*, 1715, ii; *Epist.* xxi). James's misquotation—and from his favourite Pliny (*N. H.* xxxv. (36) 10)—would show that the popular substitution of *ultra* for *supra* had been already accepted.

pantoun. Cf. Watson, 'Ἑκατομπαθία, 'To the Reader': '[say] to the second that though *Venus* be in my verse, yet her slipper is left out' (Spenser Soc. ed., p. 6).

5–13. Cf. Du Bellay, *Defense*, chap. xi; and Gascoigne, ante, p. 47 and note. See infra, p. 221, chap. vii. And cf. Wilson, *Arte of Rhetorique* [1553], fol. 3 v°: and Ben Jonson: 'But all this in vain, without a natural wit and a poetical nature in chief' (*Discoveries*, in *Works*, ed. Cunningham, iii. 421).

17. *blok*, plan, 'block out.' Cf. James's preface to the

Uranie, ' I haue put in the French on the one side of the leif, and my blocking on the other' (ed. Arber, p. 21).

24. *fete*; for *syllable*, though James uses the latter too (e. g. p. 212, l. 27; p. 213, l. 21).

211. 19–32. The characteristics of the poet here given are exclusively external and technical, as in Ronsard and Du Bellay. In some portions the resemblance may be due to direct suggestion (cf. Ronsard, *Préf. de la Franciade*; Du Bellay, *Le Poëte courtisan*, ll. 75–80, 113).

212. 5. *cullouris* (pl.), i.e. rhythm or metre—a Scots usage, to be distinguished from that other sense, 'figures,' 'ornaments,' 'rhetorical modes,' deduced from Cicero, Quintilian, and Horace, through Scaliger, *Poetice*, iii. 30. For the former sense cf., perhaps, Jonson, *Conversations*, XV; for the latter supra, p. 65, l. 32, Chaucer, *Squieres Tale*, ll. 30–1. Wilson, *Arte of Rhetorique* [1553], f. 94 v°. For the sing. form in the sense here, see p. 213, l. 11.

213. 21–4. Cf. Gascoigne, ante, p. 49, ll. 23–5.

26. This exclusive choice of the iamb may be, as has been suggested (Saintsbury, *Hist. Crit.* ii. 178), additional proof of French influence in this tract, but the limitation was already recognized. See Gascoigne, ante, p. 50, ll. 6–10, 23–7, the Spenser-Harvey correspondence, passim, and Webbe, p. 273, l. 4.

32. Cf. p. 224, l. 7.

214. 1–11. Obviously modelled on Gascoigne, ante, p. 50, l. 30– p. 51, l. 17. James's example is less happy.

12, &c. *Sectioun*, i.e. caesura.

215. 3–14. Contrast Gascoigne's placing of the caesura, ante, p. 54, § 13.

16. *monosyllabis*. Contrast Gascoigne, ante, p. 51, § 5.

26. *suppose*, though.

216. 29. Cf. Ronsard, *Abrégé de l'Art poétique*, u. s., p. 344.

217. 1–3. Cf. Gascoigne, ante, p. 48, ll. 31–3, and p. 51, § 6; Ronsard, u. s., p. 351.

10–11. James had many examples to choose from in mediaeval literature or in sixteenth-century Scots: and he may have been thinking of such passages as the opening lines of Du Bellay's *Exécration sur l'Angleterre*.

24. *Flyting.* This is a common sixteenth-century Scots form of poetic invective, allied to the older *tenson* and *estrif,* and analogous in excessive abuse to the Medicean *tenzone.*

25. *hurland ouer heuch,* i. e. dashing (driven violently) over craggy steeps.

33. *waill,* choose.

218. 1–10. *vocabula artis.* Cf. Gascoigne's 'apt vocables,' ante, p. 47, l. 12.

18–20. Cf. the Glosse on 'his name' in 'July' of the *Shepheardes Calender.* Contrast the 'indecorous' learning of the shepherds in the *Complaynt of Scotlande* (1549).

23, &c. *Tumbling verse.* See note to p. 223, l. 9.

219. 4. Orig. 'giue.'

9. *as for Comparisons.* Cf. Ronsard, *Préf. de la Franciade,* u. s., p. 188.

18. Ronsard speaks of epithets (*Abrége,* u. s., p. 350), but against those which are unnecessary (e. g. *rivière courante*).

28. *corruptit wordis.* Cf. Sidney, supra, note to p. 204, l. 18.

220. 20–8. Cf. Gascoigne, ante, p. 48, ll. 9–23.

30-2. An anacoluthon : 'that . . .*ye*' or ' [that] . . . to.'

221. 1. As James does in his *Phoenix,* e. g. p. 45 (ed. Arber).

5. *Inuention.* Cf. p. 210, ll. 5–13 (note).

10. Cf. Du Bellay, *Vers traduits* (*Epistre*), p. 4.

12, &c. Cf. ii. p. 33, ll. 18–19.

26. Cf. Gascoigne's 'ryding rime' and remarks thereon, ante, p. 56, § 16. Also Puttenham, Campion, and Daniel, by the Index.

222. 21. *learnit.* The example chosen will be found among James's poems in the *Lusus Regius* (ed. Rait, p. 17).

22. *Ballat Royal,* ballade royal, originally of seven lines of ten syllables, *a b a b b c c,* as in the *Kingis Quair* of James I, King of Scots ; later, according to James VI, as here, with an additional line inserted between the sixth and seventh, *a b a b b c b c.* This is not the true *ottava rima* ; nor is it the true *rhyme-royal,* though it frequently bears the name, and is historically related through it to the older French *chant-royal.* See next note.

32. *Troilus verse,* so-called from Chaucer's use of the seven-lined stanza in his *Troilus,* is the true *rhyme-royal.* This is Gascoigne's *rythme royall,* defined ante, p. 54, § 14. Chaucer,

it should be noted, uses *three* rhymes (*a b a b b c c*). James's
example is from Alexander Montgomerie's *Echo* (S. T. S. edit.
p. 138).

223. 9. *Rouncefallis or Tumbling verse.* The origin of the
term *rouncefal*, which James VI here applies prosodically, is
not clear. Stanyhurst uses it in the same sense, 'to tumble'—

> 'thee tree
> At leingth with rounsefal, from stock vntruncked, yt harssheth'

(*Aen.*, ed. Arber, p. 63: see also p. 92). Dekker has 'Dost roare ?
th'ast a good rouncivall voice to cry Lanthorne and candle-light'
(*Satiromastix*, 1602, p. 243). T. Heywood in the *Golden Age*
(ii. 1) speaks of a 'bona roba, a rounceval, a virago, or a good
manly lass'; and Gayton in 1654 (*Notes upon Don Quixote*, III.
ii. 72) describes a certain woman as a 'more rare sight then we
exhibit at Bartholomew Faire (take in to help it the reaking
sweating Rouncifolds of Py-Corner too).' The underlying notion
of a hoydenish, rough-and-tumble, 'falling-away' manner is well
expressed in the line, and in the rush and bob of the stanza.
I am indebted to Mr. W. A. Craigie for the above quotations
from the collections for *N. E. D.*

The example is from Montgomerie's *Polwart and Montgomerie's Flyting* (S. T. S. edit. p. 69).

26-7. Cf. Gascoigne, ante, p. 55, l. 16.

31. *Commoun verse.* This stave is Gascoigne's *Ballade*
(ante, p. 54, l. 35), which he also gives to 'matters of loue' (ib.
p. 57, l. 1).

224. 3. *this*, thus (Middle Scots usage).

7. Cf. ante, p. 213, l. 32.

9. Montgomerie's *Cherrie and the Slae* (S. T. S. edit. p. 6).

WEBBE (pp. 226-302).

227. 27. *deuises.* Sir Egerton Brydges would find here an
allusion to *The Paradyse of Daynty Deuices* (1578). See his
edition, p. xxiv.

229. 16. *beeing not the firste.* Webbe refers (infra) to the
critical opinions of, among others, Ascham, Gascoigne, Spenser,
and Harvey; and has, indeed, small claim to originality in any
portion of his Treatise.

30. *censure*, judgment, criticism (not necessarily adverse).
Cf. p. 301, l. 21, note.

34. *thys reformed versifying.* See pp. 278 et seq.

230. 6. ποετρια. This impossible variant of ποίησις is the
M. Lat. word *poetria* printed in Greek letters; the Greek word
ποιήτρία means a poetess. *Poetria* was given currency by
Geoffrey de Vinsauf's *Nova Poetria*, c. 1200. Webbe's scholarship throughout is not of the best, though he ventures on
translation.

Cf. Sidney, ante, p. 155: and 'E. K.'s gloss to 'April' in the
Shepheardes Calender.

18. *Phormio*, Prol. 18. Cf. also *Heaut*. Prol. 23. See infra, ii.
p. 329, ll. 9–10, and ' E. K.'s gloss to 'December' of *The Shepheardes Calender*: 'Musick, that is Poetry, as Terence sayth
. . ., speking of Poetes.'

24. *Panegeryca*, i. e. πανηγυρικά (συμπόσια, δεῖπνα). The whole
passage (l. 20–p. 231, l. 5) is taken direct from ' E. K.'s gloss
to ' October' of *The Shepheardes Calender.* Webbe omits 'E.K.'s
clue to the passage in Plato (*Laws*, i).

231. 2. *Vates.* See ante, p. 154, l. 5, note. Webbe distinguishes
between *Vates* and *Poeta*: just as Ronsard makes a further
distinction between the original poets who conversed with
oracles and prophets, and 'les seconds Poëtes' who were
' plus enflez d'artifice et labeur que de divinité' (*Abrégé*).

16. *Orig.* Pʹιθμος. Cf. p. 267, ll. 6–15.   20. *Orig.* λοητεία.

34. *Tusc.* i. 26 'sine caelesti aliquo mentis instinctu.' Cf.
Webbe's words on the next page, ll. 2–3.

232. 5. *Fasti*, vi. 5. The emblem in ' October' of *The Shepheardes Calender*, from which Webbe quotes below.

7. *late*, recently.

10–11. *Shepheardes Calender*, ' October.'

21. *English Poet.* Cf. p. 246, l. 4, and note to p. 192, ll. 15–18.
' E. K.'s reference to this unknown work will be found in the
argument to ' October' in *The Shepheardes Calender.* Grosart's
' soupçon of suspicion' that it is 'incorporated or adapted' in
Sidney's *Apologie* (ed. Spenser, i. pp. 99, 453) is probably of little
value ; and Collier's discovery of a reference to it in Nicholas
Breton's ' Epitaph on Spenser' in his *Melancholike Humours*
(ed. Spenser, i. cxlviii) is based on a misunderstanding of the

text. See Schelling's *Poetic and Verse Criticism of the Reign of Elizabeth*, Philadelphia, 1891, pp. 31–3.

234. 6, 7. *Orig.* ' made houses, and kept.'

235. 15. *delight . . . commoditie.* Cf. supra, p. 158, ll. 5–6, note, and p. 197, l. 3, note.

33. *none woorth the reading twyce* is said by Cicero of the plays of Livius Andronicus in particular (' Livianae fabulae vix satis dignae quae iterum legantur,' *Brutus*, 71): but his general drift in the passage is substantially what Webbe makes it.

236. 14. Aristotle, *Poetics*, i. 8. Webbe probably takes this at second-hand, as elsewhere in his references to the Aristotelian canon. He follows Horace not merely in the theory but in the historical illustrations, e.g. l. 24, where, with Lodge (supra, p. 81), he reproduces the order of *Sat.* i. 4 (though Cratinus is senior to the other two), and l. 26, where he recalls the association of Plato and Menander in *Sat.* ii. 3. In these examples he copies Fabricius Chemnicensis *verbatim*, whom he translates, infra, p. 295.

31. *Theagines.* Probably for the tragic poet Theognis (by confusion with the better known name of the hero in the *Aethiopica* of Heliodorus, supra, p. 388), of whose work but two words, φόρμιγξ ἄχορδος, survive. These are mentioned in Aristotle's *Rhetoric*, and in Demetrius, *De Elocutione*, 85. Aristophanes refers to him once or twice as a poet so dull and frigid (ψυχρός) that it snowed in Thrace when he brought out a play at Athens (Smith's *Class. Dict.*).

237. 20. Cf. Lodge, supra, p. 82.

30. Propertius ii. 32. 66. Quoted by Meres, infra, ii. p. 316, l. 3 (see note).

238. 15. C. Silius Italicus, author of the *Punica*.

239. 14. *Pallengenius.* See p. 30, l. 10, note.

Baptista Mantuanus. See p. 244, ll. 11–12, note.

15–16. Christopher Ocland, Master of Southwark and Cheltenham Schools, whose Latin poems appeared in 1582, in a volume entitled *Anglorum Praelia ab anno* 1327 . . . *vsque ad annum* 1558. *Item De Pacatissimo Angliae Statu imperante Elizabetha compendiosa Narratio.* The book was ordered by the Privy Council to be taught ' in all grammar and free schools within this realme.' Alexander Neville's *Kettus, sive de furoribus*

Norfolciensium Ketto Duce is included in the volume. Cf. Hall's *Satires* (ed. Grosart), iv. 3, ll. 16-17 :—

> 'Or cyte olde *Oclands* verse, how they did weild
> The wars in *Turwin*, or in *Turney* field.'

240. 14. See supra, p. 29, ll. 31, &c.; p. 32, l. 21.

241. 4-5. Now in the edition by Mr. G. C. Macaulay, 4 vols., Oxford, 1899–1902.

10. *the God of English Poets*, &c. So Spenser, 'The God of Shepheards, *Tityrus*, is dead' (*Sh. Cal.*, 'June'); and ' E. K.' in his gloss '. . . by Tityrus is meant Chaucer, . . . whom he calleth the God of Poetes for his excellencie.'

242. 9. *quantity.* Webbe's description of Langland's verse is not clear. If he be using 'quantity' as in p. 281, l. 1, his account is not less inadequate.

23. *ninth* ; an error for the *eleventh* eclogue ('November') of the *Shepheardes Calender* (q. v.).

31. *the olde Earle of Surrey.* (See p. 126, l. 2, note.) The first collection of his poems appeared in *Tottel's Miscellany* (1557). See the editions by Nott (1815–16), Yeowell ('Aldine,' 1866), and Arber (1870, &c.).

32. L. Vaus, i.e. Thomas Vaux, second Baron Vaux of Harrowden (1510–56), whose poems appeared posthumously in *Tottel's Miscellany* (1557) and *The Paradyse of Daynty Deuises* (1576). See ii. p. 413.

Thomas Norton of Bristow. See supra, p. 30, l. 8, note.

33. Richard Edwardes (? 1523–66), Master of the Children of the Chapel Royal (1561), author of *Palamon and Arcite* (1566), and of the comedy *Damon and Pithias* (1571).

Thomas Tusser (? 1524–80), author of the popular *Hundreth Good Pointes of Husbandrie* (1st edit. 1557).

Thomas Churchyard (?1520–1604), a contributor to *Tottel's Miscellany*, and chiefly known by his occasional booklets or broadsheets (*Churchyardes Chippes*, 1575, &c.).

William Hunnis (*d.* 1597), Master of the Children of the Chapel Royal (1566), author of *A Hyve full of Hunnye* (1578), and some metrical psalms. Webbe quotes from him on p. 277.

Haiwood. This may be either John Heywood the epigrammatist (see Index) or Jasper Heywood (1535–98), who contributed to the *Paradyse of Daynty Deuises*, and to the English *Seneca*. The context favours the latter ascription.

34. *Sand*. The 'D. S.' and 'D. Sand' of the *Paradyse of Daynty Deuises* have been identified, on slender evidence, with Dr. Edwin Sandys (? 1516–88).

Hyll. Perhaps the 'R. Hill' (also printed 'Hall') of the *Paradyse of Daynty Deuises*.

S. Y. Is this the 'M. Yloop' (perhaps for Pooly), one of the contributors to the above (see title-page of edit. 1576)?

M. D. Is this 'Master Dyer' (see p. 89, l. 7, note)?

243. 7. *Earle of Oxford*, i.e. the seventeenth Earl (1550–1604). See notes to ii. p. 63, l. 32; p. 65, l. 26.

14. *D*. Phaer: an error for T[homas] Phaer, repeated on p. 256, l. 25. For Phaer and Twyne see note to p. 137, l. 29.

27. Arthur Golding's translation of the *Metamorphoses* appeared in 1565 (*The Fyrst Fower Bookes*) and in 1567 (*The XV Bookes*).

35. *Googe . . . Pallengenius*. See supra, p. 30, l. 10, note.

244. 3. Abraham Fleming (? 1552–1607). Cf. also p. 266, l. 1.

5. *one of hys name*. Is Webbe alluding to Samuel Fleming of King's College (see ii. p. 425)? Or, if he refers to the Christian name, can he be thinking of Abraham Fraunce?

11–12. *Seneca in English*. See note to p. 312, l. 1.

the other partes of Ouid, i.e. *The Heroycall Epistles*, by George Turberville, 1567 (see p. 315, l. 11, note), and the first three books of the *De Tristibus*, by Churchyard (1580).

Horace, by Drant (see note on p. 373).

Mantuan. *The Eglogs of the Poet B. Mantuan Carmelitan*, by George Turberville (1567). See p. 315, ll. 11–12, note.

29. *Whetstone*. See p. 58.

31. Anthony Munday (1553–1633). Cf. the allusion in ii. Appendix, p. 490, l. 13.

245. 2. Iohn Graunge (fl. 1577), author of *The Golden Aphroditis* (1577). Webbe quotes from him on p. 277.

Knyght. Mr. H. Morley suggests *Edward Knight*. 'Little is known of Edward Knight, whose initials "E. K., Gentleman," are before commendatory verses prefixed to Munday's *Mirror of Mutabilitie*, "Ed. Knight" being signed at the end. This must be Webbe's "Knyght" in the list of good poets—the only known person who might be the "E. K." of Spenser's *Shepheardes Calendar*, if he was not Edward Kirke' (*English Writers*, ix. 152).

Robert Wylmott (fl. 1568-1608), was to bring out, in 1591, a second edition of the Tragedy of *Tancred and Gismund* (written by 'The Gentlemen of the Inner Temple' and acted in 1568), in which the older decasyllabic rhymed quatrains are 'polished according to the decorum of these daies,' i.e. in blank verse. Webbe was interested in Wilmot's venture, and wrote an epistle for the revised version. There he speaks of the play as 'a work, either in stateliness of shew, depth of conceit, or true ornaments of poetical art, inferior to none of the best in that kind : no, were the Roman Seneca the censurer.' And again : 'Your commendable pains in disrobing him of his antique curiosity, and adorning him with the approved guise of our stateliest English terms (not diminishing, but more augmenting his artificial colours of absolute poesy, derived from his first parents) cannot but be grateful to most men's appetites, who upon our experience we know highly to esteem such lofty measures of sententiously confused tragedies.' (Dodsley, ed. 1825, ii. 160-4.)

Darrell? This can hardly be the antiquary William Darell (*d.* 1580). Googe's wife was a Darrell of Scotney, Kent.

F. C. Mr. H. Morley suggests that this is a misprint for *F. G.*, i.e. Fulke Greville.

F. K. ? Francis Kinwelmersh (*d.* ?1580), who collaborated with Gascoigne and contributed to the *Paradyse of Daynty Deuises*.

G. B. Perhaps G. Bucke, who adds a Quatorzain in commendation of Thomas Watson in the 'Εκατομπαθία (Spens. Soc. edit. p. 11). A George Buc or Bucke (*d.* 1623), a minor poet, knighted in 1603, was Master of the Revels from 1608. Or is he the ' M. Bewe ' who contributes to the *Paradyse of Daynty Deuices*, which Webbe has much in mind ?

10. *Master Sp.* See note to p. 112, l. 12.

17. *Gabriell Haruey.* See note to p. 284, l. 4.

31-5. Cf. p. 284, ll. 3-5.

246. 3-4. *his Dreames, his Legends*, &c. See p. 100, l. 24 (note) ; p. 133, l. 7 (note) ; and p. 232, l. 21 (note).

8. *hys two brethren* : John Harvey (1564-92), and Richard Harvey (1560-1623).

246. 28-34. Probably a reference to Elderton. See ante, p. 125, l. 28 (note). With the pun in l. 30 cf. Nash, infra, p. 333, l. 35.

247. 3-16. Quoted from ' E. K.', ante, p. 131.

248. 26, &c. Webbe here repeats the mediaeval distinction between tragedy and comedy borrowed from Donatus and the neo-classical critics. Cf. Puttenham, infra, ii. p. 33 et seq. On the question of the influence of the *Iliad* and *Odyssey* in defining these kinds, see Scaliger, *Poetice*, i. 4.

250. 19-20. *Ars Poet.* ll. 333-4.

26-27. ib., ll. 343-4.

251. 4. ib., l. 338.

31. *Ep.* ii. 1. 126. [Orig. *fugitat.*]

35. Sir Thomas Elyot (1490 ?-1546).

252. 1-8. See Mr. Croft's edition of Elyot's *Gouernour*, i. 123. The third line reads ' Pullyng their eares from wordes unclene.'

17. Orig. ' but it is were.'

253. 3. *inconueniences.* Cf. p. 65, l. 32 (note).

255. 22, &c. Webbe's definition of the Epic may be compared with Puttenham's, infra.

256. 19. Quintil. x. 1 (514).

25. *D.* Phaer. See note to p. 243, l. 14.

257. 15, &c. *Aen.* i. 201-13. Webbe does not give the extracts from Phaer quite *verbatim.*

258. 15. *Aen.* iv. 1.

259. 9. Ib., l. 589.

260. 16. Ib., ix. 664.

261. 8-9. *towardes the end.* Not so ; l. 181.

262. 4. *Golding.* See note to p. 243, l. 27.

15, &c. *Eglogues.* Cf. The General Argument of *The Shepheardes Calender.*

23. *Titus Calphurnius,* i.e. T. Julius Calpurnius, Sicilian, whose volume *Eclogae Septem* was printed first at Parma in 1478, and in many later editions with the Eclogues of Nemesianus. See Fabricius, *Bibl. Lat.* p. 554 et seq.

24. *Mantuan.* See p. 239, l. 14 (note), and p. 244, l. 12 (note).

263. 4. *Sp.* See p. 245, l. 10 (note).

29. See ante, p. 128, ll. 1-7.

264. 25-265. 5. Cf. ' E. K.' in Gloss to ' January' of *The Shepheardes Calender.*

265. 12–13. Cf. p. 279, l. 21. Webbe's wisdom is but Horace's, *Ars Poet.* 9 &c. and 465.

22. Tusser. Supra, p. 242, l. 33 (note).

27. Googe. Supra, p. 243, l. 35 (note).

29. Heresbachius, Conradus (1496–1576), author of *Rei Rusticae Libri Quatuor* (Cologne, 1570), Englished in 1577 by Googe in his *Foure Bookes of Husbandrie.*

266. 1. *Flemming.* Supra, p. 244, l. 3 (note).

4–16. There is no record of the separate publication of Webbe's pirated verses. He himself gives his version of the First and Second Eclogues, infra, p. 284.

27. Supra, p. 240.

267. 6–15. Cf. p. 231, l. 16. Cf. also Gascoigne, ante, p. 50, ll. 4–5, 27.

22, &c. Borrowed from Ascham, ante, p. 32. See also Willes, ante, p. 47 (footnote).

268. 5. The 'three speciall notes' are taken from Gascoigne. See ante, p. 49, §§ 3 and 4.

270. 9–10. 'January' eclogue.

271. 9. See the 'April' eclogue, before the 'Song.'

11–19. Repeated on p. 286.

28. 'August' eclogue.

272. 3–11 'November' eclogue.

19. *Rogero . . . Trenchmore.* Cf. Gosson, *Schoole of Abuse,* 'neyther pyped *Rogero* nor *Turkelony*' (ed. Arber, p. 26).

30. *Powlters Measure*: borrowed from Gascoigne, ante, p. 56, l. 8.

273. 4. *the old Iambicke stroake.* See note to p. 213, l. 26.

10–13. Cf. Gascoigne, p. 51, and James VI, p. 214.

29. See ante, p. 268, l. 11 (and note).

274. 1. *chouching,* couching. See *N. E. D.,* s. v. *Couch* v.¹ § 15. It is difficult to account for this form.

15. *anothers* (orig. *Authors*).

275. 10, &c. A tardy acknowledgment to Gascoigne's *Certayne Notes,* printed supra, pp. 46–57. The passage here referred to will be found on p. 52.

276. 16–17. See Puttenham, infra, Book ii.

24. 'August' eclogue.

27. Orig. *pact.*

34. Iohn Graunge. See p. 245, l. 2.

277. 18. W. Hunnis. See p. 242, l. 33.

279. 21. *without any prescription of rules.* Cf. p. 265, ll. 12–15. Perhaps a sly reference to the much-talked-of ' Rules of Master Drant' (supra, p. 90, l. 13, note).

280. 18. *Choreus*: called later *Trochaeus*, which Webbe reserves for the tribrach. See next note.

21. *Tribrachys.* By a well-intentioned error of the press, this has been substituted for 'Trochaeus' in Webbe's text. The foot is a tribrach, but Webbe adopts the alternative usage allowed by Cicero (*Or.* 57. 193) and Quintilian (ix. 4. 82) by which *trochaeus* is a name of the tribrach. Puttenham and others follow the accepted rule.

25-6. For the reverse definition of *Bacchius* and *Palimbacchius* see Quintil. ix. 4 (484). See also Scaliger, *Poetice*, ii. 3, and Fabricius Chemnicensis, Bk. VI (p. 265 a).

33. *Tallœus.* Audomarus Tallaeus or Talaeus, editor of Cicero's *De Oratore* (1553), published his own *Rhetorica* at Paris in 1552. For other references see notes, infra, p. 309, l. 11 ; ii. p. 245, ll. 6 and 10.

281. 15. *Position.* Cf. Harvey (p. 118, l. 20; p. 121, l. 4, note, 22-33). For the place of ' Position' &c. in academic criticism, see Fabricius, *De Re Poetica*, i. 1, from which Webbe borrows the *Catholica*, infra, p. 290.

282. 7–8. From this it would appear that Webbe had not seen Stanyhurst's volume, where long 'I' is common. (See the article by Mr. R. B. McKerrow, in *The Modern Language Quarterly*, V. i. 7.)

283. 3. See the complete verse on p. 284.

9. This is a wrong-headed reference to Surrey's Virgil ' drawn into a strange meter' (ante, p. 32, l. 24).

12-20. Watson's lines were certainly ' in the mouthes of all men.' Cf. Ascham's *Scholemaster* (ed. Mayor, 71) ; Spenser and Harvey, supra, p. 118, l. 13 ; Kendall's *Flowers of Epigrammes* (1577). See Sidney's commentary on the Latin quotation in the letter to his brother Robert (*Correspondence*, ed. Pears, pp. 196–7).

28-9. See p. 99, ll. 21-2, and note.

284. 4. Cf. Webbe's passage on p. 245. See the specimens

in the Spenser-Harvey correspondence, ante, p. 87 et seq., and ' E. K.'s Postscript, ante, p. 134, and note.

284. 13. See note to p. 266, ll. 4–16.

285. 20–1. Ovid, *Amores*, iii. 8. 3–4.

26–7. Ovid, *Epist. ex Ponto*, iv. 3. 35–6.

30. Orig. *Phalocium*.

286. 2, &c. The verses are quoted by Webbe on p. 271.

289. 18. Orig. *Chores*: Webbe's (or his printer's) confusion with *Chore*, &c. on p. 286.

290. 13. *the Cannons . . . gathered by Georgius Fabricius Chemnicensis* (orig. *Cremnicensis*, in error). These are a translation of the concluding section of the 6th Book of the enlarged edition of Fabricius's *De Re Poetica Libri Septem* (printed in 1560). See pp. 300 a–305 b of the 1584 Paris edition, reprinted infra, as an Appendix to the Notes to Webbe (pp. 417–21). George Fabricius (1516–71) must not be confused with Jo. Albertus Fabricius who is referred to supra and infra. His Life (with a portrait) by Schreber appeared at Leipzig in 1717.

292. § 12. Cf. Arist. *Poetics*, xv.

293. 8–9. Cic. *De Opt. Gen. Orat.* 5 (14). Cf. Horace, *Ars Poet.* 133.

15. *In a Comedie* : ' In genere Dramatico ' (G. Fabricius).

23–5. Cicero, *De Deorum Natura*, i. 20. 53.

294. 9. *inconuenience*. Cf. note to p. 253, l. 3.

295. 17–21. Cf. Scaliger, *Poetice*, i. 7.

297. 1. *A Poet is*, &c. Cf. Sidney, supra, p. 195, l. 23, and note.

299. 5. *Angellius*. Nic. Angellius edited Macrobius in 1515 (Basle). See J. A. Fabricius, *Bibl. Lat.* p. 622.

8. *Mummius*. Webbe follows the text of Fabricius in reading *Memmius*.

12. C. Sollius Apollinaris Sidonius (*d.* 482), Bishop of Auvergne (Clermont), whose *Carmina XXIV* and *Epistolarum libri IX* are extant (1st edit. Milan, 1498). See J. A. Fabricius, u.s., pp. 634–6.

21. *De Orat.* ii. 78.

300. 2. See Quintil. iv. 2. 191. Scaliger, *Poetice*, iii. 32.

301. 8. Webbe repeats the error in the text of Fabricius (κρῆψιν).

14. *Ars Poet.* l. 322.

21. *exquisite censure*, exact (careful) criticism.

Appendix to Notes on Webbe.

(See note to p. 290.)

Q. HORATII FLACCI DE *ARTE POETICA*
CATHOLICA.

Ex Epistola ad Pisones.

I. *Inuentio sit ad materiam accommodata, non dissidens, non aliena, non monstrosā. Nam mulieris caput, ceruix equi, corpus auis varie coloratum, membra e variis animantibus collecta, pedes in caudam piscis exeuntes, in pictura monstrum deforme faciunt: quod si eadem sit in oratione diuersitas, quid potest dici mendosius?*

II. *Ornamenta nec nimia sint, nec temere quaesita, nec vbique adhibeantur aut ostententur.*

III. *Forma dicendi obseruanda, ne grauia tenuiter, prolixa breuiter dicantur, hoc ad decorum pertinet & ad materiam, vt cum rebus magis verba grandia consentiant.*

IV. *In descriptionibus poëticis, fidem ne excedat oratio, neve sit plane contra naturam inducta fictio.*

V. *Dispositio talis sit, ne peccetur exquisita sedulitate, aliqua omitti possunt, aliqua prolixitate nocent: nec est vna pars excolenda, & relinquenda altera. Id probat exemplo fabri, qui caput & superiorem corporis partem exprimebat artificiose, reliquum opus absoluere non poterat. Probat idem suo iudicio, quod nollet corporis parte reliqua esse pulcher, & naso esse adunco deformis. Omnia membra similia & composita sint oportet, in integro & bene formato corpore.*

VI. *Videndum est, num quis par esse possit ei materiae, quam tractandam suscipere cogitat. Ingenii enim vires saepe imprudentem vel incautum destituunt.*

VII. *Elocutio in verbis posita est, & in verborum formis. Verba sunt aut simplicia aut coniuncta, vetera aut noua, propria aut translata. In singulis vtendum iudicio & prudentia, & vsitatorum praecipuus honor est. Eadem enim ratio verborum, quae nummorum, vt vsitata & probata magis valeant.*

VIII. *Considerandum genus carminis, & accommodandum argumentis, & qui numeri sint ad quoduis genus accommodati magis. Carminum genera vsitatissimorum quatuor, Heroicum, Elegiacum, Iambicum, Lyricum.*

IX. *Non vno orationis genere in omnibus scriptis est vtendum. Insurgunt interdum Lyrici, interdum Comici. Conueniunt autem grandia proprie tragicis, humilia comicis. Fit autem vt ideae misceantur, pro ratione temporis aut loci.*

X. *Affectuum habenda ratio est: aliud decet hilares, aliud tristes: aliud iracundos, aliud lenes, quare cum industria tractandi sunt. Requiruntur autem tria in carmine, pulchritudo, suauitas, animorum affectio. Theophrastus scripsit, pulchritudinem esse quandam deceptionem, & Aristoteles eam vocat τυραννίδα ὀλιγοχρόνιον. Suauitas retinet lectorem, affectus mouent.*

XI. *Personis danda sunt sua conuenientia, vt oratio sit bene morata.*

*In hac parte consideranda dignitas, aetas, sexus, fortuna, conditio, pro-
uincia, patria.*

XII. *Personae sumuntur aut a poëtis aliis, aut finguntur a nobis. Si
sumuntur ab aliis, obseruandum est* τὸ ὅμοιον, *hoc est, vt sequamur eum
auctorem exacte, quem ad imitandum proposuimus, cuius rei ponuntur
exempla. Sin finguntur nouae a nobis retinendum est* τὸ ὁμαλόν, *id est,
aequale, vt ita personas introducamus, vt vbique sibi conueniant, & vt
extrema primis respondeant, ne hominem modo audacem introducamus,
modo prudentem, & cautum: id enim viciosum est. In vtroque seruan-
dum* τὸ ἁρμόττον, *quod hoc loco vertit conuenientiam, vt conueniens est,
virum esse fortem, mulierem timidam, seruum callidum, adolescentem
ingenuum.*

XIII. *Quae communia sunt: ita tractentur, vt propria fiant. Materiae
communes sunt, de quibus omnes possunt dicere, quas si ita quis tractet, vt
praecipuam laudem consequatur, facit eas proprias & suas, vt multi scripserunt de bello Troiano, sed quod commune fuit, id sibi proprium fecit
Homerus.*

XIV. *De Graecis quia sumenda multa, vt Latini omnes sumpserunt,
non eadem verba vt interpreti sunt exprimenda, sed libertate quadam vtendum
est, ingenii atque iudicii, qualis esse solet imitatoris.*

*Hoc praeceptum de Cicerone transtulit, qui inquit, Non verbum verbo
necesse est reddere.*

XV. *Exordium ne sit ineptum, hoc est, alienum, aut tumidum.*

XVI. *Propositio vel narratio e propinquo petita & verisimilis sit. In
narrando decorum aetatum ne negligatur.*

XVII. *In genere Dramatico, non necessarium est omnia facta palam
exhibere, vt sunt crudelia, turpia, monstrosa: sed ea narrare ut gesta sunt,
oratione commoda & pudica, multo rectius & speciosius est.*

XVIII. *In comoedia plures esse actus, quam quinque, molestum, pauciores
illepidum.*

*Deorum personas inducere non decet, nisi in rebus maximis. Cicero:
'Poëtae Tragici cum explicare argumenti exitum non possunt, ad Deum
confugiunt.'*

Plures personae quam quatuor ne loquantur propter confusionem.

*Chori sint morati, in quibus aut admoneantur homines, aut reprehen-
dantur, aut instituantur ad virtutem.*

*Chori materia eligatur eiusmodi, quae sit argumento praesenti apta atque
congrua.*

Instrumenta & cantus referantur ad simplicitatem vetustam.

*Musica cum intheatralis, & cantuum licentia, quae cum opibus Romanorum
creuit, est perniciosa disciplinae & moribus.*

XIX. *In Satyra grex rusticus, & dii agrestes producuntur ad tempe-
randam ludo & iocis Tragoediae tristiciam. In iocis tenendum, ne sint
lasciui, scurriles, maledici, quod praeceptum in genere ad alia scripta omnia
pertinet.*

*In satyra habenda ratio est loci, vt diei festi, personarum, vt Bacchi,
Sileni, Satyrorum: argumenti ne misceantur inconuenientia: verborum, vt
sint apta personis: decori, ne qui in Tragoedia fuit heros, in Satyra intro-
ducatur ardelio: auditorum denique, ne offendantur, si misceantur ridiculis
foeda, turpibus lasciua, iocosis probrosa.*

XX. *Eligendi pedes carminis vniuscuiusque proprii, in eoque nimia
licentia non est vtendum.*

Veteres in Iambico vsi puris iambis, deinceps assumptus est spondeus in locis inaequalibus.

Secuta postea talis licentia est, vt & spondeo liberrime, & pedibus aliis peregrinis, nequaquam festiue vterentur.

XXI. *Adhibenda in carmine scribendo cura & attentio.*

Quae ex tempore fiunt carmina, tanquam operae leues habentur, quae sine arte fiunt, eiiciuntur vt ineptae. Hoc quamuis multi non curant, tamen incuria auditoris, esse non debet causa negligentiae & erroris.

Qui scribere digna eruditis auribus cupit, auctores Graecos studiose legat, nec vnquam deponat de manibus.

XXII. *Artes habent sua incrementa, vt caeterae in natura res. Ita Tragoedia, quae primum rudis fuit auctore Thespi, posteris temporibus ornamenta accepit ab Aeschylo, primum acta ruri in vicis, deinde in theatris vrbium magnarum.*

XXIII. *Artes quaedam oriuntur, quaedam intercidunt, naturali quadam vicissitudine. Intercidit Comoedia vetus, propter maledicentiam, qua aperte lacerabantur homines : ei petulantiae statuta poena est, ne nimium acerbitas progrederetur. In eius locum Satyra successit apud Latinos. Veteris Comoediae auctores fuerunt Eupolis, Cratinus, Aristophanes : mediae, Plato Comicus : recentioris, Menander, quae in vsu mansit, & celebris facta est.*

XXIV. *Non simus contenti aliorum inuentis, sed & ipsi exemplo veterum aliquid nostra industria proseramus, quod laude sit dignum. Hoc fecerunt, qui scripserunt apud Latinos Togatas, quae habebant argumenta Graeca : vel qui scripserunt Praetextatas, quae argumenta Latina.*

XXV. *Vt carmen sit perfectum, id efficit cura & compositio : ideo quod tale non est, merito reprehenditur. Ingenii facultas artem superat.*

XXVI. *Poëta vt perfectus fiat, eget cognitione eius philosophiae, quae mores efficit meliores. Quae ad naturam spectat, minus plausibilis est, & minus ornamentorum habet & minus est vtilis.*

XXVII. *Ad philosophiam maior addenda est poëtae scientia, vt nouerit mores hominum, & ingenia populorum : id fit peregrinando, vt quae scribenda sunt, ita exprimat, atque variet, vt fiant narrationes speciosae.*

XXVIII. *Finis poëticae est, vt scribantur iucunda & vtilia. Iucundum est, quod delectat, nempe quod non nimis prolixum, quodue memoria teneri potest, itaque quod verisimile, & non plane ficticium. Vtile est quod animos incitat doctrina & sapientia.*

XXIX. *Ignoscendum est delictis quibusdam, praesertim in magno opere. Errores committuntur aut in arte propria, aut in aliena. Errare poëtam in praeceptis, turpe est : in aliena arte errorem committere, magis ferendum, vt a Virgilio in aditu Africae fingitur Aeneas ceruos iaculatus, cum Africa ceruum non habeat. Errores iisdem contingunt, aut incuria, cum peccatur negligentia, aut communi hominum fragilitate, quia nemo inuentus, qui nouerit omnia. Itaque hi postremi errores etiam non sunt exagitandi.*

XXX. *Bonus poëta hoc agat, vt semper delectet, & auditorem lectoremue detineat. In pictura quaedam delectant longius posita, quaedam adhibita propius. Contra, poëta & in vmbra & in sole delectationem asserat.*

XXXI. *In poëta nihil admittitur mediocre, qui nisi excellentissimus sit, deterrimus est.*

XXXII. *Poema nisi sit dulce & aequale, ingratum est : id probatur sensibus duobus, vt auditu & gustatu in cibis iucundis. Ita igitur sit poema, vt suauitate sit gratum, & sui simile sit, vsque ad finem, ne quem a legendo moretur & absterreat.*

XXXIII. *Qui scripturus est aliquid posteritate dignum, ne id aggre-*
diatur, natura non adiuuante.

Non e ligno omni fit Mercurius, vt est in prouerbio, nec omnium studiis
aut laboribus fauet Minerua. Praestantissima est in omni arte, natura, &
poetam non tam fieri, quam nasci sermone eruditorum dicitur.

XXXIV. *Nemo tam doctum se existimet, quin aliorum iudiciis sua scripta*
subiiciat, & ea domi sapius retractet atque corrigat.

XXXV. *Vtilitas poëticae inde propagata est, quia veteres scripserunt*
optima, ad hominum videlicet vitam, mores, & felicitatem pertinentia, suaque
scripta longo tempore examinata, iam senes protulerunt. Vsus poëticae quis
olim fuerit, exemplis hominum doctissimorum constat. Orphei, qui primum
villas condidit: Amphionis, qui vrbes: Tyrtaei, qui bella fortiter gessit:
Homeri, qui scripsit sapienter.

XXXVI. *In poëta artifice tria requiruntur, natura, ars, & diligentia.*

XXXVII. *Discendum a peritis, & erroris confessio scribenti necessaria, vt*
quod malum est vitet, & meliora discat facere.

Erroris confessio animi magni est & ingenui.

De Hippocrate medico scribunt Celsus & Quintilianus, quod errores
quosdam, ne posteros deciperet, sit confessus, more scilicet magni viri, &
fiduciam rerum magnarum habentis. Leuia enim ingenia, quia nihil
habent, nihil sibi detrahunt, vt idem Celsus ait.

XXXVIII. *In eligendis amicis, qui verum nos doceant, & scripta emen-*
dent nostra, acri iudicio vtendum est: ne eligantur imperiti, adulatores
fraudulenti, imperiti iudicare nesciunt, adulatores metuunt offendere, fraudu-
lenti non laudanda solent commendare.

XXXIX. *Nemo se ipse fallat, aut falli se ab aliis patiatur, sed ad emen-*
dationem scriptorum adhibeat grauem virum iudicem, eiusque consilio mutet
ac deleat, quae corrigenda & expolienda videbuntur.

XL. *Qui adulator non est, & post scriptionem iudicare nouit, rei nulli*
magis incumbat, quam emendationi, idque faciat graui studio & iudicio
exquisito. Id qui non facit, & hac in re qui peccat sponte, & famam temere
prostituit: is pro insano & furioso & cer[r]ito habeatur.

XLI. *Vicia versuum sunt septem, vt eorum qui carent arte, facilitate,*
ornatu: item eorum, qui sunt superflui, obscuri, ambigui, otiosi.

Ex Epistolis ad Maecenatem, Augustum, Florum.

XLII. *Imitatio non sit seruilis nec superstitiosa, quasi non audeas ab*
exemplo decedere, neque eadem sit fatua & imprudens, vt etiam imiteris non
imitanda & viciosa.

XLIII. *Alienis vestigiis non semper insistendum, viam enim interdum*
non tritam ab aliis & inusitatam, ingredi licet.. Horatius carmen Iambicum
mutuatus ab Archilocho est, eiusque numeros & elegantiam expressit: turpi-
tudinem in verbis, & in conuiciis dicacitatem vitauit prudenter.

XLIV. *In carmine aura popularis non captanda, sed videndum, vt do-*
ctorum iudiciis probentur, ea quae scripta sunt.

XLV. *Iudicium vulgi de poëtis raro verum, ideo non est sequendum.*
Iudicauit autem vulgus Romae, quod Pacuuius esset doctus, Accius grandi-
loquus, quod Afranius imitator Menandri, Plautus Epicharmi, quod Teren-
tius arte esset superior, Caecilius grauitate: sed non idem periti sentiebant.
Extat apud Macrobium nescio an Angellium, de iis qui scripserunt epigram-
mata, simile iudicium, de Rhetoris Antonii Iuliani sententia, quod Catullus

& Caluus bona pauca, Neuius implicata, Hortentius inuenusta, Cinna ille-pida, Mummius dura scripserit.

XLVI. *Antiqui ita sunt laudandi ne nouis detrahatur, nec aliis putetur iter interclusum ad magna peruemiendi. Scite Sidonius ad Eucherium, Veneror antiquos, non tamen ita, vt meorum aequaeuorum virtutes aut merita postponam.*

XLVII. *Nouitas grata est, si sit erudita : nam artes non simul inchoari & perfici certum est, sed tempore & studio excoluntur : quae tamen si ad summum peruenerint, rursus minuuntur & quasi decrescunt.*

Cic. de Orat. Nihil est in natura rerum omnium, quod se vniuersum pro-fundat, & quod totum repente euolet.

XLVIII. *Artem nemo exercere audet in primis periculosam, qui eam non bene didicerit : id faciunt gubernatores, faciunt idem medici : sed hoc minime fecerunt poëtae quidam Romani, quos calor & impetus tantus tulit, vt scribendis carminibus fere omnes gloriam quaererent, pauci tamen assequerentur.*

XLIX. *Poëta affectuum tractandorum non sit minus peritus, quam funambulus aut magus artis suae esse solet : tum ea euidentia res describat, vt lector non audire, sed ipsis locis & negociis, vbi quid agitur, interesse videatur. Eam facultatem* ὑποτύπωσιν *Fabius,* πρὸ ὀμμάτων θέσιν ἢ ποίησιν *vocat Aristoteles.*

L. *Poëtae aut in theatris placere cupiunt, vt Comici & Tragici : aut in bibliothecis student reponi.*

Theatrales affectuum animi habeant rationem, vt permoueant spectatorum aures & oculos. Ii vero qui intra parietes placere expetunt, sumant ad scri-bendum otium, & ad expoliendum tempus, vt possint satisfacere politis virorum sapientissimorum iudiciis in vmbra.

LI. *Poëta non sit importunus, vt auditu intempestiuo offendat : non difficilis, vt aliorum admonitiones spernat, non ambitiosus, vt sua scripta nimis admiretur : non morosus vt satis praemiorum tribui sibi non posse existimet : non superbus denique, vt honorari vltra modum velit.*

LII. *Necessaria poëtae est emendatio, vt obscuris lucem, splendorem vul-gatis addat. Omnia impropria, leuia, parum decora tollat atque deleat, antiquos, cum iudicio imitetur, nimis ambitiosa rescindat, aspera leuiget, sanitate sermonis in toto scripto vtatur, quae virtute carent, ea arte & ordine corrigat.*

LIII. *Suscipiat primum partes actoris poëta, vt sic habeatur, quasi non scribat attente, nec scripta sua expoliat, vt quiuis putet, se similia posse efficere, propter simplicitatem. Suscipiat praeterea partes histrionis, vt videatur vulgaria & vsitata agere : non tamen eadem agere propter varietatem : nec laborasse, sed lusisse, nec sudasse, sed exercuisse videatur. Nam artem sic celare, vt nihil appareat laboriosum aut exquisitum, cum tamen studio & cura expolita sint omnia, maxima virtus est, quam Aristoteles* κρύψιν *appellat.*

LIV. *Sapientia non ea sola est, vti verbis multis & elegantibus, sed ea etiam scire ac dicere, quae ad vitam bene beateque agendam pertinent, vnde artem poëticam sine cognitione & scientia philosophiae, nugas canoras supra nominauit. Itaque poëtam bonum & legitimum, oportet esse ornatum verbis, & sententiis sapientem, & oratori si non parem, certe maxime pro-pinquum & philosopho amicissimum.*

FRAUNCE (pp. 303–6).

Fraunce's *Arcadian Rhetorike* and his earlier *Lawier's Logike* (1588), his other prose work in English, probably owe something, if only in inception, to Thomas Wilson's popular *Arte of Rhetorique* (1553) and his earlier *Rule of Reason, conteinyng the Arte of Logique* (1551). They belong to the same class, though, like Richard Sherry's *Treatise of Schemes and Tropes* (1550), or William Fulwood's *Enimie of Idlenesse* (1568), they are more exclusively devoted to the collection of illustrative passages from ancient and modern authors. *The Arcadian Rhetorike* shows an advance on these in respect of its wider range of comparison, and it is for this, and its incidental references to Spenser, rather than for any critical value, that it is remembered. The *Returne from Parnassus* (Pt. i, Act 4, Sc. 1) pokes fun at these books, perhaps at Fraunce's own title-page.

Fraunce's books of verse, *The Lamentations of Amintas*, a translation of Thomas Watson's *Amyntas* (1587), *The Countesse of Pembrokes Yvychurch*(Parts I and II, 1591 ; Part III, 1592), and *The Countess of Pembrokes Emanuell* (1591), are written in hexameters, but they do not contain any critical observations, even on their metrical form. In these, according to Ben Jonson (by Drummond's report), Fraunce 'was a foole,' but perhaps not a greater than many of his contemporaries who experimented in the ' English hexameter.'

303. ll. 20, &c. *Countesse of Pembroke*, &c. See the titles of the poems named above. Fraunce was Sidney's friend. In his *Lawier's Logike* he tells us that the book had grown out of an early discourse on logic in presence of Sir Philip Sidney. He gives passages from Sidney's *Arcadia* and *Sonnets* in the *Rhetorike* : and the title is probably a direct compliment to his hero.

305. 26. *forme of an egge*, &c. See ante, p. 32, l. 11, note ; p. 47, note.

27. *Willy*. See p. 47, footnote, and p. 126, l. 17.

32. *Sheph. Cal.* In his *Lawier's Logike*, Fraunce says 'because many loue logike that neuer learne Lawe, I haue reteyned those ould examples of the new Shepheards Kalender which I first gathered.'

Nash (pp. 307-37).

I.

307. 11. *sine linea.* The proverbial *nulla dies sine linea,* explained in Pliny, xxxv. 10. 36, § 84.

308. 5-8. Nash's sarcasm generally contains covert attacks on individual authors and books (cf. p. 311, l. 31, &c.). Here, strangely enough, he appears to be referring to a passage in Greene's *Menaphon*: 'Wee had, answered *Doron,* an Eaw amongst our Rams, whose fleece was as white as the haires that grow on father *Boreas* chinne, or as the dangling deawlap of the siluer Bull, . . . her face like *Mars* treading vpon the milke white cloudes.' Nash may be implying that 'better pens,' such as Greene's, are 'outbraued' by the 'bumbast' of the tragedians. Studioso in the *Parnassus* Plays delights to bring in Boreas.

13. *bumbast . . . blanke verse.* Cf. the phrase in the famous Shakespearian passage in Greene's *Groatsworth of Wit* ('as well able to bumbast out a blanke verse as the best of you'), probably written in 1592.

14. *kilcow,* bragging, bullying. See *N. E. D.*

31. Cic. *Orat.* 28. Cf. *De Orat.* ii. 60.

309. 11. *Peter Ramus . . . his pettie Logique.* The well-known logic of Pierre de La Ramée (*Dialecticae libri duo, A. Talaei praelectionibus illustrati.* Paris, 1560) was Englished in 1574 '*per M. R. Makylmenaeum Scotum.*' William Temple, afterwards Sir Philip Sidney's secretary, published an edition in 1584. See also ii. p. 245, l. 6, note; and *The Pilgrimage to Parnassus,* Acts 2 and 3.

35, &c. *Sus Mineruam.* This adage (a favourite with Cicero) is explained in Pompeius Festus (Müll., p. 310): 'Sus Mineruam in prouerbio est, ubi quis id docet alterum cuius ipse inscius est.' *Asinus ad Lyram,* spoken of a doltish or awkward person, is noted by Gellius, p. 3, l. 16. Nash is probably borrowing in both cases from school-day memories.

310. 7. *Amomum* (ἄμωμον), a fragrant herb, not carefully determined in older literary usage, though now restricted to the genus 'Zingiberaceae.' Turner, in his *Herbal* (1551), reports that it is sometimes identified with the Christmas Rose. Cf. *Euphues* (ed. Landmann, p. 85).

23-4. *Iyl of Braintford's Testament* was printed by Robert Copland, c. 1525.

furmentie, frumenty, a spiced dish of hulled wheat boiled in milk.

Brainford (Brentford), a holiday resort of the lower classes, frequently referred to in the Jest-Books and popular tracts. Cf. *The Jests of George Peele, with foure of his companions at Brainford* (*Shaks. Jest-Books*, ii), and Dekker, *Works*, ii. 322, iii. 130.

27-8. Note Nash's 'euphuistic' alliteration. See p. 322, ll. 28-34, note.

28-9. Cf. ii. p. 227, ll. 31-2.

33, &c. Cf. infra, p. 325, ll. 16, 28.

311. 8. *Pasquil*. See ii. p. 56, l. 29.

9. A reference to the Martinist controversy.

11. *friplers*, i.e. fripperer's, old-clothes man's.

15. *tapsterlie*. Cf. supra, p. 125, l. 28, note ; p. 317, &c.

30, &c. Nash's reference to *triuiall translators*, and the allusions which he strews throughout the following sentences (down to l. 29 on p. 312), are now explained as an attack on Thomas Kyd. (See G. Sarrazin's *Thomas Kyd und sein Kreis* (1892), J. W. Cunliffe's *Influence of Seneca on Elizabethan Tragedy*, 1893, and the Introduction to F. S. Boas's edition of Kyd's *Works*, 1901.) Kyd had produced, in 1588, *The Householders Philosophie*, a translation of Tasso's *Padre di Famiglia* (printed by Boas, u. s., pp. 231-84). His *Cornelia* (Boas, u.s., pp. 101-60) was a translation, with modifications, of Garnier's *Cornélie*, as it appeared in the edition of 1585.

33. *Nouerint*. From the opening phrase of a scrivener's document : *Nouerint uniuersi per praesentes*, &c., as given infra ii. p. 238, l. 31, and in *The Returne from Parnassus*, Pt. ii. 4. 2, l. 1624. The usage is common. Cf. Greene's *Groatsworth of Wit* : ' for he had good experience in a *nouerint*' (l. 16).

35. This would appear to be a satirical exaggeration. (See Boas, u.s., p. lxv.)

312. 1. *English Seneca*, i.e. the translation of the *Tenne Tragedies*, which was issued by Thomas Newton in a collected edition in 1581, consisting of Jasper Heywood's version of the *Troas* (first printed 1559), the *Thyestes* (1560), the *Hercules Furens*

(1561), Alexander Nevyle's *Oedipus* (wr. 1560, pr. 1563), Thomas Nuce's *Octavia* (wr. 1562, pr. 1566), John Studley's *Medea and Agamemnon* (1566), Henry Denham's *Hippolytus* (lic. 1556), and Thomas Newton's *Thebais* (1581).

3–4. A reference to the earlier *Hamlet*, ascribed to Kyd, on which Shakespeare founded his play. (See Cunliffe, u. s., p. 5; Boas, u. s., pp. xlv–liv.)

10. Mr. Boas (u. s., p. xxiii) suggests that Nash borrowed the image not from Aesop but from the *Shepheardes Calender*. The likeness of Nash's phrase to Spenser's line, 'He was so enamored with the newell' (276), is striking.

13. *Italian.* See note to p. 311, l. 30.

18. Nash's charge of 'home-born mediocritie' is supported by Kyd's editor. (See Boas, u.s., xx.)

19–20.   'The middle path
  Which brought me to the faire Elizian greene . . .
  Here finding Pluto with his Proserpine
  I shewed my passport . . .'
                       The Spanish Tragedie, i. 1. 73–7.

Marlowe's line 'For he confounds hell in Elysium' (*Doctor Faustus*, iii. 60) had been connected by R. Simpson (*New Shaks. Soc. Trans.*, 1875–6, 168, note) with Nash's gibe: but the allusion to the foregoing passage is clear.

20–22. 'The sneer at those who "haue not learned the iust measure of the Horizon without (i.e. without the aid of) an hexameter" is directed (with a probable pun upon the various senses of "measure") at Kyd's borrowing the details of his picture of the lower world from the Sixth Book of the *Aeneid*.' (Boas, u. s., p. xxix.)

22–3.

'*Lorenzo.* Yet speake the truth, and I will guerdon thee,
  And shield thee from what euer can ensue,
  And will conceale what ere proceeds from thee;
  But if thou dally once againe, thou diest.
Pedringano. If Madame *Bel-Imperia* be in loue—
Lorenzo. What, Villaine, ifs and ands?'
                      The Spanish Tragedie, ii. 1. 72–7.

Nash's 'bodge up' is, of course, unjust.

26. *French Doudie.* See note to p. 311, l. 30. Mr. Boas suggests that there may be here a more special reference to Kyd's imitation in the Lord General's narrative (*Sp. Tr.* i. 2. 22 *et seq.*) of the Messenger's account in *Cornélie*, Act V, of the Battle of Thapsus (u.s., p. xxix).

313. 1. *Sadolet,* Cardinal Jacopo Sadoleto. See ii. p. 248, ll. 5-13, note.

2. *Plantine,* Christoffel Plantin, the famous printer.

6. *William Turner (d.* 1568), Dean of Wells, physician and writer on botanical subjects.

9. *Sir Thomas Eliot.* Ante, p. 413.

10-11. *with his Comicall wit,* in his *Utopia* ('Libellus vere aureus'), Louvain, 1516; afterwards translated, London, 1551 ('A fruteful and pleasaunt worke').

13. Cf. Ascham, supra, p. 21, and the passages printed in Mayor's edition, p. 162, &c. See also Ascham's letter to the Duke of Somerset, Nov. 21, 1547 (Giles, I. i. p. 138). Nash obviously knew his Ascham well; he refers to the *Scholemaster,* infra, pp. 336-7.

27. *Colona.* Read *Colonia,* as in Ascham (ed. Mayor, p. 162). 'Colony,' not 'Colonist,' is intended.

30. Sir John Cheke. Ante, i. p. 9, l. 30, &c.

31. Sir John Mason (1503-66), ambassador and statesman. Doctor Watson. See i. p. 21, l. 31, note.

32. Redman, John (1499-1551). See note to p. 21, l. 31.

Grindall. This is less likely to be the more notorious Edmund (? 1519-81), Archbishop of Canterbury, the 'Algrind' of the *Shepheardes Calender,* than William Grindal (*d.* 1548), Ascham's favourite pupil, who was a Fellow of St. John's, Cambridge, in 1543, and tutor to Queen Elizabeth. See Grant's *Vita Aschami* (Giles's *Ascham,* III).

Leuer, Thomas (1521-77), Fellow of St. John's, Cambridge, 1548.

Pilkington, James (? 1520-76), Master of St. John's, Cambridge, 1559, and first Protestant Bishop of Durham, 1561.

314. 14. *manuarie,* manual. Cf. *manuary craftes* (=handicrafts) in *Euphues* ('To the Gentlemen Schollers in Athens').

19. *Scythians.* Cf. note, supra, p. 75, l. 33.

315. 9. Gascoigne's *Supposes* (acted 1565) was an adaptation of Ariosto's *I Suppositi*.

10. *as Tullie.*   See *Acad. Quaest.* i. 3. 10 ; *De Fin.* i. 3 ; *Tusc. Quaest.* i. 1, &c.

11–12. Turberuile (George), translator of Mantuan (1567), Ovid's Epistles (1567–8), Mancinus (1568), and the *Tragical Tales* from the Italian (1576). He tried blank verse in six of the Ovidian Epistles.

14. Golding.   See p. 243, l. 27, note.

15. *editions of Diuinitie . . . out of the French tongue.*   He completed Sidney's translation of De Mornay (1589), and translated sermons and commentaries of Calvin, Beza, &c.

17. *Phaer,* supra, p. 137, l. 29, note.

23. *Stanihurst,* supra, p. 135.

30. *as neere as I can.*   Nash takes great liberties with Stanyhurst's text. See the *Conceites,* pp. 137–8, in Arber's edition.

316. 4. *triobulare,* trifling, of small account (lit. 3 *oboli*, or a ½-drachm).

5. *huffe snuffe,* braggart.   Nash is gibing at Stanyhurst in his own words—'Linckt was in wedlock a loftye Thrasonicai huf snuffe'(ed. Arber, p. 143). See the parody in ii. p. 241, ll. 4–5. Cf. Hall's *Sat.* i. 3, 17: 'Graced with huf-cap termes and thundring threats ', and Peele's *Old Wives Tale* (Bullen, i. p. 333).

8, &c. *France.*   See Fraunce, supra, p. 303, note.

Thomas Watson (? 1557–92) is best known as the author of the Ἑκατομπαθία, *or a Passionate Centurie of Loue* (1582). His Latin translation of the *Antigone* appeared in 1581 (see ii. p. 322, l. 29, note) ; his Latin poem *Amyntas* in 1585. The last was ' paraphrastically translated ' into English by Fraunce (see notes to i. p. 303, and ii. p. 321, ll. 7 and 11).

21. *Haddon, Walter.*   See i. p. 21, l. 31. Cf. this list of names with Meres's, ii. p. 315, l. 14, &c.

23. *Carre, Nicholas* (1524–68), Regius Professor of Greek at Cambridge, 1547.

24. *Thomas Newton with his Leyland.*   Thomas Newton (? 1542–1607) contributed in 1589 *Illustrium aliquot Anglorum Encomia* to Leland's *De Rebus Britannicis Collectanea.*

317. 13. *vndermeale,* afternoon.

16. *Tam Marti*, &c.   A common motto : used by Gascoigne on his title-pages.   See *The Returne from Parnassus*, Pt. i. 3. 1 (l. 951).   Cf. the other form *Tam armis quam ingenio*, as in Kyd, *Sp. Trag.* ii. 1. 107.

18. Hor. *Epist.* i. 5. 19.

34–5. Hor. *Epist.* i. 18. 82.

318–19. Cf. Meres's lists, infra, ii. p. 319.

318. 12. Livio Celiano. (Cf. Meres, infra, ii. p. 319.)   His *Rime* appeared in 1587.   A paraphrase of one of his madrigals, as printed in John Wilbye's *Madrigals*, 1598, will be found in Mr. Bullen's *Lyrics from Elizabethan Song-books*, p. 64.

33. As yet Spenser had published only the *Epigrams* and *Sonnets* (the *Visions of Petrarch* and the *Visions of Bellay* of 1591), and the *Shepheardes Calender*.

319. 6, 9. *Mathew Roydon* (fl. 1580–1622).   His *Elegie, or Friends passion for his Astrophill*, is printed in Spenser's *Colin Clout* (1595).   See the 'Globe' *Spenser*, p. 568.

7. *Thomas Atchelow*, the 'ingenious Atchlow' of Dekker's *Knights Coniuring* (1607).   Not in *D. N. B.*

George Peele's first work, the *Araygnement of Paris*, is dated 1584.

Roydon, Atchelow, and Peele are three of the five writers of commendatory verses in Watson's Ἑκατομπαθία (1582).

320. 1. *blankes*, i. e. blank verse.   See note to l. 18.

5. William Warner (? 1558–1609).   The first edition of his *Albions England* (Pt. I) is dated 1586; the second (Parts I and II), 1589.

10. *Abcie*, i. e. A B C.   Cf. *Abscedarie*, infra, p. 328, l. 4, note.

18. *blankes*.   Cf. l. 1.   Is a pun intended here (*blank*, a small coin) ?

II.

321. Grosart has endeavoured to explain the title of Nash's pamphlet as 'more likely fetched from Greene's *Anatomie of Flatterie* or from his *Arbasto, or Anatomie of Fortune* than from the *Anatomie of Abuses*,' because of 'his relations to and admiration of Robert Greene, and contrariwise his detestation of Stubbes as a grim Puritan.'   The argument is, however, double-

edged : and we have sufficient evidence to prove that he has the Puritan in mind. See note to p. 324, l. 16.

1–5. This favourite story is given by Cicero, *De Invent.* ii. 1.

2. Cf. Ariosto, *O. F.* c. 11, st. 71; *The Complaynt of Scotlande,* ed. Murray, p. 11.

11. *duncerie*, a common word with Nash (cf. p. 331). See also *The Returne from Parnassus,* Pt. ii. 3. 1 (l. 1111). *N. E. D.* gives only later examples.

12. *Nigrum theta,* (Θ), a conventional critical mark indicating censure of a passage, derived from the Θ (the initial of Θάνατος), placed on the Greek voting-tablets. See ii. p. 376, l. 4.

16. Orig. πουεσοπολις.

322. 27. *Idlebies*, idle fellows.

28–34. A direct hit at the Euphuistic vogue. Cf. Sidney, supra, p. 202, l. 33, note, and ii. p. 269. Note also *loue, lust . . . vice, visard.* Cf. p. 310, ll. 27–8. See also the list of names on p. 323, l. 33, &c., and also p. 337, ll. 12–13.

323. 1. Sir Egerton Brydges sees here an allusion to the title-page of *The Paradyse of Daynty Deuices : Conteyning sundry pithy preceptes, learned Counsels, and excellent inuentions, right pleasant and profitable for all estates . . .* (1578).

9–10. Ovid, *Ars Amat.* i. 1.

15–21. Cf. Ascham, supra, pp. 3–4. See Nash, p. 329, *Abbie-lubber.* Cf. *Euphues* (ed. Landmann, p. 83).

33, &c. Cf. the parallel passage in *Euphues* (‘To the graue Matrones and honest Maydens of Italy ’).

324. 16. An obvious allusion to Philip Stubbes's *Anatomie of Abuses* (1583). See note to p. 321.

26. *Nullus,* &c. Ovid, *Tristia,* i. 9. 6. Quoted by Greene in *Menaphon* (ed. Arber, p. 30), and as a motto in the *Paradyse of Daynty Devices* (ed. Brydges, p. 30*, No. 40).

325. 16 and 28. See note, supra, p. 310, l. 33, &c.

35. *boate, boote.* See note, p. 322, ll. 28–34.

326. 1. *Ne sutor.* See note, supra, p. 210, ll. 1–4.

16–20. See Lodge, supra, p. 63, ll. 1–4.

21. *A small ship.* A common Elizabethan metaphor.

35. *rednose Fidler. . . . Ale Knight.* Cf. note to p. 125, l. 28.

327. 12. The *De Asino Aureo* of Apuleius supplies the figure.

17. *Campanus.* Cf. Lodge, p. 65, l. 21.

328. 4. *abscedarie*, illiterate (med. Lat. *abecedarium*, an alphabet or primer—'A B C D').

7. i. e. Alabandensis Apollonius.   See Cic. *de Orat.* i. 28. 126.

21. *Aen.* ii. 274.

33. In the opening paragraphs of the *Tusculan Disputations*.

329. 18. *Poetry a daintie dish*.   A common metaphor.   See Introduction.

23. Cf. the list of Romances on p. 323.

331. 1. *duncerie*.   See note, p. 321, l. 12.

12. Cf. Lodge, p. 65, l. 16.

16. *sixt*.   It is in the *Fourth*, line 7.

332. 17. Cf. p. 59, l. 15 ; p. 79, l. 31, and ii. p. 309, l. 13.

19–23. Cf. Ascham, passim, and Webbe, pp. 254–5.

23. *haune*, awn.

333. 35. *potman . . . Poet*.   Cf. Webbe, supra, p. 246, l. 30.

334. 9. Cf. p. 312, l. 10.

13. *Cherillus*, Choerilus, referred to by Horace, *Epist.* ii. 1. 233, and *Ars Poet.* 357. 'I rather take vpon me to write better then *Choerilus*, then once suppose to imitate Homer,' Thomas Watson Ἑκατομπαθία, 'To the Reader' (Spenser Soc. edit., p. 6). For other references, see Index.

16. *Ramus*, supra, p. 309, l. 11, note.

335. 12. *his*.   Nash has confused his grammatical number.

336. 33. Mulcaster's *Positions wherein those primitiue circumstances be examined, which are necessarie for the training vp of Children, either for skill in their booke or health in their bodie* was printed in 1581.   His *First Part of the Elementarie which entreateth chefelie of the writing of our English tung* followed in 1582.

The Bodleian text is missing after 'bethinke.' The concluding portion is added to the copy in a later hand.

35. See note to p. 313, l. 13.

337. 1. See *Eduardi Grant Oratio de Vita et Obitu R.A.* (printed by Giles, iii. pp. 294–355).

23. *of Women*.   See supra, p. 324, ll. 6–9.

Appendix (pp. 341-4).

Sir Edward Hoby (1560–1617), son of Sir Thomas Hoby, the translator of Castiglione's *Cortegiano* ('The Courtyer').

342. 11. *Viues*, Ioannes Ludovicus (1492–1540), frequently referred to throughout these volumes (in text and notes). His English reputation was probably helped by the fact that he had been tutor to the Princess Mary, daughter of Henry VIII. He was a Fellow of Corpus Christi College, Oxford (see *D. N. B.*). Cf. ii. p. 245, l. 6, note.

28-9. See note to p. 158, l. 8.

38. See note to p. 71, l. 18.

END OF VOLUME I